Introduction to
Family Law

DELMAR CENGAGE Learning

Options.

Over 300 products in every area of the law: textbooks, online courses, CD-ROMs, reference books, companion websites, and more – helping you succeed in the classroom and on the job.

Support.

We offer unparalleled, practical support: robust instructor and student supplements to ensure the best learning experience, custom publishing to meet your unique needs, and other benefits such as Delmar Cengage Learning's Student Achievement Award. And our sales representatives are always ready to provide you with dependable service.

Feedback.

As always, we want to hear from you! Your feedback is our best resource for improving the quality of our products. Contact your sales representative or write us at the address below if you have any comments about our materials or if you have a product proposal.

Accounting and Financials for the Law Office • Administrative Law • Alternative Dispute Resolution • Bankruptcy Business Organizations/Corporations • Careers and Employment • Civil Litigation and Procedure • CLA Exam Preparation • Computer Applications in the Law Office • Constitutional Law • Contract Law • Court Reporting Criminal Law and Procedure • Document Preparation • Elder Law • Employment Law • Environmental Law • Ethics Evidence Law • Family Law • Health Care Law • Immigration Law • Intellectual Property • Internships Interviewing and Investigation • Introduction to Law • Introduction to Paralegalism • Juvenile Law • Law Office Management • Law Office Procedures • Legal Nurse Consulting • Legal Research, Writing, and Analysis • Legal Terminology • Legal Transcription • Media and Entertainment Law • Medical Malpractice Law Product Liability • Real Estate Law • Reference Materials • Social Security • Sports Law • Torts and Personal Injury Law • Wills, Trusts, and Estate Administration • Workers' Compensation Law

---

DELMAR CENGAGE Learning
5 Maxwell Drive
Clifton Park, New York 12065-2919

For additional information, find us online at:
www.delmar.cengage.com

Introduction to
Family Law

N. R. Gallo

DELMAR
CENGAGE Learning

Australia • Brazil • Japan • Korea • Mexico • Singapore • Spain • United Kingdom • United States

DELMAR
CENGAGE Learning™

Introduction to Family Law
N. R. Gallo

Career Education Strategic Business
Unit: Vice President: Dawn Gerrain

Director of Editorial: Sherry Gomoll

Acquisitions Editor: Pamela Fuller

Developmental Editor: Melissa Riveglia

Editorial Assistant: Sarah Duncan

Director of Production: Wendy
A. Troeger

Production Manager: Carolyn Miller

Production Editor: Betty L. Dickson

Technology Project Manager: Joseph
Saba

Director of Marketing: Wendy
Mapstone

Cover Design: Dutton and Sherman
Design

For product information and technology assistance, contact us at
Cengage Learning Customer & Sales Support, 1-800-354-9706

For permission to use material from this text or product,
submit all requests online at **www.cengage.com/permissions**
Further permissions questions can be emailed to
permissionrequest@cengage.com

Library of Congress Control Number: 2004043808

ISBN-13: 978-1-4018-1453-3

ISBN-10: 1-4018-1453-0

Delmar
Executive Woods
5 Maxwell Drive
Clifton Park, NY 12065
USA

Cengage Learning is a leading provider of customized learning
solutions with office locations around the globe, including Singapore,
the United Kingdom, Australia, Mexico, Brazil, and Japan. Locate your
local office at **international.cengage.com/region**

Cengage Learning products are represented in Canada by
Nelson Education, Ltd.

For your course and learning solutions, visit **delmar.cengage.com**

Visit our corporate website at **cengage.com**

Notice to the Reader

Publisher does not warrant or guarantee any of the products described herein or perform any independent analysis in connection with any of the product information contained
herein. Publisher does not assume, and expressly disclaims, any obligation to obtain and include information other than that provided to it by the manufacturer. The reader is
expressly warned to consider and adopt all safety precautions that might be indicated by the activities described herein and to avoid all potential hazards. By following the
instructions contained herein, the reader willingly assumes all risks in connection with such instructions. The publisher makes no representations or warranties of any kind,
including but not limited to, the warranties of fitness for particular purpose or merchantability, nor are any such representations implied with respect to the material set forth
herein, and the publisher takes no responsibility with respect to such material. The publisher shall not be liable for any special, consequential, or exemplary damages resulting,
in whole or part, from the readers' use of, or reliance upon, this material.

Printed in the United States of America
4 5 6 7 8 9 13 12 11 10

Contents

Chapter 9   **Child Custody   271**

Chapter 10 Child Support 315

Chapter 11   Divorce and Tax: No Shelter for the Weary   352

Cases

Cases adapted and reprinted courtesy of Cengage Learning.

Exhibits

Preface

INTRODUCTION

Over a decade ago I was asked to teach a Family Law course in our local college's paralegal program. Having worked as a paralegal and then as an attorney, I wanted to share with my students the legal theory and practical tips I had learned in several law practices. I spent weeks pondering the teaching methods I would use for that course. My primary goal was to convey information in a way that would not turn my students into robotic note-takers, but would make them excited participants in applying recently learned theory to real-life cases.

Looking back, I realize the germination of this textbook began while preparing to teach that first course. Back then, my law office began to take on the appearance of a packrat's hideout. I was intent on gathering materials that would help me cohesively blend legal theory with practical hands-on experience.

I knew firsthand just how important practical application of legal theory would be to my students once they hit the job market. Prior to going to law school, I had managed to find a job as a paralegal *in training* at a local law firm. My intent was to earn real-life experience before hitting the law books. At the risk of sounding like an antique, this was before the creation of most American paralegal education programs. Back in the not-so-good "good old days," one of the only ways to train as a paralegal was on the job.

My second goal was to help build the confidence of my students before they entered the job market. I wanted to prevent them from having the same nerve-wracking experiences I'd had after being thrown head-first into the fire of a busy law office. I wanted my students to make a less fiery and more comfortable progression from student to practicing paralegal. How would I do this? I felt I needed to convey the drama, pathos, and humor that occurs every day in a busy family law practice, in conjunction with plenty of theory and practical application. These goals of mine were not being addressed by the textbooks being offered at the time, so I knew I would have to write a text to help me bring the reality of a law practice into the classroom.

My idea was that students reading a family law textbook would have greater interest in the material if they could imagine themselves in the role of a newly graduated family law paralegal. That was how this textbook's main character of Susan, a paralegal working at her first law firm, was born. I wanted my students to feel like they were experiencing the material through Susan's eyes. After all, wouldn't the natural result be students retaining more material if they were interested in finding out what was going to happen next to Susan and her firm's clients?

The inclusion of Susan's various job assignments was a response to my students' natural curiosity about life on the job. At the start of each semester, students always ask me what a typical family law paralegal does. My answer is usually, "That depends," because there really is no typical job description. A paralegal's work might include dealing with the personality conflicts of warring spouses. Domestic violence can intrude into a practice. A day's assignments might involve preparation for an adoption hearing, or tracking down a non-paying parent for child support. The list goes on.

It has been suggested that the name of this textbook could have been *Introduction to Domestic Relations,* since so many of our twenty-first century domestic units are created without the DNA connection that historically was thought to be necessary in order for a group of people to be called a family. I disagree. Instead, I propose that our basic human need to be a member of a family unit transcends biology. We may be born with the only DNA we will ever have, but this genetic identifier should never be a prerequisite to being part of a family unit. An accurate definition of a contemporary family cannot be found in any dictionary, nor, perhaps, should one be found there. Americans in the twenty-first century have created families as diverse as their DNA and are redefining the traditional notion of what a *family* is and how it is created.

The diversification and realignment of our collective psyche does not happen without societal and judicial conflict. It is here, amidst this conflict, that the law refuses to remain static. It is a fundamental tenet that evolution is expected in the law, but nowhere else is the yin and yang of the human condition played out so dramatically as it is in family law.

I have chosen material for this textbook that reflects the "meat and potatoes" of today's family law practice, plus more controversial topics that keep arriving at law office doors with greater regularity. Such controversial topics as surrogacy births, same-sex marriage, and palimony once floated along the legal sidelines but must now be included in any thorough discussion of family law practice. This is why I have also included a chapter on the once-whispered-about subject of domestic violence and how it is being more forcefully dealt with in the courts and in our legislatures.

I have a special message to the family law student reading this right now. The knowledge you gain in your Family Law class could prove to be the most *personally* valuable knowledge you will gain of any legal subject. This benefit should not be overlooked. Many of my students have stated that *anyone* who plans to cohabit (married or unmarried) should first take a Family Law course. Some have also insisted that if you have a family, you should be informed about family law. I agree. It is an unfortunate fact of life that many American marriages will end in divorce. Breaking up is never easy, particularly for any children from the union, but a divorcing couple will find the process much less daunting if they are knowledgeable about the workings of the legal system.

ORGANIZATION OF THE TEXT

Each chapter begins with introductory material on its particular topic. Next, the on-the- job experiences of Susan are shared. Susan meets clients with all types of pressing legal problems and admirably fulfills her role as researcher, writer, interviewer, motion and pleadings preparer, and shoulder to cry on. Throughout the textbook, Susan's experiences are mingled with informative legal theory, pertinent case briefs with follow-up discussion questions, and practical exhibits. In order to give students a flavor of the legal trends across the country, cases have been carefully chosen from a wide spectrum of states. Studying and discussing these cases is an invaluable tool for developing a student's analytical skills.

Additionally, all the chapters include an *Ethics Alert* scenario for the students to ponder because no one should enter a law firm without a firm grounding in the ethical rules that apply to legal practice in the twenty-first century. Every chapter concludes with a *Chapter Summary* that contains a repetition of key points to help students retain information. *Review Questions* are then provided. They cover the important questions students should be able to answer after reading the chapter. Also provided is a list of *Key Terms* that are defined in each chapter and in the Glossary because vocabulary building is an intrinsic part of learning the law. Finally, illuminating Internet sites appropriate to the subject matter of each chapter are provided and described in *Surfing the Web.* The appendices include several pertinent statutes for referral, suggested ethical guidelines for paralegals, a list of paralegal organizations across the country, and a list of state child support offices.

Chapter 1 begins with the focus on Susan's efforts to find her first paralegal position. Like so many students, regardless of age, Susan is inexperienced, but ready to gallop headlong into practice. This excitement to get started on a new career led me to include the first chapter, *Life on the Job,* in the text. All the learned theory and practical application will not matter one iota if the student cannot land that first job. In Chapter 1, Susan creates a portfolio of her best Family Law coursework and learns job interviewing techniques. She is hired by the law firm of Johnson & Webster to support two of the firm's attorneys whose practices concentrate on family law matters. Attorneys Alyssa Jensen and J. D. Dombroski will initiate Susan into the mysterious world of memorandums of law, appellate briefs, motions, pleadings, and human emotions pushed to their limits.

Chapter 2 emphasizes research techniques and is provided as a handy resource. It may be referred to when needed or studied as a chapter. Analytical skills will be developed through research assignments designed to emphasize the prevailing law in a student's home state. So, while students will learn the legal trends across the nation, they will also learn the law in the state in which they are studying and in which they will very likely work once they have finished their schooling.

Students can fill a dozen family law notebooks with theory, but be frustrated on the job if they cannot successfully research a legal issue. The question of whether to include Chapter 2, *Legal Research and Writing,* which deals exclusively with research within a Family Law office, was answered by my own students. Fresh from a semester break, a class of Family Law students voted enthusiastically for the inclusion of the research and writing chapter. Why? Some students felt a need for a legal research refresher. Some wanted me to share any hints I had gathered over the years. Still other students pointed to how much they related to Susan's apprehension when she was asked to assist with her first official appellate brief.

Chapter 3 covers the growing American trend of cohabitation without marriage. Americans from 18 to 80, are living together without following the traditional path to marriage. Unfortunately, cohabitants can face legal dilemmas unique to their chosen living situation. These legal dilemmas and their possible solutions are discussed in detail in the chapter by following the unexpected love story of Susan's cousin, Joanna, who is a business-minded accountant and her musician boyfriend.

Chapter 4 covers the legal essentials that must be included when writing a prenuptial, post-nuptial, or reconciliation agreement. The legal requirements are introduced by following the second-time-around love story of a middle-aged Romeo and Juliet. Madly in love, the couple is trying to balance a lifetime of experience, two nasty divorces, and grown children who are worried their future inheritances will be left to a new spouse. Susan's boss decides to take a few days off and leaves Susan to fly solo, interviewing two couples who plan to sign prenuptial agreements.

Chapter 5 shares the interesting history of our marriage rituals, clarifies anecdotal knowledge of common law marriages and annulments, and explains the numerous marriage requirements that must be fulfilled across the country. An interesting historical remnant called the breach-of-promise cause of action is explained by following the story of Susan's friend, Tara, a broken-hearted fiancée left to deal with the wedding bills.

Chapter 6 explains the ramifications of claiming and denying paternity. The story of Michelle, an unexpectedly expecting feisty mom-to-be seeking every legal option to make her baby's doubting father face up to parenthood, adds a dose of reality to paternity issues. Once again, Susan brings a client to the firm.

Chapter 7 reviews each step of the adoption process, the numerous types of adoptions, and the different approaches to adoption across the country. The story of a 40-something couple yearning for a child to call their own concentrates on their efforts to complete an independent adoption using a personalized Web site. Susan and Alyssa share a heartwarming adoption experience with their clients.

Chapter 8 is the longest chapter in the textbook. The length can be justified because the subject, *Divorce and Separation,* is really the main focus of many family law practices. Susan's neighbor, Libby, chooses the Johnson & Webster law firm to represent her in her divorce. The human drama of divorce is evident in the frustration and dashed dreams displayed by angry spouses forced to split property and custody of their children. Libby's divorce experience, from initial interview to final judgment, is detailed with pleadings personalized to her case.

Chapter 9 concentrates on child custody issues. A wife's affair turns a reasonable man unreasonable in his heated pursuit of sole custody. Susan is shocked by the animosity between the "Battling Baxters" who appear to have momentarily forgotten what is best for their children while each fights for sole custody of the children.

Chapter 10 delves deeply into child support issues. Extensively discussed are the federal and state laws that have been enacted in an effort to promote payment of child support. A client's post-divorce financial troubles lead Susan on a search for a deadbeat parent. Using available legal resources, she tries to obtain monetary relief.

Chapter 11 explains in simple steps the often-confusing tax ramifications of divorce. Susan gets a lesson in just how complicated tax issues can be following a divorce. She also witnesses one attorney's wily effort to avoid higher taxes for his client.

Chapter 12 is included because no family law textbook should forget the unfortunate occurrence of domestic violence in our society. The available state and federal statutory protections may appear to be a maze for the victim. The efforts of Maggie, Susan's childhood friend, a victim trying to break free from an abusive relationship and navigate the available federal and state protections, puts a human face on the reality of this part of family law.

The final chapter, Chapter 13, concentrates on the emerging field of alternative dispute resolution. Susan's boss, J. D. Dombroski, decides to expand into family mediation and explains the numerous benefits (and some of the negatives) of this alternative method of handling the divorce process to Susan. One divorcing couple's experience is followed through five mediation sessions with J. D.

ABOUT THE AUTHOR

A member of the American Association of Paralegal Educators Family Law Syllabus Task Force (2003) and the American Bar Association's Family Law Section, the author is licensed to practice law in both Florida and New Jersey, has volunteered as an Early Settlement Panel member for Sussex County Superior Court, Newton, New Jersey, and is a frequent public speaker. A newspaper reporter and editor prior to studying law, the author's law practice has included family mediation. A cum laude graduate of William Paterson University, the author attended Nova Southeastern University and was a recipient of a National Endowment for the Humanities funded grant for the study *Paul Robeson, 20th Century Humanist and Lawyer.* The author is an associate professor and Legal Studies program coordinator at Sussex County Community College, Newton, New Jersey.

SUPPLEMENTAL TEACHING MATERIALS

- The **Instructor's Manual** is written by the author and contains the following:
  - A suggested course syllabi that follows the format of the text
  - Answers to the chapter Review Questions within the text
  - Suggestions for teaching each of the chapters in the text
  - Further discussion of the cases following each boxed legal case
  - Multiple-choice, true and false, fill in the blank, and mix and match vocabulary questions for each of the chapters
  - Discussion of the Ethics Alert scenarios provided in each chapter
- **On-line Companion™**—The On-line Companion™ is meant to complement the textbook and the instructor's lectures and classroom activities. Students may take the opportunity to test their growing knowledge by deciding the real-life outcomes of the numerous case scenarios provided. The On-line Companion™ is a no-cost benefit that is not intended as a substitute for the textbook and classroom experience.
- **Webtutor™**—The author has written an accompanying Webtutor™ on Web CT and Blackboard platforms to facilitate active engagement with the course content. The Webtutor encourages review of lecture material, expands the depth of course content, and promotes self-directed learning. The Webtutor will provide *immediate feedback* from quizzes, and its contemporary format will appeal to today's student.
- **Web page**—Come visit our Web site at **www.paralegal.delmar.cengage.com**, where you will find valuable information such as hot links and sample materials to download, as well as other Delmar, Cengage Learning Paralegal products.
- **Westlaw®**—West's on-line computerized legal research system offers students "hands-on" experience with a system commonly used in law offices. Qualified adopters can receive ten free hours of Westlaw®. Westlaw® can be accessed with Macintosh and IBM PC and compatibles. A modem is required.
- **Strategies and Tips for Paralegal Educators**, a pamphlet by Anita Tebbe of Johnson County Community College, provides teaching strategies specifically designed for paralegal educators. A copy of this pamphlet is available to each adopter. Quantities for distribution to adjunct instructors are available for purchase at a minimal price. A coupon on the pamphlet provides ordering information.
- **Survival Guide for Paralegal Students**, a pamphlet by Kathleen Mercer Reed and Bradene Moore, covers practical and basic information to help students make the most of their paralegal courses. Topics covered include choosing courses of study and note-taking skills.
- **West's Paralegal Video Library**—Delmar, Cengage Learning Paralegal is pleased to offer the following videos at no charge to qualified adopters:
  - *The Drama of the Law II: Paralegal Issues Video*
    ISBN: 0-314-07088-5
  - *The Making of a Case Video*
    ISBN: 0-314-07300-0
  - *ABA Mock Trial Video-Product Liability*
    ISBN: 0-314-07342-6
  - *Arguments to the United States Supreme Court Video*
    ISBN: 0-314-07070-2

- **Court TV Videos**—Delmar, Cengage Learning Paralegal is pleased to offer the following videos from Court TV for a minimal fee:
  - *New York v. Ferguson—Murder on the 5:33: The Trial of Colin Ferguson*
    ISBN: 0-7668-1098-4
  - *Ohio v. Alfieri*
    ISBN: 0-7668-1099-2
  - *Flynn v. Goldman Sachs—Fired on Wall Street: A Case of Sex Discrimination?*
    ISBN: 0-7668-1096-8
  - *Dodd v. Dodd—Religion and Child Custody in Conflict*
    ISBN: 0-7668-1094-1
  - *In Re Custody of Baby Girl Clausen—Child of Mine: The Fight for Baby Jessica*
    ISBN: 0-7668-1097-6
  - *Fentress v. Eli Lilly & Co., et al—Prozac on Trial*
    ISBN: 0-7668-1095-x
  - *Garcia v. Garcia—Fighting over Jerry's Money*
    ISBN: 0-7668-0264-7
  - *Hall v. Hall—Irretrievably Broken—A Divorce Lawyer Goes to Court*
    ISBN: 0-7668-0196-9
  - *Maglica v. Maglica—Broken Hearts, Broken Commitments*
    ISBN: 0-7668-0867-x
  - *Northside Partners v. Page and New Kids on the Block—New Kids in Court: Is Their Hit Song a Copy?*
    ISBN: 0-7668-9426-7

Please note the Internet resources are of a time-sensitive nature and URL addresses may often change or be deleted.

Contact us at delmar.help@cengage.com

DEDICATION

I dedicate this effort to my family. My parents, the children of immigrants, were the first members of their families to go to college and instilled a *can-do* American spirit in their children. My father, Dr. James M. Gallo, college professor, health professional, entrepreneur, and author, lives by the saying *the harder you work, the luckier you get.* My mother, Nancy V. Gallo, library director and educator, shared and nurtured in me her love of reading.

If my words are fulfilling my goals, it is in no small part because of the moral support from and the second set of eyes of my sister, Andrea R. Gallo. In an extraordinary act of kindness and commitment of time, she signed on as a much appreciated reader and editor of my words. My sister Jamie may have been thousands of miles away, but I always felt her close by, supporting my efforts every step of the way.

My beloved aunt, Josephine Gallo Sczcomak, defined her life by her family connections. Her continued interest in this text was a motivating force when lethargy overtook my muse. My appreciation goes to John M. Sczcomak, CPA and devoted son of Michael and Josephine. John generously shared his tax expertise. Thanks, cousin.

When the task seemed endless, I soon learned that a play break with James, our now 3-year-old fountain of energy, would revive my spirits. James is blessed to have two amazing and talented big sisters, Alyssa and Tara. My loves, I share this book with all three of you.

Finally, this text would never have made it to paper if not for my extraordinary spouse. Dale, I thank you for always putting family first, for holding down the fort throughout the seemingly endless process of producing this text, and for making our home my favorite place to be.

ACKNOWLEDGMENTS

The monumental task of writing this textbook was made less so because of the assistance of my extraordinary students. Many students have kindly given the review and test questions dry runs and have generously provided feedback on the text. In particular, students Patricia O'Grady and Nancy Kalipetis put into exemplary practice the skills learned in the classroom.

This text would never have made it into a student's backpack if not for the wonderful crew at Delmar, Cengage Learning Paralegal. Thank you all for your hard work and dedication to producing the best text possible.

Additionally, I would like to acknowledge the invaluable contributions of the following reviewers for their suggestions and attention to detail:

Henry H. Arnold, III
Aiken Technical College
Aiken, South Carolina

Richard T. Martin
Washburn University
Topeka, Kansas

Michele Bradford
Gadsden State Community College
Gadsden, Alabama

Gayle V. Mozee
Graham & James
Palo Alto, California

Bob Diotalevi
Florida Gulf Coast University
Fort Myers, Florida

Buzz Wheeler
Highline Community College
Des Moines, Washington

David J. Hallett
Pioneer Pacific College
Wilsonville, Oregon

Catherine Dunn Whittinghill
College of Saint Mary
Omaha, Nebraska

AVENUE FOR FEEDBACK

I look forward to hearing from students and educators with questions, suggestions, or comments about the text, the *Instructor's Manual,* or the Webtutor. You may reach the author at **ngallo@sussex.edu**.

Chapter 1

Life on the Job

INTRODUCTION TO FAMILY LAW PRACTICE

The typical family law practice may handle cohabitation agreements, prenuptial agreements, paternity claims, and adoptions. Unfortunately, the law firm's staff may also encounter clients dealing with the harsh reality of domestic violence. Generally, though, the largest part of a typical family law practice involves the representation of clients going through the often-traumatic divorce process. Statistically, over half of all marriages end in divorce in the United States.[1] Frankly, what may be bad news for America's marriages is good news for a law firm's business. More than in most other areas of the law, attorneys who practice family law must balance the client's *legal needs* with *sensitivity* to the client's emotional state. A well-trained **paralegal** can have a vital and important role in assisting the attorney with this dual responsibility.

Many of you already know the definition of a paralegal provided by the American Bar Association (ABA). The ABA defines a paralegal, also called a **legal assistant,** as *a person qualified by education, training or work experience, who is employed or retained by a lawyer, law office, corporation, governmental agency or other entity and who performs delegated substantive legal work for which a lawyer is responsible.*[2]

Although the ABA deftly defines the paralegal's role, there really is no typical workday for a paralegal. Your schedule will be as varied as the attorneys, clients, and the multiple areas of practice that you will encounter. If you know the area of law you would like to concentrate on after completing your paralegal education, you are most likely one step ahead of the majority of people who are studying to be paralegals. You will be following the experiences of just such a student throughout this textbook.

SUSAN'S STORY

Susan knew as soon as she finished her Family Law course that she wanted to work as a paralegal in a busy family law practice. Now that she has graduated, she is still confident in her decision. However, she is still searching for an ideal position in which to begin her new professional life.

Susan Searches for a Job

Susan stepped out of her car, deeply breathing in the familiar summer smells of freshly mown grass and hamburgers being grilled, and walked down her driveway. Nancy, Susan's mother, eagerly opened the screen door for Susan and welcomed her with a big hug. "You're late! I was getting worried."

Returning the hug, Susan commented, "Umm, something smells good."

Nancy chuckled, "That's your lunch. I told your dad we should wait until you got back from your interview to start the grill, but he just couldn't wait. You know how mowing the lawn makes him hungry. The burgers should be almost ready." Then, tilting her head inquisitively, she gently asked, "So? How did it go?"

Susan was not in the mood to talk about her difficulties in getting a job. "It came and it went," she snapped.

Seeing her mother's worried look, Susan was immediately sorry about her shortness. "I'm sorry," she explained with a sigh. "It's just that I've been to quite a few interviews since I graduated, and so far I'd describe the opportunities as running the gamut from bad to ugly. I'm beginning to wonder if a good offer will *ever* come my way."

Nancy put a comforting arm around Susan as they walked together toward the home's cozy kitchen, and said, "Let's get lunch on the table, and then I want the three of us to review how you should approach your future interviews."

As the screen door slammed behind them, Susan slumped against the kitchen counter with a less-than-enthusiastic look on her face. Deciding that now was not the time to tell her daughter to stand up straight, Nancy decided to let it go, and announced, "Ice cream cake from Cliff's Parlor for dessert!"

Beaming with renewed energy, Susan eagerly asked, "With cookie crumbs and chocolate?"

Nancy smiled and responded, "Of course, what else? Let's go outside and see what Dad is up to."

Sitting on the deck around the family's old redwood picnic table, mother, father, and daughter companionably enjoyed the day. As they looked out at the pretty yard where flowers were just starting to bloom, Susan's dad, Jim, turned, smiled at his youngest daughter, and inquired, "So, does the world look a little rosier after that gourmet lunch?"

Susan responded, "Well, it is kind of hard to be depressed after one of your famous half-pound burgers."

Jim, an analytical man by nature, said, "That's exactly right, my girl, but now—more to the matter at hand—I think the key with your job search is to determine exactly the methodology you're using, and then tweak it to success."

Nancy thought her daughter would respond with, "Oh, Dad, you just don't understand"—but instead, Susan replied, almost whispering, "I don't know what I'm doing wrong."

Moving his expansive girth to a comfy, cushioned chair, Jim asked, "What exactly *are* you doing to get a job as a paralegal?"

Susan jumped right in with a reply. "I'm sending the *resume* I prepared during my last semester at school to every paralegal or legal assistant position advertisement I see in the paper or on the Internet," she said. "The resume details my education and job experience. I've also sent my resume to every law firm in the telephone book with a short *cover letter*. The cover letter explains why I am interested in working for the firm. In my cover letter, I told the law firms how much I want a job to get experience so that I can grow in my field." Taking a much-needed breath, Susan looked expectantly at her mom and dad.

Without much expression, Jim asked, "And what type of interviews have you been able to get from your methodology?"

Susan dejectedly responded, "The pits is what I've gotten. I've been on four interviews. One interviewer asked if I would work for free until I had some experience. One interviewer really wanted a glorified gofer and thought my comment about moving ahead meant I'd train on their time and then look for another job. The other two jobs were for areas of the law that I'm not the least bit interested in."

Jim and Nancy looked at each other knowingly. Jim asked, "Nance, may I go first?"

"Be my guest," she nodded.

Effective Job Search Techniques

Clearing his throat, Jim began, "Well, I have quite a few suggestions. First, it's a good idea to do a little research about a firm before you attend the first interview. I think your interviewer would be impressed with your professionalism. You told me awhile ago that the county library has a large set of books that lists lawyers by town all over the country, along with their area of expertise, and even a partial list of clients." Jim paused, "I don't remember the name, but you looked up that workers' compensation lawyer for your cousin. Remember, Susan?"

Susan interjected, "Oh, you mean the reference books called *Martindale-Hubbell*."[3]

Jim smiled, "Yes, that's it! I remembered the name had a hyphen, but I couldn't think of it." He continued, "Secondly, I'd take advantage of the convenience of word processing by revising your resume and cover letter for each job to describe how your experience matches the particular law firm's needs."

Hunching forward, Susan asked, "But, how do I do that if I've never had a legal job before?"

Jim answered, "You've had other jobs that required qualities similar to those the law firms are probably looking for, plus you completed your legal internship with excellent reviews by your supervising attorney." When Susan did not look convinced, he pressed, "Right?"

Susan agreed, "Well, I guess so."

Jim was not finished, "And I have another suggestion. Where did you put all your college papers?"

Susan answered, "I have them in a box, ready to go into the attic."

Shaking her head, Nancy smiled and interjected, "Remember when your sister graduated with her graphic design degree and she didn't even have an internship to talk about? She created a portfolio of her work to bring with her to interviews." Realizing she had piqued Susan's interest, Nancy continued, "She got a great job once she really showed what she could do and decided to market herself." Susan remembered that, and how her college advisor had suggested that Susan save her papers, but she had been shy about showing actual schoolwork with grades and comments by the instructor.

Jim added one more suggestion: "If I were you, I'd only apply to law firms that practice in the areas of law that you have a particular interest in."

Susan nodded at that suggestion. "You're right, Dad. I interviewed with those two firms that handled cases I'd rather not deal with, just because they called. I've always wanted to work in a family law practice. I do think the interviewing experience with those other firms was valuable, though."

Nancy had quietly cleared off the table as Jim and Susan were talking, but now she spoke up and said, "It's getting pretty chilly out here, guys; let's go in."

As they were moving inside, Susan broke out into her biggest smile of the day. "Thanks so much for your suggestions," she said. "I'm going to go upstairs and look through my papers to see if I can create a portfolio of my legal work to dazzle a future boss with!"

Susan Lands a Job

Several weeks later Susan pulled into the driveway, jumped out of her car, and ran up the walkway. Pulling the front door open, she yelled, "Hey, everybody! Anybody! I got it! They want me!"

Simultaneously, Jim, Nancy, Jamie (Susan's older sister), and Snuggles, the family golden retriever, converged to find out what all the commotion was about. Jim, Nancy, and Jamie all spoke at once: "Susan, what happened?" "Susan, what's wrong?" "Quit that barking!"

Making her announcement while being furiously licked by Snuggles, Susan laughed, "I got the job at Johnson & Webster. I'll start in a week as a paralegal working with two attorneys who handle family law matters exclusively!" After a celebratory group hug that included Snuggles, Susan added, "You were so right. They loved the portfolio. They saw that I had research experience and that I learned some solid basics in my Family Law college class. I'm so glad I kept all those papers."

PLANNING NOW FOR A SUCCESSFUL JOB SEARCH

Do you already know you would like to work in a family law practice? Perhaps you are not as sure about it as Susan, our recent graduate, was, but you think it may be a possibility in the future. The next question you should ask yourself is:"What can I do *right now* to help propel myself into a successful job search while I'm still a student in this Family Law class?"

Although you may be taking a Family Law course months, or even years, before a job search begins, it is never too early to prepare a *sample portfolio*. A portfolio is a collection of your work gathered together for review by prospective employers. Prospective employers are never happier than when they see physical proof that a prospective employee already knows how to do at least some of the work that would be required for the job. The portfolio should include samples from completed coursework, for example, pleadings, a case information statement, motions, client letters, a memorandum of law, and an appellate brief. You will read more about these documents later in this text.

If you are taking your Family Law class early in your legal education, you may want to revise your work product as you get closer to graduation. After all, you do not want earlier (and less-experienced) work samples to land in your portfolio and hurt, rather than help, your chances of landing a job upon graduation. All of your Family Law coursework should be kept on a computer disk for fine-tuning as your knowledge and abilities improve. In fact, *all* coursework should be word processed and saved to a disk.

Perhaps you are not sure that working in a family law practice is for you. If so, perhaps that is because you are unfamiliar with what a family law paralegal's job encompasses. No one list of paralegal job duties will fit every firm. So where can you learn more about the possible job responsibilities of a family law paralegal? You can begin to learn about the position in Family Law class. Ask your instructor to describe what the daily work life of a family law paralegal is like in your geographical area. You can also attend local paralegal association meetings. Association meeting dates are usually announced in area newspapers. Look in Appendix A for a list of paralegal and legal assistant associations in your area. Speaking with paralegals who are working in the field can give a student an invaluable, real-world look at life in the trenches. Association meetings are also a great place to begin networking with paralegals already working in the field. You may hear about a job opening before a law firm advertises the position, and best of all, you may gain a different perspective on a prospective employer from a paralegal who is already working in that firm.

YOU HAVE LANDED THE JOB—NOW WHAT?

Once you have landed a job with a family law practice, or in any area of practice for that matter, you will quickly learn two things: (1) the relationship the firm maintains with clients is the foundation of the practice, and (2) first impressions count.

Scheduling Appointments

The first step in dealing with a prospective client usually occurs when the prospective client telephones the law office to request an appointment with an attorney. While many larger law firms may have a receptionist or secretary in charge of making appointments, everyone in a law firm should know the proper procedure for setting up appointments. It may sound easy enough to just check the attorney's schedule and set up an appointment, but then a problem may arise later. A conflict of interest may occur. For example, what if a prospective client seeking representation for a divorce calls for an appointment with an attorney, but the attorney is already representing the prospective client's spouse? Ethically speaking, the attorney should not be representing both spouses. Such representation would be a **conflict of interest.** Any employee of the law firm who sets appointments should know how to check the names of prospective clients against the law firm's client list. Cross-checking can be most efficiently done by utilizing a computer program. Computer programs are available that are designed to ensure that neither the attorney requested by a prospective client nor any other attorney in the law firm is already representing the prospective client's spouse. If a prospective client passes the cross-checking, then the appointment can be arranged.

Preparing the Client for the First Appointment

The prospective client's first appointment is especially important because the first impression is usually the most lasting. The client should not be allowed to walk into the appointment unprepared. During the initial telephone call, the client's address and telephone number should be taken. Unless the client asks that a letter from the law firm not be sent to the address given, the telephone call should be followed with a letter detailing the date and time of the appointment and directions to the office. The client may be willing to share the purpose of the appointment. For example, if a new client knows that he wants the attorney to begin divorce proceedings, then the letter may list paperwork that should be brought to the first appointment. If possible, copies of bank records, income tax forms, a list of property owned, a list of debts owed, and a list of living expenses should be brought to the first meeting along with any other pertinent information that is available. Sometimes, though, the first appointment may just be a consultation to see if the person wishes to become a client and the attorney wants to be hired by the person.

The Client's First Appointment

During the first meeting, the attorney will usually spend most of the time listening to the prospective client's issues and concerns. As soon as the client and attorney have made the decision to work together, the attorney may ask the client to read and sign a **fee agreement,** often called a *retainer.*

A **retainer** should explain (in easily understood language) the rights of the client, and the duties the attorney has to the client. The retainer is essentially a contract between the client and the attorney. Failure of either party to comply with the retainer agreement may be the basis for a breach of contract by the client or attorney, or even legal malpractice by the attorney. A **breach of contract** is defined as a failure, without legal excuse, to live up to a significant promise made in a contract. **Legal malpractice** is defined as professional misconduct or unreasonable lack of skill. This word is usually applied to bad, incomplete, or unethical work or behavior of an attorney or other professional.

The retainer agreement should clearly describe the work that the attorney is being hired to do, the hourly fee the attorney is charging, and the costs involved. For example, the work may be described generally as "dissolution of marriage," and the attorney's fee may also include a description of the hourly fee for any work done by paralegals or other attorneys in the firm. Usually the client will be asked to make a lump-sum payment to the attorney up-front upon signing the retainer agreement. The hourly fees, and any costs, will be paid from the lump sum.

The possible costs involved could include filing a petition or complaint with the court clerk, as well as paying for the services of a court reporter, accountant, or experts. The terms **petition** and **complaint** both refer to the initial pleading in a legal case, but some states use one term or the other. A complaint is the first main paper filed in a civil lawsuit. It includes, among other things, a statement of the wrong or harm done to the plaintiff by the defendant, a request for specific help from the court, and an explanation of why the court has the power to do what the plaintiff wants. The **court clerk** is the official responsible for filing all court papers, scheduling court appearances, and the general running of the local county or circuit court. A **court reporter** is a person trained to input verbal statements into a machine that then allows the court reporter to transcribe the statements into a written document. **Experts** are persons who are highly trained in their particular field and are utilized by attorneys to supply information pertaining to the case and to testify on behalf of clients. For example, mental health professionals are often hired when there is a custody dispute.

All 50 states prohibit a contingency fee arrangement in family law matters. A **contingency fee** arrangement is defined as an attorney's fee based upon the amount won by the attorney's client from the opposing party at the successful conclusion of the case. A contingency fee arrangement is not typically allowed in family law matters, as it is thought that such a payment arrangement could encourage an adversarial relationship between the parties.

Once the retainer and financial matters are dealt with, the next step is to create a client file. This would also be a good time to input the new client's name into the firm's client roster.

Creating a Client File

Creating a client file is usually called *opening a file.* This may sound simple, but the importance of efficiently opening a client file cannot be underestimated. The word *opening* is used to describe the process of setting up a new client's office file. Following the official opening of the new client file, every member of the firm, from senior partner to receptionist, should be able to pick up that file and find whatever they need within its contents.

Each firm has its own particular way of organizing client files. When client files are organized in the same way, any member of the law firm staff can pick up the file and immediately know where certain items are located. For example, a case file folder may be divided into parts consisting of the correspondence, pleadings and motions, discovery—including interrogatories, deposition transcripts, and produced documents, plus a section for orders, agreements and judgments, memorandums of law, case notes, and exhibits. Each attorney within a firm may also have particular methods of organizing files that the staff will follow.

The **pleadings** are the initial case documents filed with the court, for example, the complaint and answer, or the petition and response. The **answer** or **response** is defined as the first pleading by the defendant in a lawsuit. A **motion** is a request that a judge make a ruling or take some other action.

The **discovery** section consists of any information gathered during the investigation stage of the case. For example, produced documents could include financial records and expert reports. **Interrogatories** are written questions sent from one side in a lawsuit to the other, attempting to get written answers to factual questions or seeking an explanation of the other side's legal contentions. A **deposition transcript** is the written record of a **deposition,** which is a process whereby attorneys for both parties have an opportunity to ask the opposing party and any witnesses supporting the opposing party's case questions under oath.

An **agreement** is an intention of two or more persons to enter into a contract with one another combined with an attempt to form a valid contract.

An **order** is a written command of direction given by a judge. A *judgment* is the official decision of a court about the rights and claims of each side in a lawsuit. A *memorandum of law* (memo of law) is a legal analysis of the case. It may be used only by the firm to analyze the merits of the case, or it may also be written for submission to the court in support of a motion. An **exhibit** is any object or document offered and marked as evidence in a trial, hearing, or deposition. An exhibit can also be attached to a pleading or other formal paper.

The outside of the file should have the client's name, address, and telephone and fax numbers. It should also have the name, address, and numbers of either the opposing counsel or the *pro se* opposition. **Pro se** is Latin and is defined as "for self." A *pro se* party is not represented by an attorney, but rather represents himself.

STARTING A CASE

The legal document that initiates all lawsuits, regardless of subject matter, is the complaint. The purpose of the complaint is basically what it sounds like it would be: to list the problems that the **plaintiff,** the initiator of the lawsuit, has with the **defendant,** the person who is being sued. Some states use the terms **petitioner** and **respondent** instead of *plaintiff* and *defendant.*

If the complaint involves a request for a divorce, the problems listed cannot be just a litany of annoying habits. Although hanging hosiery in the tub or leaving the seat up on the toilet may be incredibly annoying to some, those problems do not rise to the legal level of sustaining a legitimate cause of action. A **cause of action** is the legal reason the request was made by the plaintiff. All 50 states have statutes that list the allowable causes of action that can be used by a plaintiff who is requesting a divorce or dissolution of marriage in a particular state. A *divorce* or *dissolution of marriage* is defined as the ending of a marriage by court order. For example, let us review the reasons a California resident can request the end of a marriage. California uses the term *dissolution.* The allowable causes of action for dissolution of marriage or legal separation include: *(a) Irreconcilable differences, which have caused the irremediable breakdown of the marriage; or (b) incurable insanity.*[4] A *legal separation* is official recognition of a couple's intention to no longer live as man and wife, but to do so without legally ending the marriage. *Irreconcilable differences* are those grounds that are determined by the court to be substantial reasons for not continuing the marriage and that make it appear that the marriage should be dissolved. So, a plaintiff in California would have to list either reason (a) or (b) in the complaint as the reason the plaintiff wants a dissolution of marriage to be granted by a court.

Proper Service Required

You have read that a lawsuit is initiated by a plaintiff by the filing of the complaint with the court clerk. The complaint is filed along with a paper called a *summons.* The summons should list the defendant's name, residence, and, often, place of employment. The summons, along with a copy of the complaint, is usually given by the court clerk to a sheriff's officer or *process server.* For a fee, which varies depending on the distance traveled, the sheriff's officer or process server is to personally give a copy of the complaint and summons to the defendant. This serving of the defendant is known as **service of process.** The summons is actually *summoning* the defendant to court to answer the claims made by the plaintiff in the complaint.

The defendant has three options after being properly served. The defendant's options are as follows: (1) file an answer, (2) file an appearance, or (3) ignore the complaint. The first two options get the case rolling. Alternatively, defendants may sign a waiver of service when they are given a copy of a complaint. The waiver of service is often used in amicable divorces. It saves the expense of paying for formally serving the defendant. The defendant may still respond to the plaintiff's complaint by denying all or some of the statements made by the plaintiff in the complaint. The **waiver of service** is an acknowledgment by the defendant, or the defendant's attorney, that she has received the complaint and agrees to the court's jurisdiction without requiring the official service of process.

The responding document to the complaint is the answer. The answer is a legal pleading that responds to each allegation made by the plaintiff. Instead of filing an answer, a second option is to file what is generally known as an appearance. The **appearance** is a document that allows the defendant to recognize that the complaint has been served and that there is no real disagreement by the defendant with what is stated within the complaint. The defendant can also file a **counterclaim** along with the answer. For example, suppose a plaintiff filed for a divorce based on mental cruelty and demanded alimony and the marital home in the complaint. The defendant could file an answer that included a counterclaim asking for a divorce based on the plaintiff's adultery and also asking for marital home. The third option is to ignore the complaint. Failure to file an answer will end with a default judgment being entered against the defendant. A **default judgment** is defined as the result of failing to take a required step in a lawsuit.

WHICH COURT HAS PROPER JURISDICTION?

The majority of the 50 states are split into counties with county court systems that use various names for their trial level courts, for example, superior court, district court, and circuit court. New York's trial court is called the Supreme Court, while Ohio and Pennsylvania call theirs the Court of Common Pleas. Arkansas, Mississippi, and Tennessee use the name Chancery Court. In some states, family matters may be heard in state courts called Family Court or Domestic Relations Court.

County courts have jurisdiction to hear cases involving parties who reside within the county, to hear cases involving property located within the county, and to hear all legal disputes that originate within the county. The Latin term for a court's jurisdiction over a person is *in personam* **jurisdiction.** The Latin term for a court's jurisdiction over property is *in rem* **jurisdiction.**

A county with a large population usually has a correspondingly large number of judges who work in the county court system. The judges may be split among several areas of the law. Certain judges may hear only family matters. Counties with smaller populations usually have a correspondingly smaller number of judges who hear every type of case filed in the county court system.

The act of serving the summons upon the defendant gives the court *in personam* jurisdiction over the defendant because he has been properly notified that he is being sued. If a court has *in personam* jurisdiction, then the court has the authority to hear a case involving a defendant. The court can make decisions involving the defendant and can also punish the defendant for failing to appear in court if the defendant has been ordered by the court to appear. Punishment for failing to appear when ordered can involve a judge issuing a **bench warrant,** which is an order by a judge to have the party named in the bench warrant picked up by the police and brought before the judge for punishment. Punishment could mean time in the county jail or monetary fines.

For most divorcing spouses, the question of what court has proper jurisdiction to hear the divorce case is relatively simple. For example, when both parties and the children reside in the same county, the local county court will hear the matter. Unfortunately, jurisdictional issues are not always that simple.

Dealing with Jurisdictional Difficulties

Sometimes a party attempts to file a case in a county or state that neither party involved in the dispute lives in, or where the dispute in question has no reasonable connection. Why would anyone want to file a case with a court that has little or no connection to the legal dispute? The filing party may be trying to find a judge or another state that is more sympathetic to the filing party's legal position. The act of one party searching for a more sympathetic court is known as **forum shopping.** In the American legal system, forum shopping is not permitted. Another reason may be that the filing party is trying to make it more difficult for the defendant to efficiently respond to the plaintiff's complaint by keeping the defendant away from witnesses and making it more expensive for the defendant to mount a defense.

When a case is filed in what appears to be an inappropriate court system, two things can happen. The judge hearing the matter may make a self-initiated determination that the parties are in the wrong court system due to a lack of proper jurisdiction, or the defendant in the case can present a motion to the judge hearing the matter to ask that the case be dismissed because the court lacks proper jurisdiction.

Necessary Information

Most states require a **case information statement (CIS)** to be attached to every complaint and answer filed in the state. The amount of information required differs with the type of case. For example, the case information statement for a divorce can be an incredibly detailed run-down of the plaintiff's and defendant's financial budget. Such a statement may be called a **financial affidavit** by some states. This financial information should provide the judge assigned the case with enough information to determine what the financial needs of the parties are both temporarily and in the long term. You should always look to your state's court rules to ascertain the state's requirements.

Docket Numbers

The act of filing a complaint with a court system results in a **docket number,** sometimes called a **case number** or a **calendar number** by some states, being assigned to the case. The docket number is the case's identifier within the court system where it was filed. Like fingerprints are to people, there should not be a duplicate number.

SUSAN'S FIRST DAY ON THE JOB

"So, as I was saying, this is Ms. Jensen's office, and this is Mr. Dombroski's office," Andrea announced, as she motioned a manicured hand to the left and right of the spacious paneled corridor.

Since this was her first day at Johnson & Webster, Susan was being given the grand tour by Andrea, the office manager. Andrea continued, "As you know, you'll be working exclusively with Ms. Jensen and Mr. Dombroski on their family law cases."

A response did not seem necessary, so Susan just nodded and hoped she did not look like one of those toy dogs in the back of her dad's Buick. "Now, let me think," Andrea said, still managing to look elegant while chewing on the tip of a pen, "I don't think I forgot anyone." She continued, "You've met the secretaries, the other paralegals, except for Pat who is on vacation, the partners, the associates who are in the office this morning, and, of course, you met Ms. Jensen and Mr. Dombroski during your interview." Susan knew that the partners were attorneys who had an ownership interest in the firm. The associates were also attorneys and were employed by the law firm.

Susan had patiently waited to see her office for the last hour and now hesitantly said, "I haven't seen where I'll be working."

Andrea chewed on her pen a bit more and then, stifling a nervous giggle, announced, "I was afraid that would come up. The truth is, your help is really needed here in the office immediately, but the office space hasn't quite grown with the firm." She added, "It's only temporary; we'll be moving early next year."

Andrea and Susan walked down the carpeted corridor and stopped at a closed door at the rear of the office near the small office kitchen. Andrea opened the door and a broom promptly fell out. This was not that surprising, since the new office had been the broom closet until that morning. Looking slightly embarrassed, Andrea picked up the broom and firmly said, "I promise it will look a lot better after the painters finally get here, and we figure out how to squeeze a desk in here." Seeing the disappointment on Susan's face, Andrea tried to comfort her by adding, "Look on the bright side. No one else's office has a utility sink!"

"Where will I work until the painting is done?" Susan politely inquired.

Andrea answered, "The library. It's big and sunny and all yours until we get this admitted mess up to speed." She gently asked, "Okay?"

Placated, Susan smiled and said, "Okay."

Walking together toward the library, Andrea and Susan encountered Ms. Jensen. "You're back from court already?" Andrea asked Ms. Jensen.

"A very quick motion and back in the office before 10:30 A.M. works for me," Alyssa Jensen announced. Turning to Susan, she continued, "Hi, glad to see you again, and welcome to Johnson & Webster." She offered her hand to Susan.

Shaking hands, Susan answered, "Thank you for the opportunity, Ms. Jensen."

Alyssa responded, "Please, call me Alyssa. We don't stand on formality around here." Alyssa thanked Andrea for showing Susan around the office and asked, "So, Susan, are you ready to start working?"

"Absolutely!" was Susan's eager response.

Andrea smiled and said, "You seem to be all set, so I'll get back to work. Just stop by my office to fill out your benefits form before you leave today."

"Thanks, Andrea," Susan responded, "I'll see you later."

Susan promptly gave Alyssa her undivided attention as Alyssa began, "Now, as we told you during your interview, J. D. and I—that's J. D. Dombroski—share most of our cases. That way one of us can always cover for the other." Looking at Susan, Alyssa explained, "J. D. is at a deposition this morning and asked me to get you started on a **notice of motion.** We will need a Notice of Motion and Application for *Pendente Lite* Relief as soon as possible."

Searching her memory, Susan recalled that a support *pendente lite* application was defined as a request to the court for temporary support while the final judgment for divorce was pending and that a certification would have to be prepared as well. The certification would consist of the client's statement and signature attesting to the truth of the statement. Alyssa continued, "We're representing Mrs. Gladys Vander in her divorce, but she needs immediate temporary support from her husband. We'll also need a **certification of plaintiff** and an order. Do you think you can prepare a Certification of Plaintiff in Support of the *Pendente Lite* Motion and an Order?" Alyssa asked.

"I'll do my best," Susan nervously responded, wondering how on earth she was going to prepare the documents.

Susan regained her composure when Alyssa nonchalantly mentioned that the Miller file had a good sample *pendente lite* package to work from while preparing the Vander documents. The audible sigh of relief escaping from Susan's lips made Alyssa smile and say, "Please ask all the questions you need to, and especially, remind J. D. and me to give you samples for the work we ask you to do. Is that a deal?"

Susan returned the smile and answered with relief, "That's a deal."

Susan Gets Up Close and Personal with Her First Motion

Later that same day, Susan was putting the finishing touches on her first real motion for a Johnson & Webster client when Alyssa sauntered into the library. "I thought I'd pop my head in to see how things are going," Alyssa said while eating a protein bar. "Sorry about the munching, but it's 3:30 P.M., and this is my lunch."

Anxious, but pleased to have finished, Susan said, "Perfect timing. I'm just finished and ready for you. It took longer than I expected, since I'm getting used to the computer network here."

"No problem," Alyssa responded, "Let's give it a look and see what you did."

Susan Produces Documents

You can read a typical Notice of Motion and Application for *Pendente Lite* Relief in Exhibit 1.1. The Certification of Plaintiff in Support of the *Pendente Lite* Motion can be read in Exhibit 1.2. Finally, the Order for *Pendente Lite* Relief can be read in Exhibit 1.3. The documents Susan prepared for Mrs. Vander are provided because you will very likely be required to prepare similar documents for your future clients. Remember, the temporary support documents might be called by different names in your state, and you will have to strictly follow the specific court rules of your state when preparing all legal documents.

Susan Receives Feedback on Her Work

"It looks like they are all ready to go," Alyssa remarked. "Writing your first real motion is always a little scary. I'm pleased to see you produced some excellent documents."

Relieved, Susan responded, "Well, the best thing was being given some sample documents to work from."

Nodding in agreement, Alyssa said, "I always say, there's no use reinventing the wheel every time you write something. We'd never get things done on time or make any money!" She added, "You can call Mrs. Vander and have her come in to sign the documents."

Nodding her head, Susan answered, "Right away."

DISCOVERY

As previously discussed, the process of gathering information to support your client's case is called the discovery phase. It can involve interrogatories, demands for production, depositions, experts, private investigators, and anything else that assists an attorney with the preparation of her case.

The First Step in Discovery

The first step in discovery is usually the preparation of interrogatories. Interrogatories are written questions sent from one side in a lawsuit to another. They attempt to get written answers to factual questions or an explanation of the other side's legal contentions. The interrogatories are prepared by the attorney for each party, and then sent to the opposing party's attorney, who then answers them with his clients. In your role as a paralegal, you can be extremely helpful in assisting attorneys with both the preparation of interrogatories to be sent to the opposition, and the gathering of information needed to answer interrogatories received from opposing parties.

Typically, a law firm will have a set of standard interrogatories that are always used for each type of case. In a divorce case, name, address, employment status, salary, and retirement benefits information is always requested in the interrogatories. Usually, additional interrogatories are also created that apply to the specific facts of a particular case. For example, what if your client's husband runs a cash business, and she knows that he makes more money than he will admit to her—or to the Internal Revenue Service? Questioning your client's spouse on the amount of business equipment owned, workers employed, and expenses he manages to pay, versus the profit he will admit to, will be of great help in tracking down net profit figures.

Usually, the answers to interrogatories received from the opposition are not completely satisfactory. The opposition may not have completely answered the interrogatories as requested, or may have refused to answer certain interrogatories. There must be a legally valid reason for refusing to respond, or only partially responding, to interrogatories. Some legally valid reasons for not answering interrogatories include: (1) the

---

EXHIBIT 1.1 Notice of Motion
and Application for *Pendente Lite* Relief

J. D. Dombroski, Esq.
Johnson & Webster, Esqs.
123 Main Street
Newton, New Jersey 12345
973-555-1212
Attorney for Plaintiff

GLADYS VANDER,	) SUPERIOR COURT OF NEW JERSEY
	) CHANCERY DIVISION-FAMILY PART
Plaintiff,	) SUSSEX COUNTY
	) Docket No. FM-19-12345-03
v.	) CIVIL ACTION
	)
HEINRICK VANDER,	) NOTICE OF MOTION AND
	) APPLICATION FOR *PENDENTE LITE*
	) RELIEF
Defendant.	)
	)

TO: Max Justice, Esq.
102 Legal Lane
Newton, New Jersey 07860
Attorney for Defendant

SIR:

    PLEASE TAKE NOTICE that on Tuesday, April 24, 2004, at 9:00 A.M. or as soon thereafter as counsel may be heard, the undersigned attorney for the plaintiff shall move before the Honorable Judge Comfort, Superior Court of New Jersey, Chancery Division, Family Part, Sussex County, at the Courthouse in Newton, New Jersey, for an order:

1. Requiring defendant to pay a reasonable amount for the *pendente lite* support and maintenance of the plaintiff and the minor children born of the marriage, namely, Albert Vander and Rena Vander, ages 9 and 5, respectively.
2. Directing defendant to maintain medical insurance *pendente lite* for the plaintiff and the children and requiring defendant to be responsible for all medical, dental, hospital, and prescription drug expenses.
3. Requiring defendant to maintain life insurance on his life, with the plaintiff named as beneficiary, in the amount of $150,000.
4. Restraining defendant from selling any assets pending final determination of this matter.
5. For counsel fees and costs of this application.
6. For such further relief as the Court may deem equitable and just.

PLEASE TAKE FURTHER NOTICE that annexed hereto is a certification in support hereof.

PLEASE TAKE FURTHER NOTICE that annexed hereto is a form of Order pursuant to R. 1:6-2.

PLEASE TAKE FURTHER NOTICE that oral argument with regard to this motion is requested, given the nature of the relief sought and the complexity of the issues involved.

                                    By: _____
                                             J. D. Dombroski, Esq.
                                           Attorney for Plaintiff

DATED: April 10, 2004

The undersigned hereby certifies that the within pleading was signed within the time permitted by the rules.

_____
J. D. Dombroski, Esq.

EXHIBIT 1.2 Certification of Plaintiff in Support of *Pendente Lite* Motion

J. D. Dombroski, Esq.
Johnson & Webster, Esqs.
123 Main Street
Newton, New Jersey 12345
973-555-1212
Attorney for Plaintiff

GLADYS VANDER,
 	
               Plaintiff,
 	
v.
 	
HEINRICK VANDER,
 	
               Defendant.
	)
	)
	)
	)
	)
	)
	)
	)
	)
	)
	)
	)
	)
	)
		SUPERIOR COURT OF NEW JERSEY
		CHANCERY DIVISION-FAMILY PART
		SUSSEX COUNTY
		Docket No. FM-19-12345-03
		CIVIL ACTION
		
		CERTIFICATION OF PLAINTIFF IN
		SUPPORT OF *PENDENTE LITE*
		MOTION

I , Gladys Vander, do hereby certify that:

1. I am the plaintiff in the foregoing action.

2. I reside at 13 Main Street, Newton, New Jersey. The defendant resides at 19 First Street, Sparta, New Jersey.

3. The marriage between the defendant and me took place on June 6, 1990.

4. There were two children born of the marriage: Albert Vander, born July 19, 1995, aged 9, and Rena Vander, born October 24, 1998, aged 5, both of whom are presently in my custody.

5. I am presently unemployed, and I have been unemployed throughout the marriage.

6. The defendant is presently employed by Lewton Trust Company, as Accounts Receivable Officer, and earns approximately $65,000 per year.

7. My age is 40 years, and the age of the defendant is 42 years.

8. The major asset of the marriage is the marital residence, which was purchased in 1990 for $150,000 with a down payment of $30,000, and which I now estimate is worth $175,000. The only other major assets are two automobiles, one of which is worth $16,000 with an outstanding loan of $8,000, and the other of which is worth $2,000; both are driven only by the defendant and myself.

9. I am presently living in the marital residence with the unemancipated children of the marriage and need funds from the defendant in order to provide the basic necessities for the children and myself. Since the time that the defendant separated himself from me on November 1, 2002, he has been voluntarily paying the sum of $300 per week, has been maintaining the life insurance offered through employment in the approximate amount of $150,000, and continues to name me as the beneficiary. The defendant also continues to maintain the medical insurance offered through his employment for the children and me.

10. I have paid my attorney, J. D. Dombroski, the sum of $2,000 as and for a retainer against his fees based on $200 per hour plus disbursements.

11. A budget form listing the monthly expenses for the children and myself is attached to the Case Information Statement filed herewith.

12. The allegations of the complaint are made part hereof and incorporated herein as if set forth at length herein.

13. This certification is made in support of my application for *pendente lite* relief.

14. I certify that the foregoing statements made by me are true. I am aware that if any of the foregoing statements made by me are willfully false, I am subject to punishment.

                                                                _____
                                                                   Gladys Vander

DATED: April 30, 2004

EXHIBIT 1.3 Order for *Pendente Lite* Relief

J. D. Dombroski, Esq.
Johnson & Webster, Esqs.
123 Main Street
Newton, New Jersey 12345
973-555-1212
Attorney for Plaintiff

GLADYS VANDER,	) SUPERIOR COURT OF NEW JERSEY
	) CHANCERY DIVISION-FAMILY PART
Plaintiff,	) SUSSEX COUNTY
	) Docket No. FM-19-12345-03
v.	) CIVIL ACTION
	)
HEINRICK VANDER,	)
	) ORDER FOR *PENDENTE LITE*
	) RELIEF
Defendant.	)
	)

This matter having come to the attention of the court of April 24, 2004, on application of the plaintiff, J. D. Dombroski, Esq., attorney for plaintiff, and in the presence of counsel for the defendant, Max Justice, Esq., and the court having read the papers filed on behalf of the respective parties, and the court having heard argument of counsel, and the court having considered same and for good cause shown:

It is, on this 30th day of April, 2004,

ORDERED, as follows:

(1)   That the plaintiff shall have temporary custody of the unemancipated children of the marriage, subject to the liberal and reasonable visitation rights by the defendant, the exact times and dates to be determined between the parties;

(2)   That the defendant shall pay to the plaintiff the sum of $450 per week, effective as the 24th day of April, 2004, which sum shall be unallocated alimony and child support;

(3)   That the payments required shall be made through the Sussex County Probation Department in accordance with the rules and procedures established therefore, and further that two copies of the within order shall immediately be filed by the attorney for the plaintiff with the said probation office, together with information concerning the addresses of both the parties and their telephone numbers and the place of employment of the defendant;

(4)   That the defendant shall continue to maintain such medical insurance and life insurance as is offered through his employment, without change of beneficiary or other status thereof, and, in addition thereto, the defendant shall be responsible for all reasonable and necessary medical expenses not covered by the insurance on the plaintiff and the une mancipated children of the marriage, provided that the plaintiff shall not incur any such medical expenses in excess of $200 per injury, incident, or illness, without first giving notice to the defendant, giving him an opportunity to investigate the necessity therefore and the reasonableness of the proposed cost thereof, except in cases of emergency;

(5)   That the defendant shall pay to J. D. Dombroski, Esq., attorney for the plaintiff, a *pendente lite* counsel fee in the sum of $1,000 within 5 days of the entry thereof.

_____
S. Comfort, J.S.C.

The undersigned hereby consents to the
form of the within order.

_____
Max Justice, Esq.
Attorney for Defendant

question is too burdensome to answer; (2) the information is irrelevant to the action; (3) the information requested intrudes upon the attorney-client privilege; or (4) the information is unknown to the party.

An attorney who receives incomplete answers to interrogatories generally has three options: (1) accept the answers as received; (2) again request that the interrogatories be answered; or (3) submit a motion to the court asking that the court intervene and order that the original interrogatories be answered.

Motions Take Practice

A motion is a request for a judge to take some action. For example, suppose you have sent interrogatories to the opposing party's attorney, but no answers have been sent back to you within the time allowed by your state's court rules. You ask for them once more, but again, no response. The next step would be to file a motion asking the court to order that the interrogatories be answered. The motion must be sent both to the court and to the opposing attorney. The opposing attorney then has a certain number of days to respond to the motion, depending on the court rules in that state. The response is an opportunity for the opposing attorney to explain why the interrogatories were not answered, or were answered less than satisfactorily. The response to the motion must then be filed with the court, and a copy sent to the attorney who filed the motion. The attorney who filed the original motion then has a certain number of days, determined by his particular state's court rules, to file a response to the initial response. The two attorneys ultimately have an opportunity to orally argue their motion and responses before a judge in open court.

Alternatively, the attorneys can request that the issue be decided by the judge solely *on the papers*. In other words, the judge can make a decision by reading the documents filed with the court without oral argument by the attorneys. Either way, the result will be an order issued by the judge in favor of one of the parties.

Failure to comply with any order can result in **sanctions** by the court. For example, the judge could ultimately dismiss a case, order fines paid, or sanction an attorney for failing to adhere to an order.

Produce Documents or Else

Another method of gathering information is to send a formal request for documents to the opposing party's attorney. This formal request for documents is generally known as a Demand for Production of Documents. This demand may sound deceptively simple, but remember, in a hotly contested matter, the opposing party's attorney often refuses to comply with such a demand.

As with the refusal to answer interrogatories, attorneys can refuse to produce requested documents for several legally valid reasons. The most common reasons used include: (1) providing such documents would take so much effort it would be unduly burdensome; (2) the documents are not in the party's possession or under the party's control; (3) the documents requested intrude upon the attorney-client privilege; and (4) the documents are the result of the attorney's work on the case and come under the attorney work-product privilege. The **attorney-client privilege** is defined as the right of a client, and the duty of that client's lawyer, to keep confidential the contents of almost all communication between them. Exceptions may include discussions of possible future crimes and discussions knowingly held in front of others. The **attorney work-product privilege** is defined as the principle that a lawyer need not show the other side in a case any facts or things gathered for the case, unless the other side can convince the judge that it would be unjust for these things to remain hidden and that there is a special need for them.

Again, as with the motion in response to the opposing party's refusal to answer interrogatories, the attorney can file a motion with the court in response to the opposing party's refusal to produce documents. The result of a Motion for Production of Documents being filed with the court is either the issuance of an order demanding the production of the requested documents, or an order denying the request for the documents.

The Deposition Process: On the Record

Once interrogatories and demands for production have been exchanged, the next step is usually the scheduling of depositions. The purpose of depositions was discussed earlier in this chapter. Even though most depositions are held in one of the attorney's offices, remember that the testimony is given under oath and on the record. Every word of testimony is recorded by a court reporter. The court reporter is usually hired by the attorney who has requested the deposition. The court reporter takes the oath of any party and witnesses who testify and also prepares a deposition transcript, which is the word-for-word testimony of the individuals who are deposed.

The paralegal often gets involved with the deposition both before and after the fact. Before the deposition, a paralegal can provide significant assistance by drafting an outline of questions and identifying exhibits. Once the deposition transcript is sent to the attorney, a paralegal may be given the job of creating a **deposition summary.** A deposition summary is created by picking out pertinent testimony and summarizing it line by line for the trial attorney. In order to facilitate this process, each sentence in the deposition transcript is numbered. Review Exhibit 1.4, which shows part of a deposition transcript.

The Truth and Nothing But?

The sample deposition transcript in Exhibit 1.4 involves Mrs. Julie Jones, the defendant-wife in a divorce complaint, and J. D. Dombroski, the plaintiff-husband's attorney. Following is a brief summary of the facts. Mr. Bobby Jones has been home taking care of the Jones' children and has not worked outside the home for several years, while Mrs. Jones has been working to keep up with the proverbial Smiths. Mr. Jones wants a share of Mrs. Jones's business or, at the very least, a substantial amount of alimony until he can be retrained in a lucrative field. The problem is that Mrs. Jones claimed in her interrogatories that she grosses approximately $100 per day in her hair salon business. J. D., Mr. Jones's attorney, will try during Mrs. Jones's deposition to lead her to admit to having a higher income than what she has claimed.

As shown by the partial deposition transcript in Exhibit 1.4, Mr. Dombroski has now taken Mrs. Jones to a point where her interrogatories say one thing, but her testimony says another. Mrs. Jones has claimed that she makes $100 per day, and has also testified that she sees at least eight clients per day. Do the math. Mrs. Jones must be making more than $100 per day. Depending on the attorney's evaluation of the situation, he may call Mrs. Jones on the discrepancy right there during the deposition, or he may wait to spring it on her in court if the case goes to trial. The benefit of waiting is that Mrs. Jones would look less than truthful while explaining her income in the witness box.

THE TRIAL PROCESS

Most cases filed in the United States do not conclude with a trial. Rather, a huge majority of cases are settled between the parties without the help of a judge. Although most family law cases are settled before reaching the trial stage, it is still necessary for a family law paralegal to know each of the steps in a trial in order to assist the attorney and client. Some attorneys believe in preparing every case as if it were going to trial. This may not always be feasible in a busy office, but it is a good goal for which to reach.

The Judge Hears the Case

When a case does go to trial, a trial judge, without a jury, will hear most family law cases. Everything else about a family law trial is similar to other civil trials. The lack of a jury usually means somewhat less dramatic presentations by the participating attorneys.

EXHIBIT 1.4 The Julie Jones Deposition

1. Mr. Dombroski: Mrs. Jones, you wrote in your interrogatories that you run the Julie Jones Hair Salon and Scalp Massage Parlor. Are you sole owner of your business?
2. Mrs. Jones: Yes, I am.
3. Mr. Dombroski: How many hair clients do you see per day?
4. Mrs. Jones: On average, I see eight clients per day for haircuts or styles or perms, and maybe two for scalp massages.
5. Mr. Dombroski: What are your service fees?
6. Mrs. Jones: Do you want to know *all* the fees?
7. Mr. Dombroski: Yes, I do.
8. Mrs. Jones: Well, all right, but it's a long list. For example, haircuts range in price from $26 to $45, perms are $60, coloring can be anywhere from $35 to $64, a wash and set without blow dry can be $25 Chair massages are $10 for 15 minutes.
9. Mr. Dombroski: You answered your interrogatories yourself?
10. Mrs. Jones: Absolutely. Yes.
11. Mr. Dombroski: The last page of your interrogatory packet was a certification. Do you recall this last page?
12. Mrs. Jones: Yes.
13. Mr. Dombroski: In fact, do you recall this certification in the interrogatories stating that you would *tell the truth, the whole truth in the interrogatories, and nothing but the truth, so help you God?*
14. Mrs. Jones: Yes.
15. Mr. Dombroski: I'm showing you the certification page with what appears to be your signature. Is this your signature, Mrs. Jones?
16. Mrs. Jones: Yes, that's my signature.

Pretrial Work

The attorneys will usually begin with *pretrial hearings,* also known as *pretrial conferences.* This type of hearing or conference is a meeting of the lawyers and the judge to narrow the issues in a lawsuit, agree on what will be presented at the trial, and make a final effort to settle the case without a trial. For example, the defendant's attorney may wish certain evidence to be admitted to the trial, and the plaintiff's attorney may want the evidence blocked. The judge can make a determination during a pretrial hearing. This determination can also be made during the trial, but it will interrupt the flow of the trial.

Road Map of the Case

The plaintiff presents his case first. The plaintiff's attorney begins the trial with an opening statement. The **opening statement** is an outline for what will be presented during the trial and what the plaintiff hopes to prove. The defendant's attorney then follows the plaintiff's attorney with the defense's opening statement. The defense paints a picture of what evidence it will present during the trial.

Following the opening statements, the plaintiff calls witnesses to the stand. For example, the witnesses in a divorce case can range from the parties themselves, to the parties' children, to experts hired for their expertise. Such experts could include an accountant to analyze a couple's finances, or a psychologist to evaluate their suitability for child custody. Experts are usually deposed outside the courtroom prior to their testifying at trial in order to familiarize opposing counsel with the experts' opinions. They also usually write their opinions in written reports that are exchanged between the attorneys prior to their depositions. However, when there is a serious dispute between the parties, the judge may appoint additional experts to analyze a couple's finances, or an additional psychologist to evaluate their suitability for child custody. Additional experts mean more financial costs to the parties.

Usually, both the plaintiff and the defendant will have witnesses whose testimony will help support their cases. Remember, some states use the terms *petitioner* and *respondent* instead of *plaintiff* and *defendant.* During the plaintiff's presentation, the plaintiff's attorney will ask questions of witnesses, aiming for testimony beneficial to the plaintiff's case. The process of the plaintiff's attorney asking such beneficial questions is called **direct examination.** Following direct examination, the defendant's attorney then has an opportunity to ask questions of the same witnesses.

The process of the defendant's attorney asking questions of the plaintiff is called **cross-examination.** The main point of cross-examination is to lessen the impact of a witness's direct examination. For example, Exhibit 1.4 provides the part of a deposition transcript that involves the income of Mrs. Jones, a defendant in a divorce case. Mrs. Jones's attorney may ask Mrs. Jones questions regarding her income during his direct examination. The plaintiff's attorney may recognize the discrepancies between the income testified to at trial, testified to at the deposition, and provided by Mrs. Jones in her interrogatories. These discrepancies should lead the plaintiff's attorney, upon cross-examination of Mrs. Jones, to question the truthfulness of all of Mrs. Jones's testimony.

The cross-examination is followed by an opportunity for the plaintiff's attorney to ask **re-direct** questions, which are designed to lessen any negative impact the cross-examination may have had upon the plaintiff's case. Re-direct is followed by **re-cross** by the defendant's attorney. It can be described as a last shot at questioning the plaintiff. All of these steps are then repeated in the opposite order for the defendant's case.

Finally, both parties take turns at presenting a closing argument. The closing arguments are supposed to review the entire case and explain how the testimony and evidence presented clearly provide reasons for the court to decide the case in favor of one of the parties.

It's Not Over Until the Judge Decides

Following the defendant's closing, the family law judge will conclude the trial and take the time she needs to review the testimony. When the judge is ready to announce her decision, she has her bailiff call the parties and their attorneys into the courtroom—or, alternatively, the decision is given in a written opinion to the parties. The decision may come hours, days, or even weeks after the last day of the trial.

The judge then signs what is known as a *final order* or, in some states, a *final judgment.* The order is filed with the court clerk, and then the case is officially closed.

Post-Judgment Matters: All Said and Done?

Post-judgment activities can also be a significant part of a law practice. You are probably wondering how a *final* judgment can be changed without going through the appeals process. After all, the issuing of a final judgment usually means the end of the case, unless an appeal is undertaken. However, a judge's final judgment in a divorce case is never really final when spousal support, child support, and child custody are part of the mix.

Generally, support and custody issues can be revisited and changed at a later date if there has been a significant change in circumstances or certain facts were not known to the court at the time of the final judgment. Requesting such a change is known as requesting a **modification.** For example, a client who has changed jobs and now makes much less income than when the original judgment was signed may attempt to modify the judgment downward by filing a motion for modification. On the other hand, if the paying parent is now making more money, the receiving parent may want to return to court for a recalculation upward. You will read much more about modifications in the chapters on divorce and separation, child custody, and child support.

WEAVING ETHICS INTO YOUR WORKDAY

The professional lives of attorneys and paralegals/legal assistants are guided by rules of professional conduct. These include rules created by the group or organization that has jurisdiction over such matters in each state. Typically, a state's bar association or an arm of state government (e.g., the judiciary) has jurisdiction over the behavior of attorneys and their staffs. State rules of professional conduct are usually based upon the American Bar Association's Model Rules of Professional Conduct, as well as requirements of each state's judicial system and legislature.

Paralegals may find additional guidance in the ethical codes promulgated by the National Federation of Paralegal Associations (NFPA) and the National Association of Legal Assistants (NALA). Numerous national and state organizations have been created to foster professionalism and the exchange of information for practicing paralegals and paralegal students. The *Model Standards and Guidelines for the Utilization of Legal Assistants* (Model Standards) produced by NALA is just one example of ethical guidelines available for the paralegal. Another example is the NFPA's *Model Code of Ethics and Professional Responsibility* (Model Code). You should be aware that the Model Standards and the Model Code are not codified law but, rather, are intended to outline for the paralegal professional a suggested course of acceptable conduct. The Model Standards and Model Code provide detailed descriptions of how the services of paralegals/legal assistants may be best utilized.

You have already read the ABA's definition of a paralegal/legal assistant at the beginning of this chapter. If you are studying this material in college, you are probably fulfilling the educational requirements suggested by NALA. You can learn about NALA's educational requirements by reading the Model Standards in Appendix B. Another section of the Model Standards that will probably be of great interest to all working paralegals covers the duties that paralegals should be allowed to undertake. The "Surfing the Web" section at the end of this chapter includes several Web sites for state and national paralegal organizations.

At the end of each chapter of this text, a section entitled "Ethics Alert" is presented. These sections describe situations involving Susan, clients, or Susan's coworkers at the Johnson & Webster law firm. You may want to refer to the Model Standards when answering the questions in these sections about ethical dilemmas that Susan must face.

CHAPTER SUMMARY

A paralegal, also called a legal assistant, is defined by the ABA as *a person qualified by education, training or work experience, who is employed or retained by a lawyer, law office, corporation, governmental agency or other entity and who performs delegated substantive legal work for which a lawyer is responsible.*[5]

Preparing for your career at your first family law firm can begin with preparation for the interview process while you are still in school. As a paralegal student, you should keep copies of your coursework and make corrections to that work product as suggested by your instructors. Preparing a portfolio of your best work may convince a prospective employer that you are the right person to hire.

Once you have landed a position with a family law practice, you will quickly learn that you will play a large role in the success of the law firm. Your professional relationship with clients helps to promote your firm's good reputation in the community. Working as a family law paralegal, you will find yourself dealing with cases reflecting the human experience. Cases dealing with divorce, domestic violence, adoption, and the newest trends in society may pass through your firm's doors. As a paralegal, you will often find yourself in the role of office liaison when dealing with clients and the staffs of other law firms. This will especially be so when your supervising attorney is away at depositions or in court.

The first thing to do when dealing with a prospective new client is to cross-check to see if there is a conflict of interest. Once a new client has signed a retainer agreement, your duties may involve opening a new file. It is essential that the file be consistent and arranged in an orderly manner.

You will have to become familiar with the process of preparing complaints, answers, interrogatories, deposition transcript summaries, case information statements, and motions. The work you produce for your supervising attorney will usually fall under the attorney work-product privilege.

The vast majority of cases are settled prior to reaching a trial, but a client's case should be prepared to go to trial if necessary. The steps in a trial include: the plaintiff's opening statement, the defendant's opening statement, the plaintiff's direct examination, the defendant's cross-examination of the plaintiff's witnesses, the re-direct of plaintiff's witnesses, the re-cross of the defendant's, the defendant's direct examination, the plaintiff's cross-examination, the defendant's re-direct examination, the plaintiff's re-cross, the plaintiff's closing argument, and then the defendant's closing argument. A judge in most states makes the final decision and writes the decision in an order. However, decisions on spousal support, child support, and child custody can usually be modified at a later date.

As a paralegal, you are required to follow ethical guidelines. Those guidelines are provided by each state's court rules and legislation. Model guidelines are also provided by the ABA and numerous state and national paralegal organizations.

Key Terms

paralegal
legal assistant
conflict of interest
   fee agreement
retainer
breach of contract
legal malpractice
petition
complaint
court clerk
court reporter
expert
contingency fee
pleading
answer
response
motion
discovery
interrogatory
deposition transcript

deposition
order
exhibit
pro se
plaintiff
defendant
petitioner
respondent
cause of action
service of process
waiver of service
appearance
counterclaim
default judgment
in personam jurisdiction
in rem jurisdiction
bench warrant
forum shopping
case information statement
   (CIS)

financial affidavit
docket number
case number
calendar number
notice of motion
pendente lite
certification of plaintiff
sanction
attorney-client privilege
attorney work-product
   privilege
deposition summary
opening statement
direct examination
cross-examination
re-direct
re-cross
modification

Surfing the Web

http://www.advocateparalegal.com Interesting Canadian company offering paralegal services directly to the consumer. Do you think such a company would be legally sanctioned in the United States?

http://www.paralegals.org Lengthy list of paralegal organizations across the country.

http://steve.drh.net Informative networking site run by a paralegal.

http://www.hg.org Listing of law firms worldwide, plus an extensive legal resource center.

http://www.lectlaw.com Easily accessible site offering information and products.

http://www.law.cornell.edu Cornell Law School's site, which provides federal and state constitutions, codes, and court opinions and also highlights recent U.S. Supreme Court decisions.

http://www.law.com Regional and national legal news and information.

http://www.nala.org Continuing education and professional development programs for the nation's paralegals.

ETHICS ALERT

Susan's classmate, Wanda, called Susan to catch up on gossip. Happily, she told Susan that she, too, has been hired by an attorney specializing in family law. Wanda's boss has offices in two different states. Wanda is really excited about her job because her boss is letting her run the office in one state while he is busy in the office located about fifty miles away.

Originally Wanda's boss reviewed all of her work. He knew, however, that Wanda was an A student, and as he saw what excellent work she was doing, his faith in her grew. Eventually he told her he no longer needed to review her work, and that she should just go ahead and sign his name on documents she prepared. Wanda remembered from her classes that this is not a good idea, but when she brought up the subject with her boss, he gave her a signature stamp and instructed her to use it on all of the office work.

Wanda told Susan that she was really enjoying being in charge in her office, but Susan became concerned about the ethical implications of the situation. She dug out her textbooks and checked her copy of the NALA Model Rules, which confirmed that she had reason to be concerned. She wondered whether she should mail her copy of the Model Rules to Wanda and her employer.

Can you find the portion of the NALA Model Rules in Appendix B that applies to this situation? What do you think? Should Susan burst Wanda's bubble by sharing her ethical concerns with Wanda?

Review Questions

1. What types of cases are represented in a family law practice?
2. What is the American Bar Association's definition of the work a paralegal or legal assistant can do?
3. Name some effective job search techniques.
4. Where can you find the names of lawyers, along with their areas of expertise and their locations?
5. What would a sample portfolio include?
6. Where can you learn about a paralegal's responsibilities?
7. Why is it essential for a prospective client to be checked against the firm's client list prior to scheduling an appointment?

8. How can a client be best prepared for a first meeting with his attorney?
9. (a) What is a retainer agreement?
   (b) Describe its contents. (c) What may happen if the retainer agreement is not adhered to?
10. Why are contingency fees not allowed in family law matters?
11. What does a typical legal file consist of?
12. What does *pro se* mean?
13. What is a cause of action?
14. When a person receives service of process, what three options are available, and what are their likely results?
15. Describe the purpose of a *pendente lite* motion, certification, and order.
16. What is included in the discovery phase?
17. How are cases identified within the court system?
18. (a) What are interrogatories?
    (b) What are valid reasons for not answering interrogatories?
19. Once answers to interrogatories are received from opposing counsel, what option does an attorney have if a response to an interrogatory is not adequate?
20. What can happen if a court order is not complied with?
21. (a) What is involved in a deposition?
    (b) What tasks might a paralegal perform following a deposition?
22. (a) Do the majority of cases go to trial?
    (b) What are the typical steps in a trial?
23. Can a final judgment ever be changed?
24. Where can a description of the suggested proper conduct for attorneys and paralegals be found?

Endnotes

1. U.S. Census Bureau, *Current Population Survey* (2000).
2. *Guidelines for the Approval of Paralegal Education Programs—General Purposes, Procedures, and Definitions* G-103 (American Bar Association, 2002).
3. *Martindale-Hubbell Law Directory*, 121st ed., (Summit, New Jersey, 1989).
4. CAL. STAT. ANN. § 2311 (West 2003).
5. *Guidelines* G-103 (ABA, 2002).

Chapter 2

Legal Research and Writing

DEVELOPING YOUR SKILLS

This chapter is designed to help those of you, whether first-time legal researchers or experienced students, who wish to fine-tune your legal research and writing skills. You will be following Susan as she receives her first official legal memorandum of law office assignment at Johnson & Webster. A **legal memorandum of law** is a document that explains a client's legal issues and details the law that the writer and researcher believes is applicable to a client's particular set of facts.

Following a review of our legal system and some essential research techniques, you will read about Susan's next assignment. Later, you will share Susan's surprise as she hears that she will take part in researching and writing an appellate brief. An **appellate brief** is a written statement prepared by one side in a lawsuit to explain its case to an *appellate level* court. An appellate level court is the court above the trial court level. Typically, the party writing the brief has lost her case at the trial level and is appealing the lower court's decision. Despite its name, appellate briefs are rarely brief.

SUSAN'S FIRST RESEARCH AND WRITING ASSIGNMENT

Several days after joining Johnson & Webster, Susan finally met Pat, the most experienced paralegal at the firm who was now, thankfully, back from her vacation. Around Johnson & Webster, she was known as the person to go to if you needed a question answered, a client's history recalled, or, if you were a new employee, your nerves steadied.

"So, you must be the new recruit," Pat proclaimed as she purposefully strode into Susan's makeshift office. "Glad to make your acquaintance!" she added, stretching out her hand.

Susan stood to shake Pat's hand. Pat quickly offered to help Susan with her recent memorandum of law assignment. "So, I heard you've been given your first memo," Pat announced as she visually surveyed Susan's attempts to civilize an office that had only recently been a broom closet. "I'd be happy to help you with it." Smiling, she added, "If you wouldn't think I'm butting in."

"Oh no, are you kidding?" Susan exclaimed. " I would be grateful for the help. Mr. Dombroski knows I did a lot of research at school, but my last semester internship experience was kind of weak in that area," Susan admitted. "It's been a few months since my last research assignment, and—if you don't mind—I could use a push in the right direction."

"No problem," Pat generously responded. "Research is like riding a bicycle. Once you learn it, you never really forget it." That said, Pat literally rolled up her sleeves to get to work. "Okay, what's the client's problem?" she asked.

Susan sat down and looked at her notes. "Well, our client, Ricky Ricardi, came in yesterday to see Mr. Dombroski. His problem is that his wife, Lucie, took their two kids and left New Jersey to move to Seattle," Susan read. "Furthermore, Mrs. Ricardi wanted child support sent to Seattle. Oh, and Mr. Ricardi filed for divorce last October. The real problem is that Mrs. Ricardi also filed for divorce in Washington and began a custody proceeding there."

Pat had listened intently while Susan explained the facts. She took a sip of her double espresso and asked Susan where she planned to start her research.

"I thought I'd go to the digest, which would, of course, lead me to case law. I was also going to look at the statutes to see what they say about custody," Susan said confidently.

Pat smiled, "Good places to start, but I have a short-cut suggestion first."

Susan's interest was piqued, and she replied, "I'm all for short-cuts if you still get to a valid conclusion."

"I learned years ago that in law, and in the typical law office, there really is very little that is new under the sun," Pat said conspiratorially. She took in Susan's baffled expression. "You know, most every legal problem has been seen before," Pat explained. "I'd ask around the office to see if a memo with these same issues has been researched before." Tapping her chin, she recalled, "As a matter of fact, Mr. Ricardi's problem does sound awfully familiar." She looked at her watch and said, "I have a complaint to prepare that has to be filed today, but why don't you ask around?" Pat then walked out of Susan's cramped office as purposefully as she had entered it.

Susan took Pat's suggestion and began inquiring around the office. She thought that Pat was probably right. In an office of eight attorneys and three paralegals, a custody issue like Mr. Ricardi's had to have come up before.

Sure enough, Cheryl, Mr. Johnson's paralegal, recalled a similar situation. Armed with a somewhat dated memo but plenty of places to begin researching, Susan stopped at Pat's desk to thank her. "You were right," Susan happily stated. "Cheryl recalled a memo that was done awhile back."

Pat responded, "Great. Use it as a starting point, and don't forget the all-important Shepardizing."

Susan answered, "Of course not. I remember my research professor reminding us that Shepardizing is extremely important—and that it has nothing to do with sheep and a man in a caftan!"

Later, after a very long day of research and writing, Susan sat at her office computer and put the finishing touches on the Ricardi memo. When Pat stopped by to say goodnight, Susan looked up from her computer and said, "Thanks again for your help today."

"No problem," Pat answered, as she stifled a yawn. "The first day back is always the longest." Chuckling, she continued, "I'll probably forget I had a vacation before my suntan starts fading! Oh, by the way, we have an especially interesting appellate brief we're going to start working on tomorrow."

Her eyes as big as proverbial saucers, Susan squeaked in panic, "What we—me?"
Pat laughed. "We'll have to write something that sounds better than that!" she joked. "Don't stay too late, now, tomorrow's another day."

You can read Susan's first official efforts at writing a legal memorandum of law in Exhibit 2.1. While you are reading, take notice of the memorandum's legal points regarding jurisdictional issues. Susan's memo provides a general overview of how jurisdiction is determined. See if you can pick out any errors in the memo. You will read more about jurisdiction and custody in later chapters.

EXHIBIT 2.1 Susan's First Memorandum of Law

Memorandum of Law

TO: Mr. Dombroski
FROM: Susan, Paralegal
DATE: October 30, 2003
SUBJECT: Ricky Ricardi, Client #54321

Statement of Facts

Ricky and Lucie Ricardi were married on June 26, 1994, in Lovely Town, Apex County, New Jersey, where they resided together until March 10, 2002. There were two children born of the marriage, Little Ricky, born in 1994, and Little Lucie, born in 1996.

On March 10, 2002, Mrs. Ricardi left a note for our client stating that she loved him, but was frightened by his temper—and his bongo drum playing was driving her nuts. Mrs. Ricardi informed Mr. Ricardi that she was moving to Seattle, Washington, and taking the children with her. She apparently said she would advise him when she arrived so that he could send money for child support.

Mr. Ricardi was hurt, outraged, and extremely confused by this action. He advised us that he waited this long to seek advice because he was without funds and not sure what to do. However, he did have a friend who finally passed the bar exam on the tenth try and helped him out. Newly minted attorney Teddy Mertz, Esq., prepared and filed a complaint for divorce in New Jersey on Mr. Ricardi's behalf, but Mr. Ricardi is not sure Teddy knows what to do next, so Mr. Ricardi came to Johnson & Webster. Mr. Ricardi is also seeking custody. He filed his complaint on October 19, 2003, in Apex County, New Jersey.

Prior to the complaint being filed in New Jersey, Mr. Ricardi advised Mr. Mertz that his wife had begun a custody proceeding in the State of Washington on September 26, 2002, which sought both custody of the children and child support.

Our client feels that because the children were born and raised in New Jersey, New Jersey should retain jurisdiction over this case. He does not want to travel to Washington for resolution of any legal issues, nor does he want a Washington court to have jurisdiction over child support.

Issues Presented

1. Does New Jersey or Washington retain jurisdiction for custody of the children of the marriage and for child support?
2. Was Mrs. Ricardi's unilateral removal of the children from the home wrongful?

Discussion

Our client has not provided us with enough information. We have no information about whether he has had any visitation with his children or, indeed, has had any communication with them. Is there a schedule for telephone calls to the children? Does he have reports from the children's teachers and school indicating whether their performance and behavior has improved or declined? This affects jurisdiction insofar as the best interests of the children are concerned. In moving the children such a great distance, Mrs. Ricardi also interfered with any normal visitation, including midweek parenting time, that Mr. Ricardi might be able to schedule. Does he even know where his children are? Has Mrs. Ricardi provided him with a physical location or merely advised him about where to mail the support payments?

There are two provisions in this case under which New Jersey may retain jurisdiction: N.J.S.A. § 2A:34-31(2) and N.J.S.A. § 2A:34-37.

The first provision deals with significant connection with New Jersey and the best interest of the children. Pursuant to N.J.S.A. § 2A:34-31(2): *It is in the best interest of the child that a court of this state assume jurisdiction because (i) the child and his parents, or the child and at least one contestant, have a significant connection with this State; (ii) there is available in this State substantial evidence concerning the child's present or future care, protection, training, and personal friendships.*

Mr. Ricardi maintains that since both of the children were born in New Jersey, lived in New Jersey for eight and six years respectively, attended schools and made friends in New Jersey, and had a history in the state, that New Jersey should hold jurisdiction on this matter. We need to have our client provide additional information that supports a significant connection, for example, grandparents, cousins, or other close relatives with whom the children have close connections.

(continued)

EXHIBIT 2.1 *continued*

The second provision is that pursuant to N.J.S.A. § 2A:34-37, the statute provides: *Jurisdiction may be declined by reason of conduct of the parties.* If the petitioner for an initial decree has wrongfully taken the child from another state, or has engaged in similar reprehensible conduct, the court may decline to exercise jurisdiction if this is just and proper under the circumstances.

Mrs. Ricardi unilaterally removed the children from the marital home and relocated in another state that is 3,000 miles distant. We do not know her reasons for choosing Washington. We do not know if she has family or other close connections there. We do not know if she has a means of support there. We do not even know her true reasons for leaving Mr. Ricardi, other than the vague allegation contained in her note of March 10, 2002, since we have not been provided with a copy of her complaint. We do know that she planned to advise Mr. Ricardi where he could send his child support, but she gave no indication of when or where he might contact his children.

In *Bowden v. Bowden,* 440 A.2d 1160, 182 N.J. Super. 307 (1982), the plaintiff-wife presented that the defendant-husband did not care that she had removed the children until she filed an action against him in Nebraska for maintenance and support. The defendant claimed that she unilaterally and surreptitiously removed the children. The court concluded that there was a genuine issue of material fact and that a plenary hearing was required to make a final determination.

Mr. Ricardi did not file his papers until some time after Washington was considered the "home state" of the children. In *Bowden,* the court held that where simultaneous jurisdiction had occurred, there had to be communication between the states to determine jurisdiction. The *Bowden* case appears to be similar to our case in that Mrs. Ricardi removed the children of the marriage from their home state.

In N.J.S.A. § 2A:34-30(e), home state is defined as the state in which the child immediately preceding the time involved lived with his parents, a parent, or a person acting as parent, for at least 6 consecutive months. Periods of temporary absence of any of the named persons are counted as part of the 6-month or any other period. N.J.S.A § 2A:34-31(c) states: *Physical presence of the child, while desirable, is not a prerequisite for jurisdiction to determine his custody.* These two provisions allow for simultaneous jurisdiction to occur, and both of these provisions apply in this case, based on the information provided.

In *Stevens v. Stevens,* 177 N.J. Super. 167, 427 A.2d 620 (1981), the Appellate Division held that the mother's removal of the child from an Arizona babysitter's care without notice to the father, and bringing the child to this state [N.J.], was "reprehensible" conduct, and thus warranted the court's declining jurisdiction under the UCCJA.

In *G.C. v. N.Y.,* 651 A.2d 110, 278 N.J. Super. 363 (App. Div. 1995), one of the grounds on which New Jersey established jurisdiction was that when the mother filed for custody in New Jersey, the father withdrew his initial objection to jurisdiction and affirmatively invoked New Jersey jurisdiction through his cross-application for custody. The matter was ultimately remanded for further proceedings. He did file a complaint for divorce and custody in New Jersey, causing him to, in effect, decline jurisdiction in Washington, and giving New Jersey jurisdiction. However, N.J.S.A. § 2A:34-36, which deals with simultaneous proceedings, nullifies the foregoing in that jurisdiction by a court of this state is precluded where the court of another state has already properly established such jurisdiction. N.J.S.A.§ 2A:34(a) states: *A court of this State shall not exercise its jurisdiction under this act if at the time of filing the petition a proceeding concerning the custody of the child was pending in a court of another state exercising jurisdiction substantially in conformity with this act, unless the proceeding is stayed by the court of the other state because this State is a more appropriate forum.*

Two different arguments could be made based on this statute. One argument is that New Jersey cannot hold jurisdiction, since jurisdiction has already been established in Washington. The alternative argument is that Washington, when notified by the New Jersey court that this state is a more appropriate forum and that Mrs. Ricardi willfully removed the children from their home state and their father, should refuse jurisdiction.

However, Mr. Ricardi is clearly in violation of N.J.S.A. § 2A:34-31A (1)(i), in that he does not meet the requirement that this state be the *home state of the child[ren] at the time of commencement of the proceeding, or (ii) had been the child's home state within 6 months before commencement of the proceeding.* Mr. Ricardi did not file his papers until more than 18 months had passed after the removal of the children. Sufficient time has passed to nullify his contention that the children were wrongfully taken from the state. His reasons for waiting until after Mrs. Jackson filed her papers in another state need to be examined.

Conclusion

In view of the foregoing, and without sufficient information regarding the best interests of the children, it seems unlikely that Mr. Ricardi's application for New Jersey jurisdiction would be granted. He waited more than 18 months before filing his papers for divorce and custody. Indeed, he did not file them until after his wife filed. This works against his declaration that the children were willfully removed from the state. His delay in taking any action provides the basis for the state of Washington to be considered the home state for the children. He took no action until after his wife filed her applications in Washington. Only then did he file a complaint for divorce and custody. Without the additional information, we cannot determine if Mr. Ricardi's allegations, or indeed Mrs. Ricardi's, causes either of them to qualify under the Uniform Child Custody Jurisdiction and Enforcement Act, and if so, which parts. We need this information in order to complete research in support of Mr. Ricardi's application for New Jersey jurisdiction and for custody of his children.

Discussion of Susan's Research and Writing Assignment

What do you think of Susan's first official attempt at a memorandum of law? Do you think you would have answered the issues differently? What do you think about the list of questions Susan had? Would you have made an attempt to get your questions answered before sitting down to write the memorandum? It may appear to you that Susan had more questions than answers. It is not always possible to have all questions answered before sitting down to write, but the time and effort a paralegal spends in having as many questions answered as possible is appreciated and makes the results more useful. Do you think Susan is ready to move on to an appellate brief?

Ready or not, Susan has been assigned by Alyssa Jensen to assist Pat with the research and drafting of an appellate brief. Alyssa will review their work, fine-tune the writing, and give final approval before the brief is filed with the court. When it comes to appellate briefs, paralegals are likely to serve in a supporting role to an attorney writing the brief. Paralegals may, for example, summarize transcripts, review citations, Shepardize, write factual information, and obtain exhibits. Before examining Susan's appellate brief, however, we will review how our legal system was created and some essential research techniques.

HOW OUR LEGAL SYSTEM WAS CREATED

Our American legal system is essentially an English import stemming from the time when America was an English colony. The English legal system emphasized a judge's role in creating law. English judges were empowered to determine the outcome of a legal case, and their decisions became the law. The English also empowered Parliament—England's version of Congress—to create law. The founders of the United States did not change much of the existing legal structure, but they did put an emphasis on a new-fangled legal concept known as the United States Constitution. This is why the two-pronged approach of empowering both judges and legislators to create law is still in existence today.

Common Law

Let us review in detail how the American legal system creates law in two distinct ways. One way is the common law method. Common law is based on the written opinions of judges. When a judge has determined that present law does not adequately apply to a case before the court, he may find it necessary to *create* law by deciding the case before the court in a way that has not been done before. This judicial process of creating law is typically referred to as *judge-made law, case law,* or *common law.*

Written opinions rarely come from the trial level. Usually, they result from appellate court level and *supreme court* level decisions. The appellate courts are immediately above the trial level and typically have three judges hearing an appeal from a trial level case. The state supreme courts usually have seven to eleven judges hearing the appeal of case decisions from the appellate level immediately below them.

When more judges are involved, differences of opinion usually arise. An appellate or supreme court level opinion may consist of one to three parts. The three possible parts are the majority, the dissent, and the concurrence. The **majority opinion** is the written opinion of the majority of judges, and that is considered the official case law. The **dissenting opinion** is written when one or more judges disagree with the majority and feel the need to write the legal reasons for their disagreement. The **concurring opinion** is written by one or more judges who agree with the majority but feel the need to further explain their reasons for doing so.

When a judge decides that previous judicial decisions apply to a particular case before the court, that judge follows the legal decisions made in past cases and applies them to the present case. This is known as following precedent. **Precedent** is defined as a court decision on a question of law that has binding authority on lower courts in the same court system that are deciding cases involving a similar question of law. This concept of following case law precedent is known as the **doctrine of *stare decisis.***

In the American common law system, a judge has a responsibility to follow precedent. However, a judge does not have to follow a precedent if he makes a determination that the precedent was based on faulty legal reasoning. Here is a classic example. The United States Supreme Court decided, in the case of *Brown v. Board of Education,* 347 U.S. 482 (1954), that the long-standing legal precedent of separate but equal schools for African-American students was based on faulty reasoning and did not properly interpret the United States Constitution. Thus, the Supreme Court judges created new law and did not follow precedent because they decided that separate could never mean equal. The bottom line is that judges' written opinions are an integral part of the American legal system because when those opinions are in the majority, precedent is established.

Statutory Law

A second and equally important way that law is created in the United States is by our legislative bodies. Our federal system has a Congress that consists of the Senate and the House of Representatives. Like the federal system, all states also have two such elected bodies (called by a variety of names), with the exception of Nebraska, which has only one elected body. For example, New Jersey has a Senate and an Assembly. The laws created within your state's elected bodies are generally called *statutory laws.* An individual law is called a **statute.** The state and federal statutes are compiled in multivolume sets of books called **codes.** All statutes are given different numbers so they can be easily located within the codes.

HOW THE COURT SYSTEM IS SET UP

First, you need to know how your state's court system is designed. Generally, each state's court system has the highest level of state court located in its state capital. This highest level is usually known as the state supreme court, but there are exceptions. For example, New York State calls its highest level of court the Superior Court and calls its trial level court the Supreme Court.

The lower levels of courts are usually split between the counties in the state. Often, each of these *county courts,* also known as *circuit, district,* or *superior* courts in some states, is then divided even further by subject matter. For example, the county court may be split between civil and criminal matters, with certain judges hearing only certain types of cases. This splitting depends greatly on the population of the county and the number of judges on the bench. Most county courts also have a section of the court that handles only cases concerning small amounts of money. The court that handles cases involving a limited amount of monetary damages is usually known as the *small claims court.*

If the monetary amount in dispute is higher than the amount the small claims court is allowed to handle, then a different court within the county system handles the case. This court is usually known as the *trial court* and is the part of the county court that most of you are familiar with from television or from your own participation in a trial as a juror or a party. It is at this trial court level that most domestic relations matters are heard. Many county courts have a trial court section that hears only domestic relations matters. Most domestic relations matters are heard before a judge without a jury.

All parties who have cases heard at the trial court level have the opportunity to appeal that trial court decision to an appeals court, also known as an appellate court. The appeals court is located between the trial court level and the highest court level in the state. Just as each state is divided into county court sections, each state is also divided into appellate court sections. There are fewer appellate courts than trial courts, since the appellate courts hear fewer cases than the trial courts. The opportunity to appeal is not granted automatically. The party appealing a decision must claim specific permissible reasons for appealing. For example, a **legal error** could have been made during the trial. A legal error may involve a claim by the appealing party that the judge allowed evidence into the trial that should not have been admitted. An application to appeal is made to the particular appellate court that hears appeals from the county court that conducted the appealing party's trial.

If a party appeals to the appellate level and is unhappy with the result, that party then has the opportunity to appeal the appellate court's decision to the highest court of the state. Again, an appeal to the highest court can be made only if the party who is appealing a decision can show specific permissible reasons for the appeal. If a party who appeals to the state's highest court is unhappy with that court's decision, there is the possibility of appealing the case to the federal courts. However, this usually is only done if the party appealing the matter to the federal courts can show that the state court system violated federally guaranteed constitutional rights. This happens, but not often.

The Judge's Job

The job of every federal and state court judge is to *interpret* case law precedent and statutes. The work is made easier by the fact that the judges are required to apply only the case and statutory law that applies to their jurisdiction. **Jurisdiction** is defined as the geographical area within which a court has the right and power to operate. For example, a judge working within the Illinois state judicial system need apply only the case law decided by Illinois judges and the statutory law that has been created by the Illinois Legislature. A particular state's case and statutory law is known as **primary authority** within that state. A judge has to apply only primary authority to the cases before her. Case and statutory law from another state is known as **secondary** or **persuasive authority.** Secondary or persuasive authority may be applied when there is no applicable case or statutory law to apply from a court's home state. Federal law takes precedence over state law, however, so all state judges must respect the federal case law and statutes that apply to the facts of the cases before them.

LEARNING THE LAW

Let us start at the beginning. Long before a lawyer has researched a legal issue for his first client, that lawyer was a student learning all aspects of the law, including family law. Law is usually taught in law schools via the casebook method. A casebook is a book of judicial opinions gathered from cases that have been decided all over the United States pertaining to a particular subject (e.g., family law). These opinions, all of which are from the appellate level and above, are included for the law students to read and then be prepared to discuss in class. The typical law school professor leads the discussions among students by asking numerous questions about the cases they have read. This teaching method, known as the *Socratic method,* was named after the great Greek teacher and ultimate questioner, Socrates.

The Socratic method is the opposite of the lecture method. You are probably very familiar with the lecture method. You know the drill: The instructor talks, the students write notes, and those same notes are then given back as closely as possible to the instructor on the final exam. Since undergraduate Family Law courses are generally taught by lawyers who were trained in the Socratic method, you will very likely find yourself being trained in the Socratic method as well. The main purpose of the Socratic method is to make you, the student, think for yourself and begin to think more analytically.

If you have taken a legal research course, you know the basics of finding the case and statutory law that you need to support a client's case. If you have not taken such a course or you need a refresher, the next sections offer the basics of legal research.

Learning Legal Research

When you begin research on a case, you will want to find out how your particular state has decided cases similar to one on which you are working. To do this, you will need to follow certain steps. First, be aware that most attorneys and paralegals conduct the majority of their litigation work on the trial court level, and generally these cases are not reported. What does *reported* mean? For both the appellate and the Supreme Court level, judges write *judicial opinions* that contain explanations of their judicial decisions. These written judicial opinions are then gathered and reported in chronological order in a set of hardbound volumes called **reporters.** Each state has its own individual set of reporters. For example, in Pennsylvania, the set of volumes is called the *Pennsylvania State Reports.* In addition, each hardbound volume of the reporter may have a supplement bound volume, a pocket part, and an advance sheet pamphlet. A *supplement bound volume* includes cases that were decided after the hardbound volume was published. A **pocket part** literally fits into a pocket inside each hardcover reporter volume. The pocket part is not as large as the supplement bound volume nor as small as the advance sheet. The **advance sheet** pamphlet includes cases so recent that the publisher has not had time to include them in the last pocket part. Once a number of reporter volumes have been filled with reported cases, the publisher will begin a new series.

Additionally, another set of reporters contains all appellate and Supreme Court cases for particular geographic areas of the United States. These reporters are known as **regional reporters.** The 50 states are split into sections that reflect each state's geographical location. For example, the *Southwestern Reporter* includes reported cases from Arkansas, Kentucky, Missouri, Tennessee, and Texas.

You may be wondering why anyone would go to the trouble of reporting a particular case in two separate sets of reporters. To understand, you must recall the case precedent concept. A state court has a responsibility to follow the precedent created previously by the courts in that state. However, if the facts and legal issues of a particular case have never been decided upon by a court in that state, then the court may look to other state courts that have already decided cases with similar facts and issues. The law in other states is known as secondary or persuasive authority; it can be considered, but does not have to be followed, by judges in the state. Cases that concern issues that have never been decided in a state before are known as **cases of first impression.**

Do Statutes Apply to Your Case?

You will also have to decide whether your client's case involves federal or state issues, or both. Although family law historically has fallen under the rule of the states, there has been a movement toward more federal involvement in family law issues. However, most family law matters that you will be involved with in a family law office will require research of your state's law. This means that, besides using your state's reporters, you will need to access information in your state's statutory code.

Are You Researching Procedural or Substantive Law?

You need to know whether you are researching a question that involves substantive or procedural law. **Substantive law** is defined as the basic law of rights and duties, as opposed to **procedural law,** which is defined as the rules for carrying on a legal case. For example, Mr. Ricardi's custody issue is a substantive law question. The question of what legal documents need to be prepared and filed with the court on his behalf is a procedural law question.

Finding the Right Books for Research

How do you find the reported cases that will help you to support your client's position? The first step is to visit the nearest law library. Whether one is easily available will depend on the size and financial abilities of your law office. Most law firms maintain a law library that contains at least the essential volumes needed to conduct research. If your firm does not have such a library, the usual alternative is the county courthouse library, a nearby law school's library, a law library in your state's legislative building, or the library of a school that contains a paralegal program. You will probably need special permission to use any library that is not open to the public.

An easy alternative to visiting a law library is to take advantage of the Internet as a research resource. Most modern law firms have joined the computer age and have at least some research sources that can be accessed through an on-line research service. You will read more about resources that are alternatives to books later in this chapter.

Essential Sources for Legal Research

What are the *essential* research sources you need to conduct your legal research? These sources may include your state's statutory code, the case reporters for your state, the case reporters for your geographic region, the **court rules book** for your state's courts, the **case digest** for your state and geographic region, any **practice manuals** that are published for your state, and the **legal newspaper** for your state. Many of these resources are available in both paper form and on-line.

You have already read about codes and reporters, but you may be wondering how the other sources function. Each state has a court rules book that is used in every court in that state. The court rules book provides a description of required court procedures. For example, if you want to know how to file a pleading with the court, the answer will be in the court rules. Your state's case digest is an alphabetically arranged and annotated listing of all the reported cases for your state by subject matter. This is an invaluable resource when you are relatively clueless about where to begin your research. Practice manuals provide guidance and sample documents for the legal professional. A legal newspaper is typically published by each state's bar association, or the state's court system, and emphasizes legal trends, groundbreaking cases, and, often, disciplinary actions involving the state's attorneys. A classified section is usually included, and will be a useful resource for you when you start looking for employment.

You Have Found the Right Books, but Now What?

The idea of actually using any of these research sources efficiently and comfortably may appear daunting at first. However, once you learn the rudimentary steps of research, retrieving information becomes less problematic. Everyone who begins a research assignment begins with a question, for example: *What are the statutory reasons a citizen of your state can request a divorce?* Look at this sample question and ask yourself: What is the main subject area in my state's statutory code that would contain the answer to this question? The subject that jumps out in this example is *divorce,* but if no words jump out at you, write down all the words you can think of that may lead you to the right research source.

If available, you may find a legal thesaurus or a set of books called ***Words and Phrases*** helpful. *Words and Phrases* is basically a legal thesaurus. In the example given earlier, you would go to the statutory code of your state and look up the word *divorce* in the *index.* Each state's statutory code has an index that appears in a separate volume of the state's code and is organized alphabetically. You must also remember to look in the back of each volume for a pocket part containing any recent additions to the code. The most recent changes to codes are collected in advance sheetserefore, follow this process for checking to see whether there have been any changes to the code: (1) Check the advance sheets; (2) check the supplemental pocket parts; and (3) check the hardcover statutory code volume. Remember, the hardcover code volumes are updated periodically, but due to the constantly changing nature of a statutory code, the pocket parts are the only way to economically keep the code current, unless you have access to computer-assisted legal research (CALR).

Unfortunately, maintaining an up-to-date library involves plenty of effort to ensure that the pocket parts and advance sheets are placed with the right volumes of reporters and digests and not left apart from the bound reporter volume. Fortunately, computer-assisted legal research provides practically up-to-the-minute materials and requires very little upkeep.

A Brave New World: Computer-Assisted Legal Research

Two of the best-known services that offer online databases for **computer-assisted legal research (CALR)** are WESTLAW and Lexis-Nexis. Each database is extensive and detailed. They offer the codes, reporters, digests, practice manuals, and law reviews you have read about. The difference is that each is current and, rather than searching through books, the researcher searches through databases. Both of these services require passwords and charge fees to access the system and download the information.

Another available option is a *CD-rom based library.* Here, the researcher accesses the electronic information through a compact disc (CD). These CDs are frequently updated, but they will not provide up-to-the-minute research. Still another option is performing research on the Internet through a *search engine.* This type of CALR allows the researcher to type in a word (or words), and the search engine will respond with as many sites as it finds on the Internet. The only cost involved here is the cost of the Internet service provided. See Exhibit 2.2 to review a list of Internet sites that may be helpful in your legal research. You should be aware that Internet sites are often running one day but gone the next. All the sites listed in Exhibit 2.2 were accessible at time of publication.

How to Locate a State Statute

Each state statute is given a two-part number to make locating the statute in the code easier. The first number in the code refers to the chapter; the second number refers to the section of the chapter in which the statute is located. The section is provided to make it easier to find a particular statute within the chapter. An example from Texas is provided for your review. It is typical of our nation's statutes because it provides plenty of information for the reader. The Texas statute explains its purpose, defines the terms used in the act, reviews the jurisdictional aspects of the act, and provides the legislative history of the act. You can read excerpts of Chapter 152 of the *Texas Family Code* in Exhibit 2.3. Exhibit 2.3 will also provide you with a good introduction to custody and jurisdictional issues. You will be studying custody and jurisdictional issues in depth in later chapters.

Statute Analysis

Did you notice the lengthy definitions provided by the Texas statute? These definitions are provided so that every individual looking at the statute uses the correct terminology, and hopefully, confusion will be avoided. Importantly, the purpose of the statute is clarified so that it is applied correctly to cases. An intrinsic part of every case is determining which court has proper jurisdiction to hear a dispute. This Texas

---

EXHIBIT 2.2 The Internet as a Resource

Type of Information	Web Sites
Federal resources include:	
United States Supreme Court opinions	http://findlaw.com
Divorce information	http://www.divorceinfo.com
Various law forums	http://lawstreet.com
Federal resources	http://www.firstgov.gov
General law links	http://www.lawyerfinder.com
State and federal resource links	http://www.p-law.com
New Jersey court system	http://www.judiciary.state.nj.us
Federal laws, courts, public offices	http://www.icle.org
United States Department of Justice	http://www.usdoj.gov

---

statute, courtesy of the Texas legislature, has provided needed guidance to Texas courts determining the primary issue of what court has proper jurisdiction. If you look at its last lines, you will see a description of the **legislative history** of the statute. A statute's legislative history is always included because it provides the background behind the legislature's intention in enacting the law.

Needle in a Haystack: Finding the Applicable Case Law

Equally as important as finding the pertinent statutes that apply to your client's case is finding the sometimes elusive cases in your state, among the thousands of them, with facts and issues of law that are similar to the case you are working on.

First, you must thoroughly review your client's situation. For example, where would you begin your research if the following client scenario arrived at your office door? Your firm represents a single father who wants custody of a child he never knew he had until recently. This client's son has already been given up for adoption by your client's estranged girlfriend, but the client wants custody of his son. The main legal issue is clear: *Does your client/father have a right to his newly discovered son after the child has already been placed for adoption?*

Next, analyze your research question to discover its main subject areas. The *big picture* question involves *adoption*, and a smaller subissue of adoption involves the *proper notification* of a father that his child is being adopted. You should know now that you have to go to your state's reporters. Since the cases are published chronologically, how do you find particular cases that are scattered throughout numerous volumes?

This is where the case digest system comes in handy. Each state's reporters have an accompanying set of volumes known as a digest, which is set up by topics found in the state's cases. The case digest system allows a researcher equipped with a question, and not much else, to become more familiar with her topic. Unlike the reporter system, which is set up chronologically, the digest is set up *alphabetically.* All digests have an *A* to *Z* index of topics. For example, the first volume of the *New Jersey Digest* starts with *Abandonment,* and the last volume ends with *Zoning.* In our research example involving the Ricardis, the first step could be to look up the more general topic, *divorce,* or the more specific topic, *child custody* within a divorce scenario. The index is cross-referenced. For instance, if you looked up the topic *sole parent child custody,* you would be directed to a volume and page within the case digest system for *divorce.*

EXHIBIT 2.3 *Texas Family Code* Chapter 152

Chapter 152. Uniform Child Custody Jurisdiction Act

Section 152.001. Purposes; Construction of Provisions.

(a) The general purposes of this chapter are to:

   (1) Avoid jurisdictional competition and conflict with courts of other states in matters of child custody that have in the past resulted in the shifting of children from state to state with harmful effects on their well-being;
   (2) Promote cooperation with the courts of other states to the end that a custody decree is rendered in the state that can best decide the case in the interest of the child;
   (3) Ensure that the litigation concerning the custody of a child takes place ordinarily in the state where the child and the child's family have the closest connection and where significant evidence concerning the child's care, protection, training, and personal relationships is most readily available. The courts of this state should decline the exercise of jurisdiction when the child and the child's family have a closer connection with another state;
   (4) Discourage continuing controversies over child custody in the interest of greater stability of home environment and of secure family relationships for the child;
   (5) Deter abductions and other unilateral removals of children undertaken to obtain custody awards;
   (6) Avoid relitigation of custody decisions of other states in this state insofar as is feasible;
   (7) Facilitate the enforcement of custody decrees of other states;
   (8) Promote and expand the exchange of information and other forms of mutual assistance between the courts of this state and those of other states concerned with the same child; and
   (9) Make uniform the law of those states that enact it.

(b) This chapter shall be construed to promote the general purposes stated in this section.

Added by Acts 1995, 74th Leg., ch. 20, Sec. 1, eff. April 20, 1995.

Section 152.002. Definitions.

(a) In this chapter:

   (1) "Contestant" means a person, including a parent, who claims a right to custody or visitation rights with respect to a child.
   (2) "Custody" means managing conservatorship of a child.
   (3) "Custody determination" means a court decision and court orders and instructions providing for the custody of a child, including visitation rights, but does not include a decision relating to child support or any other monetary obligation of any person.
   (4) "Custody proceeding" includes a proceeding in which a custody determination is one of several issues, such as an action for divorce or separation, and includes child neglect and dependency proceedings.
   (5) "Decree" or "custody decree" means a custody determination contained in a judicial decree or order made in a custody proceeding and includes an initial decree and a modification decree.
   (6) "Home state" means the state in which the child, preceding the time involved, lived with the child's parents, a parent, or a person acting as parent for at least six consecutive months and, in the case of a child less than six months old, the state in which the child lived from birth with any of the persons mentioned. Periods of temporary absence of any of the named persons are counted as part of the six-month or other period.
   (7) "Initial decree" means the first custody decree concerning a particular child.
   (8) "Modification decree" means a custody decree that modifies or replaces a prior decree, whether made by the court that rendered the prior decree or by another court.
   (9) "Physical custody" means actual possession and control of a child.
   (10) "Person acting as parent" means a person, other than a parent, who has physical custody of a child and who either has been awarded custody by a court or claims a right to custody.
   (11) "Visitation" means possession of or access to a child.

Added by Acts 1995, 74th Leg., ch. 20, Sec. 1, eff. April 20, 1995.

Section 152.003. Jurisdiction.

(a) A court of this state that is competent to decide child custody matters has jurisdiction to make a child custody determination by initial decree or modification decree or order if:

    (1) This state:

        (A) Is the home state of the child on the date of the commencement of the proceeding; or
        (B) Had been the child's home state within six months before the date of the commencement of the proceeding and the child is absent from this state because of the child's removal or retention by a person claiming the child's custody or for other reasons, and a parent or person acting as parent continues to live in this state;

    (2) It appears that no other state would have jurisdiction under Subdivision (1) and it is in the best interest of the child that a court of this state assume jurisdiction because:

        (A) The child and the child's parents or the child and at least one contestant have a significant connection with this state other than mere physical presence in this state; and
        (B) There is available in this state substantial evidence concerning the child's present or future care, protection, training, and personal relationships;

    (3) The child is physically present in this state and:

        (A) The child has been abandoned; or
        (B) It is necessary in an emergency to protect the child because the child has been subjected to or threatened with mistreatment or abuse or is otherwise neglected or there is a serious and immediate question concerning the welfare of the child; or

    (4) It is in the best interest of the child that the court assume jurisdiction and:

        (A) It appears that no other state would have jurisdiction under prerequisites substantially in accordance with Subdivision (1), (2), or (3); or
        (B) Another state has declined to exercise jurisdiction on the ground that this state is the more appropriate forum to determine the custody of the child.

(b) Except under Subsections (a)(3) and (4), physical presence in this state of the child or of the child and one of the contestants is not alone sufficient to confer jurisdiction on a court of this state to make a child custody determination.

(c) Physical presence of the child, while desirable, is not a prerequisite for jurisdiction to determine the child's custody.

(d) Except on written agreement of all the parties, a court may not exercise its continuing jurisdiction to modify custody if the child and the party with custody have established another home state unless the action to modify was filed before the new home state was acquired.

(e) A court that has jurisdiction of a suit under Subsection (a)(3) for which a court in another state may exercise jurisdiction under prerequisites substantially in accordance with Subsection (a)(1) or (2) may enter only a temporary order to protect the child. The suit shall be dismissed in this state on the date a court of competent jurisdiction in another state signs an order in the suit or on the 91st day after the date the court in this state exercised its jurisdiction, whichever date occurs first. This subsection does not apply to a suit brought under Chapter 262.

Added by Acts 1995, 74th Leg., ch. 20, Sec. 1, eff. April 20, 1995. Amended by Acts 1995, 74th Leg., ch. 751, Sec. 24, eff. Sept. 1, 1995. Amended by Acts 1997, 75th Leg., ch. 575, Sec. 7, eff. Sept. 1, 1997.

Under the topic *sole parent child custody,* the digest provides a short description of *every* New Jersey case that dealt with a sole parent custody issue. This short description of cases dealing with a particular fact pattern is called an **annotation.** The typical annotation is no larger than a paragraph and is very helpful in determining which cases you wish to look up in their entirety in your state's reporters.

Remember, when conducting legal research, you should always look for cases with a factual history similar to your client's case. The annotations provide a short-cut for comparing your client's facts to a reported case's facts. If the reported case has a similar factual history, then the law applied in the older case may very well be the law that would be applied in your client's case. When a court applies the decision from an older case to a new case before the court, this is the doctrine of *stare decisis* in action.

Additional Research Help Available

Especially helpful to the legal professional are subject-specific practice manuals that provide step-by-step guidance for creating legal documents such as complaints and motions. Another particularly useful tool are CDs that provide templates for legal documents, although no template will completely fill your needs when you need to write a legal memorandum of law or a brief. Additionally, the American Bar Association publishes both the monthly general legal interest *Law Journal* and the family law specific *Family Advocate* filled with general interest articles detailing recent changes to law as well as upcoming trends in all areas of the law.

Not to be forgotten are the informative materials that can be found in legal encyclopedias, law reviews, and treatises. Two encyclopedias that provide a national overview are ***Corpus Juris Secundum*** **(CJS)** and ***American Jurisprudence*** **(Am Jur).** Both are used for general knowledge. Several states have state-specific encyclopedias that are much more helpful for those doing research pertaining to those states. A visit to your law library will quickly answer the question of whether you are lucky enough to work in a state with its own encyclopedia.

Citations: No Two Alike

All legal materials—cases, statutes, treatises, law reviews, and so on—have a **citation.** The word *citation* is also shortened to *cite.* A citation or cite can be compared to an address because no two are exactly alike, and it leads you to where you want to go. It is the case citation that directly leads the researcher to the complete case in the reporter. Let us use the case of *Baehr v. Lenin,* 74 Haw. 645, 852 P.2d 44 (1993), as an example. The first words tell the researcher the name of the case. *Baehr v. Lenin* means Baehr *versus* Lenin. In this case, Baehr is a party who is bringing an appeal after losing at the trial level, and Lenin is now defending the appeal after winning at the trial. The party's names were reversed in the case at the trial level, and they could reverse again if the loser at the appellate level appeals to the Supreme Court. The first set of numbers, 74 Haw. 645, means that the case can be found in the 74th volume of the *Hawaii Reports* on page 645. The second set of numbers is known as the *parallel citation* and directs you to the same case opinion, but in the geographic region reporter—in this case, the reporter for the Pacific region. The citation 852 P.2d 44 directs you to volume 852 of the second series of the *Pacific Reporter* on page 44.

Once you begin conducting research, you will find it especially convenient if your law library has both state and regional reporters. If the volume you need in the state reporter is not available, you can still find your case in the regional reporter. With CALR, both sets of reporters are accessible via the on-line database.

Shepardize or Suffer the Consequences

Once you have found statutes and cases **on point,** which is the term used when you locate cases and statutes that involve the same legal issues your client is dealing with, you still have one more important research step to complete. This essential step is called **Sheparding.** The term *Sheparding* is derived from a set of published books known as *Shepard's Citations*. It may be hard to believe it could be done, but every time a judicial opinion mentions any other case or statute, *Shepard's Citations* lists them. For example, suppose you have read a judicial opinion for Case A and want to use Case A to argue a client's case. *Shepard's Citations* will tell you whether the Case A you think is applicable law has been overruled, reversed, explained, affirmed, or distinguished by other cases that have mentioned Case A in their judicial opinions.

Remember, a statute that is no longer valid law will eventually be removed from your state's statutory code, but the removal does not happen immediately. The removal of the outdated statute will not happen until a new set of statutes is printed—unless you are utilizing CALR. However, the fact that the statutes have been altered or removed from the code will be noted in the pocket parts of the statutory code. In the case of the reporter systems, cases that have been overruled will *never* be removed from the reporters. So remember, it really is a matter of researcher beware!

Every law library that contains a set of state statutes and state reporters should have the accompanying sets of *Shepard's Citations* in either book form or available with CALR access. This cannot be emphasized enough: *Use statutes and cases only after you have Shepardized them.* Imagine the scenario of an attorney appearing in court to argue a client's case, but to support his client's legal position, he uses a case that has been overturned. You can see the problem with not Shepardizing—especially if you were the paralegal who did the research!

Analyzing a Case: Learning How to Read—Again?

One of the most important skills you can acquire is the ability to compare the cases you research to the facts of your client's case. This chapter has discussed the available resources and the importance of Shepardizing, but learning how to effectively read legal cases is extremely important. Learning to read a legal opinion is akin to learning a foreign language. Most legal opinions seem a bit cumbersome and long-winded to the uninitiated. However, a note-taking process called **case briefing** is a good way to break a long legal opinion into manageable segments. Briefing the lengthy cases you read will help you to remember the important points of each case. Case briefing will aid your memory whether you are out in the real world researching for a memorandum of law, or in class trying to remember a new point of law for an exam.

How to Brief a Case

The first step in briefing is to determine the key *facts* of the case. The journalistic credo that emphasizes *who, what, when, where,* and *how* is effective in deciphering the essential facts. The second step involves reading the case carefully, which should point the reader to the primary *legal issues* in the dispute. The appellate judges who heard the case had the job of answering the legal issues presented by the parties. The appellate judges' written answer to these legal questions is known as the judicial opinion. Including a summary of the *court's reasoning* is the third step in case briefing. You may have noticed that the plural *judges* was used. Remember, the appeals level has more than one judge and no jury. The final step in the case briefing process is the simplest. It involves determining the *holding* of the case. In other words, what was the judges' decision?

All of the cases included in this textbook have been case-briefed from their original length in order to include as many pertinent cases as possible. The original text of these cases ranges from a few pages to over 100 pages. You can see how the case briefing process is extremely helpful with the longer cases. However, all case citations for the cases in this text have been provided so you can read the cases in their entirety.

Unless you have access to a law library that is national in scope, though, you will need CALR access because the cases have been chosen from across the country.

SUSAN'S FIRST APPELLATE BRIEF

"Morning, morning," Pat repeated through the long office corridor filled with offices to the right and left. Susan heard the cheerful greeting coming closer to her office, and then Pat appeared at her door. "I picked up a muffin for you," Pat announced. "They only had blueberry left—I hope you like it."

Susan was touched by Pat's thoughtfulness. "I love blueberries, but I should be the one getting you the muffin after all the questions you've answered for me this past week."

Pat waved Susan's comment away and said, "Look, asking questions means you're learning, and for the last two days you've held your own working with me on the Yanov brief."

Susan beamed while she bit into the huge muffin. "You know, in my advanced research class, we covered the writing of an appellate brief, but there really isn't anything like working on the real thing," she said between bites.

"Exactly," Pat responded, "Mr. Yanov's predicament really hit home when I met him. I was glad Ms. Jensen was representing him and shocked when she lost the trial." She paused to carefully sip her steaming coffee.

Susan took the opportunity to ask, "Do you think the appeal has a chance?"

"I feel pretty good about this one. You know, I've been reviewing our work every day with Ms. Jensen, and she thinks Mr. Yanov has a chance—but you never know how those three judges are going to rule."

Writing Your First Appellate Brief

The appellate brief Susan and Pat worked on with Alyssa Jensen is included in Exhibit 2.4 to give you an opportunity to read the material and review the format of an appellate brief. The fictitious characters in the appellate brief are based on the real-life *Baby Richard* case located in the chapter on adoption. (See the *Baby Richard* case brief in the adoption chapter, or use CALR to look up the appellate decision in its entirety: *In re Petition of John Doe and Jane Doe,* 159 Ill. 2d 347 (1994), *cert. denied* 115 S. Ct. 499 (1995).) In our *Yanov* case, as in the *Baby Richard* case, years have gone by while the biological father and adoptive parents dispute the legality of the adoption.

If your firm was representing Oliver Yanov, our fictional client and appellant, the attorney of record would have a specified amount of time allowed by the court rules for filing the appeal. The decision to appeal would be acknowledged in a *notice of appeal* filed with the court that heard the trial. The appellant would order a copy of the trial transcript for use in the appellate brief. Yanov, the plaintiff at the trial, becomes known as the **appellant** when he appeals his loss. The fictional couple, Mr. and Mrs. Williams, the defendants and winners at the trial level, become known as the **appellees** at the appellate level. Some states may use the word *petitioner* for the appellant and the word *respondent* for the appellee.

Each state has specific rules that must be followed when appealing a lower court decision. Court rule books provide directions and detailed requirements for every step and kind of court matter—from small claims cases to cases presented to the Supreme Court. Although each state has particular procedural rules to follow when writing an appellate brief, an appellate brief typically begins with a cover sheet and Table of Contents. The Table of Contents generally consists of the following: (1) Table of Authorities; (2) Statement of Issues; (3) Statement of Facts; (4) Argument section; and (5) Conclusion. The *Table of Authorities* is a

(continues on p. 66)

EXHIBIT 2.4 Appellate Brief
(Courtesy of Patricia O'Grady, author's student)

OLIVER YANOV and ANNETTE YANOV,	:	SUPERIOR COURT OF NEW JERSEY
	:	APPELLATE DIVISION
Plaintiff - Appellants	:	DOCKET NO. A-12345-02
	:	
vs.	:	
	:	ON APPEAL FROM FINAL JUDGMENT
JUDY WILLIAMS and KEVIN WILLIAMS	:	DATED MAY 16, 2002
	:	
Defendant - Respondents	:	SAT BELOW
	:	HONORABLE JOHN L. SUSSEX, J.S.C.

BRIEF ON BEHALF OF PLAINTIFF-APPELLANT

A. Jensen, Esq.
Johnson & Webster, Esqs.
123 Main Street
Newton, New Jersey 12345
(973) 555- 1234
Attorney for Plaintiff - Appellant

(continued)

EXHIBIT 2.4 *continued*

Table of Contents

Page

TABLE OF AUTHORITIES

Page

(continued)

EXHIBIT 2.4 *continued*

RULES OF CIVIL PROCEDURE

Statement of Issues

1. Did the Superior Court of New Jersey interpretation of notice under N.J.S.A. § 9:3-45 culminate in an unjust result and violation of Oliver Yanov's 14th Amendment right to due process by denying him the notice of the adoption proceedings as he was entitled to receive as the natural parent of Baby Mary?

2. Did the Superior Court of New Jersey err in not vacating the Judgment of Adoption by not allowing Oliver Yanov, the child's natural father, the notice he is entitled to under N.J.S.A. § 9:3-46?

3. Did the Superior Court of New Jersey apply the wrong standard of evidence in determining the best interest of the child which culminated in an unjust result?

(continued)

EXHIBIT 2.4 *continued*

STATEMENT OF FACTS

Annette Couric Yanov was born in Yugoslavia on July 4, 1973 and immigrated to the United States of America in December of 1991. Currently, she has permanent residency status. **(Aff. Annette Yanov, p. 23, L 1-3.)** Since her arrival in this country, Annette had lived with her only surviving family members who had left civil war torn Yugoslavia, her aunt and uncle. **(Aff. Annette Yanov, p. 23, L 3-6.)** In 1993, Annette met Oliver Yanov, also born in Yugoslavia, who had immigrated with his family as a small child. Oliver is a naturalized citizen since 1982. **(Aff. Oliver Yanov, p. 25, L 1-5.)** Shortly thereafter they began living together. In December of 1999 Annette became pregnant. **(Aff. Annette Yanov, p. 23, L 8-13.)** She worked until April, 2000. **(Aff. Annette Yanov, p. 23, L 27.)**

In late June, 2000, Oliver Yanov was notified of a family emergency in Yugoslavia and had to leave the country. **(Aff. Oliver Yanov, p. 25, L 22-23.)** The baby was due at the end of July or early August. Oliver promised Annette that he would return in time for the birth of the baby. **(Aff. Annette Yanov, p. 23, L 29-32; Aff. Oliver Yanov, p. 25, L 24-25.)**

During that time, Oliver tried to contact Annette, by both letter and telephone. He was unable to reach her by telephone, partly because the phone system in war torn Yugoslavia was unreliable; and partly because he was unable to leave a message because Oliver and Annette did not have an answering machine in the apartment they shared. **(Aff. Oliver Yanov, p. 25, L 30-33.)** Oliver became concerned and contacted Annette's aunt and uncle Mickey and Mickey Couric. **(Aff. Oliver Yanov, p. 25, L 32.)** The Courics promised Oliver that they would inform Annette of his call.

(5)

Oliver was unable to return to the United States before the birth of the baby as he had promised because of his grandmother's subsequent death for which he had to tend to her medical and funeral bills and the difficulty of getting a flight to the United States. (**Aff. Oliver Yanov, p. 25, L 4-6.**)

Oliver had supported Annette throughout her pregnancy. He paid the household bills, her college tuition, her medical expenses and anything else Annette needed. (**Aff. Annette Yanov, p. 23, L 19-28.**) The obstetrician, Dr. Whitaker, helped them by reducing the amount of her fee because Oliver and Annette did not have insurance. (**Aff. Annette Yanov, p. 23, L 22-24.**)

Annette became extremely concerned, due to the war in Yugoslavia, when she had not heard from Oliver for several days. She called Oliver's aunt in Yugoslavia who falsely told her that Oliver had married and was on his honeymoon. (**Aff. Annette Yanov, p. 23, L 34-37.**)

Believing she had been abandoned and deserted by Oliver, Annette moved out of the apartment they had shared and into a shelter for women. She did not want to see Oliver and no longer felt she could adequately care for the baby. A friend at that shelter advised her that she could give the baby up for adoption. Annette consulted with Dr. Whitaker and asked for advice about adoption. (**Aff. Annette Yanov, p. 23, L 39-43.**)

Annette met with the representatives of the Wilson Adoption Agency and did not tell them who the father was because she did not want Olivier to know about the adoption. Although she was told to hire an attorney, Annette did not do so because she could not afford one. The baby was born on August 1, 2000. Annette kept the baby until August 15, 2000 when she signed papers giving permission for the adoption to proceed and gave the baby to the representative from the Wilson Agency for temporary custody. (**Aff. Annette Yanov, p. 23, L 44-51.**)

(6)

(continued)

EXHIBIT 2.4 *continued*

Oliver Yanov returned from Yugoslavia in September 2000 to find that Annette had moved out of their apartment. He contacted Annette's aunt and uncle who informed him that they didn't know where Annette was and that the baby died. During the following two weeks Oliver contacted St. Peter's hospital where Annette was expected to deliver. There was no record of the birth. He also checked with the Bureau of Vital Statistics to verify a birth or death of the child and he checked all the hospitals within the vicinity. **(Aff. Oliver Yanov, p. 25, L 37-45.)**

Oliver didn't see Annette until January 2001. After many months, they reunited and resumed their relationship, which culminated in marriage on July 4, 2001. They purchased a home, and retained an attorney in an attempt to regain custody of their child. **(Aff. Oliver Yanov, p. 25, L 4-26; Aff. Annette Yanov, p. 24, L 9-29.)**

Judy and Kevin Williams are the adoptive parents of baby Mary. They married on May 6, 1989 and for the past five years had resided at the same address. She works full time as an assistant dental hygienist. Kevin has been laid off and is having a hard time finding a job. **(Aff. Judy Williams, p. 31, L 1-10.)** Every potential employer that Kevin has interviewed with had an excuse for not hiring him. Judy thinks it goes back to the trouble he got into while attending college. Kevin was charged with possession of a controlled substance. **(Aff. Judy Williams, p. 31, L 12-16.)** The only job Kevin ever held was the one he was just laid off from. McDonnell Douglas hired him because he had interned with them the previous two years. **(Aff. Judy Williams, p. 31, L 22-25.)**

Judy Williams wanted the adoption more than Kevin Williams did. Judy stated that he didn't seem like he cared. **(Aff. Judy Williams, p. 31, L 47-48.)** On October 18, 2000,

Temporary Custody of Baby Mary was granted to the Williams'. **See, Judgment of Adoption, dated August 1, 2001 Judge Blank, NJ Superior Court.**

Judy Williams stated that regarding this adoption she vaguely remembers some type of problem about the father's name and that: "Our lawyer originally told us it might have been a problem because New Jersey requires both natural parents to consent to the adoption." **(Aff. Judy Williams, p. 32, L 6-11.)**

Mary was left unattended on the sofa and she rolled off and required a visit to the emergency room for the cut on her head. **(Aff. Judy Williams, p. 32, L 24-27.)** Kevin was becoming angry about all the money spent on the baby. Judy started working more hours because their savings were depleted and now they had another mouth to feed. Kevin started working more hours and so Baby Mary was being shuttled between baby sitters. According to Judy, Kevin acted like he didn't care about Judy or Mary. A final screaming match has brought about the Williams' separating. **(Aff. Judy Williams, p. 32, L 12-40.)**

The Williams are concerned with who will reimburse them for all that they invested in Baby Mary. **(Aff. Judy Williams, p. 32, L 50.)**

Chris Hilliard the director of the Yale University Child Study Center in New Haven Connecticut states that he never met Baby Mary, or her parents, Annette and Oliver Yanov, or the adoptive parents for whom he is an expert witness. Yet he has reached a conclusion--based upon the information provided to him by Williams' counsel--that the child should stay with the adoptive parents. **(Aff. Chris Hilliard, p. 36, L 1-18, p. 37, L 2.)** Mr. Hilliard also believes that the facts surrounding his own personal life brought no bias to his conclusions. Mr. Hilliard

(8)

(continued)

EXHIBIT 2.4 *continued*

stated he hasn't seen his two adopted sons since 1990 when they learned of their birth parents and went to live with them. (**Aff. Chris Hilliard, p. 37, L 14-17.**)

Ms. Pat Wells, the Yanovs' expert witness, is director of the Children and Family Justice Center of the University of Pennsylvania. There they train lawyers, physicians and other professionals to assist in the advocacy of parental and child rights, and also to lobby the State Legislature. (**Aff. Pat Wells, p. 27, L 1-5.**) Ms. Wells is familiar with both the facts and legal issues, has read all of the sworn depositions, pleadings and briefs submitted by both parties, and has met personally with Oliver and Annette. Her staff has spent over 20 hours interviewing the Yanovs and administering psychological profile tests. (**Aff. Pat Wells, p. 27, L 14-17.**)

It is Ms. Wells' professional opinion that Oliver and Annette possess the qualities necessary to raise Baby Mary. They appear to be responsible individuals with strong moral values. Both are employed and are capable of providing the necessary material support for Baby Mary. The results of the psychological tests predict the Yanovs to be well rounded individuals, capable of performing the parental functions necessary to raise Baby Mary. (**Aff. Pat Wells, p. 27, L 37-46.**)

Oliver and Annette Yanov are in the ninety-fifth percentile of established guidelines relating to parental success as set out by the children and Family Justice Center of the University of Pennsylvania. (**Aff. Pat Wells, p. 28, L 1-2.**)

ARGUMENT

POINT I

DID THE SUPERIOR COURT OF NEW JERSEY'S INTERPRETTION OF NOTICE UNDER N.J.S.A.§ 9:3-45 CULMINATE IN AN UNJUST RESULT AND VIOLATION OF OLIVER YANOV'S 14th AMENDMENT RIGHT TO DUE PROCESS BY DENYING HIM HE NOTICE OF THE ADOPTION PROCEEDINGS AS HE WAS ENTITLED TO RECEIVE AS THE NATURAL PARENT OF BABY MARY?

Oliver Yanov, the birth parent and plaintiff-appellant in this matter, was not properly noticed of the intended adoption of his child, Baby Mary, prior to adoption hearings pursuant to *N.J.S.A.* § 9:3-45, nor did he ever consent to the adoption.

The trial court followed *N.J.S.A.* § 9:3-45(b)(2) in which notice was not required because the statute states:

B. Notice pursuant to subsection (A) shall not be required on any parent;

(1) who has executed a Parent's Surrender and Consent to Adoption;

(2) whose identity and whereabouts are unknown.

Although he was not named as the father in the adoption suit, there were individuals with personal knowledge of his interest and participation, including the birth mother's attending physician, but none came forward and none were inquired of.

The Trial Court erred in its interpretation because Oliver Yanov was still entitled to notice under *N.J.S.A.* § 9:3-45(a)(2), which states:

A.   In any adoption proceeding, notice of the Complaint may not be waived

and a Notice of Hearing shall be served on each parent of the child to be adopted.

For purposes, of this section, "parent" includes (1) the husband of the mother of a

(10)

(continued)

EXHIBIT 2.4 *continued*

child born or conceived during the marriage and (2) a putative or alleged natural mother or father of a child.

In the Judgment of Adoption, in a Preliminary Hearing held by Order of the Court, it is stated that the Petitioners, Judy and Kevin Williams had fulfilled all statutory requirements. See *Judgment of Adoption*, Exhibit "1." But in fact, they had not.

It is required under the *Rules Governing The Courts of the State of New Jersey*, R. 5:10-5(b) to give notice of the proceeding to the natural parents of the child, unless on proof by affidavit of diligent inquiry, which is also required under *R.* 4:4-5, that the location of a natural parent cannot be ascertained or a court of competent jurisdiction has, on notice to the natural parents, terminated their parental rights pursuant to *N.J.S.A.* § 9:3-37.

In *Armstrong v. Manzo*, 380 U.S. 545, 550; 85 S. Ct. 1187; 14 L. Ed. 2d 62; (1965) U.S. LEXIS 1348, the Supreme Court of the United States reversed the decision on certiorari and stated that the failure to notify the father of the pendent adoption proceedings deprived him of due process and rendered the adoption decree constitutionally invalid. "Failure to give petitioner notice of the pending adoption proceedings deprived him of his rights without due process of law." [T]he basis of *R.* 5:10-5(b) is that it "provided a stricter notice requirement in conformance with due process rights of natural parents." *R.* 5:10-5(b).

"[E]ffective September, 1971, to provide even stricter and more clearly stated notice requirements, as a matter of constitutional compulsion as expressed in *Armstrong, supra.*" the State of New Jersey amended notice again to state … "the rule now makes clear … that the natural parents must be noticed in every case except as provided in *N.J.S.*[*A.* §] 9:3-45." *R.*10-5[2].

(11)

One of these requirements is "a court of competent jurisdiction has terminated the parental rights of such parent or parents." Which implies certain fundamental findings have been made as to the natural parent's unfitness, abandonment or neglect ... justifying permanent severance of the parental relationship ... see *N.J.S.[A §]* 9:3-37 et seq." *R.* 5:10-5[1].

It is important to note that Yanov's parental rights were never terminated in a court of law.

The Trial Judge did not expand upon what the Court considered proof of due diligence. In *Cf. Lutheran Social Services of NJ v. Doe*, 172 N.J. Super. 343; 411 A.2d 1183; (1979) N.J. Super. LEXIS 1014, it was decided that where a mother refused to disclose the father's identity as stated in *R.* 5:10[2] further notice was required by publication. The Williams had not published notice.

Dr. Whitaker, the attending physician throughout Annette Couric Yanov's pregnancy, not only knew who the father was, and all the details in Annette Couric and Oliver Yanov's lives, but he arranged the adoption of Baby Mary with the Wilson Adoption Agency. (*Aff. Annette Yanov*, p 23, L 19-28, 39-43, Exhibit "2.") Dr. Whitaker had Oliver Yanov's home address in his records and should have provided it to the agency and the Williams so that Yanov could be notified. All of the parties were obligated by law to do all in their powers to attempt to notify.

It is stated in *N.J.S.A.* § 9:3-45(c):

c. If personal service of the notice cannot be effected because the whereabouts of

   a parent of a the child to be adopted are unknown, the court shall determine

   that an adequate effort has been made to serve notice upon the parent if the

(continued)

EXHIBIT 2.4 *continued*

plaintiff immediately prior to or during the placement and not more than nine

months prior to the filing of a complaint has:

(1) Sent notice by regular mail and by certified mail return receipt requested,

to the parent's last known address;

(2) Made a discreet inquiry as to the whereabouts of the missing parent among

any known relations, friends and current or former employers of the

parent;

(3) Unless otherwise restricted by law, made direct inquiries, using the party's

name and last known or suspected address, to the local post office, the

Division of Motor Vehicles, county welfare agency, the municipal police

department, the Division of State Police, the county probation office, the

Department of Corrections, and any social service and law enforcement

agencies known to have had contact with the party, or the equivalents in

other states, territories or countries. Failure to receive a response to the

inquiries within 45 days shall be a negative response.

Although "Lutheran Services was granted leave to proceed by way of notice through

publication and such notice was published..." *Cf. Lutheran Social Services*, 172 N.J. Super. 343,

345, the court further stated "*R.* 4:4-5 is applicable ... the rule provides that its alternative

methods of service are "consistent with due process of law," but it should be noted that service

by publication is not generally favored ... and for this reason resort to such service is only

permitted after diligent inquiry has failed to locate the defendant." *Supra.* 343, 1186.

The Williams took no such steps in locating Oliver Yanov, the father of Baby Mary. Judy Williams by her own affidavit knew that there would be "a problem because New Jersey requires both natural parents to consent to the adoption." (See *Aff. Judy Williams*, p. 32, L 6-11. Exhibit "3.")

Had the Wilson Adoption Agency checked on Annette Couric Yanov's residence prior to her moving into a woman shelter, the agency would have found that Annette and Oliver had shared the same address. Had the Wilson Adoption Agency requested Doctor Whitaker to provide the basic knowledge necessary to the adoption of the child regarding the birth mother, the agency would have reached the same result. By simply sending notice in accordance with *N.J.S.A.* § 9:3-45(c) by regular mail and by certified mail return receipt requested, Oliver would have learned of the adoption proceeding upon his return from war-torn Yugoslavia, the month after baby Mary's birth because his regular mail would have been at the apartment and a notice from the post office that stated they possessed a "return receipt letter" for him to sign for at the Post Office.

Judy and Kevin Williams, along with the Wilson Adoption Agency, did not fulfill their obligation to diligently search for Baby Mary's father. The Williams allowed the Judgment of Adoption, to falsely reflect that they, the Petitioners, had fulfilled all statutory requirements. See *Judgment of Adoption*, Exhibit "1." This act has deprived Oliver Yanov of his 14th amendment right to due process and has wrongfully deprived him of his child.

(14)

(continued)

EXHIBIT 2.4 *continued*

ARGUMENT

POINT II

THE SUPERIOR COURT OF NEW JERSEY ERRED IN NOT VACATING THE JUDGMENT OF ADOPTION BY NOT ALLOWING OLIVER YANOV, THE CHILD'S NATURAL FATHER, THE NOTICE HE IS ENTITLED TO UNDER N.J.S.A. § 9:3-46.

Oliver Yanov is entitled to notice pursuant to *N.J.S.A.* § 9:3-45 as the natural father of

Baby Mary. Failure of the Court to provide notice to Oliver denied him the right to object to the

adoption of his daughter.

The Court held no hearing to find that Oliver failed to perform the regular and expected

parental functions and support of the child; nor that he was unable to provide these functions

presently or in the future as stated in *N.J.S.A.* § 9:3-46(a)(1)(2).

N.J.S.A. § 9:3-46(a)(1)(2) states:

A.   A person who is entitled to notice pursuant to *N.J.S.A.* § 9:3-45 shall have

the right to object to the adoption of his child. A Judgment of Adoption

shall not be entered over an objection of a parent communicated to the

court unless the court finds:

(1)   that the parent has substantially failed to perform the regular and

expected parental functions of care and support of the child,

although able to do so; or,

(2)   that the parent is unable to perform the regular and expected

parental functions of care and support of the child and that the parent's inability to perform those functions is unlikely to change

in the immediate future; or,

(3)   Granting the judgment of adoption over the objections of the

parent will not be inimical to the best interests of the child.

Oliver Yanov has no debilitating infirmities in his present or past that would render him

unable to care for his child. Unlike the father who suffered and recovered from his illness in *In

the Matter of the Adoption of Children by GPB. Jr.,* 161 N.J. 396; 736 A2d 1277; (1999) N.J.

LEXIS 1367, where the child, R.M., "was young enough to remember his father's uncontrolled

mental illness [***403] and had been left with feelings of anxiety and insecurity about the

stability of his family [***1281], whereby the Appellate Division reversed because the

appropriate test was whether continuation of the father's parental rights would result in imminent

danger of serious harm to the children, and finding no such danger, reversed the judgment of

adoption." Unlike these children Baby Mary is in no such danger from her father and is too

young to form a cognitive recollection of what a parent is much less who her parents are while in

custodial care.

"The bond between parent and child remains society's most fundamental relationship."

See *Santosky v. Kramer*, 455 U.S. 745, 102 S. Ct. 1388, 71 L. Ed. 2d 599 (1982) and *Stanley v.

Illinois*, 405 U.S. 645, 92 S. Ct. 1208, 31 L. Ed. 2d 551 (1972). "Parents who forsake their

children run the risk that others may take their place. Abdication of parental responsibilities can

lead to the loss of parental rights and to the adoption of a child." See *G.P.B., supra,* at 8. Oliver

did not forsake his child.

(16)

(continued)

EXHIBIT 2.4 *continued*

"Before authorizing the adoption of a child, a court must terminate parental rights of the

biological parent." See *In re P.S.*, 315 N.J. Super. 91, 107, 716 A.2d 1171 (App. Div. 1998).

Terminating parental rights implicates fundamental liberty interests that are protected under the

United States Constitution." See *Santosky*, supra, 455 U.S. 745, 753.

"The termination of parental rights involves consideration of the nature of the right, the

permanency of the threatened loss, and an evaluation of parental unfitness." See *L.A.S.*, 134 N.J.

127, 132-33, 631 A.2d 928 (1993). "Merely showing that a child would be better off with an

adoptive parent rather than with the biological parent is not enough." See *New Jersey Div. Of*

Youth and Family Services v. A.W., 103 N.J. 591, 603, 512 A.2d 438 (1986). See also *G.P.B.*,

supra, at 9.

"The New Jersey Legislature has responded to those concerns by repeatedly amending

the relevant statutes … [T]he statute controlling termination of parental rights simply stated that

such rights could not be terminated unless the court found that the parent "failed to perform the

regular and expected parental functions of care and support of the child, [including] maintenance

of an emotional relationship." *N.J.S.A.* § 9:3-46(a) (amended 1994). Courts interpreted that

version of the statue to mean that termination of parental rights depended on a finding that the

biological parent had abandoned or neglected the child." See *L.A.S.*, *supra*, at 134. "To find

abandonment or neglect, courts required conduct showing a settled purpose to forsake parental

responsibilities." *Id.*, at 135.

The 1994 amendment provided an objective definition of "regular and expected parental

functions" that specified three activities constituting "the core values of parenthood." See *In the*

Matter of the Adoption of a Child By W.P. and M.P., 308 N.J. Super. 386, 385, [*406] 706 A.2d 198 (App. Div. 1998). Those functions included:

    (a) The maintenance of a relationship with the child such that the child perceives the person as his parent;

    (b) Communicating with the child or person having legal custody of the child and parenting time rights [***12] unless having parenting time is impossible because of the parent's confinement in an institution, or unless prevented from so doing by the custodial parent or other custodian of the child or a social service agency over the birth parent's objection; or

    (c) Providing financial support for the child unless prevented from doing so by the custodial parent or other custodian of the child or a social service agency.

"In determining whether a parent has affirmatively assumed the duties of a parent, the court shall consider … the fulfillment of financial obligations for the birth and care of the child, demonstration of continued interest in the child, demonstration of a genuine effort to maintain communication with the child … and the establishment and maintenance of a place of importance in the child's life." See *G.P.B., supra,* at 18.

Oliver Yanov affirmatively assumed the duties encompassed by the role of being a parent. While the child was in the womb, he provided the financial means to support the mother of his child, Annette f/k/a Couric, and not only provided her with, but was an active part of her prenatal care under Dr. Whitaker. Oliver's interest in his child's well being did not wane after Baby Mary's birth in fact he searched diligently for the record of her birth (and possible death) at hospitals, the Bureau of Vital Statistics and by contacting Annette's relatives.

(18)

(continued)

EXHIBIT 2.4 *continued*

For months he searched using every means possible, such as friends, family, and modeling agencies, looking for clues to find Annette and his child. He loved her; he loved his child. He wanted his family united. See *Aff. Oliver Yanov*, p 25, L 39-48, p 26, L 1-20, Exhibit "4."

He demonstrated through his actions a genuine effort to maintain communication and establish a place of importance in his child's life despite the deliberate deceit and treachery of those knowing the truth surrounding the birth of his daughter. Had he not been prevented by the Wilson Adoption Agency and the custodians of Baby Mary, Oliver would have been able to maintain a parental relationship with his daughter, and provided financial support.

(19)

ARGUMENT

POINT III

THE SUPERIOR COURT OF NEW JERSEY APPLIED THE WRONG STANDARD OF EVIDENCE IN DETERMINING THE BEST INTEREST OF THE CHILD WHICH CULMINATED IN AN UNJUST RESULT.

At the time of the hearing on the Motion to Vacate Judgment of Adoption the Superior Court stated the following on the record regarding Oliver and Annette Yanov that: "Plaintiffs have not established by the **preponderance of the evidence** [emphasis added] that the best interests of Baby Mary are not being served by permitting the judgment of adoption to remain in effect." See *Motion to Vacate Judgment of Adoption*, hearing transcript, Exhibit "5."

It was during the pendency of the appeal, *In the Matter of the Adoption of Children By G.P.B., JR.*, 161 N.J. 396; 736 A.2d 1277; (1999) N.J. LEXIS 1367 that Legislature amended the governing statute N.J.S.A. § 9:3:46 to underscore that the dominant consideration was the best interest of children rather than the rights of their biological parents. "Fairly read, the amendment reflects decreasing legislative tolerance for biological parents who engage in the act of procreation, but do not assume the responsibilities of parenthood [***17] ... [I]n an action to terminate parental rights, the statute expressly states that "the best interests of the child requires that a parent affirmatively assume [*409] the duties encompassed by the role of being a parent." L. 1998, c.20, sec.2 (effective September 11, 1998). n1."

Oliver Yanov, has for all intended purposes affirmatively assumed the duties encompassed by the role of being a parent while his child was in the womb because he provided the financial means to support the mother of his child, Annette f/k/a Couric, and provided her

(20)

(continued)

EXHIBIT 2.4 *continued*

with and was an active part of her prenatal care, and took extraordinary action to reunite his

family.

[T]he statute controlling termination of parental rights simply stated that such rights

could not be terminated unless the court found that the parent "failed to perform the regular and

expected parental functions of care and support of the child, [including] maintenance of an

emotional relationship." *N.J.S.A.* § 9:3-46(a) (amended 1994). Courts interpreted that version of

the statue to mean that termination of parental rights depended on a finding that the biological

parent had abandoned or neglected the child." See *L.A.S.*, 134 N.J. 127, 132-33; 631 A.2d 928

(1993). The Court held no hearing to determine if Oliver Yanov had abandoned or neglected his

child.

When the Trial Court denied the motion to vacate the judgment of adoption it erred in its

interpretation of the standard that was to be used. In its reason, the Court stated that Oliver

Yanov had not established by the preponderance of the evidence the best interests of the baby.

The Court has shown in the past whereby terminating the parental rights of natural fathers

found by **clear and convincing** [emphasis added] evidence to have failed to satisfy his

obligations to the child. See *In re Adoption of Children by D.*, 61 N.J.89 (1972); *In re Mercado

Ado*ption, 182 N.J. Super. 628 (App. Div. 1982); *In re Adoption by J.J.P.*, 175 N.J. Super 420

(App. Div. 1980); In *re Adoption of a Child by J.R.D.*; 246 N.J. Super. 619 (Ch. Div. 1990); and

Matter of Adoption of a Child by R.K., 303 N.J. Super, 182; 198 (Ch. Div. 1997). *See also R.*

5:10-5[3.10].

Under *N.J.S.A.* § 9:3-46(a) no time limit applies to the determination of the best interest

of the child. In contrast, the time to determine whether an objecting parent has "failed to perform

(21)

the regular and expected parental functions of care and support" is "the six month period prior to the placement of the child for adoption." *N.J.S.A.* § 9:3-46(a)(2)(c). See *G.P.B., supra,* at 7.

"[*412] Under Title 30, the "best interests" test continues to concentrate on whether the parent has harmed or is likely to continue to harm the child. *N.J.S.A.* § 30:4C-15.1(a), … sets forth a four-prong test to determine a child's best interest; three of the four prongs focus on harm to the child. …In Title 9 proceedings, the Legislature has redirected the focus from harm to the child to the discharge of parental functions. Although the failure of a parent to [***24] discharge parental functions often will harm the child, Title 9 proceedings are less concerned with such harm and more with the parent's willingness and ability to provide [**1286] effective parenting. To that end, *N.J.S.A.* § 9:3-46 directs courts to consider whether the objecting parent has affirmatively assumed his or her parental duties and has fulfilled the "regular and expected parental functions of care and support." See *G.P.B., supra,* at 7-8. In considering those factors, the court should avoid a comparative analysis of the birth parent with the adoptive parent. As we have noted, the question is not whether the child would be better off with the adoptive parent, [***26] but whether the biological parent has failed to fulfill his or her duties.

"When the child's biological parent resists termination of parental rights, our function is to decide [***9] whether the parent can raise the child without causing harm." See *In re Guardianship of J.C.*, 129 N.J. 1, 10, 608 A.2d 1312 (1992). "The cornerstone of our inquiry is not whether the parent is fit, but whether he can become fit to assume the parental role within time to meet the child's needs." Ibid. "The analysis of harm entails strict standards to protect the statutory and constitutional rights of the natural parents." Ibid. "The burden rests on the party seeking to terminate parental rights "to demonstrate by clear and convincing evidence" that risk

(22)   *(continued)*

EXHIBIT 2.4 *continued*

of "serious and lasting [future] harm to the child" is sufficiently great as to require severance of parental ties." Ibid. *See also In the Matter of the Adoption of a Child By W.P. and M.P.,* 308 N.J. Super. 376, 379; 706 A.2d 198 (App. Div. 1998).

In *In re Adoption of Children by D.,* 61 N.J. 89, 94 (1972) the case held in discussing *N.J.S.A.* § 9:3-24(c), permitting a termination of the right of a parent to custody of a child sought to be adopted if the parent has forsaken parental [***6] obligations, held that where the parent had not forsaken obligations, the adoption could not be approved even if in the best interests of the child. *See also Sorentino v. The Family and Children's Society of Elizabeth,* 72 N.J. 127, 131; 367 A.2d 1168; (1976) N.J. LEXIS 225.

"While the prospective adopting parents have a great stake in this matter, their interests are necessarily subordinate to the rights of the natural parents." *Sorentino, supra,* 72 N.J. 127, 131 (1976).

In *Santosky v. Kramer,* 455 U.S. 745, 102 S. Ct. 1388, 71 L. Ed. 2d 599 (1982) the Supreme Court clearly held:

1. Process is constitutionally due a natural parent at a state-initiated parental rights termination proceeding.

    (a) The fundamental liberty interest of natural parents in the care, custody, and management of their child is protected by the Fourteenth Amendment, and does not evaporate simply because they have not been model parents or have lost temporary custody of their child to the State. A parental rights termination proceeding interferes with that fundamental liberty interest. When the State

(23)

moves to destroy weakened familial bonds, it must provide the parents with fundamentally fair procedures.

(b) The nature of the process due in parental rights termination proceedings turns on a balancing of three factors: the private interests affected by the proceedings; the risk of error created by the State's chosen procedure; and the countervailing governmental interest supporting use of the challenged procedure. *Mathews v. Eldridge*, 424 U.S. 319, 335; 96 S.Ct. 893, 903, 47 L.Ed.2d 18.

2. The "fair preponderance of the evidence" standard . . . violates the Due Process Clause of the Fourteenth Amendment. *Id.* at 1396 - 1402.

(b) A preponderance standard does not fairly allocate the risk of an erroneous fact-finding between the State and the natural parents. . . . Coupled with the preponderance standard, these factors create a significant prospect of erroneous termination of parental rights. . . . which leave the child in an uneasy status quo, and an erroneous termination, which unnecessarily destroys the natural family, does not reflect properly the relative severity of these two outcomes. *Id.* at 1398 - 1401.

3. Before a State may sever completely and irrevocably the rights of parents in their natural child, due process requires that the State support its allegations by at least clear and convincing evidence. A "clear and convincing evidence" standard adequately conveys to the factfinder the level of subjective certainty about his factual conclusions necessary to satisfy due process. Determination of the precise burden equal to or greater than the standard is a matter of state law properly left to state legislatures and state courts. *Id.* at 1402 - 1403.

(24)

(continued)

EXHIBIT 2.4 *continued*

Failure to apply the correct standard not only affects the rights of Oliver Yanov but, his child, Baby Mary. "The child has an outcome of the hearing independent of that of the parent. To be sure, 'the child and his parents share a vital interest in preventing erroneous termination of their natural relationship.'" *Santosky, supra*, 455 U.S. 745, 790 (1982). "For a child, the consequences of termination of his natural parents' rights may be well far-reaching ... 'The child loses rights inherent in the parent-child relationship, not just for [a limited] period ..., but forever.'" *Id.*, at 762.

(25)

CONCLUSION

For all the foregoing reasons, petitioner respectfully requests this court to reverse the order of the Judgement for Adoption of the court below.

complete listing of all the cases, statutes, constitutional provisions, and rules of civil procedure applied in the appellate brief. The *Statement of Issues* consists of the questions of law posed to the appellate court by the appellant. The *Statement of Facts* contains all the pertinent details of the case thus far. The *Argument* applies the law to the issues and facts, and presents the reasons why the appellant should prevail. The *Conclusion* ties up all the issues and the argument for a final push for the appellant's case. The appellee will have a designated amount of time to write a responsive brief. The briefs are read by the appellate court, which may decide the case *on the papers* (no oral argument) or after listening to oral argument. Most states have strict rules and time limits for oral arguments.

Appellate Brief Analysis

What did you think of the appellate brief in Exhibit 2.4? The word *long* probably comes to mind, but the length is necessary to argue all the points. You should pay careful attention to the details of the appellate brief, since you may be asked to work on one soon. Remember, you can find out the real-life results of the *Baby Richard* case in the chapter on adoption.

CHAPTER SUMMARY

Legal research and writing are intrinsic parts of most legal practices. Paralegals may be asked to assist in writing all types of documents, including correspondence, pleadings, motions, memorandums of law, and appellate briefs. Most legal documents have an accepted format that should be followed by the writer, especially legal documents that are to be filed with the court. You can find the rules for legal writing in your state's court rules.

The American legal system is based on the English legal system. Because of this, our country's laws are created with a two-pronged approach. The two-pronged approach includes common law and statutory law. The legal system is designed to allow the courts to follow precedent, which is based on the doctrine of *stare decisis*. The role of the judge is to interpret case law and statutes. Judges should apply primary authority first, and then secondary authority.

A judge can only hear a case over which the judge has jurisdiction. Jurisdiction is extremely important. There are different types of jurisdiction. There is *in personam* (over the person) jurisdiction and *in rem* (over the thing) jurisdiction. Each state has a court system. The federal government also has a national court system. The state courts hear cases in which the particular court has jurisdiction. The federal courts may have jurisdiction if the case involves a person or subject over which a federal court has jurisdiction.

Learning the law often involves the Socratic method of teaching. Conducting your legal research often involves utilizing a significant number of written materials and computer-assisted legal research (CALR). The written materials include, but are not limited to, the following: state reporters, regional reporters, codes, digests, supplement bound volumes, pocket parts, advance sheets, court rules books, practice manuals, legal newspapers, legal encyclopedias, treatises, and law journals. The use of CALR has steadily increased, and online resources are readily available.

Law may be either substantive or procedural. Legal research involves gathering information in two main areas: statutes and case law. A third area, administrative rules, may also be a good source for answering certain legal questions. The first area you should check for the answer to your legal issue is your state's statutes, and the second area is the case reporters for your state. You can determine which cases in the reporters to look up by utilizing a digest for your state. Both digests and state statutes can be found in annotated versions. The annotations, which are short descriptions of statutes or cases that may involve fact scenarios similar to your client's fact pattern, are a great tool for the researcher.

Each case and statute has a citation unlike any other. The citation can be compared to an address for finding the legal information it refers to. Once you have found reported cases with fact patterns similar to those of your clients, you will never forget the Shepardizing process. Failing to Shepardize cases or statutes could mean that the attorneys will depend on a statute or case that is no longer good law.

Key Terms

legal memorandum of law
appellate brief
majority opinion
dissenting opinion
concurring opinion
precedent
doctrine of *stare decisis*
statute
code
legal error
jurisdiction
primary authority
secondary authority

persuasive authority
reporter
pocket part
advance sheet
regional reporter
case of first impression
substantive law
procedural law
court rules book
case digest
practice manual
legal newspaper
Words and Phrases

computer-assisted legal
   research (CALR)
legislative history
annotation
Corpus Juris Secundum (CJS)
American Jurisprudence (Am
   Jur)
citation
on point
Shepardizing
case briefing
appellant
appellee

Surfing the Web

Refer to Exhibit 2.2 for a list of Web sites that may help you in your legal research.

ETHICS ALERT

Susan has been told by Pat, the old pro, that she should take advantage of all the memos and briefs that have been written at Johnson & Webster over the years. Pat also has suggested that Susan keep a file of memos and briefs that she prepares for future reference, in addition to gathering as much help as possible from the memos and briefs written in the past by the firm's attorneys and paralegals. Susan wonders whether client confidentiality should be a concern, and also whether it is fair to charge one client for work that may be shared by another client in the future. Should Susan be concerned?

Review Questions

1. What is a legal memorandum of law?
2. Why is there a two-pronged approach to law in the United States?
3. What is common law based on?
4. (a) What is precedent? (b) What is the Latin term for the concept of following precedent?
5. When does a judge *not* have to follow precedent?
6. (a) The laws created by a state's elected bodies are called what? (b) Where can you find these laws?

7. (a) If you do not win a case at the trial level, where can you appeal?
   (b) Is the opportunity to appeal automatically granted in family law matters?
8. If you lose your first appeal, can you appeal again?
9. What is a judge's main job?
10. What is jurisdiction? Why is it important?
11. What is the difference between primary and secondary authority?
12. What does *reported* mean when talking about legal research?
13. What are the parts of a reporter volume?
14. What is the name of the set of books that lists all reported cases from a particular geographic region?
15. What is a case of first impression?
16. What are the essential resources needed to conduct legal research?
17. How do you begin a research assignment?
18. What is the process for checking statutory or case law changes?
19. What are the options for CALR?
20. What is the case digest system, and why is it important to the legal researcher?

Chapter 3

Living Together

THE GROWING TREND OF COHABITATION

Americans love the white lace and promises of a wedding. In fact, we love marriage so much that nine out of ten of us marry in our lifetimes.[1] Another fact of American life is that those marriages are not lasting. The divorce rate for first-time marriages hovers at just over 50 percent, and it is even higher for those who marry twice or more. One of the fastest-growing segments of society consists of unmarried partners sharing a household. More than three in seven adults are not currently married but share their home with a partner.[2] A significant number of unmarried partners sharing a household are gay and are not legally permitted to marry even if they wish to, although the Massachusetts Supreme Court found the ban against same-sex marriage unconstitutional as this text was going to print. There is an exception in Vermont, where a limited civil union is legal. You will read more about civil unions in a later chapter.

Being an unmarried partner sharing a household can create far-reaching emotional and financial ramifications. In the following, you will read about some of the pitfalls of such a relationship and how to legally prevent possible turmoil.

JOANNA'S STORY—BUT MOTHER, I LOVE HIM!

"That's it!" Joanna practically screamed. "I don't want to hear anymore about my so-called ridiculous relationship!"

Eleanor Hill, Joanna's usually extraordinarily patient mother, was as exasperated with Joanna as Joanna was with her. "In all your 32 years, you *never* raised your voice to me," Eleanor responded. "Of course, that was *before* meeting William and deciding that you're—I can't even believe I'm saying this— actually going to *live* with him."

Breathing rhythmically as instructed by her new yoga instructor, Joanna leaned against her mother's spotless white counter in her equally spotless kitchen. With a deep breath, Joanna looked at her mother and said, "Mom, I love you, but you can't try to control my life anymore. I'm going to live a freer life." Joanna could see her mom was not buying it, so she added, "Look, you can control organizing your schedule and your antiseptic house, but I'm old enough to do what *I* need to do." Having said that much, Joanna continued, now on a roll, "Maybe I've never raised my voice to you because I've always done what you wanted and never felt strongly enough to disagree, but I do feel strongly about William. You may feel comfortable with plastic all over the *good* living room furniture, but I won't have your plastic attitude suffocating me any longer!"

Eleanor slumped speechlessly into a kitchen chair as Joanna escaped out the back door, letting it bang shut behind her.

For the first time in 20 years, most of the Hill clan, including Eleanor and Frank, Joanna's father, and even the women in Eleanor's bridge club, all held the same opinion: Joanna had gone crazy from love. The difference between the views held by the bridge club and those of Joanna's family, however, was that the bridge club ladies could understand Joanna's attraction to William.

William was a 26-year-old sometime bartender aspiring to be a rock star. He had wooed the 32-year-old reticent accountant with his humor and genuineness. Joanna had been unlucky in love for so long that she had given up on dating. She met William when she was hired as the accountant for the club where he often performed. Joanna had tussled with the age difference in the beginning, but William's kindness and maturity had given her the strength to deal with the admonitions of friends and family who warned her to "be careful" about William.

Always the businesswoman first, Joanna recently decided—on her own—to give her younger cousin Susan, a paralegal, a call to see about visiting an attorney before William moved into her hard-earned first house.

Preventing Cohabitation Disaster—J. D.'s Advice

A few days later, Joanna sipped the law firm's three-hour-old coffee and waited for Susan's boss to finish with another client. "I'm terribly sorry about this," Susan whispered to Joanna. "Unfortunately, a client had an emergency because of a domestic violence incident with her soon-to-be-ex-husband, and J. D. just *had* to see her this afternoon."

Joanna nodded nervously and whispered into Susan's ear, "It's fine. I appreciate your getting me in to see your boss, and I don't mind waiting in such comfy chairs—I just wish the coffee tasted better." Susan smiled at her cousin as J. D. escorted a teary-eyed client out the firm's front door.

Turning toward the waiting cousins, J. D. Dombroski offered his hand to Joanna and invited her into his office. "Welcome to Johnson & Webster. I can see the resemblance between you two."

Susan said with a smile, "Well, I'll leave you to it. I have to go finish a deposition summary for Alyssa." Joanna thanked Susan and followed J. D. into his office.

After asking Joanna to make herself comfortable in one of the office's leather wing chairs, J. D. went right on to business. "Ms. Hill, Susan has explained to me that you are here for a consultation regarding the pros and cons of living with your boyfriend without getting married."

Joanna responded, "That's exactly it. *Everyone* I know is telling me it's a bad idea to live with William. So, I wanted to hear what an attorney had to say about it."

J. D. began, "Well, number one, while your situation is increasingly more common these days, it *does* have great risks. It would be extremely unwise for you not to protect your assets and the financial stability you've worked so hard to achieve." He paused, and then added, "But, I'm not going to tell you not to live together with your boyfriend."

Joanna smiled, and J. D. continued by saying, "However, I do want to point out that your beau may be a nice young man who is very much in love with you, but he has nothing to lose and everything to gain. You stand to lose a great deal—excuse me for saying this—if your romance *fizzles* and ends acrimoniously."

Joanna was no longer smiling, but J. D. went on, "Your significant other could conceivably make claims on assets earned by you if the both of you don't take the precaution of entering an agreement, or in other words, a contract, that clearly outlines the assets and responsibilities each of you have to the other. This type of contract is usually called a **cohabitation agreement.**"

Joanna was convinced. She nodded and asked, "What's my next step?"

J. D. handed her a sample cohabitation contract and said, "Take a look at this. I think you'll agree there isn't any clause that wouldn't be described as good common sense by a reasonable person. If you were marrying William, I would make sure you were completely honest in listing all your assets and liabilities in what is called a prenuptial agreement, but a complete listing is not required in a cohabitation agreement." Leaving Joanna to her reading, J. D. left the office. He returned a few minutes later with more coffee. "Thought you'd like another cup of mud," he offered.

Returning his smile, Joanna responded, "I'll take you up on the cohabitation agreement, but—if you don't mind—I think I'll pass on the coffee." Agreeing that the sample cohabitation agreement basically covered the points that were important, Joanna decided to discuss the agreement with William and then get back to J. D.

A Cohabitation Contract Makes Good Sense

After reading the contract, Joanna realized just how much she stood to lose if her relationship with William took the proverbial "nose dive." She also realized that it was grounded in good old-fashioned common sense and that if William *really* loved her, it would make good sense to him as well. More than anything else, however, Joanna wanted their relationship to be rooted in honesty and openness, and she felt that this agreement could only help, not hinder, their relationship. She was sure she would be able to show William that this was the way to go.

The next morning Joanna called J. D.'s office and spoke with Susan. "Hi, Susan," Joanna opened. "It's a go. I spoke with William, and he's fine with the contract." She added, "You know my family—he's especially hoping that by signing this contract, they'll get off his back."

Susan agreed, "I'm sure J. D. is right and it's all for the best."

A week later the cohabitation agreement was ready for Joanna and William's review and signatures. You can read the cohabitation contract signed by the contractually bound couple in Exhibit 3.1. See if you agree with J. D.'s description of the cohabitation contract being "good *common sense*." Every cohabitation contract should be written with the specific couple in mind, and any sample contract should be used only as a suggested guideline. The cohabitation contract can be as simple or as complicated as the property and lives of the parties necessitates it to be. The term **addendum** is used in the contract and is defined as an attachment to the contract that is considered a part of the contract.

Happy Couple Adheres to Contract

As it turned out, William was a sensible young man who saw the merits of such an agreement. Moreover, because he hoped it would give him the incentive he needed to jump-start his own career, he entered into it wholeheartedly. William also hoped Joanna's family would become a little more warm and fuzzy toward him when he visited them. He soon moved into Joanna's upscale townhouse, and they proceeded to make beautiful music together for two happy years. William became a very successful rock musician who was much in demand. His income soon became double, and then triple, the amount of Joanna's. Eventually, it appeared that the sky would be the limit. The couple's favorable financial position allowed them to acquire a house, two cars, a boat, and various other symbols of economic success. Adhering strictly to their cohabitation agreement, they added those items bought jointly and independently to their addendums. Furthermore, now that their mutual honesty and openness had paid off and their relationship was ripe with trust and respect, they felt ready to graduate to a more serious commitment to each other—marriage.

COME LIVE WITH ME AND BE MY LOVE

Joanna and William's plans to marry are opposite of the national trend, which is moving away from marriage. (You will read more about the couple and their plans in Chapter 4 on prenuptial agreements.) This trend is reflected in statistics showing that between 1990 and 2000, there was an increase of 72 percent in unmarried partners living together.[3] This is obviously a huge jump, and Americans are not alone. Marriage rates also

EXHIBIT 3.1 Joanna and William's Cohabitation Contract

Cohabitation Contract of Joanna Hill and William Lovejoy

The parties entering this cohabitation contract are Joanna Hill, to be known as Party A, and William Lovejoy, to be known as Party B. The Parties will reside together at 1 Loveboat Lane, Bucolic Borough, State of Bliss.

The Parties enter this Cohabitation Contract with the intent that the Parties' relationship and cohabitation will be conducted with clarity and fairness. In pursuit of this intention, the Parties agree to the following:

A. The Parties understand this agreement will not survive in the event the parties marry.

B. The Parties each separately own real and personal property. This real and personal property is listed under Party A and Party B's names on the attached addendums. The addendums are made a part of this agreement.

C. In the event of separation or death, each party understands that this agreement is designed to prevent any claims from being made by one party against the property of the other party.

D. Each party will retain his or her own name.

E. Each party will maintain separate bank accounts, investments, credit or charge accounts, and any other type of financial accounts.

F. Household Expenses: The parties will each contribute equally to such household expenses as food, sundries, and entertainment. The mortgage and utilities will be paid by Party A. *[In the alternative, a couple whose incomes are disparate may wish to divide expenses according to a percentage of their incomes. For example, one party may earn twice as much as the other and, therefore, would pay a proportionately higher percentage of the household expenses.]* Both Parties agree that subsequent to the signing of this agreement, all of their separately purchased property valued over $250.00 *[or any amount agreed by the Parties]* will be listed on additional addendums and made a part of this agreement.

G. Additions to the attached addendums will include the name of the owner of the property and be signed and dated by both Parties.

H. Both Parties agree that joint purchases made subsequent to the signing of this agreement will be listed on additional addendums and be made a part of this agreement. The additional addendums will include the value of the item, the percentage of ownership of each party, and the disposition of the item in the event the Parties split up. Any additional addendums pertaining to this paragraph will be signed and dated by both Parties.

Joanna Hill _____

William Lovejoy _____

Witness _____

DATED: _____

have fallen in Australia, Austria, Belgium, Bulgaria, China, France, Germany, Greece, Ireland, Israel, Italy, Portugal, Spain, Switzerland, and the United Kingdom. Recently, the marriage rate in Switzerland reached the lowest rate in 80 years, with an 85 percent drop.[4] You can review interesting statistics pertaining to the living arrangements of American citizens in Exhibit 3.2.

Why Are Couples Living Together?

Why is this trend toward cohabitation happening? There are no definitive reasons, but some cohabiting partners may live together to avoid the possibility of divorce or to keep alimony from a previous marriage. As previously mentioned, same-sex partners who wish to marry are not legally allowed to marry except for a limited civil union exception in Vermont and a pending final outcome in Massachusetts. Another reason for cohabitation may be that disabled citizens and citizens receiving public assistance would lose financial benefits if they married, and so some of them remain in unmarried partnerships.

Why Is Granny Living with Her Boyfriend?

Senior citizens face similar financial fears and are part of the new statistic. According to the United States Census Bureau, unmarried opposite-sex couples age 65 and older rose 73 percent from 1990 to 1999.[5] A senior receiving financial benefits from a deceased spouse may lose those benefits upon remarriage. If a widowed spouse remarries before turning 60, her Social Security benefits stemming from the previous marriage are forfeited. Remarriage after 60 has no effect on Social Security eligibility.[6] Another reason is that hospitals and Medicaid cannot look to a cohabiting partner to pay the other partner's medical bills, but a person *can* be required to pay a spouse's medical bills. Actually, spouses can be required to pay *any* of their spouses' unpaid bills.

NEW PROTECTIONS ON THE HORIZON FOR COHABITING PARTNERS

The increasing numbers of cohabiting partners, along with society's increasing acceptance of cohabitation without marriage, has made cohabiting partners a force to be reckoned with. Some countries—such as Canada, France, and Sweden—are taking the lead in protecting partners in unmarried cohabiting relationships. Unmarried but cohabiting citizens of those three countries are allowed to register and gain marital-type rights as domestic partners. The term **domestic partner** usually refers to a person who has been designated as another's life partner outside marriage and who, because of such designation, may receive benefits of some kind. Some cities and states in the United States allow cohabiting residents to register as domestic partners. Refer to Chapter 5, Exhibit 5.4 for a list of states and cities that offer such registration.

Landmark Cohabitation Case: *Palimony* Added to Dictionary

One of the best-known cases concerning a cohabiting but unmarried couple involved the late actor Lee Marvin and Michelle Triola Marvin. The case became infamously known in the media as a *palimony* case. The plaintiff, Michelle Triola Marvin, was awarded the property and support historically received only by a divorcing spouse, not a former lover. That did not last long, though, once Lee Marvin appealed the trial court's decision.

The California case of *Marvin v. Marvin,* 122 Cal. App. 3d 871, 176 Cal. Rptr. 555 (1981), added the word *palimony* to the English language. It also added new legal ramifications for unmarried couples living together. **Palimony** is defined as financial support paid between persons who are not, and never were, married.

EXHIBIT 3.2 Living Arrangements of Americans (Courtesy of the U.S. Census Bureau)

Living Arrangements of Younger and Older Adults: March 2000 (In thousands)

Characteristic	Number		Percent	
	Men	Women	Men	Women
Younger Adults				
18 to 34 years old				
Total	31,854	32,464	100.0	100.0
Living alone	2,830	2,156	8.9	6.6
Married spouse present	10,603	13,298	33.3	41.0
Not married spouse present—child of householder	9,737	6,661	30.6	20.5
None of the above	8,684	10,349	27.3	31.9
18 to 24 years old				
Total	13,291	13,242	100.0	100.0
Living alone	551	588	4.1	4.4
Married spouse present	1,305	2,332	9.8	17.6
Not married spouse present—child of householder	7,497	5,629	56.4	42.5
None of the above	3,938	4,693	29.6	35.4
25 to 34 years old				
Total	18,563	19,222	100.0	100.0
Living alone	2,279	1,568	12.3	8.2
Married spouse present	9,298	10,966	50.1	57.0
Not married spouse present—child of householder	2,240	1,032	12.1	5.4
None of the above	4,746	5,656	25.6	29.4
Older Adults				
65 years old and over				
Total	13,886	18,735	100.0	100.0
Living alone	2,355	7,427	17.0	39.6
Married spouse present	10,084	7,743	72.6	41.3
None of the above	1,447	3,565	10.4	19.0
65 to 74 years old				
Total	8,049	9,747	100.0	100.0
Living alone	1,108	2,983	13.8	30.6
Married spouse present	6,170	5,156	76.7	52.9
None of the above	771	1,608	9.6	16.5
75 years old and over				
Total	5,837	8,988	100.0	100.0
Living alone .	1,247	4,444	21.4	49.4
Married spouse present	3,914	2,587	67.1	28.8
None of the above	676	1,957	11.6	21.8

Lee Marvin was a well-known actor best remembered for his Academy Award–winning roles in *Cat Ballou* and *The Dirty Dozen*. Michelle Triola Marvin was a little-known singer and actress who became well known when she sued Lee Marvin for support and maintenance after he ended their six-year relationship in 1970. Michelle claimed that she gave up her career as a singer and actress to be Lee's companion and that, except for benefit of clergy and an $8 marriage license, they lived together as man and wife in every way. Ms. Marvin, who legally changed her surname to Marvin shortly before their relationship ended, alleged in her suit that they had a verbal agreement to share any property they acquired during their relationship and, therefore, she was entitled to half of his earnings during the six years they lived together as a "married" couple. She sought $100,000 for sacrificing her career and half of the $3.6 million he earned while they lived together.

Originally, the trial court dismissed Ms. Marvin's complaint, without hearing any arguments, on the grounds that enforcing such a contract between unmarried persons was tantamount to promoting prostitution and was, therefore, illegal. This decision was upheld on appeal. However, in 1976, the California Supreme Court overruled the two lower courts. It remanded the case back to trial court, stating that the plaintiff had provided a suitable basis for her breach-of-promise suit for which the trial court could give damages and, furthermore, that her complaint could be amended to state a cause of action for breach of implied contract. An **implied contract** is a contract with existence and terms determined by the *actions* of the persons involved, not by their words. In explaining its decision, the court declared that society no longer views cohabitation as morally reprehensible and that enforcing judicial rules based on moral considerations now ignored by most of society would not be just.[7]

The sensational 11-week trial attracted international attention, not only because Mr. Marvin was a major movie star who was supported by many of his equally famous colleagues, but also because it was the first legal test of palimony, or the property rights of unmarried couples. On April 18, 1979, the Superior Court of California again rejected Ms. Marvin's claims, saying they found no legal basis for her claim that she had either an express contract or an implied contract with the actor to share his assets. An **express contract** is defined as a contract with terms stated in oral or written words. However, under the legal principle of equitable remedy, the judge awarded Ms. Marvin the sum of $104,000 to be used primarily for her economic rehabilitation. An **equitable remedy** is defined as a solution that is just, fair, and right for a particular situation. The $104,000 amount was equivalent to $1,000 a week for two years, which was based on the highest salary Ms. Marvin earned in her career as a singer.

Lee Marvin appealed the rehabilitative award, while Michelle Triola Marvin challenged the amount of the award. The Court of Appeals for the Second District of California affirmed the lower court's decision that Ms. Marvin was not entitled to any of Mr. Marvin's earnings. The court stated that she had benefited both economically and socially from their relationship, while Mr. Marvin had never acquired anything of value from Ms. Marvin, was not unjustly enriched by their relationship because of any wrongful act, and was under no obligation to pay a reasonable sum for her support. The court also reversed the $104,000 rehabilitative award on the basis that it was not within the issues framed by the pleadings. Ms. Marvin appealed to the state supreme court to have the $104,000 rehabilitative award reinstated, but was denied a hearing.[8]

The plaintiff sued the defendant for property and support that she believed she was entitled to after six years of living together. Do you think the plaintiff's motivating force could have been a need for public recognition of her alleged role in the defendant's success? In the *Marvin* case, did the court take on the role of protector of the institution of marriage, follow basic contract law, or combine these two elements? Do you think that expanding the rights of an unmarried cohabitant to include some or all of the rights of a spouse is an expansion whose time will come in the twenty-first century?

On a *technical* note, when you initially refer to a case, include the entire citation. After that you may use only the first name or, if referring to a particular page in the case, the first name and the page number.

Marvin Case Has Long-Term Effect

The decision in *Marvin* very likely inspired scores of live-in lovers to think seriously about the financial ramifications of falling out of love. Although Michelle Triola Marvin lost the rehabilitative award and any share in the property or assets of her cohabitant, the precedent was established that unmarried couples could now sue each other, and the word *palimony* was added to the English vocabulary.

Both the famous and the unknown have been inspired by the contractual issues and palimony concepts of the *Marvin* case. For example, the former maid and mother of three of Marlon Brando's children sued the actor for $100 million in damages. Her April 2003 complaint claimed:

> *Brando expressed to Plaintiff at the commencement of, and throughout the course of, the parties' relationship that she and Brando were in fact equal partners together in their mutual endeavors, and that she would always be financially compensated and secured for the rest of her life and the lives of their children.*

Furthermore, she claimed:

> *Brando agreed that in the event of the dissolution of their relationship by death, separation or otherwise, that all of Defendant Brando's property, including that acquired during the time of the parties' relationship, would be divided equally for the benefit of Plaintiff and the parties' children.*[9]

The parties confidentially resolved issues of custody, support, and palimony.

Another well-known palimony case involved actor Clint Eastwood and longtime costar and companion Sondra Locke. Their case created such a media frenzy that a Los Angeles County judge closed the courtroom to the press, igniting a constitutional law battle. Ultimately, the California Supreme Court ruled that the public has a right under the First Amendment to attend a civil trial. Although the public already clearly had the right to attend *criminal* trials—a right that had been long upheld by the U.S. Supreme Court—the California Supreme Court's ruling was one of the first major rulings in which a high court affirmed the right of the public to attend a *civil* trial. The parties who stirred up all this fuss, Eastwood and Locke, ultimately settled their palimony suit for an undisclosed amount.[10]

Palimony After Death Do Us Part

The palimony concept continues to be expanded, as evidenced by a recent New Jersey Supreme Court case that allowed palimony claims to be made against a deceased cohabitant's estate. The case involved a 30-year relationship that ended with the death of one of the partners. The surviving partner was left practically destitute while the deceased partner's estate was left to a wife and children he had not lived with for over 25-years. The court explained that if one of the partners is lured into cohabitation by a promise of support given by the other, that promise will be enforced.[11] According to the court, the deceased partner had made a promise, *clearly implied, if not expressed, that he would see to it that she was adequately provided for during her lifetime.* The decision ordered the apportionment of the estate between the partner, wife, and children of the deceased.

So, What Is an Unmarried Couple to Do?

It was not so long ago that unmarried but cohabiting American couples risked criminal prosecution because of statutes that made fornication (sex outside of marriage) illegal. This is still the case in some countries. For example, Nigeria and the United Arab Emirates discourage unmarried partners from living together by imposing on cohabiting couples sentences of public floggings, imprisonment, and even death.

Although the risk of being criminally prosecuted for fornication is small in the United States, some courts have been slow to completely accept unmarried cohabitation. So, although cohabitants may no longer be subject to criminal charges, they may still face pressures. In 1978, a Pennsylvania court decided to uphold the dismissal of two employees of a public library who lived together without marriage and had a child together. The court observed that the living arrangement of the two employees might impair the ability of the employees (a janitor and a librarian) to interact with the public in the course of their work.[12] Surprisingly, this decision was made despite the 1972 repeal of Pennsylvania's criminal fornication and adultery statutes.

More recently, the Michigan Supreme Court, in a 1998 decision, rejected a landlord's argument that he had a constitutional right to refuse to rent an apartment to an unmarried couple. The landlord argued that it was against his religion.[13] The Michigan case resulted in a positive outcome for the cohabitants. Just to confuse you a bit, however, the Ninth Circuit Court of Appeals in 1999 heard a similar case that originated in Alaska and decided the case in a different manner. The unmarried cohabiting couple in Alaska was denied an apartment by a landlord who claimed that for religious reasons he could rent to an unmarried couple. The court decided that Alaska's marital status antidiscrimination law could not be enforced against landlords who, for religious reasons, refuse to rent to unmarried couples.[14] Yes, you read that correctly. These two courts made opposite decisions on cases that were basically identical in terms of facts.

Cohabiting Couples Must Create Their Own Legal Protections

The first point an unmarried but cohabiting couple should realize is that married couples take vows that gain them access to an extensive legal arsenal. Each of the 50 states has statutes and well-established case law pertaining to just about every marriage scenario that could be imagined. Unmarried and cohabiting couples are largely on their own in crafting legal protections that fit their particular partnership.

Other protections come from some state courts that are now using equitable remedies to prevent a formerly cohabiting but unmarried partner from facing financial hardship after the living-together arrangement ends. *Equitable remedies* are used by the courts to apply fairness in a particular situation. A court has the power to do justice where specific laws do not cover the situation. The unclear legal ramifications of living together without marriage continues to make the creation of a cohabitation agreement a good idea. The alternative to having created a valid cohabitation agreement may mean that an impersonal court system will be determining a dispute between a formerly happy couple. This is what happened in the case discussed in the next section.

Contract Law to the Rescue

In *Alderson v. Alderson* (see Case 3.1), the court essentially ignored the sexual relationship of the parties and decided the property settlement based on contract law principles. After a rather bumpy start, Steve and Jonne Alderson had little difficulty settling issues regarding their children. Those issues were decided by a **stipulation**, which is defined as an agreement between lawyers on opposite sides of a lawsuit. However, the financial issues were not settled without a fight.

In *Alderson*, Jonne claimed that Steve used duress to force her to sign deeds. **Duress** is defined as the unlawful pressure on a person to do what she would not otherwise have done. The classic contract law principle of estoppel was used by Steve to try to circumvent Jonne's claims. **Estoppel** is defined as being stopped, by your own prior acts, from claiming a right against another person who has legitimately relied on those acts. Steve made the estoppel claim as part of a set of **affirmative defenses,** which are the parts of the defendant's answer to a complaint that go *beyond* denying the facts and arguments of the complaint. Affirmative defenses set out new facts and arguments that might win the case for the defendant, even if everything in the complaint is true. The term *amended complaint* is also used in the *Alderson* case. An

amended complaint is a complaint that has been altered after it was first filed because of a change of some kind in the case. The amended complaint will be refiled with the court and served on the defendant again. Recall from your earlier reading that when a party has sufficient facts to support a valid lawsuit, that party has a cause of action. A party filing a complaint is not limited to claiming a certain number of causes of action. The court in *Alderson* bifurcated the claims made by the parties. **Bifurcated** means that there will be separate hearings for different causes of action in the same case. The *Alderson* case involved multiple causes of action, but the burden was still on the plaintiff to prove all her claims. The term **without prejudice** is used to describe a right given to one of the parties that prevents the court from denying the party the right to return to court to appeal.

The *Alderson* case is a good example of how people who were once in love can end up sitting at different tables in a courtroom. As you read the case, try to think of ways the entire matter could have been handled without all the litigation.

Unjust Enrichment Theory Applied

The court in the *Alderson* case clearly looked to contract theory to support its findings in favor of Jonne Alderson. This was not the theory used in a relatively recent Wisconsin case in which the Wisconsin Fourth District Court used the unjust enrichment theory. **Unjust enrichment** is defined as obtaining money or property unfairly, and at another's expense. The court wanted to avoid the unjust enrichment of two former cohabitants who had lived together without a cohabitation agreement. The court affirmed a jury award of $7,000 to Linda Walsh for the housework and cooking she performed, and for money she spent (mostly on groceries) during the more than eight years she lived with Harlan Ray. Harlan also received an award of $1,289 on his counterclaim. He claimed that Linda and her children had been unjustly enriched by the housing he provided to them, and by the repairs he made on her car.[15]

Creating the Optimum Cohabitation Agreement

When unmarried couples decide to create a cohabitation agreement, both parties should be completely aware of the agreement's ramifications. Such an agreement should not be negotiated over glasses of wine and signed on a whim to make one of the parties happy. Both parties should clearly state their intentions to each other to ensure there is mutual understanding as to the content of the agreement. They should then memorialize their intentions in a written agreement that is signed and witnessed. It is always advisable to have separate legal representation, particularly when there is unequal wealth between the parties. No one wants to face a disgruntled former partner who claims he was not properly advised by his own legal counsel. There are legal guidelines for creating a cohabitation agreement, but they are not as stringent as those covering prenuptial agreements.

A **prenuptial agreement** is a contract created between two engaged individuals prior to their marriage. The requirements of a prenuptial agreement will be studied in detail in the next chapter. Unlike a prenuptial agreement, in which the parties are required to give each other a complete listing of their assets and liabilities, there are *no such legal requirements* for a cohabitation agreement. The only legal restriction is that none of the state courts will enforce any portion of a cohabitation agreement that involves the exchange of sexual favors.

When a couple contemplates the creation of a cohabitation agreement, they must first ask themselves *why* they want to create such an agreement. In most cases, the couple is attempting to circumvent any hard

CASE 3.1 *Alderson v. Alderson,* 180 Cal. App. 3d 450, 225 Cal. Rptr. 610 (1986)

Facts: Jonne Koenig and Steve Alderson first met in December 1966 in Reno, Nevada. Jonne was living with her parents at the time and was employed at a local bank. During the ensuing year, Jonne and Steve fell in love and talked of marriage.

In September 1967, Jonne moved from Reno to Portland, Oregon, for the purpose of marrying Steve, who had moved there a month earlier. However, the marriage plans, for various unspecified reasons, did not materialize. Instead, Jonne and Steve embarked on a period of nonmarital cohabitation that lasted for 12 years.

Steve worked as a civil engineer. The parties' earnings were placed in joint bank accounts. The two filed a joint federal income tax return as a married couple in 1967.

In September 1968, the couple moved to Eugene, Oregon, because of Steve's job. There they purchased their first home. The decision to purchase a home was made jointly. The parties intended the acquisition to be both a home and an investment. Title was taken in Steve's name only; nevertheless, the down payment on the property came from the parties' joint savings account, and according to Jonne's testimony, it was her understanding that she and Steve owned the property together. Jonne became a receptionist, and Steve continued to work as a civil engineer. The couple had the first of their three children in December 1969.

Between 1968 and 1979, the two acquired a total of 14 properties, most of which were purchased purely for investment purposes. Down payments for these purchases came from the couple's joint savings account and/or loans from Jonne's parents. Jonne and Steve acquired title to seven of the properties as husband and wife or as married persons. With three of the properties, they acquired joint title without designation as to marital status. The other properties were purchased in Steve's name only.

Jonne, who continued to work off and on during this period, contributed her earnings toward these real estate purchases. Additionally, she collected the rents, paid the bills, and kept the books for all the rental properties. She also helped to repair and fix up the properties. She later testified that she viewed the properties as

> *our houses. We both worked and sacrificed different things so that we had the money to buy them and to keep them. We had higher expectations than some because we wanted property. We wanted investments. We wanted things for the future of our kids.*

During the entire 12-year period that Jonne and Steve lived together, they held themselves out as a married couple to everyone, including family and friends. Jonne assumed Steve's surname of Alderson as her own, as did the three children.

At the end of this period, in December 1979, the parties separated. Jonne moved from the family home because, she testified, *Steve told me to get out.* Prior to leaving, Jonne signed deeds for all of the houses. She said she did so under *duress.* She testified that Steve made various threats concerning what he would do to her if she did not sign. She testified, *Steve told me that I would never get any property. He would see me dead before I got any of them.* Jonne said she was afraid for her own safety, and so she *just signed the deeds to get out.* Jonne received no payment for signing the deeds.

(continued)

CASE 3.1 *continued*

On October 14, 1980, Jonne filed an amended complaint against Steve. The first cause of action alleged that Steve was the father of Jonne's three minor children and sought child support and attorneys' fees. The second and third causes of action alleged that Jonne and Steve lived together as husband and wife for a 12-year period, although they were not married. According to the complaint, the parties agreed to equally share the property acquired during the course of their relationship. The second cause of the action also alleged that Steve had coerced Jonne into signing deeds to the real property. This complaint sought to set aside the deeds and to equally divide the property.

In the third cause of action, Jonne alleged that Steve had recently committed assault and battery against her and had broken her arm. The assault apparently took place some time after the filing of the first amended complaint. Steve was later convicted of having committed a misdemeanor, based on this assault. The complaint sought compensatory and punitive damages. In the fourth cause of action, Jonne sought injunctive relief against her alleged harassment by the appellant.

In his answer to the complaint filed on November 10, 1980, Steve denied paternity of two of the three children. He also denied all the other material allegations of the complaint. Steve set forth affirmative defenses asserting that (1) Jonne had sexual intercourse with other men; (2) the alleged agreement to share property violated the statute of frauds; (3) estoppel; and (4) self-defense.

On February 18, 1982, an Order Specifying Issues Without Substantial Controversy was filed, in which the following issue was deemed established against Steve: *On or about September 7, 1980, defendant Steve Colden Alderson did willfully and unlawfully use force and violence upon the person of plaintiff.* This order was based upon Steve's municipal court conviction for the misdemeanor.

All of the issues concerning paternity, child support, and child visitation were settled by stipulation, including an acknowledgment by Steve that he *was* the father of all three children. After hearing the evidence, the court rendered judgment for Jonne on the property issues. The court declared that Jonne was entitled to an undivided one-half interest in the parties' property and set aside the previous deeds. By stipulation, the court reserved jurisdiction to divide the property. In a stipulated order filed on May 25, 1982, the parties equally divided the property. The stipulation was made without prejudice to Steve's right to appeal from the judgment. On June 16, 1982, Steve filed a notice of appeal regarding the division of the property.

On July 9, 1982, the trial of the bifurcated third and fifth causes of action was held. Judgment was rendered again in favor of Jonne and included $15,000 in compensatory damages, plus $4,000 for punitive damages. The July 9, 1982, judgment was not the subject of the appeal.

In her complaint, Jonne, in essence, alleged an implied contract between the parties to equally share the property acquired during the course of their relationship. In ruling in her favor, the trial court found this allegation to be true.

In this appeal, Steve did not appear to dispute the court's finding. Nevertheless, he maintained that the trial court's ruling upholding the contract must be overturned because the contract was illegal and, thus, unenforceable. Quoting from *Marvin v. Marvin,* 18 Cal. 3d 660, 134 Cal. Rptr. 815, 557 P.2d 106 (1976), he claimed:

> *[I]t is clear that a contract between two married persons living together will not be enforced if an inseparable part of consideration for the contract is an agreement to provide sexual services. The record below is uncontradicted that the agreement between appellant and respondent integrally contemplated that the parties would provide sexual services to each other.*

Issue: Whether the parties' sexual relationship voided their contractual agreement.

Court's Reasoning: We find no merit in Steve's contention. In *Marvin,* the court stated, *a contract between non-marital partners, even if expressly made in contemplation of a common living arrangement, is invalid only if sexual acts form an inseparable part of consideration for the agreement.* In summary, we base our opinion on the principle that adults who voluntarily live together and engage in sexual relations are nonetheless as competent as any other persons to contract respecting their earnings and property rights.

Holding: The March 31, 1982, judgment dividing the subject properties equally between the parties, and the January 28, 1993, order appointing a receiver, are accordingly affirmed.

Case Discussion: What differences did the court find between Jonne Alderson's situation and Michelle Triola Marvin's situation? Do you think contract principles can be applied fairly in a case of a couple's breakup, or do the emotions involved in a breakup muddy the legal waters? Do you think that a cohabiting couple's sexual relationship should limit the contract rights of the parties involved? Other than marrying Steve, what could Jonne have done at the beginning of her relationship with Steve to protect herself?

feelings they may feel toward each other if they break up. Truthfully, it is doubtful that a legal document will prevent such hard feelings from occurring, but what a cohabitation agreement *can* do is clearly define the property that each person is bringing, or brings in the future, into their new home together. A cohabitation agreement also can be the vehicle through which a couple defines their expectations. A cohabitation agreement will not ensure that a lawsuit will not be filed by one party against the other; however, if a lawsuit *is* filed, the cohabitation agreement can be used by the court as evidence to determine the intentions of the parties when they became cohabitants. If the court finds the cohabitation agreement to be a valid contract, the court cannot ignore it. The agreement will be used as a guideline in determining how the parties should be treated.

The parties to the agreement may come to a law office together. The attorney who is hired should be hired by only one party. The other party should have the agreement reviewed by her own attorney. A paralegal's role in the creation of a cohabitation agreement begins the minute a client enters a law office. As a paralegal, you may be involved in the interviewing process and may be given the responsibility of creating the agreement with the assistance and oversight of an attorney.

On a *technical* note, when creating any type of agreement, each paragraph of the agreement should be delineated by either a letter or a number. This allows readers to easily locate any paragraph that is being discussed.

Same-Sex Couple Faced Prosecution

In a later chapter, you will read about the efforts that have been made to make same-sex marriages legal. Right now, if a same-sex couple wants to begin a new chapter in their life together, one way to do that is to establish a home together. It was not too long ago that a same-sex couple faced a serious possibility of prosecution. *Bowers v. Hardwick,* 478 U.S. 186 (1986), is a classic example of a same-sex couple who faced criminal prosecution (see Case 3.2). At its most obvious, this case is about the state of Georgia's right to

CASE 3.2 *Bowers v. Hardwick*, 478 U.S. 186 (1986)

Facts: In August 1982, Bowers, the respondent, was charged with violating the Georgia statute criminalizing sodomy by committing that act with another adult male in the bedroom of the respondent's home. After a preliminary hearing, the District Attorney decided not to present the matter to the grand jury unless further evidence developed. Respondent then brought suit in federal district court, challenging the constitutionality of the statute insofar as it criminalized consensual sodomy. He asserted that he was a practicing homosexual and that the Georgia sodomy statute placed him in imminent danger of arrest. He also asserted that the statute violated the federal Constitution. The district court granted the state of Georgia's motion to dismiss Bower's lawsuit for failure to state a claim against the state, relying on *Doe v. Commonwealth's Attorney for the City of Richmond,* 403 F. Supp. 1199 (E.D. Va. 1975), which the United States Supreme Court summarily affirmed, 425 U.S. 901 (1976).

Bowers appealed the granting of the motion to dismiss. A divided panel of the Court of Appeals for the Eleventh Circuit reversed. The Eleventh Circuit Court of Appeals held that *Doe* was distinguishable from the *Bowers* case. Relying on the decisions in *Griswold v. Connecticut,* 381 U.S. 479 (1965), *Eisenstadt v. Baird,* 405 U.S. 438 (1972), *Stanley v. Georgia,* 394 U.S. 557 (1969), and *Roe v. Wade,* 410 U.S. 113 (1973), the court went on to hold that the Georgia statute violated the respondent's fundamental rights because his homosexual activity is a private and intimate association that is beyond the reach of state regulation by reason of the Ninth Amendment and the due process clause of the Fourteenth Amendment.

The case was remanded for trial. In order to prevail, the state would have to prove that the statute supported a *compelling state interest* and that *the statute was the most narrowly drawn* means of achieving the state's interest. The United States Supreme Court granted the Attorney General's petition for *certiorari* because other courts had arrived at judgments contrary to that of the Eleventh Circuit in this case. The Attorney General asked the Supreme Court to answer whether the antisodomy statute violated the fundamental rights of homosexuals.

Issue: Whether the United States Constitution confers a fundamental right upon homosexuals to engage in sodomy and, hence, invalidates the laws of the many states that still make such conduct illegal.

Court's Reasoning: Precedent aside, the respondent would have us announce, as the Court of Appeals did, a fundamental right to engage in homosexual sodomy. This we are quite unwilling to do. Proscriptions against that conduct have ancient roots. Sodomy was a criminal offense at common law and was forbidden by the laws of the original 13 states when they ratified the Bill of Rights. In 1868, when the Fourteenth Amendment was ratified, all but 5 of the 37 states in the Union had criminal sodomy laws. In fact, until 1961, all 50 states outlawed sodomy, and today, 24 states and the District of Columbia continue to provide criminal penalties for sodomy performed in private and between consenting adults.

The respondent asserts that where the homosexual conduct occurs in the privacy of the home, he relies on *Stanley v. Georgia,* 394 U.S. 557 (1969), where the Court held that the First Amendment prevents conviction for the possession and reading of obscene material in the privacy of one's home. *Stanley* was firmly grounded in the First Amendment. Victimless crimes, such as the possession and use of illegal drugs, do not escape the law when they are committed at home. Even if the conduct at issue here is not a fundamental right, Respondent asserts that there must be a rational basis for the law, and that there is none in this case other than the presumed belief of a majority of the electorate in Georgia that homosexual sodomy is immoral and unacceptable. This is said to be an inadequate rationale to support the law. The law, however, is constantly based on notions of morality, and if all law representing essentially moral choices is to be invalidated under the due process clause, the courts will be very busy indeed.

Holding: Reversed.

Case Discussion: Recently, the United States Supreme Court was contemplating *Lawrence v. Texas,* No. 02-102 (2003), a similar case from Texas, and overturned *Bowers.*[a] The Supreme Court stated in the *Lawrence* opinion that *Bowers* was *not correct when it was decided, and it is not correct today. It ought not to remain binding precedent.* The Court went further and stated that *when homosexual conduct is made criminal by the law of the state, that declaration in and of itself is an invitation to subject homosexual persons to discrimination both in the public and in the private spheres.* You can test your Shepardizing skills by checking to see that *Bowers* was overturned. Interestingly, this case again proves that all types of law overlap and that you cannot adequately study one area of the law without reading cases involving all areas of the law.

---

[a]Biskupic, Joan, "Justices Hear Texas Anti-Sodomy Case," *Daily Record,* March 27, 2003, A9.

criminalize behavior occurring between two consenting adults in the privacy of their home. The case is also about the courts' and society's role as moral arbiters.

In this case, Bowers sued the state of Georgia to invalidate a Georgia statute that made sodomy between two consenting adults a criminal offense. The United States Supreme Court, responding to a *writ of certiorari,* explained that such conduct had been prohibited since ancient times, and the court saw no reason to prohibit Georgia from criminalizing the behavior. A *writ of certiorari* is Latin and literally means *to make sure.* A *writ of certiorari* is a request for an appeal, but one which the higher court is not required to take for decision. Often the Supreme Court will hear such *certiorari* requests only if they involve issues of general public importance.

Before you read *Bowers,* be aware that the opinion discusses the concept of how a court determines whether a statute is constitutional. Courts look to see if the attorneys for the state can prove that the statute in question serves a *compelling state interest* and is *the most narrowly drawn means of achieving a state's objective.* If the interest and means cannot be proved, then the statute may be considered *overly burdensome* to the citizens of the state and, therefore, in violation of the United States Constitution.

CHAPTER SUMMARY

The number of unmarried couples who are cohabiting has increased dramatically in the last decade. This large increase crosses all social, economic, age, and sex lines. The fear of divorce and loss of financial benefits is believed to be the main reason for this increase.

Married couples, because of their marital status, have access to more than 1,000 benefits that are not available to unmarried cohabiting couples, who are basically on their own when it comes to fashioning personal protections. An unmarried couple who plans to cohabitate should prepare and sign a cohabitation agreement to deal with the financial questions that inevitably arise when a couple lives together. An attorney and a paralegal may assist in the preparation of such a document, but cohabiting unmarried couples can also prepare their own agreements, since the legal requirements for such an agreement are not as strict as those covering prenuptial agreements. However, it *is* best if both parties have their own legal representation. Another option available in some cities and states is for a cohabiting couple to register as domestic partners with a domestic partner registry.

One of the best-known cases concerning a cohabiting couple, the *Marvin* case, added the word *palimony* to our dictionaries. The *Marvin* case has had a long-term effect. Palimony cases continue to be brought by disgruntled formerly cohabiting lovers who think their former partners owe them something. The trend in the courts is to determine if promises, either implied or expressed, were clearly made that one partner would provide for the other after a breakup. Some courts have also looked to the unjust enrichment theory to award financial settlements to former cohabitants.

Key Terms

cohabitation agreement	equitable remedy	bifurcated
addendum	stipulation	without prejudice
domestic partner	duress	unjust enrichment
palimony	estoppel	prenuptial agreement
implied contract	affirmative defenses	*writ of certiorari*
express contract	amended complaint	

Surfing the Web

http://www.singlemomz.com An interesting site that provides information for and from single mothers. Living together information is listed under relationships.

http://www.equalityinmarriage.org Provides information, resources, and support for couples before, during, and after marriage.

http://www.center4civilrights.org Site originating in Pennsylvania and offered by The Center for Lesbian and Gay Rights.

http://www.bcfamilylawresource.com Canadian site offering a comprehensive survey of family law written in plain language.

http://www.palimony.com This sites states that its goal is to provide a one-step source of information for unmarried couples living together.

ETHICS ALERT

You may have noticed that while Susan waited with her cousin for Joanna's appointment with J. D., Susan mentioned that another client was distraught over a domestic violence incident. Would you admonish Susan for telling her cousin what the topic of the distraught client's visit with J. D. was, or do you think Susan was just being polite in giving her cousin the reason J. D. was running late and that her remarks were nothing to be concerned about?

Review Questions

1. What is a cohabitation agreement? What is an addendum?

2. Is there a legal requirement that parties entering into a cohabitation agreement must be completely honest in providing a list of their assets and liabilities?

3. Why would any romantically involved couple want to tarnish their romance with a little reality by entering into a cohabitation agreement?

4. What are some reasons that Granny may be living with her boyfriend?

5. What is a domestic partner?

6. Why did the *Marvin* case become nationally known as a palimony case?

7. What was the long-term effect of the *Marvin* case?

8. Read the following fact pattern and answer the questions at the end.

   Despite the fact that Gary and Gloria took pains to enter into a cohabitation agreement that listed the property each brought to their new home and clearly defined the responsibilities and the expectations they had of each other, Gary failed to live up to his end of the bargain when he got fired from his job and did not bother to find another one. Gloria became overly burdened by their bills and did not feel romantically inclined toward Gary. When she increasingly refused to have sex with him, Gary accused her of not living up to her end of their agreement to have sex no less than twice a week. Feeling disgruntled and sexually unfulfilled, Gary absconded from their apartment with all their furnishings, including all the items Gloria had so painstakingly paid for.

   (a) How might their cohabitation agreement help Gloria? (b) Does their agreement help Gary?

9. Why are some courts now applying equitable remedies to situations involving formerly cohabiting couples?

10. What is the importance of *Bowers* being overturned?

Endnotes

1. Solot, Dorian, "No Ring to It: Considering a Less Married Future," *Jewish Public Forum Archive* 25 (August 2002): 1–9.

2. U.S. Census Bureau, *Current Population Survey* (2000).

3. *Id.*

4. Solot, *supra* note 1, at 4.

5. U.S. Census Bureau, *Current Population Survey* (2000).

6. Espinoza, Galina, "There Goes the Bride," *AARP Journal* (July/August 2002): 13.

7. "Lee Marvin to Fight Suit of Ex-Companion Over Promise of Life Support," *New York Times*, January 9, 1979, 4.

8. "Court Reverses $104,000 Award for Ex-Companion of Lee Marvin," *New York Times*, August 13, 1981, 12.

9. Smoking Gun Archive, October 2002, http://www.thesmokinggun.com/

10. Barnes, Patricia G., "Fame No Bar to Press Coverage," *ABA Journal* January, 11, 1999): 43.

11. Booth, Michael, "Palimony After Death Do Us Part," *New Jersey Law Journal*, (October 28, 2002): 1, 14.

12. *Hollenbaugh v. Carnegie Free Library,* 436 F. Supp 1328 (W.D. Pa. 1977), aff'd, 478 F.2d 1374 (3d Cir.), *cert. denied,* 439 U.S. 1052, 99 S. Ct. 734, 58 L. Ed. 2d 713 (1978).

13. France, Steve, "Not Under My Roof You Don't," *ABA Journal* (April 1999): 25.

14. *Thomas v. Anchorage Equal Rights Commission,* No. 97-35220 (1999).

15. Presser, ArLynn, "Palimony Award for Housework," *ABA Journal* (March 22, 1993): 39.

Chapter 4

Prenuptial Agreements

LOVE AND CONTRACTS: AN UNLIKELY PAIR

This chapter highlights the stories of three loving couples who are planning to wed, but are seeking the assistance of attorneys to help them create *prenuptial agreements* prior to beginning their lives of wedded and *protected* bliss.

A p**renuptial agreement**, also known as an **antenuptial agreement,** is a contract made between two individuals *before* their marriage to each other, but the contract does not take effect until *after* the individuals are married to each other. Such an agreement could be described as an insurance policy in the case of a marital demise.

For example, you are probably familiar with the concept of life insurance. A life insurance policy is a contract between the life insurance company and the owner of the policy who chooses the insured person and the beneficiary. When the insured person dies, the insurance company will pay a previously agreed-upon monetary sum to the designated beneficiary. Similarly, a prenuptial agreement is also a contract, but it is between two individuals who *both* want to be financially insured against the marriage ending. Just as the life insurance policy defines the payout prior to the insured's death, both parties to a prenuptial agree to the details of any post-divorce financial settlement *prior* to a divorce occurring.

Parties who create their own prenuptial agreements are defining their own rights and responsibilities to their future spouses, and turning their backs on one-size-fits-all state laws that list statutorily imposed rights and duties of spouses. Because the parties are stepping outside specific statutory requirements, they must comply with other requirements in order for a prenuptial agreement to be considered binding and valid.[1]

Historically, many states have frowned upon prenuptial agreements because they were thought to promote divorce. Judges in such states declared the agreements void and against public policy, and would not enforce them. Interestingly, even in the most stridently antiprenuptial states, most courts have upheld the portions of prenuptial agreements that dealt with the rights given to each spouse in the event of either spouse's death.

Each state's requirements for creating a valid prenuptial agreement is different, based upon whether the state has enacted the **Uniform Premarital Agreement Act,** which is also known as the **UPAA.** Twenty-five states and the District of Columbia have enacted the UPAA. The remaining 25 states have legislation and case law applicable to their individual states. However, the general requirements for all states include: (1) a written agreement; (2) contractual capacity of the parties; (3) voluntary agreement free of *fraud, duress,* and *undue influence;* (4) the agreement must not be unconscionable; and (5) *full disclosure of assets.*[2] **Fraud** is any kind of trickery used to cheat another of money or property. As noted earlier, *duress* is unlawful pressure on a person to do what she would not otherwise have done. **Undue influence** is pressure that takes away a person's free will to make decisions. A *full disclosure of assets* is a complete listing of all real and personal property in which the parties have ownership interest. Refer to Exhibit 4.1 to see if your state has enacted the UPAA, or if it follows a more state specific combination of case and statutory law.

ENGAGED COUPLES COMBINE MARRIAGE AND BINDING CONTRACTS

In the previous chapter you discovered that William was a sensible young man who saw the merits of signing a cohabitation agreement with Joanna, Susan's cousin. William hoped that living with Joanna, who had made living together contingent upon William signing a cohabitation agreement, would give him the incentive he needed to jump-start his career. The contractually bound couple moved into Joanna's upscale townhouse and

---

EXHIBIT 4.1 Uniform Premarital Agreement Act Guide

Is There a Uniform Premarital Agreement Act in Your State?

State	Valid in State	State	Valid in State
Alabama	No	Montana	Yes
Alaska	No	Nebraska	No
Arizona	Yes	Nevada	Yes
Arkansas	Yes	New Hampshire	No
California	No	New Jersey	Yes
Colorado	Yes	New Mexico	No
Connecticut	No	New York	No
Delaware	No	North Carolina	Yes
District of Columbia	No	North Dakota	Yes
Florida	No	Ohio	No
Georgia	No	Oklahoma	No
Hawaii	Yes	Oregon	Yes
Idaho	Yes	Pennsylvania	No
Illinois	Yes	Rhode Island	Yes
Indiana	Yes	South Carolina	No
Iowa	Yes	South Dakota	Yes
Kansas	Yes	Tennessee	No
Kentucky	No	Texas	Yes
Louisiana	No	Utah	Yes
Maine	Yes	Vermont	No
Maryland	No	Virginia	Yes
Massachusetts	No	Washington	No
Michigan	No	West Virginia	No
Minnesota	Yes	Wisconsin	No
Mississippi	No	Wyoming	No
Missouri	No		

proceeded to live happily together for two years. Now that their mutually honest relationship is ripe with trust and respect, they feel ready to graduate to a more serious commitment to each other—marriage. An added bonus is that William is now a Hill family favorite, not to mention an honorary bridge club member!

The tables have turned, however, and now it is William who fears that much of his financial success will be at stake should his future marriage fall apart. His lawyer, I. M. Sharkey, Esq., keeps repeating that he should consider a prenuptial agreement that not only would protect his *assets,* but also would help avoid a long, bitter fight over their possessions in the event of a divorce. **Assets** are money, property, and money-related rights, such as money owed by another. William felt confident that Joanna would agree to sign a prenuptial agreement. Remembering her fears and how the cohabitation agreement acted as a catalyst to their success as a couple, Joanna did agree. William and Joanna have made certain, though, that the prenuptial agreement will provide a comfortable financial future for Joanna in the unfortunate case of a divorce.

William's increasing wealth and celebrity status make him a typical candidate to propose a prenuptial agreement for his future spouse and himself. Prenuptial agreements are especially useful when one future spouse is extremely well-off and the other future spouse is not, but it should be noted that the courts will not validate a prenuptial agreement that leaves an ex-spouse destitute.[3]

Atypically, our second couple, Jack and Diane, are young and without current assets. However, the future looks financially bright, so a prenuptial agreement might be a good idea for them as well. You will read more about why such an agreement might be a good idea for them later in the chapter.

A more common prenuptial scenario involves an engaged couple who have children from previous marriages. While such a couple may not have the kind of wealth enjoyed by William and Joanna, they often want to protect what they *do* have for their children's futures. This is the case with our third couple, Bridget and Robert, both AARP card-carrying senior citizens. Although their love for each other makes them feel younger than springtime, both Bridget and Robert have children in their thirties. Neither Bridget nor Robert, not to mention their kids, wants their children to be forgotten.

Unfortunately for Johnson & Webster's profit line, the now-wealthy William and Joanna have moved to sunny Los Angeles and will be using two attorneys in California for their prenuptial agreement instead of using Susan's firm. However, both couples—Bridget and Robert, and Jack and Diane—have scheduled appointments with Alyssa in anticipation of their upcoming nuptials.

Seeking Legal Advice

When an engaged couple makes the decision to create a prenuptial agreement, they often seek legal advice. Frequently, the couple will see one attorney together to have the agreement written, and then one party will go separately to another attorney to have the agreement reviewed before signing it. While the attorneys are responsible for explaining to clients the legal ramifications of signing a prenuptial agreement, a paralegal may be given the responsibility of handling the prenuptial agreement interview. Following the client interview, the paralegal should be able to present an accurate picture of the client's financial status to the attorney who is working with the paralegal on the creation of the prenuptial agreement.

SUSAN CONDUCTS PRENUPTIAL AGREEMENT INTERVIEWS

Sitting in Alyssa's firm office chairs, Susan and her boss were sharing a few rare moments together over coffee. "Sue, I'd like to have you try your hand at interviewing some clients scheduled to see me this week," Alyssa announced.

"Sure. What type of interviews?" Susan asked.

"I have two couples coming in for possible prenuptial agreements," Alyssa continued. "Well, wait a minute, *you* arranged the one appointment for your friend—Polly, I think, or is it Sally?"

Confused for a minute, Susan asked, "Do you mean Diane?"

Laughing, Alyssa replied, "See, my brain is fried after the last trial. I'm going to escape for a couple of mental health days before I forget my *kid's* name."

A little worried about the responsibility, Susan remarked, "Obviously, I've never handled prenup interviews. What do you want me to do?"

Alyssa sipped her coffee while simultaneously signing letters and kicking off her high-heeled shoes. "Well, I'll leave you with the prenuptial interview questions list that J. D. and I use when interviewing," she explained. "J. D. will be here, of course, but just ask the questions, and tell them I'll be reviewing the material, writing up a draft, and discussing it with them at their next office visit. It'll be a piece of cake."

Susan muttered a weak "okay" and returned to her office to call the clients. She did not have a chance to worry for long about the interviews. Bridget and Robert were scheduled for 10 A.M. and Jack and Diane for 2 P.M. the next day. After speaking with Alyssa, Susan called both couples and explained that Alyssa would be unavoidably out of the office, but that they could still come in and at least get the interview completed with her, and then they could schedule another appointment with Alyssa. Susan was surprised when both couples agreed to come in and see her even though Alyssa would not be there.

AN OLDER COUPLE PLANS TO WED

Susan could see that Bridget Beaumont and Robert Smith were in love. Following introductions, the couple held hands as they followed Susan into Alyssa's office for the interview. An obviously talkative person, Bridget began by saying, "Everyone knows we're in love, but my son says it's because we announce it to anyone standing within five feet." Laughing, she continued, "We want everyone to know how great it is to find love again at our ages, but my grown son is such a grouch." After a reflective pause, she continued excitedly, "A friend of mine is a family therapist, and she told me she thinks there are four steps adult children must take in dealing with a parent's remarriage."

"That sounds very interesting," Susan politely commented, "What are they?"

Bridget was more than happy to share. "She said children need to recognize a parent's right to happiness, remember that they have a unique relationship with their parent, seek help, and deal with the money issues. We can't personally do the first two items for our children, but we did come here for help in dealing with our finances."[4]

A pragmatic Robert picked up the story, saying, "I guess our grown children from our previous marriages are tired of hearing Bridget and me go on and on about true love. It's probably because the kids remember our previous marriages as being less than happy."

Bridget loudly chimed in, "*That's* the understatement of the year!"

Robert smiled, and then explained the situation knowledgeably: "Susan, like we told your boss, we're here because we know there are two possible scenarios that could happen to us, unless we're careful. First, our marriage could end in divorce, and any financial position we've resurrected after our first burnout marriages will be ruined. Secondly, even if the marriage with my life's soulmate turns out to be the success I know it's going to be, one of us could die. Then, instead of individual assets going to each of our surviving children, the inheritance would go to the surviving spouse and, eventually, the surviving spouse's offspring."

Bridget added, "We don't want to do that to our kids. My only son and I have talked for years about his sweat equity in my house having a twofold purpose. He's helping his mom and working on a house that he'll inherit one day. Robert understands that."

Nodding in agreement, Robert said, "We want everyone to live peacefully without worrying."

Robert and Bridget had obviously done their homework and paid attention during their initial telephone conversation with Alyssa. Neither scenario was a pretty picture, but both provided excellent reasons for creating a prenuptial agreement. Robert and Bridget knew the prenuptial agreement, if enforced by the court, should circumvent any future legal confrontations.

Susan was starting to relax and actually welcome her task of interviewing such a friendly and knowl-edgeable couple. She asked, "Why don't we start with the questions that Alyssa left for us to cover?"

"Okay," Bridget answered, "I *do* have a question or two first, though."

Susan smiled and waited patiently as Bridget dug some notes out of her purse. With a deep breath, Bridget began, "Which one of us does Alyssa represent? Should one of us hire our own lawyer, or can Alyssa take care of us both, since we're a happy couple and not a divorcing couple?" Before Susan could open her mouth, Bridget quickly continued, "Are there certain clauses that should always be included? How long after the agreement is signed can we be married? Does it matter? Can I write some-thing in there about not wanting to share a bathroom? Should we rewrite our wills?"

Completely stunned by Bridget's machine-gun questioning style, Susan answered, "Those are great questions, and I want to write each one down and have Alyssa answer them for you. However, I can tell you right now that it would be advisable for you to revise your wills to reflect the prenuptial agreement."

Before the couple had a chance to respond, Susan smiled and quickly said, "If there are no more questions, let's do the interview."

A sample of typical questions that are asked during a prenuptial agreement interview is provided for your review in Exhibit 4.2.

Susan's Summary of Bridget and Robert's Interview

After the interview with Bridget and Robert, Susan wrote a summary of the information she had gathered during the interview and placed it in the file. The previous marriages of Bridget and Robert both ended in acrimonious divorces. Bridget is 57 years old and has returned to work as a real estate agent. Due to fluctu-ations in the market, her income in the last three years has ranged from $23,000 to $37,000. Robert is

---

EXHIBIT 4.2 Prenuptial Agreement Interview Questions

1. Full name of bride:
2. Address of bride:
3. Age of bride:
4. Social Security number of bride:
5. Full name of groom:
6. Address of groom:
7. Social Security number of groom:
8. Is this the first marriage for bride?
9. If not, how many times has bride been married?
10. List the name(s) of previous husbands of bride:
11. Is this the first marriage for groom?
12. If not, how many times has groom been married?
13. List the name(s) of previous wives of groom:
14. Where is bride employed?
15. What is bride's job title?
16. What is bride's yearly salary?
17. Does bride have a pension and/or investment plan of any type at her employment?
18. If so, describe and list the value of any pension or investment plan:

19. Where is groom employed?
20. What is groom's job title?
21. What is groom's yearly salary?
22. Does groom have a pension and/or investment plan of any type at his employment?
23. If so, describe and list the value of any pension or investment plan:
24. List all real property owned solely or otherwise by bride:
25. List the assessed value and purchase price of any real property listed:
26. List all real property owned solely or otherwise by groom:
27. List the assessed value and purchase price of any real property listed:
28. List all personal property valued over $100 owned by bride:
29. List the assessed value and purchase price of any such personal property valued over $100 and owned by bride:
30. List all personal property valued over $100 owned by groom:
31. List the assessed value and purchase price of any such personal property valued over $100 and owned by groom:

61 years old and is an administrator for a pharmaceutical company with which he has been employed for 21 years. He is now earning $64,000. Although Bridget's income is not as large as Robert's, she is the proud owner of a home she purchased seven years ago with the lump-sum settlement from her divorce. Bridget purchased the tired fixer-upper for $120,000, but after spending seven years working on the house, with help from her only son, Bridget thinks she could sell it for $220,000. There is a small mortgage on the home in the amount of $25,000. Bridget also inherited from her aunt, Helen Goodanty, an annual annuity in the amount of $10,000.

Robert rents a very glamorous and expensive apartment overlooking the ninth hole of the local country club's golf course. Robert's previous marriage, or rather his divorce, was so nasty and expensive that the home Robert and his first wife owned was sold to pay for both of their attorneys' fees. His first wife did not work outside the home and, therefore, could not afford to pay for her own attorney. The profit remaining after their legal fees were paid was left to his wife, instead of her taking a share of Robert's pension. Robert's only asset is $100,000 in his pension account. Robert is also paying $22,000 in annual alimony to his ex-wife.

A LITTLE STORY ABOUT JACK AND DIANE

Susan was glad she had some time between interviews. "How do Alyssa and J. D. deal with the constant questions?" she wondered. Coming up next was Jack and Diane. "That shouldn't be so bad," Susan thought hopefully. "I know they haven't acquired much of anything yet."

Jack and Diane were right on time for their appointment. Diane was a longtime friend of Susan's, so Susan greeted the couple enthusiastically. "Hey, you guys!" Susan exclaimed, "Welcome to Johnson & Webster." The old friends gave each other quick hugs and moved into Alyssa's office.

Diane Maguire and Jack Hill are in love and are planning to marry. Neither Diane nor Jack has been married before. Diane is a 24-year-old schoolteacher who has been working for three years at the local elementary school. Jack is also 24 years old and will begin his medical school studies very soon. Before the happy couple decided to marry, Diane had planned to return to graduate school, but now she has put the idea on the back burner.

Jack began, "Well, you know why we're here."

Susan responded, "Why don't you tell me what you want Alyssa to do for you, and I'll take notes?"

"Well, economics dictate that Diane continues working to help pay my way through medical school, or we'll have to apply for school loans," Jack said, sounding a little embarrassed.

Diane picked up the story, saying, "If I continue working, all the loans won't be necessary. Once Jack starts practicing, though, I'll return to school for my master's degree, and perhaps even my doctorate in education."

Jack remarked, "Then, it will be *my* turn to pay for Diane's education."

The plan made sense, but what if Jack and Diane's marriage ended before Diane had her turn? Jack and Diane knew that graduate school can be especially draining for students and hard on marriages. Diane's cousin, Peter, financially supported his wife's college and law school education, and when she graduated from law school the first case she handled was her own divorce!

Jack commented, "Hey, I know Diane trusts me to keep my word, but I decided after hearing about her poor cousin Peter that I would put Diane's mind to rest by suggesting we create a prenuptial agreement, and Diane agreed."

"Sounds great to me," Susan commented. "I just have to go through this list of questions, and then we'll make another appointment for you guys to sit down with Alyssa." A short 20 minutes later Susan was walking her friends to the door. Susan had been right; Jack and Diane did not have many assets to discuss.

When Alyssa returned on Monday after her long weekend at a spa, she was full of zip. "Good morning, Sue," she bubbled. "How did the interviews go?"

Amazed at Alyssa's mood transformation, Susan smiled and answered, "Great. I asked the questions you left for me and dodged a few questions I thought were best left to you. Both couples are scheduled to return and meet with you."

"Wonderful," Alyssa replied. "I saw the questions in the file. I'll go over them with you so you'll know the answers, too. Each party to a prenuptial should have their own attorney, and they should always have a fair amount of time between the signing of the prenuptial agreement and the marriage ceremony so it doesn't look like a rush job." Smiling, she added, "I read that Bridget wants to include a clause about not sharing a bathroom. I wish I'd thought of that with my husband. Courts usually smile at clauses like that, but rarely give them legal weight in deciding issues in a divorce matter. By the way, you were right to advise Bridget and Robert to revise their wills. There's no reason to have conflicting documents hanging around. When are they scheduled to come back in?"

"I gave us a week to get the drafts done," Susan answered.

Alyssa commented, "During my initial phone consultation with the couples, I figured that Jack and Diane's agreement might be short and sweet—a one-pager—but that Bridget and Robert's would end up being longer." She had reviewed Susan's notes and was eager to get to work on preparing drafts for both couples. "I think you should try preparing some drafts for practice, too," Alyssa announced. "Later, we can compare our versions. Does that sound good?"

"Yes, it does, Susan replied." "I'll get right on it."

Later, Susan beamed as Alyssa reviewed her drafts and said, "I'm impressed with your effort."

"Thanks, Alyssa," Susan said gratefully. "I made sure to follow your list of required clauses for prenups, and then I referred to past agreements to make sure I had samples of each of the clauses I wanted to include. I also made sure to attach an addendum listing each person's individually owned assets."

"Good job. I think both of our couples will be satisfied," Alyssa said, turning away to begin her next project.

A week later, both couples returned to the office and met with Alyssa, reviewed their drafts, and had their remaining questions answered. Alyssa again advised that each person should be separately represented by counsel, or should sign letters waiving the right to separate counsel. You will read more about the specific legal requirements of writing prenuptial agreements next, but first, review the material prepared for the happy couples. Read Exhibit 4.3, the Prenuptial Agreement prepared for Bridget and Robert. There would also be an addendum attached to agreement listing each individually owned asset. Then read Exhibit 4.4 to review a pertinent prenuptial clause prepared for Jack and Diane.

LOOK TO THE CONTRACT

Whatever the factual scenario in a particular case, all prenuptial agreements should clearly state what each individual understands he is to receive or give to the other spouse if the marriage fails. To understand what the necessary elements of a prenuptial agreement are, you must understand some basic contract law. A **contract** is defined as an agreement or covenant between two or more persons, in which each party binds himself to do or not to do an act, and in which each acquires a right to what the other promises. When broken down, the definition of a *contract* includes these basic elements: an *offer, acceptance, mental intent to make a contract,* and *consideration.* An **offer** is defined as making a proposal and presenting it for acceptance or rejection. An **acceptance** is defined as agreeing to an offer. **Consideration** is the promise to do or forbear from doing (that means *not do*) some act that a party otherwise would have the right to do, such as sue for a larger share of any marital property. In a prenuptial agreement, the

EXHIBIT 4.3 Prenuptial Agreement for Bridget and Robert

Prenuptial Agreement of Bridget Beaumont and Robert Smith

A. This is a Prenuptial Agreement between Bridget Beaumont, to be known as Party A, and Robert Smith, to be known as Party B. The intention of the parties is to maintain their respective estates for the benefit of children born of prior marriages.

B. Party A and Party B enter this Agreement with full knowledge of the approximate value of each other's estate and of all the rights and privileges to each other's estate that would be conferred by marriage if this Agreement had not been entered into; and

C. Upon separate legal advice, both parties have agreed to waive any rights to each other's estate upon death of either or both parties, or in the event of the separation or dissolution of their marriage; and

D. Both Parties, by virtue of this Agreement, desire to determine, fix and establish the rights that will accrue to each of them in the property and estate of the other upon the death of either or both of them, or in the event of separation or dissolution of their marriage; and

E. The Parties do hereby acknowledge that Party A is the sole owner of the property located at 25 Forever Young Drive, Soultown, Bliss, U.S.A., with such property acquired by her prior to marriage to Party B and without any contribution from Party B, and Party B acknowledges that he has no rights to said property nor any future rights that may occur by marriage to Party A, or any rights in event of death of Party A, or separation or dissolution of marriage to Party A.

F. The Parties do hereby acknowledge that Party B has exclusive right to his retirement pension account with Drugs R Us Pharmaceuticals and Party A acknowledges that she does not own any rights in said pension upon marriage to Party B, or any rights incurred upon the death of Party B, or upon separation or dissolution of their marriage; and

G. Party B acknowledges that Party A is the sole owner of the annual annuity from Helen Goodanty and hereby waives any rights to said annuity in event of the death of Party A, or upon separation or dissolution of their marriage; and

H. The Parties acknowledge that whatever debts they incurred prior to their marriage are their sole responsibility and they shall indemnify and hold harmless the other party for any such indebtedness, to wit Party A acknowledges sole responsibility for the $25,000 equity mortgage on her home, and Party B acknowledges sole responsibility for the $22,000 yearly alimony to his ex-wife.

I. The Parties acknowledge that they each received independent legal counsel in the preparation of this Agreement and are satisfied as to its contents.

J. Any property, real, personal, or mixed, which shall now or hereafter be held in the joint names of the parties shall be owned in accordance with the title of joint ownership and barring any other designation, shall be presumed to be held equally by the parties with survivorship rights, if any, as may be specifically designated by the title ownership.

K. Nothing in this agreement shall prevent or limit either party from making provisions for the other by Last Will and Testament, in which case provisions of the Last Will and Testament shall prevail.

L. The Financial Statements and List of Assets of both parties are attached in an Addendum.

M. In the event of a divorce, dissolution, or annulment of the marriage between the parties, Robert Smith will vacate the home owned by Bridget Beaumont. In the event of Bridget Beaumont's death, Robert Smith will vacate the home within six months of Bridget's death. All expenses of maintaining the marital home during this period of occupancy by Robert shall be his sole obligation.

N. This agreement has been executed and delivered in the State of Bliss and the provisions shall be construed and enforced in accordance with the law of Bliss, regardless of either party's change of domiciliary.

O. The fact that this agreement was prepared by counsel for one of the parties shall create no presumptions and specifically shall not cause any ambiguities to be construed against that party.
   On this _____day of 2003, before me personally came Bridget Beaumont and Robert Smith, known to me as the individuals described in and who executed this instrument.

Witness _____

DATED: _____

Bridget Beaumont _____

DATED: _____

Robert Smith _____

DATED: _____

EXHIBIT 4.4 Prenuptial Clause for Jack and Diane

It is understood between the Parties that Party A, Joseph (Jack) Hill, will begin his medical school studies as a full-time student subsequent to his marriage to Party B, Diane Maguire, on July 15, 2004.

Party B will continue in her teaching position and will be the sole provider for the couple. Party B's income will support Party A's living expenses, as well as Party A's tuition expenses. Party A acknowledges Party B's assistance and agrees that in the event that the Parties divorce, Party B will be entitled to remuneration for the outlay made for Party A. Party B agrees such remuneration will consist of payment by Party B of Party A's living expenses and tuition while Party A undertakes a master's degree and doctorate. The expenses are not to exceed the cost paid for Party B's tuition and living expenses calibrated to the cost of living increase, if applicable.

This agreement does not limit Party A and B's right to any other assets or rights acquired during their marriage.

---

consideration is often the promise of Party *A* not to sue and ask for a larger or different property settlement from Party *B,* and in return, Party *B* promises to give a clearly defined amount to Party *A* in the event of a divorce between Party *A* and Party *B.*

In the American legal system, courts hesitate to push aside a contract. A fundamental principle of contract law is that judges will look within the "four corners of the contract," which means that if there is a dispute, the judge will first read the actual contract to determine what the parties to the contract intended when they created the contract. The courts do not like to go outside the agreement to hear testimony explaining what the parties meant when they wrote the contract. Such testimony is known as **parole evidence,** and with a few exceptions, it is usually frowned upon by the courts. Occasionally, in an effort to keep the contract in effect, the courts will hear testimony to bring some clarity to an ambiguous contract. Another reason the court may hear parole evidence is if such evidence will prevent an inequity.

Creating a prenuptial agreement is the responsibility of both the attorneys representing the parties *and* the parties themselves, since they must comply with the agreement. Judges are hesitant to rewrite contracts that have turned out unsatisfactorily for one or both parties. However, if the parties to the contract mutually agree to such a rewriting, then the legal term by which that rewriting is known is **rescission.** Also, an unhappy party may go to court to set aside a prenuptial agreement if she can prove that all the legal requirements for preparing such an agreement have not been met. As discussed at the beginning of this chapter, not all state requirements are the same. Therefore, state-specific research must be conducted.

What Should Be Included in a Prenuptial Agreement?

Although an individual may reside in a state that does not require full disclosure of assets, it is still advisable to be completely honest in listing assets and liabilities. A complete listing is necessary so that both parties to a prenuptial agreement will be aware of the other's financial position *before* signing the agreement. It is also a good idea to list liabilities. The complete listing is necessary because each person who is married in any of the 50 states has certain rights that are given only upon marriage, and if a person signs a contract giving up those rights, that signer must be aware of exactly what he is giving up. For example, in California, a **community property** state, a person has a right to 50 percent of all his spouse's earnings from the day the couple is married. The opposite side of that coin is that a person can also be held 50 percent responsible for all his spouse's debts from the day of marriage. A prenuptial agreement circumvents the state's law as long as both the bride and groom (or, less romantically stated, both parties to the contract) are put on notice of all the facts.

As stated earlier, 25 states have enacted the UPAA, and the other 25 states have dealt with prenuptial agreements by enacting statutes particular to their individual states.[5] A sample of state-specific statutes pertaining to prenuptial agreements is provided in Exhibit 4.5 for your review.

No Two Prenuptial Agreements Are Alike

Each prenuptial agreement is different from the next because each agreement is negotiated by the parties involved. Typically, most prenuptial agreements include an introductory paragraph that describes *why* the couple is entering into the agreement. This paragraph allows the couple to make their intentions clear and supports the validity of the prenuptial agreement if one of the parties to the agreement attempts to have a court declare the agreement invalid. For example, a couple (like Bridget and Robert) with children from previous marriages might state that their intent is to protect assets earned during prior marriages for the children of those marriages.

Usually, a prenuptial agreement describes the rights each party has to property or spousal support in the event the marriage ends in divorce. For example, a prenuptial agreement may include a clause that designates a certain amount of property or spousal support that a divorcing spouse would be entitled to after a certain number of years of marriage. Many settlements are tied into the number of years of marriage. So, a spouse who is entitled to a certain lump-sum settlement after two years of marriage may then be entitled to an increase in the monetary amount of the lump-sum settlement after each succeeding year of marriage. Perhaps a certain yearly monetary sum of spousal support would be tied to the marriage lasting at least five years, and so on. Some prenuptial agreements include warnings that proof of adultery by the *payee spouse* will lead to a reduction in the financial settlement for the payee spouse, and proof of adultery by the *payor spouse* will lead to a larger financial settlement for the payee spouse. The **payee spouse** is the spouse receiving the money, and the **payor spouse** is the spouse paying the money. Some states may consider such contingencies against public policy, in which case those clauses pertaining to the contingency, or perhaps the entire agreement, will be void.

Certain key items should be included in the agreement: (1) a list of all assets, liabilities, income, and expectations of gifts and inheritances; (2) a description of how premarital debts will be paid; (3) a description of what happens to each party's premarital property in reference to appreciation, gains, income, rental, dividends, and proceeds of such property in the event of death or divorce; (4) a decision about who will own the marital or secondary homes in the event of death or divorce; (5) a specification of the status of gifts, inheritances, and trusts that either spouse receives or benefits from, whether before or after the marriage; (6) clarification of what will happen to each type of property, such as real estate, artwork, furniture, and jewelry; (7) a decision on the amount allocated for alimony, maintenance, or spousal support, or a provision for a waiver or property settlement instead of support; (8) details of death benefits, stating what each party will provide for the other; and (9) a decision about medical, disability, life, and long-term care insurance.[6]

Just How Specific Should the Prenuptial Agreement Be?

A prenuptial agreement can be as specific as the parties desire; for example, the agreement might designate the household duties each party will undertake once the couple is married (Party *A* will take the trash out on even days, and Party *B* will do it on odd days). A relatively recent prenuptial phenomenon is the very specific *no-children clause*. For example, the *New York Times* quoted one Manhattan couple's no-children clause as follows:

EXHIBIT 4.5 Sample of Prenuptial Statutes

Prenuptial Statutes

State	Citation	Grounds
California	CAL FAM. CODE §§ 1611–1615	Must be in writing and signed by both parties; enforceable without consideration; burden of proof on party against whom enforcement is sought to prove either of the following: (1) agreement was not voluntary; (2) was *unconscionable* at the time it was executed, and before execution, all of the following applied to that party: (a) party was not provided fair and reasonable disclosure of property or financial obligations of other party, (b) party did not voluntarily and expressly waive, in writing, any right to disclosure of property or financial obligations of other party beyond the disclosure provided, (c) party did not have, or reasonably could not have had, adequate knowledge of property or financial obligations of other party. Unconscionability of agreement decided by court as matter of law.
Florida	FLA. STAT. § 732.702	Any written contract, agreement, or waiver, before or after marriage must be signed by waiving party; no disclosure for agreement, contract, or waiver executed before marriage. *Lutgert v. Lutgert,* 338 So. 2d 1111 (Fla. 2d DCA 1976). Any antenuptial agreement benefiting one party in a grossly disproportionate manner, together with evidence of coercion, raises presumption of undue influence or overreaching when validity of agreement is contested in dissolution of marriage. *Edsell v. Edsell,* 464 So. 2d 1197 (1985). However, presumption of undue influence or overreaching does not apply to agreements contested in probate.
New Jersey	N.J. STAT. ANN. §§ 37:2-32 TO 37:2-41	Must be in writing and signed by both parties; enforceable without consideration; must be full and fair disclosure of earnings, property, and financial obligations of both parties. Burden of proof is on party seeking to set aside agreement, who must prove (1) party executed agreement involuntarily, or (2) agreement was unconscionable at time enforcement was sought, or (3) before execution of agreement, party was not provided full and fair disclosure of earnings, property, and financial obligations of other party.
NEW YORK	N.Y. DOM. REL. LAW § 236, part A(3)	Valid and enforceable when agreement is in writing, signed by both parties, and acknowledged or proven in the manner required to entitle a deed to be recorded; provisions must be fair and reasonable at time agreement was made and not unconscionable at time of entry of final judgment.
Pennsylvania	*Simeone v. Simeone,* 525 Pa. 392, 581 A.2d 162 (1990)	(1) Prenuptial agreements are contracts and should be evaluated as such; absent fraud, misrepresentation, or duress, spouses should be bound by terms of agreement; (2) must be full and fair disclosure of each party's financial position; absent such disclosure, party seeking to set aside agreement must prove by clear and convincing evidence that assets were understated; (3) reasonableness of prenuptial agreement is not a proper subject for judicial review.
Texas	TEX. FAM. CODE ANN. ch. 5, § 5.46	Must be in writing and signed by both parties; enforceable without consideration; and there must be fair and reasonable disclosure of earnings, property, and financial obligations of both parties. Burden of proof is on party seeking to set aside agreement to prove: (1) party executed agreement involuntarily; (2) agreement was unconscionable at time enforcement was sought; or (3) party, before execution, was not provided fair and reasonable disclosure of property or financial obligations of the other party; or (4) did not voluntarily and expressly waive, in writing, any right to disclosure of property or financial obligations of other party beyond disclosure provided; and (5) did not have, or reasonably could not have had, an adequate knowledge of property or financial obligations of other party.

The parties have discussed their future plans and desires relating to having or adopting children once they are married. Both parties hereby acknowledge that after careful deliberation they agree that they shall not have or adopt children once married. This decision is not made out of a limitation of commitment to the other, but rather this provision is based upon an analysis of the parties' present and anticipated family structure, financial situation, and the lifestyle the parties anticipate having upon and during their marriage.[7]

It is questionable, though, whether a no-children clause will be upheld by the courts.

Courts Rule Concerning Children

Prenuptial agreements often cover the issue of children born to a couple during their marriage and the child support to be paid in the event of a divorce, but courts in all 50 states retain the right to nullify any portion of the prenuptial agreement that pertains to child custody or support. Although the courts usually respect contracts created between two adults, they still retain jurisdiction and final say on the issue of child custody and support, it is unlikely that a party who agreed to a no-children clause would be released from paying child support because of it.

Helpful Practice Tips

Attorneys may ask their clients for a list of goals the clients are trying to achieve by creating a prenuptial agreement. This may help the clients to focus on the purpose of the agreement. It is best for both parties that they have a reasonable amount of time to contemplate the agreement and that they seek individual legal advice prior to marrying. A spouse who signs a prenuptial agreement that is unexpectedly sprung on her may have regrets about it later. Even if a client wants to hand-deliver the agreement to his fiancée, it is advisable to have a dated letter, completed agreement, and a list of all assets sent to the fiancée's attorney in order to prove that the timeline of events allowed reasonable notification before the wedding. Attorneys should also emphasize that if a prenuptial agreement is not adhered to but is just tossed in a drawer and forgotten, a court may later decide that, based on the parties' actions, the agreement has been abandoned and should not be enforced.[8]

Historical Prenuptial Case

The case of *Posner v. Posner* (see Case 4.1) was decided in Florida in 1970. It is somewhat historical because it was one of the first to recognize that prenuptial agreements should *not* be considered void as against public policy. The case involved divorcing spouses who were both unhappy with the trial court's decision. Both appealed the judgment. The appellate court's decision did not make them any happier. They both appealed again—this time to the Florida Supreme Court.

The Florida Supreme Court granted a petition for *certiorari* to review the appellate decision. In the case, the Supreme Court took the time to carefully explain that a contract within the institution of marriage is vastly different from a contract entered into in the commercial marketplace. Note that the court uses the terms *quash* and *vacate* to describe its action. **Quash** means to overthrow or completely do away with the decision. **Vacate** means that the court is setting aside the decision. The term *judicial notice* is also used by the court. **Judicial notice** is when the judge recognizes the existence or truth of certain facts without requiring one side in a lawsuit to prove them.

CASE 4.1 *Posner v. Posner*, 233 So. 2d 381 (1970)

Facts: The three appellate judges who considered the appeals agreed that the couple had created a valid prenuptial agreement, that the husband should be granted a decree of divorce, and that the child support award should be $1,200 per month. However, each took a different position respecting the prenuptial agreement's terms concerning alimony. The wife's view was that she should receive more than that which she agreed to in the prenuptial agreement. The three judges' disparate views were as follows: (1) the parties may validly agree upon alimony in an prenuptial agreement, but the trial court is not bound by their agreement; (2) a prenuptial agreement is void as against public policy; and (3) a prenuptial agreement's clause respecting alimony should be just as binding as a prenuptial agreement's clause settling the property rights of the wife in her husband's estate upon his death.

Issue: Whether a prenuptial agreement as it pertains to alimony is binding upon the parties.

Court's Reasoning: At the outset, this court recognizes that there is a vast difference between a contract made in the marketplace and one relating to the institution of marriage.

A prenuptial agreement by which a prospective wife waives or limits her right to alimony, or to the property of her husband in the event of a divorce or separation, regardless of who is at fault, has been in some states held to be invalid.

A husband could, through abuse and ill treatment of his wife, force her to bring an action for divorce and thereby buy a divorce for a smaller cost than he would otherwise have to pay.

Prenuptial, or so-called marriage settlement, contracts, by which the parties agree upon and fix the property rights each spouse will have in the estate of the other upon the other's *death,* have long been recognized as being conducive to marital tranquility and in harmony with public policy. Such an agreement has been upheld after the death of the spouse, even though it also contained a provision settling their property rights in the event of divorce or separation.

This court can take judicial notice of the fact that the ratio of marriages to divorce has reached a disturbing rate in many states. A new concept of divorce in which there is no guilty party is being advocated by many groups and has been adopted by the state of California, providing for dissolution of a marriage upon pleading and proof of irreconcilable differences between the parties, without assessing the fault for the failure of the marriage against either party.

With divorce being such a commonplace fact of life, it is fair to assume that many prospective marriage partners might want to consider and discuss, and agree upon if possible, the disposition of their property and alimony rights of the wife in the event their marriage fails.

In summary, we hold that a prenuptial agreement, if entered into in good faith, is a valid and binding agreement between the parties at the time and under the conditions it was made, but *subject to be increased or decreased under changed conditions.*

Holding: Accordingly, the decision under review is quashed with instructions to the District Court of Appeal, Third District, to vacate that portion of the final decree of the trial court relating to alimony and support money and remand same for further proceedings in the trial court not inconsistent with this opinion.

Concurring Opinion: The question of alimony was agreed upon by the parties prior to marriage in an agreement that we here hold to be valid. In arriving at that conclusion, the court is unconcerned with whether the husband was initially able to pay more alimony than the amount agreed to in the prenuptial agreement, since the very purpose of such an agreement is to provide a mutually satisfactory substitute for such determination of ability.

Case Discussion: We might as well face it: This case is really about a wife being sorry she agreed to a certain sum of alimony prior to her marriage. In reading the *Posner* case, did you get the feeling that the court was "speaking out of both sides of its mouth"? The prenuptial agreement is being upheld and respected as the contract it is. However, on the other hand, the court appears also to be saying that the amount of alimony apparently agreed to in the prenuptial agreement can be modified by the court. Isn't the point of a prenuptial agreement to have the parties create a mutually satisfactory substitute for having the court determine the financial settlement? What do you think?

How to Prove the Invalidity of a Prenuptial Agreement

While attorneys are usually hired to create a prenuptial agreement, they are also hired to prove that such an agreement should be found invalid by a court. In order to determine whether a prenuptial agreement is valid or invalid, the courts apply the state's divorce statutes pertaining to property division and spousal support.

The state statutes are typically more generous than the average prenuptial agreement.

A prenuptial agreement can fail a validity test in several ways. One way is if the prenuptial agreement does not follow all the requirements of the state's prenuptial statutes. For example, failure to provide full and fair disclosure of the financial condition of each signer, if it is required by state law, will invalidate a prenuptial agreement. If there is no specific statute pertaining to prenuptial agreements, the spouse seeking to invalidate the agreement can show proof that required contract standards were not met. A spouse who can also prove that there was *fraud* (any kind of trickery used to cheat another of money or property) committed by one spouse to induce the other spouse to sign the agreement will also have a better chance of success when seeking to have it declared invalid.

The case of *Nanini v. Nanini* (see Case 4.2) provides a good explanation of when a *summary judgment* voiding a prenuptial agreement may be granted and sustained. **Summary judgment** is defined as a final judgment for one side in a lawsuit without trial, when the judge finds—based on pleadings, depositions, affidavits, and so on—that there is no genuine factual issue in the lawsuit or a portion of the lawsuit. In this case, the petitioner, Mrs. Nanini, claimed that fraud was committed to induce her to sign the prenuptial agreement. She also attempted to prove that a full and fair disclosure of her husband's financial condition was not provided to her prior to her signing the agreement.

Constructive Trust Created for Husband

The case of *Martin v. Farber* (see Case 4.3) places the court in the role of protector of Mr. Farber. Apparently he was a loving and trusting husband to Nettie Sue Farber for over 40 years. The court created a *constructive trust* on Mrs. Farber's estate to financially provide for Mr. Farber following Mrs. Farber's death. A **constructive trust** is defined as a remedy employed by a court to convert the legal title of property into a trust, held by a trustee, for the benefit of a third party who in good conscience should have reaped the benefits of the possession of the property put into the constructive trust. The term *intestate* is used to describe how Mrs. Farber died. **Intestate** is defined as dying without a will. The lack of a valid will then requires that the distribution of inheritances to heirs be according to a state's laws regarding who should collect such inheritances.

CASE 4.2 *Nanini v. Nanini,*
166 Ariz. 287, 802 P.2d 438 (1990)

Facts: This is an appeal from the granting of a partial summary judgment, entered in the husband's favor, in an action for dissolution of marriage. The parties met in Chicago, Illinois, in the mid-1960s and ultimately were married there on March 22, 1969. It was the second marriage for each. The husband was in the construction business, and the wife had a successful clothing store in Chicago for about 20 years prior to the marriage. She was well-educated, and claimed she had never required the services of an attorney in the time she had been in business.

Five days before the marriage, the husband took her to his lawyer's office. She had no idea why they were going there until she was presented with a document identified as a prenuptial agreement. The agreement provided that the property then owned by each party, together with the rents and profits, would remain the sole and separate property of each party after the intended marriage, and that neither party had any right, title, or interest to the other's property. It also provided that if either party died without leaving a will, the estate of such party would go to the heirs-at-law of the deceased party as though the parties had never been married. In addition, the provisions indicated that each party would retain as his sole and separate property all earnings from his personal service or efforts after the marriage, including rents and profits. The parties also agreed that the contract would be construed in accordance with, and governed by, the laws of the state of Illinois.

Although the agreement stated that the wife was represented by attorney Richard T. Ryan of Chicago and bore the signature of this attorney, the wife testified during her deposition that nobody ever explained the agreement to her in detail or counseled her concerning its significance. However, she admits that she was advised to read it, had the opportunity to read it, and did, in fact, read enough of it to understand that it provided that each party's property was going to be maintained as his own separate property after the marriage—which she felt was fair enough.

Financial statements of both parties that were initialed and attached to the agreement showed the wife's net assets to be $264,868, and husband's net assets to be $1,158,385.37. However, the wife claimed in her deposition that no financial statements or other documents were attached to the agreement when she signed it. She testified at her deposition that she signed it as she was instructed to do because she was in love with her future husband and would have signed whatever he put in front of her. In her deposition, she stated that she assumed that at the time of the marriage, her husband was worth *in excess* of the amount reflected in the financial statement that she claims was not attached to the agreement. Another financial statement prepared for another purpose, and dated 10 days later, showed the husband's net worth to be $3,182,731.13.

Throughout the marriage the parties kept separate banking accounts, with the exception of one joint account for household purposes. The money was placed in the joint account by the husband. The husband also funded a joint stock account. In addition, each party had separate stock accounts. There was no evidence of commingling among the separate accounts or between the separate accounts and the joint account. The wife refused to allow her stockbroker to tell her husband how much her separate stock account contained, and for a time she even had the account statements sent to a friend's address so the husband would have no idea of her financial worth.

Since the husband paid the couple's ordinary expenses out of his separate property, including a $2,000 monthly allowance to the wife and payment of their joint taxes, the wife was able to amass a tax-free stock portfolio in her separate account worth more than $2,000,000, yielding approximately $140,000 per year. She also had joint ownership of land worth more than $1,000,000 and other securities.

The parties executed written agreements whenever they did purchase anything jointly, and when the husband borrowed money from the wife, he paid it back from his separate funds.

Issue: Whether the granting of a partial summary judgment was in error based on an unrebutted presumption of fraud.

Court's Reasoning: An appeal of a summary judgment must review the facts and evidence in the light most favorable to the party against whom the summary judgment was entered. If there is any doubt as to whether an issue of material fact exists, summary judgment is inappropriate. Even if there is no factual dispute, summary judgment is not warranted if possible inferences to be drawn from the circumstances are conflicting. The inferences must be viewed in the light most favorable to the party opposing summary judgment. However, the rule mandates the entry of summary judgment after adequate time for discovery, and upon motion, against the party who fails to make a showing sufficient to establish the existence of an element essential to the party's case, and on which that party will bear the burden of proof at trial. The wife contends that, because she did not know the total amount of her husband's net worth, there is a presumption of fraud in the inducement to have her enter into the agreement. The husband has not rebutted this. She also contends that she could not have intelligently signed the agreement because she did not have the advice of counsel. We do not agree with either of these contentions.

The Illinois law regarding the validity of prenuptial agreements is that prenuptial agreements are generally enforceable. The rules governing construction of other contracts are applicable to prenuptial agreements. Where the parties enter into such an agreement without fraud, duress, or coercion, the agreement is valid. However, where the parties are engaged to be married before the contract is signed, a *confidential relationship* (i.e., one involving a special relationship of trust) exists. If the provisions made for the wife are disproportionate to the extent and value of the husband's estate, the presumption is raised that the husband intentionally concealed his assets.

The presumption of intended concealment vanishes as soon as contrary evidence is produced. The wife admitted that she knew the nature and extent of her husband's property. The fact that all the ramifications of the agreement were not explained by a lawyer to the wife does not support the setting aside of the agreement.

The trial court rejected the wife's argument, holding that one who has had *an opportunity to read* a contract before signing, but signs before reading, *cannot later plead a lack of understanding.* Here the wife did read through the agreement enough to understand what it provided, as she stated in her deposition, *what was mine was mine, and what was his was his.*

Holding: We affirm the court's partial summary judgment and order that the parties shall bear their own attorneys' fees for this appeal.

Case Discussion: Do you think having the representation of an attorney at the time of the signing of the agreement would have placed the wife in any better position at the end of the marriage? Do you think that the wife must have been a savvy businesswoman in order to amass the assets that she had by the end of her marriage? Do you agree with the decision?

CASE 4.3 *Martin v. Farber,*
68 Md. App. 137, 510 A.2d 608 (1986)

Facts: Three days prior to their marriage on June 22, 1939, Nettie Sue Farber, then Nettie Sue Goldberg, and Morris W. Farber entered into a prenuptial agreement. The agreement provided, in essence, that Mrs. Farber would retain sole control of the property she acquired either prior to or during the marriage. Mr. Farber relinquished all rights in the property and the estate of Mrs. Farber.

At the time of the execution of the agreement, Mrs. Farber was 39 years old, a widow, and the mother of two boys. Her first husband, Dr. Chester Goldberg, died in 1936. Mrs. Farber inherited property from him, which included real estate located in Baltimore City. She also received more than $20,000 from insurance proceeds.

Mr. Farber, although steadily employed as an electrician, had no accumulated wealth at the time of his marriage to Mrs. Farber. However, he did continue to work until his retirement in 1967. During his 44-year marriage to Mrs. Farber, Mr. Farber turned his paychecks over to his wife. Mrs. Farber, meanwhile, remained at home and managed the couple's household and financial affairs.

When Mrs. Farber died intestate in August 1983, she had accumulated, in her own name, assets valued at approximately $275,000. The Orphans Court for Baltimore County appointed Mr. Farber as personal representative of his deceased wife's estate. Mrs. Farber's grandchildren filed a petition in the Circuit Court for Baltimore County to remove Mr. Farber from that position. They asserted that he had signed a valid prenuptial agreement in which he renounced any claim to Mrs. Farber's estate. In response, Mr. Farber filed a petition for relief alleging that the prenuptial agreement was invalid and that, under Maryland's intestacy laws, he was entitled to his share of the estate.

Following a trial, the judge concluded:

> It is true that many, many years ago Morris released any claim that he might have to Nettie's property or estate. After some forty-four years of a seemingly happy marriage, in which Morris turned everything he owned over to Nettie without question, and also upon her assurances that she would take care of Morris, it would not only be unjust, but unconscionable for the court to enforce the agreement.

The trial judge determined that a constructive trust should be imposed upon Mrs. Farber's estate for the benefit of Mr. Farber during his life, with the remainder to be distributed equally to Mrs. Farber's heirs. Dissatisfied with the decision of the trial court, both sides appealed.

Issues: (1) Whether the prenuptial agreement entered into by Morris W. Farber and Nettie Sue Farber in 1939 was still valid and enforceable. (2) Whether the imposition of a constructive trust on the estate of Nettie Sue Farber was proper.

Court's Reasoning: The grandchildren claimed that the prenuptial agreement was valid and enforceable and that Mr. Farber was precluded from obtaining any interest in Mrs. Farber's estate. Mr. Farber contended that since the agreement was not to be enforced, the proper action of the lower court should have been to order that the intestacy law would determine the distribution of assets of the estate. Proceeding from that premise, Mr. Farber further asserted that he was entitled to the first $15,000 plus half the residual of his wife's estate.

The trial judge erred in ruling that the agreement was unconscionable. It was not. The trial judge was particularly concerned by the fact that Mr. Farber turned everything he earned over to Mrs. Farber, and that she repeatedly assured her husband that she would take care of him. No matter how disturbing those facts may be, they do not afford an adequate basis for the court's ruling. Yet to be determined is whether, under the circumstances of the case, a constructive trust was properly imposed.

Ordinarily, before a constructive trust can be imposed by a court, there must be *clear and convincing* evidence of wrongdoing, coupled with circumstances that render it inequitable for the holder of legal title to retain the beneficial interest. When a confidential relationship exists, different rules are applicable.

In order to establish the existence of a confidential relationship, it must be shown that one party is under the domination of another or that the circumstances are such that one party is justified in assuming that the other will not act in a manner inconsistent with the party's welfare. Once it is demonstrated that a confidential relationship exists, a presumption arises that a confidence was placed in the dominant party, and the presumption shifts the burden to the dominant party to show, by clear and convincing evidence, that the transactions entered into were fair and reasonable.

The record before us revealed that throughout the Farber's 44-year marriage, Mrs. Farber stayed home attending to the domestic chores and the couple's financial matters. Mr. Farber continued to work outside the home. He regularly earned wages, which he diligently turned over to his wife. Those facts, when viewed in light of Mrs. Farber's repeated assurances to her husband that she would take care of him, lead us to the conclusion that a confidential relationship existed between the Farbers, and that Mrs. Farber was the dominant of the two.

Based on the evidence presented to support Mr. Farber's assertion that his wife abused that confidential relationship by using his earnings to acquire assets that she titled, or placed, solely in her own name, we agree that the imposition of a constructive trust was proper. We think, however, that the trust should only be imposed to the extent that Mr. Farber's funds were used to acquire assets that were not a part of, or attributable to, the assets in Mrs. Farber's estate prior to the marriage of the couple. In limiting the scope of the constructive trust, we are mindful that a primary purpose of that form of trust is to prevent unjust enrichment. Therefore, the constructive trust should be limited to the extent that Mr. Farber is able to trace his funds into his wife's estate. The imposition by the trial court of a constructive trust over the *entire* estate, without regard to the amounts actually contributed by Mr. Farber, was in error.

Holding: Judgment affirmed in part and reversed in part. Case remanded for further proceedings in accordance with this opinion. Costs to be divided between the parties.

Case Discussion: The appellate court's decision has now put Mr. Farber in the position of proving how much he contributed to the acquisition of property by Mrs. Farber. Do you think Mrs. Farber intended the prenuptial agreement to be used by her *grandchildren* after a 44-year marriage to Mr. Farber?

Deceased Spouse's Honesty Questioned

When it comes to prenuptial agreements, most states require the prospective spouses entering into the agreement to be completely honest about their financial positions. Alternatively, some states simply look to whether the prenuptial agreement is essentially fair in how it treats the less economically secure spouse in the event the marriage fails. This difference between states is important because if one spouse fails to be completely candid in a state that requires candid admissions, the prenuptial agreement may be considered invalid, thereby necessitating the application of that particular state's laws on the division of property and spousal support.

The case of *In re Estate of LeRoy A. Hillegass* (see Case 4.4) essentially concerns an attempt by a widowed spouse to have a prenuptial agreement found invalid because of her spouse's alleged lack of truthfulness about the state of his financial resources at the time of their marriage. As you read the case, note whether the court required complete candidness regarding each spouse's finances. The court described the legally

CASE 4.4 *In re Estate of LeRoy A. Hillegass,* 431 Pa. 144, 244 A.2d 672 (1968)

Facts: LeRoy A. Hillegass died at the age of 76, leaving an estate inventoried at $265,876. He was survived by his widow, Esther V. Hillegass, who was 60 years old, to whom he had been married for five years before his death. He was also survived by David Hillegass, his son by a former marriage; Bradford LeRoy Hillegass, a grandson; and Alda M. Holtzman, his sister. Mr. Hillegass left a will dated March 19, 1964, and a codicil dated April 15, 1965. In his will, which was executed over a year before his marriage to Esther, he bequeathed a legacy to his son and to his sister conditioned upon their surviving him. He also created a trust of $40,000 for the benefit of his grandson. Finally, he gave his residuary estate in trust to pay the net income to his son for life, with the remainder to certain charities. Thirteen days after his marriage on April 15, 1965, Mr. Hillegass executed a codicil bequeathing Esther property valued at approximately $30,000.

LeRoy A. Hillegass and Esther V. Cassel, his intended wife, had entered into a prenuptial agreement, under seal, that raises the most important question in this case. The Hillegass prenuptial agreement stated:

> *Whereas, it is the purpose of this agreement to give each of the parties hereto the free and absolute control and disposal of his or her separate property or estate; and Whereas, it is the intention of the intended wife to waive, relinquish and bar all her inchoate interest and other rights or interests, either as wife or widow of the First Party, in and to any property now owned or hereafter acquired by the First Party, including her right of election to take against the Will of the First Party.*
>
> *Now, Therefore, in consideration of the said marriage and the covenants of the Second Party, the First Party agrees to pay the Second Party, the sum of Ten Thousand Dollars ($10,000.00) immediately after April 1, 1965; and in consideration of the said marriage and covenants of the First Party, the Second Party agrees to pay the First Party the Sum of One Dollar (1.00) immediately after April 1, 1965. She hereby releases unto the First Party, his heirs, personal representatives and assigns forever all of her interests, rights and claims in and to the said property of every nature and kind.*
>
> *Leroy A. Hillegass released all his rights in and to the property of his intended wife in provisions identical with those provisions for the wife hereinabove quoted.*

Issue: Whether the wife presented clear and convincing evidence of material misrepresentations or nondisclosure prior to her signing the prenuptial agreement.

Court's Reasoning: In compliance with the prenuptial agreement, Hillegass paid Esther the sum of $10,000 on April 15, 1965, which was 13 days after they were married. Moreover, he gave Esther gifts that totaled approximately $30,000.

In spite of the prenuptial agreement, Esther filed an election to take against her husband's will. The executor of the will, David Hillegass, joined in by other heirs, filed a petition to set aside Esther's election. The lower court granted the petition and set aside Esther's election to take against her husband's will. A prenuptial agreement calls for the highest degree of good faith and a reasonable provision for the surviving spouse or, in the absence of such a provision, a full and fair disclosure of all pertinent facts and circumstances.

Reasonableness will depend upon the totality of all the facts and circumstances at the time of the Agreement, including: (a) the financial worth of the intended husband; (b) the financial status of the intended wife; (c) the age of the two parties; (d) the number of children of each; (e) the intelligence of the parties; (f) whether the survivor aided in the accumulation of the wealth of the deceased spouse; and

(g) the standard of living the survivor had before marriage and could reasonably expect to have during marriage. Full and fair disclosure *does not* require one to disclose the exact amount of one's property.

We shall now consider the facts in the light of the aforesaid principles. In this case, there was no clear and convincing evidence by the wife of material misrepresentations or nondisclosure, and consequently we need not consider whether the provision for the intended wife was, or was not, reasonable.

Holding: Decree affirmed, appellant to pay the costs.

Case Discussion: Do you think that if Mrs. Hillegass could have proved by clear and convincing evidence that Mr. Hillegass had misrepresented his estate, the amount in the prenuptial would have been considered unreasonable by the court?

---

permitted option of the widow taking an **election** against her late husband's estate. The law permits the spouse of a deceased person to elect to take a statutorily provided percentage of a deceased spouse's estate if the amount bequeathed in a will is less than the amount provided for by statute, or if there is no will.

THE STATUS OF PRENUPTIAL AGREEMENTS: WHERE ARE THEY NOW?

You have read about the history of prenuptial contracts and how courts all over the country deal with such contracts. Although the majority of courts once refused to accept them, all 50 states now accept the legitimacy of prenuptial contracts.

The somewhat surprising Pennsylvania case of *Simeone v. Simeone,* 525 Pa. 392, 581 A.2d 162 (1990), is at the tough-love end of the legal spectrum when it comes to how a court will view prenuptial contracts. The court in the *Simeone* case threw out any special treatment of the parties because of their marital relationship. Instead, they decided to use the case to declare that all contracts, whether prenuptial or commercial, should be treated the same. The *Simeone* judges did not want to hear that the validity of the prenuptial agreement Mrs. Simeone signed should be affected by her ignorance, lack of counsel, the fact that the agreement was presented to her by her much older husband on the eve of the wedding, or that her current financial situation was severely affected by the divorce. The majority looked to the equal status of women in society and refused to invalidate the agreement *absent fraud, misrepresentation, or duress.*

The dissenting judge's opinion in the *Simeone* case is more typically mainstream in that he refused to disregard the familial ties between the two key parties. The dissent discussed the court's traditional role *to protect and not to undermine those institutions and interests which are vital to our society.* Today, most courts balance their concern for validating prenuptial agreements as the contracts they are, with consideration of the often unequal status and confidential and familial connection of the parties.

RECONCILIATON AGREEMENTS

The parties in *Curry v. Curry* (see Case 4.5) jumped all over the legal arena. They married, divorced, allegedly remarried, and filled the court system with pleadings from both sides. This case provides a good analysis of the difference between a prenuptial agreement and a *reconciliation agreement.* A **reconciliation**

CASE 4.5 *Curry v. Curry,*
260 Ga. 302, 392 S.E.2d 879 (1990)

Facts: The parties were married in 1975, divorced in 1977, and allegedly remarried by common law later in 1977. The husband filed for divorce in 1981, but the couple reconciled before the divorce was final. The husband filed for divorce again in 1984. In 1984, the parties signed a reconciliation agreement that dismissed the pending action without prejudice, provided for certain payments by the husband to the wife, and barred the wife from future claims for alimony or equitable division of property. In 1989, the husband filed a new complaint for divorce and sought an order enforcing the terms agreed to in the reconciliation agreement if a divorce occurred. A hearing was held before the wife filed defensive pleadings or a counterclaim, and the trial court entered a final judgment to enforce the agreement. The appellate court granted the wife's application for appeal.

The wife contends that the trial court erred in granting a final judgment following what she described as a temporary hearing. The record shows that counsel for the wife agreed that the sole purpose of the hearing was to determine the validity of the reconciliation agreement, and that if the agreement was determined not to be valid, then another hearing would be set to resolve issues of support. The wife's counsel participated fully in the hearing, raised no objections to its timeliness, and requested that the court rule upon the enforceability of the agreement. After a three-hour hearing, the trial court held that the reconciliation agreement was valid. The sole issue in the case having been resolved, there was nothing left to be decided according to the trial court.

Issue: Whether the judge improperly failed to provide a hearing for jury issues and instead resolved those issues himself.

Court's Reasoning: A trial judge should employ basically three criteria in determining whether a prenuptial agreement should be enforced: (1) Was the agreement obtained through fraud, duress, or mistake, or through misrepresentation or nondisclosure of the material facts?; (2) Is the agreement unconscionable?; and (3) Have the facts and circumstances changed since the agreement was executed, so as to make its enforcement unfair and unreasonable? We know of no reason why a reconciliation agreement should stand on a different footing from a prenuptial agreement. A trial judge shall determine whether or not to enforce the agreement. There was no error.

This marriage would have terminated in 1984, but for such a reconciliation agreement. There has been no change in circumstances that was not foreseeable at the time that the agreement was entered into. The deteriorating disability of Mr. Curry was foreseeable. The increase in the value of the nonmarital assets was foreseeable, as well as Mrs. Curry's graduation from nursing school and having an independent source of earnings. Substantial performance has occurred under the reconciliation agreement. The parties were represented by counsel and bargained for what they received in the reconciliation agreement. Without a showing of fraud, mistake, duress, or misrepresentation of fact, the court does not have the authority to set aside or ignore such contract. Mr. and Mrs. Curry are both bound by those terms.

Holding: Judgment affirmed.

Case Discussion: This case should make you wonder what the wife was thinking when she signed the reconciliation agreement. The husband had filed twice for divorce and orchestrated the reconciliation agreement for the wife's signature. Do you think the husband was being savvy enough to hedge his bets in the event of yet another breakup? Can you imagine the wife feeling pressured to sign such an agreement if she wanted to reconcile?

agreement is an agreement made between spouses who have reunited following a separation. Another type of marital agreement is called a **post-nuptial agreement,** which is an agreement between spouses. It is different than a reconciliation agreement, since typically the married couple has not separated and reconciled. The content and circumstances surrounding the creation and signing of a post-nuptial agreement will be strictly reviewed by the courts. This strict review is due to the even more confidential relationship between the parties after their marriage. The term *substantial performance* is used in the *Curry* opinion to refer to the contract between the parties. **Substantial performance** occurs when a party to a contract has completed a valuable and significant percentage of a contract's requirements.

CHAPTER SUMMARY

Prenuptial, post-nuptial, and reconciliation agreements are types of contracts that may be entered into by an engaged or married couple. They detail a couple's understanding of their rights in the event of divorce. A prenuptial agreement (also known as an antenuptial agreement) is a contract entered into by two individuals before their marriage to each other, but which doesn't take effect until after the marriage. A post-nuptial agreement is a contract entered into by a married couple after their marriage. It is less typical than a prenuptial agreement, as is a reconciliation agreement, which is a contract entered into by a married couple after they have been separated and have decided to reconcile. All of these agreements usually include some mutual agreement detailing financial settlements in the event of divorce or death. Nonfinancial matters may be predetermined as well but, depending on the subject matter, may not be enforced by the courts. Each state's requirements for creating a valid prenuptial agreement is different and based upon whether or not that particular state has enacted the Uniform Premarital Agreement Act (UPAA). Twenty-five states and the District of Columbia have enacted the UPAA, and the remaining states each have individual legislation and case law. However, general requirements include: (1) a written document; (2) contractual capacity of the parties; (3) a voluntary agreement free of fraud, duress, and undue influence; (4) an agreement that is not unconscionable; and (5) full disclosure of assets.

Parties to a prenuptial agreement should understand that they cannot waive rights to child support. Certain key items should be included in the agreement: (1) a list all assets, liabilities, income, and expectations of gifts and inheritances; (2) a description of how premarital debts will be paid; (3) a description of what happens to premarital property in reference to appreciation, gains, income, rental, dividends, and proceeds of such property in the event of death or divorce; (4) decision on who will own the marital or secondary homes in the event of death or divorce; (5) a specification of the status of gifts, inheritances, and trusts that either spouse receives or benefits from, whether before or after the marriage; (6) clarification of what will happen to each type of property, such as real estate, artwork, furniture, and jewelry; (7) a decision of the amount allocated for alimony, maintenance, or spousal support, or a provision for a waiver or property settlement instead of support; (8) details of death benefits, stating what each party will provide for the other; and (9) a decision on medical, disability, life, and long-term care insurance.

Although the spouses can include child custody and support issues in the prenuptial agreement, the courts have the ultimate decision-making authority over such issues, and any predetermined issues concerning child custody and support will ultimately have to be approved by the court.

Key Terms

prenuptial agreement	fraud	offer
antenuptial agreement	undue influence	acceptance
Uniform Premarital Agreement Act (UPAA)	assets	consideration
	contract	parole evidence

rescission	vacate	election
community property	judicial notice	reconciliation agreement
payee spouse	summary judgment	post-nuptial agreement
payor spouse	constructive trust	substantial performance
quash	intestate	

Surfing the Web

http://www.allLaw.com Are you puzzled about where to begin? Try this site to get started.
http://www.legalforms.com Do you need a legal document? This is the site to try.
http://www.findlaw.com Are you looking for more information on a topic? Try findlaw for all types of legal assistance.
http://www.lectlaw.com Have you been looking for law in all the wrong places? Try lectlaw.
http://www.divorceinfo.com Legal assistance by state.

ETHICS ALERT

Susan has been asked to handle the interview of a client who wants to have a prenuptial agreement written prior to his marriage. The client, Thurston Howell IV, inherited loads of cash from his granny, Lovey Howell. He really does not want to share any of it with his starlet fiancée, Nutmeg, in case marriage number four goes sour. Susan has been asked by J. D. to conduct the interview and to get all the financials from Thurston. Susan has read Thurston's files and doubts Thurston's truthfulness during the interview. In the nicest way possible (after all, Thurston *is* a wealthy client), Susan questions the completeness of Thurston's answers. Thurston replies by winking at Susan and stating, "I don't know what you mean. Anyway, what my little cupcake doesn't know won't hurt her." Thurston the Fourth is being very generous to Nutmeg in the prenuptial agreement. Should Susan still be concerned?

Review Questions

1. Define a prenuptial and antenuptial agreement.
2. What is the UPAA? Has your state enacted the UPAA?
3. What are the general requirements of a prenuptial agreement? How are the general requirements of a prenuptial agreement different from those for other kinds of contractual agreements?
4. When are prenuptial agreements especially useful?
5. What elements of a valid contract should one look for in a prenuptial agreement?
6. What is consideration? What is the usual consideration in any prenuptial agreement?
7. What is the *four corners of the contract?*
8. Would parole evidence be welcomed by most courts?
9. What is the legal term for the parties mutually agreeing to rewriting a contract?
10. Certain key items should be included in a prenuptial agreement. What are they?
11. Would a no-children clause release a parent from paying child support?
12. What precautions should be taken and under what circumstances should the signing of a prenuptial agreement be done?
13. What happens if a prenuptial agreement is found to be invalid?
14. What is a post-nuptial agreement? What is a reconciliation agreement?
15. How do most courts today view the intimate nature of the relationship of the parties to a prenuptial contract?

Endnotes

1. Podell, Peggy L., "Before Your Client Says 'I Do,'" *ABA Journal* (August 1999): 80.
2. Weidel, Cecile C., "Love on the Dotted Line," *ABA Journal* (May 2000): 125.
3. Newsome, Lynn Fontaine, "Premarital Agreements," *Sidebar* 2, no. 2 (May 1998): 1.
4. Paul, Pamela, "Mom's in Love Again," *Connections,* Time Bonus Section (April 2003): 5.
5. "Premarital Agreement," *Family Advocate* (1995): 8.
6. Baskies, Jeffrey A. "Time to Change Your Will," *Family Advocate* 18, no. 3 (1996): 27.
7. Brook, Jill. "A Promise to Love, Honor and Bear No Children," *New York Times,* section 9, October 13, 2002, 1, 11.
8. Walther, Michael, "Do You Need a Premarital Agreement?" *Family Advocate* 18 no. 3 (1996): 46.

Chapter 5

Marriage

DEFINING MARRIAGE

The American concept of marriage has changed form with the times and has evolved to become a union defined by love with a legal arsenal of over one thousand laws pertaining to it. Each state has attempted to define marriage. California's *Family Code* definition is typical. It defines **marriage** as *a personal relationship arising out of a civil contract between a man and a woman, to whom the consent of the parties capable of making that contract is necessary. Consent alone does not constitute marriage. Consent must be followed by the issuance of a license and solemnization.*[1] However marriage may be defined, the majority of Americans do marry. Refer to Exhibit 5.1 to review marriage statistics provided by the United States Census. These statistics highlight selected years between 1970 and 2000.

Defining Marriage Around the World

Generally, the marriage ceremony is regarded as a religious rite or includes religious features, although the religious element is not always regarded as necessary to the validity of the union. Marriage under the early Christians was a religious act of the very highest kind, namely, one of the seven sacraments.

Martin Luther, the Catholic priest who created the Protestant Reformation when he broke with the Roman Catholic Church in 1517, declared that marriage was not a sacrament, but a *worldly thing*. Owing to the influence of the Protestant Reformation and the French Revolution, the nonreligious *civil marriage* has been instituted in almost all the countries of Europe and North America, as well as in South America.

A **civil marriage** is defined as a government-sanctioned union that is created when a government employee officiates at a marriage ceremony, after which the participants are declared husband and wife. In some countries it is essential to the validity of the union that the couple first completes a civil marriage, even if a religious ceremony is planned. In the United States, a civil marriage ceremony is merely another way a marriage may be conducted.

Marriage Customs

The American marriage you are familiar with today has developed from a long line of interesting legends, customs, and religious rites.[2] For example, you may have attended weddings in the past and wondered why fellow guests tied shoes to the newlyweds' car bumper prior to their departure from the reception. This

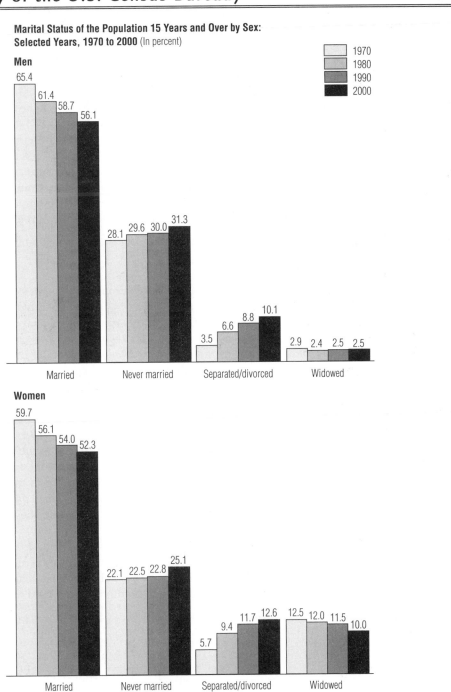

EXHIBIT 5.1 Marital Status of Americans (Courtesy of the U.S. Census Bureau)

Marital Status of the Population 15 Years and Over by Sex: Selected Years, 1970 to 2000 (In percent)

Legend: 1970, 1980, 1990, 2000

Men

	Married	Never married	Separated/divorced	Widowed
1970	65.4	28.1	3.5	2.9
1980	61.4	29.6	6.6	2.4
1990	58.7	30.0	8.8	2.5
2000	56.1	31.3	10.1	2.5

Women

	Married	Never married	Separated/divorced	Widowed
1970	59.7	22.1	5.7	12.5
1980	56.1	22.5	9.4	12.0
1990	54.0	22.8	11.7	11.5
2000	52.3	25.1	12.6	10.0

Source: U.S. Census Bureau, Current Population Survey, March Supplements: 1970 to 2000.

unusual American custom can apparently be credited to the ancient Egyptians. The ancient Egyptian custom was for the father of a newlywed daughter to exchange sandals with his new son-in-law to symbolize the passing of her care over to the groom.

Another firmly entrenched American custom is the exchange of wedding rings. Have you ever wondered why newlyweds place their wedding rings on their third finger of their left hand? One version is that the ring was placed on the third finger of the left hand because of an ancient belief that a delicate nerve began in the ring finger and ran straight to the heart.

What wedding would be complete without a cake? The first wedding cakes may have originated in England. Guests would first throw wheat at the bride as a symbol of future bounty for the happy couple, and then pick up the wheat and eat it. Hundreds of years after the first wheat was thrown, bakers decided to make cakes from the gathered wheat stalks.

Honeymoons also have a particularly interesting history. While you may imagine a honeymoon as a blissful escape, long ago it was likely a period when the groom, having bought or captured a bride, disappeared with her so that her family could not rescue her. By the time they reappeared, the bride was often pregnant. Why the term *honeymoon?* In Germany and Scandinavia, a moon was a month. Couples would typically retreat for a month. Then during the sixteenth century, the term *honeymoon* began to be used to refer less to a time period and more to a feeling. The newly married were considered to be in the honey or full phase of their love.[3]

Monogamy to Multiple Marriages

Along the winding road that is the story of marriage are deviations from the two-person marriage concept known as **monogamy.** Although monogamy is the rule in Western society, many other cultures allow plural marriage, or **polygamy.** In many traditional African, Arab, and Asian societies, men are allowed to have more than one wife at one time. The earliest books of the Old Testament contain many references to polygamy. In fact, pointing to the Old Testament as their resource, some members of the Mormon faith followed the polygamy concept until it was outlawed by the United States government in the early twentieth century. At that time, the federal government forced polygamous Mormon men to declare one woman as a legal wife. A small minority of Mormons still practice polygamy without the official approval of their church or the government.[4]

The **polyandry** marriage is the union of several husbands with one wife. It has been practiced at various times by a considerable number of groups. It existed among the ancient Britons, the primitive Arabs, the inhabitants of the Canary Islands, the Aborigines of America, the Hottentots, and the inhabitants of India, Ceylon, Tibet, Malabar, and New Zealand. In the great majority of these instances, polyandry was the exceptional form of conjugal union. In fact, even with polyandry, the wife typically belonged not to several entirely independent men, but to a group united by the closest ties of blood. In other words, she was married to one family rather than to one person.

People involved in plural marriages generally have sought benefits in marriage that are different from those sought in a monogamous union. For example, in various polygamous cultures of Africa and the Middle East, if a man has many heirs from multiple wives, his social position is enhanced. In addition, when a woman married a man with many wives, often the result was greater cooperation in both farming and other domestic work.[5]

Arranged Marriages

Historically, marriages often have been arranged between families, usually with some right of veto by the bride or groom. Arranged marriages dominate primarily in societies that place great importance on property inheritance and linkages between families, or in which elders think that young people are unable to make sound choices. China, India, and the Middle East are among the areas of the world where societies traditionally have practiced, and in some instances still practice, arranged marriage. In such societies, careful attention is usually paid to the health, work habits, character, and family background of the bride and groom so as to ensure a successful match.

Until Death Do Us Part?

Throughout history, marital unions that endured until the death of one of the spouses appear to have been in the minority. Most ancient cultures authorized husbands to divorce their wives whenever they felt so inclined. Such early Christian emperors as Constantine, Theodosius, and Justinian legalized divorce.

By the tenth century, though, the Catholic teachings on the indissolubility of marriage had become embodied in the civil legislation of every Catholic country. In all the countries that adopted the Catholic religion, divorce was very soon abolished.[6] However, the churches that separated from Rome, including the Greek Orthodox Church and all the Protestant sects, have permitted divorce in varying degrees.

Until relatively recently, divorce continued to be forbidden in countries that recognized the Catholic religion as their official religion. For example, it was only on February 27, 1997, that the Republic of Ireland made divorce legal. Irish couples seeking a divorce must live apart for four out of the last five years of their marriage, must claim that there is no prospect of reconciliation, and must make provisions for dependent family members.[7]

Is Marriage Really a Contract?

Although the expression "the marriage contract" is used in everyday speech, marriage is technically known as an *anomalous contract,* and from a legal standpoint is not to be confused with other forms of contract. Describing marriage as an anomalous contract is another way of saying that it is an unusual contract. American marriages are considered a matter of family law, not contract law. Family law dictates whom one can marry and sets forth minimum ages for marriage. It also governs divorce and, to some degree, ownership of property, but it stops short of dictating what personal details the marital relationship will entail. For example, if spouses wish to make a contract that includes the details of their division of labor, they may do so, but it should be understood that stipulations such as those setting out details on who will clean the house and watch the children are almost never enforceable at law. However, terms of prenuptial and postnuptial contracts concerning property settlement and spousal support are enforceable.

In colonial New England, all marriages were performed by justices of the peace until 1692, when clergy were made officials of the state for that purpose. When the Constitution of the United States was drawn up, control over marriage law was placed under the jurisdiction of the individual states. Today a constitutional amendment would be required to allow federal law to alter marriage and divorce laws of the states. Such laws are written and revamped in state legislatures in response to pressures brought by changing customs.[8]

LEFT AT THE ALTAR

For the time being, all these interesting marriage customs no longer matter to Tara, one of Susan's oldest friends. Tara's fiancé has called it quits, and she is suffering from both a broken heart and pain concerning her pocketbook. She turns to Susan in search of a sympathetic ear and free legal advice. Read about Tara's expensive troubles in the following text.

> "Hello, Susie?" Tara sniffed tearfully into the phone.
>
> "Hi, this is Susan. I can't come to the phone right now, but your message is important to me. Please leave your name and number, slowly, and I will return your phone call."
>
> "Oh, I thought it was the real you for a minute. I hate these machines," Tara mournfully complained into the inanimate message machine. She then proceeded to use up most of Susan's tape. "Well, anyway, you won't believe this, but Bud has backed out of the wedding. He feels he wants to have more time to get to know his inner child. So, he's quitting his job and traveling around the world. I can't believe it. Dad has spent so much already on the preparations, and I've spent so much time and money of my own." Tara paused, then huffed into the tape, "What am I suppose to do now? We paid a down payment on the hall and deposits on the dress, the limo, and the flowers." After pausing again, she added morosely, "Oh my, I nearly forgot: I paid for the honeymoon deposit because Bud was saving up for the rest of the trip and. . . ."
>
> At this point, Susan's tape ran out. Several hours later Susan returned home and retrieved the message. After listening to it, she knew that her friend Tara was going to ask her for legal advice. Later, as she relaxed in the tub, Susan reflected to herself, "If I had a dollar for each time I'm asked for a legal opinion I can't ethically or legally give as a paralegal, I'd own a brand-new sports car." Nevertheless, Susan decided that when she went to work on Monday she would ask one of the firm's attorneys about Tara's legal options.
>
> Meanwhile, Susan planned to make two phone calls. The second call would be to her friend to commiserate. The first call would be the local bridal shop to stop the order for her bridesmaid's dress. "With any luck," Susan thought, "I won't be stuck with that hot-pink satin and lace bridesmaid's dress that would be useless for anything else!"

History of the Breach-of-Promise Action

The English common law system successfully transplanted to American soil the *breach-of-promise* cause of action. **Breach of promise** is short for a breach of promise to marry. Historically, England's breach-of-promise actions were brought solely by the wronged party to an ecclesiastical court, which is a religious court. These courts could not order the breaching party to pay monetary damages; however, with the power of the church behind them, they could heavily influence the breaching party to go through with the wedding—or suffer the consequences. These consequences could be extremely serious, for example, the court could order that the breaching party be excommunicated from the church.

By the 1600s, the English law courts had gotten into the act and were awarding monetary damages if the breaching party had acted in a fraudulent way toward his intended. So, if a deceitful cad lied to his intended, and that lie was the basis of the promise to marry, he could be sued for the actual money spent in reliance upon that lie.

The sixteenth-century Englishman understood the significance of a marriage proposal to society and the courts. William Shakespeare's 1583 betrothal was typical for his era. Nineteen-year-old Shakespeare married Anne Hathaway, the daughter of a well-to-do farmer. She was seven or eight years his senior. Their first child, a daughter, was born six months after the marriage. Note that in sixteenth-century England, an agreement to marry was often made in the presence of witnesses and, though not recorded, was enough to constitute a formal betrothal and, to all intents and purposes, a marriage. In many cases, the final sanction of the Church was not sought until a child was imminent. There is no evidence that Shakespeare's courtship, marriage, and child's birth were unusual.[9]

Suing for a Broken Promise

The American courts have based the cause of action for a breach-of-promise suit solidly in contract law. As stated earlier, a contract is defined as a legally enforceable agreement between two or more parties that is created when one of those parties makes an offer that the other accepts, and for which there is a legal exchange of *consideration*. Legally speaking, consideration is anything of value, monetary or otherwise.

The nineteenth-century plaintiff claiming a breach of promise to marry was typically a female. The average nineteenth-century American woman depended on marriage for her very survival, and the breaking of an engagement promise often left the aggrieved female less desirable in the marriage market. Thus, it is understandable that society and the courts, given those social conditions, allowed women to make breach-of-promise claims that would place them in the financial position in which they would have been had the marriage taken place. In effect, the courts treated the plaintiff as if the marriage had taken place and failed, and the court was now figuring out what *alimony* should be paid. **Alimony** is money paid by a divorced spouse to the ex-spouse for ongoing personal support.

The plaintiff in a breach-of-promise action in nineteenth-century America was allowed by the courts to request three types of damages: (1) *expectation damages;* (2) *reliance damages;* and (3) *pain and suffering damages.* A plaintiff's **expectation damages** were damages that, if awarded, would place the plaintiff in the same position she would have been in had the wedding taken place. The nineteenth-century plaintiff in a breach-of-promise action was often awarded the amount of damages a twentieth-century *divorcing spouse* would claim.

The type of damages that are still awarded by the courts in *both* breach-of-promise actions and heartbalm statute actions (discussed later in this chapter) are typically known as reliance damages. Reliance occurs when a *promisee*—usually the jilted fiancée—takes an action she otherwise *would not* have taken, or refrains from taking an action she otherwise *would* have taken, because of a presumption that a promise will be honored. Examples of actions the promisee might take in preparing for an imminent marriage include renting a wedding hall, buying a dress, and even refraining from taking a new job in another town. A breaching fiancé can be sued for reliance damages, in such an instance, for the cost of the hall, the dress, and the lost wages. **Reliance damages,** which are often requested, and often granted, compensate for the expenditures the plaintiff has reasonably made in reliance on the broken promise of the defendant. These reliance damages can be based on the actions the wronged party took or did not take because of her reliance on the promise.

The nineteenth-century plaintiff also could often prove that the broken promise caused her emotional pain and suffering, and could recover **pain and suffering damages.** When making this claim, she was using *tort law* to deal with the breach of a contract. A **tort** is defined as a personal wrong by one party against another. Tort law allows damages to be paid to the injured party.[10]

Interestingly, the defendant in a breach-of-promise action in the nineteenth century could defend himself by claiming that the plaintiff was unchaste. It was a wise defendant, however, who refrained from arbitrarily using the unchaste claim just to reduce damages. If the jury did not believe the unchaste claim, they could add more damages because of the defendant's attack on the plaintiff's good name.

Breach-of-Promise Backlash

By the early twentieth century, excessive use of the court system to deal with broken marriage promises resulted in a backlash against the breach-of-promise claim. The public interest in lurid and sensational evidence regarding the romantic lives of litigants, and the social ostracism resulting from these types of cases, also helped bring about this backlash. Critics of the breach-of-promise cause of action suggested that a party who broke off an engagement prior to the marriage ceremony should be *commended* for refusing to enter a loveless marriage and should not be punished by the court system. Furthermore, these early twentieth-century critics often suggested that monetary damages were not an effective remedy for the brokenhearted. The chief argument against the traditional breach-of-promise action, however, was that it approached matters of the heart as if they were property transactions. This argument rang true to many, because by the twentieth century, the majority of Americans who married did so for love, and not because of arranged financial alliances.

Heart-Balm Statutes Change Law

The gradual change of opinion away from the common law breach-of-promise action ushered in the first American **heart-balm statutes** in the 1930s. At that time, one judge memorably described the statutes using the poetic name *heart-balm* to refer to the financial soothing of the victim's pocketbook in compensation for an unfortunate affair of the heart. These early 1930s heart-balm statutes essentially dismantled the old-fashioned breach-of-promise action and were enacted by legislatures in 25 states as a replacement for the common law breach-of-promise action.

The traditional breach-of-promise action entitled a jilted party to expectation damages aimed at compensating the jilted fiancée for her loss of the financial and social position she would have been in had the marriage taken place. The states that passed heart-balm statutes no longer allowed expectation damages and limited the jilted fiancée to reliance damages. The remaining states still allowed breach-of-promise actions and still have not, with the exception of Washington, abolished the expectation damages available to the aggrieved betrothed, although expectation damages are rarely awarded these days.

The Issue of the Ring

One material item important to most American brides and grooms is the engagement ring. The romantic custom of the ring is thought to have originated with King Charles VII of France, who gave diamonds not to his future wife, but to his mistress! The engagement ring is now America's traditional symbol of a couple's commitment to marry. It is also often a very expensive item. Who gets the ring when an engagement is called off? The answer depends on which state the star-crossed couple lives in.

Some states have decided that the person who does not keep the promise is not entitled to keep the engagement ring. If the receiver of the ring calls off the wedding, she has to return the ring. Some states insist that *all* gifts made in contemplation of marriage be returned, *regardless of who broke off the engagement,* because the gifts were made *contingent* upon the wedding taking place. Most courts, however, consider a ring given as a holiday or birthday gift exactly as that—an **irrevocable gift.** Even if the gift was intended by both parties to also be an engagement ring, the courts usually look at the ring as a present and forget about the engagement aspect.

Now that you have read the legal history of the breach-of-promise action and learned about the more recent heart-balm legislation, what do you think Tara's options will be? In the following text, you will find the answer to that question, along with Susan when she depends on the good nature and knowledge of one of the firm's young associates in seeking information for her friend.

OPTIONS FOR A JILTED FIANCÉE:
ADVICE TO THE LOVELORN

"I'm the last person you should ask about relationships," Jameson said in response to Susan's questions about breach of promise and broken engagements. He exclaimed, "Who do you think I am, Miss Lonelyhearts?"

After working for several months with Jameson, a second-year associate, Susan knew he would get around to answering her questions eventually. He had been helpful in the past when Susan had come to him because she was confused.

"No, I don't think Miss Lonelyhearts is sporting a full beard this season," Susan smiled back.

"Okay, okay," Jameson said, "Tell me again, I'll listen."

Susan moved from the doorway into Jameson's small office and sat down. "First, I'm sorry to bother you, but my friend is really in a mess," she began. "She and her father have paid for almost the whole wedding." Susan continued sarcastically, "And now the groom has announced that his *inner child* needs to roam, and he's changed his mind about settling down."

Jameson listened patiently and looked concerned when Susan mentioned Tara. "Is this the same Tara I met at your housewarming party?" he inquired. Susan nodded. Jameson recalled how sweet Tara had been to his young daughter, and how she had played with her when the four-year-old became bored at the grown-up party. Jameson said, "You were right to come to me. In this state, we no longer have the breach-of-promise statute that would allow Tara to recover expectation damages for what she's losing out on by not becoming the wife of *Mr. In-Touch-with-His-Inner-Child.*"

"But what can she do about the money she's put out before the marriage?" Susan anxiously inquired.

Jameson leaned forward and tapped the desk with his pen. "I'm getting to that. The courts in our state *will* generally hear lawsuits stemming from a broken engagement *if* the damages requested are based on the expenditures made in the reasonable anticipation of a marriage."

Susan looked relieved. She asked, "So basically, Tara and her dad have a chance of getting their money back from her fiancé if she can prove the breakup wasn't *her* decision, and that she was truly engaged prior to spending all that money on the wedding preparation?"

Jameson nodded and said, "Yeah, but of course, if *Mr. Needs-to-Roam* doesn't have the money, Tara could sue him and receive a judgment she won't be able to collect."

Susan made a sound showing disgust, but then she brightened as a new thought came to her. "What if Tara uses the sale of her engagement ring to offset her expenditures?"

"Good idea," Jameson concurred. "The courts in our state will sometimes allow the so-called *jilted* party to keep the ring if it was given as an irrevocable gift, and not solely as a condition of marriage. Of course, to prove the ring was an irrevocable gift, Tara would have to prove there was a voluntary delivery of the ring, and that it was her fiancé's intention to relinquish title and control immediately to her."

Susan purposefully rose from her chair. "That's great, because I know that Tara was given the ring as a birthday gift before the engagement was official. Since it was so expensive, Bud didn't want to buy another ring. Thanks so much for the info."

Jameson was happy to have helped. "No problem. I *did* wonder about those two at your party, but I didn't want to mention that they didn't seem like a match made in heaven." He shyly commented, "Since my divorce, it's been hard to meet nice women like Tara. They're always taken. Do you think she'd go out with me?" He quickly added, "After a decent period of adjustment, of course."

Breaking into a big grin, Susan answered, "I couldn't think of a nicer pair!"

THE LEGAL REQUIREMENTS OF MARRIAGE

Most people know how to define a marriage and know that a marriage license is required. There is also a lengthy list of additional prerequisites that are equally important. All 50 states have their own legal requirements that must be met by a couple intending to marry in the state. Although the requirements vary slightly from state to state, they are basically similar. The bride and groom's requirements generally include eight prerequisites: (1) a license; (2) different sexes; (3) not being already married; (4) acceptable degree of consanguinity; (5) mental capacity; (6) intent to marry; (7) an age requirement; and (8) a solemnization ceremony.

Another way to view these prerequisites is to consider them as conditions that must be met in order for the marriage vows to create a valid and binding marriage contract with all its duties and benefits. Such legally required essential elements are more technically known as *conditions precedent*. A **condition precedent** is an event that creates or destroys rights and obligations. For example, if a certain future event happens, a right or obligation ends. Generally, the failure of a bride and groom to meet these essential elements will render their marriage invalid. If a state considers the lack of an essential element especially important, the attempted marriage contract is often considered ***void ab initio.*** This term translated from Latin means *void from the very beginning.* A person who is involved in a void marriage contract can honestly say, *I have never been married.* Review the marriage requirements for all 50 states in Exhibit 5.2, which also provides details of the legal significance of the eight prerequisites for a valid marriage.

License Requirements

Fairly typical across the nation is the requirement that a bride and groom apply for a marriage license. For example, if you want to get married in Texas, you need to go to a county clerk to buy a license, and the license should be obtained in the county in which you plan to marry. Furthermore, each applicant should submit the following: (1) proof of identity; (2) proof of parental consent if under 18 years of age; (3) proof that any prior marriage has been dissolved; (4) Social Security numbers; and (5) a signed application and printed oath.

Different-Sex Requirement

All 50 states require that the bride and groom planning to marry be different sexes. A slight deviation from the different-sex requirement occurs in Vermont. The Vermont Legislature has approved persons of the same sex committing to each other in what are called *civil unions.* A **civil union** is a government-approved legal commitment that creates the rights and obligations of same-sex partners to each other. Lawsuits fighting the different-sex requirement for marriage continue to be brought throughout the United States, and there are several movements aimed at getting states to accept and acknowledge the civil union concept. Same-sex partners in Vermont have essentially the same benefits and responsibilities as opposite-sex couples who marry. An extensive review of the legal status of same-sex marriage proposals throughout the United States is provided later in this chapter.

Bigamy

All 50 states require that the bride and groom cannot be already married to other persons. A person who marries two or more times without legally dissolving prior valid marriages is committing **bigamy.** Such a person is known as a *bigamist.* An exception to this existed in the Utah Territory until the end of the nineteenth century because of the Mormon religion's acceptance of polygamy. In 1890, the leader of the

EXHIBIT 5.2 Marriage Requirements

Marriage Requirements by State
Age and Costs

State	Statute	Consent Age W/WO	Cost
Alabama	30-1	14/18	$25.00
Alaska	25.05	14/18	$25.00
Arizona	25-101 through 25-122	14/18	$50.00
Arkansas	9-11	male 17; female 16/18	$35.00
California	300–500	no age limit/18	$50.00–$80.00
Colorado	14-2-105 through 14-2-110	16/18	$20.00
Connecticut	815e-460-29	16/18	$30.00
Delaware	13-1	male 18; female 16/18	$30.00
District of Columbia	30-1	18/18	$35.00
Florida	741.04 through 741.09	16/18	$85.50; $56.00 if couple takes 4-hour course
Georgia	19-3-1 through 19-3-68	16/18	$30.00 average
Hawaii	572	15/18	$50.00
Idaho	32-301 through 32-501	16/18	$28.00
Illinois	750 ILCS 5/	16/18	$15.00–$30.00
Indiana	IC 31-11-2; IC 31-11.5; IC 31-11-4	17/18	$18.00
Iowa	595.2	16/18	$30.00
Kansas	23-106	male 14; female 12/18	$50.00
Kentucky	402	18/18	$34.00
Louisiana	235	18/18	$25.00
Maine	23:652	16/18	$20.00
Maryland	2-201 through 2-503	16/18	$35.00
Massachusetts	207-28A	male 14; female 12/18	$4.00
Michigan	551.51	16/18	$20.00
Minnesota	517.01	16/18	$70.00
Mississippi	93-1	male 17; female 15	$20.00
Missouri	451	15/18	$50.00
Montana	4-1	16/18	$30.00
Nebraska	42-104	17/19	$15.00
Nevada	122	16/18	$35.00
New Hampshire	457	male 14; female 13/18	$45.00
New Jersey	37:1	16/18	$28.00
New Mexico	40-1-1	16/18	$25.00
New York	14-1-2	16/18	$25.00–$30.00
North Carolina	51	16/18	$40.00
North Dakota	14-03	16/18	$35.00
Ohio	3101	male 18; female 16/18	$30.00
Oklahoma	43-3	16/18	$25.00
Oregon	106	17/18	$60.00
Pennsylvania	Title 23, part 1	16/18	$25.00–$40.00
Rhode Island	15-1-1	male 18; female 14/18	$24.00
South Carolina	20-1	male 16; female 16/18	$25.00
South Dakota	25-1-2	16/18	$40.00
Tennessee	36-3	16/18	$31.00–39.00
Texas	2.101	14/18	$31.00
Utah	30-1	14/18	$40.00

(continued)

EXHIBIT 5.2 *continued*

Vermont	5142	16/18	$20.00
Virginia	20-2	16/18	$20.00
Washington	26-4	17/18	$51.00
West Virginia	48-1	18/18	$23.00
Wisconsin	765 through 767	16/18	$50.80
Wyoming	20-1	16/18	$25.00

Waiting Periods and Blood Tests

State	Waiting Period After Applying to Receive License	Expiration of License After Receipt	Blood Test Required	Waiting Period to Marry After Receiving License
Alabama	None	30 days	Yes	None
Alaska	3 days	3 months	No	None
Arizona	None	1 year	No	None
Arkansas	None	60 days	No	None
California	None	90 days	No	None
Colorado	None	30 days	No	None
Connecticut	None	65 days	Yes	None
Delaware	None	30 days	No	1 day if resident
District of Columbia	3 days	None	Yes	None
Florida	None	60 days	No	3 days/Florida residents only
Georgia	None	None	Yes	None
Hawaii	None	30 days	No	None
Idaho	None	1 year	Yes	None
Illinois	None	60 days	No	1 day
Indiana	None	60 days	Yes	None
Iowa	3 days	20 days	No	None
Kansas	3 days	6 months	No	None
Kentucky	3 days	30 days	No	None
Louisiana	None	30 days	Yes	3 days
Maine	3 days	90 days	No	None
Maryland	2 days	6 months	No	None
Massachusetts	3 days	60 days	Yes and medical	None
Michigan	3 days	33 days	No	None
Minnesota	5 days	6 months	No	None
Mississippi	3 days	90 days	Yes	None
Missouri	3 days	30 days	No	None
Montana	None	30 days	Yes	None
Nebraska	3 days	3 months	No	None
Nevada	None	1 year	No	None
New Hampshire	None	60 days	No	3 days
New Jersey	None	90 days	No	None
New Mexico	None	30 days	No	None
New York	None	65 days	No	1 day
North Carolina	None	30 days	No	None
North Dakota	3 days	None	No	None
Ohio	None	60 days	No	None
Oklahoma	None	None	Yes	None
Oregon	None	30 days	No	None

Pennsylvania	None	1 year	No	None
Rhode Island	None	60 days	No	None
South Carolina	None	60 days	No	None
South Dakota	3 days	20 days	No	None
Tennessee	3 days	6 months	No	None
Texas	3 days	30 days	No	72 hours
Utah	None	30 days	No	None
Vermont	3 days	90 days	No	1 day
Virginia	2 days	6 months	No	None
Washington	3 days	33 days	No	None
West Virginia	3 days	60 days	Yes	3 days
Wisconsin	5 days	6 months	No	None
Wyoming	3 days	90 days	No	None

Mormon Church rejected the practice of polygamy. This was soon after the United States Supreme Court upheld a series of federal laws making polygamy illegal. Bigamy is now a crime in every state. Thus, "one person, one marriage" is another essential element. The following typical definition of bigamy comes from Pennsylvania's statute found at 18 Pa. C.S. § 4301, which states:

> *(a) A married person is guilty of bigamy, a misdemeanor of the second degree, if he contracts or purports to contract another marriage, unless at the time of the subsequent marriage: the actor believes that the prior spouse is dead; the actor and the prior spouse have been living apart for two consecutive years throughout which the prior spouse was not known by the actor to be alive; or a court has entered a judgment purporting to terminate or annul any prior disqualifying marriage, and the actor does not know that judgment to be invalid. (b) Other party to bigamous marriage. A person is guilty of bigamy if he contracts or purports to contract marriage with another knowing that the other is thereby committing bigamy.*

The Consanguinity Factor

Consanguinity is defined as having a blood relationship or kinship. Thus, the question of whether a bride and groom are blood relatives is a question regarding the couple's consanguinity. A minimal degree of separation by blood relatives is an essential element that must be present in order to validate a marriage as legal and binding. Although the minimal degree of separation varies by state, each state prohibits marriage between close blood relatives. In fact, 24 states prohibit marriage between first cousins despite the fact that the *Journal of Genetic Counseling* has published information showing that the increased risk of birth defects to children born of first cousins is nominal; the American legal system and our social psyche considers first cousins as being blood relatives who are too close in kinship to marry. The state of Mississippi provides a good example of a state code dealing with consanguinity issues.[11] It says:

> *The son shall not marry his grandmother, his mother, or his stepmother; the brother his sister; the father his daughter, or his legally adopted daughter, or his granddaughter; the son shall not marry the daughter of his father begotten of his stepmother, or his aunt, being his father's or mother's sister, nor shall the children of brother or sister, or brothers and sisters intermarry being first cousins by blood. The father shall not marry his son's widow; a man shall not marry his wife's daughter or his wife's daughter's daughter, or his wife's son's daughter, or the daughter of his brother or sister; and the like prohibition shall extend to females in the same degrees. All marriages prohibited by this subsection are incestuous and void.*

Notice that this Mississippi statute includes in its prohibition the marital union between some individuals who would conceivably have no blood relationship. The statute suggests that it is society's aversion to even the *thought* of intermarrying that led Mississippi to prohibit marriages between men and women who are not blood relations but are related by marriage or adoption.

Illinois has an interesting requirement for a resident who wants to marry her first cousin.[12] Generally, marriage between cousins of the first degree is prohibited in Illinois; however, first cousins may marry if: *(1) Both parties are 50 years of age or older; or (2) either party, at the time the couple applies for a marriage license, presents to the county clerk of the county in which the marriage is to take place a certificate signed by a licensed physician stating that a party to the proposed marriage is permanently and irreversibly sterile.*

Mental Capacity

One of the most essential elements required before marriage is that the parties have the **mental capacity** to marry. If either party is incapable of knowing the type of contract he is entering, this essential element is not present. For example, what if Leila Lonelyhearts drinks a pint of tequila during her vacation in Mexico and suddenly decides to marry the handsome pool guy at her hotel? Since Leila's mental faculties have been influenced by a large dose of liquor, the question that must be asked is: *Does Leila understand that once she marries, she will have rights and subsequent responsibilities regarding her new husband?* Realistically, if Leila is so drunk she does not realize what she is doing, the required mental capacity requirement is not met. If Leila's predicament seems far-fetched, consider the following facts regarding the Dennis Rodman and Carmen Elektra Las Vegas nuptials.

Rodman and Electra were allegedly married on November 14, 1998. Rodman filed for separation on the same date. He followed up on November 29, 1998, by filing a formal Petition for Annulment. Rodman's petition, filed in California's Superior Court, claimed that his one-day marriage should be nullified because of *fraud* and *unsound mind.* However, any hope of proving his marriage had never completed *ratification* was essentially gone when Rodman and Electra held a press conference on February 7, 1999, to tell the world they were still happily married. **Ratification** is the confirmation and acceptance of a previous act done by oneself or another person. The epilogue: Electra filed for divorce on April 4, 1999, and the couple was arrested on November 5, 1999, for alleged acts of domestic violence against each other in a Miami Beach hotel room. The couple's divorce was finalized by the end of November in 1999.[13]

Drug intoxication, alcohol intoxication, or mental illness usually prevents a person from forming the requisite intent to enter a valid marriage. However, there is an interesting exception. In some states, a person who comes to her mental senses and then clearly indicates that the intent is to be married, in effect, ratifies the marriage. A ratified marriage then becomes a valid legal marriage. So, a person who is intoxicated when she marries and goes to bed but wakes up sober and decides to have sexual relations with her new spouse *ratifies* her marriage.

Intent to Marry

If one of the marrying parties takes the marriage vows without the intent to fulfill the responsibilities of marriage, the marriage may be considered a **sham marriage.** For example, if a 25-year-old adult male marries a 15-year-old minor female, knowing full well that such a marriage does not meet the legal age requirements, the 25-year-old cannot come back from the honeymoon and relieve himself from his responsibilities toward his wife by seeking an annulment. However, the 15-year-old wife is given the option of seeking an annulment because of the *voidable* status of the marriage. A **voidable** marriage is a marriage that a party can legally get out of because of some defect in the creation of the marriage, but it will be effective and binding if one or both parties do not choose to get out of it. So, if the 15-year-old does not choose to get out of the marriage, the 25-year-old will have to go through the divorce process to get out of the marriage. It is unlikely, however, that he could as easily get out of trouble with the police for his involvement with an underage female whom he married without parental permission.

Some marriages are based upon one spouse perpetrating a fraud upon the other. In this situation, again, there would be no valid intent to marry. *Fraud* is defined as any kind of trickery used to cheat another of money or property. Here is an example of a marriage involving fraud. Suppose a financially challenged woman named Helen learns that if she marries a soldier in the U.S. military she will be entitled to a free college education as the soldier's spouse? Assume further that Helen later learns that, even if she divorces, she will still be entitled to the free education. So, Helen travels to an Army base, meets G.I. Joe, and marries him with the intent of quickly divorcing him and going to college. In this example, Helen does not have the requisite intent to marry. G.I. Joe should seek an annulment and foil Helen's financial aid plan.

In order to further understand how fraud can occur within the context of marriage, you must first understand how marriage has been historically viewed by society and the courts. The fundamental purpose of marriage historically has been to ensure the birth of children. Along with procreation, society viewed sexual relations between spouses to be an intrinsic part of any marriage. These two fundamental purposes of marriage have been considered so important that the failure of a prospective spouse to be perfectly honest about any sterility or impotence problems gives legal recourse to the other spouse. This means that if one spouse marries while *knowing he is sterile* and does not tell the other spouse prior to the marriage, the unwitting spouse can seek an annulment based on fraud. However, if both spouses know about the sterility prior to their marriage, an annulment will not be granted. In that case, the only way to end the marriage would be by divorce.

Impotence Leads to Fraud Claim

The case of *T. v. M.* (see Case 5.1) reflects the situation in the majority of states that allow annulment in the case of impotence only if the couple has never had sexual intercourse since their marriage. The court politely described such post-nuptial sexual relations as *ratification of the marriage.* The husband in this case sought an annulment based on allegations that the wife knew she was impotent prior to the marriage. This was a case of first impression. Recall from your earlier reading that a case will be considered one of first impression when the subject matter of the case has never before been decided by a court in a particular state.

Age Requirement

Each state allows anyone at least 18 years old who has met all the other essential elements to marry. There are some variations across the country regarding anyone under 18 years of age who is planning to wed. Georgia's statute is typical in how it handles the underage scenario. In Georgia, 16-year-old and 17-year-old marriage license applicants may receive a license *if* the parents of both appear, present identification, and consent in writing to the marriage. Underage marriage applicants also may receive a marriage license *without* their parents' consent upon presenting proof of pregnancy, signed by a licensed physician, or proof that the bride and groom are the parents of a child born out of wedlock.

Will Newlyweds' Age Spoil Honeymoon?

A possible problem exists for two soon-to-be newlyweds named Bobby and Stella. Bobby and Stella are both 16 years old, and both have their parents' permission to marry. Everyone wants to make sure all the legal requirements are fulfilled, but Bobby and Stella think they have hit a snag. They want to go camping on their

CASE 5.1 *T. v. M., falsely called T.,* 100 N.J. Super. 530, 242 A.2d 670 (1968)

Facts: This action to annul a marriage on the ground of impotence was a case of novel impression in New Jersey and, perhaps, in this country. The wife, while still a virgin with an intact hymen, suffered a miscarriage during the marriage. The husband sought the annulment, charging his wife with being physically and incurably impotent. The parties were married in New Jersey on July 25, 1964. Efforts at sexual intercourse proved to be impossible because of the inability of the female organ to permit penetration to the slightest degree. On one occasion, the husband used force in his attempt to penetrate. This resulted in his ejaculation against the wife, causing pregnancy.

The husband urged his wife to see a doctor. At first, she refused to do so. She asked him to give her time, saying that she was nervous and that eventually everything would work out fine. Although they continued to try to solve the problem, the situation did not change, and the parties separated. At that time, neither of them were aware that the conception had taken place.

A few months later, the wife advised the husband that she was prepared to see a doctor because she thought she was pregnant. In November of 1965, they both went to see Doctor George Massell, an obstetrician and gynecologist, because the wife was spotting. The doctor attempted to examine her pelvically by manual examination. He testified that this proved to be impossible. Two days later the doctor learned that her bleeding had progressed, and he admitted her to the hospital. He again found it impossible to examine her physically, but her symptoms indicated early miscarriage. It was the doctor's opinion that there had been no penetration by the husband beyond the hymen, and that the wife was suffering from a firm, fixed, deep-seated psychological problem. When asked how a pregnancy could occur in a woman whose hymen was intact, he testified that this is *possible* and that it is not unknown in medical science. To use the doctor's term, it was a *splash pregnancy.*

Issue: Whether a virgin wife, capable of procreation, can be legally declared to be impotent so as to warrant an annulment of the marriage.

Court's Reasoning: Impotence is a ground for nullity of marriage in New Jersey. The pertinent statute provides as follows: *The parties, or either of them, were at the time of marriage physically and incurably impotent, provided the party making the application shall have been ignorant of such impotency or incapability at the time of the marriage, and has not subsequently ratified the marriage.* Vaginismus, physical or psychological, is a recognized cause of incurable impotency in New Jersey, and the annulment of a marriage may be granted where one or both of the parties are, at the time of the marriage, physically or incurably impotent. When the impotency was known before the marriage but was not disclosed, the marriage may be annulled at the suit of the innocent party for the fraud inherent in the nondisclosure. The court was not able to find a reported opinion in this country where a dissolution of marriage was sought because of an impotent wife who was not able to copulate and yet was capable of procreation. The wife in this case had initially filed an appearance seeking to be heard as to certain property rights, which claims were withdrawn by her attorney at the final hearing. The husband's annulment was affirmed.

Holding: T., the husband, wins.

Case Discussion: Do you question the husband's claim that he was completely ignorant of his wife's impotency? Do you think the wife deserved a right to any marital property for having suffered a miscarriage?

honeymoon in another state, but they know that the state they want to travel to requires everyone to be 18 years old in order to be considered validly married. They do not want to travel together unless they will be considered husband and wife wherever they go.

Do Bobby and Stella really have a serious problem? If these two young people stay in school, they will eventually learn about a part of the United States Constitution that specifically discusses interstate relations. Article IV of the United States Constitution includes the *full faith and credit clause,* which is applied to questions of interstate relations. Section I of the full faith and credit clause states: *Full Faith and Credit shall be given each State to the public Acts, Records, and judicial Proceedings of every other State.* In other words, the full faith and credit clause was designed to provide assurances to all citizens that one state must respect the laws and judicial proceedings of another state. In Bobby and Stella's case, this means that if State *A* has allowed them to legally marry, then all the other states must respect State *A*'s decision and acknowledge their marriage as valid and legally binding. So it looks like Bobby and Stella can proceed with their honeymoon as planned.

Solemnization Ceremony

The **solemnization ceremony** is the occasion where a bride and groom verbally state their intention to be married and have their statements witnessed by a legally sanctioned individual who pronounces the bride and groom married. All 50 states require a solemnization ceremony and provide a listing of which public officials and clergy may conduct marriage ceremonies.

For example, New York's state guidelines provide a lengthy list of public officials and clergy who may conduct marriages ceremonies in that state. The list includes: the mayor of a city or village; the city clerk or one of the deputy city clerks of a city of more than one million inhabitants; and a marriage officer appointed by the town or village board or the city common council. Also able to conduct marriage ceremonies are justices or judges of the following courts: the United States Court of Appeals for the Second Circuit, the United States district courts for the Northern, Southern, Eastern, and Western Districts of New York, the New York Court of Appeals, the Appellate Division of the New York Supreme Court, the New York Supreme Court, the Court of Claims, the Family Court, a Surrogates Court, the Civil and Criminal courts of New York City (including housing judges of the Civil Court), and other courts of record. In addition, the following people are authorized to conduct such ceremonies: a village, town, or county justice; a member of the clergy or a minister who has been officially ordained and granted authority to perform marriage ceremonies from a governing church body in accordance with the rules and regulations of the church body; a member of the clergy or a minister who is not authorized by a governing church body but who has been chosen by a spiritual group to preside over their spiritual affairs; and other officiates as specified by § 11 of New York's Domestic Relations Law.

This long list is typical of that found in most states' solemnization ceremony statutes. Given this many choices, engaged citizens of New York and the other 49 states certainly should not have any problem finding a designated official to marry them.

COVENANT MARRIAGE: THIS ONE'S FOR KEEPS?

The **covenant marriage** concept is best defined by the Louisiana Legislature, which created and enacted the first such legislation in the United States in 1997.[14] Louisiana's statute states:

> *A covenant marriage is a marriage entered into by one male and one female who understand and agree that the marriage between them is a lifelong relationship. Parties to a covenant marriage have received*

counseling, emphasizing the nature and purpose of marriage and the responsibilities thereto. Only when there has been a complete and total breach of the marital covenant commitment may the non-breaching party seek a declaration that the marriage is no longer recognized.

What do you think of this statute? If your initial response is to wonder what is new here, that is exactly the point: There really is not anything new about covenant marriage in the sense that it sounds like a throwback to the old-fashioned concept that marriage should be a lifelong commitment. However, the difference appears in the situation of a divorce. A covenant marriage is not for the fainthearted, because even though a couple who enters a covenant marriage in Louisiana can still divorce, the requirements for divorce are stricter than those for a conventionally married couple. These requirements include: adultery; a sentence of death or imprisonment for a felony; abandonment of the marital home for a year; physical or sexual abuse; or living separate and apart continuously without reconciliation for two years. In contrast, a couple who has entered into a conventional marriage in Louisiana can divorce after living apart for only six months.

Residents of Louisiana may support the covenant marriage concept, but less than 10 percent of the couples marrying in Louisiana have chosen this option. Nevertheless, Arizona has passed similar covenant marriage legislation, and more states are considering implementing such legislation.

COMMON LAW MARRIAGE

A **common law marriage** is a legally binding marriage that typically occurs without a license or ceremony under the laws of many states when a man and woman hold themselves out as married or live together as if married. A popular misconception about this type of marriage is that a couple must live together for seven years before a common law marriage can occur.

Historically, a common law marriage could be created in most of the states, but the majority has abolished this methodology. A minority of 12 states and the District of Columbia still have this legal relic. However, a couple who becomes legally bound in a common law marriage in a state that recognizes such a marriage *will* have that marriage recognized by the other states. As stated earlier, a couple who is considered legally married in one state will be considered legally married in the other states.

Generally, the required elements of a common law marriage consist of the following: (1) A man and woman must mutually intend to be husband and wife; (2) the man and woman must let it be commonly known they are husband and wife; and (3) in some states, the man and woman must live together. Review Exhibit 5.3 to see if your state is a common law marriage state.

PUTATIVE MARRIAGE

Based on what you have learned so far, it may seem that a marriage that is void would leave the two spouses not married and, therefore, without any of the legal rights earned through marriage, but this is not always so. What about the spouse who enters a marriage honestly, but finds out later that the marriage is not legal? For example, suppose Sally married Ed in good faith, and then learned a few years later that Ed had never legally divorced his first wife. Sally and Ed may have spent the years they were *supposedly married* buying a family home and having children. It certainly would be a hardship on Sally and the couple's children to suddenly learn that the marriage was void. Sally would be ineligible for any of the benefits normally associated with marriage; for example, she would not have the inheritance rights a wife normally possesses. In the event of Ed's death, she would not be eligible to receive Social Security survivor benefits, nor would she inherit property owned solely by Ed.

EXHIBIT 5.3 Is There Common Law Marriage in Your State?

Common Law Marriage by State

State	Valid in State	State	Valid in State	State	Valid in State
Alabama	Yes	Kentucky	No	North Dakota	No
Alaska	No	Louisiana	No	Ohio	No
Arizona	No	Maine	No	Oklahoma	Yes
Arkansas	No	Maryland	No	Oregon	No
California	No	Massachusetts	No	Pennsylvania	Yes
Colorado	Yes	Michigan	No	Rhode Island	Yes
Connecticut	No	Minnesota	No	South Carolina	Yes
Delaware	No	Mississippi	No	South Dakota	No
District of Columbia	Yes	Missouri	No	Tennessee	No
Florida	No	Montana	Yes	Texas	Yes
Georgia	No	Nebraska	No	Utah	Yes
Hawaii	No	Nevada	No	Vermont	No
Idaho	No	New Hampshire	Yes	Virginia	No
Illinois	No	New Jersey	No	Washington	No
Indiana	No	New Mexico	No	West Virginia	No
Iowa	Yes	New York	No	Wisconsin	No
Kansas	Yes	North Carolina	No	Wyoming	No

The apparent unfairness to men or women in Sally's position has motivated the courts and legislatures in the majority of states to make a special exception when dealing with spouses who entered a void marriage in good faith, believing they were entering a legally valid marriage. Such an exception effectively turns an invalid marriage into a valid one only for purposes of property settlements and spousal support. When a court of competent jurisdiction declares that an invalid marriage was entered into by either one or both spouses in good faith, the invalid marriage becomes what is legally known as a **putative marriage.**

California's statutory definition of a putative marriage is fairly typical.[15] California's legislature defines a putative marriage as *a marriage which has been solemnized in due form and celebrated in good faith by both parties, but which by reason of some legal infirmity is either void or voidable.* The essential element of such a marriage is a belief that it is valid. A putative marriage may arise from either a common law marriage or a ceremonial marriage that was entered into honestly. The majority of courts have found that a putative marriage ends as soon as both spouses are aware of the impediment to the validity of their marriage.

In our example, obviously Sally and Ed cannot be considered to be legally married because Ed is already married to another woman. Even though Sally's position is tenuous because of Ed's first marriage, she may still be entitled to some of the rights that are conferred upon legal spouses. However, until Ed and his first wife are legally divorced, Sally's rights will be superceded by the rights of Ed's first wife. If Sally and Ed were to break up, Sally *would* be entitled to go to court and ask the court to apportion any property and provide spousal and child support in the fairest way possible under the circumstances. If circumstances warranted, Ed could face criminal charges for bigamy.

Is a Putative Marriage Punishing?

The case of *Garduno v. Garduno* (see Case 5.2) shows the difficulties a court may have in determining whether a couple's marriage is a putative marriage or a legally valid marriage, based on the state's common law marriage statute.

CASE 5.2 *Garduno v. Garduno,* 760 S.W.2d 735 (1988)

Facts: Roberto Garduno (appellant) appealed the trial court's finding that he and Margarita Garduno (appellee) had entered both putative and common law marriages to each other between 1980 and 1986. The trial court's finding resulted in an award to the appellee of the personal property and cash in her possession, a 1986 Volkswagen, a 25 percent interest in the husband's certificates of deposit, stock, a vacation time-share plan, and the couple's condominium unit. The 25 per-cent share was based on the appellant's half-interest in the property. The appellant's former wife owned the other half.

In Texas, the elements of a common law marriage are: (1) a present agreement to be husband and wife; (2) living together as husband and wife; and (3) holding each other out to the public as such. A putative mar-riage is one that was entered into in good faith by at least one of the parties, but which is invalid by reason of an existing impediment on the part of one or both parties. However, since there is no legally recognized marriage, property acquired during a putative marriage is not community property, but *jointly owned sep-arate property.* The trial court found the couple cohabitated and held themselves out to the public as a mar-ried couple from the middle of 1980 to May of 1986.

Issue: Whether the parties entered into a good faith putative marriage and subsequent common law marriage.

Court's Reasoning: The good faith of the putative spouse is generally a fact question. However, when the putative spouse is aware that a former marriage existed at one time, the question becomes one of the rea-sonableness of that party's belief that the former marriage has been dissolved. In this case, the wife saw what she believed to be a valid Mexican divorce decree in 1984. However, shortly thereafter she learned from the appellant's lawyer that the divorce decree was set aside by the Mexican courts. She testified that she did not believe this to be true. When reliable evidence of an impediment to marriage comes to a party, that party cannot simply declare disbelief of this information and continue as if it were untrue. The party has a duty to investigate the situation further. In the present case, the appellee was no longer acting in good faith after learning that the Mexican divorce had been set aside. At this point, any putative marriage that may have arisen came to an end.

The next question is whether there was sufficient evidence to show that after the appellant's *valid* divorce from his first wife in 1986, the parties entered a valid common law marriage. We find that there was sufficient evidence to show a common law agreement after the parties continued to cohabitate and hold themselves out as married after the appellant's 1986 divorce.

Holding: We reverse and render that portion of the trial court's judgment finding a putative marriage before January 3, 1986, and that portion awarding a 25% interest in the 1,500 shares of stock to appellee. The remainder of the judgment is affirmed.

Case Discussion: You can see from the appellate court's decision that the first Mrs. Garduno received a larger share of the pie than the second Mrs. Garduno. Can you make an argument that only licensed mar-riages should be allowed because common law marriage and putative marriage concepts are too compli-cated to apply fairly in each case? Can you make an argument that the common law marriage and putative marriage concepts should continue because they allow legal protections for the parties involved?

ANNULMENT

An **annulment** is the official recognition by a court of law that a marriage never legally existed. The term *void ab initio* can be used to describe a marriage that should be annulled. Translated from the Latin, *void ab initio* literally means *void entirely and completely since the start.* Failing to request an annulment of a void marriage can lead to legal problems down the road. A validly married spouse can be held financially responsible for the debts of the other spouse. For example, if Spouse *A* buys goods on credit and fails to pay for the goods, Spouse *B* can be held responsible for the goods unless Spouse *B* can point to the invalidity of the marriage as a reason for not being responsible for the creditor's bill. A court's judgment of annulment will help convince the creditor of the truth.

In contrast to an annulment, a **divorce** or **dissolution of marriage** is the official recognition by a court of law that a valid marriage did exist, but that it will now legally cease to exist. All the states make some exceptions to a marriage being considered automatically void—even if the essential elements of marriage have not been met. In some instances, a marriage may be considered legally valid, but *voidable,* until a court with competent jurisdiction over the parties declares that the marriage is not valid and grants an annulment. So, while a court may *eventually* determine that a marriage is void, the marriage is called a *voidable* marriage until that judicial determination is made.

Religious Annulment

A *legal* annulment should never be confused with a *religious* annulment. A religious annulment has no legal standing and is granted by an ecclesiastical court. Ecclesiastical courts are defined as religious courts. A religious annulment provides that the couple is considered not to have been validly married according to the rules of whatever religious group is granting the annulment. It cannot be assumed that because an annulment is granted by a court of law, the annulment will be valid according to an ecclesiastical court, and vice versa. For example, the Catholic Church may grant the Church's version of a religious annulment, called a *declaration of nullification.* The Catholic Church's declaration of nullity says that what looked like a marriage never was one. A declaration of nullity is granted when it can be shown that some defect made a particular marriage invalid from the beginning despite outward appearance, the good faith of the partners, or the birth of children. It should be underscored that a declaration of nullity does *not* affect the legitimacy of the children of such a marriage. Plus, according to the law of all 50 states, a couple seeking a religious annulment—whatever their religious affiliation—would still need to seek a legal divorce to deal with custody and financial issues, and before legally marrying again.

Religious Divorce

The Jewish and Muslim faiths also make provisions for spouses who wish to end their marriages. Unlike the Catholic faith, which requires proof of a marriage's invalidity from the beginning, the religious courts of the Jewish and Muslim faiths provide that spouses in valid marriages may be granted a *religious divorce.* The Jewish faith's special court that grants a religious divorce is called a *Beth Din.* The husband submits a document called a *get,* and fault by either party does not have to be shown. Receiving the get insures the spouses can be remarried by a rabbi. The Muslim faith's rules for being divorced are interpreted differently, depending on the country. Typically, a husband will perform a *Talak* three times. Talak means *I divorce you.* Wives do not have the option of performing a Talak and must go to court to request a divorce. Again, all 50 states require that spouses seek a legal divorce in addition to any religious divorce or annulment.

Taking the Husband's Name: What's in a Name?

Traditionally, there was never any question that a new wife would take the family name of her husband. In the past, a woman effectively became the property of her husband upon marriage, and she had little choice but to become known as Mrs. Whomever. The case of *In re Change of Name of Polly Christine (Brewer) Miller* (see Case 5.3) discussed the question of name choice. The lower court that originally heard the case in 1978 based its decision on the archaic notion that a woman loses her power of choice upon marrying.

CASE 5.3 *In re Change of Name of Polly Christine (Brewer) Miller*, 218 Va. 939, 243 S.E.2d 464 (1978)

Facts: Petitioner, Polly Christine Miller, formerly Brewer, petitioned the court below to change back to her maiden name. The petition was denied, and petitioner contends that the trial court abused its discretion in denying her application. Mrs. Miller claims that the Code states: *Any person desiring to change his own name, or that of his child or ward, may apply therefore to the circuit court of the county or city in which the person whose name is to be changed resides.*

Petitioner alleged that the change of name was not sought for any dishonest, illegal, or fraudulent purpose. She stated that she desired to resume her maiden name of Brewer because that is the surname by which she is commonly known. She has also embarked on a career in accounting and is known among her colleagues and clients by her maiden name. A number of creditors extended credit to the petitioner and her husband in the surname of Miller, but Polly stated that she intended to notify all her creditors of the change of name. The trial court, in a memorandum opinion, gave several reasons for denying the petitioner's application. First, even though the petitioner announced her intention to notify her creditors of the change of name, the creditors would not have adequate protection if she inadvertently failed to notify them and thereafter changed her residence. Secondly, there is no compelling need for a change of name. Thirdly, the proposed name change contravenes society's substantial interest in the easy identification of married persons. Fourth, the petitioner's as-yet-unborn children would be substantially burdened in explaining to their peers why they did not have their mother's name and why their mother and father had different names. Fifth, the petitioner could satisfy her desire for a separate professional career under the provisions of the Code relating to the transaction of business under an assumed name.

Issue: Whether the lower court abused its discretion in refusing to grant the petitioner's name change request.

Court's Reasoning: Under the common law, a person may adopt any name he wishes provided it is not done for a fraudulent purpose or does not infringe upon the rights of others. Although a married woman customarily assumes her husband's surname, there is no statute requiring her to do so. The trial court abused its discretion in denying the applicant's petition to resume her maiden name.

Holding: Judgment of the trial court is reversed, and the case is remanded for entry of an order granting the application for the change of name.

Case Discussion: If you did not know this case was decided in 1978, would you have thought the decision was from the nineteenth century?

ALIENATION OF AFFECTION AND CRIMINAL CONVERSATION

As far back as twelfth-century England, a master could recover damages for physical injury to a servant if loss of services resulted. Since a wife was viewed as a servant, a husband could also sue for the loss of the wife's services when she was injured. Later, to meet the labor crisis caused by the Black Death epidemic in fourteenth-century England, a remedy was created for any employer who had a servant enticed away from service.[16] The use of the **enticement action** for lost servants was followed by husbands using the action against a defendant who had allegedly enticed a wife away from her husband. Enticement actions had little to do with the emotional state of a marriage, but sought to protect a husband's right to his wife's consortium. **Consortium** was traditionally defined as a wife's services, companionship, and sexual relations, but now includes a husband's services, companionship, and sexual relations as well.

The right of a husband to sue for loss of his wife's affection was first discussed in the 1745 English case of *Winsmore v. Greenbak*. Later, American cases followed the line of reasoning begun in *Winsmore,* and the enticement tort evolved into he *alienation of affection* action in mid-nineteenth-century America. **Alienation of affection** is the taking away of the love, companionship, or help of a person's husband or wife. The tort of alienation was first recognized in New York in 1866 in *Heermance v. James,* 47 Barb. 120 (N.Y. App. Civ. 1866) and was eventually adopted in all states except Louisiana.

Generally, to establish a cause of action in an alienation of affection case, there were three elements needed: (1) a valid marriage; (2) loss of affection or consortium; and (3) wrongful and malicious conduct of the defendant who caused the loss of affection. Adultery was *not* required to support a cause of action for alienation of affection. The alienation of affection action has been used by wronged spouses not only against alleged lovers of their spouses but also against interfering in-laws and friends!

Alternatively, the tort action of *criminal conversation* mainly required that adultery had occurred. **Criminal conversation** is the causing of a married man or woman to commit adultery. Interestingly, the term *conversation* probably derives from the former life of this type of action as an ecclesiastical crime. The term *conversation* was used euphemistically for sexual intercourse. The true essence of the criminal conversation cause of action is the husband's exclusive right to sexual relations with the wife. This was based on both a need to maintain pure bloodlines for inheritance purposes and the principles of morality. By the way, the idea of allowing a husband to seek retribution from his wife's lover dates back from as early as the ancient Teutonic tribes. Most tribes required the wife's lover to pay compensation to the husband. Some tribes also authorized the husband to kill the lover, the wife, or both.[17]

Remember that the nineteenth-century husband was, according to prevailing law, in a legally superior position to his wife. A husband's own adultery, or the post-event condoning of his wife's behavior, did not limit his right to sue for criminal conversation. The only available defense to a criminal conversation claim was the husband's consent or connivance in the affair. The fact that the wife had consented to the adultery would not be a defense for her lover, and the husband could still sue for his loss of marital rights.

During the last half of the nineteenth-century, all the states enacted statutes generally known as the **Married Women's Property Acts,** which removed the majority of a wife's legal disabilities. Consequently, married women were allowed to acquire, own, and transfer property; to make contracts; to be employed and keep their earnings; and to sue and be sued. Historically, the alienation of affection and criminal conversation actions were viewed not only as tools to pay damages to a spouse for a personal loss, but also as devices to promote family harmony. American courts often found the two actions claimed together. However, in 1890, the Massachusetts legislature was the first to reject the alleged benefits of the alienation of affection action. The action was found to have a potential for abuse and lacked a deterrent effect. The alienation of affection cause of action has now been abolished by statute in 35 states, by common law in 4 states, and was never recognized in one state. The criminal conversation cause of action has been similarly viewed as a historic remnant of the past. It has been abolished by statute in 29 states and by common law in 4 states.

How the majority of states view the tort of criminal conversation was stated well in *Hunt v. Hunt,* 309 N.W.2d 821 (S.D. 1981). The *Hunt* court did not believe criminal conversation to be a viable legal remedy, but rather

> *an outmoded holdover from an era when wives were considered the chattel of their spouse rather than distinct legal entities. Wives are not property. Neither are husbands. The love and affection of a human being who is devoted to another human being is not susceptible to theft. There are simply too many intangibles which defy the concept that love is property.*

Case Led to Demise of Criminal Conversation Claim

Society traditionally supported the institution of marriage by frowning upon extramarital affairs. The courts and legislatures went a step further when they provided a legal remedy for the injured spouse by creating the tort of criminal conversation. Usually, this protection was available only to the husband. This was true in Pennsylvania. Such uneven paternalistic protection supported the chauvinistic view of women as the property of their husbands. Thus, a man who became sexually involved with a married woman was in effect damaging the property of another man. The national trend in the middle of the twentieth century was to allow the use of the criminal conversation cause of action by injured wives. The modern trend away from the courts taking a paternalistic role led to the tort of criminal conversation becoming part of our legal history in most states. The 1976 case of *Fagden v. Lenkner* (see Case 5.4) exemplifies the reasons for the demise of the criminal conversation cause of action.

LEGAL DUO: CIVIL RIGHTS AND NEGLIGENCE?

The 1971 case of *Gates v. Foley* (see Case 5.5) involved a legal duo: *civil rights law* and *tort law.* A tort is a private wrong, and when a person is unintentionally injured by another person, the result is often a *negligence* claim by the injured party. **Negligence** is defined as the failure to exercise a reasonable amount of care in a situation that causes harm to someone or something. This case added a civil rights twist. Civil rights are the rights of all citizens that are guaranteed by the Constitution and other laws.

In *Gates v. Foley,* the plaintiff was the wife of a man who was severely injured in a car accident by the defendant. The plaintiff claimed that due to the defendant's negligence, she had suffered a loss of consortium with her husband. A problem arose for the plaintiff when the defendant argued at trial that only a husband could make a loss of consortium claim. The defendant claimed that the law, cloaked in centuries-old tradition, did not give equal status to both a husband and wife's claim of loss of consortium.

PRIVACY ISSUES WITHIN MARRIAGE

The case of *Griswold v. Connecticut* (see Case 5.6) exposed the state of Connecticut's statutory intrusion into its citizens' marriages and their private relationships. In this case, the statute in question involved the state's ban on any person's use of contraception that prevented anyone, including doctors, from counseling people about contraception. You may be surprised to learn that the case is relatively recent, having been decided by the United States Supreme Court in 1965.

CASE 5.4 *Fagden v. Lenkner,*
469 Pa. 272, 365 A.2d 147 (1976)

Facts: Appellee, James T. Fagden, brought an action against the appellant, George Lenkner, based upon the theory of criminal conversation. The complaint alleged that the appellee and one Bonnie Hoch Fagden were married in 1972, and that during the period of this marriage, the appellant, without the consent of the appellee, criminally conversed with Ms. Fagden. Pursuant to Rule 1037(c) of the Pennsylvania Rules of Civil Procedure, the appellee asked the trial court to enter judgment against the appellant on the issue of liability based upon the latter's written admission that he had engaged in sexual intercourse with the appellee's wife. The court did so.

Issue: Whether the cause of action based upon the theory of criminal conversation retains validity in light of modern legal and societal changes.

Court's Reasoning: The criminal conversation cause of action is made out upon the appellee's proof that while married to the appellee, his wife and the Appellant engaged in at least a single act of sexual intercourse without the consent of the appellee. There are but two possible complete defenses to the action: an outright denial by the appellant of having had any such relation with the appellee's spouse, and proof that the appellee consented to the adulterous relation. It is no defense to the action, however, that the appellee's spouse consented or that the wife was the aggressor or seducer. It was thought at common law that a wife was not competent to give her consent so as to defeat her husband's interest. It has been written that *a man who has sexual relations with a woman, not his wife, assumes the risk that she is married. Even her misrepresentation that she is single affords the offender no defense to liability for criminal conversation.*

Those actions for interference with domestic relations that carry an accusation of sexual misbehavior— that is to say, criminal conversation, seduction, and to some extent alienation of affection actions—have been peculiarly susceptible to abuse. Together with the action for breach-of-promise to marry, they have afforded a notoriously fertile field for blackmail and extortion by means of manufactured suits in which the threat of publicity has been used to force settlements.

Under our new Crimes Code, the Pennsylvania legislature has seen fit to abolish the crime of adultery, serving to decriminalize the very behavior upon which an action in criminal conversation rests. The total abolition of this cause of action is well within the bounds of our judicial powers.

Holding: The appellant, Lenkner, wins.

Dissenting Opinion: The majority totally abolishes the cause of action for criminal conversation without any statutory or other authority for doing so, other than its own inclinations that the tort is an *anachronism.* Justice Roberts stated: *I cannot agree that the marital relationship which has been protected in this commonwealth for more than two centuries is no longer deserving of the protection of our law.*

Case Discussion: Justice Roberts made an excellent point. The American courts had been protecting the nation's marital relationships for two centuries. Should the courts have ended that protection, as the court did in the *Fagden* case? Do you think that now, more than ever, society needs to protect the institution of marriage, or do you think that the courts should refuse the thankless role of protector of our nation's morals?

CASE 5.5 *Gates v. Foley,* 247 So. 2d 40 (1971)

Facts: The plaintiff, Hilda I. Gates, claimed that the defendant negligently operated his auto-mobile, causing a collision with an automobile operated by her husband. It was further alleged that, as a result of the accident, the plaintiff's husband was rendered totally disabled, and the plaintiff claimed damages for the loss of consortium and other services from her husband.

A motion to dismiss the complaint was granted on the ground that it failed to state a cause of action. The plaintiff appealed from the final judgment of dismissal, and the District Court of Appeals affirmed the judgment. This case is here on petition for writ of *certiorari* supported by a certificate of the District Court of Appeals, Fourth District, that the decision reported is one that involves a question of *great public interest.*

Issue: Whether the wife has a valid cause of action against the defendant for loss of consortium due to her husband's injuries.

Court's Reasoning: At common law, a wife could not maintain such an action. In 1950, the United States District Court of Appeals for the District of Columbia updated the common law of the District of Columbia by acknowledging a cause of action in the wife for loss of consortium. However, this court rejected the District of Columbia's reasoning. A flood of authorities in other jurisdictions have overturned the common law rule and, on various grounds, allowed the wife to recover for loss of consortium. We are being asked to follow the trend, which has been definitely in the direction of approving the wife's cause of action for harm to the marriage relation resulting from negligent injury to her husband.

Note that the suit is for *loss of consortium,* and not for loss of support or earnings that the husband might recover himself. We are only concerned with the loss of consortium, which is the companionship and fellowship of husband and wife and the right to each to the company, cooperation, and aid of the other in every conjugal relation. Consortium means much more than mere sexual relation and consists, also, of that affection, solace, comfort, companionship, conjugal life, fellowship, society, and assistance so necessary to a successful marriage.

The law is not static. It must keep pace with changes in our society, for the doctrine of *stare decisis* is not an iron mold that can never be changed.

The unity concept of marriage has, in large part, given way to the partner concept whereby a married woman stands as an equal to her husband in the eyes of the law. Medieval concepts that have no justifica-tion in our present society should be rejected. We therefore hold that deprivation to the wife of the hus-band's consortium constitutes a real injury to the marital relationship, and one which should be compensable at law if due to the negligence of another.

Holding: Wife has a valid loss of consortium claim.

Case Discussion: Can you believe that as late as 1971, the issue of whether the loss of a wife's con-sortium should be treated equally with the loss of a husband's consortium was a burning issue that was of "great public interest"? This case is a good example of the flexibility seen in the doctrine of *stare deci-sis.* Yes, the court must look to precedent for guidance, but as the court in this case stated, *precedent is not an iron mold which can never be changed.* The *Gates* decision effectively cracked the mold on the consortium issue.

CASE 5.6 *Griswold v. Connecticut,* 381 U.S. 479, 85 S. Ct. 1678 (1965)

Facts: This case involved the Planned Parenthood League of New Haven, Connecticut. The parties were Griswold, the director of Planned Parenthood, League of Connecticut, and Buxton, a licensed physician, professor at the Yale Medical School and director of Planned Parenthood, League of New York. The initial problem was that both Griswold and Buxton were found guilty under Connecticut law as accessories and fined for providing contraception and information regarding contraception. The statutes whose constitutionality was questioned in the appeal provided:

Any person who uses any drug, medicinal article or instrument for the purpose of preventing conception shall be fined not less than fifty dollars or imprisoned not less than sixty days nor more than one year or be both fined and imprisoned.

Additionally, the statutes included: *Any person who assists, abets, counsels, causes, hires, or commands another to commit any offense may be prosecuted and punished as if he were the principal offender.*

Issue: Whether Connecticut's law prohibiting anyone from promoting and disseminating information about birth control is unconstitutional.

Court's Reasoning: We do not sit as a superlegislature to determine the wisdom, need, and propriety of laws that touch economic problems, business affairs, or social conditions. This law, however, operates directly on an intimate relation of husband and wife and their physician's role in one aspect of that relation.

The Fourth and Fifth amendments were described in *Boyd v. United States,* 116 U.S. 616, as protection against all governmental invasions in the *sanctity of a man's home* and the *privacies of life.* We recently referred, in *Mapp v. Ohio,* 367 U.S. 643 (1961), to the Fourth Amendment as creating a *right of privacy, no less important than any other right carefully and particularly reserved to the people.*

The present case, then, concerns a relationship lying within the zone of privacy created by several fundamental constitutional guarantees. And it concerns a law which, in forbidding the use of contraceptives rather than regulating their manufacture or sale, seeks to achieve its goal by means that have a maximum destructive impact upon that relationship. Such a law cannot stand in light of the familiar principle, so often applied by this Court, that *a governmental purpose to control or prevent activities constitutionally subject to state regulation may not be achieved by means which sweep unnecessarily broadly and thereby invade the area of protected freedoms.*

We are dealing with a right of privacy older than the Bill of Rights—older than our political parties and older than our school system. Marriage is a coming together for better or worse, hopefully enduring, and intimate to the degree of being sacred.

Holding: Reversed.

Concurring Opinion: It should be said of the Court's holding today that it in no way interferes with a state's proper regulation of sexual promiscuity or misconduct. As my Brother Harlan stated so well in his dissenting opinion in *Poe v. Ullman,* 367 U.S. 497, at 553:

(continued)

CASE 5.6 *continued*

[A]dultery, homosexuality and the like are sexual intimacies which the State forbids ... but the intimacy of husband and wife is necessarily an essential and accepted feature of the institution of marriage, an institution which the State not only must allow, but which always and in every age it has fostered and protected. It is one thing when the State exerts its power either to forbid extramarital sexuality ... or to say who may marry, but it is quite another when, having acknowledged a marriage and the intimacies inherent in it, it undertakes to regulate by means of the criminal law the details of that intimacy.

Dissenting Opinion: Justice Black, with whom Justice Stewart joined, dissented. In order that there may be no room at all to doubt why I vote as I do, I feel constrained to add that the law is every bit as offensive to me as it is to my brethren of the majority and my Brothers Harlan, White, and Goldberg who, reciting reasons why it is offensive to them, hold it unconstitutional.

Had the doctor-defendant here, or even the nondoctor defendant, been convicted for doing nothing more than expressing opinions to persons coming to the clinic that certain contraceptive devices, medicines, or practices would do them good and would be desirable, or for telling people how devices could be used, I can think of no reasons at this time why their expressions of those views would not be protected by the First and Fourteenth amendments, which guarantee freedom of speech. But speech is one thing; conduct and physical activities are quite another. The two defendants here were active participants in an organization that gave physical examinations to women, advised them what kind of contraceptive devices or medicines would most likely be satisfactory for them, and then supplied the devices themselves, all for graduated fees, based on the family income. Thus, these defendants admittedly engaged with others in a planned course of conduct to help people violate the Connecticut law.

Case Discussion: Do you think the appellants' behavior was an appropriate way to deal with Connecticut's anticontraception statute? Can you think of another way to influence legislators to change a law, *without* getting arrested and appealing the case all the way to the United States Supreme Court? Perhaps the appellants could have organized a grassroots campaign to have the state legislature change the anticontraception statute. What do you think?

SOCIETAL TRENDS AFFECT MARRIAGE VOWS

The accepted standard throughout most of history was that once a woman married, society placed her rights secondary to her husband's. The marriage vow to *love, honor, and obey* spoken by the wife vested certain rights in her husband. While society placed responsibility for the wife's economic support upon her *protector* and husband, it also gave her husband control of any property the wife owned before or acquired during her marriage.

Through marriage, the husband's power was not only limited to his economic supremacy, but also reached to his physical control over his wife. Society's acceptance of that physical control led to the creation of the commonly used phrase "rule of thumb." Developed in medieval England and transplanted to the

American lexicon, *rule of thumb* was the Medieval English legal standard by which a man could be judged for physically controlling his wife: A husband was to use a piece of wood no wider than his thumb to beat his wife, or else he could face charges of unfair punishment.

A *New York Times* newspaper article published in 1925 was short but spoke volumes on a woman's place in Moultrie, Georgia, society circa 1925. The article was entitled, "Court Upholds Right to Spank a Wife." According to the article, Judge Ogden Persons ruled in Superior Court that Fred Bannister, a young farmer, indicted on a charge of assault and battery, was not guilty. Judge Persons ruled: *A man has a right, under certain circumstances, to place his wife across his lap and spank her.*

It is understandable, then, that such societal acceptance of a husband's physical control led to the courts' refusal to recognize that a rape could occur between a husband and wife. The wife's vow to *obey* her husband was seen as a lifetime acquiescence to all of her husband's wishes.

The majority of states codified society's acceptance of the husband's dominant position by creating a marital rape exemption in their rape statutes. Strangely, a woman's right to her separate property was recognized by the courts long before the same courts recognized that the crime of rape occurred when a husband forced a sexual act upon an unwilling spouse. As the twentieth century came to a close, all 50 states finally recognized that the crime of rape can occur between spouses.

Rape: Why a Marital Exemption?

Historically, under the criminal code, a married man ordinarily could not be convicted of forcibly raping or sodomizing his wife. This was the so-called marital exemption for rape. Although a marital exemption was not explicit in earlier rape statutes, an 1852 treatise stated that a man could not be guilty of raping his wife.[18] The assumption, even before the marital exemption was codified, that a man could not be guilty of raping his wife is traceable to a statement made by the seventeenth-century English jurist Lord Hale, who wrote, *The husband cannot be guilty of a rape committed by himself upon his lawful wife, for by their mutual matrimonial consent and contract the wife hath given up herself in this kind unto her husband, which she cannot retract.*[19] Although Hale never cited any authority for his statement, it was relied on by state legislatures that enacted rape statutes with the marital exemption and by courts that established a common law exemption for husbands.

The first American case to recognize the marital exemption was decided in 1857 by the Supreme Judicial Court of Massachusetts, which stated that it would *always be a defense to rape to show marriage to the victim.* Decisions to the same effect by other courts followed, usually with no rationale or authority cited other than Hale's view of a wife's implied consent. As stated earlier, however, this trend changed in the late twentieth century, and the *People v. Liberta* case (see Case 5.7) was a part of that change.

SUPREME COURT AIDS LOVING COUPLE

The case of *Loving v. Virginia* (see Case 5.8) is a good example of how the federal government can step in when a state's laws have not kept up with the vast changes in society. Virginia had *antimiscegenation laws* dating back to the time of slavery. **Antimiscegenation laws** are laws that prohibit interracial relations, including a ban on marriage. Prior to *Loving,* the state of Virginia had expanded its earlier laws barring interracial sexual relations to prohibit racial intermarriage as well.

CASE 5.7 *People v. Liberta,* 64 N.Y.2d 152, 474 N.E.2d 567, 485 N.Y.S.2d 207 (1984)

Facts: At the time the incident in this case took place, a married man could not ordinarily be prosecuted under the New York Penal Law for raping or sodomizing his wife. The defendant, Mario Liberta, though still married at the time of the incident, was treated as an unmarried man under the Penal Law because of a Family Court restraining order. On this appeal, he contended that because of the exemption for married men, the statutes for rape in the first degree and sodomy in the first degree violated the equal protection clause of the federal Constitution. The defendant also contended that the rape statute violated equal protection because only men, and not women, could be prosecuted under it.

The defendant called his wife, Denise Liberta, to ask if he could visit his son on March 24, 1981. Denise would not allow the defendant to come to her house, but she did agree to allow him to pick their son and her up and take them both back to his motel after being assured that a friend of his would be with them at all times. When they arrived at the motel, the friend left. As soon as only Mario, Denise, and their son were alone in the motel room, Mario attacked Denise, threatened to kill her, and forced her to perform a sexual act on him and engage in sexual intercourse with him. The son was in the room during the entire episode, and the defendant forced Denise to tell their son to watch what the defendant was doing to her.

The defendant allowed Denise and their son to leave shortly after the incident. Denise, after leaving her son with her parents, went to a hospital to be treated for scratches on her neck and bruises on her head and back, all inflicted by her husband. She also went to the police station, and on the next day, she swore out a felony complaint against the defendant. On July 15, 1981, the defendant was indicted for rape in the first degree and sodomy in the first degree.

For purposes of the rape and sodomy statutes, a husband and wife were considered to be *not married* if at the time of the sexual assault they were living apart pursuant to a valid and effective: (1) order issued by a court of competent jurisdiction, which by its terms or in its effect required such living apart; (2) decree or judgment of separation; or (3) written agreement of separation.

The defendant moved to dismiss the indictment, asserting that because he and Denise were still married at the time of the indictment, he came within the *marital exemption* to both rape and sodomy. The state opposed the motion, contending that the temporary order of protection required Mario and Denise to live apart, and that they in fact were living apart, and thus were *not married* for purposes of the statutes. The trial court granted the defendant's motion and dismissed the indictment, concluding that the temporary order of protection did not require Mario and Denise to live apart from each other, but instead required only that he remain away from her, and therefore the marital exemption applied.

On appeal, the Appellate Division reversed the trial court, reinstated the indictment, and remanded the case for trial.

The defendant was then convicted of rape in the first degree and sodomy in the first degree, and the conviction was affirmed by the Appellate Division. The defendant asserts on this appeal that the temporary order of protection is not the type of order that enables a court to treat him and Denise as not married, and that thus he is within the marital exemption.

Issue: Whether the appellant's conviction was improper under the marital rape exemption.

Court's Reasoning: We find that there is no rational basis for distinguishing between marital rape and non-marital rape. The various rationales that have been asserted in defense of the exemption are either based upon archaic notions about the consent and property rights incident to marriage or are simply unable to withstand even the slightest scrutiny. We therefore declare the marital exemption for rape in the New York statute to be unconstitutional. The other prerequisite for finding a husband and wife to be *not married* based on an order of protection is that they were in fact living apart at the time of the incident. This is a question of fact that was resolved against the defendant by the jury and will not be disturbed by this court.

Rape is not simply a sexual act to which one party does not consent. Rather, it is a degrading, violent act that violates the bodily integrity of the victim and frequently causes severe, long-lasting physical and psychic harm. To imply consent to such an act is irrational and absurd. Other than in the context of rape statutes, marriage has never been viewed as giving a husband the right to coerce intercourse on demand. A marriage license should not be viewed as a license for a husband to forcibly rape his wife with impunity. A married woman has the same right to control her own body as does an unmarried woman.

Accordingly, the defendant was properly found to have been statutorily *not married* to Denise at the time of the rape.

Holding: Appeal denied.

Case Discussion: The traditional justification for the marital exemption was the common law doctrine that a woman was the property of her husband and that the legal existence of the woman was *incorporated and consolidated into that of the husband.* Can you believe that as little as 20 years ago a woman's right to claim a rape had occurred would be stymied by such an archaic notion as a marital rape exemption? There are no longer any marital rape exemptions. When *Liberta* was decided, nine states still provided a complete exemption to rape as long as there was a valid marriage. Those states included Alabama, Arkansas, Kansas, Montana, South Dakota, Texas, Vermont, Washington, and West Virginia. In other states, statutes provided for a marital rape exemption, but with certain exceptions. Typically those exceptions were in cases where the spouses were living apart pursuant to either a court order or a separation agreement. These states included Alaska, Arizona, Colorado, Idaho, Indiana, Nevada, New Mexico, New York, North Carolina, North Dakota, Ohio, Oklahoma, Pennsylvania, Rhode Island, South Carolina, Tennessee, Utah, Wisconsin, and Wyoming. In Connecticut, Delaware, Hawaii, and Iowa, there was a marital exemption for some, but not all, degrees of forcible rape. During this same time, four other states—Georgia, Mississippi, Virginia, and Nebraska—and the District of Columbia still had a common law exemption.

SAME-SEX MARRIAGE AROUND THE WORLD

Courts throughout the United States continue to deal with the constitutional issue of same-sex marriage. Many countries around the world also have dealt with the question of same-sex marriage. Just after midnight on April 1, 2001, four couples shared a wedding ceremony uniting six men and two women in the world's first same-sex marriages. The four sets of new spouses tied the knot in The Netherlands, which became the first country to allow same-sex marriages. Belgium was the next to join The Netherlands by extending equal marriage rights to gays and lesbians. Nearer to the United States, the Canadian Supreme Court recently decided that same-sex couples should have rights that are identical to those given to heterosexual couples.

An alternative to marriage is the concept of a **registered partnership** created in Scandinavia. Sometimes called a *civil union* as well, these partnerships fall short of having full equal status with marriage, but they do provide some of the benefits and protections of civil marriage. The registered partnership concept has been recognized in Denmark, France, Greenland, Hungary, Iceland, Norway, Spain, and Sweden, beginning first in Denmark in 1989. The extent of the acceptance of the same-sex

CASE 5.8 *Loving v. Virginia*, 388 U.S. 1 (1967)

Facts: A black woman and a white man, both residents of Virginia, were married in the District of Columbia. When they returned to Virginia, they were arrested, convicted of violating the state's ban on interracial marriage, and had their one-year jail sentence suspended for 25 years on the condition that they would leave the state and not return to Virginia for 25 years.

Issue: Whether Virginia's antimiscegnation law barring racial intermarriage violates the equal protection clause of the Fourteenth Amendment.

Court's Reasoning: The state's argument is that the legitimate purpose of the antimiscegenation laws *to preserve the integrity of its citizens, and to prevent the corruption of blood, a mongrel breed of citizens,* and the *obliteration of racial pride.* This argument is obviously an endorsement of the doctrine of white supremacy. The state does not contend that its powers to regulate marriage are unlimited, but argues that the equal protection clause simply requires that the state's criminal laws apply equally to all races, in the sense that members of each race are punished to the same degree. The clear and central purpose of the Fourteenth Amendment was to eliminate *all* official state sources of invidious racial discrimination in the states. The fact that Virginia prohibits only interracial marriages involving white persons demonstrates that the racial classifications must stand on their own as measures designed to maintain white supremacy. There can be no doubt that restricting the freedom to marry solely because of racial classifications violates the central meaning of the equal protection clause.

Holding: Reversed.

Case Discussion: The Fourteenth Amendment is referred to by the Supreme Court in explaining why Virginia's antimiscegenation statute was declared unconstitutional. The Fourteenth Amendment was added to the Constitution to ensure that *any* civil rights given to citizens in the federal Constitution could not be taken away by the individual states. Can you think of other examples of state laws that have been struck down by the United States Supreme Court as violating the Fourteenth Amendment?

partnership was evident when Norway's conservative Finance Minister, Per-Kristian Foss, announced he was marrying his longtime male companion in January 2002. The wedding took place at the Norwegian Embassy in Sweden.

In Germany, the federal government has passed a law allowing gay and lesbian couples to exchange vows at a local government office. Couples who exchange such vows would need to go to court for a divorce. The same-sex couples in Germany receive some of the benefits that are automatically given to heterosexual couples, such as inheritance rights and health insurance coverage. However, they have not been granted the right to adopt children, and they do not receive the same tax benefits as heterosexual couples.

Same-Sex Marriage in the United States

This section explores the status of same-sex marriage in the United States at the start of the new millennium. A well-known same-sex couple, musician Melissa Etheridge and Julie Cypher, willingly shared their story and their wish to have children together in many magazine articles in the late 1990s.[20]

In 1993, rock star Melissa Etheridge announced to the world that she was a lesbian, and she followed that announcement in 1996 with the news that she and her longtime partner, Julie Cypher, were going to have a baby. Cypher had been artificially inseminated with semen contributed by musician David Crosby (of Crosby, Stills, Nash, and Young musical fame). A sibling again fathered by Crosby later joined the first child. Domestic life for Etheridge and Cypher had all the traditional trimmings of the American family. The couple had their kids and a home. Julie was even a stay-at-home mom.

If Etheridge and Cypher had wanted to marry, they could not have done so legally in the United States. By the way, Etheridge and Cypher have since split up, following the birth of the couple's second child.

Before exploring the status of same-sex marriage in the United States, a question should be asked: Is the attainment of a same-sex legal marriage a valid goal when over 50 percent of all American marriages end in divorce? Consider your views on this question as you read the following text.

A valid marriage automatically confers legal recognition upon the relationship of the husband and wife. This legal recognition is accompanied by a long list of rights and duties that it confers upon the spouses. Some of those rights and duties include the following: the ability to make medical or other decisions for each other in times of crisis or incapacity, the ability to share parental rights and responsibilities for children, the ability to obtain joint insurance to transfer property without being taxed and to file joint returns, the ability to seek tort damages if the other is seriously injured or killed, and the ability to inherit without a will. Two other benefits provided to married heterosexual couples under the federal law include benefits a spouse can receive from the Social Security Administration and the Veterans Administration after the death of a wage earner or veteran. There are many more examples of benefits that spouses enjoy. In fact, the United States General Accounting Office conducted an audit that found 1,049 different ways the law favors married partners.[21]

Some states, cities, and private companies have begun to offer limited recognition of the same-sex partnership. This recognition comes in the form of benefits, such as health insurance and family leave traditionally offered to married couples. For example, the Western branch of the Salvation Army, which covers 13 states, recently announced that it would extend health benefits to same-sex partners of employees. California has been joined by a growing number of municipalities that now have domestic partner registries. Review the list of municipalities with such registries in Exhibit 5.4. California and Hawaii are currently the only states that have established domestic partner registries at the state level.

The **California Couples Registry** provides the following rights to same-sex couples. As domestic partners, these couples have the right to:

- ❏ visit each other in the hospital, as marital spouses can
- ❏ make medical decisions for each other if either is incapacitated
- ❏ use sick leave to care for one's domestic partner or partner's children, and be exempt from state income tax on health benefits one's employer provides for one's partner
- ❏ collect unemployment insurance if one has to give up one's job to relocate with one's domestic partner, as marital spouses can
- ❏ file for disability benefits on behalf of one's incapacitated partner
- ❏ receive notice of conservatorship proceedings about one's domestic partner, participate in the proceedings, and have preference in being designated as conservator for one's partner
- ❏ sue for the wrongful death of one's partner, or for emotional distress for witnessing a serious injury inflicted upon one's partner
- ❏ use a newly designed statutory will form, which has a box to indicate intent to leave property to one's partner

EXHIBIT 5.4 Municipalities with Domestic Partner Registration (Courtesy of the State of California)

States and Municipalities with Domestic Partner Registries

Employer Name	Year Registry Enacted	Employer Name	Year Registry Enacted	Employer Name	Year Registry Enacted
California		Key West, City of	1998	**New York**	
Berkeley, City of	1991	**Georgia**		Albany, City of	1996
Cathedral, City of	1997	Atlanta, City of	1993	East Hampton, Town of	2002
Davis, City of	1994	**Hawaii**		Ithaca, City of	1990
Laguna Beach, City of	1990	State of Hawaii	1997	New York, City of	1993
Long Beach, City of	1997	**Illinois**		Rochester, City of	1993
Lost Angeles, County of	1999	Oak Park, Village of	1997	Southampton, City of	2003
Marin, County of	1993	**Iowa**		Westchester, City of	2002
Oakland, City of	1996	Iowa City, City of	1994	**North Carolina**	
Palm Springs, City of	2000	**Louisiana**		Carrboro, City of	1994
Palo Alto, City of	1995	New Orleans, City of	1993	Chapel Hill, City of	1995
Petaluma, City of	1999	**Maine**		**Oregon**	
Sacramento, City of	1992	Portland, City of	2001	Ashland, City of	1999
San Francisco, City of	1990	**Massachusetts**		Eugene, City of	2002
Santa Barbara, City of	1997	Boston, City of	1993	Multnomah, County of	2000
Santa Barbara, County of	1999	Brewster, City of	1995	**Pennsylvania**	
Santa Monica, City of	1995	Brookline, City of	1993	Philadelphia, City of	1998
State of California	1999	Cambridge, City of	1992	**Texas**	
West Hollywood, City of	1985	Nantucket, City of	1996	Travis, County of	1993
Colorado		Provincetown, City of	1993	**Washington**	
Boulder, City of	1996	**Michigan**		Lacey, City of	2000
Denver, City of	2000	Ann Arbor, City of	1991	Olympia, City of	2000
Connecticut		**Minnesota**		Seattle, City of	1994
Hartford, City of	1993	Minneapolis, City of	1991	Tumwater, City of	1999
District of Columbia		**Missouri**		**Wisconsin**	
Washington, City of	1992	Jackson, County of	2003	Madison, City of	1990
Florida		Kansas City, City of	2003	Milwaukee, City of	1999
Broward, County of	1999	St. Louis, City of	1997		

❐ obtain health insurance benefits if one's partner is a public employee, with benefits continuing after the partner's death

❐ use the step-parent adoption procedure to adopt each other's children

Such registration still does not provide same-sex couples with inheritance rights or community property rights, nor does it provide them with access to family courts if the relationship breaks up. However, the fight for equal protections for same-sex couples continues across the country. As noted earlier, the Massachusetts Supreme Court decided in late 2003 that same-sex couples have a constitutional right to marry. The Massachusetts Legislature will have to decide next how to deal with that decision. A registered partner should always notify the registry when a relationship ends. Review California's domestic partner registry's Notice of Termination of Domestic Partnership in Exhibit 5.5.

EXHIBIT 5.5 Notice of Termination of Domestic Partnership (Courtesy of the State of California)

State of California
Kevin Shelley
Secretary of State

FILE NO: _____

(Office Use Only)

NOTICE OF TERMINATION OF DOMESTIC PARTNERSHIP
(Family Code Section 299)

Instructions:

1. Complete and send by <u>CERTIFIED</u> mail to:
    Secretary of State
    P.O. Box 942877
    Sacramento, CA 94277-0001
    (916) 653-4984

2. There is no fee for filing this Notice of Termination

I, the undersigned, do declare that:

Former Partner:_____ and I are no longer Domestic Partners.
   (Last)   (First)   (Middle)

Secretary of State File Number: _____.

If termination is caused by death or marriage of the domestic partner please indicate the date of the death or the marriage: _____.
                  (month/day/year)

This date shall be the actual termination date for the Domestic Partnership as provided in Family Code Section 299.

_____   _____   _____   _____
Signature   (Last)   (First)   (Middle)

_____   _____   _____   _____
Mailing Address   City   State   Zip Code

NOTARIZATION IS REQUIRED
State of California
County of _____

On _____, before me,_____, personally appeared

_____

personally known to me (or proved to me on the basis of satisfactory evidence) to be the person whose name is subscribed to the within instrument and acknowledged to me that he/she executed the same in his/her authorized capacity, and that by his/her signature on the instrument the person executed the instrument.

_____   [PLACE NOTARY SEAL HERE]
Signature of Notary Public

SEC/STATE LP/SF DP-2 (Dec 1999)

History of Same-Sex Marriage Movement

Advocacy for same-sex marriage began in the 1970s with the emergence of the gay rights liberation movement. Same-sex couples seeking to marry brought losing legal challenges in Minnesota, Kentucky, and Washington state. The legal argument supporting the challenges pointed to the United States Supreme Court's reasoning in the 1967 case of *Loving v. Virginia.* Recall that in *Loving* the Court struck down race-based restrictions on marriage. The same-sex marriage advocates argued that the same reasoning should be applied to remove the restrictions on same-sex marriage. In 1993, a case in Hawaii, *Baehr v. Lewin* (see Case 5.9) brought the issue to national attention. After the trial court dismissed the case with little explanation, the Hawaiian Supreme Court gave the proposition serious review.

The Defense of Marriage Act

While a Hawaiian trial court was hearing new evidence in *Baehr,* there were rumblings in Washington, D.C. Members of Congress presented the Defense of Marriage Act at the federal level. The **Defense of Marriage Act (DOMA)** was designed to allow individual states to decide separately whether the full faith and credit and the equal protection clauses of the United States Constitution allow same-sex marriages. Such a decision by the states would place them in a better position to deny recognition to same-sex marriages if Hawaii allowed them. The Defense of Marriage Act also included approval for the federal government to deny recognition of same-sex marriages for the purpose of applying the more than one thousand benefits and protections usually provided to married couples. The act quickly passed in both the Senate and House of Representatives, and President Clinton signed DOMA into law in 1998.

While the outcome of the *Baehr* case was pending, the Hawaiian state legislature created a law permitting any two adults who are barred from marrying each other to register as **reciprocal beneficiaries.** The benefits of being reciprocal beneficiaries fall short of the benefits incurred through marriage; however, the reciprocal beneficiaries legislation expanded benefits to same-sex couples, blood relatives, and housemates.

The Hawaiian voters responded to the possibility of Hawaii being the first state to legalize same-sex marriage by passing a referendum to add a constitutional amendment to the Hawaiian state constitution banning same-sex marriage. The amendment effectively nullified the decision of the trial court who had heard the *Baehr* case on remand, which had decided that the different-sex marriage requirement was not supported by a compelling state interest and that same-sex marriage should be permitted.

Civil Unions: Bumper Crop for Vermont

The question of whether the constitution of the state of Vermont granted lesbians and gay men the right to marry was answered by the Vermont Supreme Court shortly after *Baehr* in *Baker v. State,* 170 Vt. 194, 744 A.2d 864 (1999). The popular press quickly announced the court's decision, declaring that Vermont was the first state to give lesbians and gay men the right to marry, but that announcement missed the legal mark. Yes, the Vermont Supreme Court did conclude that lesbians and gay men must have equal legal rights under the state's law. However, instead of ending sex discrimination in the marriage laws, the Vermont Legislature created a new legal concept called a *civil union.* Like marriage, a civil union conveys comprehensive protections under civil law; however, at present civil unions are not recognized by the federal government, and it is unclear to what extent they will be recognized by other states. In fact, 34 states have created laws to negate all civil unions and domestic partnerships. Between July 1, 2000, and January 4, 2002, the state of Vermont issued 3,471 civil union licenses. Of those, 2,291 were for female couples, and 1,180 were given to male couples.[22]

CASE 5.9 *Baehr v. Lewin,* 74 Haw. 530, 852 P.2d 44 (1993)

Facts: Plaintiffs filed their complaint for injunctive and declaratory relief on May 1, 1991. The plaintiffs' complaint alleged that on or about December 17, 1990, the defendant denied the applications for marriage licenses presented by Plaintiffs Baehr and Dancel, Plaintiffs Rodrigues and Pregil, and Plaintiffs Lagon and Melillo, respectively, solely on the ground that the couples were of the same sex. Plaintiffs sought a judicial declaration that the construction and application of Hawaii Revised Statutes § 572-1 denying an application for a license to marry because an applicant couple is of the same sex is unconstitutional.

In 1993, the Hawaii Supreme Court vacated the lower court's order and judgment in favor of the defendant and remanded the case for further proceeding, with the burden of proof on the defendant. The defendant would have to prove there was sufficient credible evidence that the public interest in the well-being of children and families, or the optimal development of children, would be adversely affected by same-sex marriage.

Issue: Whether there is compelling state interest to deny the plaintiffs marriage licenses because they are of the same sex.

Court's Reasoning: The court found as a matter of law that the defendant failed to sustain his burden to overcome the presumption that HRS 572-1 is unconstitutional by demonstrating or proving that the statute furthers a compelling state interest.

The sex-based classification in HRS 572-1, on its face and as applied, was unconstitutional and in violation of the equal protection clause of Article I, § 5, of the Hawaii Constitution and the Department of Health. The State of Hawaii and its agents are enjoined from denying an application for a marriage license solely because the applicants are of the same sex.

Holding: The case is remanded to give the plaintiffs an opportunity to present evidence.

Case Discussion: Following the Hawaiian Supreme Court's decision that Hawaii's limitation of marriage licenses to different-sex couples appeared to violate the state constitutional ban on sex-based discrimination, the court ordered that there be a trial to test whether the state could justify the law. The case was sent back to the trial court because when the trial court first heard the case back in 1991, the trial judge had dismissed the case without the plaintiffs' having a chance to present evidence to support their case.

The plaintiffs did not specifically win the right to same-sex marriage, but did win the right to return to the trial court and have the state attempt to prove a compelling state interest in keeping the state statute that barred same-sex marriage. Can you think of reasons to argue both for and against there being a compelling state interest in banning same-sex marriages?

Transgender Issues in Marriage

The issue had to come up. What sex is a person after the person has had sex reassignment surgery? Should the person always be considered to be the sex he was born as, and which was designated on his birth certificate, or should the person be legally redesignated as being the sex that his body reflects? These were the legal issues in a case presented to the Kansas Supreme Court in early 2002. The court was asked to answer these questions because of a family dispute involving a $2.5 million inheritance. The Kansas Supreme Court ruled that the transsexual wife was legally male because her birth certificate said she was male, and therefore, she was never legally married to her late husband. The husband had died without a will, and under state law, his wife would automatically receive half of his estate, and his children would receive the other half. The husband's son from his first marriage, however, went to court in an attempt to invalidate the marriage.[23] The wife lost her appeal.

The Kansas decision was similar to one made in Texas in 1999. In the Texas case, the wife was prevented from filing a wrongful death suit against the doctors she claimed had committed negligence in treating her late husband. The wife had been designated as a male on her birth certificate prior to her sex-change operation. This case led several lesbian couples living in Texas to seize the opportunity to legally marry because one of the women in each couple was born male prior to having sex-change surgery and, therefore, could marry her female partner according to the Texas court's theory that the sex you are born is the sex you are legally.

CHAPTER SUMMARY

American marriage customs and laws pertaining to marriage have a long history that is rooted in ancient, multicultural traditions. Societal changes are reflected in the status of twenty-first-century women in American marriages. Women's role in marriage and society has drastically changed. These changes have included the demise of the marital rape exemption, the acknowledgment of a woman's right to choose her own name, and the nineteenth-century married women's property acts. No longer considered the property of their husbands, women have earned multiple rights as evidenced by numerous judicial decisions.

A marriage may not be considered valid unless all the essential legal elements of a marriage are met. These requirements include: (1) a marriage license; (2) different sexes; (3) not being already married; (4) acceptable degree of consanguinity; (5) mental capacity; (6) an intent to marry; (7) some sort of solemnization ceremony; and (8) an age requirement. These eight requirements must be met unless a couple resides in one of the states where common law marriages are still legally recognized.

In order for common law marriage to be recognized, an individual state's requirements must be met. These may include: (1) a man and woman living together for a statutorily required number of years; (2) the man and women letting it be commonly known that they are husband and wife; and (3) neither being legally married to anyone else. A major shift in societal mores has seen a movement away from courts providing paternalistic protection to engaged individuals who may be faced with unwanted breakups. A minority of states may still provide some monetary relief to a jilted fiancée left with justifiable expenses following a breakup. Along with the growing number of rights women have gathered in the last two hundred years has come the expected demise of legal actions that are now seen as historical *legal remnants,* such as the criminal conversation and alienation of affection actions which are no longer used in most states.

The United States Supreme Court has played an important role in reviewing the constitutional ramifications of state statutes, including the Court's finding that a ban on interracial marriage was unconstitutional. Another evolving trend in family law is the changing definition of family to a more inclusive definition. Hawaii was the first state to set an example by supporting same-sex marriage, until its state constitution was changed to prevent such marriages. Vermont stepped up next and allowed civil unions, which are the closest thing to a legal same-sex marriage in the United States. In late 2003, the Massachusetts Supreme Court decided that same-sex couples have a constitutional right to marry. The United States appears to be several steps behind some European nations that allow more expansive civil unions and The Netherlands, Belgium, and Canada, which allow same-sex marriage with all the rights and responsibilities inherent in a different-sex marriage.

Key Terms

marriage
civil marriage
monogamy
polygamy
polyandry
breach of promise
alimony
expectation damages
reliance damages
pain and suffering damages
tort
heart-balm statute
irrevocable gift
condition precedent

void ab initio
civil union
bigamy
consanguinity
mental capacity
ratification
sham marriage
voidable
solemnization ceremony
covenant marriage
common law marriage
putative marriage
annulment

divorce
dissolution of marriage
enticement action
consortium
alienation of affection
criminal conversation
Married Women's Property Acts
negligence
antimiscegenation laws
registered partnership
California Couples Registry
Defense of Marriage Act
    (DOMA)
reciprocal beneficiaries

Surfing the Web

http://www.lambdalegal.org This site provides information on the nation's oldest and largest legal organization working for the rights of lesbians and gay men.

http://www.usmarriagelaws.com Provides marriage requirements and laws in the United States and selected countries.

http://www.equalityinmarriage.com This site describes itself as educating women and men about the importance of equality in marriage and divorce.

http://www.law.cornell.edu Very informative site with a wide variety of links.

http://www.go4marriage.com Matchmaking site that also provides informative descriptions of Hindu, Muslim, and Christian marriage laws.

http://www.cuddleinternational.org This site takes a proactive approach to defending marriage between cousins.

ETHICS ALERT

Susan is at work one day and sees two neighbors, Jamie and Bill, come into the Johnson & Webster office. Thinking nothing of it, Susan continues her current assignment in the library. Later that afternoon, Alyssa comes into the library and asks Susan to use the answers on a prenuptial questionnaire to put together a draft of a prenuptial agreement for the neighbors. Susan cannot believe what she reads. The neighbors are planning to be married in a Las Vegas wedding the next week. Susan knows the two neighbors are both men, but the questionnaire does not have any questions regarding the sex of clients. Susan has known the guys for years, and Jamie has always dressed like a woman and acted like the perfect lady of the house. Should Susan share her knowledge with Alyssa? In a law firm, one never wants to send a client away if one can avoid it. Can you think of an alternative to a prenuptial agreement for Jamie and Bill?

Review Questions

1. What is a typical definition of marriage?
2. A marriage ceremony that has no religious affiliation is called what?
3. What is the difference between monogamy, polygamy, and polyandry?
4. Why is marriage technically known as an anomalous contract?
5. What is the history behind the breach-of-promise cause of action?
6. What three types of damages might a nineteenth-century plaintiff have requested in a breach-of-promise action?
7. What are the heart-balm statutes?
8. What would be the best scenario in which to receive an engagement ring if you wanted to keep it after your breakup with your fiancé or fiancée?
9. What are the eight prerequisites for a valid marriage?
10. What is a civil union?
11. What would be an example of ratification of a voidable marriage?
12. What is a covenant marriage?
13. What is a common law marriage? Does your state have common law marriage?
14. What would a court have to declare to recognize a putative marriage?
15. What is an annulment? Does the term *void ab initio* have anything to do with an annulment?
16. What is the difference between a religious annulment and a legal annulment?
17. Is a woman required to take her husband's name when she marries?
18. What is a loss of consortium claim?
19. What did the married women's property acts do for women?
20. What privacy issue did *Griswold* discuss?
21. Why was there a marital rape exemption?
22. What are antimiscegenation laws?
23. What is a registered partnership?
24. Does your municipality have a domestic partners registry?
25. What is the purpose of the Defense of Marriage Act?
26. What new legal concept did the Vermont Legislature create after the state supreme court concluded that lesbians and gay men must have equal legal rights under state law?

Endnotes

1. Cal. Fam. Code Ann. § 4100(1) (2003).
2. http://www.virginiabrides.com.
3. http://msuinfo.ur.msstate.edu.
4. History of Polygamy, April 30, 2003, http://www.polygamy.org.
5. *Catholic Encyclopedia 1913,* Electronic Version (New Advent, Inc., 1977), 465.
6. *Id.* at 468.
7. Divorce in Ireland, April 30, 2003, http://www.divorceuk.com.
8. Bohannon, Paul, and John Middleton, eds., *Marriage, Family, and Residence,* (1968), 257–264.
9. *Selected Plays of William Shakespeare* (Fine Editions Press, 1952), 17.
10. Prosser, W., *The Law of Torts,* 4th ed., 124.
11. Miss. Code Ann. ch. 301, § 93-1(1) (1997).
12. Ill. Comp. Stat. 750, § 5 (1999).
13. Smoking Gun Archive, July 27, 2002, http://www.thesmokinggun.com.
14. La. Rev. Stat. Ann. § 9.272–274 (2003).
15. Rajan, Raj, "The Putative Spouse in California Law," *Contemporary Legal Issues* 11 (2000): 95.
16. "Alienation of Affections and Criminal Conversation: Unholy Marriage in Need of Annulment," *Arizona Law Review* 23 (1981): 323.
17. *Columbia Law Review* 30 (1930): 651.
18. Barbour, *Criminal Law of the State of New York,* 2d ed. (1890), 69.
19. Hale, *History of Pleas of the Crown* (1870), 629.
20. "We're a Family and We Have Rights," *Newsweek,* November 4, 1996, 72–78.
21. http://www.lambdalegal.org, April 29, 2002.
22. http://www.gay.com, April 29, 2002.
23. Wilgoren, Jodi, "Suit Over Estate Claims a Widow Is Not a Woman," *New York Times,* January 13, 2002, 18.

Chapter 6

Paternity

PROVING PATERNITY

Paternity is the legal recognition of a man as the father of a child. Maternity is the legal recognition of a woman as the mother of a child. Not surprisingly, maternity is rarely an issue, but the question of how to prove paternity and ensure a child's right to financial support from her biological father is an age-old problem. Understanding the historical context of how the courts once dealt with paternity issues is important in order to put yesterday's and today's legal standards in perspective.

Historically, children born outside of marriage were described as **illegitimate.** The law dealt harshly with such children and generally would not recognize legitimization of them, even if their parents married later. Such harshness was not reserved for the children.[1] Parents could also bear a negative stigma.

Colonial America's courts dealt harshly with the father in the arcanely named *bastardy criminal trial.* This harshness can be attributed to laws reflecting a society that supported the concept that sexual relations should occur solely *within* the confines of marriage. An additional priority at that time, and still today, was to get financial support from the father of the child so as to lessen any burden on the state.

Legally speaking, the child born outside of marriage was typically excluded from most, if not all, of the rights normally given to children of married parents. Two examples of such rights include the right to inherit from a parent according to state *intestacy laws,* and the right to sue for *wrongful death* of a parent. State **intestacy laws** detail the distribution of inheritances to heirs according to the state's laws about who should collect an inheritance. A wrongful death action is a lawsuit against a person who caused a death.

In 1968, this legally sanctioned exclusionary behavior was found by the United States Supreme Court to violate the United States Constitution's equal protection clause, in the landmark case of *Levy v. Louisiana.*[2] The Court in *Levy* found that state statutes supporting the unequal treatment of so-called legitimate and illegitimate children were discriminatory. The **equal protection clause** provides a constitutional requirement that a state government not treat equals unequally, set up illegal categories to justify treating persons unfairly, or give unfair or unequal treatment to a person based on that person's race, religion, disability, color, sex, age, or national origin.

ONE SIDE OF THE STORY: MICHELLE'S EXPECTING

Susan's friend Michelle is currently dealing with a paternity experience. When she explained her situation to Susan, she had to choke out her words between intermittent sobs.

"I'm so upset," Michelle told her sympathetic friend. "Can you believe Johnny isn't answering my phone calls anymore and refuses to believe the baby is his?"

Susan put her arm around Michelle's shoulder and whispered, "Don't worry, don't worry," as if speaking to a babe in arms.

"I should have listened to my friends and family and never dated the jerk in the first place," Michelle said shaking her head. "But I wouldn't take any advice." Hitting the kitchen table with her fist and nearly spilling the coffee in their cups, she loudly vented, "I can't let Johnny think he can get away with this behavior!"

Susan pondered the problem. First, she knew from her Family Law class that, with the right evidence, Johnny would *not* get away with ignoring his responsibility. Secondly, Susan knew that she was in no position to offer legal advice, even if she felt she really knew the answers to her friend's questions.

Michelle dried her tears, looked hopefully at Susan, and asked, "Susan, I know you're working in a family law firm and that you got an A in Family Law at school. I was wondering if maybe you could handle this mess with Johnny for me?" Before a startled Susan had time to speak, Michelle quickly added, "It's just that I can't afford a lawyer."

Sighing, Susan said, "Michelle, I'd love to help you, but ethically—and legally—I really can't give you legal advice about your problem with John."

"Oh come on, we've been friends for years," Michelle reminded Susan. Shrugging her shoulders and looking at Susan slyly, she said, "Besides, we're sitting in my kitchen. Who will know?"

Despite Michelle's urging, Susan stood firm. She told her friend, "At the risk of making you angry, I can't give you legal advice, but I *can* suggest a lawyer who was a guest speaker in our class on just this question of establishing paternity, or you can come in to speak with one of the lawyers at the firm."

Michelle had known Susan for years and knew she was not likely to change her mind. In a softer voice, Michelle responded, "Okay, don't give me the look. I'll take *both* lawyers' names." She apologetically concluded the conversation, saying, "Thanks for pointing me in the right direction and, especially, for having the patience to listen to me."

The Other Side of the Story: Johnny's Denying

Meanwhile, Johnny was visiting his Cousin Vinny, a criminal lawyer, to look for some legal advice of his own.

"Vinny, it's like this," Johnny told his cousin. "I'm not the father of Michelle's kid. I only kissed her!"

Vinny responded suspiciously, "You only kissed?"

"Well, we didn't exactly have real sex," Johnny answered with an embarrassed laugh and a bright red face. "Besides, I don't think we'd hooked up yet at the time she must have gotten pregnant."

None too happy with his cousin's answer, Vinny replied, "Johnny, I'm an expert *criminal* lawyer, but I know *zilch* about paternity claims." Shaking his head and dreading long hours in the library, Vinny added in resignation, "But, you are my cousin. So, I'll give you a call after I've had a chance to do some legal research."

DNA: To Test or Not to Test

Cousin Vinny was a man of his word. He reviewed statutes, case law, and law journal articles on the subject of proving paternity. A week later he called Johnny. "Hey Johnny, it's me," said Vinny. "It doesn't look good. You'll have to face the music and get a **DNA test.**"

Shocked, Johnny asked, "What's that?"

Vinny replied, "Here, I'll read from the lab's brochure:

DNA stands for deoxyribonucleic acid and it's the nucleic acid of our chromosomes. The DNA molecule carries in its biochemical structure the genetic information passed from generation to generation and specifies the amino acid sequence of the polypeptide chains of proteins.

Apparently, every human being gets two copies of DNA from each parent. It's like a huge genetic alphabet of chemical combinations. There are over three billion combinations in our genetic makeup."[3]

Overwhelmed with that much science, Johnny asked, "Huh? Are you kidding me?"

"No, really," Vinny answered. "It's pretty interesting. You see, the DNA test gives science the ability to establish a genetic link between people. And get a load of this—they even used DNA testing to prove that the descendants of a slave woman owned by Thomas Jefferson were genetically related to Jefferson." He continued, "Our state is like all the rest. We have a statute that provides rules for proving paternity, and then we have clear guidelines for determining how to get child support from the fathers."

"Well, I'll just refuse to get the test and that will get me out of it," Johnny thought to himself.

Vinny was one step ahead of Johnny. He declared, "And if you're thinking of just refusing to take the test, forget about it. The law then switches the burden to the alleged father who refuses the DNA test to prove he's not the father." The silence from Johnny's end of the telephone told Vinny he'd gotten through to his cousin. Vinny asked, "So, if you still don't think you're the father, should I go ahead and schedule the test?"

"Go ahead," Johnny answered. "You know, maybe it might not be so bad having a little Johnny Junior running around."

PROVING PATERNITY AND GETTING SUPPORT

During the last 80 years, the National Conference of Commissioners on Uniform State Laws has been creating suggested uniform legislation to deal with the intertwined issues of paternity and support. Unfortunately, during the twentieth century, the majority of states failed to enact the Conference's uniform legislation. The Conference did experience some success, however, with the Uniform Parentage Act of 1973 (UPA). The UPA of 1973 was in effect in 19 states as of December 2000.

The UPA of 1973 was different from previous Conference attempts because of its emphasis on all children being treated equally, without regard to the marital status of the parents. Importantly, the Act established a set of rules for presumptions of parentage, shunned the term *illegitimate,* and employed the new term *child with no presumed father* to describe a child born to an unmarried mother. Part of UPA's success with the 1973 version can be attributed to numerous United States Supreme Court decisions including and following the *Levy* case you read about earlier. The *Levy* decision invalidated state inheritance, custody, and tort laws that put children of unmarried parents at a disadvantage.

Law reflects society's constant changes. The Conference believed the Uniform Parentage Act as proposed in 2000, and amended in 2002, should be their official recommendation because of the many changes occurring in society. Essentially, the amended version was designed to have the law treat a child of unmarried parents more equally. In addition, changes in the UPA (2002) include: (1) meeting the challenge of adapting to recent scientific reproduction developments; (2) providing guidelines for state *registries of paternity* to deal with the rights of a man who is neither an *acknowledged, presumed,* or *adjudicated father;* (3) providing comprehensive coverage of genetic testing; and (4) bringing more consistency between the UPA and the 1996 and 2001 versions of the **Uniform Interstate Family Support Act (UIFSA).**

The **registries of paternity** are designed for states to use in providing unmarried fathers with a place to go and voluntarily declare themselves as the biological father of a child. When a father registers, or when the mother places the biological father's name on a child's birth certificate, the biological father becomes an **acknowledged father.** A man is considered a **presumed father** if he is married to the biological mother. An **adjudicated father** is a man who has been declared the father by a court of law.

Since January 1998, the federal government has required each state to adopt the UIFSA, which supersedes any previous state statutes concerning child support enforcement. The requirement was connected to whether the federal government would provide a state with funding to help offset the cost of state-provided child support. The previously applicable statutes were the original and revised **Uniform Reciprocal Enforcement of Support Act,** abbreviated as **URESA** and **RURESA.** The intent behind the newer UIFSA is to create a more effective framework for child support enforcement in interstate cases. UIFSA can also be used to establish and enforce a support order, modify a support order, and *determine parentage*, with or without an accompanying establishment of support.

Specifically, UIFSA's article 70.1, entitled the Proceeding to Determine Parentage, states:

> *A tribunal of this State may serve as initiating or responding tribunal in a proceeding brought under the Act to determine that the petitioner or respondent is a parent of a child. In a proceeding to determine parentage, a responding tribunal of the State shall apply the Uniform Parentage Act.*

You will read more about the UIFSA, URESA, and RURESA in later chapters.

Location, Location, Location: Proving Paternity Across America

All 50 states have been encouraged by the federal government to create statutes to deal with paternity questions. All the states have now created such statutes, but with some differences. For example, California law is very pro-family. California law provides that a man is considered a *presumed father* if any of the following occurs: (1) The man and the natural mother are married to each other, or were married 300 days before the child was born; (2) before the birth of the child, he and the natural mother attempted to marry each other; or (3) following the child's birth, he and the natural mother are married and (a) he consents to be named as the child's father, (b) he signs a voluntary promise to support the child as his natural child, or (c) he openly acknowledges the child as his own.[4]

If Michelle and Johnny were Californians, would Johnny be considered a *presumed* father? Johnny never married Michelle, nor does he apparently intend to be married to Michelle. The conclusion is that Johnny would not be considered a presumed father according to California's law. This does not mean that Michelle cannot sue Johnny to have his paternity declared and make him pay child support.

If Michelle had become pregnant with Johnny's baby while married to another man, Johnny also would not be considered the presumed father under California law. Michelle's marital status would hinder Johnny's rights to sue to declare himself the father of Johnny Junior. California's courts have historically been strong supporters of the family and have held that a nonmarital biological father *does not have standing* to sue an intact family to assert his rights of fatherhood.

Suppose, however, that Johnny lived in Texas and Michelle became pregnant with his baby while married to another man. Texas has declared that a biological father *cannot be denied standing* to have a court acknowledge his parental rights, even if the mother is married to another man. As far as DNA testing is concerned, state statutes in Texas clearly provide that if Johnny refused to submit to parentage testing, the burden of disproving that he is the father would fall on him.[5] Johnny would more than likely be declared the father, since he would not be able to disprove that he was the father without submitting to parentage testing.

If Johnny lived in Illinois and refused to submit to the DNA test, the state would take his refusal very seriously.[6] Illinois courts could resolve the question of paternity against him and declare his paternity without the DNA test if the facts supported such a decision.

Suppose Johnny lived in Florida. Florida's law provides that if Johnny voluntarily acknowledged Michelle's baby as his own, then Johnny could sign and have notarized an affidavit acknowledging paternity, but he would still have the right to rescind the acknowledgment within 60 days of the date of the acknowledgment.[7]

You can see from the variety in just these few examples that each state has to be researched for specific statutory requirements.

Procedure Must Be Followed

The reason the federal government became involved in telling the states—or rather the state agencies that provide financial support for needy children—how to go about establishing paternity is because the federal government provides funding to the states for such child support programs. The state agencies that distribute this funding are known as *Title IV-D* agencies because Title IV-D is part of the name of the federal statute that provides funding for state child support programs.

Each state is required by federal law to have *a simple civil process for voluntarily acknowledging paternity and a civil procedure for establishing paternity in contested cases.* The requirements for how a state must establish this process and procedure are clearly stated. Federal law also provides that if paternity *is* established in a contested case and genetic tests were performed, the Title IV-D agency must attempt to obtain a judgment for the costs of performing the genetic tests from the party who denied paternity. Each state is also required by the federal code to do its best to secure support for a child from any person who is legally liable for such support by using *state law and reciprocal arrangements adopted with other states.*

Bottom Line

Vinny was right to tell Johnny that all 50 states require alleged fathers to participate in a medical test to determine paternity, or face the consequences. Additionally, all 50 states have some sort of system for pursuing child support from declared fathers. If Johnny really is *not* the father of Michelle's baby, his best plan of action is to volunteer to take a DNA test. The DNA test would almost conclusively determine that Michelle's baby is not Johnny's.

Make Room for Daddy

What Johnny *told* Vinny he would do and what he actually *did* turned out to be two different things. Johnny put off taking the test for weeks. Meanwhile, Michelle got more and more angry. She was tired of waiting around for Johnny to make up his mind. At this point, Michelle can request a judicial determination declaring Johnny as the father of her child. To do so, she would have to bring a complaint for paternity. A **complaint for paternity** is a legal action filed with the court system asking a judge to make an official determination of paternity. Michelle wants to get the DNA test over with, move on with plans for her life with a baby, and just generally aggravate Johnny, so she makes an appointment to visit Johnson & Webster.

Susan chatted with Michelle in the waiting room while Alyssa was finishing another consultation. "Have you heard anything about Johnny taking the DNA test yet?" Susan inquired.

Visibly annoyed, Michelle reported, "He was plenty interested in me before the baby, but so far he hasn't volunteered to take the test or acknowledged that he's the father."

Susan was just about to make a sarcastic comment at Johnny's expense when the receptionist notified them that Alyssa was ready to see them in her office. Michelle had asked earlier if Susan could be present during the meeting to give her moral support.

Susan and Michelle exchanged pleasantries with Alyssa, and then Alyssa started the interview by asking Michelle what she thought Johnny's responsibilities should be.

"I want Johnny to face up to the facts of life," Michelle began. "I want to keep my baby, and I'll need him to help pay for stuff."

Alyssa answered, "I went through this information during our initial telephone consultation, but I want to repeat—you *can* request a formal acknowledgment of his paternity, child support, a portion of the medical costs, and attorneys' fees."

"I even told him all of that when I cornered him at the dance club last weekend, but he just said good luck and ran off with his new girlfriend," Michelle responded morosely.

Alyssa replied, "I know you were hoping he'd step up to his responsibilities, but I think it's time we filed a complaint and got that cousin Vinny you told me about into this. Maybe he'll be able to talk some sense into Johnny before the baby arrives."

Michelle agreed to filing the complaint and was told Susan would call her in a day or so, at which time she could return to the office to sign the pleading.

As soon as Michelle left, Alyssa needed to leave in order to get to a deposition on time. She asked Susan to try writing the paternity complaint by following a sample complaint she provided. Read the draft of the Complaint for Paternity that Susan prepared for Michelle's case in Exhibit 6.1.

Motivation Spelled *Lawsuit*

Alyssa was right. The complaint motivated Vinny to get on Johnny's case. Vinny finally convinced Johnny that he really had no a choice about the test—he *had* to take it.

So Johnny finally went to a local laboratory and took the dreaded DNA test, still stubbornly refusing to acknowledge that he was the father. The results came as no surprise to Michelle. The paternity evaluation laboratory report showed a 99.99 probability that Johnny was the father. Review the highest test score Johnny ever received (in school or out) in Exhibit 6.2.[8] Then review the results that Johnny would have received had the test been negative and showed zero probability for paternity in Exhibit 6.3.

What's the Next Step After a Positive DNA Test?

The next step is really up to Johnny. He can voluntarily agree to help to support his child *or* Michelle can go to court and ask a judge to sign an order that clearly provides the following: (1) a determination of parentage; (2) reasonable expenses for Michelle's pregnancy and post-partum disability; (3) child support for Johnny Junior; and (4) attorneys' fees and court costs.

Some firm advice from his lawyer convinced Johnny to face up to his responsibilities toward Michelle and the baby. In the end, Alyssa and Vinny negotiated a settlement that was approved by the court. Johnny agreed to acknowledge paternity, share medical costs not covered by Michelle's insurance, and pay child support. This negotiated settlement was presented to a judge who wrote the settlement into a court order. Included in the court order was Michelle's agreement to pay her own attorneys' fees—and to call the baby Johnny Junior if it is a boy!

EXHIBIT 6.1 Michelle's Complaint for Paternity

Alyssa Jensen, Esq.
Johnson & Webster, Esqs.
123 Main Street
Newton, New Jersey 12345
973-555-1212
Attorney for Plaintiff

MICHELLE MONROE,	)	
	)	
Plaintiff,	)	
	)	SUSSEX COUNTY SUPERIOR COURT
v.	)	CHANCERY DIVISION-FAMILY PART
	)	Docket No. 711711
JOHNNY ROMEO,	)	
	)	
	)	COMPLAINT FOR PATERNITY
Defendant.	)	
	)	

1. The Plaintiff resides at 2 Regrets Avenue, Green, New Jersey.
2. Defendant resides at 4 Lover's Lane, Green, New Jersey.
3. The Plaintiff had sexual intercourse with the Defendant from July 4, 2002, ending on or about July. 30, 2002. The intercourse resulted in a pregnancy.
4. The Plaintiff is now pregnant.
5. The Plaintiff has never been married.
6. The Defendant has refused to acknowledge the child as his own.
7. The Defendant has refused to undergo DNA testing.
8. Neither the Plaintiff nor the Defendant is Native American.

WHEREFORE, Plaintiff requests that this Court order the Defendant to undertake DNA testing, enter a declaration of paternity, order child support, order that medical costs associated with the pregnancy and birth be paid, and order any other relief as the Court deems fit. Alyssa Jensen, Esq.

_____
Alyssa Jensen, Esq.
Attorney for Plaintiff

DATED: _____

Certification of Verification of Plaintiff

I, Michelle Monroe, am the Plaintiff in the foregoing Complaint. The allegations of the Complaint are true to the best of my knowledge and belief. The said Complaint is made in truth and in good faith and without collusion, for the cause set forth above.

_____
Michelle Monroe

EXHIBIT 6.2 Johnny's DNA Results (Sample report provided by Orchid GeneScreen)

ORCHID
GENESCREEN

GENETIC TEST REPORT

GS Case/Test Set:184208/496427
Customer Number:

Michelle Monroe
2 Regrets Avenue
Green, New Jersey 90210

	Race	Specimen ID	Specimen Collection
Mother: Monroe, Michelle	Caucasian	900002	04/24/2003
Child: Monroe, Baby		900001	04/24/2003
Alleged Father: Romeo, Johnny	Caucasian	900000	04/24/2003

> Combined Paternity Index = 10,944 to 1
> Probability of Paternity = 99.99%

Conclusion

The alleged father, Johnny Romeo, cannot be excluded as the biological father of Baby Monroe. Based on the genetic testing results, the probability of paternity is 99.99% when compared to an untested random man of the North American Caucasian population. (Prior Probability = 0.5). At least 99.99% of the North American Caucasian population is excluded from the possibility of being the biological father of the child.

System	Mother	Child	Alleged Father	Paternity Index
D16S539	11, 13	11, 12	12, 13	1.71
D18S51	15, 17	17, 16	16, 23	2.69
D19S433	14	14	14	3.06
D21S11	31	28, 31	28, 30	3.05
D2S1338	17, 18	17, 18	18, 25	1.89
D3S1358	14, 15	15, 16	16, 18	2.12
D8S1179	14	13, 14	13	3.03
FGA	18, 20	20	20, 26	3.21
TH01	6, 7	7	6, 7	2.67
vWA	16, 20	18, 20	17, 18	2.45

Sworn to and subscribed in my presence on April 29, 2003.

I certify that the foregoing testing was conducted in accordance with the standard protocol and the results contained herein are true and correct to the best of my knowledge.

Joy Johnson, Ph.D., Associate Director

Accredited by the American Association of Blood Banks

5698 Springboro Pike Dayton, Ohio 45449   800-443-2383

How Paternity Testing Works

Paternity testing is based on a simple principle of biology: Children inherit genetic factors from both biological parents, with each parent passing on half of a child's genetic factors. Testing a mother and child provides information first about the factors passed from the mother to the child. Factors that are not inherited from the mother *must* come from the biological father. An alleged father's typings are then evaluated to determine if he possesses *all* of the genetic factors that the child must inherit from the biological father. If he does not possess all of these factors (excepting the rare possibility of a mutation), he is genetically *excluded* from paternity. If he does possess all of them, he is *included,* and a probability is calculated that he is the father. This is based on how rare the factors are that the alleged father and child share.

Technology and Results

GeneScreen uses DNA testing exclusively for paternity tests. The primary type of testing utilizes a technique called polymerase chain reaction. Polymerase Chain Reaction (PCR) is a technique used to make many copies of specific sections of an individual's DNA. One person's DNA differs from another's by the length of these specific sections. These sections are passed from parents to children, as explained above. The lengths are expressed as numbers, like 4.0 or 12.0. Everyone has two numbers in each genetic system (if a number is only shown once, like 6.0, it means that both numbers are the same, in this case 6.0, 6.0). A child always inherits one number from its mother and one from its biological father.
If an alleged father is not excluded in a genetic system, a *paternity index* is calculated. This is a number that compares an alleged father's chance of passing the genetic factor that the child had to receive from the biological father (this factor is called the *obligate allele*), as opposed to receiving it from a random man. For example, a paternity index of 3.23 means that the alleged father is 3.23 times more likely to pass the obligate allele than a man chosen at random from the population at large of similar ethnic origin. The more rare the obligate allele, the higher the paternity index.

If an alleged father is excluded in a particular genetic system, the paternity index for that system is 0. Since the genetic systems tested are independent of each other, the paternity indexes of the individual genetic systems can be multiplied together to provide a *combined paternity index.* This number shows how much more likely it is for the alleged father to pass *all* of the obligate alleles together than for a random man to pass them. The combined paternity index is converted into a percentage number, called the *probability of paternity.* Calculation of this number can take non-genetic evidence into consideration (as *prior probability*), but this is almost always chosen so as to be a neutral assessment of the non-genetic evidence (prior probability = 0.5).

The Report

The results for each party tested are shown for each genetic system, under columns labeled "Mother," "Child," and "Alleged Father." The paternity index for each system is shown in the column labeled "Paternity Index." If an alleged father is excluded in two or more genetic systems, as defined above, he is considered excluded, and the combined paternity index is 0. A probability of paternity of 99% or greater indicates a strong likelihood that the alleged father is the biological father of the child.

Note: This explanation is for guidance and informational purposes only, and is not intended to provide all scientific details or theoretical possibilities. Please consult GeneScreen if additional information is needed.

VOLUNTARY ACKNOWLEDGMENT OF PATERNITY

Not every biological father is as hesitant as Johnny was to voluntarily acknowledge his paternity. Federal law provides that an **acknowledgment of paternity** should be filed with the state registry of birth records, and that the registry may not charge for filing an acknowledgment or denial of paternity. Such an acknowledgment may be withdrawn within 60 days of filing or by the date of the first paternity hearing, but if the person who made the acknowledgment or denial of paternity moves to withdraw the acknowledgement within two years of the child's birth, that person must prove that fraud, duress, or material mistake of fact led to the original acknowledgment.[9] Review the Voluntary Declaration of Paternity in Exhibit 6.4.

The new UPA promotes the importance of a parentage registry. A **parentage registry** allows an unmarried father to register his acknowledgment of parentage and request that he be notified of any legal

EXHIBIT 6.3 Example of Test with Zero Probability (Sample report provided by Orchid GeneScreen)

ORCHID GENESCREEN

GENETIC TEST REPORT

Michelle Monroe
2 Regrets Avenue
Green, New Jersey 90210

GS Case/Test Set:184208/496427
Customer Number:

	Race	Specimen ID	Specimen Collection
Mother: Monroe, Michelle	Caucasian	900002	04/24/2003
Child: Monroe, Baby		900001	04/24/2003
Alleged Father: Romeo, Johnny	Caucasian	900000	04/24/2003

Combined Paternity Index = 0
Probability of Paternity = 0.00%

Conclusion

The alleged father, Johnny Romeo, cannot be the biological father of Baby Monroe, since he and child do not share necessary paternal markers in multiple genetic systems.

System	Mother	Child	Alleged Father	Paternity Index	
DD16S539	11, 13	11, 12	10, 11	0.00	EXCLUSION
D18S51	15, 17	17, 23	15, 18	0.00	EXCLUSION
D19S433	14	14	14	3.06	
D21S11	31	28, 31	28, 30	3.05	
D2S1338	17, 18	17, 22	22, 25	13.16	
D3S1358	14, 15	15, 16	14	0.00	EXCLUSION
D8S1179	14	13, 14	13	3.03	
FGA	6, 7	7	6, 7	40.00	
TH01	22, 24	20, 22	21, 23	0.00	EXCLUSION
vWA	16, 20	18, 20	17, 18	2.45	

Sworn to and subscribed in my presence on
April 29, 2003.

I certify that the foregoing testing was conducted in accordance with the standard protocol and the results contained herein are true and correct to the best of my knowledge.

Joy Johnson, Ph.D., Associate Director

Accredited by the American Association of Blood Banks

5698 Springboro Pike Dayton, Ohio 45449   800-443-2383

EXHIBIT 6.4 Voluntary Declaration of Paternity (Courtesy of the State of California)

STATE OF CALIFORNIA - HEALTH AND HUMAN SERVICES AGENCY   CALIFORNIA DEPARTMENT OF CHILD SUPPORT SERVICES

DECLARATION OF PATERNITY

SEND ORIGINAL (White Copy) To: DCSS
PATERNITY OPPORTUNITY PROGRAM
P.O. BOX 419070
RANCHO CORDOVA, CA 95741-9070

SECTION A

Child

NAME OF CHILD - FIRST	MIDDLE	LAST
DATE OF BIRTH (Month, Day, Year)	SEX	FOR STATE USE ONLY

Place of Birth

HOSPITAL NAME		CITY
COUNTY	STATE	

Father

NAME OF FATHER - FIRST	MIDDLE	LAST
SOCIAL SECURITY NO.	DATE OF BIRTH (Month, Day, Year)	PLACE OF BIRTH (STATE OR COUNTRY)

☐ BY CHECKING THIS BOX I CERTIFY I DO NOT HAVE A SOCIAL SECURITY NUMBER

CURRENT ADDRESS (NUMBER, STREET, CITY, ZIP)

Mother

NAME OF MOTHER - FIRST	MIDDLE	LAST
SOCIAL SECURITY NO.	DATE OF BIRTH (Month, Day, Year)	PLACE OF BIRTH (STATE OR COUNTRY)

☐ BY CHECKING THIS BOX I CERTIFY I DO NOT HAVE A SOCIAL SECURITY NUMBER

CURRENT ADDRESS (NUMBER, STREET, CITY, ZIP)

SECTION B - READ OTHER SIDE BEFORE SIGNING

I declare under the penalty of perjury under the laws of the State of California that I am the biological father of the child named on this declaration and that the information provided is true and correct. I have read and understand the rights and responsibilities described on the back of this form. I understand that by signing this form I am consenting to the establishment of paternity, thereby waiving those rights. I am assuming all the rights and responsibilities as the biological father of this child. I wish to be named as the father on the child's birth certificate.

I have been orally informed of my rights and responsibilities.

SIGNATURE OF FATHER	DATE SIGNED

I declare under the penalty of perjury under the laws of the State of California that I am the natural mother of the child named on this declaration and that the information provided is true and correct. I have read and understand the rights and responsibilities described on the back of this form. I certify that the man signing this form is the only possible father of this child. I know that by signing this form I am establishing the man signing this form as the biological father of this child with all the rights and responsibilities of a biological father under the laws of California. I consent to the establishment of paternity by signing this form.

I have been orally informed of my rights and responsibilities.

SIGNATURE OF MOTHER	DATE SIGNED

SECTION C - TO BE COMPLETED BY WITNESS AT THE HOSPITAL, AGENCY OR CLINIC (PLEASE PRINT)

DECLARATION WITNESSED BY (SIGNATURE AND PRINTED NAME)	DATE

NAME OF AGENCY (HOSPITAL, CLINIC OR OTHER)

ADDRESS (ADDRESS, CITY AND ZIP CODE)

SECTION D - TO BE COMPLETED BY NOTARY PUBLIC IF NOT WITNESSED ABOVE

State of _____

County of_____

On_____before me, _____, personally

appeared_____

personally known to me (or proved to me on the basis of satisfactory evidence) to be the person(s) whose name(s) are subscribed to the within instrument and acknowledged to me that he/she/they executed the same in his/her/their signature(s) on the instrument the person(s), or the entity on behalf of which the person(s) acted, executed the instrument. WITNESS by hand and official seal.

CS 909 (1/03) DECLARATION OF PATERNITY

DISTRIBUTION: ORIGINAL WHITE COPY - DCSS
YELLOW & PINK COPIES - PARENTS
GREEN COPY - LOCAL CHILD SUPPORT AGENCY

(continued)

EXHIBIT 6.4 *continued*

WHAT IS THE PURPOSE OF A DECLARATION OF PATERNITY?

A declaration of paternity form is used to legally establish the paternity *(the father)* of a child when the mother and father are not married to each other. It should be signed only by the biological mother if she is not married. It may be signed by the biological father regardless of his marital status. **Signing this form is voluntary. If any part of this form does not make sense to you, talk to your local Child Support Agency or a lawyer before signing the form.**

HOW WILL YOU AND YOUR CHILD BENEFIT IF YOU SIGN THIS FORM?

When both parents sign this form it will:

- Legally establish a parent-child relationship between the biological father and the child. Your child has the right to know his or her mother and father and to benefit from a relationship with both parents.

- Allow the father's name to be added to the birth certificate. Your child will benefit by having both of your names appear on his or her birth certificate. If the form is signed after the child's birth certificate is prepared, there will be a fee to amend the birth certificate to add the father's name.

- Legally establish the man as the child's father without going to court. This will give the father parental rights such as the right to seek child custody and visitation through a court action and to be consulted about the adoption of the child.

- Make it easier for your child to learn the medical histories of both parents, to benefit from the father's health care coverage, and to receive Social Security or Veterans' dependent or survivor's benefits, if eligible.

WHAT DOES IT MEAN IF YOU SIGN A DECLARATION OF PATERNITY?

- A correctly completed signed declaration of paternity filed with the California Department of Child Support Services will have the same effect as a court order establishing paternity for the child. If your child does not live with you and a court action is filed, you may be ordered by the court to pay child support. A court action must be filed to deal with the issues of custody, visitation or child support.

- By signing this declaration, you are, by your choice, giving up all of the following rights, as they relate to paternity establishment: the right to a trial in court to decide the issue of paternity; to notice of any hearing on the issue of paternity; to have the opportunity to present your case to the court, including the right to present and cross examine witnesses; to have an attorney represent you; or to have an attorney appointed to represent you if you cannot afford one in an action filed by the local child support agency.

- If either of you later change your mind about signing this form, you must complete a *Rescission Form For the Declaration of Paternity (CS 915)* to rescind or cancel the declaration of paternity **and** file it with the California Department of Child Support Services within 60 days from the date you sign this form. You can get a rescission form from your local Child Support Agency, or Local Registrar of Births and Deaths.

- A Declaration of Paternity may be challenged in court only in the first two years after the child's birth by using blood and genetic tests that prove the man is not the biological father. It also may be overturned if the father or mother is able to prove that he/she signed the form because of fraud, duress, or material mistake of fact.

- If either or both of you are under the age of eighteen, a declaration of paternity will not establish paternity until sixty days after both of you are age eighteen or are legally emancipated. If you wish to legally establish paternity before both of you become adults, you should consult an attorney.

IF YOU CHANGE YOUR MIND AFTER YOU SIGN A DECLARATION OF PATERNITY?

- If either of you later change your mind after you sign this form, you must complete a *Rescission Form for the Declaration of Paternity* (CS 915) to cancel or rescind the declaration of paternity. You must file the rescission form with the California Department of Child Support Services within 60 days from the date you signed the declaration of paternity. You can get a rescission form from your local child support agency, local registrar of births and deaths or family law facilitator's office. Rescinding this form will not remove the father's name from the birth certificate.

- For further questions contact the State POP Coordinator at (866) 249-0773.

STATE OF CALIFORNIA - HEALTH AND HUMAN SERVICES AGENCY   CALIFORNIA DEPARTMENT OF CHILD SUPPORT SERVICES

IMPORTANT NOTICE TO UNMARRIED PARENTS

If the parents of the child are not legally married, the father's name will not be added to the birth certificate unless you: (1) sign a declaration of paternity in the hospital or (2) sign the form later or legally establish paternity through the courts and pay a fee to amend the birth certificate.

WHAT IS THE PURPOSE OF A DECLARATION OF PATERNITY?

A declaration of paternity form is used to legally establish the paternity (the father) of a child when the mother and father are not married to each other. **It should be signed by the biological mother only if she is not married.** It may be signed by the biological father regardless of his martial status. **Signing this form is voluntary. If any part of this form does not make sense to you, talk to your local Child Support Agency or a lawyer before signing the form.**

HOW WILL YOU AND YOUR CHILD BENEFIT IF YOU SIGN THIS FORM?

When both parents sign this form it will:

- Legally establish a parent-child relationship between the biological father and the child. Your child has the right to know his or her mother and father and to benefit from a relationship with both parents.

- Allow the father's name to be added to the birth certificate. Your child will benefit by having both of your names appear on his or her birth certificate. If the form is signed after the child's birth certificate is prepared, there will be a fee to amend the birth certificate to add the father's name.

- Legally establish the man as the child's father without going to court. This will give the father parental rights such as the right to seek child custody and visitation through a court action and to be consulted about the adoption of the child.

- Make it easier for your child to learn the medical histories of both parents, to benefit from the father's health care coverage, and to receive Social Security or Veterans' dependent or survivor's benefits, if eligible.

WHAT DOES IT MEAN IF YOU SIGN A DECLARATION OF PATERNITY?

- A correctly completed and signed declaration of paternity filed with the California Department of Child Support Services will have the same effect as a court order establishing paternity for the child. If your child does not live with you and a court action is filed, you may be ordered by the court to pay child support. A court action must be filed to deal with the issues of custody, visitation or child support.

- By signing this declaration, you are, by your choice, giving up all of the following rights, as they relate to paternity establishment: the right to a trial in court to decide the issue of paternity; to notice of any hearing on the issue of paternity to have the opportunity to present your case to the court, including the right to present and cross examine witnesses; to have an attorney represent you; or to have an attorney appointed to represent you if you cannot afford one in an action filed by the local child support agency.

- A declaration of paternity may be challenged in court only in the first two years after the child's birth by using blood and genetic tests that prove the man is not the biological father. It also may be overturned if the father or mother is able to prove that he/she signed the form because of fraud, duress, or material mistake of fact.

- If either or both of you are under the age of eighteen, a declaration of paternity will not establish paternity until sixty days after both of you are age eighteen or are legally emancipated. If you wish to legally establish paternity before both of you become adults, you should consult an attorney.

IF YOU CHANGE YOUR MIND AFTER YOU SIGN A DECLARATION OF PATERNITY

- If either of you later change your mind after you sign this form, you must complete a *Rescission Form for the Declaration of Paternity* (CS 915) to cancel or rescind the declaration of paternity. You must file the rescission form with the California Department of Child Support Services within 60 days from the date you signed the declaration of paternity. If you signed the declaration of paternity when you were under the age of 18 years old, you must file the rescission form within 60 days after you reach the age of 18 years old. You can get a rescission form from your local child support agency, local registrar of births and deaths or family law facilitator's office.

- **For further questions contact the State POP Coordinator at (866) 249-0773.**

(continued)

EXHIBIT 6.4 *continued*

STATE OF CALIFORNIA—HEALTH AND HUMAN SERVICES AGENCY   CALIFORNIA DEPARTMENT OF CHILD SUPPORT SERVICES

PATERNITY OPPORTUNITY PROGRAM
PATERNITY DECLARATION - INSTRUCTIONS FOR COMPLETION
(THIS FORM IS TO BE COMPLETED BY UNMARRIED PARENTS ONLY)

GENERAL INFORMATION

The attached declaration form is to be used by unmarried parents to declare the father of the child. Paternity means legal fatherhood. Completing and signing this form is voluntary. **THIS IS A LEGAL DOCUMENT. PLEASE CAREFULLY READ THE REVERSE SIDE OF THE FORM BEFORE YOU SIGN IT.** There is important information about what it means to you and your child when you sign this form. In order for the Declaration of Paternity to be valid, both parents must complete and sign this form. The form must be signed in the presence of a witness from the hospital or agency accepting the form. If not signed at a hospital, prenatal clinic or public agency, you must sign the form in the presence of a Notary Public. If you are the biological father and you wish to have your name entered on the child's birth certificate, you must sign this form. Otherwise, you must go to court to establish legal paternity and pay a fee to amend the child's birth certificate to add your name. Please see section "Filing This Form" below for more details.

PLEASE USE BLACK INK WHEN FILLING OUT THE ATTACHED FORM. PRINT ALL INFORMATION, EXCEPT FOR YOUR SIGNATURE. PLEASE PRESS FIRMLY AND PRINT CLEARLY WHEN FILLING OUT THE FORM. THIS FORM MUST BE SIGNED IN THE PRESENCE OF AN AUTHORIZED REPRESENTATIVE OR A NOTARY PUBLIC.

SECTION A

This section identifies the mother, biological father, child and the place of the child's birth. Your social security number may be used to find parents so child support, and other benefits your child may need, may be collected. If you write down your social security number, it will be on any copies made of this form.

SECTION B

In this section, both parents declare they are the mother and biological father of the child named on this form. Both parents must sign and date the form, for this form to be legal. **PLEASE READ THE REVERSE SIDE OF THE FORM BEFORE YOU SIGN IT.**

SECTION C

This section is to be completed by the person who is a witness to the parents' signatures on the form. The witness must be an official representative of the hospital or agency accepting the form.

SECTION D

This section is to be completed ONLY when the form is witnessed by a Notary Public. If parents do not complete the form at a hospital, prenatal clinic or public agency, they can only sign it before a Notary Public. This section is to be completed and stamped by a Notary Public.

FILING THIS FORM

The original of this form MUST be sent to:

> **California Department of Child Support Services**
> **Paternity Opportunity Program**
> **P. O. Box 419070**
> **Rancho Cordova, CA 95741- 9070**

THE ORIGINAL OF THIS FORM MUST BE SENT WITHIN 20 DAYS OF DATE IT WAS SIGNED.
If you did not complete this form at the hospital *(or when you registered your child's birth)*, and you want to add the father's name to the birth certificate, you must contact the State Department of Health Services, Office of Vital Records, 304 S Street, P.O. Box 730241, Sacramento, CA 94244-0241 or your Local Registrar of Births and Deaths. They will provide you with the additional forms you need to complete. You will be charged a fee to have your child's birth certificate changed to include the father's name.

Both parents will be given a copy of this form. This form is an important legal record. Parents should keep their copies in a safe place.

CANCELING OR RESCINDING THIS FORM

To rescind or cancel this form, either parent must complete and sign a *Rescission Form for the Declaration of Paternity (CS 915).* This form must be filed with the California Department of Child Support Services POP Unit *(see address above)* within sixty days of the date the paternity declaration was signed. If you signed the declaration of paternity when you were under the age of 18 years old, you must file the rescission form within 60 days after you reach the age of 18 years old. To obtain a form to rescind or cancel this form, contact the local child support agency, local registrar of births and deaths, or family law facilitator's office. Evidence that a copy of the form has been provided to the other parent must also be provided with the rescission form. Rescinding this forms will not remove the father's name from the birth certificate.

CS 909 (1/03) COVERSHEET   PAGE 2

proceedings involving his child. The registry concept was discussed in *Lehr v. Robertson.*[10] In *Lehr,* the Supreme Court upheld a New York statute that required the father of a child born out of wedlock to register with the parentage registry if he wished to be notified of a termination of parental rights hearing or adoption proceedings. **Termination of parental rights** is the court-ordered extinguishment of a parent's right to his child. Men who are married to a biological mother have always had the right to be properly notified of any termination of parental rights hearings or adoptions proceedings, but this New York statute was opposed by unmarried fathers because it placed an additional burden on them that was not placed on married fathers. The *Lehr* case supported registries as an efficient means to ensure notification. Unmarried fathers are not always easily located. The parental registry requirement removes the burden of locating the father for proper notification. Without this requirement, the courts could never be certain that a biological father had received notification of a termination of parental rights hearing or an adoption proceeding. At least 28 states had developed paternity registries as of May 2000.

Fighting the Biological Father: Hit the Road, Jack!

In some cases, the biological father has wanted to acknowledge paternity and to support and connect with his child, but the mother has had other ideas. This is what happened in one California case. Recall that California is *extremely* pro-family and supportive of the presumed father. In *Michael H. v. Gerald D.,*[11] the mother, Carol, was married to Gerald when she became pregnant and gave birth to Michael's child. Although Carol and Michael had a rollercoaster-type relationship, Michael still developed a familial relationship with his child. For years, Carol continued relationships with both her husband and Michael. Finally, Michael filed a paternity action to have his status as the child's father protected. Gerald was not happy about this at all and opposed the action on the basis of his position as the *presumed* father.

In *Michael H. v. Gerald D.,* Michael argued that his true biological connection to the child gave him standing to sue for a declaration of paternity. The California Supreme Court, however, did not agree. They declared that Gerald, the presumed father, was entitled to that recognition because he was married to Carol when she became pregnant and had remained in the lives of Carol and the child. Michael was essentially declared an usurper within the marital relationship.

If you think the unwed father was treated harshly in the *Michael H.* case, you may truly lose your patience with the legal system when you read about the custody problems of another unwed father from Illinois. Peter had lived with Joan somewhat regularly for 18 years, and they had three children together. When Joan died, the state moved to have the children declared wards of the state of Illinois because *the state claimed they lacked a surviving parent.* Peter was *presumed* by the state to be an unfit parent because he was not married to his children's mother. By the way, this case is not from 1872, but from 1972.

Peter fought Illinois's presumption of unfitness all the way to the United States Supreme Court.[12] The Supreme Court ultimately agreed with Peter that marital status does not prove fitness, nor does nonmarital status prove unfitness. Unwed fathers *should* have the right and standing in the courts to fight for a connection to their children.

Today, most states allow unwed fathers to make paternity claims, even when the biological mother is married to another. Depending on the state, however, an unwed father may have additional hurdles to jump. While some states place few restrictions on the unwed father who wants to formalize his relationship with his biological child, other states still require the biological father to prove that an acknowledged relationship with his biological child would be in the best interests of the child or that he has developed a connection beyond biology with the child. This last requirement is extraordinarily difficult to prove if the mother and the presumed (but not biological) father are fighting the biological father's attempts to establish such a connection. Often, though, the mother chooses not to fight the connection, since the court's acknowledgment of the father's paternity will lead to child support responsibilities being imposed on him.

No Facts in Dispute?

The case of *Department of Public Aid ex rel. Vicki Galbraith v. Jeff Jones* (see Case 6.1) substantively deals with a paternity claim. Procedurally, this case provides a good explanation of the legal standard by which a court may grant a summary judgment motion. A **summary judgment motion** claims that there is a ***prima facie*** case, which is Latin for *there are no facts in dispute,* because both parties agree to all the pertinent facts of the case. If a summary judgment motion is denied, the case continues to be litigated. This case also provides an excellent explanation of what is considered *clear and convincing evidence* when dealing with a question of paternity. **Clear and convincing evidence** is stronger evidence than a *preponderance of the evidence,* but not as strong as *beyond a reasonable doubt.* **Preponderance of the evidence** is defined as the greater weight of evidence, not as to quantity of evidence, but as to quality: Meaning, believability, and the more important facts have been proved. **Beyond a reasonable doubt** is the level of proof required to convict a person of a crime. It does not necessarily mean that the court or jury is 100 percent convinced, but it comes close to that meaning.

DNA Wins over Vasectomy

The Pennsylvania case of *Kesselring v. Kesselring* (see Case 6.2), clearly shows that DNA is mightier than a vasectomy when a putative father attempts to extricate himself from paternity and child support. Describing a man as a **putative father** is an alternate way of saying *presumed* father. In this case, Mr. Kesselring was the putative father because he was married to Mrs. Kesselring when she became pregnant and gave birth.

Biological Father Battles Presumed Father

The status of a presumed father is so strong in California that one trial court reviewed scientific evidence that appeared to clearly determine that the biological father was not the mother's husband, and *still* decided in favor of the presumed father over the almost-certain biological father. In the case of *J.W.T.* (see Case 6.3), the court used the term *prima facie,* which is a Latin term that translates literally as *on the face of it.* A *prima facie* case is a case that one party will win because the evidence so clearly supports it—unless the other side comes forward with evidence to disprove it. As you read the *J.W.T.* case, note how the court used the term *prima facie.*

CASE 6.1 *Department of Public Aid ex rel. Vicki Galbraith v. Jeff Jones,* 666 N.E.2d 12, 216 Ill. Dec. 844 (1996)

Facts: The Department of Public Aid is involved in this case because the Department filed a petition to request a Chicago court to declare that Jeff Jones was the father of Vicki Galbraith's baby boy, K.G., born February 3, 1993. The Department filed the petition because the state might have to carry the burden of supporting Vicki's son if the father fails to do so. The Department's initial trial-level petition to the court requested via a *summary judgment motion* that the court declare Jeff the father and order child support payments. The summary judgment motion was won by the Department, and Jeff decided to appeal.

Jeff's main argument on appeal was that the summary judgment was improper because there still were facts in dispute. These facts included the following: (1) Jeff alleged he had not had sexual relations with Vicki for two years prior to K.G.'s birth; (2) Jeff alleged Vicki had told him she slept with a man named Trokey; and (3) Jeff alleged Vicki had told him she'd slept with Trokey around the time of conception. Jeff failed to convince the trial court and was found to be the father of the child in question. He appealed again.

Issue: Whether respondent's rebuttal evidence as set forth in his affidavit and interrogatories was clear and convincing enough to disprove the paternity claim.

Court's Reasoning: It should be noted that attached to the Department's Motion for Summary Judgment were the results of the court-ordered blood tests, which revealed a combined paternity index of 611 to 1 and a probability of paternity of 99.84%. Also attached to the Motion for Summary Judgment was the affidavit of Vicki Galbraith, which stated: (1) She was the mother of K.G.; (2) she became pregnant with K.G. between May 9 and May 18, 1992; and (3) she had sexual relations only with the respondent between April 27, 1992, and June 2, 1992. The respondent generally denied paternity, but also gave some inconsistent statements regarding whether he had sexual relations with the child's mother during the probable time of conception. The respondent testified that he was sterile *without providing any evidence.* The trial court reasoned that a presumption of paternity existed due to a combined paternity index of 611 to 1, but also that the respondent failed to present any rebuttal evidence that was more than speculation, let alone clear and convincing.

During this appeal, the respondent did present some rebuttal evidence generally denying paternity, and indicating that Galbraith admitted having sexual relations with another man soon after the time of conception. The respondent's affidavit also indicated that Galbraith told him the father of the child was a man other than himself. This evidence fails to constitute the clear and convincing evidence necessary to rebut the presumption of paternity.

Galbraith's affidavit states she had sexual relations exclusively with the respondent from April 27, 1992, to June 2, 1992. Galbraith did not deny having sexual relations with Trokey, but she claimed those occasions happened soon after she was pregnant, between June 7, 1992, through July 1, 1992. The respondent does not deny that the date of probable conception given by Galbraith is correct, nor does he deny the accuracy of the time of commencement of the relationship between Trokey and Galbraith. The respondent has presented no evidence to indicate that the time of conception could have been during the time Galbraith was seeing Trokey. Apparently, the respondent was given several continuances to attempt to locate Trokey but was unable to do so. Without some evidence to support his claim that Trokey could be the father of the child, the respondent has failed to rebut the presumption of paternity.

Holding: Affirmed.

Case Discussion: Does it seem to you that paternity claims are all about science today? The respondent took blood tests, but today he would have taken a DNA test. Can you imagine the type of evidence that had to be presented to the court before DNA testing became available? The respondent's failure to find Trokey and have him either volunteer or be court-ordered to complete a paternity test was really the undoing of his case.

CASE 6.2 *Kesselring v. Kesselring,*
455 Pa. Super. 57, 686 A.2d 1343 (1996)

Facts: Mr. Kesselring had a vasectomy prior to his wife becoming pregnant. Some time later, the Kesselrings decided to divorce. Mr. Kesselring then filed a complaint to determine the paternity of his wife's child and to argue the amount of child support payments.

Issues: (1) Whether the presumption of legitimacy clearly and convincingly is overcome by evidence that the mother's husband had undergone a vasectomy. (2) Whether the child's actual expenses determine the amount of child support.

Court's Reasoning: The DNA tests revealed a 99.9% probability that the appellant was the father of the appellee's son. The appellant is clearly paying more than reasonable expenses. However, the court finds that it was not until he was faced with divorce and child support that the putative father raised the issue of paternity. Further, the court, finding both the timing and the argument to be weak, decided there was not clear and convincing evidence to disprove paternity.

On the issue of child support, we find that Mr. Kesselring was paying more than reasonable expenses.

Holding: Mr. Kesselring loses.

Case Discussion: If DNA testing was not available, do you think Mrs. Kesselring may have lost this case? The DNA testing was invaluable in proving Mr. Kesselring's paternity. Without the DNA results, the proof that Mr. Kesselring had had a vasectomy might have convinced the court that the child was not biologically connected to Mr. Kesselring. This case demonstrates that vasectomies are not foolproof.

CHAPTER SUMMARY

Historically, illegitimate children and their parents were dealt with harshly by the legal system and society. The Uniform Parentage Act of 1973, revised in 2000 and 2002, was successful in large part due to a series of United States Supreme Court decisions invalidating state inheritance, custody, and tort laws that put children of unmarried parents at a disadvantage. The UPA (all versions) has firmly established a set of rules for presumption of parentage, shunned the term *illegitimate,* and employed the term *child with no presumed father.*

All 50 states are required under federal law to have statutory guidelines for determining paternity. Registries of paternity allow a father to register his claim of being the biological father of a child. The terms used to identify a father may include *acknowledged father, presumed father, putative father,* or *adjudicated father.* All 50 states are required under Title IV to follow federal guidelines in providing the legal mechanism for pursuing child support both within and outside a claimant's state of residence.

The primary test used for proving paternity is the deoxyribonucleic acid test generally known as the DNA test. The DNA test is 99.8 conclusive. Scientifically speaking, the paternity of a child can be disproved only by genetic testing, and nothing less. The majority of states shift the burden of disproving

CASE 6.3 *In the Interest of J.W.T., a minor child,* **945 S.W.2d 911 (1997)**

Facts: While living together, Larry G. and Judy T. conceived a child. Though still married to her husband, Randy T., Judy intended to marry Larry after her divorce and to raise the child with Larry. Judy and Randy T. reconciled and withdrew their divorce action. Larry brought an action alleging his paternity, acknowledging responsibility for child support payments, and requesting a judicial declaration of paternity and recognition of visitation rights prior to the child's birth. After the child's birth, a court order was issued to have all parties submit to scientific paternity testing. The results showed a 99.41% probability that Larry G. was the biological father, but the trial court still determined Randy T. to be the child's father. Larry G. appealed the trial court's decision.

Issues: (1) Whether a positive paternity test is sufficient evidence to support a legal standing requirement for a lawsuit. (2) Whether a burden is placed upon the mother and her husband to prove the paternity of the putative father.

Court's Reasoning: Since the paternity test clearly and convincingly establishes a *prima facie* fact of paternity of the alleged father, the paternity test is sufficient to support the legal standing requirement for a lawsuit. The assumption that a child born during a marriage is the result of marital relations can be disputed only with clear and convincing evidence. Paternity tests excluding the putative father's paternity and including another's paternity shifts the burden to the mother and putative father to prove his paternity.

Holding: The Court of Appeals determines the evidence from the paternity testing to conclusively establish the putative father's paternity and remands to the lower court.

Case Discussion: Do you agree with the appellate court's decision to remand the case back to the trial court to give Judy and Randy T. an opportunity to prove that the child in question was their biological child? Does it seem to you that with the obvious results of the DNA test available, the remanding of the case is needlessly time-consuming? Do you think that the presumed father, that is, the spouse of the biological mother, should automatically be assumed to be the father in order to respect the sanctity of the marriage?

paternity to a defendant who refuses to take a DNA test. A father may also file a voluntary acknowledgment of paternity.

Individual states have their own requirements for determining parental rights for fathers. These approaches that states take vary from pro-family (biology is not as important as marital status and the presumed father's role in a child's life) to pro-biology (biological connection is of paramount importance). Each state allows the filing of a Complaint or Petition for Paternity to have a court make an official determination of paternity. The result of a positive decision can include a determination of parentage, with a birth certificate being issued, and recovery of expenses for the birth of the child, child support, and attorneys' fees and costs.

Key Terms

paternity
illegitimate
intestacy laws
equal protection clause
DNA test
Uniform Interstate Family
    Support Act (UIFSA)
registries of paternity

acknowledged father
presumed father
adjudicated father
Uniform Reciprocal
    Enforcement of Support
    Act (URESA)
complaint for paternity
acknowledgment of paternity

parentage registry
termination of parental rights
summary judgment motion
prima facie
clear and convincing evidence
preponderance of the evidence
beyond a reasonable doubt
putative father

Surfing the Web

http://www.nccusl.org Electronic version of UPA (2002).

http://www.aaml.org This American Academy of Matrimonial Lawyers Web site contains the model paternity statute.

http://www.paternityinfo.com The source for paternity laws.

http://www.paternitytestingassociates.com Check this site for information on paternity testing and DNA testing.

http://www.dnacenter.com For further information on paternity testing, surf this site.

http://www.dnatestingusa.com Do your children not look alike? Click here to find out how you can obtain a paternity test to prove they have the same father.

http://www.lawsource.com To find information on the uniform state laws, check here.

ETHICS ALERT

Michelle decides she does not want to use Susan's law firm because the hourly fees are more than she can afford. Instead, Michelle has found a law firm that charges a lot less. The law firm employs paralegals to handle the filing of paperwork, and then sends clients off to represent themselves *pro se*. Michelle is thrilled that the paralegal seems really happy to help. Apparently, the paralegal who answered the phone when Michelle called will get a *cut of the fee charged to Michelle for bringing in Michelle's business.* Does this arrangement seem like a good idea to you? You may want to review the *NALA Model Standards and Guidelines* in Appendix B to answer this ethical dilemma.

Review Questions

1. Historically, how were the children of unmarried parents treated by the American legal system?
2. What genetic test provides paternity results?
3. How was the equal protection clause applied by the United States Supreme Court in the landmark *Levy* case?
4. Why was the *Levy* case so important?
5. What was the first somewhat successful uniform paternity legislation?
6. What is the purpose of the registries of paternity?
7. What is an acknowledged father?
8. (a) What is a presumed father? (b) What is a putative father? (c) What is an adjudicated father?
9. Since January 1998, the federal government has required each state to adopt what act?
10. What would you include in the typical paternity complaint?

Endnotes

1. "Exploring Paternity Issues" (seminar, New Jersey Institute for Continuing Legal Education, March 22, 2003).
2. *Levy v. Louisiana,* 391 U.S. 68 (1968).
3. Gutendorf, Robert W., "DNA Testing and Gene Screen" (Exploring Paternity Issues seminar, New Jersey Institute for Continuing Legal Education, March 22, 2003).
4. CAL. FAM. CODE ANN. ch. 2, § 7611 (2003).
5. TEX. FAM. CODE ANN. ch. 207, § 160 (Vernon 2003).
6. ILL. STAT. ch. 750, § 45-11 (2003).
7. FLA. STAT. § 63.053 (2003).
8. GeneScreen, Dayton, Ohio.
9. 42 U.S.C. § 666(a)(5)(D)(iii) (2003).
10. *Lehr v. Robinson,* 463 U.S. 248 (1983).
11. *Michael H. v. Gerald D.,* 110 S. Ct. 22, 105 L. Ed. 2d 91 (1989).
12. *Stanley v. Illinois,* 405 U.S. 645, 92 S. Ct. 1208, 31 L. Ed. 2d 551 (1972).

Chapter 7

Adoption

THE PURPOSE OF ADOPTION

A family unit can consist of people with no biological connection to one another. One way this happens is through adoption. **Adoption** is the formal, voluntary process by which adults are legally declared as parents of children who are not their own. American families adopt more than 40,000 children into their homes each year.[1] Adoption law can be traced back to 285 B.C. in the Babylonian Code of Hammurabi. The primary purpose of adoption in the Code of Hammurabi was to meet the needs of prospective parents. The opposite is true today. The intended purpose of adoptions today is to meet the needs of the child who is being adopted. American adoptions are conducted in a staggering number of ways. However, the needs of the child should always be the primary focus, regardless of how an adoption is conducted.

Types of Adoption

During the mid-twentieth century, the majority of adoptions were conducted through adoption agencies. This is no longer true. Now less than half of all adoptions are conducted through agencies.[2] If an adoption *is* done through an agency, the agency may be either a public or a private adoption agency. A **public adoption agency** is supported by tax dollars and is responsible for the adoption of all children under the guardianship of the child's home county or state of residence. A **private adoption agency** is supported by the fees it collects and donations. However, both public and private agencies must be licensed by the state to conduct adoptions. The courts usually place children with agencies following either voluntary parental surrender of parental rights or the involuntary termination of the parental rights of a child's biological parents. The act of surrendering parental rights to another is known as **relinquishment.** Termination of parental rights occur until after a court hearing in which the parents are given an opportunity to contest the termination.

International adoption is typically handled through an agency. An **international adoption** occurs when the child and the adoptive parents are from two different countries. Legal work through immigration services must be done in order to authorize an international adoption.

The independent adoption is a form of adoption being used by a growing number of people. In the case of an **independent adoption,** the biological mother often creates the requirements she wants met by the adoptive parents of her child. Often the birth mother then places her child *directly* with the adoptive parents. This type of adoption is also known as an **identified, designated**, or **collaborative adoption.** The biological mother's requirements must be within the guidelines mandated by each individual state's adoption statutes, and the adoption (like *all* adoptions) must be finalized by a judge.

The manner in which adoptions are conducted has changed over the years. Agencies used to arrange primarily closed adoptions. A **closed adoption** is an adoption whereby the adoptive parents and the biological parents do not know each other's identity. Additionally, the closed adoption does not allow information about the adopted child and the biological parents to be given to either of them. Today, the open adoption concept is much more prevalent.

Open adoption is typically an adoption whereby the biological parents and the adoptive parents meet each other and exchange information. Legislatures in almost all states now have statutes that specifically allow the release of information to adoptive children and their biological parents. This information is usually nonidentifying. Some states have opened mutual registries for adoptive children and biological parents who are interested in identifying each other. Mutual agreement is necessary before any information can be released. A small number of open adoptions also allow for continued limited involvement of the biological parents in the life of the adopted child. One open adoption concept is kinship adoption. **Kinship adoption** is a form of adoption where the adoptive parents are biologically related to the child to be adopted (e.g., grandparents, uncle and aunt, or other relatives).

In this chapter, Alyssa and Susan become an integral part of one couple's personal quest to adopt a child through an independent and open adoption.

THE STORY OF AN ADOPTION

Lauren and James Mahoney married in their late 30s and have been happily married for nine years. Their happiness, however, has been marred by the fact that they have tried unsuccessfully to have a child. Following years of expensive fertility treatments, the Mahoneys have decided adoption is the only answer left for them. The Mahoneys are both fitness buffs and quite healthy, but many adoption agencies have rules limiting the age of prospective adoptive parents. The Mahoneys are concerned about working with either a private or a public agency because these rules often cut off prospective adoptive parents over 40. Even though the Mahoneys may be the happiest and most well-adjusted and financially secure couple to arrive at an agency's door in years, most agencies would abide by the age-restrictive rules. An independent adoption is probably the best opportunity for a couple like the Mahoneys, since independent adoptions typically have few rules that are "carved in stone."[3]

The Mahoneys have decided to present their story to an attorney at the Johnson & Webster law firm because they have heard through friends that the firm has handled quite a few successful adoptions. The Mahoneys scheduled their appointment with Alyssa Jensen as soon as they made the decision to ask an attorney for help. On the morning of their appointment, Alyssa announced to Susan that prospective new clients were coming in for a consultation regarding an adoption.

Surprised, Susan commented, "I didn't think you handled adoptions anymore."

"Actually, we do still handle adoptions—but, as you've seen in the last month, the real meat and potatoes of our practice is divorce," Alyssa explained. "Often, we can't facilitate an adoption because there just aren't that many infants available to our clients. Plus, clients often come to our office with a preconceived picture of the child they wish to adopt."

"You mean they come to you asking for a 'child with my husband's blue eyes and my hair coloring?'" Susan asked.

"Exactly. Unfortunately, I haven't been too successful at matching a client's mental picture with an available child," Alyssa lamented.

"What do you need me to help with?" Susan inquired. She was curious to see how this kind of thing was handled.

Alyssa explained that a form questionnaire was used to create a file for clients wanting to adopt, and that the answers were used to create an interesting ad and Web site.

The mention of the Web site made Susan decidedly cautious. "I hope *I'm* not going to be expected to create Web sites for new clients. Am I?" she asked with trepidation. "I'm just now getting up to speed with our computer system!"

"We *have* sort of expected a lot out of you so soon—but no, we subcontract the creation of the Web site to an independent consultant," Alyssa laughingly assured Susan. "Don't worry. I'll do the initial interview and introduce you once I've explained about the ad and the Web site. I want you to ask them the questions on the Web site questionnaire." Alyssa added, "By the way, we usually don't do the ad or Web site when clients are willing to go outside the United States for a child because foreign infants are more available. "So, you may be off the hook. Just remember that adoption is a many-step process, both legally and emotionally."

Susan inquired, "Now, I'm really interested. What do you consider those steps?"

Alyssa seemed pleased at Susan's interest. She answered, "There are essentially three steps in the adoption process. The first stage is identifying a child who is in need of adoption and the prospective parents for that child. The second stage is ensuring that all the legal requirements are met for terminating the existing parental rights. The third stage has very little to do with us. It's the successful incorporation of the child into her new family."[4]

Last Hope for First-Time Clients?

Later that same day, the Mahoneys met with Alyssa and shared their problem with her. "So, you see, Ms. Jensen," Lauren Mahoney concluded, "You and your firm really are our last hope for adopting a child."

Alyssa had patiently listened to the Mahoneys tell the story of their lengthy struggle to have children, but now she was uncomfortable with being described as their "last hope," especially when the couple was looking for an American child. Alyssa did not like the odds of trying to adopt only inside the United States. "Well, I appreciate both of you being so honest with me," Alyssa told the couple. "And I'm going to be just as honest in return." Taking a deep breath, she began, "I'd love to tell you that I know definitely how a happily married, loving, and financially secure couple can be *guaranteed* a child, but the odds aren't good." The Mahoneys looked crushed, so Alyssa quickly added, "Look, I'm not saying it's impossible, but you simply must go into this with realistic expectations."

"Can't you do anything to help us?" Jim Mahoney pleaded. "The public and private agencies have either restricted us or placed us lower on their lists because of our age."

"Well, yes," Alyssa said. "Our firm deals with *independent* adoption, which means that the biological parents have much more to say about who the adoptive parents will be." She continued, "For example, an adoptive mother might not care that you're both in your late 40s; she may, instead, look at your maturity, readiness, and financial security."

The Mahoneys' faces had perceptively brightened. "What's next?" they asked together.

"I'd like to put together a file on both of you," Alyssa answered. "My paralegal, Susan, will assist by asking you both some questions, creating an ad, and gathering the information and photographs for a Web site, if you agree."

"What goes into the ad and Web site?" Jim asked excitedly.

"They're designed to attract expecting parents who are thinking about adoption," explained Alyssa. "They include your description of yourselves and your lifestyle. You have an opportunity to explain why you'd make great parents and how their child would have a wonderful life with you—things like that."

Still disappointed, Lauren asked, "So, you don't have a list of babies waiting for adoption?"

Alyssa shook her head, "I'm afraid not, but we *have* had some success attracting expecting parents because we support biological parents who want to have as open an adoption as possible. Would you have a problem with the biological parents knowing who you are?"

Lauren and Jim looked at each other. Answering for both, Lauren declared, "Jim and I have spoken about this. We'd understand a biological parent's desire to know who their baby's parents were going to be. We would even provide photographs for the parents if they wished to see pictures of the child growing up. But, what we *don't* want is the biological parents showing up at birthday parties."

Nodding, Alyssa responded, "That's totally understandable. Most biological parents don't want to keep that tight a connection either, after making such a hard decision as adoption." She brought the meeting to a close with a review and the signing of a retainer agreement, and then introduced the Mahoneys to Susan.

Susan Interviews the Mahoneys

"Mr. and Mrs. Mahoney, I'd like you to meet our paralegal Susan," Alyssa stated, motioning toward Susan.

Trying her best to sound like she had been creating Web sites for years, Susan shook hands with the Mahoneys and said, "It's nice to meet you. I'm looking forward to gathering the information that will make your Web site outstanding. We've set the conference room aside for our interview." Saying good-bye to Alyssa, the Mahoneys followed Susan to the conference room.

"What I'd like to do is ask you some questions about your life together," Susan began. "Can you explain why you wish to adopt?"

Lauren looked at Jim, so he answered. "We've been happy together for years and know in our hearts that we can provide a child with much love and stability."

Lauren smiled and continued, "We have many great years ahead of us, and we want our child to know that life can be a wonderful, joyful experience."

Susan was starting to think that any child would be lucky to have these two nice people for parents. Smiling back, she asked, "What would a typical day be like once you adopted a child?"

Lauren was quick to answer, "Well, first, we've decided that I would take a leave of absence from my job. Next, I'd have to say there wouldn't be a typical day because there isn't anything typical about a baby. For example, if the baby discovered a fascinating butterfly or how wonderfully his toes worked, then we'd spend the time following the butterfly or playing footsie."

Jim smiled at his wife and added, "Part of being more mature is having the patience we may not have had at 25."

Susan asked several more questions about their lifestyle, hobbies, friends, and family. The information would help her write copy that would best reflect the Mahoneys. "Well, that should do it for now," Susan said. "Do you have any questions?"

Lauren asked, "How long do you think it might take to get a response?"

Susan remembered Alyssa's comments on the difficulty of adoption. She stated, "I'm sorry to say, the process really can't be put on a timeline." As the Mahoneys got up to leave, Susan offered her hand and said, "I hope we'll be able to call you soon." She really meant it, too.

Will the Stork Deliver to a Law Office?

A law office may not be the first place a couple visits when they want to have a child, but attorneys and their staffs are a resource for couples who wish to become parents through adoption. As a paralegal working in a law firm handling adoptions, you may experience, right along with clients, the emotional highs and lows that are inherent in the adoption process.

While attorneys can help make dreams come true for childless couples by locating expectant mothers who wish to place their children for adoption, there *can* be problems. Unfortunately, an emotional high point can become an emotional low point when an apparently smooth adoption is interrupted because a biological mother has changed her mind and wants to keep her child. This kind of emotional rollercoaster is part of everyday life at law firms that handle adoptions.

An attorney should come into the picture when there is no agency to guide the adoption through the legal system. Attorneys vary in terms of the role they play in an adoption, but most of them enlist support from their paralegals. Some attorneys concentrate only on preparing legal papers and representing parents at adoption hearings once prospective adoptive parents have found biological parents willing to have their child adopted. Sometimes attorneys are instrumental in finding available children for prospective adoptive clients. These attorneys, through their contacts with physicians or agencies, help expectant mothers find biological parents who are willing to place their child for adoption. Like Alyssa, they may place ads and create Web sites.

An attorney often handles the details of any financial support that is given to the biological mother by the prospective adoptive parents. State laws place limits on how much financial support a biological mother may receive from prospective adoptive parents. A parent who agrees to her child's adoption for profit commits a criminal act, as do adoptive parents who agree to pay a biological mother an amount that is beyond the state limits. An attorney who is involved with such payments also commits a criminal act. Attorneys must ensure that state laws are strictly followed.

Generally, state courts require that a record of all financial support given to the biological mother by the adoptive parents be provided to the court before the adoption can be finalized. This is a safeguard against adoptions that amount to no more than the purchase of a child. Financial support is generally considered legally permissible if it is given to assist with costs relating to the mother's pregnancy. Some states do not allow the mother's prebirth living expenses to be paid on the basis that providing living expenses gives the appearance that the child is being purchased.

All 50 states have statutory requirements to follow when dealing with an adoption. Exhibit 7.1 lists the state statutes you may refer to when beginning your research on your state's statutory adoption requirements.

Meanwhile . . . Back with the Mahoneys

The Mahoneys are glad they made the decision to defy the odds and try to adopt a child. Alyssa carefully explained the legal requirements for, and possible problems involved in, an independent adoption so that the Mahoneys could make an informed decision. Through her contacts and the Web site created with the answers provided to Susan during the Mahoneys' interview, Alyssa has now located an unmarried biological mother who wishes to have her child adopted by a loving and responsible couple. After months of waiting and telephoning Susan frequently to check on whether there were any leads, the Mahoneys may now be able to fulfill their dream.

The meeting between the Mahoneys and the biological mother, a 19-year-old college student named Amy Sinclair, convinced Amy to consent to the adoption of her soon-to-be-born child. Amy and her 18-year-old boyfriend, Larry Smith, believe the best thing for their child is adoption. They both want to finish their education, and neither Amy nor Larry has family that can help with the financial and emotional support they would need to raise a child. While still adhering to their state's adoption guidelines, the Mahoneys have agreed to pay Amy's living expenses and all of her medical bills. Amy and Larry have agreed to let the Mahoneys take the baby home directly from the hospital.

The Mahoneys Take the Required Steps

The Mahoneys learned firsthand that once an adoption decision is made, a number of legal requirements must be met. The statutory requirements of the state in which the adoption will occur should always be followed. As discussed, each state provides specific requirements regarding the biological mother's and father's consent, as well as limitations on what financial support a biological mother and father may receive from the adoptive parents.

In order for the Mahoneys' adoption to go forward, a **petition for adoption** must be filed with the county in which the adoption will occur. Generally, and the Mahoneys' case is no different, most states require the following: (1) name and address of the biological mother; (2) a statement that the biological mother consents to the adoption; (3) name and address of the adoptive parents; (4) a statement that the

---

EXHIBIT 7.1 Beginning Your Adoption Research

State	Where You May Begin	State	Where You May Begin
Alabama	ALA CODE § 26-10A-7 (2003)	Montana	MONT. CODE § 42-1-102 (2003)
Alaska	ALASKA STAT. § 25.23 (2003)	Nebraska	NEB. REV. STAT. § 43-101 (2003)
Arizona	ARIZ. REV. STAT. ANN. § 8 (2003)	Nevada	NEV. REV. STAT. § 127.230 (2003)
Arkansas	ARK. CODE ANN. § 9-9 (Michie 2003)	New Hampshire	N.H. REV. STAT. § E:25 (2003)
California	CAL. FAM. CODE § 222.20 (2003)	New Jersey	N.J. STAT. ANN. § 9:3-38 (2003)
Colorado	COLO. REV. STAT. § 19-5 (2003)	New Mexico	N.M. STAT. ANN. § 32A-5-3 (Michie 2003)
Connecticut	CONN. GEN. STAT. § 45a-725 (2003)	New York	N.Y. SOC. SERV. § 372-f (McKinney 2003)
Delaware	DEL. CODE tit. 13, § 902 (2003)	North Carolina	N.C. GEN. STAT. § 48-2-206 (2003)
District of Columbia	D.C. CODE ANN. § 4-114 (2003)	North Dakota	N.D. CENT. CODE tit. 14, ch. 15, § 01 (2003)
Florida	FLA. STAT. § 63.172 (2003)	Ohio	OHIO REV. CODE ANN. § 3107.68 (2003)
Georgia	GA. CODE ANN. § 19 (2003)	Oklahoma	OKLA. STAT. ANN. tit. 10 § 7501.2 (2003)
Hawaii	HAW. REV. STAT. § 578-1 (2003)	Oregon	OR. REV. STAT. § 309 (2003)
Idaho	IDAHO CODE § 16-1501 (2003)	Pennsylvania	PA. CONS. STAT. § 2535 (2003)
Illinois	ILL. REV. STAT. ch. 750, para. 850/8 (2003)	Rhode Island	R.I. GEN LAWS § 15-7.2-2 (2003)
Indiana	IND. CODE § 31-19-12 (2003)	South Carolina	S.C. CODE ANN.§ 20-7-1650 (2003)
Iowa	IOWA CODE § 600 (2003)	South Dakota	S.D. CODIFIED LAW ANN. § 25-12 (2003)
Kansas	KAN. STAT. ANN. § 59-2112 (2003)	Tennessee	TENN. CODE ANN. § 36-1-102 (2003)
Kentucky	KY. REV. STAT. ANN. § 199.01 (2003)	Texas	TEX. FAM. CODE ANN. § 162.005 (2003)
Louisiana	LA. REV. STAT. ANN. ch. C., art. 281.7 (2003)	Utah	UTAH CODE ANN. § 78-3–4.13 (2003)
Maine	ME. REV. STAT. ANN. tit. 18-A, § 9-313 (2003)	Vermont	VT. STAT. ANN tit. 15A, § 2-401 (2003)
Maryland	MD. CODE ANN. FAM. LAW § 85-301 (2003)	Virginia	VA. CODE ANN. § 63.2-1200 (2003)
Massachusetts	MASS. GEN. L. ch. 210, § 6 D (2003)	Washington	WASH. REV. CODE ANN. § 26.33.090 (2003)
Michigan	MICH. COMP. LAWS § 700.2114 (2003)	West Virginia	W. VA. CODE § 48-4-1 (2003)
Minnesota	MINN. STAT. § 259.21 (2003)	Wisconsin	WIS. STAT. ANN. § 48.434 (2003)
Mississippi	MISS. CODE ANN. § 93-17 (2003)	Wyoming	WYO. STAT. § 1-22-109 (2003)
Missouri	MO. REV. STAT. § 453.090 (2003)		

---

adoptive parents intend to adopt the child; (5) name and address of the biological father, if known; (6) a statement that proper notice has been given to the father and whether he has consented to the adoption; (7) name, birth date, and birth location of the child; (8) notification made to any social services agencies involved in the matter; and (9) a certification by the adoptive parents that all of their statements are true. You can read the Mahoneys' fairly typical Petition for Adoption in Exhibit 7.2.

Along with the petition for adoption, Susan has prepared other necessary documents. In Susan's jurisdiction, Amy Sinclair's judicial surrender and an affidavit from Larry Smith also need to be prepared. The **judicial surrender** states the biological parent's intention to have her child adopted. The **affidavit** states the biological father's intention and approval of the adoption. The names of the documents differ, depending on the jurisdiction, but the necessity and intention of the documents are the same in all adoption cases. You can read Amy Sinclair's Judicial Surrender and Larry Smith's Affidavit in Exhibit 7.3 and Exhibit 7.4, respectively. Exhibit 7.5 shows the **Notice** to Larry Smith of the upcoming hearing, and Exhibit 7.6 contains the order for a preliminary and final hearing of adoption.

Typically, a preliminary hearing is held by a judge. This hearing gives both the biological and the adoptive parents an opportunity to appear in court, although they may choose not to do so. Careful attention must be given to seeing that the biological parents receive adequate notice of the preliminary hearing. The

EXHIBIT 7.2 The Mahoneys' Petition for Adoption

Alyssa Jensen, Esq.
Johnson & Webster, Esqs.
123 Main Street
Newton, New Jersey 12345
973-555-1212
Attorney for Petitioners

In the Matter of AN ADOPTION BY JAMES MAHONEY AND LAUREN MAHONEY, HIS WIFE.	)))))))))	SUPERIOR COURT OF NEW JERSEY CHANCERY DIVISION-FAMILY PART SUSSEX COUNTY Docket No. 2003-1234 CIVIL ACTION COMPLAINT FOR ADOPTION

Petitioners, James Mahoney and Lauren Mahoney, his wife, state:

1. The subject of this Petition is a male child, Samuel Sinclair, born on April 7, 2003, at St. Chilton's Hospital, Maytown, New Jersey.

2. It is the intention of the biological mother, Amy Sinclair, to consent to the adoption of Samuel Sinclair by the Petitioners.

3. The Petitioners, James Mahoney and Lauren Mahoney, husband and wife, reside at 56 Side Street, Maytown, County of Sussex and State of New Jersey. They are emotionally and financially able to fulfill the needs of the minor child, Samuel Sinclair, and intend to treat the minor child as their own child for all purposes.

4. The biological father, Larry Smith, has been duly notified of the intention of the Petitioners to adopt Samuel Sinclair and consents to the adoption of Samuel Sinclair by the Petitioners.

5. It is in the best interests of the minor child, Samuel Sinclair, that this court approves of his adoption by the Petitioners.

6. Petitioners have fulfilled all requirements for the adoption with the Department of Human Services, County of Sussex, State of New Jersey.

7. The child to be adopted has no property.

WHEREFORE,

Petitioners respectfully request this court to grant the adoption of the minor child, Samuel Sinclair, by the Petitioners. Hereafter the minor child shall be known as James Mahoney, Jr., and shall have all the legal rights and provileges of a child who is the legal relation of the Petitioners.

Certification

James Mahoney and Lauren Mahoney do solemnly swear that we are the petitioners in the above Petition of Adoption. We have read the above Petition and attest to the truthfulness of the Petition. We attest to the truthfulness under penalty of perjury. Sworn and signed the 25th day of March, 2003, in Sparta, New Jersey.

_____ Lauren Mahoney	_____ James Mahoney

EXHIBIT 7.3 Amy Sinclair's Judicial Surrender

Alyssa Jensen, Esq.
Johnson & Webster, Esqs.
123 Main Street
Newton, New Jersey 12345
973-555-1212
Attorney for Petitioners

In the Matter of THE ADOPTION OF A CHILD BY JAMES MAHONEY AND LAUREN MAHONEY, HUSBAND AND WIFE.	)))))))	SUPERIOR COURT OF NEW JERSEY CHANCERY DIVISION-FAMILY PART SUSSEX COUNTY Docket No. 2003-1234 CIVIL ACTION JUDICIAL SURRENDER

1. I, Amy Sinclair, residing at 199 College Crest, Hootenville, NJ, birth mother of Samuel Sinclair, do hereby consent to the adoption of my son, Samuel Sinclair, born on April 7, 2003, at St. Chilton's Hospital, Maytown, New Jersey, by James Mahoney and Lauren Mahoney.

2. I am unable to care for my child, Samuel Sinclair. I feel that it is in his best interests for him to be placed with the adoptive parents for the purpose of adoption.

3. I have been advised that the surrender becomes irrevocable when executed or acknowledged before a Judge, and therefore no action or proceeding may be maintained by me for the custody of the child. I recognize and understand that my parental rights are hereby terminated as to the child in favor of the adoptive parents. I do this knowingly, voluntarily, and of my own free will.

4. I understand that by termination of my rights in favor of the adoptive parents, I will have no rights in, or authority over, the child. I understand the adoptive parents will have full authority and control over the child, with the ability to make decisions about medical, legal, and social matters concerning the child, including the future maintenance, keeping, care, and education of the child.

5. I have been fully apprised of my rights and all alternatives to adoption, and I fully understand these rights. I have been offered the option of counseling through a licensed adoption agency and have declined the same. I understand and recognize that under the laws of the State of New Jersey, once I execute and sign this surrender, I will receive no further notification of the filing of a Complaint for Adoption or of any court proceedings or hearings in regard to the adoption. I know that by signing this document I am voluntarily waiving and giving up my right to be notified of any legal proceedings in regard to the adoption.

6. I understand that under the laws of the State of New Jersey this surrender is valid and binding. I understand that this termination of parental rights and surrender of custody will be recognized by the State of New Jersey and be binding upon me.

7. I am not under the influence of alcohol, medication, or illegal drugs. I am competent and fully understand this Surrender and its contents.

8. I have also been advised that before I acknowledge or execute this Surrender, I have the right to be represented by a lawyer of my choosing, and, if I am financially unable to obtain the same, a lawyer will be assigned at public cost.

DATED: _____

_____
Amy Sinclair

STATE OF NEW JERSEY	)
	) SS.
COUNTY OF SUSSEX	)

On this _____day of April, 2003, before me personally came Amy Sinclair, the person described in and who executed the foregoing instrument, and she acknowledged that she executed the same. I am satisfied that such a person has been appraised of her rights, has executed this Surrender willfully and voluntarily, and understands that the same is irrevocable upon execution and permanently affects her parental rights to the child placed for adoption. I have given a copy of this Consent upon the execution thereof.

_____
S. Comfort, J.S.C.
Judge of:

EXHIBIT 7.4 Larry Smith's Affidavit

Alyssa Jensen, Esq.
Johnson & Webster, Esqs.
123 Main Street
Newton, New Jersey 12345
973-555-1212
Attorney for Petitioners

In the Matter of	) SUPERIOR COURT OF NEW JERSEY
THE ADOPTION	) CHANCERY DIVISION-FAMILY PART
OF A CHILD BY JAMES MAHONEY	) SUSSEX COUNTY
AND LAUREN MAHONEY, HUSBAND	) Docket No. 2003-1234
AND WIFE.	) CIVIL ACTION
	)
	) AFFIDAVIT OF LARRY SMITH

LARRY SMITH, being of full age, and duly sworn according to law, upon his oath deposes and says:

1. I am the biological father of Samuel Sinclair, who was born on April 7, 2003, in the Town of Maytown, County of Sussex, and State of New Jersey.

2. Samuel Sinclair's biological mother is Amy Sinclair.

3. I understand a complaint for adoption will be instituted by Mr. and Mrs. Mahoney's counsel, Alyssa Jensen, Esq., upon my execution of this Affidavit.

4. I understand the nature of the relief sought by the Mahoneys, which includes extinguishing forever any and all rights, duties, privileges, and relations which I have, or may ever have, with Samuel Sinclair as his biological father.

5. Ms. Jensen has advised me to consult with an attorney prior to executing this document.

6. After much careful consideration, and believing it to be in the best interests of the child, I do hereby consent to this adoption freely and voluntarily and, further, waive and relinquish any and all rights, duties, privileges, and relations which I have, or may in the future ever have, with Samuel Sinclair.

7. I agree that from the date of the decree of adoption, this child, for all legal intents and purposes, be the child of the person adopting the child and any and all rights, duties, privileges, and relations which I have, or would ever have, with Samuel Sinclair by virtue of being his biological father will forever be extinguished and ended.

_____

Larry Smith

Subscribed and sworn to before
me this _____ day of _____, 2003.

_____
A Notary Public of New Jersey

preliminary hearing is usually an opportunity for the adoptive parents to have the child officially placed at home with them. The next judicial step will be the final hearing. Following the final hearing, the judge will sign the order of adoption, which, will legally declare the Mahoneys the adoptive parents of Amy Sinclair's and Larry Smith's biological child.

Home Sweet Home?—Not Without a Home Study Report

Whether an adoption takes place through a public or a private agency or is an independent adoption, all 50 states require that at least one home study report be conducted after a child has been placed with prospective parents and before the adoption is finalized. This is done to ensure the adoptive child's safety. A **home study report** is usually prepared by a local social services agency after a social worker has interviewed the adoptive parents and visited their home to assess the home environment and the child's acclimation to the family. Agencies often interview the adoptive parents' employers and other references the agencies have requested as well. The social worker usually asks a wide variety of questions of the prospective adoptive parents. The questions concentrate on the prospective parents' attitudes, beliefs, and plans for raising the child.

The majority of states require agency and independent adoptions to go through both a preplacement home study and a post-placement home study. A minority of states require only a post-placement home study in the case of an independent adoption. Since the biological mother usually makes the decision about who will adopt her child in an independent adoption, some states do not require a post-placement home study for fear of treading on the mother's ultimate right to choose her child's adoptive parents.

The Final Hearing for the Mahoneys

Generally, the biological parents do not appear at the final hearing. A social worker from the county typically appears in court to testify that all the proper procedures were followed during the adoption process. For example, the signing of the final order usually cannot be done until the child has lived with the adoptive parents for a statutorily designated period of time. Usually, during this same period, a social worker visits the adopted child in his new home before the final order is signed. Following testimony by the social worker and the adoptive parents, the judge will sign the final order of adoption. Once this is done, an amended birth certificate can be issued reflecting the adoptive parents as the child's legal parents. The Mahoneys' case was typical in that neither of the biological parents attended the final hearing. In fact, both Amy and Larry were back in residence at their respective colleges and attending classes before the final hearing took place. During the hearing, Alyssa questioned the social worker who had visited the Mahoneys' home to assess how the little boy, soon to be legally named James Mahoney, Jr., was acclimating to life with Lauren and James, Sr. The Mahoneys' testimony followed.

Tears of Joy

When Lauren and James Mahoney left the courthouse after the judge signed the final order, their eyes were full of happy tears. As Alyssa bid farewell to the Mahoneys and James, Jr., at the foot of the courthouse stairs, she offered her best wishes to the newly *legal* family. She announced, "I'm so happy I could help to make little James, Jr., a reality, and I know he'll have a wonderful life with both of you."

Fighting back tears, James, Sr., replied, "I never thought I'd appreciate someone's help so much."

Lauren added, "You've changed our lives. We can't thank you and Susan enough."

A little teary-eyed herself, Alyssa responded, "Unlike a lot of what we do, this case was our plea-sure. Susan will be so happy to hear that everything went well today."

Lauren gave James, Jr., a hug and told Alyssa, "We'll invite you to his first birthday party."

EXHIBIT 7.5 Notice to Larry

Alyssa Jensen, Esq.
Johnson & Webster, Esqs.
123 Main Street
Newton, New Jersey 12345
973-555-1212
Attorney for Petitioners

In the Matter of	)	SUPERIOR COURT OF NEW JERSEY
THE ADOPTION OF A CHILD, SAMUEL	)	CHANCERY DIVISION-FAMILY PART
SINCLAIR, BY JAMES AND LAUREN MAHONEY,	)	SUSSEX COUNTY
HUSBAND AND WIFE.	)	Docket No. 2003-1234
	)	CIVIL ACTION
	)	
	)	
	)	NOTICE

TO: Larry Smith
      567 College Crest
      Hootenville, NJ 00000

SIR:

PLEASE TAKE NOTICE that on Tuesday, April 9, 2003, at 9:00 A.M. in the forenoon, at the Sussex County Court House, 4347 High Street, Newton, New Jersey, a hearing will take place in the above-entitled matter wherein the Plaintiff is seeking the adoption of Samuel Sinclair, born on April 7, 2003, in Maytown, New Jersey, and wherein it has been determined that you are the birth father of the child to be adopted; and

TAKE FURTHER NOTICE that you have a right to appear at that hearing and object to the proposed adoption; and

TAKE FURTHER NOTICE that at the hearing on Tuesday, April 9, 2003, the Plaintiff will seek to terminate any parental rights you may have with respect to Samuel Sinclair; and

TAKE FURTHER NOTICE that you have a right to be represented by an attorney at said hearing.

Alyssa Jensen, Esq.
Attorney for Plaintiffs

DATED: April 7, 2003

"Thanks. I'd love it!" exclaimed Alyssa as she got into her car, waved good-bye, and drove off. She thought to herself, "Now this kind of case really makes all our hard work worth it!"

WHAT ARE THE BIOLOGICAL MOTHER'S RIGHTS?

EXHIBIT 7.6 Order for Preliminary and Final Hearing

Alyssa Jensen, Esq.
Johnson & Webster, Esqs.
123 Main Street
Newton, New Jersey 12345
973-555-1212
Attorney for Petitioners

In the Matter of THE ADOPTION OF A CHILD, SAMUEL SINCLAIR, BY JAMES AND LAUREN MAHONEY, HUSBAND AND WIFE.	)))))))))	SUPERIOR COURT OF NEW JERSEY CHANCERY DIVISION-FAMILY PART SUSSEX COUNTY Docket No. 2003-1234 CIVIL ACTION ORDER FOR PRELIMINARY AND FINAL HEARING

A duly verified Complaint in the above matter having been presented by James and Lauren Mahoney for adopting Samuel Sinclair, an infant child, and for changing his name to James Mahoney, Jr., in accordance with the provisions of the Statute:

IT IS on this _____ day of _____, 2003;

ORDERED that the child sought to be adopted shall be a ward of this court and that Plaintiffs, James Mahoney, and his wife, Lauren Mahoney, shall have custody of said child, subject to the further order of this Court; and it is further

ORDERED that the Court requests an agency investigation pursuant to N.J.S.A. 9:3-48, and will take direct evidence at the final hearing of the facts and circumstances surrounding the adoption; and it is further

ORDERED that the biological father, Larry Smith, will be notified via both regular mail and certified mail, return receipt requested, of the date of the hearing.

ORDERED that the _____ day of _____, 2003, at _____ o'clock, before this Court in Newton, New Jersey, be fixed as the date of the preliminary and final hearing in accordance with the Statute.

_____
S. Comfort, J.S.C.

While prospective adoptive parents may suffer deep disappointment when a biological mother changes her mind, the biological mother's right to choose adoption, or not, is one of our country's most important individual constitutional protections. On the other hand, the legal rights of prospective adoptive parents differ slightly in each state. The guidelines for the adoption process are found in the statutes of each state.

In Massachusetts, for example, once a biological mother signs a consent to adoption that is witnessed and notarized, she has given her irrevocable consent to the adoption. The only valid claim the biological mother can then make to retract her consent is to prove that she signed under *fraud* or *duress.* As stated earlier, fraud is any kind of trickery used to cheat another, and duress is unlawful pressure on a person to do what she would not otherwise have done.

Alternatively, North Carolina's statutes provide the biological mother with up to 30 days to change her mind or until the court issues an interlocutory decree of adoption. *Interlocutory* is defined as a provisional or temporary court order. The **interlocutory decree of adoption** precedes a final order of adoption. Following the interlocutory decree, North Carolina's law states that the biological mother's consent is irrevocable, absent fraud or duress.

WHAT ARE THE BIOLOGICAL FATHER'S RIGHTS?

Although all 50 states clearly give the birth mother the right to consent or not to consent to her child's adoption, the father's rights are not as clear-cut. The first step is to determine whether the father is married to the biological mother. If the biological parents are married, there is a presumption that the husband is the father of any child born to the biological mother. (See Chapter 6 on paternity.) This presumption means that, even if the husband is not the father of the child, he *still has a say* in whether the biological child of his wife can be adopted. The husband's consent is required in order to go forward with the adoption.

Consent of the biological father is not always required when he is *not* married to the biological mother. Although most states do give an unmarried biological father the right to be notified of any impending adoption, the right is not automatic. As you may recall from Chapter 6, a majority of the states have paternity registries wherein the burden is placed on the biological unmarried father to register his claim of paternity. The registered father is then provided with notice of an impending adoption, called the notice of alleged paternity. The **notice of alleged paternity** should inform the biological father not only of the upcoming adoption, but also of the date, time, and place of any scheduled adoption hearing.

Florida uses a particularly unusual method to ensure that the biological father is notified. Under Florida law, any mother who does not know who fathered her child must share her sexual history in a newspaper advertisement before an adoption becomes final. Apparently, the goal is to find the father and prevent any of the custody battles that can break up adoptive families. The law requires a mother to list her name, age, and description, along with descriptions of any men who may have fathered the child. The ads must be placed in a newspaper in the city where the child was conceived.[5] Can you imagine seeing someone you know featured this way in your hometown newspaper?

If the biological mother does not know the identity of the biological father, Florida law requires the mother to testify to that fact in court before an adoption can take place. If the biological mother believes that several men could be the father of her child, all the possible candidates should be notified via a notice of alleged paternity. If any one of the possible paternal candidates comes forward to oppose the adoption, a DNA test can be taken to ensure that the opposing party is truly the biological father. While the best interests of the child must be of paramount importance to everyone involved in an adoption, fulfilling the legal requirements is extremely important as well.

Across the country, it is usual, except in a case where the mother has abandoned or abused her child, for adoptions to be prevented from going forward without the biological mother's written consent. However, most states do not require the biological father's written consent. Nonetheless, the majority of states *do* require that the biological father be given the opportunity to contest the adoption. In most states this is done by notifying the biological father that the biological mother has consented to an adoption. This notification is generally given to the father anywhere from one to two months after the child's birth. As provided by individual statute, the biological father then has a certain number of days from the notification to step forward and contest the adoption.

Notification Problems

Several problems can arise when attempts are made to notify the biological father of an adoption. For example, the biological mother may not know the identity of her child's father. If the identity is unknown, then the biological mother must attest to this fact before the adoption can continue. On the other hand, if the biological father is known but cannot be located, most states require that every reasonable effort be made to locate him. At this point, it is advisable to have proof of the effort. Proving that a thorough search has been conducted is easier if the law firm handling the adoption makes an honest attempt to do the following: (1) conduct a post office search; (2) search the driver's registration rolls; (3) request a search of all the military branches and then prepare proof that the search resulted in no father being in the military; (4) search voter's registration rolls; and (5) place notices in newspapers in the area where the biological father is known to have lived last. All five steps can be handled by a paralegal in the law office.

Father Fights Adoption

An attorney's expertise and assistance can help to prevent the emotionally draining experience of adoptive parents learning, after they think the adoption is finalized, that their child's biological father is fighting the adoption by claiming that he was never properly notified. The legal technicalities of proper notice can be very tricky, but they must be followed, since great heartache can occur down the line if notice is not given properly.

An example is the case popularly known as the *Baby Richard* case.[6] This case (see Case 7.1) involved a claim by the biological father that he was not given sufficient notice of the adoption of his son. Multiple appeals by the adoptive parents ultimately failed, and the nation witnessed the traumatizing act of a crying 4-year-old child being taken from his adoptive mother's arms and handed over to the child's biological father. Legislators across the nation, recoiling from the sight of the 4-year-old child being taken from the only family he had ever known, reacted by creating legislation that demands speedier court appeals when dealing with the welfare of a growing child. Eventually the *Baby Richard* custody battle involved a governor, the General Assembly, and judges all the way to the United States Supreme Court. Moreover, Illinois Supreme Court Justice J. Heiple was vilified by a famous newspaper columnist, along with the governor of Illinois, for overturning two lower court rulings that Justice Heiple believed wrongly granted the adoption of the child when the biological father had been erroneously informed the child died at birth.[7]

The Baby Richard case was formally named *In re Petition of John Doe and Jane Doe* in an ultimately fruitless effort to protect the parties' privacy. Recall from Chapter 2 that Susan assisted with the preparation of the Yanov brief. The Yanov brief was based on the factual scenario and legal rulings of the *Baby Richard* case.

Biological Parent Versus Adoptive Parents

Many adoptive parents imagine the nightmare of a biological parent stepping forward to dispute the pending adoption before the adoption is finalized but *after* the adoptive parents have grown to love their soon-to-be adopted child. This nightmare became reality for the prospective adoptive parents in the case of *In the Matter of Baby Girl Clausen* (see Case 7.2). The prospective adoptive parents, Jan and Roberta DeBoer, decided to fight the biological parent in what eventually turned into another media frenzy.[8] The terms "*ex parte* order" and "preliminary injunction" are used in the case. An ***ex parte* order** is Latin for an order granted *with only one side present in court.* A **preliminary injunction** is a judge's order to a person to do or to refrain from doing a particular thing until the issue can be fully tried in court.

CASE 7.1 *In re Petition of John Doe and Jane Doe, 159 Ill. 2d 347 (1994)*

Facts: When his fiancée, Daniela Janikova, was eight and one-half months pregnant, Otakar Kirchner was called back to his native Czechoslovakia to attend to his dying grandmother. While he was there, Daniela received a call from Otakar's aunt saying that Otakar had taken up with an old girlfriend. Believing Otakar had abandoned her and their baby for another woman, Daniela moved out of their apartment and into a women's shelter. At the shelter, she was advised by a social worker to give her baby up for adoption. Angry and upset with Otakar, and thinking she had no other choice, she agreed. The social worker called her personal attorney who, in turn, contacted the adoptive mother. The adoptive mother just happened to be a friend and employee of the attorney. At the urging of the adoptive parents, John and Jane Doe, along with their attorney, Daniela gave birth at a different hospital from the one she and Otakar had originally planned in order to avoid any intervention on his part. Baby Richard was born on March 16, 1991. Still extremely hurt and angry at Otakar, Daniela executed a surrender and consent form on March 20, 1991, while refusing to divulge the identity and whereabouts of the father. However, the adoptive parents and their attorney were well aware there was a father out there who had been denied any knowledge of his son's existence.

When Otakar returned to Chicago, he discovered that Daniela had moved out. Extremely concerned for Daniela and the baby, Otakar contacted Daniela's uncle who informed him that he had no idea where Daniela was, and that the baby died at birth. Not believing him, Otakar immediately began an intensive and persistent search to find his family. His search even included going through Daniela's uncle's garage for evidence of diapers. Otakar eventually met up with Daniela, and they reconciled. On Mother's Day, *57 days after the birth* of their son, Daniela admitted to Otakar that their baby was alive, and that she had given him up for adoption. He immediately hired a lawyer and contested the Does' adoption of his son on the basis of *lack of proper notification and consent.*

The trial court declared Otakar an unfit parent under section 1(D)(b) of the Adoption Act because he did not show sufficient interest in the baby during the first 30 days of the child's life. Despite evidence of his support and concern throughout her pregnancy, and his frustrated efforts to find and locate his child after his birth, the trial court declared his consent was unnecessary under section 8(a)(1) of the Adoption Act. Otakar appealed, and the appellate court affirmed the lower court's ruling holding that Otakar's parental rights could be lawfully terminated, without regard to whether he was unfit, when the court perceived that such termination of parental rights would be *in the best interests of the child.* In other words, the appellate court found that the child's best interests would prevail over any consideration of a parent's rights. Not one to give up, Otakar appealed to the Illinois Supreme Court.

Issue: Whether a child's best interests should prevail over consideration of the biological father's right to consent to the adoption of his child.

Court's Reasoning: On June 16, 1994, the unanimous decision of the Illinois Supreme Court held that there was insufficient evidence that the father had not shown a reasonable degree of interest in the child within the first 30 days of his birth and ordered the child removed from the home of the adoptive parents and returned to his biological father, Otakar Kirchner. In explaining the decision of the court, Justice Heiple declared, "To the extent that it is relevant to assign fault in this case, the fault here lies initially with the mother, who fraudulently tried to deprive the father of his rights, and secondly, with the adoptive parents and their attorney, who proceeded with the adoption when they knew that a real father was out there who had been denied knowledge of his baby's existence. When the father entered his appearance in the adoption proceedings 57 days after the baby's birth and demanded his rights as a father, the petitioners should have relinquished the baby at that time."

In referring to the best interests of the child standard, Justice Heiple explained that this standard can never be used *before* the proper termination of a parent's rights. *The adoption laws of Illinois are neither complex nor difficult to apply. Those laws intentionally place the burden of proof on the adoptive parents in establishing both the relinquishment and/or unfitness of the natural parents and the fitness and the right to adopt of the adoptive parents.* In addition, Illinois law requires a good faith effort to notify the natural parents of the adoption proceedings. These laws are designed to protect natural parents in their pre-emptive rights to their own children wholly apart from any consideration of the so-called best interests of the child. If it were otherwise, few parents would be secure in the custody of their own children. If the best interests of the child were a sufficient qualification to determine child custody, anyone with superior income, intelligence, education, and so on might challenge and deprive parents of their right to their own children. The law is otherwise and was not complied with in this case.

Justice Heiple further explained:

> The adoptive parents should have relinquished the baby at the fifty-seventh day. Instead of that, however, they were able to procure an entirely erroneous ruling from a trial judge that allowed the adoption to go forward. The father's only remedy at that stage was a legal appeal, which he took. He is not the cause of the delay in this case. It was the adoptive parents' decision to prolong this litigation through a long and, ultimately, fruitless appeal. Now, the view has been expressed that the passage of time warrants their retention of the child; that it would not be fair to the child to return him to his natural parents, now married to each other, after the adoptive parents have delayed justice past the child's third birthday.

Holding: Biological father's appeal granted.

Case Discussion: Unfortunately, the case did not end there. Justice Heiple's strong words did not deter the adoptive parents from prolonging and delaying the inevitable. They petitioned the Illinois Supreme Court for a rehearing. On July 12, 1994, the Illinois Supreme Court rejected their request, setting off a round of personal attacks on Supreme Court Justice J. Heiple by a famous newspaper columnist and the state's governor, who tried to enter the case on behalf of the adoptive parents.[a] The very next day, however, the same court granted a stay allowing the adoptive parents to keep custody of the child while they appealed to the United States Supreme Court.

In the meantime, all the publicity elicited such a public outcry on behalf of the adoptive parents that the legislature overwhelmingly passed a bill to help the adoptive parents keep Baby Richard. The governor eagerly signed it into the law. The law provided for a hearing to consider a child's best interest in custody proceedings when an adoption is denied or revoked on appeal, as in this case.

On November 7, 1994, the United States Supreme Court refused to hear the adoptive parent's case. On January 25, 1995, the Illinois Supreme Court gave custody of the almost 4-year-old boy to his biological father after rejecting the adoptive parents' appeal, which was based on the law that was hastily passed on their behalf. The lawyer for the adoptive parents declared that he would ask the Illinois Supreme Court to delay the effect of its ruling while he, again, appealed to the United States Supreme Court. On January 28, 1995, United States Supreme Court Justice John Paul Stevens refused to delay the Illinois Supreme Court ruling. The lawyer for the adoptive parents said they would approach other United States Supreme Court justices for a stay, or ask the entire Court to hear the case. In a 7-to-2 vote, the United States Supreme Court turned down their requests for a delay. Finally, on April 30, 1995, Baby Richard was returned to his biological father, Otakar Kirchner. The adoptive parents' final appeal was rejected by the United States Supreme Court on June 19, 1995.[b]

What do you think of the governor's efforts to help the adoptive parents? Do you think legislation that would put a limit on how long an adoption dispute could continue would be a good idea?

---

[a]Don, Terry, "Baby Ruling sets the Stage for New Fight," *New York Times,* November 8, 1994, A15.

[b]"The Supreme Court: Parental Rights; Adoptive Parent Rebuffed by High Court in Last Plea," *New York Times,* June 20, 1995, B7.

CASE 7.2 *In the Matter of Baby Girl Clausen, DeBoer v. Schmidt,* 199 Mich. App. 10, 501 N.W. 2d 193 (1993)

Facts: This highly publicized case concerns a dispute over the rights of a child. In February 1991, Baby Girl Clausen (BGC) was born to Clara Clausen in Iowa. On February 10, 1991, Clausen signed a release-of-custody form, relinquishing her parental rights to BGC. Clausen, who was unmarried at the time of the birth but who married Daniel Schmidt in April 1992, had named Scott Seefeldt as the father. Seefeldt executed a release-of-custody form, on February 14, 1991.

Clara Clausen filed a request in the Iowa juvenile court to revoke her release of custody on March 6, 1991. In an affidavit accompanying the request, Clausen stated that she lied when she named Seefeldt as the biological father of BGC, and that the child's biological father was Daniel Schmidt. Schmidt filed an affidavit of paternity on March 12, 1991. At a hearing in juvenile court, attended by both Clausen and the adoptive parents, the court dismissed Clausen's request to revoke her release of custody on the ground that it lacked subject matter jurisdiction. This was because a petition for adoption had been filed. The court also dismissed Schmidt's attempt to claim custody. The DeBoers and BGC returned to Michigan.

Schmidt filed a petition on March 27, 1991, in the Iowa District Court seeking to intervene in the adoption proceeding initiated by the DeBoers. He asserted that he had not given consent for the adoption. The court ordered blood tests. The DeBoers objected, and as a result, it was not until September 1991 that the child's test results were available. They showed a 99.9 percent probability that Schmidt was the father of BGC, and a zero percent probability that Seefeldt was the father.

The DeBoers filed a petition on September 24, 1991, in the Iowa District Court to terminate Schmidt's parental rights. The Iowa District Court conducted a trial with regard to the issue of paternity, termination of parental rights, and adoption beginning on November 4, 1991. On the basis of these findings, the court concluded that the termination proceeding was void with respect to Schmidt, and that the DeBoers' petition to adopt BGC must be denied. The court ordered that the DeBoers return physical custody of the child to Schmidt no later than January 12, 1992, at 6:00 P.M. The court retained jurisdiction under its general equitable powers in order to complete any matters necessary to protect the interests of BGC.

In the meantime, the Iowa Court of Appeals reversed the termination of Clara Clausen's parental rights and remanded the case to juvenile court proceedings. The Iowa Supreme Court granted further review of the decision and allowed the DeBoers to appeal the district court's decision. The Iowa Supreme Court stayed the district's court's order changing physical custody of BGC. They also consolidated its review of the court of appeals decision concerning Clara Clausen's parental rights with the appeal filed by the DeBoers.

On November 20, 1992, the Iowa Supreme Court denied the DeBoers' motion for reconsideration and remanded the case to the district court for issuance of an order changing physical custody of BGC from the DeBoers to Schmidt.

The Iowa District Court ordered the DeBoers to appear on December 3, 1992, with BGC. The DeBoers did not appear at the hearing. In an order entered on December 3, 1992, the district court terminated the DeBoers' rights as temporary guardians and custodians until further order of the court. Schmidt was given authority to proceed by any legal means to enforce the order requiring the DeBoers to relinquish possession of the child. The court found that the DeBoers had no legal right or claim to physical custody of the child, and that they were acting outside any legal claim to custody or possession of the child. The court scheduled a hearing for December 18, 1992, for the DeBoers to show cause why they should not be held in contempt. The court also found that the DeBoers should be assessed attorney fees and costs.

On December 3, 1992, the same day the DeBoers' rights were terminated in Iowa, they filed a petition in Washtenaw Circuit Court in Michigan pursuant to the Uniform Child Custody Act. The petition sought modification of the Iowa order granting custody of BGC to Schmidt. The DeBoers argued that Michigan had jurisdiction under the Uniform Child Custody Jurisdiction Act (UCCJA) because BGC had resided in Michigan for all but approximately three weeks of her life, and Michigan was the *home state* of BGC as that term was defined by UCCJA. The petition alleged that it would be in the best interests of BGC for Michigan to assume jurisdiction. On December 3, 1992, the Washtenaw Circuit Court entered an *ex parte* order that ordered Schmidt not to remove BGC from Washtenaw County.

On December 11, 1992, Schmidt filed a motion for summary disposition in Washtenaw Circuit Court to dissolve the preliminary injunction and to recognize and enforce the Iowa judgment in this case. In a hearing on January 5, 1993, the Washtenaw Circuit Court denied Schmidt's motion for summary disposition, and directed that BGC was to remain with the DeBoers until further order. The court entered a written order on January 11, 1993.

Following this, an Iowa District Court's hearing, held on January 22, 1993, resulted in the DeBoers being held in contempt of court and bench warrants being issued for their arrest.

Issue: Whether the Washtenaw Circuit Court had jurisdiction to intervene in this case.

Court's Reasoning: We find the Washtenaw Circuit Court lacked jurisdiction to intervene in this case. The UCCJA has been enacted by every state, including Michigan. Its primary purpose is to avoid jurisdictional competition between states by establishing uniform rules for deciding when states have jurisdiction to make child custody determinations. Under the UCCJA, the Washtenaw Circuit Court was precluded from intervening in this case and was obligated to recognize and enforce the Iowa order of December 3, 1992.

The DeBoers filed their petition in the Washtenaw Circuit Court on December 3, 1992. On that date, the Iowa District Court entered an order terminating the DeBoers' rights as temporary guardians and custodians of BGC, and scheduled a hearing for the DeBoers to show cause why they should not be held in contempt. The Iowa District Court correctly concluded that the DeBoers' petition for adoption should be dismissed. The Iowa District Court order of December 3, 1992, implemented the decision of the Iowa Supreme Court and stripped the DeBoers of any legal claim of custody to BGC. The grant of temporary custody was rescinded. The DeBoers became third parties with respect to BGC, and no longer had a basis on which to claim a substantive right to custody. A right to legal custody cannot be based on the fact that a child resides or has resided with a third party. The DeBoers had no further legal rights to BGC. The DeBoers had attempted to use the UCCJA and the Washtenaw Circuit Court to create a new right that the Iowa court had extinguished. The DeBoers initiated a custody dispute in a state in which they had no standing to do so.

We do not find the DeBoers' conduct reprehensible under UCCJA, or that it violated the parental kidnapping statute. Therefore, we decline to make an award of attorney fees and costs in this case, or to remand the case to the Washtenaw Circuit Court for a hearing with regard to this issue. We find that the Iowa order of December 3, 1992, must be enforced, and that the custody of the child must be transferred to her father, Daniel Schmidt. The transfer of custody is stayed for 20 days from the date of the certification of this opinion to afford the parties an opportunity to appeal.

Holding: The Washtenaw Circuit Court's denial of Schmidt's motion for summary disposition and to dissolve the injunction is reversed.

Case Discussion: This case caused quite an uproar in the media. The lengthy proceedings became an issue because the child in question was growing older and more attached to the DeBoers each day. Did you follow all the legal maneuvering that occurred in the two states practically simultaneously? Can you list the mountain of pleadings filed by the lawyers in this case? The epilogue to this case was unfortunate: The DeBoers faced bankruptcy and ended their 17-year marriage after losing the case. The DeBoers' divorce was eventually followed by reports that the Schmidts had separated.[a]

---

[a]"Couple in Baby Jessica Battle Divorce," *Sunday Star-Ledger,* October 24, 1999, 1–22.

TERMINATION OF PARENTAL RIGHTS

The biological parents of the child in the Mahoney vignette in this chapter *voluntarily relinquished* their parental rights. Some states provide that the act of **voluntary parental surrender** of a child to an adoption agency effectively terminates the parents' legal rights. Other states require that the voluntary relinquishment be followed by a court order. The opposite of such voluntary relinquishment is **involuntary termination of parental rights,** which occurs when a judge finds that the parents have failed to properly care for their child to the extent that the child's physical and/or mental welfare has been gravely compromised. Following involuntary termination of parental rights, custody of the child moves to the state, and then from the state to adoptive parents.

The case of *Kingsley v. Kingsley* (see Case 7.3) involved the involuntary termination of a biological mother's parental rights to her son. The fact that the media described the case as involving the request by a child to *divorce* his mother resulted in a flurry of publicity, and even a made-for-television film. Technically speaking, a child and his parents cannot be *divorced* from each other, but this case *was* different in that the child filed suit for termination of his mother's parental rights on his own behalf, rather than the more typical scenario in which the state alone requests such a termination.

THE ROLE RACE PLAYS IN ADOPTION

Until the mid-twentieth century, race played very little part in adoption in the United States. The written laws and unspoken policies of many states were clear by their lack of support and intolerance for interracial adoption. This dark-ages philosophy was slowly whittled away as the nation's courts began to obliterate racial discrimination at all levels of society, which was followed by a period in which many people of one race adopted children of another. By the 1970s, however, a backlash against interracial adoption occurred based on the fear that the predominantly white adoptive parents would not be able to foster racial identification in nonwhite children. The arguments, both pro and con, concerning interracial adoption were effectively silenced by a federal law that prohibited the denial of any adoption or foster placement because of race, color, or national origin. Teeth were given to the act because federal funding was connected to the prohibition.

An exception to this prohibition of prejudicial treatment is another federal law called the Indian Child Welfare Act. The **Indian Child Welfare Act** was created at the urging of the Indian Nations that wished to curtail the adoption of Indian children by non-Indian adoptive parents. This act gives power to the tribes to approve or disapprove the adoption of an Indian child by non-Indian parents.[9]

FEDERAL INFLUENCE ON ADOPTION

The **Interstate Compact on the Placement of Children,** a federal statute, was designed to protect children who are born in one state and taken to another state to be adopted.[10] The Compact provides that in both the birth state and the state of adoption, fundamental guidelines must be followed to ensure the safety and best interests of the adoptive child. The attorney handling an adoption should assist the adoptive parents with filling out the Interstate Compact application in the state where the child is born *if* the child is to be removed to another state by his adoptive parents.

CASE 7.3 *Kingsley v. Kingsley*, 623 So. 2d 780 (1993)

Facts: Eleven-year-old Gregory Kingsley filed a petition for termination of the parental rights of his natural parents on June 25, 1992. This was highly unusual because a minor is not normally considered to have the legal capacity to file legal documents on his own behalf. He also filed a separate complaint for a declaration of his rights and adoption by his foster parents. The trial court declared that Gregory, although a minor, had the capacity to file all the legal documents. Gregory's foster parents also filed a petition for Gregory's adoption with his consent, along with three additional petitions filed on Gregory's behalf by his foster mother, Gregory's guardian *ad litem,* and the Department of Health and Rehabilitative Services. There was a two-day trial. All the petitioners testified, as well as Rachel Kingsley, Gregory's mother. The trial court, against Rachel Kingsley's wishes, terminated her parental rights. In a separate written judgment, the court granted Gregory's adoption by his foster parents. Rachel Kingsley appealed on several issues.

Issues: (1) Whether the court erred in allowing a minor to bring a termination of parental rights proceeding on his own behalf. (2) Whether the trial court erred in hearing the termination and adoption proceedings simultaneously, and thereby violated Rachel Kingsley's rights to procedural due process. (3) Whether the finding of abandonment of Gregory by Rachel Kingsley lacked clear and convincing evidence.

Court's Reasoning: Rachel argued that the trial court erred in holding that Gregory had the capacity to bring a termination of parental rights proceeding on his own behalf. Specifically, Rachel argued that being a minor prevented him from legally initiating or maintaining an action for termination of parental rights. Rachel also argued that trying the termination and adoption proceedings simultaneously violated her rights to procedural due process. She claimed that the focus of the proceedings shifted from the issues of abandonment and neglect to a comparison of Rachel's parenting skills with those of the potential adoptive parents. Rachel argued that this procedure resulted in unduly placing upon her the burden to overcome this comparison, and this resulted in an interference with her fundamental liberty interest as Gregory's mother.

The evidence presented was clear and convincing. The mother was satisfied to permit the State of Florida to care for her child for six months and failed to make even marginal effort to have the child rejoin her. This court will defer to the trial court's evaluation of the credibility of the witnesses and the weight to be given their testimony. We agree that Gregory lacked the capacity to bring the petition in his own right. We agree with Rachel that trying these two cases simultaneously constituted error and that the better practice would have been to separate these two cases. However, additional petitions were filed by adults on his behalf. Both of these issues resulted in errors, but we find the errors to have been harmless. Rachel failed to show that comparisons between the foster parents and her parenting skills were the focus of the trial. Rather, the issues of abandonment and neglect were emphasized.

However, Rachel's attorney filed an oral appeal in open court immediately following the trial court's oral pronouncement terminating her parental rights. This appeal superseded the adoption proceedings. At that point, the trial court was without subject matter jurisdiction to proceed and clearly erred in granting the foster parents' petition for adoption.

Holding: The final judgment granting adoption is reversed and remanded to the trial court.

(continued)

CASE 7.3 *continued*

Case Discussion: The bottom-line issue in this case, popularly known as *Gregory K.,* was whether the court would recognize Gregory, a minor, as a person who had legal standing. This case answered that question in the negative. Minors do not have standing to initiate a termination of parental rights case themselves. The reversal of the adoption was called *a terrible blow to youth rights.*[a] However, Gregory K.'s case was later *successfully* presented by Social Services on Gregory's behalf. His mother's parental rights were terminated, and the foster parents returned to court and successfully adopted Gregory.

Should children be able to bring their parents to court? Do children know what is best for them? What do you think?

---

[a]"Gregory K. Win Reversed," *Freedom Voice* 9, no. 1 (Winter 1994).

Congress passed the Adoption and Safe Families Act in 1997. The purpose of this act is to require states to hold hearings on the issue of parental ability and to seek the termination of parental rights if warranted. The goal of the act is to put an end to the long-term foster care of children and make the children eligible for adoption.[11]

ADULTS ADOPTING ADULTS

The definition of *family* continues to evolve in today's society. Many individuals have created their own definitions of family; however, without a biological connection, the American legal system provides few protections for these individuals. In an attempt to provide legal protections, some adults have attempted to adopt other adults. Adult adoption has not been accepted in many states.

SAME-SEX ADOPTIVE PARENTS

The changes in family structure that have occurred in society have been reflected in the increase in the number of adoptions of children by same-sex partners. In the not-so-distant legal past, a prospective parent's same-sex sexual orientation negatively affected that person's chances of adopting a child. In fact, unmarried heterosexuals also were denied the right to adopt. Same-sex couples were typically denied the right to adopt a child together because of their unmarried and homosexual status, despite proof of being part of a cohesive family unit. Today the emerging trend throughout the nation is to focus on a child's best interests and to allow such adoptions when they are in the best interests of a child. A significant number of states still deny adoption based on same-sex sexual orientation, but courts in New York, New Jersey, Washington, D.C., Massachusetts, and Vermont have ruled that unmarried couples, both heterosexual and homosexual, may adopt if the adoption can be proved to be in the best interests of the children in question.[12]

SAFE HAVENS FOR ABANDONED INFANTS

The unfortunate fates of infants abandoned by their mothers have resulted in new laws being passed in a majority of states. An increase in abandoned newborn infants in their state led the Texas legislature in 1999 to enact legislation that would allow a parent of an unwanted newborn to drop the baby off at a safe haven center without fear of legal reprisal. The purpose was to have the newborns protected and eventually adopted. The so-called safe haven laws have since been enacted in 31 states.[13]

CAN ADOPTION BE UNDONE?

The majority of states provide that an adoption is irrevocable once a judge signs the final order of adoption. **Irrevocable** is legally defined as incapable of being called back, stopped, or changed. This assurance is provided because the child's biological parents' parental rights must be severed before an adoption can go forward. If the courts allowed revocation of an adoption, the child would then legally become an orphan without parents. Revocation of an adoption would make the child a ward of the state, and that is exactly opposite of the purpose of adoption.

The question has arisen regarding what adoptive parents can do if the children they adopt have inherent mental or physical conditions they were not aware of when they adopted the children. The law on this issue is relatively clear. Just as parents who give birth are not able to "return" a child, adoptive parents do not have the right to return a child who is "flawed." There *is* an exception, however. If the agency or biological parent *knew* of a major medical condition and *failed to inform* the adoptive parents, the adoption may be able to be revoked.

This is the type of situation that was discussed in the case of *Roe v. Catholic Charities* (see Case 7.4). The case explains the adoption agency negligence cause of action. The **adoption agency negligence** cause of action requires the defendant to have breached a duty in its failure to supply plaintiffs with the information the defendant possessed and had available regarding the adoptable children. The breach must be the direct and proximate result of the damages sustained by the plaintiffs.

CASE 7.4 *Roe v. Catholic Charities,* 225 Ill. App. 3d 519, 588 N.E.2d 354 (1992)

Facts: This case involved three adoptions and several adoptive parents—John and Mary Roe, Betty Doe and Carol Boe, and the three children they adopted through the adoption agency, Catholic Charities. The adoptive parents each stated they wanted to adopt a *normal and healthy child.* The parents claimed they were told by the social worker employed by the agency that their children were mentally and physically normal. They also claimed that the social worker said the agency would tell them everything they knew about the children, and that the parents would incur no unusual expenses.

While making these statements, however, the defendant knew that Jane Roe had seen mental health professionals for violent and uncontrollable behavior, as well as intellectual, social, and emotional retardation. The defendant also knew that Billy Doe had exhibited severe abnormal behavior, such as smearing feces on the interior walls of past foster homes, and had exhibited other uncontrollable behavior in those homes as well. In addition, the defendant knew that Joe Boe displayed destructive behavior in past foster homes, such as stomping a foster family's dog to death. The adoptive parents obtained a court order to review the defendant's files and learned of the medical problems. The parents filed a lawsuit claiming fraud, breach of contract, and negligence. The circuit court dismissed the case because the state of Illinois did not recognize a cause of action for malpractice in adoption. The plaintiffs appealed.

(continued)

CASE 7.4 *continued*

Issues: (1) Whether Illinois recognizes a cause of action for fraud based upon an adoption agency's intentional misrepresentation of a child's health and psychological background. (2) Whether the facts were sufficient to establish a cause of action for social worker malpractice.

Court's Reasoning: This is a case of first impression in Illinois. The defendants fear that recognition of a cause of action for fraud in the adoption setting will force agencies to guarantee that adopted children will mature into happy and healthy children. We require no guarantee of future health and happiness. To do so would place an unbearable burden upon the adoption agencies. We merely require adoption agencies to follow the law. Although at the time of the adoption there was no statute requiring disclosure, the agency was prohibited from committing fraud. The defendant argues that such recognition will hinder its efforts to place handicapped children with families. We believe that a policy to tell the truth, rather than fraud, will actually help in the placing of handicapped children.

Regarding the second issue, we believe that the facts alleged and admitted in the case are sufficient to establish a cause of action for social worker malpractice. The plaintiffs must plead that the defendant owed them a duty, that the defendant failed to perform or breached that duty, and that the breach was the cause of the plaintiffs' injuries and damages. We find specifically that a duty was owed to the plaintiffs by the defendant. The defendant had a duty to give an honest and complete response to the plaintiffs' specific request concerning the characteristics of the potentially adoptable children. The defendant breached that duty in its failure to supply the plaintiffs with the information the defendant possessed and had available. The breach was the direct and proximate cause of the damages sustained as alleged by the plaintiffs. Given the factors, we recognize the tort of adoption agency negligence and hold that the plaintiffs in this case have adequately pleaded a cause of action.

Holding: Plaintiffs win appeal.

Case Discussion: The court did not mention it, but do you think the adoptive parents might have had a suspicion about the true well-being of the children before the adoptions became final? Adoptive children typically reside with their adoptive parents prior to the final order of adoption being signed. If the adoptive parents *did* have some growing awareness that the children had previously undisclosed problems, do you think they should have gone through with the adoptions? If they did have suspicions, should the adoptive parents have the continuing responsibility for the children despite the agency's behavior?

CHAPTER SUMMARY

Adoption creates a legal relationship between a child and a person who is not the biological parent of the child. All 50 states have statutes that provide guidelines for completing a legal adoption. Adoptions may be done by working with a public or private agency, or through a private and independent arrangement between the biological parents and the adoptive parents. Adoptions may be either open or closed. An international adoption involves adoptive parents and a child from two different countries. An independent adoption is also known as an identified, designated, or collaborative adoption. If there is a biological connection between the adoptive parents and the child, the adoption is called a kinship adoption. Attorneys may act as the facilitator for either the biological or adoptive parents in arranging a private adoption. Attorneys also may represent the adoptive parents in all types of adoption proceedings.

The legal standard used by the courts for adoption is *the best interests of the child* test. The legal procedures for adoption differ from state to state, but the fundamental constitutional guidelines apply in all states. Constitutional protections require that any parent whose child is in the adoption process must be properly notified before his rights are terminated. Following the proper biological parent notification, both biological parents must sign a consent form agreeing to the adoption. If the consent of one biological parent is unavailable, the court may then terminate the biological parent's parental rights following a hearing— if, following proper notification, a parent has failed to step forward to contest the adoption. In such a case, a hearing will be held to put that fact on the record. Biological parents do have statutory rights specific to each individual state. Any evidence of fraud or duress may nullify a biological parent's permission or a court's order of adoption. Many states have created paternity registries that put the burden on the biological and unmarried father to register his claim of paternity.

The proper legal procedure for an adoption includes filing an adoption petition on the part of the prospective adoptive parents. Minors do not have the right to petition a court to terminate their biological parents' rights. The biological parents may file an affidavit or certification detailing approval of the termination of parental rights and adoption by the designated adoptive parents. Following the filing of a petition and an adoption hearing, which includes testimony on the adoptive parents' fitness and usually a home study, the court typically issues an interlocutory decree, which becomes final at a designated time depending on state statute. The final adoption order provides the adopted child and adoptive parents with all the rights of biological children and parents. Adoptions are typically irrevocable, but there are exceptions. For example, if the adoption involved fraud being perpetrated upon the adoptive parents, the adoption may be nullified.

Key Terms

adoption	open adoption	*Ex parte* order
public adoption agency	kinship adoption	preliminary injunction
private adoption agency	petition for adoption	voluntary parental surrender
relinquishment	judicial surrender	involuntary termination of
international adoption	affidavit	parental rights
independent adoption	notice	Indian Child Welfare Act
identified adoption	home study report	Interstate Compact on the
designated adoption	interlocutory decree of	Placement of Children
collaborative adoption	adoption	irrevocable
closed adoption	notice of alleged paternity	adoption agency negligence

Surfing the Web

http://www.abcadoptions.com Do you want to find details on adopting a baby? Read adoption postings.

http://www.adoptionlawsite.org The goal of this site is to provide a single online resource for all who seek adoption information.

http://www.law.cornell.edu This site provides links to the adoption laws of the 50 states.

http://www.bastards.org Do you have difficulty understanding the "legal lingo" of adoption? This site promotes open access to adoption records.

http://www.chask.org If you are looking to combine religion and adoption, look no further.

ETHICS ALERT

Annie, an old friend from Susan's high school days, has called Susan for help. Annie has heard through the grapevine that Susan is working for a law firm, and she wants Susan to arrange an adoption of her soon-to-be-born baby. Susan explains to Annie that she cannot personally represent Annie in the adoption and that an attorney would have to represent her. Susan further explains that Annie cannot legally accept payment for her child. Annie asks Susan if Susan can "just look in the office files and connect me up with some clients who are good and kind and really want a baby."

During the phone call, Annie brings Susan up-to-date on what has been going on in her life for the last few years. Annie tells Susan she needs at least $50,000 to pay off bills and start a new life out of the state. Susan feels very sorry that Annie has had so much hard luck and believes that Annie *can* start life fresh and give her baby a better life with adoptive parents. Should Susan help her old friend?

Review Questions

1. What is the definition of adoption?
2. What should be the primary focus of an adoption?
3. What is a public adoption?
4. What is a private adoption?
5. List the types of adoptions described in this chapter.
6. What are the three basic steps in the adoption process?
7. How can an attorney facilitate an adoption?
8. What type of financial support of the biological mother is usually permissible?
9. Who must consent to an adoption according to your state statutes?
10. When is revocation of consent permitted according to your state statutes?
11. What should be included in a petition for adoption?
12. What usually occurs during a preliminary adoption hearing?
13. What usually occurs during a final adoption hearing?
14. What is a home study report?
15. What rights does the biological father have?
16. What steps should be taken in making a reasonable effort to locate the biological father?
17. Following the involuntary termination of parents' rights, who has custody of the child?
18. What is the purpose of the Indian Child Welfare Act?
19. What is the purpose of the Interstate Compact on the Placement of Children?
20. When may adoption be revocable?

Endnotes

1. Jervey, Gay, "Priceless," *Money* 161, no. 4 (April 2003): 119.
2. Hicks, Randall B., *Adopting in America* (Sun City, CA: Wordslinger Press, 1993).
3. Lancaster, Kathy, *Keys to Adopting a Child* (New York: Barron, 1994).
4. *Id.*
5. *Daily Record,* August 14, 2002: 5.
6. *In re Petition of John Doe and Jane Doe,* 159 Ill. 2d 347 (1994).
7. Don, Terry, "Storm Rages in Chicago over Revoked Adoption," *New York Times,* July 15, 1994, A1.
8. "Couple in Baby Jessica Battle Divorce," *Sunday Star-Ledger,* October 24, 1999, 1–22.
9. 42 U.S.C.A. § 5111 (2003).
10. 25 U.S.C.A. § 1915 (2003).
11. 42 U.S.C.A. § 671 (2003).
12. Boskey, James B., and Toby Solomon, "Reconsidering Adoption: The New New Jersey Adoption Statute," *New Jersey Family Lawyer* XIV, no. 3 (April 1994).
13. Tebo, Margaret Graham, "Texas Idea Takes Off," *ABA Journal* (September 2001): 30.

Chapter 8

Divorce and Separation

BIG BUSINESS

Weddings are expensive and are big business these days, but the legal costs of divorce in the United States amount to more than $30 billion per year. Each year more than 1.8 million people divorce, and the issue of custody for more than 1 million children is decided.[1]

MICHAEL AND LIBBY: TILL DIVORCE DO US PART

Susan's longtime neighbors Michael and Libby Smith hoped that their self-described *perfect* courtship and *perfect* wedding would lead to the *perfect* marriage. Unfortunately, somewhere in the midst of having two children, renovating a home, and pursuing careers, their perfect marriage began to unravel. According to Michael, Libby is so wrapped up in renovating their home and being an artist that she puts the children third, and he comes last, *after* decorating their home.

Libby denies that the children are next to last on her list, but admits that Michael might not even be fourth. She has lost interest in Michael and finds him "boring." According to Libby, she and Michael no longer have any mutual interests aside from the children, and she claims he never did want to develop mutual interests. She says Michael left the renovation of the 100-year-old barn into their dream home to Libby while he worked on getting ahead in his career.

Unfortunately, Michael's career involves traveling several weeks out of the month. This leaves Libby to deal with the children, her career, and the renovations. Libby did not feel she could complain much before her artwork began earning her a profit. When she did complain, Michael said he felt he could not change his schedule and refused to go to a marriage counselor. Michael now says he always hated the idea of living in a renovated barn and thought Libby would have gotten over that "harebrained" idea. Michael insists that if the barn was sold and Libby did not concentrate on her art so much, everything would go back to the way it was.

The bottom line: Although Michael and Libby are both good people, as a couple, they can hardly be in the same room without bickering so loudly the neighbors can hear them fighting. Michael and Libby have decided to give their neighbors a break and call it a day. Michael is planning to move out of the barn he has come to hate.

Hiring an Attorney: A Law Firm Enters the Picture . . . Almost

The day after their decision to divorce, Libby decided to visit an attorney while Michael was off on yet another business trip. Libby was in an attorney's office only once before, and that was to have wills written for her and Michael. During a chat with a recently divorced girlfriend, Libby learned that if she acted as her own attorney instead of hiring an attorney, she would be representing herself *pro se*. However, Libby knew she would be more comfortable hiring an attorney than trying to represent herself *pro se*. Libby believes she and Michael can get divorced in a civilized manner; however, Michael *does* have more business acumen, and Libby is sure that Michael's business experience will work against her if she does not hire a professional.

Although they have mutually agreed to get a divorce, neither spouse has told the other of any immediate intentions to seek legal advice. Libby decided to make an appointment with the same attorney who wrote their wills.

Sitting anxiously in the law firm's waiting room, Libby was approached by the attorney who wrote the wills. Embarrassed, he apologized to Libby for wasting her trip to his office, but unfortunately, the new receptionist was not aware that Michael had already called the attorney to discuss the couple's impending divorce. The attorney told Libby that he was already representing Michael, so he could not take her case, as it would be a conflict of interest.

Efficient Appointment Procedures and Avoiding Conflict-of-Interest Problems

How should Libby have been treated when she first telephoned the law firm for an appointment? In Libby's case, the unnecessary confusion could easily have been averted if an efficient appointment procedure had been in place. First, who was answering the telephone at the law firm? If it was a receptionist, the receptionist should be taught the fundamentals of setting up appointments. The receptionist should have easy access to a list of each of the law firm's clients, and if there is more than one attorney in the firm, the list should include which attorney is handling which case. The easiest way to access client names is by using a computer program designed to cross-check possible conflict-of-interest problems. Numerous computer programs are designed to make law office management an easier task. Alternatively, some attorneys make themselves available for short telephone consultations prior to the first appointment.

Once any possible conflicts are avoided, the person who makes appointments for the firm's attorneys should ask why the appointment is being made. Knowing *why* an appointment is being made will alert the attorney to the subject matter and help him prepare for the upcoming appointment. Asking the client for the reason for the interview also gives the receptionist an opportunity to send the new client a letter that clearly lists the pertinent documents and financial records the client should gather. The first appointment in a divorce case is much more productive and everyone's work is made a lot easier if the client brings such documents and financial records to the meeting. Alternatively, some attorneys use the first interview as a consultation to see if the individual wishes to retain the attorney—and if the attorney wants the person as a client!

First Impressions, Lasting Impressions

The first contact a client has with a law firm very likely will produce in the client a lasting impression of that firm. During a client's initial interview, some attorneys prefer to have a paralegal present if the paralegal will be participating in preparing the client's case. However, some attorneys prefer to see clients alone during the first interview in order to develop a rapport with them. Other attorneys prefer to see clients alone first, and then to ask their paralegals to complete an extensive client questionnaire with the clients.

The first meeting with a client seeking a divorce is typically the first legal step toward ending the marriage, and for most clients, it is a huge emotional drain. Clients who are seeking a divorce typically speak with the attorney about their fears, concerns, and reasons for seeking a divorce.

For the attorney, this an excellent opportunity to explain the steps taken when seeking a divorce, the attorney's hourly fee, and the work that a paralegal will be doing on the client's case. The description of the paralegal's work should emphasize the cost savings when a paralegal works on a client's case under the supervision of the attorney. While reviewing the applicable state law, including custody, support, and property division, the attorney should take the opportunity to further explain how long it typically takes for a divorce to be finalized in that particular state. An explanation of the process for initiating temporary spousal and child support may be discussed, and finally, the attorney will give the client a list of documents the client must gather in order to assist the attorney with the preparation of the case (if these documents have not been gathered already). Once the decision has been made, the client is given a retainer agreement to read and then sign, along with the attorney.

Meeting the Client's Needs

Libby cannot believe that Michael got himself together and called an attorney already. This surprising turn of events leaves her in the position of finding another attorney. Paralegals need to realize that when a new client approaches a law firm, she may have seldom—or perhaps *never*—had the need to seek the advice of an attorney before. A fine-tuned sensitivity to a client's emotional state before, during, and after closing the case will help the paralegal develop a rapport with the client. In the paralegal role, you often will have more contact with the client than the attorney handling the case, since attorneys are often out of the office (e.g., attending court or depositions).

The paralegal's relationship with a new client can influence whether that client comes back to the law firm when other types of legal work are needed. A satisfied client usually means a returning client and referrals. There is no better advertising than that by word of mouth. A loyal client helps to ensure the financial stability of the law firm and, therefore, the paralegal's position.

SUSAN TRAINS FOR DIVORCE PRACTICE

All the attorneys at Johnson & Webster believe their staff can help to make or break a law firm's reputation. Alyssa and J. D. decided years ago that training their support staff in every detail of their family law practice would result in happier and more satisfied clients *plus* reduce the stress of practicing law in such a busy practice.

Alyssa and J. D. decided to have lunch outside the office to discuss Susan's progress. They chatted about their spouses and children, and eventually the conversation shifted back to work. "You know J. D., I'm glad Susan studied the Family Law basics in college, but I *definitely* want to completely train her in the way we work all our cases," Alyssa commented. J. D. nodded agreeably while munching on the Rose Cafe's blue-plate special. She continued, "She's really been quick to pick up our methods, and I'm happy with this rookie's work."

"Yeah, I am, too—but remember that *dog* of a first memorandum of law?" J. D. interjected.

Alyssa laughed and replied, "That *was* pretty bad, but Pat guided her on the appellate brief and that worked out well. Now, she has worked on a paternity case, a few prenuptial agreements, the Mahoney adoption, and a smattering of just about everything else we are doing. Remember, too, she has brought several clients to the firm."

Finishing with lunch, J. D. pushed his chair back from the table and said, "I know what you're getting at. You want me to play teacher and train her from start to finish with a divorce case."

Alyssa answered, "You know me too well, but you're a great teacher, and I have the patience of a toddler sometimes."

Laughing, J. D. teased, "Don't insult toddlerdom—you can be far worse."

Alyssa chuckled and replied, "I know. But, seriously, I think Susan needs to be trained in a methodical way, and it should come from you, Teach."

"Okay, okay, let's get out of here before you ask me to do something else," J. D. remarked.

SUSAN IS ASSIGNED TO HER FIRST DIVORCE CASE

Susan's boss, J. D. Dombroski, seemed to be in the mood to lecture. He said, "So you see, Susan, when a marriage breaks up, there are *three* versions of the story of why *happily ever after* ended in a visit to our law office." Pausing for dramatic effect, J. D. concluded, "The *true* story of why a marriage goes bust usually lies somewhere between *his* version and *her* version of the breakup." J. D. suddenly remembered why he had asked Susan to come into his office. "Listen to me. I'm starting to sound like a philosopher. I asked you in to tell you about your newest assignment," he announced. "I know you studied Family Law in college, but we'd like to begin training you in the way our firm handles our divorce cases. So, I'm putting you on a new divorce case. The client is coming in today." Looking through his papers for the details, he continued, "I believe you know her. Her name is Elizabeth Smith. She mentioned to the receptionist that you referred her to our firm."

Susan nodded and thought of her neighbors, Mike and Libby Smith. Both seemed like perfectly nice people separately, but when they were together, *nice* was not a word that popped into Susan's mind, or into the mind of anyone else within hearing distance. She told J. D., "My parents know the Smiths better than I do. I don't really know them very well, but Mrs. Smith knows I work at a law firm, and she needs help." Susan paused, and then continued, "So I suggested she call the firm if she was serious about a divorce. I think there's a lot of anger between the Smiths, and I just wonder how they can be like they are together, when they are such nice people individually."

Seeing that Susan was asking for an answer, and not just posing a rhetorical question, J. D. replied, "Sue, I wish I could tell you that, but I learned years ago that I do not do the client justice if I play at being a psychiatrist. Mrs. Smith is coming in at two o'clock. I'd like you to attend the interview session. She actually asked if you could assist with the case." Pausing, he added reflectively, "Susan, the best thing you and I can do for Mrs. Smith is to make sure she has the best legal assistance we can provide and to try to be a strong shoulder for her to lean on."

Susan left J. D's office and headed back to the library to finish some research she had been working on for the last day and a half. Walking down the firm's expansive paneled corridor, Susan thought, "This may be my first real-life divorce case, but I'm going to take this opportunity to be a human sponge and learn everything I can."

MEETING THE NEW CLIENT

During a client's first appointment with a new attorney, she should get an opportunity to meet any support staff who will be working on her case. Hopefully, she has brought financial records if she was asked to do so when she made the appointment. The client will very likely appreciate having an opportunity to explain why she has reached the difficult point of wanting to file for a divorce and what she wants from the divorce with respect to financial matters and custody, if applicable.

A client's emotions are likely to alternate between anger, frustration, resignation, and sadness during the initial interview with a divorce attorney. While the attorney should be ready with tissues and empathy, he should also make sure that the interview stays on track concerning the legal issues that must be discussed.

The list of *essential* questions to ask a divorce client is lengthy. For example:

❐ Has the client separated from her spouse?
❐ Are there children involved?

❏ How are the client and the children surviving financially?

❏ Are the children staying with the mother, but also visiting their father?

❏ Is there mutually owned property that needs to be protected?

❏ Does the client understand the financial costs involved in filing for divorce and completing the dissolution of marriage process?

❏ Does the client know what kind of work a paralegal can do on her case?

The list of client questions could continue for pages.

The list of questions to be asked of Elizabeth Smith was typical in its number and variety. A transcript of Elizabeth Smith's interview with J. D. is provided in Exhibit 8.1. The exhibit demonstrates what a client interview is like in a relatively uncomplicated (or so it may seem at first) divorce scenario. A client's interview would be more extensive than Elizabeth Smith's if large financial matters were at issue or a possible custody dispute existed. Mrs. Smith's meeting was designed to familiarize J. D. with the needs and circumstances of a client he had never met before. Read the interview in Exhibit 8.1 to see what Mrs. Smith hopes J. D. and Susan can do to help her.

EXHIBIT 8.1 The Interview: Libby Tells It Like It Is (for Her)

J. D.: Mrs. Smith? Good afternoon. How are you?

Libby: Good, thank you. Well, actually, I've been better. I'm here because I think it's time for a divorce. Please call me Libby. I heard about your office from my neighbor's daughter, Susan. Is Susan going to be here during our meeting? I'd be much more comfortable with Susan in the office. I'm hoping she can work with you on the divorce. That's why I decided to come to you.

J. D.: Yes, of course. The receptionist is calling Susan in now. Oh, here she is.

Susan: Hi Lib. How are you? Mr. Dombroski said it would be okay for me to sit in and take notes.
Typically at this point the client has been seated, and perhaps coffee or water has been offered. There should be tissues in the office and plenty of them because more than likely there will be emotional reaction to some of the questions. If a client has insisted on coming into the law office as soon as possible, there may not have been enough time for the client to gather all the records and supporting documents the attorney will need for the case.

J. D.: Yes, Susan will definitely be working with me on your case. So, I have quite a long set of questions I'd like to ask you—if you are sure you want to move forward with the filing of a divorce complaint.

Libby: I'm sure. I didn't come in here without thinking about it long and hard. I think it's best for me and for the children. So, I don't want to be rude, but if we could just move ahead, I'd appreciate it.

J.D.:   Okay. What was your maiden name, and what is your date of birth?

Libby: Moore, and I was born on October 3, 1963.

J. D.: Your husband's name and date of birth?

Libby: My husband's name is Michael Smith, and he was born December 9, 1961.

J. D.: And your address?

Libby: We live on Main Street in the town of Newton.

J. D.: The house number?

Libby: 55

J. D.: Is that in Sussex County?

Libby: Yes.

(continued)

EXHIBIT 8.1 *continued*

J. D.: Do you recall if our firm ever represented you or your husband before?

Libby: No, your receptionist asked me that. I've personally never been represented before. I've never had a legal problem before this came up. My husband's attorney is Howard Hughey of Dewey, Hughey & Lewey. Do you want me to tell you my story?

J. D.: Yes, that is exactly what I was going to ask you to do.

Libby: Okay. Well, I'm here because Michael and I just can't agree on anything. I can't live with him. It's reached a point where he says terrible, cruel things to me. I'm afraid of him sometimes. I really don't like the way he treats me or the children. And he came from such a fine, upstanding family.

J. D.: Do you think you or the children are in any danger?

Libby: No, I don't think we're going to be the next *Law and Order* episode. He just seems so mad at me all the time. It's horrible at our house—very tense.

J. D.: Has Michael been diagnosed with any medical or psychological conditions?

Libby: He just sits in his chair and watches television. So, unless being lazy is such a condition, the answer is no. I am afraid because he smokes and I'm afraid that he's going to fall asleep with a lit cigarette. I can't get him out of a recliner we bought him for Father's Day last year. My husband will not be parted from it. He loves it; he never leaves it. But the thing is, he's becoming a terrible example to the children. He's not healthy. It's been like this ever since he went into therapy to deal with his feelings about hitting 40. I think he was trying to get in touch with himself, but he should have just left himself alone.

J.D.: How long has your husband been like this?

Libby: Well, I'd say for the last year, it's gotten worse. He's always been a little cold and distant. But I was young when I met him, and I just thought he was something different and exciting from my family who are not cold and distant at all—just the opposite. Well, frankly, I thought he'd change. I thought having children would warm him up, but it didn't.

J. D.: Do you still have a physical relationship with your husband?

Libby: No, not really. He's been very cold and distant for months.

J. D.: Is your husband employed?

Libby: Well, he works for an accounting firm. He was so good. He used to be their best fellow, but I think he's lost interest in his work, too.

J. D.: Does he know you're here?

Libby: No, he doesn't know I'm here. To be honest, I went to another lawyer first, over at Dewey, Hughey & Lewey. They'd done our wills and that's when I found out Hughey was already representing my husband in the divorce. I didn't even know about a divorce yet.

J. D.: That must have been very hard for you, hearing the news that way.

Libby: Yes, but I've really made up my mind now.

J. D.: Okay, let's continue. When were you married?

Libby: We were married in Sparta, New Jersey, on Valentine's Day 1986.

J. D.: How long have you been living in your home?

Libby: We've been living there for 10 years.

J. D.: How much is your house worth?

Libby: Our house is probably worth around $200,000 after all the work we have put into it.

J. D.: Is the checking account in both of your names?

Libby: Well, it is, but the money I put in there just seems to go away. I think that he's buying a lot of lottery tickets, but he just denies it. Where's the money going otherwise? Well, I don't know; I hate to say that about my husband.

J. D.: Is the house in your name *and* his name?

Libby: Yes, we bought it together.

J. D.: Do you have children together?

Libby: We have two children, Alphonse and Brianna.

J. D.: How old are they?

Libby: Al is 10 years old, and Bri is 12 years old. I really want them out of this whole situation. I can't stand it anymore.

J. D.: Do your children attend public or private school?

Libby: They're in public school. We're a basic middle-class family. Anyway, we were—until his gambling gave him his high. I believe—I'm not a psychologist of course—but I believe having read all the books (and I do read magazines every month) that his gambling gave him a high that helped with his undiagnosed depression. I think he always had untreated depression and that the gambling helped him forget his problems. He *said* he's stopped, but I don't know for sure.

J. D.: I assume that you are still living in the same residence.

Libby: For now, yes. That's basically it. Can you file for divorce right away? Can you get him out of the house? I don't know what else to tell you. I'm not a therapist. I'm not his mother. I'm supposed to be his wife, but I've just had it. My Aunt Josephine used to have a saying when she was exhausted. I finally understand what she meant. She'd say, "I feel like a piece of meat and I'm done, so put a fork in me." I'm done with Michael. A divorce is the only thing that might get him out of that recliner!

J. D.: I'll need to ask very specific questions about your financial picture. What has your joint and individual income been the last year?

Libby: Well, I made about $16,000 from my art. I can't believe its finally selling after all these years, but it isn't a sure thing. Michael's salary is $50,000 per year. There have been ups and downs, and we've used that money for renovations, and the kids have lots of lessons and lots of different things. We spent the money. There was all that gambling for quite a while. I'm not going to say that we didn't spend the money. We spent the money. We went on family vacations and had nice clothes. But now we don't have much. I'm not complaining about having nothing, though—I'm complaining about the fact that I can't take him anymore.

J. D.: I understand. Do you have other investments?

Libby: We have a $15,000 IRA in my name and Michael's 401K with a face value of $35,000.

J. D.: Is there any chance of reconciliation from your aspect?

Libby: Maybe in heaven.

J. D.: Susan told me you have a small farm. I'd like to know the costs of maintaining it. What do you have on this farm?

Libby: We have chickens, rabbits, a goat, two horses, and a llama named Snowflake.

J. D.: What money was used for the down payment on the farm? Whose money?

Libby: I guess it was *our* money. I mean, I was so busy being a mother and making dinner until I found myself with my art. Michael was always the center of my existence until my art. It was really Michael who wanted the farm and the animals—you know, the whole Currier and Ives thing. The truth is that he's never had the time to care for the animals. He hasn't been much interested in the reality of just how much work fixing up the place really is. And now, believe it or not, he blames *me* for wanting to buy it and take the work on.

J. D.: How much does it cost to maintain a little farm—you know, to feed the animals and to hire help around the place?

Libby: Oh, I would say that feed for the animals is about $300 a month. I clean the horses. I clean the llama. I clean the chickens. I do everything. I do all the cleaning of the house. I take care of everything.

J. D.: After the divorce, do you want to keep the animals or sell everything?

Libby: *I* never wanted the animals in the first place! I'll give all the pets away to good homes, and with the chickens, we'll have a barbecue, J. D. The whole gang here at the office can come, and that will be the end of Michael's chickens.

J. D.: How much is left on the mortgage?

Libby: Well, the mortgage is $1,250 a month, but we still have 20 years to go, so about $170,000 is what is left on it.

J. D.: Do your children have extra expenses?

Libby: They attend public school, but they do take some private lessons in music.

J. D.: How much is that?

Libby: About $100 a month for the two children.

J. D.: How much does it cost to maintain your lifestyle, business, and your personal expenses?

Libby: Well, I'll give you my list here. Your secretary told me to bring the list that she faxed to me. I'd say repairs and maintenance are about $150 a month. Heat is about $150 a month because we're wood-heated. We've got a lot of wood on our property.

J. D.: Who cuts the wood?

Libby: I do. I really was into the *Little House on the Prairie* thing when I was a girl.

(continued)

EXHIBIT 8.1 *continued*

J. D.:   How much is the electric?

Libby: Oh, electric is about $100 a month. It is expensive because a lot of my artwork is done by welding.

J. D.:   Phone?

Libby: Phone is about $80 a month, and cable is $45 a month.

J. D.:   Food?

Libby: Food is $800 a month.

J. D.:   How about health insurance?

Libby: Oh yes, we're very well-insured through Michael. He's very good that way.

J. D.:   Do you have a cell phone?

Libby: No.

J. D.:   Do you grow a lot of your own food?

Libby: Some.

J. D.:   How much does it cost to do that?

Libby: Well, I use the manure from the horses and I really think that's the way to go and I will continue to grow some food. But it still costs us about $300 a month because we only do organic and we donate a lot to the local shelter.

J. D.:   Was there ever a time that you said you wanted to go back to work full-time?

Libby: I can honestly say that I have never said that. I was always an artist. In the beginning of our marriage, I worked in Macy's as a perfume sample girl, and later I worked in a school nursery. I was the craftperson. I was very happy. I *had* thought about becoming an art teacher years ago.

J. D.:   So your husband never said anything to you like "Honey, you need to get a job?" He was happy with the arrangement you had?

Libby: He was happy because he wanted the house always perfect and for me to be available to entertain. I had to make dinner for clients and be available to go out for client dinners. I also had to make dinner for him every night that he was home. He had certain dietary needs. He's very strict on his organic eating. His worst habit is smoking.

J. D.:   He gave you money for the children's lunches for school?

Libby: Oh, the children's lunches are $50 a month. I imagine that my clothing isn't much. I wear a lot of natural fabrics that I weave myself.

J. D.:   How much does the yarn cost?

Libby: The yarn is from the llama. I also have club dues for the gym. That's about $600 a year. I have an orthodontist for Alphonse. Unfortunately, he started to look like one of our rabbits, so we thought it was necessary to get him braces.

J. D.:   How much is that?

Libby: That's $350 a month. Oh, and my greatest indulgence is my hair. I must have natural boar bristle brushes and I must have my hair professionally cut. My haircuts are $40.

J. D.:   How often is that?

Libby: Every six weeks, religiously.

J. D.:   How about the children?

Libby: My youngest—she has long hair that I trim for her, but my son does need a haircut every six weeks at $12 a haircut.

J. D.:   What about their clothes?

Libby: Oh, the children's clothing is expensive. Well, you know, you have to dress them in a certain way. Otherwise they just won't be accepted at school. So I would say that the children's clothing is at least $560 per kid for two seasons.

J. D.:   That's $2,240 per year.

Libby: Wow, I guess so.

J. D.:   All right, we have discussed the house; now, what about the bank accounts?

Libby: The savings account has about $2,000, and the checking account has about $3,000.

J. D.:   What about vacations?

Libby: Well, I like them. Is that your question?

J. D.:   Actually, I meant, how often do you vacation as a family?

Libby: Well, say we have the week in Florida at my mom's. That's about $400 and we always have at least two weeks at the lake. That's about $2,000.

J. D.:   You'll also have to bring all tax forms for the last three years, insurance information, and bank accounts. Do you think that he'll try to get custody of the kids?

Libby: No, I don't think so. I think that they should stay with me and continue going to school where they are. A divorced friend said I should ask for *joint legal custody,* but I should have *physical custody.*

J. D.:   And do you think he would be agreeable to that?

Libby: I think that he wants to continue to see the children, but would be agreeable.

J. D.:   Do you have any credit cards?

Libby: Yes, we have two credit cards each.

J. D.:   What are the balances on them?

Libby: About $6,700.

J. D.:   After these proceedings go through, how do you plan to provide for yourself?

Libby: Well, I guess if my artwork keeps going the way it has been, I'll be all right. Like I said, I made $16,000 this last year. It's the first time that I've ever made any money with my artwork, I can't believe it. But I can't guarantee that it's going to continue. So, I think, I obviously can't support the children on that income.

J. D.:   Do you have any type of domestic help, such as a cleaning service?

Libby: No, I'm a woman of the hearth. I do my own cleaning, my own gardening, and my own growing of food.

J. D.:   Do you have a pool?

Libby: No, we swim in the pond.

J. D.:   Do you have a landscaper?

Libby: Yes, you are looking at her.

J. D.:   Snow removal?

Libby: You are looking at the snow remover, too. Michael has a bad back, so I am a woman of all trades. However, I do need help with maintenance stuff. That's about $200 a month for repairs on the old place.

J. D.:   Do you eat at restaurants at all?

Libby: Only the Organic Garden.

J. D.:   How often?

Libby: Twice a month I meet a girlfriend there. It costs about $20 or $30 a month. Oh, and I make my own wine.

J. D.:   You have a lot of talents. It's your husband's loss.

Libby: I could be the Martha Stewart of Newton.

J. D.:   Absolutely. Now, the wine-making has got to be expensive. How much does that cost?

Libby: You take a grape and a foot. Haven't you seen the *I Love Lucy* wine-making episode? The only thing I did want to mention to you is that our furniture is pretty expensive. It's a lot of lovely inherited pieces of mine and Michael's in the mission style. Very nice, have you ever heard of Stickley?

J. D.:   Yes, of course, Stickley designed furniture is incredibly expensive. Didn't a Stickley table go for $30,000 at auction last year?

Libby: Well we don't have any of that. We do have some Pickley. It was a knock-off, 80 years ago, of Stickley. Even a knock off is worth something, though, so we think our furniture is worth about $25,000.

J. D.:   How about jewelry—do you have any?

Libby: I just have my wedding band.

(continued)

EXHIBIT 8.1 *continued*

J. D.:   Have either one of you received an inheritance or financial settlement of any kind?

Libby: Well, actually Michael had an inheritance, but we put it all into the barn. Was that a bad thing to do?

J. D.:   How much was it?

Libby: $30,000. We spent it renovating our kitchen, three years ago. Was that a good thing?

J. D.:   For you, yes.

Libby: So, I don't have any other expenses that I can think about. Oh, magazines and periodicals—I do read a lot of them, you know. We're out there in the country, and there's not much to do. I buy *Llama Life* and *Living with Fowl.* I would say they cost about $13 a month.

J. D.:   How about your car? How much does it cost to maintain it?

Libby: Oh, I'm under a prepaid plan. We're both under warranty.

J. D.:   Okay, how about gas?

Libby: For my car, about $20 a week.

J. D.:   You don't have other things, like motorcycles, four-wheelers, or boats, do you?

Libby: No, we have a tractor, though—does that count? The tractor is worth only about $1,000.

J. D.:   How about car insurance? How much do you pay just for your car?

Libby: The car insurance is $60 a month. You also have to think about the tires and oil changes. This has been very tiring for me. I really don't want the children to spend Christmas with anyone but me at the barn. It's very important to me—Christmas is *my* holiday.

J. D.:   Out of everything that we have discussed, what is it that you really want?

Libby: I want my children, I want my barn, and I want to maintain my lifestyle. I guess I need to get child support and I also need some money for myself—I think some spousal support. Seventeen years of marriage should mean something—that's what I think.

J. D.:   It should.

Libby: Thank you. It feels so good to hear you say that.

J. D.:   As far as your health, do you have anything that might require medical attention?

Libby: No, I'm a workhorse.

J. D.:   How will you be paying your legal fees?

Libby: I make beautiful metal sculptures out of old railroad pieces. I could trade you one for your work. Do you think that you would be interested in doing that?

J.D.:   Usually we don't do that. The partners don't allow it.

Libby: Well, I guess there's some money in the savings. I can pay with that. That's our joint account. I hope there won't be that much argument with this case. Michael doesn't like to spend a lot of money, unless he's gambling, if he doesn't have to. I don't think he'll want to drag this out.

J. D.:   That's good to hear. Well, Libby, that's it for now. I'll have Susan call you with any follow-up questions I have.

Libby: Thanks. I feel better for having gotten all this off my chest. What's next?

J. D.:   The process goes something like this. First, you'll read and sign the retainer agreement and pay our retainer fee. Next, we'll put together a *pendente lite* package for you and hopefully that will lead to some temporary support. We'll have to have a hearing on that motion at the courthouse. We'll write up your complaint and a case information statement and file them along with your motion. We'll also send a courtesy copy to your husband's attorney with interrogatories.

J. D.:   *(Libby had been following J. D., to this point, but now looked confused, so J. D. explained what he meant.)* Interrogatories are legal questions we ask the opposition to answer and these questions begin our discovery process. Okay?

Libby: I'm with you. Go ahead.

J. D.:   If this doesn't settle easily, we'll probably have to move on to depositions. Depositions are oral questions and answers.

Libby: I've seen those done on television with a court reporter.

J. D.:   Exactly. Anyway, the court system requires that we show up at the courthouse periodically for case management and case settlement conferences if we don't settle this quickly. Eventually, you'll have a final hearing to receive the official judgment of divorce. Everything we end up agreeing to goes into the final order of divorce, which is then filed with the court clerk. We'll ask that all support payments be made through the probation department. That's pretty much it. Do you have any other questions?

Libby: Not right now, but thank you for giving me an idea of where we're going with this.

J. D.: I'm glad I can help you. It's been a pleasure meeting you. I'll let Susan show you out.

SUSAN'S REACTION

As she escorted Libby to the firm's lobby door after the interview, Susan's head was swimming. She could not wait to get back to the office and talk to J. D. about the interview, but she wanted to be polite to Libby. Interrupting Susan's thoughts, Libby said, "Susan, thanks for sitting through the interview with me. I'm glad I know someone here at the office."

"No problem, I'm glad to help during a tough time," Susan responded, as Libby waved good-bye. Heading back to J. D.'s office, Susan tried to remember all the steps of a typical divorce that she had learned about in her Family Law course.

Knocking on J. D.'s door, Susan was greeted by J. D.'s cheery question, "So, what did you think of your first client interview?"

Susan quickly answered, "I forgot how extensive the questions have to be, and to tell you the truth, I was a little confused regarding the proper steps to follow right up to the final judgment. I'm glad you went over them with Libby. It was a good refresher for me."

Smiling, J. D. responded, "I'll need you to set up the client file for Libby's case, and I'll let you try your hand at the *pendente lite* motion and the case information statement."

Excited, but worried she would not know how to begin, Susan said, "I'll be happy to do that. I did work on Mrs. Vander's *pendente lite* motion on my first day, but I'm not quite sure about the case information statement."

"Oh, I'm definitely going to give you a push in the right direction," J. D. answered. "I learned years ago to never reinvent the wheel, so what I'll do is give you another file with the same kind of work, and you can use it as a model." J. D. shuffled some papers, and then continued, "Since this is your first case for the firm, I'll also do a motion and a case information statement, or CIS for short, to show you the correct version and for you to use in checking your work."

Relieved, Susan said thankfully, "That's great, J. D. I really appreciate your guidance."

Getting some sample files out of the file cabinet, he responded with a smile, "No problem. Hiring you means the firm has made an investment in you. It's in everyone's best interest that you learn the correct way to do things from the start. So, let's begin our review."

Read Libby's retainer agreement with J. D. in Exhibit 8.2. The standard Johnson & Webster retainer agreement is the first item J. D. will have Susan put in Libby's case file, along with the notes from the interview.

DEALING WITH A CLIENT'S IMMEDIATE FINANCIAL NEEDS

Most client interviews end with the client asking, "What's next?" J. D. knew that dealing with Libby's immediate financial needs should take first priority, and that's exactly how Libby's interview ended. He explained just how one goes about having one's financial needs met when a divorce is looming. Fortunately, Libby had not been shy about listing her immediate financial needs because she got a big shock when she went to her bank a few days after her consultation with J. D.

EXHIBIT 8.2 Retainer Agreement

J. D. Dombroski, Esq.
Johnson & Webster, Esqs.
123 Main Street
Newton, New Jersey 12345
973-555-1212
Attorney for Plaintiff   March 1, 2003

Mrs. Elizabeth Moore Smith
55 Main Street
Newton, New Jersey 12345

      Re: *Smith v. Smith*

Dear Mrs. Smith:

      The purpose of this memorandum of retainer is to confirm our understanding whereby you have retained my services for the purpose of representing you in a matrimonial matter. Our agreement includes the following:

1. *Fee Arrangement.* The fee arrangement shall be $200 per hour for attorney time required to complete the matter. The services will include appearances in the Superior Court of New Jersey through judgment and I shall not be obligated to proceed to appeal unless this agreement is extended in writing to cover such services. The fee shall include, but is not be limited to, the following types of services: office conferences; telephone conferences; court appearances; preparation of documents; review of documents and correspondence received; attendance at settlement conferences; and such other reasonable and necessary services as may be required to fully represent you. Traveling time to and from court and other meetings is included. All services will be billed to the nearest 1/10th of one hour, with that measure of time being the minimum charge per service. In representing you, it is difficult to predict the time that will be required to complete the matter, and therefore it is impossible at this time to establish a fixed fee. You should be aware that a staff paralegal may be utilized to provide services allowed by law under the supervision of a firm attorney. The services of the paralegal will be billed at $75 per hour of paralegal time. These services include preparation of documents, filing of documents, legal research and investigatory matters necessary to the adequate representation of your interests in this matter. All paralegal services will be billed to the nearest 1/10 of one hour.

2. *Disbursements.* Any and all reasonable disbursements necessarily incurred by me on your behalf shall be in addition to my fees and paid by you. Such disbursements include, but are not limited to, court costs, sheriff's fees, search fees, appraisal fees, recordation fees, long-distance telephone charges, photocopying costs, and delivery service fees. Additional fees that may be required to properly represent you in this matter include accounting fees and fees for investigative services. As to those services, you and I shall jointly decide whom shall be retained to perform such services, and you will make your own financial arrangements with the accountants or investigators, as appropriate.

3. *Retainer.* As down payment toward my final fees, I will require an initial retainer of $3,000. If the services rendered by me are completed in less than 15 hours, I will keep the full retainer as a minimum fee.

4. *Rendering of Statements.* Once the retainer has been exhausted, I will render statements to you on a monthly basis, payment for which shall be due and payable as of the due date for each monthly statement. However, if any balance remains due at the time of final hearing, then, as accurately as can be calculated at that time, the balance shall then be due. Any balance due upon the rendering of the final statement shall be paid promptly. All payments received from you shall be credited toward earned services and incurred disbursements.

5. *Payment of Fees by Spouse.* My fees, and the disbursements incurred on your behalf, are your primary and individual obligation, regardless of any court orders for your spouse to pay counsel fees. However, the court may award, or your spouse may agree to pay, all or part of my fees and disbursements. Such awards or agreements to pay counsel fees are, at this time, quite unpredictable. Further, such an award or agreement as to the payment of your counsel fees is not a guarantee that the same will actually be paid. Therefore, any court award of counsel fees or agreement by your spouse to pay the same does not affect the amount of counsel fees and costs that you are hereby obligated to pay to me, except to the extent

that such payments are actually received, in which case they shall be credited first toward any balance due to me by you, thus reducing that outstanding balance. If a payment is received by me from your spouse during the course of representation and it exceeds the balance then due from you, it shall be credited toward future services. If a payment is received from your spouse in excess of the final statement, any overage will be refunded to you. Should you be obligated to pay counsel fees and costs to your spouse as a result of a court order or your voluntary agreement to do so, such payment shall be separate and independent from any sums due to me on account of my representation of you.

6.   *Interest, etc.* To the extent that a statement has not been paid in full within 30 days of the date of the statement, interest shall apply to any outstanding balance and shall be calculated at the rate of 12% per annum on the declining balance, or such higher rate as allowed by law on judgments.

7.   *Guarantees.* There have been no representations or guarantees made by me regarding the outcome of this matter as to the obtaining of a judgment of divorce, annulment, or separate maintenance, as the case may be, or as to the nature or amounts of any awards or distributions of alimony, child support, property division, counsel fees and costs, the terms of an interspousal agreement, or any other aspect of this matter. Any discussions in this regard, past or future, are limited only to predictions of the same based on my experience and judgment, but in no event will be taken as a representation or guarantee as to the results, which might be obtainable either in a contested case or by way of negotiated settlement.

8   *Duties and Conduct.* It shall be my duty to exert my best efforts on your behalf in the course of my representation of you in this matter. It shall be your duty to cooperate with me as fully as possible in order that I may best represent you. In this regard, you will:

A.   Not sign documents without prior review by me;

B.   Promptly furnish me with information relative to the marital history and financial aspects of the case, as well as other documents when requested;

C.   Promptly notify me in the event of a reconciliation, and be absolutely truthful with me in order that I may best advise you and represent your interests.

9   *Communication.* For informational purposes, you will receive copies of all pleadings and correspondence initiated by me. In addition, you will receive copies of all pleadings and nonroutine correspondence initiated by the attorney for your spouse. Additionally, I shall be available for telephone conferences or meetings with you during normal office hours. However, if because of prior engagements I am unavailable, I shall make every attempt to communicate with you as quickly as possible.

Where appropriate, if it appears that I will be unable to do so promptly, I shall request my secretary or paralegal to communicate with you for the purpose of determining the reason for your inquiry in order that any action I might take if I were otherwise immediately available will not be delayed. It is my policy to foster as much communication between you and me as possible in order that you be kept well-informed and so that I will have the information I need in order to best represent you.

10.   *Decision Making.* Inasmuch as a decision with regard to any particular proposal for settlement of the financial aspects of this matter will undoubtedly have substantial effects upon you in the future, those substantive decisions will be made by you. Of course you will have the benefit of my advice and prediction of what I think a court would do if the matter was not settled but was instead submitted to the court for a decision. In view of your relative unfamiliarity with the workings of the court system, I will have primary responsibility for procedural decisions that affect your case.

If you fully understand the contents of this memorandum and are in agreement with the terms thereof, kindly sign one of the copies and return it to me, and retain the other copy for your records.

Very truly yours,

_____

J. D. Dombroski, Esq.

JDD/ak
Encls.

The undersigned understands and agrees to the contents hereof.

_____

Elizabeth Moore Smith

DATED: March 21, 2003

Here is what happened. After Michael returned from his business trip, he was called by his attorney. The attorney told Michael that Libby had visited his office looking for legal representation for a divorce. This prompted Michael to speed up his plans for moving out of the barn. Needing deposit money, Michael nearly cleaned out their joint checking and savings accounts Luckily, Libby had paid the current month's mortgage and J. D.'s retainer before Michael's cleaning spree. Libby knew Michael would not continue to deposit his paycheck into their joint checking account. Even though Libby was beginning to make money from her artwork, the sales were intermittent, and currently her artwork is not selling. What should Libby do now?

Libby did the right thing in this situation: She asked for help. With hundreds of variations on the same theme, Libby's situation is fairly typical. You have two people living in one residence, and one moves out. Now the two people have the same income they had before, but two residences to pay for. It is the rare divorce that does not bring some economic hardship along with it. By the time the final divorce decree is handed down in the typical divorce case, the divorcing couple has negotiated the final property settlement, possibly child and spousal support, and child custody. The problem for most couples is that it might take years to get to the moment when the final decree or order is given. Meanwhile, children still need to eat, and bills will not wait until the divorce is finalized.

Recall Susan's *pendente lite* assignment from Chapter 1. Temporary support, also known as *pendente lite* support, is the legal solution to the financial difficulties that can occur during divorce proceedings. Literally translated, *pendente lite* means during the pendency of the litigation. For a court to grant an order for temporary support, the parties will have to appear for a hearing before a judge—or in some states, a commission—to argue why such support is needed. Temporary support paid by one spouse for the other spouse's temporary support is usually granted unless both spouses are self-supporting. If one spouse has temporary custody of minor children, the other spouse is usually ordered to pay temporary child support. Any temporary order may also be called an **interlocutory decree.** *Interlocutory* means temporary and not final. The amount of temporary support does not necessarily mean that the same amount will be granted in the final decree of divorce. However, the amount of temporary support granted will typically be a factor considered by the court in awarding final alimony and child support.

Also filed with the *pendente lite* application will be a financial accounting of the couple's finances, often called a *case information statement,* although it may be called by a different name depending on the state. All 50 states require that a financial accounting for the couple be filed with the court when temporary support is requested. The financial accounting details the couple's finances and needs. Even if no temporary support is being requested, the courts still require a complete financial accounting in order to make a final decision support and the property settlement.

Courts often direct that temporary and permanent alimony, as well as child support awards, be paid through a county agency such as the probation department. The probation department then establishes probation payment accounts for the alimony and child support. The probation department is often used because it is in the best position to institute efficient contempt proceedings if payment is not made as ordered.

Each client should be asked to fill out a case information statement that will give the court an extremely detailed financial picture of the couple's assets and liabilities. Libby's completed Case Information Statement, which is fairly typical, can be viewed in Exhibit 8.3. Notice how detailed the list of expenses is. Everything the Smith family spends money on (including shampoo) is listed. Can you imagine how much effort it takes to accurately determine the average family's living expenses?

EXHIBIT 8.3 Libby Smith's Case Information Statement

Attorney(s):　　　　　　J.D. DOMBROSKI, ESQ.
Office Address & Tel.No.:　123 MAIN STREET, NEWTON, NJ 12345
Attorney(s) for:　　　　　Plaintiff

ELIZABETH SMITH, Plaintiff, v. MICHAEL SMITH, Defendant.	SUPERIOR COURT OF NEW JERSEY CHANCERY DIVISION - FAMILY PART SUSSEX COUNTY Docket No. FM-19-12345-03 CASE INFORMATION STATEMENT OF ELIZABETH SMITH

NOTICE:　**This statement must be fully completed, filed and served, with all required attachments, in accordance with Court Rule 5:5-2 based upon the information available. In those case where the Case Information Statement is required, it shall be filed within 20 days after the filing of the Answer or Appearance. Failure to file a Case Information Statement may result in the dismissal of a party's pleadings.**

PART A - CASE INFORMATION:

		ISSUES IN DISPUTE:	
Date of Statement	10/20/2003	Cause of Action	No
Date of Divorce (post-Judgment matters)		Custody	Yes
	. . . .	Alimony	Yes
Date(s) of Prior Statement(s)		Child Support	Yes
		Equitable Distribution	Yes
. . . .		Counsel Fees	Yes
Your Birthdate	10/03/1963	Other	No
Birthdate of Spouse	12/09/1961	. . . .	
Date of Marriage	02/14/1986		
Date of Separation	. . . .		
Date of Complaint	. . . .		

Does an agreement exist between parties relative to any issue?　[　] Yes [X] No. If Yes, **ATTACH** a copy (if written) or a summary (if oral).

1. Names and Addresses of Parties:

Your Name　ELIZABETH SMITH
Street Address 55 MAIN STREET　　City NEWTON　　State/Zip NJ 07860
Other Party's Name　MICHAEL SMITH
Street Address (if different) 79 CAROL STREET　City OAK RIDGE　State/Zip NJ 07438

2. Name, Address, & Birthdate of all Child(ren); Person with whom Child(ren) Reside(s):

a. Child(ren) From This Relationship

Child's Full Name	Address	Birthdate	Person's Name
ALPHONSE SMITH	55 MAIN STREET, NEWTON	03/21/1993	PLAINTIFF
BRIANNA SMITH	55 MAIN STREET, NEWTON	04/21/1991	PLAINTIFF
. . . .	. . . .	. . . .	. . . .
. . . .	. . . .	. . . .	. . . .

b. Child(ren) From Other Relationships

Child's Full Name	Address	Birthdate	Person's Name
. . . .	. . . .	. . . .	. . . .
. . . .	. . . .	. . . .	. . . .
. . . .	. . . .	. . . .	. . . .
. . . .	. . . .	. . . .	. . . .

EASY SOFT, Inc.	C.I.S.(Revised, effective 04/02/2001): Untitled	04/14/03	Page 1

(continued)

EXHIBIT 8.3 *continued*

PART B - MISCELLANEOUS INFORMATION:

1. Name and Address of Your Employer   (Provide Name & Address of Business. if Self-employed)

Name of Employer SELF-EMPLOYED ARTIST   Address 55 MAIN STREET, NEWTON NJ

Name of Employer . . . .   Address . . . .

2. Health Insurance and Life Insurance Information:

ATTACH Affidavit of Insurance Coverage as required by Court Rule 5:4-2 (f) (See Part G)

3. Additional Identification:

   Social Security Number: 888-99-6666

   State Driver's License Number: NHK5555555   Eye Color: HAZEL

4. ATTACH sheet listing all prior/pending family actions involving support, custody or Domestic Violence listing Docket Number, County, State and the disposition reached.

PART C - INCOME INFORMATION: Complete this section for self and (if known) for spouse.

ATTACH to this form a corporate benefits statement as well as a statement of all fringe benefits of employment.

1. LAST YEAR'S INCOME

	Yours	Joint	Spouse or Former Spouse
1. Gross earned income last calendar (2002)	16,000.00	66,000.00	50,000.00
2. Unearned income (same year)	. . . .	. . . .	. . . .
3. Total Income Taxes paid on income (incl. Fed., State, F.I.C.A., and S.U.I.). If Joint Return, use middle column.	. . . .	7,500.00	7,500.00
4. Net income (1 + 2 - 3)	16,000.00	58,500.00	42,500.00

ATTACH a full and complete copy of last year's Federal and State Income Tax Returns. If none has been filed, **ATTACH** W-2 statement 1099's, Schedule C's, etc., to show total income plus a copy of the most recently filed Tax Returns.

Check if attached: Federal Tax Return [ ]   State Tax Return [ ]   W-2 [ ]   Other [ ]

2. PRESENT EARNED INCOME AND EXPENSES

	Yours	Spouse (if known)
1. Average Gross monthly income (based on last 3 pay periods - **ATTACH** pay stubs)	. . . .	4,166.00

   Commissions and bonuses, etc., are:

   [ ] included*   [ ] not included*   [X] not paid to you.   Comments: . . . .

   * **ATTACH** details of basis thereof, including, but not limited to, percentage overrides, timing of payments, etc.
      ATTACH copies of last three statements of such bonuses, commissions, etc.

2. Deductions per month (check all types of withholdings):		
[X] Federal [X] State [X] F.I.C.A. [X] S.U.I. [X Other	. . . .	624.90
3. Net Average Income (1 - 2)	. . . .	3,541.10

Comments: . . . .
         . . . .

PART G - INSURANCE COVERAGE

Name and Address of Your Health Insurance Company(ies); Policy Information:

Name of Company ABC INSURANCE   Address   200 ALPHA, GREEN, NJ
I.D. Number   58496   Group Number   1K45123
Coverage Type: Single [ ]   Parent-Child [ ]   Family [X]   Optical [ ]
                      Hospital [ ]   Major-Medical [ ]   Dental [ ]   Drug [ ]   Diagnostic
Check if made available through employment [X] or personally obtained [ ]
. . . .

Name of Company . . . .   Address   . . . .
I.D. Number   . . . .   Group Number   . . . .
Coverage Type: Single [ ]   Parent-Child [ ]   Family [ ]   Optical [ ]
                      Hospital [ ]   Major-Medical [ ]   Dental [ ]   Drug [ ]   Diagnostic
Check if made available through employment [X] or personally obtained [ ]
. . . .

Name of Company . . . .   Address   . . . .
I.D. Number   . . . .   Group Number   . . . .
Coverage Type: Single [ ]   Parent-Child [ ]   Family [ ]   Optical [ ]
                      Hospital [ ]   Major-Medical [ ]   Dental [ ]   Drug [ ]   Diagnostic
Check if made available through employment [X] or personally obtained [ ]
. . . .

Name of Company . . . .   Address   . . . .
I.D. Number   . . . .   Group Number   . . . .
Coverage Type: Single [ ]   Parent-Child [ ]   Family [ ]   Optical [ ]
                      Hospital [ ]   Major-Medical [ ]   Dental [ ]   Drug [ ]   Diagnostic
Check if made available through employment [X] or personally obtained [ ]
. . . .

Name and Address of Life Insurance Company(ies); Policy Information

Name of Company REEL INSURANCE COMPANY   Address   67 EAST SHORE, SPARTA, NJ
Policy Number   MM9856   Beneficiary   ELIZABETH SMITH
Face Amount $ 500,000.00   Name of Insured MICHAEL SMITH
Policy Owner   MICHAEL SMITH   2nd Beneficiary . . . .

Name of Company . . . .   Address   . . . .
Policy Number   . . . .   Beneficiary   . . . .
Face Amount $ . . . .   Name of Insured . . . .
Policy Owner   . . . .   2nd Beneficiary . . . .

Name of Company . . . .   Address   . . . .
Policy Number   . . . .   Beneficiary   . . . .
Face Amount $ . . . .   Name of Insured . . . .
Policy Owner   . . . .   2nd Beneficiary . . . .

Name of Company . . . .   Address   . . . .
Policy Number   . . . .   Beneficiary   . . . .
Face Amount $ . . . .   Name of Insured . . . .
Policy Owner   . . . .   2nd Beneficiary . . . .

Comments: . . . .
              . . . .

EXHIBIT 8.3 *continued*

3. YOUR YEAR-TO-DATE EARNED INCOME

Provide Dates: From . . . . To . . . .

1. GROSS EARNED INCOME: $ . . . .
   Number of Weeks   . . . .

2. TAX DEDUCTIONS: (Number of dependents: . .)

   a. Federal Income Taxes   a. $ . . . .
   b. N.J. Income Taxes   b. $ . . . .
   c. Other State Income Taxes   c. $ . . . .
   d. FICA   d. $ . . . .
   e. Medicare   e. $ . . . .
   f. S.U.I.   f. $ . . . .
   g. Estimated tax payments in excess of withholding   g. $ . . . .
      actually made
   h. . . . .   h. $ . . . .
   i. . . . .   i. $ . . . .
                                            TOTAL $ . . . .

3. GROSS INCOME NET OF TAXES $ . . . .

4. OTHER DEDUCTIONS   If mandatory, check box

   a. Hospitalization/Medical Insurance   a. $ . . . .   [ ]
   b. Life Insurance   b. $ . . . .   [ ]
   c. Pension/Profit Sharing Plans   c. $ . . . .   [ ]
   d. Savings/Bond plan   d. $ . . . .   [ ]
   e. Wage Execution   e. $ . . . .   [ ]
   f. Retirement Fund Payments   f. $ . . . .   [ ]
   g. Medical Reimbursement (flex fund)   g. $ . . . .   [ ]
   h. Other: . . . .   h. $ . . . .   [ ]
                                       TOTAL $ . . . .

5. NET YEAR-TO-DATE EARNED INCOME: $ . . . .

   NET AVERAGE EARNED INCOME PER MONTH: $ . . . .

4. YOUR YEAR-TO-DATE GROSS UNEARNED INCOME

Source	How often paid	Year to date amount
. . . .	. . . .	. . . .
. . . .	. . . .	. . . .

TOTAL GROSS UNEARNED INCOME YEAR TO DATE $ . . . .

5. HISTORY OF ADDITIONAL COMPENSATION

1. Have you received a bonus(es) during the current calendar year? If so, state the date(s) of receipt and set forth the gross and net amou received.   No

2. Did you receive a bonus(es) during the immediate past calendar year? If so, state the date(s) of receipt and set forth the gross and net amounts received.   No

3. Have you received any other supplemental compensation during either the current or immediate past calendar year? If so, state the da of receipt and set forth the gross and net amounts received. Also describe the nature of any supplemental compensation received. No

   . . . .
   . . . .

Date of receipt	Gross Amount	Net Amount
. . . .	. . . .	. . . .
. . . .	. . . .	. . . .
. . . .	. . . .	. . . .

PART D - MONTHLY EXPENSES (computed at 4.3 wks/mo.) . . . .

Should reflect standard of living established during marriage, but not repeat those income deductions listed on Part C.

		Yours and children (# . .) residing with you	Expenses paid for spouse and/or children (# . .) not residing with you
SCHEDULE A: SHELTER			
If Tenant:			
Rent	. . . .	$	$ . . . .
Heat (if not furnished)	. . . .	. . . .	. . . .
Electric & Gas (if not furnished)	. . . .	. . . .	. . . .
Renter's Insurance	. . . .	. . . .	. . . .
Parking (at Apartment)	. . . .	. . . .	. . . .
Other Charges (Itemize)	. . . .	. . . .	. . . .
. . . .		. . . .	. . . .
. . . .		. . . .	. . . .
. . . .		. . . .	. . . .
If Homeowner:			
Mortgage	. . . .	$ 1,250.00	$ . . . .
Real Estate Taxes (unless included w/ mortgage payment)		. . . .	. . . .
Homeowners Insurance (unless included w/ mortgage payment)		. . . .	. . . .
Repairs & Maintenance	. . . .	150.00	. . . .
Heat (unless Electric or Gas)	. . . .	150.00	. . . .
Electric & Gas	. . . .	100.00	. . . .
Water & Sewer	. . . .	. . . .	. . . .
Garbage Removal	. . . .	. . . .	. . . .
Other Mortgages or Home Equity Loans (Specify)	. . . .	. . . .	. . . .
. . . .		. . . .	. . . .
Snow Removal	. . . .	. . . .	. . . .
Lawn Care	. . . .	. . . .	. . . .
Maintenance (Condo/co-op)	. . . .	. . . .	. . . .
Other Charges (Itemize)	. . . .	. . . .	. . . .
. . . .		. . . .	. . . .
. . . .		. . . .	. . . .
. . . .		. . . .	. . . .
Tenant or Homeowner:			
Telephone	. . . .	$ 80.00	$ . . . .
Mobile/Cellular Telephone	. . . .	. . . .	. . . .
Service Contracts on Equipment	. . . .	45.00	. . . .
Cable TV	. . . .	. . . .	. . . .
Plumber/Electrician	. . . .	. . . .	. . . .
Equipment & Furnishings	. . . .	. . . .	. . . .
Internet Charges	. . . .	. . . .	. . . .
Other (itemize)	FARM ANIMAL FOOD	300.00	. . . .
. . . .		. . . .	. . . .
. . . .		. . . .	. . . .
. . . .		. . . .	. . . .
TOTAL		$ 2,075.00	$ . . . .
SHELTER COMBINED TOTAL		$ 2,075.00	
SCHEDULE B: TRANSPORTATION			
Auto Payment	. . . .	. . . .	. . . .
Auto Insurance (number of vehicles: 2)		60.00	. . . .
Registration, License, Maintenance		. . . .	. . . .
Fuel and Oil	. . . .	20.00	. . . .
Commuting Expenses	. . . .	. . . .	. . . .
Other Charges (Itemize)	. . . .	. . . .	. . . .
TOTAL		$ 80.00	$ . . . .
TRANSPORTATION COMBINED TOTAL		$ 80.00	

(continued)

EXHIBIT 8.3 *continued*

SCHEDULE C: PERSONAL

	Yours and children (# . .) residing with you	Expenses paid for spouse and/or children (# . .) not residing with you
Food at Home & household supplies	$ 800.00	$ . . . .
Prescription Drugs	. . . .	. . . .
Non-prescription drugs, cosmetics, toiletries & sundries	. . . .	. . . .
School Lunch	50.00	. . . .
Restaurants	30.00	. . . .
Clothing	187.00	. . . .
Dry Cleaning, Commercial Laundry	. . . .	. . . .
Hair Care	49.00	. . . .
Domestic Help	. . . .	. . . .
Medical (exclusive of psychiatric)*	. . . .	. . . .
Eye Care*	. . . .	. . . .
Psychiatric/psychological/counseling*	. . . .	. . . .
Dental (exclusive of Orthodontic)*	. . . .	. . . .
Orthodontic*	350.00	. . . .
Medical Insurance (hospital, etc.)*	. . . .	. . . .
Club Dues and Memberships	50.00	. . . .
Sports and Hobbies	. . . .	. . . .
Camps	. . . .	. . . .
Vacations	200.00	. . . .
Children's Private School Costs	. . . .	. . . .
Parent's Educational Costs	. . . .	. . . .
Children's Lessons (dancing, music, sports, etc.)	100.00	. . . .
Baby-sitting	. . . .	. . . .
Day-Care Expenses	. . . .	. . . .
Entertainment	. . . .	. . . .
Alcohol and Tobacco	. . . .	. . . .
Newspapers and Periodicals	13.00	. . . .
Gifts	. . . .	. . . .
Contributions	. . . .	. . . .
Payments to Non-Child Dependents	. . . .	. . . .
Prior Existing Support Obligations		
this family	. . . .	. . . .
other families (specify)	. . . .	. . . .
Tax Reserve (not listed elsewhere)	. . . .	. . . .
Life Insurance	. . . .	. . . .
Savings/Investment	. . . .	. . . .
Debt Service (from page 7)	625.00	. . . .
Parenting Time Expenses	. . . .	. . . .
Professional Expenses (other than this proceeding)	. . . .	. . . .
Other (specify)	. . . .	. . . .
. . . .	. . . .	. . . .
. . . .		
. . . .		
	$ 2,454.00	$ . . . .

* unreimbursed only   PERSONAL COMBINED TOTAL $ 2,454.00

SUMMARY OF MONTHLY EXPENSES(computed @ 4.3 wks./mo.):

	Yours & children (# . .) residing with you	Expenses paid for spouse and/or children (# . .) not residing with you	Combined Total Expenses
Schedule A: Shelter	$ 2,075.00	$	$ 2,075.00
Schedule B: Transportation	$ 80.00	$	$ 80.00
Schedule C: Personal	$ 2,454.00	$	$ 2,454.00
Grand Totals	$ 4,609.00	$	$ 4,609.00

PART E - BALANCE SHEET OF FAMILY ASSETS AND LIABILITIES

STATEMENT OF ASSETS Description	Title to property (H,W,J)	If you contend asset is fully or partially exempt from equitable distribution, state reason:	Value $	Date of Evaluation Mo/Day/Yr
1. Real Property				
55 MAIN STREET, NEWTON	J	ESTIMATE	200,000.00	....
....	.	....	....	....
....	.	....	....	....
2. Bank Accounts, Certificates of Deposit				
SAVINGS	J	....	2,000.00	....
CHECKING	J	....	3,000.00	....
....	.	....	....	....
3. Vehicles				
HONDA PASSPORT	J	UNKNOWN	....	....
MITSUBISHI GALANT	J	UNKNOWN	....	....
TRACTOR	J	APPROXIMATELY	1,000.00	....
....	.	....	....	....
4. Tangible Personal Property				
FURNITURE AND FURNISHINGS	J	ESTIMATE	25,000.00	....
....	.	....	....	....
....	.	....	....	....
....	.	....	....	....
....	.	....	....	....
5. Stocks and Bonds				
UNKNOWN TO WIFE	.	....	....	....
....	.	....	....	....
....	.	....	....	....
....	.	....	....	....
6. Pensions, Profit Sharing, Retirement Plans, IRA, 401k, etc.				
IRA	.	....	15,000.00	....
401K	.	....	35,000.00	....
....	.	....	....	....
....	.	....	....	....
7. Businesses, Partnerships, Professional Practices				
APPLIED RESOURCES TECHNOLOGY	.	VALUE UNKNOWN	....	....
....	.	....	....	....
....	.	....	....	....
8. Life Insurance (Cash Surrender Value)				
REEL INSURANCE COMPANY	H	UNKNOWN	....	....
....	.	....	....	....
....	.	....	....	....
9. Other (specify)				
....	.	....	....	....
....	.	....	....	....
....	.	....	....	....

TOTAL GROSS ASSETS $ 281,000.00

....
....

(continued)

EXHIBIT 8.3 *continued*

STATEMENT OF LIABILITIES

Description	Name of Responsible Party (H,W,J)	If you contend liability should not be considered in equitable distribution, state reason:	Monthly Payment	Total Owed	Date of Evaluation
1. Mortgage in Real Estate					
55 MAIN STREET, NEWTON, NJ	J	. . . .	1,250.00	170,000.00	. . . .
. . . .	.	. . . .	. . . .	. . . .	. . . .
. . . .	.	. . . .	. . . .	. . . .	. . . .
. . . .	.	. . . .	. . . .	. . . .	. . . .
2. Other Long Term Debts					
. . . .	.	. . . .	. . . .	. . . .	. . . .
. . . .	.	. . . .	. . . .	. . . .	. . . .
. . . .	.	. . . .	. . . .	. . . .	. . . .
. . . .	.	. . . .	. . . .	. . . .	. . . .
3. Revolving Charges					
CHADWICK'S	J	. . . .	. . . .	200.00	. . . .
MASTERCARD	J	. . . .	. . . .	100.00	. . . .
MASTERCARD	J	. . . .	. . . .	3,200.00	. . . .
MASTERCARD	J	. . . .	. . . .	3,200.00	. . . .
. . . .	.	. . . .	. . . .	. . . .	. . . .
. . . .	.	. . . .	. . . .	. . . .	. . . .
4. Other Short Term Debts					
. . . .	.	. . . .	. . . .	. . . .	. . . .
. . . .	.	. . . .	. . . .	. . . .	. . . .
. . . .	.	. . . .	. . . .	. . . .	. . . .
. . . .	.	. . . .	. . . .	. . . .	. . . .
5. Contingent Liabilities					
. . . .	.	. . . .	. . . .	. . . .	. . . .
. . . .	.	. . . .	. . . .	. . . .	. . . .
. . . .	.	. . . .	. . . .	. . . .	. . . .
. . . .	.	. . . .	. . . .	. . . .	. . . .

Items marked with * are not included in Debt Service on Page 5

. . . .
. . . .

TOTAL GROSS LIABILITIES: (Other than Contingent Liabilities) $ 176,700.00

NET WORTH: (Other than Contingent Liabilities) $ 104,300.00

PART F - STATEMENT OF SPECIAL PROBLEMS

Provide a Brief Narrative Statement of Any Special Problems Involving This Case: As example, state if the matter involves complex valuation problems (such as for a closely held business) or special medical problems of any family member etc.

. . . .
. . . .

PART G - ATTACH AFFIDAVIT OF INSURANCE COVERAGE AS REQUIRED BY COURT RULE 5:4-2(f).

PART H - ATTACH CHILD SUPPORT GUIDELINES WORKSHEETS, AS APPLICABLE, BASED UPON AVAILABLE INFORMATION.

I certify that the foregoing statements made by me are true. I am aware that if any of the foregoing statements made by me are willfully false, I am subject to punishment.

DATED: _____ . . . . _____   SIGNED: _____

                                                              ELIZABETH SMITH

CHECK IF YOU HAVE ATTACHED THE FOLLOWING REQUIRED DOCUMENTS

1. A full and complete copy of your last federal and state income tax returns
   with all schedules and attachments.   . . . .   NO

2. Your last calendar year's W-2 statements and 1099's.   . . . .   NO

3. Your three most recent pay stubs.   . . . .   NO

4. Bonus information including, but not limited to, percentage overrides, timing of payments, etc.;
   the last three statements of such bonuses,commissions, etc.   . . . .   NO

5. Your most recent corporate benefit statement or a summary thereof, showing the nature, amount and status of retirement
   plans, savings plans, income deferral plans, insurance benefits, etc.   . . . .   NO

6. Any agreements between the parties.   . . . .   NO

7. A statement of prior/pending cases (Part B-5).   . . . .   NO

8. An Appendix IX Child Support guideline worksheet.   YES

. . . .
. . . .

Case Information Statement provided Courtesy of Easy Soft, Inc.

Motioning for Temporary Support

J. D. has a more accurate understanding of Libby's financial situation now that the budget statement has been completed. He will petition the court to order Michael to pay for temporary support of Libby and the children by serving a Notice of Motion for *Pendente Lite* Relief. Susan has prepared the legal papers under J. D.'s watchful eye. Review Susan's work in Exhibit 8.4. The notice of motion is accompanied by a *certification of plaintiff* that supports Libby's claim for temporary support. Read the Certification in Exhibit 8.5. Remember, depending on your state, the request for temporary support may vary slightly in name and filing requirements. A review of your state's court rules should answer any state-specific questions.

Do Not Forget the Order!

J. D. will also submit a ready-to-be-signed Order for *Pendente Lite* Relief at the same time the motion and plaintiff's certification are submitted asking the court to order Michael to provide temporary support. An *order* is a written command or direction given by a judge. J. D. will also submit a Certification of Lawyer's Services for *pendente lite* fees, asking the court to award counsel fees on behalf of his client. A *certification of service* is a formal statement to the court that an attorney or other individual will complete, or has completed, work on behalf of another. Submitting the order for *pendente lite* relief along with all the other documentation saves time for the judge and is an efficient way to ensure that the order includes every point made in the motion. The judge is free to sign the order as it is, make changes to the submitted order, or write a new order. Read the Order for *Pendente Lite* Relief in Exhibit 8.6 (see p. 221) and J. D.'s Certification of Lawyer's Services in Exhibit 8.7 (see p. 222).

Settlement Problems: The Plot Thickens

According to Libby, Michael did not react well to her hiring an attorney. She called J. D. as soon as she learned that Michael had cleaned out the couple's checking account. J. D. suggested to Libby that she try to talk to Michael about temporary financial support. Libby did as J. D. asked and was in for a surprise. Michael heatedly accused Libby of adultery and told her he would not pay support to a wife who "fooled around." According to Libby, she vehemently denied the accusation, but Michael, not believing her, stormed out of the barn. This prompted Libby to call J. D. once again. Usually Susan was responsible for fielding telephone calls from anxious clients, but fortunately for Susan, J. D. was in the office because of a court holiday and was able to speak with Libby himself.

Libby relayed the most current events as J. D. listened. He had heard this kind of thing many times before and knew how to respond. "Libby, I know you're shocked by Michael's behavior," J. D. said. "I believe you're not guilty of what Michael is accusing you of, but we'll just move forward with our motion and put the decision in the judge's hands. Whatever Michael thinks you did will not allow him to abandon his responsibility to his family. Okay?"

Somewhat consoled, Libby answered, "Okay, but I can see now we won't be able to settle this between ourselves."

J. D. added, "I'm going to ask for oral argument on the motion so I can be sure to explain your needs in person to the judge." Needing to wrap up the call before the next client interview, J. D. concluded, "Believe me, it'll be all right, but you'll just have to have faith. Okay?"

Libby took a deep breath and responded, "Okay, J. D. I'm in your hands."

J. D. Argues for a Temporary Support Motion: Michael Is Ordered to Pay

J. D. argued his motion for Libby's *pendente lite* relief several weeks after filing the motion. After the hearing, he called Susan at the office to check in and to share the favorable results.

EXHIBIT 8.4 Notice of Motion for *Pendente Lite* Relief

J. D. Dombroski, Esq.
Johnson & Webster, Esqs.
123 Main Street
Newton, New Jersey 12345
973-555-1212
Attorney for Plaintiff

ELIZABETH MOORE SMITH, 　　　　　　　　Plaintiff, v. MICHAEL SMITH, 　　　　　　　　Defendant.	) SUPERIOR COURT OF NEW JERSEY) CHANCERY DIVISION-FAMILY PART) SUSSEX COUNTY) Docket No. FM-12345-03) CIVIL ACTION)))) NOTICE OF MOTION FOR) *PENDENTE LITE* RELIEF)

TO: Howard Hughey, Esq.
Dewey, Hughey & Lewey, Esqs.
52 Goody Lane
Glenwood, New Jersey 07461
Attorney for Defendant

SIR:

PLEASE TAKE NOTICE that on Wednesday, April 30, 2003, at 9:00 A.M. or as soon thereafter as counsel may be heard, the undersigned attorney for the plaintiff shall move before the Honorable Judge Comfort, Judge of the Superior Court of New Jersey, Chancery Division, Family Part, located at 43-47 High Street, County of Sussex, Newton, New Jersey, for an order:

1. Requiring defendant to pay a reasonable amount for the *pendente lite* support and maintenance of the plaintiff and the minor children born of the marriage, namely, Alphonse Smith and Brianna Smith, ages 10 and 12 respectively.
2. Directing defendant to maintain medical insurance *pendente lite* for the plaintiff and the children, and requiring defendant to be responsible for all medical, dental, hospitalization, and prescription drug expenses.
3. Requiring defendant to maintain life insurance on his life, with the plaintiff named as beneficiary, in the amount of $500,000.
4. Restraining defendant from selling or dissipating any assets pending final determination of this matter.
5. For counsel fees and costs of this application.
6. For such further relief as the Court may deem equitable and just.

PLEASE TAKE FURTHER NOTICE that annexed hereto is a Certification in Support hereof.

PLEASE TAKE FURTHER NOTICE that annexed hereto is a form of Order pursuant to R. 1:6-2.

PLEASE TAKE FURTHER NOTICE that oral argument is requested with regard to this motion, given the nature of the relief sought and the complexity of the issues involved.

　　　　　　　　　　　　　　　　　　By: _____
　　　　　　　　　　　　　　　　　　　　J. D. Dombroski
　　　　　　　　　　　　　　　　　　　　Attorney for Plaintiff

DATED: April 2, 2003

The undersigned hereby certifies that the within pleading was signed within the time permitted by the rules.

_____

J. D. Dombroski, Esq.

EXHIBIT 8.5 Certification of Plaintiff

J. D. Dombroski, Esq.
Johnson & Webster, Esqs.
123 Main Street
Newton, New Jersey 12345
973-555-1212
Attorney for Plaintiff

ELIZABETH MOORE SMITH,	)	SUPERIOR COURT OF NEW JERSEY
	)	CHANCERY DIVISION-FAMILY PART
Plaintiff,	)	SUSSEX COUNTY
	)	Docket No. FM-12345-03
v.	)	CIVIL ACTION
	)	
MICHAEL SMITH,	)	
	)	CERTIFICATION OF PLAINTIFF DATED 4/02/03
Defendant.	)	

I, ELIZABETH MOORE SMITH, do hereby certify that:

1. I am the plaintiff in the foregoing action.

2. I reside at 55 Main Street, Newton, New Jersey. The defendant resides at 79 Carol Street, Oak Ridge, New Jersey.

3. The marriage between the defendant and I took place on February 14, 1986.

4. There were two children born of the marriage, to wit: Alphonse, born March 21, 1993, age 10, and Brianna, born April 21, 1991, age 12.

5. I am presently self-employed for about one year, and was unemployed for the 15 years previously.

6. The defendant is presently employed by Smith Ford, Inc., as an accountant and earns approximately $50,000 per year.

7. My age is 39 years, and the age of the defendant is 41 years.

8. The major assets of the marriage are the marital home purchased in 1993 for $125,000, which I now estimate is worth $250,000, an IRA in my name, and the defendant's 401K plan.

9. I am presently living in the marital residence with the unemancipated children of the marriage and need support from the defendant in order to provide the basic necessities for the children and myself. Since the time that the defendant separated himself from me, he has voluntarily been paying the sum of $200 per week, has paid the premiums on the life insurance offered through employment in the approximate amount of $500,000, and continues to name me as the beneficiary. The defendant also continues to maintain the medical insurance offered through his employment for the children and me.

10. I am asking the court to grant me temporary custody of our children, Alphonse and Brianna, and to grant the defendant liberal and reasonable visitation, to be worked out between us.

11. My household budget is listed on the attached Case Information Statement filed herewith.

12. This certificate is made in support of my application for *pendente lite* relief.

13. I certify that the foregoing statements made by me are true. I am aware if any of the foregoing statements made by me are willfully false, I am subject to punishment.

DATED: April 2, 2003

_____
Elizabeth Moore Smith

EXHIBIT 8.6 Order for *Pendente Lite* Relief

J. D. Dombroski, Esq.
Johnson & Webster, Esqs.
123 Main Street
Newton, New Jersey 12345
973-555-1212
Attorney for Plaintiff

ELIZABETH MOORE SMITH,	)	SUPERIOR COURT OF NEW JERSEY
	)	CHANCERY DIVISION-FAMILY PART
Plaintiff,	)	SUSSEX COUNTY
	)	Docket No. FM-12345-03
v.	)	CIVIL ACTION
	)	
MICHAEL SMITH,	)	
	)	ORDER FOR *PENDENTE LITE*
Defendant.	)	RELIEF

This matter having come to the attention of the court on April 30, 2003, on application of the plaintiff, J. D. Dombroski, Esq., attorney for plaintiff, and in the presence of counsel for the defendant, Howard Hughey, Esq., and the court, having read the papers filed on behalf of the respective parties, and the court having heard argument of counsel, and the court having considered same, and for good cause shown:

It is, on this day of April 30, 2003,

ORDERED, as follows:

(1) That the plaintiff shall have temporary custody of the unemancipated children of the marriage, subject to theliberal and reasonable visitation rights by the defendant, the exact times and dates to be determined between the parties;

(2) That the defendant shall pay to the plaintiff the sum of $450 per week, effective as the 24th day of April 2003, which sum shall be unallocated as between alimony and child support;

(3) That the payments required shall be made through the Sussex County Probation Department in accordance with the rules and procedures established therefor;

(4) That the defendant shall continue to maintain such medical insurance and life insurance as is offered through his employment, without change of beneficiary or other status thereof, and in addition thereto, the defendant shall be responsible for all reasonable and necessary medical expenses not covered by the insurance of the plaintiff and the unemancipated children of the marriage, provided that the plaintiff shall not incur any such medical expenses in excess of $200 per injury, incident or illness, without first giving notice to the defendant, giving him an opportunity to investigate the necessity therefor and the reasonableness of the proposed cost thereof, except in cases of emergency;

(5) That the defendant shall continue to maintain life insurance totaling $500,000.

_____
S. Comfort, J.S.C.

The Undersigned hereby consents to the form of the within order.

_____
Howard Hughey, Esq.
Dewey, Hughey & Lewey, Esqs.
Attorney for Defendant

EXHIBIT 8.7 Certification of Lawyer's Services

J. D. Dombroski, Esq.
Johnson & Webster, Esqs.
123 Main Street
Newton, New Jersey 12345
973-555-1212
Attorney for Plaintiff

ELIZABETH MOORE SMITH,	) SUPERIOR COURT OF NEW JERSEY
	) CHANCERY DIVISION-FAMILY PART
Plaintiff,	) SUSSEX COUNTY
	) Docket No. FM-12345-03
v.	) CIVIL ACTION
	)
MICHAEL SMITH,	)
	) CERTIFICATION OF LAWYER'S
Defendant.	) SERVICES

I, J. D. DOMBROSKI, do hereby certify that:

1. I am an attorney at law in the State of New Jersey and am personally entrusted with representation of the plaintiff in this matter.

2. Services performed by me include an initial office conference, preparation of the summons, complaint, certification of verification and noncollusion, notice of motion for *pendente lite* relief, certification of the plaintiff, the within certification and appropriate filing fee of the complaint, and $15.60 for sheriff's fees. My arrangement with my client is such that my fees are calculated at an hourly rate of $200 per hour, with paralegal fees at $75 per hour. I have been paid a $3,000 retainer. I have thus far expended 6.2 hours in the representation of the plaintiff.

3. While this matter is not unusually complex for a matrimonial matter, nonetheless, I have received indications from the defendant's attorney that an answer and counterclaim will be filed and the matter vigorously contested. Therefore, I request the court to award *pendente lite* counsel fees and costs on behalf of plaintiff.

4. I certify that the foregoing statements made by me are true. I am aware that if any of the foregoing statements made by me are willfully false, I am subject to punishment.

_____
J. D. Dombroski, Esq.

DATED: April 2, 2003

"That's great," Susan said. "I know Libby will be so relieved. Michael has been supporting the kids, but money has gotten a little tight for her. I'm sure she'll be happy to hear the news."

J. D. hurriedly asked, "Could you call and tell her? I have to run to a deposition, and I barely have time to grab lunch."

Susan replied, "Of course, it'll be my pleasure to give her some relatively good news for a change."

Right after finishing her call with J. D., Susan called Libby, who anxiously picked up the phone on the first ring. "Libby?" Susan began. "It's Susan. How are you?" Libby's sigh answered her question, and Susan commiserated, "That good, huh?"

"I'm sitting on pins and needles waiting to find out what happened today," Libby tensely stated.

Susan responded, "I'm happy to say that the news is good. The judge gave J. D. everything he asked for in the motion."

"Thank goodness," Libby said with relief. "I can't believe Michael has been so uncooperative that we've actually had go to court to argue for temporary support, rather than just stipulating through the lawyers what he'd pay for me and the kids until the final judgment."

"I know it's hard to believe, but remember what J. D. told you when we found out the motion would have to have oral argument?" Susan asked. "J. D. says sometimes people act entirely differently when they're going through a divorce. Some people say horrible things and just cannot stand to give money to a person they're divorcing."

"I know," Libby lamented. "But I never thought Michael would act this way. I guess it just really aggravates him that some of the money is coming to me."

"Has he been by to see the kids regularly?" Susan gently asked.

"Oh yes, but he's really gotten nasty with me," Libby answered with anger. "He doesn't believe I deserve any alimony, and now I think he actually might fight to have the barn sold!"

"Well, obviously, the judge doesn't agree with Michael," Susan responded firmly.

"Sue, I know I've been a bit of a pest lately, calling all the time, but you've been great to talk to me and calm me down," Libby said gratefully.

Susan did not know how to respond. Libby had been a little annoying with all her phone calls to tell Susan what Michael had said or what Libby had forgotten to add to her budget. Libby was not the firm's only client, and dealing with all her calls had been time-consuming for Susan. Then again, she was a paying client and her mother's friend, so Susan recovered and responded, "Oh Libby, I'm glad we can help you through all of this."

"Thanks again. I just wonder what Michael's next move will be. Well, I'll talk to you soon," Libby concluded.

"Take care, Libby, we'll keep in touch," Susan said, as they ended the call.

DUELING JURISDICTIONS: WHEN DIVORCING SPOUSES LIVE IN TWO DIFFERENT STATES

What happens if one separated spouse moves out of the state where he resided with his spouse, but the other spouse has remained in the state? The question of what court has jurisdiction to hear such a case is not as easy to determine as it was in Libby and Michael's divorce case. In addition, the courts look negatively toward anyone who is forum shopping. Suppose, for example, that a couple resided in New York during their marriage, but one spouse moved west to California to begin a new life. The California court will allow the spouse who is now a California resident to file for divorce in California, but the New York court may decide to keep jurisdiction over the property settlement. As you should recall from earlier reading, the New York court's jurisdiction over the property and other financial aspects of the divorce is known as subject matter jurisdiction or *in rem* jurisdiction. When the divorce proceedings are split in this way, the divorce is known as a **bifurcated divorce** or **divisible divorce.**

This is what happened in the well-known divorce of actors Burt Reynolds and Lonnie Anderson. A California court granted Reynolds and Anderson their divorce because Anderson had made California her residence after her separation from Reynolds. Reynolds remained a Florida resident. However, since Reynolds and Anderson had maintained their primary marital home in Florida and were residents of Florida during their marriage, a Florida court decided their property settlement.

Determining a Client's Domicile

A particular court's legal duty to hear a case depends upon whether that court has subject matter (or *in rem*) jurisdiction over the subject matter in the legal dispute. It is equally important to determine the jurisdiction of the court over the persons involved in the case. Jurisdiction over a person is known as *in personam* jurisdiction. The first step in determining a court's jurisdiction over a person is to ask where that person is domiciled. A person's **domicile** is determined by asking if the person intends to make a certain place his permanent home. A residence is different from a domicile because a person may have many residences, but can have *only* one domicile.

A court that has not acquired *in personam* jurisdiction may not decide a case. This jurisdictional rule was clearly explained by the United States Supreme Court in *Estin v. Estin* (see Case 8.1). In that case, the Supreme Court discussed permanent alimony, absolute and full divorce, and full faith and credit between states. **Permanent alimony** is defined as payments by a divorced spouse to his former spouse for ongoing support. An **absolute and full divorce** is defined as a complete, final, and without restriction ending of a marriage by court order. Recall the discussion in Chapter 2 of the full faith and credit clause that is included in the United States Constitution. This clause refers to the constitutional requirement that each state must usually treat as valid, and enforce where appropriate, the laws and court decisions of other states.

FINDING A CAUSE OF ACTION: FAULT VERSUS NO-FAULT GROUNDS

Historically, American courts only granted divorces in cases where one spouse could prove that the other spouse's behavior was sufficiently grievous to support the request for a divorce. Providing a description of facts sufficient to support a valid lawsuit is technically known as providing the cause of action. The inclusion in the divorce complaint (also called the *divorce petition* or *dissolution petition* in some states) of the reason the plaintiff is seeking a divorce is legally important. A plaintiff who writes a divorce complaint without an attorney might not include a statutorily permitted cause of action for the divorce. For example, a husband who wants to divorce his wife because he "just doesn't love her anymore" and "can't stand the stockings over the shower rod for one more day" is not stating a legally sufficient cause of action. Most states demand that only statutory causes of action be included in the divorce complaint. Any other information is usually considered extraneous and often will be ignored by the court.

Generally, the statutorily specified causes of action include some pretty awful reasons for wanting to end a marriage. Depending on the state, the available causes of action include adultery, alcoholism, imprisonment, and impotence.

Many states once required that the lover of a spouse who committed adultery be identified in the complaint or petition for divorce. The spouse's lover would then be named as a codefendant (or corespondent in some states) with the adulterous spouse. The need to find this codefendant created an industry for private detectives. A spouse who did not wish to divorce could utilize the law's pro-marriage stance and make it extremely difficult for the spouse wishing to be granted a divorce to get one.

Spouses who agreed they wanted a divorce, but had no legally valid fault grounds, were often tempted to conspire together to plead false grounds. If a divorce was based on such a spousal conspiracy, it was known as a **collusive divorce.**

The law's paternalistic attitude led many in the legal system to consider marriage a sacred institution. This paternalistic attitude was the standard until a trend toward the creation of no-fault divorce statutes began in the 1970s.

CASE 8.1 *Estin v. Estin,* 334 U.S. 541, 68 S. Ct. 1213 (1948)

Facts: The parties were married in 1937 and lived together in New York until the husband left in 1942. The wife brought an action against the husband for separation in 1943. The court granted the separation on the grounds of abandonment and awarded the wife $180 per month in permanent alimony. The husband went to Nevada in January 1944, and while in Nevada, he instituted an action for divorce in 1945. The wife received notice but made no general appearance.

The Nevada court granted the husband an absolute divorce in May 1945, finding that the parties had not cohabited for more than three years and that the husband had been a resident of Nevada since January 30, 1944. The Nevada decree made no provision for alimony, although Nevada had been advised of the New York decree. Following entry of the Nevada decree, the husband ceased making the alimony payments that he had been making under the New York decree. The wife then sued the husband for the back alimony. The husband responded to his wife's lawsuit by moving to eliminate the alimony provision of the New York separation decree by reason of the Nevada decree.

Issue: Whether a New York decree in a separation proceeding survived a Nevada divorce decree.

Court's Reasoning: The question is whether Nevada could, under any circumstances, adjudicate the rights of the wife under the New York judgment when she was not personally served and did not appear in the proceedings. Nevada's attempt to wipe out the wife's claim for alimony under the New York judgment was nothing less than an attempt by Nevada to restrain the wife from asserting her claim under that judgment. The Nevada court attempted to exercise *in personam* jurisdiction over a person, the respondent, who was not before the court. That may not be done. Since Nevada had no power to adjudicate the wife's rights in the New York judgment, New York need not give full faith and credit to that phase of Nevada's judgment. The divorce should be divisible. The Nevada divorce decree should be upheld, but the Nevada decision is found ineffective on the issue of alimony.

Holding: Judgment affirmed.

Case Discussion: This case includes several important legal terms and is an excellent example of the United States Supreme Court figuratively slapping the hands of a state court that was getting "too big for its britches." In reading the *Estin* case, did you understand what was meant by constructive service, *in personam* jurisdiction, full faith and credit, permanent alimony, absolute divorce, and divisible divorce? If not, review those terms. When the Nevada court allowed Mr. Estin to ignore a past order from a New York court that had proper jurisdiction in the matter, and then made a decision affecting Mrs. Estin without having jurisdiction over her, the Nevada court went too far in the eyes of the Supreme Court. What do you think would have happened in similar cases in the future if the Supreme Court had ignored the actions of the Nevada court and let the *Estin* decision stand?

The No-Fault Cause of Action: Sometimes, It Is Nobody's Fault

A **no-fault divorce statute** is a divorce statute that does not require fault to be proved by one spouse against the other spouse in order for the spouses to be granted a final judgment of divorce. Each of the 50 states now has a no-fault divorce statute available for spouses who wish to divorce without levying blame.

CHECK YOUR JURISDICTIONAL I.Q.

1. Larry and Lila Loveless lived in Lubbock, Texas. They had planned to retire to Florida and bought two acres of land there early in their marriage. However, after 25 years together, they decided not to spend their golden years with each other and went their separate ways. Larry moved to Alaska and filed for divorce there. Lila stayed in Lubbock. Which court has jurisdiction to decide the property division, and why?
2. Maureen and Murray Migraine moved to Missouri after their honeymoon. Every summer they vacationed in Maine where they had a summer home. Following six years of marital misery, Maureen decided she should have married Milton. She moved back to Mississippi and filed for divorce. Murray decided that Missouri was not for him and moved to Manhattan. Which court has jurisdiction to decide the property division, and why?

However, state legislators know that sometimes a spouse *wants* to levy blame on the other spouse. Therefore, all 50 states have retained some version of fault statutes. Assigning fault for the breakdown of a marriage can have very important consequences. If fault is proved, some courts may take such fault into consideration when deciding the final judgment pertaining to spousal and child support, child custody, and property settlement.

Deciding to divorce may be one of the most traumatic decisions in a client's life. It is a huge adjustment for the spouses, children, and families. The decision to divorce is seldom made lightly. Prior to the creation of the no-fault statutes, spouses only had fault causes of action to claim if they wanted to divorce. The search for fault in order to end the marriage did not ease the discord in a troubled marriage, and often exacerbated an already bad situation. The creation of no-fault causes of action opened a new world in divorce litigation.[2] The discord was lessened and the negative connotation of fault was eclipsed by no-fault statutes that included the new legal terms *irreconcilable differences, irremediable breakdown,* and *incompatibility.* All three terms can be defined as grounds for a divorce because the marriage has simply broken down and the spouses believe there is no possibility that they can live together in marriage. The specific term used as a no-fault cause of action for divorce is determined by individual state statute.

The no-fault statutes emphasize incompatibility and deemphasize the blaming of an individual spouse for any wrongdoing. Many states have gone so far as to replace the negative-sounding term *divorce* with the milder term *dissolution.*

A no-fault cousin to the causes of action of irreconcilable differences and irremediable breakdown is the cause of action that requires the spouses to live apart. Many states have a **living apart** cause of action that simply requires the spouses to have lived apart for a statutorily mandated amount of time before filing a complaint. Again, these statutes provide for less fuss and muss than that involved in trying to prove a fault cause of action. Nobody is held responsible for the breakup, and spouses no longer wishing to be legally joined together can cut the ties that bind without assessing blame.

Hit the Road Jack: Proving Irreconcilable Differences and Incompatibility

So, how does one prove that a couple's marital union is so bad that there is no hope for the marriage? Depending on the state, **irreconcilable differences** or **incompatibility** must be proved. Both terms define the same state of affairs within a marriage—one or both spouses think their marriage has no hope for resuscitation. In states using the term *irreconcilable differences,* the court will ask if these claimed irreconcilable differences between the spouses have caused an **irremediable breakdown** of the marriage, meaning it cannot be repaired. It is important to note that both the irreconcilable differences and incompatibility causes of action do not require that both spouses feel the same way about the marriage. It is unlikely that one spouse's claim that the marriage can be resuscitated will prevent the court from ending the marriage. In that case, though, some state courts require the couple to undergo a last-ditch effort at counseling before granting the divorce. Remember, neither the irreconcilable differences nor the incompatibility causes of action require fault to be proved. Typically, the spouse claiming irreconcilable differences or incompatibility must state in a format required by the state statue that the marriage should no longer be continued.

Living Apart

Perhaps the simplest no-fault cause of action available involves the spouses claiming that they no longer live together and that, therefore, the marriage should be ended. Obviously, it is not so simple that a spouse can move out of the marital home on Monday and be divorced by Friday. The states that provide a living apart cause of action require that the spouses live apart for a statutorily mandated amount of time before the divorce complaint can be filed. The time requirement ranges from six months to three years. The time apart must be added up consecutively. So, if Romeo and Juliet are happily married spouses for three months but then live apart for the next three months because their feelings for each other are, by then, colder than Canada in winter, they will not meet the requirements of the statute if they wish to divorce based on their living apart. Some states require that the living apart of the spouses be *voluntary* on *both* their parts. So, if Juliet were an Army sergeant who was ordered to Guam for a year and Romeo remained in the United States, Romeo cannot claim they live apart and file for divorce. Such a separation does not qualify as a living apart cause of action.

You can see from the variety in the sample divorce statutes listed in Exhibit 8.8 that some state statutes are quite explicit in listing the different reasons for which a plaintiff may seek a divorce. Review the statutory requirements for proving fault and no-fault causes of action, and then continue reading the wide variety of case briefs dealing with fault grounds contained in the rest of this chapter. Begin with the case of *Benscoter v. Benscoter,* and then read the *Hughes* and *Patzschke* cases (see Cases 8.2–8.4).

IN NAME ONLY: SEPARATION, BUT NOT DIVORCE

A husband and wife who wish to end their marriage typically have two choices. The spouses may be able to meet the criteria to be granted an annulment, or they may seek an absolute and full divorce from each other. As stated earlier, an *absolute and full divorce* is defined as the complete, final, and without restriction ending of a marriage. This absolute and full divorce is also known by the Latin term a **divorce** *a vinculo matrimonii*. However, there may be times when a divorce may not be the answer for some couples, but they still wish to live apart from each other. Some states allow spouses to legally formalize this intention of being in what amounts to almost a marriage "limbo." The legal term used to describe such a separation from one's spouse is usually *judicial separation,* although some states use other names, including *legal separation, limited divorce, divorce a mensa et thoro, separation from bed and board,* and *divorce from bed and board.*

A **judicial separation** judgment is a court judgment that provides that a husband and wife have decided to live apart by agreement instead of seeking a full and absolute divorce. It will usually make all the same provisions for spousal and child support, visitation, and property division that a divorce judgment

EXHIBIT 8.8 Sample of State Divorce Statutes

Divorce Statutes

State	Citation	Grounds
California	California Codes § 4506 et seq.	Irreconcilable differences that caused irremediable breakdown of marriage; incurable insanity.
Florida	Florida Statutes § 61-052	Marriage is irretrievably broken; mental incapacity for at least 3 years.
Illinois	Illinois Statutes ch. 40, § 401	Impotency; adultery; desertion for 1 year; habitual drunkenness for 2 years; attempt on life of spouse; extreme and repeated cruelty; conviction of felony or infamous crime; infection of spouse with venereal disease; drug addiction for 2 years; 2-year separation coupled with irreconcilable differences.
New Jersey	New Jersey Statutes § 2A:34-2	Adultery; willful desertion for 12 months; extreme cruelty; separation for 18 months; voluntarily induced addiction or habituation; confinement for mental illness for 2 years; deviant sexual conduct; imprisonment for 18 months.
New York	Domestic Relations Law § 170	Adultery; cruel and inhuman treatment; abandonment; imprisonment; separation for 1 year pursuant to either an agreement or decree.
Pennsylvania	Pennsylvania Consolidated Statutes § 3301	Willful and malicious desertion; adultery; cruel and barbarous treatment; bigamy; imprisonment for 2 years; indignities that render conditions intolerable and life burdensome; insanity or mental disorder resulting in an 18-month confinement; upon mutual consent when marriage is irretrievably broken or, if without mutual consent, after 2-year separation.
Texas	Texas Family Code § 3.01 et seq.	Insupportability because of discord or conflict of personalities; cruelty; adultery; conviction of felony and a 1-year imprisonment; abandonment; living apart for 3 years; confinement in a mental hospital for 3 years.

would make. Typically, the fact that a couple reconciles will have little effect on a judicial separation judgment. When a separated couple makes no effort to have the legal system recognize their separation, the separation will not be considered a **legal separation.**

A classic misnomer is the Latin term *divorce a mensa et thoro,* which can be misleading because the parties involved are not technically divorced. **Divorce *a mensa et thoro*** is literally defined as divorce from bed and board. This term may be used in states that have a judicial separation or a **limited divorce** available.

Not all states, however, provide their residents with the option of seeking a judicial separation. Other states not only provide a legal separation option, but also allow the legally sanctioned separation to be converted into a divorce after a specific period of time.

Another term similar to judicial separation is the action called separate maintenance. **Separate maintenance** is defined as spousal support paid by one married person to the other if they are no longer living as husband and wife. The main purpose of the separate maintenance action is to seek a court order for spousal support without getting involved with the distribution of marital property. Instead, property distribution usually is dealt with in a separate judicial separation or divorce claim. This property distribution distinction is the main difference between a separate maintenance action and a judicial separation action. The factors that generally need to be met in order to prove that a court should grant a judicial separation or order separate maintenance are similar in scope to the divorce factors discussed previously.

CASE 8.2 *Benscoter v. Benscoter,* 200 Pa. Super. 251, 188 A.2d 859 (1963)

Facts: This is an appeal from a denial of the husband's request for a divorce. The parties were married on August 21, 1946. They had four sons. The husband filed a complaint for divorce based on Pennsylvania's cause of action described as *indignities to the person.* The main indignity the husband complained of was the wife's expression of her disappointment in failing to have a female child. The husband claimed she verbally abused him and blamed him for this failure. The parties lived together for 15 years. It was not until August of 1961 that the plaintiff complained about the defendant. In August of 1958, the defendant wife was stricken with the incurable disease multiple sclerosis.

Issue: Whether the wife's alleged conduct established a legal cause of divorce.

Court's Reasoning: The wife's alleged misconduct was sporadic in nature and did not constitute a course of continual conduct as required by law. She was subjected to the frustrations that are attendant to a progressive disease. These circumstances cannot be blindly disregarded. Ill health both explains and excuses a wife's conduct. The acts of a spouse resulting from ill health do not furnish a ground for divorce. The parties to a marriage take each other for better or worse.

Holding: Appeal denied.

Case Discussion: You can see how difficult it was to get a divorce in Pennsylvania in 1963. If this case had occurred today, the husband would only need to move out of the family home for two years to fulfill the two-year separation requirement. Refer to Exhibit 8.8 to review Pennsylvania's currently available causes of action for divorce. What do you think of the court's decision in 1963? Do you think the *Benscoter* court's decision provided Mr. Benscoter with an opportunity to become a loving husband once more or a frustrated spouse?

Preparing Your Client's Divorce Complaint

In Michael and Libby's case, Michael may have retained a lawyer first, but J. D. has prepared a complaint first. Therefore, Libby is the plaintiff. Michael is the defendant who must file an answer or response to Libby's complaint. Libby's complaint has now been sent to the court located in the county where she and Michael resided during their marriage and where they both still reside. Remember, this court needs *in personam* jurisdiction over Michael and Libby, subject matter jurisdiction over the Smith's divorce case, and *in rem* jurisdiction over the property in dispute. The complaint was sent to the court clerk to be filed with the county, along with a copy of the complaint and summons to be served on Michael after it is docketed, and copies to be returned to J. D. You can review the cover letter sent by J. D. asking the court to file the complaint and then return copies to J. D. in Exhibit 8.9 (see p. 232). Libby's complaint follows in Exhibit 8.10 (see p. 233–234). The summons is shown in Exhibit 8.11 (see p. 235).

J. D. and Libby have made the decision to base the reason for the divorce on the fault cause of action dealing with mental cruelty. Libby believes, and J. D. agrees, that Michael's behavior fulfills the requirement to prove mental cruelty. J. D. has warned Libby that the *milder* cause of action involving *living apart* might create less animosity on Michael's part, but Libby does not want to wait the 18 months that is statutorily required to validate her state's living apart statute.

CASE 8.3 *Hughes v. Hughes*, 326 So. 2d 877 (1976)

Facts: Marilyn Hughes filed for divorce in April 1974, claiming that her husband, Clifford Hughes, treated her coldly and indifferently. She further alleged that they separated after he ordered her from the family home in December 1971. They were separated until November 1972 when Marilyn returned to the family home on the defendant's promise to correct his behavior. A month later she left the family home again, claiming that he had returned to his abusive behavior. The defendant denied the allegations and claimed that his wife had abandoned him. Marilyn was granted a separation from bed and board by the trial court. Clifford appealed.

Issue: Whether there was sufficient evidence to prove that the defendant treated his wife cruelly.

Court's Reasoning: The trial judge relied on the testimony of the only child of the marriage to resolve the conflicting testimony of the parties and to find that the plaintiff had proved her entitlement to a separation. The college-age daughter's testimony confirmed her mother's allegations concerning the continuation of cruel treatment by her father. The defendant had engaged in harassment by cursing his wife on many occasions and declaring that he did not love either her or his daughter.

Holding: Appellee wins. Costs to be paid by the appellant.

Case Discussion: The court stated that the wife had *proved her entitlement* to a separation. What do you think of the requirement of having the burden of proving whether you are entitled to a separation from your spouse? The no-fault statutes provided an alternative to having to show such proof.

J. D. has continued to teach Susan every step of the way. He has reviewed with Susan the complaint he prepared for Libby. Susan remembered from Family Law class that each paragraph of the complaint is included for a specific reason. For example, the domicile of the parties is included to show the court that it has jurisdiction to hear the case. Additionally, examples of alleged mental cruelty are included to help prove the mental cruelty cause of action. The very important *Wherefore* clause is included so the plaintiff may ask the court for what she wants the judge to order. J. D. explained to Susan that Libby's certification, the summons, and the cover letter should be sent to the court clerk along with the complaint.

Courtesy Is Good Policy

A client's visit to an attorney is often prompted by the client having been served a complaint or petition for divorce or having received a letter from her spouse's lawyer. J. D. had Susan prepare and send a courtesy letter to Michael to notify him that a divorce complaint had been filed and that J. D. would rather serve Michael's lawyer with the complaint than Michael personally. Even though Libby had told J. D. that Howard Hughey appeared to be representing Michael in the divorce, J. D. wanted to hear that information from Michael himself. Susan sent the letter to Michael's new apartment, since Michael has now moved out of the barn. She also sent a letter to the attorney (Howard Hughey) to confirm that he is representing Michael and to ask if Hughey will accept service on Michael's behalf. Read the letter in Exhibit 8.12 (see p. 236).

CASE 8.4 *Patzschke v. Patzschke,* 249 Md. 53, 238 A.2d 119 (1968)

Facts: The original complaint in this case was filed by the wife on August 5, 1966, charging the husband with desertion on or about July 28, 1966. The husband filed a counterclaim for divorce claiming adultery on the part of the wife. The trial court denied the wife's request and granted the husband a divorce *a vinculo matrimonii.* The wife appealed.

Issue: Whether the evidence established the husband's right to divorce on the ground of adultery by his wife.

Court's Reasoning: In this case, we have the observation of the private detectives on the night of August 13, at which time the wife and a male companion were visiting taverns and riding in an automobile at a late hour together. Although this incident might not have significance by itself, it gains more weight when coupled with the actions of the wife and the same companion on August 26, when again they were observed visiting taverns together, walking on the street holding hands, and kissing and embracing, both in a parking lot and while driving. The husband testified that the wife frequently spent evenings away from home until 2 A.M. because, she claimed, she was active in lodge work and enjoyed bowling. He further testified that "by coincidence" her diaphragm was missing from the house when she was out late. It is unquestionably true that the testimony of the private detectives is not entitled to any more weight than that of the defendant, where they conflict. The reason for this rule is that they are all interested witnesses, the detectives to justify their employment by finding what they are employed to find, and the defendant to establish innocence. What makes this case somewhat different from other cases is the fact that the evidence supplied by the detectives gains stature from the wife's patent attempt to provide herself with the *incredible* alibi witness, Mrs. Brown.

Holding: Affirmed for the husband.

Case Discussion: The *Patzschke* case was decided in 1968. It is likely that Mrs. Patzschke fought her husband's claim of adultery in order to be in a better position to have the court grant her alimony. It is unlikely that a court in 1968 would have been generous to an adulterous wife.

Contacting Opposing Counsel

When Michael receives this letter, he should contact his lawyer immediately. His lawyer, in turn, will notify Libby's lawyer as to his representation of her husband. Once J. D. is informed that Howard Hughey is definitely representing Michael, it is considered unethical for J. D. to attempt to negotiate the case with Michael personally. When Michael's lawyer is served with the summons and complaint, he should sign an **acknowledgment of service.** You can read the Acknowledgment of Service in Exhibit 8.13 (see p. 237).

Answering a Complaint

If a petition or complaint is filed by one spouse, the other spouse must respond to the complaint by filing an answer, response, or waiver. Providing an answer to the complaint within a certain number of statutorily

EXHIBIT 8.9 Letter to the Court

Johnson & Webster, Esqs.
Attorneys at Law
123 Main Street
Newton, New Jersey 12345
973-555-1212

May 19, 2003

Superior Court of New Jersey
Chancery Division, Family Part
49 High Street
Newton, New Jersey 12345

Re: *Smith v. Smith*
Docket No.: FM-12345-02

Dear Sir/Madam:

Enclosed please find the following in reference to the above-entitled matter:

(X) Complaint (1 + 2)   ( ) Stipulation of Dismissal
( ) Amended Complaint   ( ) Request to Enter Default and Certification
( ) Answer (1 + 3)   ( ) Affidavit of Nonmilitary Service
( ) Counterclaim   ( ) Answer to Counterclaim (1 + 2)
( ) Notice of Motion   ( ) Certification Supporting Motion
( ) Summons   ( ) Certification Opposing Motion
( ) Order (1 + 2)   ( ) Stipulation Extending Answer (1 + 2)
( ) Appearance   ( ) Case Information Statement
( ) Pretrial Memorandum   (X) Check in the amount of $225
( ) Affidavit of Proof   ( ) Letter Brief in Support of Motion
( ) Substitution of Attorney   ( ) Custody/Visitation Fact Sheet
( ) Early Settlement Panel Questionnaire

Would you please:

(X) File and return confirmed copies in the enc. SASE
( ) Waive fees pursuant to 1:13-2
( ) Acknowledge Service on Copy of this letter and return

Very truly yours,

_____
J. D. Dombroski, Esq.

Enc.
cc: Mrs. Elizabeth Moore Smith

EXHIBIT 8.10 Libby's Complaint

J. D. Dombroski, Esq.
Johnson & Webster, Esqs.
123 Main Street
Newton, New Jersey 12345
973-555-1212
Attorney for Plaintiff

ELIZABETH MOORE SMITH,
 	
                    Plaintiff,
 	
v.
MICHAEL SMITH,
 	
                    Defendant.
	) SUPERIOR COURT OF NEW JERSEY
	) CHANCERY DIVISION-FAMILY PART
	) SUSSEX COUNTY
	) Docket No. FM-12345-03
	) CIVIL ACTION
	)
	) COMPLAINT FOR DIVORCE
	)
	)

The Plaintiff, Elizabeth Moore Smith, residing at 55 Main Street, Newton, County of Sussex, New Jersey, by way of Complaint against the Defendant, Michael Smith, says:

1. Plaintiff was lawfully married to Defendant in a religious ceremony at St. Francis de Sales Church, in Sparta, Sussex County, New Jersey, on February 14, 1986.

2. Plaintiff was a bona fide resident of the State of New Jersey when this cause of action arose and has ever since and for more than one year preceding the commencement of this action continued to be such a bona fide resident.

3. Defendant presently resides at 79 Carol Street, Oak Ridge, County of Sussex, New Jersey.

4. The parties separated March 31, 2001, and will continue to live apart as long as they both shall live, with both parties presently residing at above-stated addresses.

5. There are two children born of the marriage, to wit: Alphonse, date of birth March 21, 1993, age 10; and Brianna, date of birth April 21, 1991, age 12.

6. Defendant has been guilty of extreme mental cruelty toward the plaintiff. Particularly specifying the acts of extreme cruelty committed by Defendant, the Plaintiff says:

    a. The Defendant and I did not share and enjoy the same mutual interests. While at the beginning of our marriage the Defendant and I both enthusiastically and energetically shared in restoring a one-hundred-year-old barn into our dream house, the Defendant now claims he no longer has the time to share in the workload. The Defendant's career involves traveling several weeks out of the month, and now I not only have to shoulder all the responsibility for the renovation, but also for raising our children while running my own business. The Defendant now says he always hated the idea of living in a renovated barn and insists it is time I got over the idea as well. Despite my repeated requests to explore new avenues of mutual interests, the Defendant has adamantly refused.

    b. The Defendant was consumed by his work. He frequently left the house at 7:00 A.M. and did not return until 9:00 or 9:30 P.M. He also worked each Saturday. Despite the fact that we lived comfortably, the Defendant believed it necessary to work long hours to acquire material possessions. I was often lonely and discouraged, and would have preferred companionship over the attainment of material possessions. I often related my sentiments to the Defendant concerning his work habits, but my pleas to either alter the Defendant's work habits or to improve the situation were left unheeded. When I suggested he change his schedule, the Defendant said it was out of the question. And when I suggested marriage counseling, the Defendant became angry and hostile.

    c. When the Defendant returned from his business trips, he would subject me to an unending stream of criticism for all my efforts on behalf of our home and our children. For example, the Defendant often made snide or sarcastic remarks regarding the manner in which I educated the children with respect to religion. He often criticized any effort undertaken by myself in this regard.

(continued)

EXHIBIT 8.10 *continued*

d. The Defendant and I did not share and enjoy the same social outlets. Whereas I was socially active and significantly more outgoing, the Defendant was more introverted and more reluctant to socialize. The Defendant was often reluctant to share in any of the activities I enjoyed and would often voice his displeasure at having to do so. The Defendant, while always enjoying an opportunity to socialize with his business acquaintances, was strongly resentful of those few occasions when I would ask him to go out with my friends or acquaintances. Often, the Defendant's resentment would place a damper on the social event we were attending by making me feel guilty for suggesting we attend.

7. By reason of these acts of extreme cruelty, Plaintiff's health and safety have become endangered and it is improper and unreasonable to expect Plaintiff to continue to cohabitate with Defendant.

8. More than three months have elapsed since the last act of extreme cruelty complained of as constituting Plaintiff's cause of action herein. The acts of extreme cruelty committed by the Defendant within a period of three months before the filing of this Complaint, as set forth, are alleged not as constituting in whole or in part the cause of action set forth herein, but as relating back to qualify and characterize the acts constituting said cause of action.

9. At the time the last act of extreme cruelty occurred, both Plaintiff and Defendant resided at 55 Main Street, Newton, County of Sussex, New Jersey, and were residents there at the time the cause of action for divorce, on grounds of extreme cruelty, arose.

10. There is no reasonable prospect of reconciliation between the parties.

11. During the marriage, the parties have acquired real and personal property and have incurred numerous debts.

12. There have been no previous proceedings between Plaintiff and Defendant respecting the marriage or its dissolution, or respecting the maintenance of Plaintiff in any court.

WHEREFORE, Plaintiff demands judgment as follows:

A. Dissolving the marriage between the parties;

B. Compelling the Defendant to pay spousal support to Plaintiff;

C. Equitably distributing all property, both real and personal, that was legally and beneficially acquired by the parties, or either of them, during the marriage and distributing all debts incurred between them during the course of the marriage;

D. Awarding Plaintiff sole residential custody and joint legal custody of the minor children born of the marriage;

E. Compelling the Defendant to pay child support to the minor children born of the marriage in accordance with the prevailing child support guidelines;

F. Permitting Plaintiff to resume her maiden name of Elizabeth Moore. Plaintiff's Social Security number is 000-12-1234.

G. Compelling Defendant to pay Plaintiff's counsel fees and costs; and

H. For such other relief as the Court may deem equitable and just.

_____
J. D. Dombroski, Esq.
DATED: May 19, 2003   Attorney for Plaintiff

CERTIFICATION OF VERIFICATION AND NONCOLLUSION PURSUANT TO R: 4:5-1

I, Elizabeth Moore Smith, am the Plaintiff in the foregoing Complaint. The allegations of the Complaint are true to the best of my knowledge and belief. The said Complaint is made in truth and in good faith and without collusion, for the cause set forth above.

_____
DATED: May 19, 2003   Elizabeth Moore Smith

EXHIBIT 8.11 Matrimonial Summons

J. D. Dombroski, Esq.
Johnson & Webster, Esqs.
123 Main Street
Newton, New Jersey 12345
973-555-1212
Attorney for Plaintiff

ELIZABETH MOORE SMITH,
 	
                Plaintiff,
 	
v.
 	
MICHAEL SMITH,
 	
                Defendant.
	)
	)
	)
	)
	)
	)
	)
	)
	)
	)
	)
	)
		SUPERIOR COURT OF NEW JERSEY
		CHANCERY DIVISION-FAMILY PART
		SUSSEX COUNTY
		Docket No. FM-12345-03
		CIVIL ACTION
		
		MATRIMONIAL SUMMONS

THE STATE OF NEW JERSEY, TO THE ABOVE-NAMED DEFENDANT:

YOU ARE HEREBY SUMMONED in a Civil Action in the Superior Court of New Jersey, instituted by the above-named Plaintiff and required to serve upon the attorney(s) for the Plaintiff, whose name and address appears above, either (1) an Answer to the annexed Complaint, or (2) a general appearance in accordance with R. 5:4-3(a), within 35 days after service of this Summons and Complaint upon you, exclusive of the day of service. If you fail to answer, or fail to file a general appearance in accordance with R. 5:4-3(a), judgment by default may be rendered against you for the relief demanded in the Complaint. You shall promptly file your Answer or your general appearance and proof of service thereof in duplicate with the Clerk of the Superior Court at the Sussex County Court House, Chancery Division, Family Part, Superior Court of New Jersey, located at 43-47 High Street, Newton, New Jersey, in accordance with the rules of civil practice and procedure.

If you do not have an attorney, you may call 1-800-555-0000 for the Sussex County Lawyer Referral Service.

_____
Clerk of the Superior Court

DATED: June 1, 2003

Name of defendant to be served: Michael Smith

Address for service: 79 Carol Street
Oak Ridge, New Jersey 07438

EXHIBIT 8.12 Letter to Defendant

Johnson & Webster, Esqs.
Attorneys at Law
123 Main Street
Newton, New Jersey 12345
973-555-1212

May 19, 2003

Mr. Michael Smith
79 Carol Street
Oak Ridge, New Jersey 07438

Dear Mr. Smith:

Please be advised that your wife, Elizabeth Smith, has retained this office to represent her in the dissolution of your marriage. Your wife indicates that there is an excellent chance of amicably resolving all outstanding issues.

I have filed a complaint for divorce on her behalf in the Superior Court of New Jersey, Sussex County. I would prefer to effectuate service upon your attorney rather than upon you, personally, as personal service necessitates the services of the Sussex County Sheriff's office. I would, therefore, suggest that you retain an attorney and have him or her call me at their earliest convenience to arrange for the service of the summons, complaint, and other related details.

Again, while I would prefer to serve the summons and complaint upon your attorney rather than upon you personally, I will nonetheless be compelled to do so if I do not hear from your legal representative within the next seven (7) business days.

I remain,

Very truly yours,

_____

J. D. Dombroski, Esq.

---

required days is absolutely necessary to avoid the plaintiff being granted a default judgment. A *default judgment* occurs when there has been a failure to take a required step in a lawsuit. Each state has its own requirements, but usually the responsive pleading must be filed with the court within 20 to 35 days. Read Michael's Answer and Counterclaim to Libby's Complaint in Exhibit 8.14. An unexpected twist has occurred. It looks like Michael and Libby's divorce will definitely not be the relatively amicable split for which Libby had hoped.

Libby Responds to Michael's Counterclaim

While Susan was working on yet another memo in the library, the receptionist's voice came over the room's intercom to announce, "Line 2 is for you, Susan."

"Thanks," Susan replied. She answered the call, saying, "This is Susan. "May I help you?"

A very agitated Libby quickly responded, "Hi Susan, it's Libby. I can't believe Michael wrote those horrible things about me in his answer. They are *not* true," she stated firmly. Pausing only a second, she added, "When was I supposed to have the *time* to have an affair? I'm so mad at him, I could spit. Why do you think he would *do* that?"

Having received a copy of answer in the office mail that very same morning, Susan had expected Libby's frantic call. Susan knew she needed to be careful not to give Libby an opinion on this recent

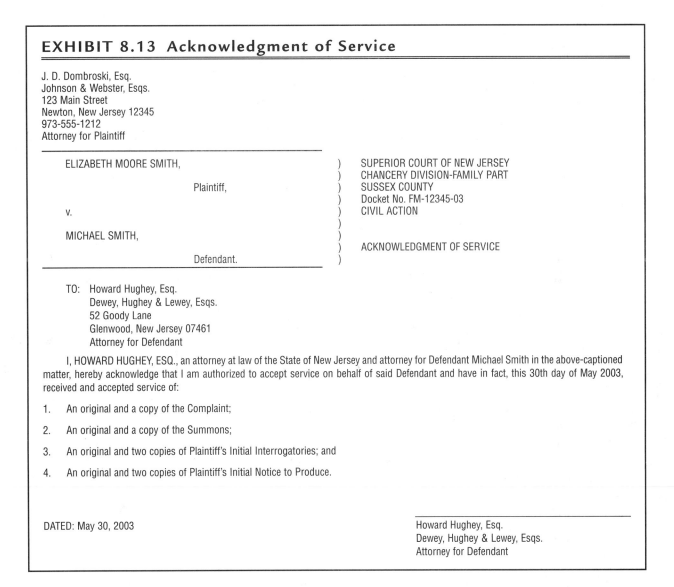

EXHIBIT 8.13 Acknowledgment of Service

J. D. Dombroski, Esq.
Johnson & Webster, Esqs.
123 Main Street
Newton, New Jersey 12345
973-555-1212
Attorney for Plaintiff

ELIZABETH MOORE SMITH,
 	
     Plaintiff,
 	
v.
 	
MICHAEL SMITH,
 	
     Defendant.
	) SUPERIOR COURT OF NEW JERSEY
	) CHANCERY DIVISION-FAMILY PART
	) SUSSEX COUNTY
	) Docket No. FM-12345-03
	) CIVIL ACTION
	)
	)
	) ACKNOWLEDGMENT OF SERVICE
	)
	)

TO: Howard Hughey, Esq.
   Dewey, Hughey & Lewey, Esqs.
   52 Goody Lane
   Glenwood, New Jersey 07461
   Attorney for Defendant

 I, HOWARD HUGHEY, ESQ., an attorney at law of the State of New Jersey and attorney for Defendant Michael Smith in the above-captioned matter, hereby acknowledge that I am authorized to accept service on behalf of said Defendant and have in fact, this 30th day of May 2003, received and accepted service of:

1. An original and a copy of the Complaint;

2. An original and a copy of the Summons;

3. An original and two copies of Plaintiff's Initial Interrogatories; and

4. An original and two copies of Plaintiff's Initial Notice to Produce.

DATED: May 30, 2003

                   Howard Hughey, Esq.
                   Dewey, Hughey & Lewey, Esqs.
                   Attorney for Defendant

turn of events. "Libby, I understand why you're so upset, but, really, the best thing for you to do is to speak with Mr. Dombroski and get his input. I know J. D. wants to talk to you, but he's in court right now."

 Audibly sighing, Libby asked, "Can't he call me from court?"

 Concerned for Libby, but needing to be watchful of what she said to her, Susan declared, "Well, I know he won't have enough time at court to give you his full attention, but I'm sure he'll call you this evening or relay a message through me."

 "Well, I guess that will have to do," Libby said dejectedly.

 "This new development will be dealt with. Is Michael still coming to the house?" Susan asked.

EXHIBIT 8.14 Michael's Answer and Counterclaim

Howard Hughey, Esq.
Dewey, Hughey & Lewey, Esqs.
52 Goody Lane
Glenwood, New Jersey 07461
973-555-9276
Attorney for Defendant

ELIZABETH MOORE SMITH,
 	
           Plaintiff,
 	
v.
 	
MICHAEL SMITH,
 	
           Defendant.
	)
	)
	)
	)
	)
	)
	)
	)
	)
	)
	)
	)

SUPERIOR COURT OF NEW JERSEY
CHANCERY DIVISION-FAMILY PART
SUSSEX COUNTY
Docket No. FM-12345-03
CIVIL ACTION

ANSWER AND COUNTERCLAIM

Defendant, MICHAEL SMITH, residing at 79 Carol Street, Oak Ridge, County of Sussex, New Jersey, by way of answer and counterclaim, says:

Answer

1. Defendant admits the allegations contained in paragraph 1 of the complaint.

2. Defendant admits allegations contained in paragraph 2 of the complaint except to deny that a cause of action arose.

3. Defendant admits the allegation contained in paragraphs 3, 4, and 5 of the complaint.

4. Defendant denies each and every allegation contained in paragraphs 6, 6(a), 6(b), 6(c), 6(d), 7, and 8.

5. Defendant admits the allegations contained in paragraphs 9, 10, and 11 of the complaint.

   WHEREFORE, Defendant demands judgment dismissing Plaintiff s Complaint together with attorney fees and costs.

Counterclaim

Defendant-counterclaimant, Michael Smith, by way of counterclaim against the Plaintiff, Elizabeth Moore Smith, herein says:

1. At the time the cause of action arose, the Defendant-counterclaimant resided at 55 Main Street Lane, Newton, County of Sussex, New Jersey.

2. The Plaintiff, Elizabeth Moore Smith, committed adultery with Gerard Goodbody, a chicken and horse feed salesman, at his residence at 77 Adventuresome Lane, Glenwood, New Jersey, on or about March 1, 2001, and has, in fact, committed adultery at other times and places presently unknown to the Defendant.

3. The Defendant-counterclaimant is now fearful that the Plaintiff was engaging in extramarital sexual relations during a period of time when they were still having sexual relations. The Defendant has, therefore, undertaken a course of testing for communicable diseases including AIDS and will have to continue to be tested for an extended period of time.

4. By reasons of these acts of adultery by Plaintiff, the Defendant's health and safety have become endangered and it is improper and unreasonable to expect Defendant to cohabit with the Plaintiff.

WHEREFORE, Defendant/Plaintiff on the Counterclaim hereby demands judgment:

A.   Dissolving the marriage between the parties;

B.   Awarding joint custody of the unemancipated children of the marriage to Defendant-counterclaimant with Plaintiff retaining physical custody.

C.   Equitably distributing all property, real and personal, owned or acquired by the parties during the course of the marriage;

D.   For counsel fees and costs to Dewey, Hughey & Lewey, Esqs.;

E.   For such further relief as the Court may deem equitable and just.

DEWEY, HUGHEY & LEWEY, ESQS.

By: _____
      Howard Hughey, Esq.

DATED: June 16, 2003

The undersigned certifies that the within pleading was served within the time permitted by the rules.

_____
Howard Hughey, Esq.
Attorney for Defendant

CERTIFICATION OF VERIFICATION AND NONCOLLUSION PURSUANT TO R. 4:5-1

1.   I am the defendant-counterclaimant in the foregoing answer and counterclaim.

2.   The allegations of the counterclaim are true to the best of my knowledge, information and belief. The said counterclaim is made in truth and good faith and without collusion for the causes set forth therein.

3.   The matter in controversy in the within action is not the subject of any other pending action in any court or a pending arbitration proceeding, nor is any such court action or arbitration proceeding presently contemplated. There are no other persons who should be joined in this action at this time.

I certify that the foregoing statements made by me are true. I am aware that if any of the foregoing statements made by me are willfully false, I am subject to punishment.

_____
Michael Smith

DATED: June 16, 2003

"No, I almost forgot to tell you. He'd been spending half his time at his new place and the other half crashed on our couch, but last night he packed up the last of his things, and this morning, this garbage arrived at my door," Libby angrily stated.

"Look, Libby," Susan began, "I know this is hard to deal with, but try to relax and let *us* deal with Michael's allegations, okay?"

Sounding a little calmer, Libby answered, "Okay, I'm going to go take some aspirin, slip into a hot bath, and follow up with a nap until the kids get home from school. You can call me back at whatever time."

Susan said, "That sounds like a good idea. Talk to you soon." Having finishing her conversation with Libby, Susan took a deep breath, and then took some aspirin herself. She thought, "What next? I can hardly keep up with all the things happening. I sure hope J. D.'s trial finishes soon so he can come in and deal with the growing pile of messages."

INTERROGATORIES: GETTING TO THE TRUTH

Read Exhibit 8.15, which contains a sample of the interrogatories sent by J. D. to Howie Hughey's office for Michael's response. Interrogatories are similar in most divorce cases. For example, the interrogatories usually ask extensively about a couple's finances. However, in special circumstances, such as with Michael's allegations, specific interrogatories have to be written. J. D. is sending the interrogatories regarding Michael's claim of adultery to see if Michael has any proof to back up his claims. The answers to all of the interrogatories will hopefully aid J. D. in preparing Libby's case for depositions and even, possibly, for trial. Unfortunately, J. D. has spoken with Hughey, and Michael is not interested in settling the case. J. D. has followed up his conversation with Hughey by calling Libby and explaining that there seems to be little chance of settling the divorce easily.

Settlement Conference Scheduled

J. D. has been sent a notification by the court that Libby and Michael's divorce case has been scheduled for a mandatory settlement conference. This conference is called by other names in some states. For example, some states use the term *case management conference*. No matter what it is called, the meeting is designed to bring the two parties and their lawyers together in one room to go over their differences and attempt to come to a settlement agreement before they reach a trial date. Across the nation, the courts are attempting to have the vast majority of cases settle before reaching trial. One reason for this is that a divorce settled by the parties will very likely be an agreement more easily accepted and adhered to by the parties. Additionally, the courts would be backlogged for years if they had to bring any more than a slim minority of cases to trial. Most state court systems have a **calendar tracking system** that follows a divorce case through the system. Many courts request that the parties come to the courthouse for a settlement conference after a certain number of days have passed since the original pleadings were filed. In Libby and Michael's case, they have been asked to appear for a settlement conference.

On the day for which Libby and Michael's settlement conference was scheduled, J. D. wanted to be completely prepared to explain Libby's position. He asked Susan to make sure the case file included both the plaintiff's and defendant's answered interrogatories, financial records, and any notes that had been made on the case. Howard Hughey still had not sent any proof to substantiate Michael's claim that Libby was fooling around with the feed salesman. The financial records were quite complete, since Libby had made copies of just about every financial paper in the barn. Depositions had been scheduled once, but fell through when Howard Hughey started a trial for another case. The depositions had been rescheduled, but J. D. really hoped

---

EXHIBIT 8.15 Sample Interrogatories Regarding Adultery Claim

1. With whom do you believe your wife had an affair(s)?
2. Where do you claim this affair occurred?
3. When do you claim this affair occurred?
4. Do you have any evidence to substantiate these claims?

---

the case would settle and the depositions would not have to happen, since depositions are an expensive undertaking involving a lot of the lawyers' time, as well as court reporter fees and transcript fees. Plus depositions can be emotionally draining for the client. J. D. believed that if he could help Michael and Libby to settle their differences and come up with a livable plan detailing their financial, custody, and visitation matters, they would both be happier in the long run.

On the day of the settlement conference, Libby, Michael, J. D., and Howard Hughey were expected to appear in Judge Comfort's courtroom at 9 A.M. Both spouses and their attorneys arrived on time and sat in the courtroom that was quickly becoming crowded. Judge Comfort walked into the courtroom as the bailiff ordered the courtroom to rise, and then announced that court was in session under the supervision of the Honorable Judge Comfort. The judge quickly reviewed his list of cases and the parties who should be appearing in court that day. Libby and Michael's case was called within 20 minutes, and the two lawyers walked to the front of the courtroom together. Howard had been sitting on one side of the courtroom with Michael, and J. D. had been sitting on the opposite side with Libby. The judge asked the lawyers if the case had been settled. Hearing a negative reply, Judge Comfort ordered Howard and J. D. to take their clients to Conference Room 4 to try to settle, and then return to inform him of their progress. When he motioned for Libby to exit the courtroom, J. D. noticed her hesitation at being in such close proximity to Michael. It was even more obvious after they were all seated in the conference room's close quarters.

Libby and Michael Hash It Out

As they seated themselves in the stuffy conference room, Libby practically growled at Michael as she said, "Hello."

"Yeah, hello," Michael muttered. "Did Al's team win his basketball game last night?"

"Yes, it was great. They won by 11 points," Libby responded in a more polite tone of voice.

Warming up, Michael remarked, "Great, I'll call him tonight."

"Good," Libby answered. Not able to restrain herself one minute more, Libby then burst out, *"Michael, how could you?"* Loudly, she added, "How could you say those things about me and the feed salesman? I am so mad at you!"

Shaking his shoulders, Michael responded, "Hey, if the feedbag fits."

"There is no feedbag fitting, and the feed salesman smells like his feed—and besides, I've never fooled around on you," Libby declared.

"Well, you always did talk with him a lot, and anyway, *you* said those things about *me* in the complaint," Michael retorted grumpily.

"They were true!" Libby responded, exasperated.

"Uh, excuse me, folks," Howard haltingly interjected. "But maybe J. D. and I should get involved here."

J. D. added, "It's okay by me if the Smiths want to hash things out." Looking at each other, the Smiths nodded.

Howard was not satisfied to sit on the sidelines. He suggested, "Well, okay, but maybe J. D. and I can referee, as long as we're here. Okay, everybody?" The clients and J. D. agreed.

"Okay, let's start with the lady," Howard announced. "You believe the statements in the counter-claim are untrue, and according to J. D., you want them withdrawn. Is that right?"

Chin held high, Libby answered, "Absolutely. *And* an apology would be nice."

Howard inquired, "Michael, you believed the statement when you made it, but would you consider withdrawing it at this time?"

Michael shrugged his shoulders and answered, "Maybe. What's in it for me?"

J. D. interjected, "Look, Mr. Smith, ask Howie. Even if your claims were true, the days of covering an adulterer in tar and feathers are long gone. The judge is not going to forego alimony with a 17-year marriage because of adultery." Realizing Michael did not believe him, J. D. added, "If you don't believe me, ask your lawyer. Attempting to prove your claim will just prolong the aggravation and expense of your divorce."

Howie responded, "Well, honestly, Michael, he's got a point, but you don't have to make a decision this minute." He added, "Think about it."

Losing patience, Libby added, "Michael, for our children's sake, do you want something like that in the public record?" Feeling like she was talking to a brick wall, she continued, "Look, I wish our state didn't require me to be specific, but other than living apart for 18 months, which I thought I just couldn't wait for, claiming mental cruelty was my only choice. It wasn't all bad, and I know we had lots of good years and we will always have the kids, but the law doesn't design complaints to include the good stuff, too." Libby's last statement seemed to sink in; both Howie and J. D. could see Michael softening.

"Okay, I'll withdraw it," Michael announced. He added, "And I'm sorry."

Libby did not speak, but instead nodded an acceptance of his apology.

"Okay, so far, so good," Howie blustered. "What would you like to see done, Michael?"

Arms crossed, Michael stated, "I want to sell the barn."

This was too much for Libby. She said loudly and firmly, "Absolutely not! I *killed* myself making that place a home. I worked like a *dog* to keep it up because you wanted to live like *Little House on the Organic Prairie.*"

"Listen to yourself," Michael retorted. "That barn is one long treadmill that you never get off. I'd like to sell the barn and split the profits. Then we can each buy a condo in town."

J. D. interjected, "The only problem is that my client doesn't have the income to afford a mortgage, and it would be unlikely she'd get one. Look, can we talk about the kids and work our way back to items that need more discussion?"

"Okay with me," Howie agreed.

Libby began, "Michael is a good dad and can see the kids anytime he wants."

Warming up, Michael announced, "You've always been a good mom."

Smiling, Libby answered, "Thanks."

"The best thing is for Libby to have the kids live with her because I travel so much," Michael said.

"How about alternating holidays, birthdays, and vacations?" J. D. asked the couple. Both Libby and Michael agreed and decided to work out the details together after the conference.

"Now, we're getting someplace," Howie announced. "J. D. and I have already figured out child support according to our state's formula for income, and we're both fine with those figures." He added, "Michael *does* want to keep his pension, but we will offset the amount with the barn, if that's agreeable. Libby will keep her IRA, and we'll have to figure out the value of the pension versus the off-set from any possible sale of the barn."

Annoyed, Libby interjected quickly, "I just said I do *not* want to sell the barn, so you'll have to get your offset from somewhere else or give me a share of the pension."

Knowing that an argument at this point could destroy everything they had accomplished so far, J. D. quickly inquired, "Shall we just leave this for a moment and go to your personal property?"

Splitting up the personal property proved to be the least difficult task, since Libby and Michael had purchased very little during their marriage, and most items were inherited pieces. Libby would keep all of her family heirlooms, and Michael would keep his family heirlooms. The questions of the barn sale and alimony for Libby still loomed when the lawyers realized it was time for them to report back to the judge. Everyone in the room knew Michael was determined not to pay alimony and would make Libby's alimony request his sticking point. Libby was being just as adamant about keeping the barn. Discussion of those points, however, would have to wait until another day. Progress had definitely been made.

Howie and J. D. shook hands as they left Judge Comfort's chambers and promised to get in touch with each other to compare notes. If Howie and J. D. could not get Libby and Michael to agree to divorce terms in the next few weeks, Judge Comfort would schedule a forced settlement conference. Both clients promised their attorneys that they would work on a visitation schedule and that they would think about alternatives and possible solutions for the problems of alimony and possible sale of the barn.

COMMUNITY PROPERTY VERSUS EQUITABLE DISTRIBUTION

The majority of states apply property division laws that utilize a legal concept known as equitable distribution. **Equitable distribution** is defined as a just and fair allocation of property acquired during the marriage between divorcing spouses. A small minority of states apply property division laws that utilize a legal concept known as community property. **Community property** is any assets acquired during a marriage. When applying the community property concept to divorcing spouses, the marital assets are equally divided.

What is the difference between community property statutes versus equitable division statutes? Generally, states using community property statutes look at *all* the earnings and losses of both spouses incurred during the marriage and *split* both between the parties. States using equitable division statutes, on the other hand, also look at the earnings and losses of both spouses during the marriage, but then *allocate* the property *based on the facts* of the individual marriage. Exhibit 8.16 provides a list of states that use the community property concept to allocate property to divorcing spouses. All other states use the equitable distribution concept.

Equitable Distribution

The legal concept of equitable distribution is based on the belief that married people should deal fairly with each other when the marriage ends. Equitable distribution does not mean that the assets of the married couple will automatically be cut down the middle so each spouse receives an equal part of the assets. Rather, the emphasis is on the court's interpretation of what is a *fair* division of the marital assets for a particular couple under a particular set of facts. Each state that uses an equitable distribution standard has a state statute listing the factors to consider in determining how a couple's assets can be equitably divided. Equitable distribution states recognize that each spouse's contributions to a marriage should be carefully considered.

The cases of *Painter v. Painter* and *Piscopo v. Piscopo* (see Cases 8.5 and 8.6) both dealt with equitable distribution. Interestingly, the *Painter* case delved into the question of whether allowing the courts to interpret the fair division of marital assets using the equitable distribution concept is constitutional. The *Piscopo* case asked the question of whether goodwill can be considered for equitable distribution. Exhibit 8.17 lists equitable distribution factors that are considered by Illinois courts; these factors are somewhat typical of those considered in all states using equitable distribution.

EXHIBIT 8.16 Community Property States

Arizona	Louisiana	Texas
California	Nevada	Washington
Idaho	New Mexico	Wisconsin

CASE 8.5 *Painter v. Painter,*
85 N.J. 196, 320 A.2d 484 (1974)

Facts: Stephen and Joan Painter were married on October 17, 1953, and lived together as husband and wife until January 23, 1967. They had three children. Stephen was ordered to pay $12,000 per year in alimony and child support plus all medical and dental bills. Stephen's problem was not with the alimony or support, but with the state's equitable distribution statute. Stephen's total assets amounted to $230,000 and Joan's total assets were approximately $98,000. Joan asked for an equitable distribution of their total property. Stephen appealed the trial court's use of equitable distribution to determine the property settlement.

Issue: Whether the use of the equitable distribution statute in determining a property settlement results in an unconstitutional deprivation of property because it deprives an individual of property without due process of law and because it is vague.

Court's Reasoning: Today, in the laws of many other states, in words very similar to those found in our statute, provision is made for the fair and equitable distribution of marital assets in the event of divorce. Many, if not most, property arrangements will probably be agreed upon between the divorcing parties, and thus will not require judicial intervention. The general purpose of the legislation is clear, and the statute is not vague or ambiguous. The courts are now empowered to allocate marital assets between the spouses, regardless of ownership. This was not the case before the enactment of the statute. Prior to this statute, it was held that the divorce statute only granted the court the power to give the wife an allowance of money in periodical installments. Clearly, any property owned by a husband or wife at the time of marriage will remain the separate property of such spouse and in the event of divorce will not qualify as an asset eligible for distribution. To the extent that any property is attributable to the expenditure of effort of both spouses or either spouse during the marriage, it clearly qualifies for distribution. We hold the legislative intent to be that all property, regardless of its source, in which a spouse acquires an interest during the marriage, shall be eligible for distribution in the event of divorce.

Holding: Case remanded for reconsideration and determination of the property distribution issue.

Case Discussion: The court in this case clearly stated that the legislature knew what it was doing when it enacted the equitable distribution concept. The legislatures in the states that have enacted equitable distribution usually have provided factors for their courts to consider when asked to make an equitable distribution decision. Refer to Exhibit 8.17 and review the equitable distribution factors that apply in Illinois. Note that these factors are quite similar to those in the list of typical alimony factors shown later in Exhibit 8.18.

EXHIBIT 8.17 Equitable Distribution Factors

1. The contribution of each spouse to the acquisition or dissipation of the marital or non-marital property, including the contribution of each spouse as homemaker to the family unit;
2. The value of each spouse's non-marital property;
3. The economic circumstances of each spouse at the time the division of property is to become effective, including the desirability of awarding the family home to the spouse having custody of the children;
4. The length of the marriage;
5. The age and health of the spouses;
6. The amount and sources of income of the spouses;
7. The vocational skills of the spouses;
8. The employability of the spouses;
9. The estate, liabilities, and needs of each spouse and the opportunity of each for further acquisition of capital assets and income;
10. The federal income tax consequences of the court's division of the property;
11. Any premarital agreement;
12. Liabilities of the spouses (including obligations from a prior marriage);
13. Whether the property award is instead of or in addition to maintenance; and
14. Any custodial provisions for the children.[a]

[a] Ill. Stat. Ann. Ch. 5, § 504 (2002).

EXHIBIT 8.18 Typical Alimony Factors

1. The actual need and ability of the parties to pay.
2. The duration of the marriage.
3. The parties' ages and their physical and emotional health.
4. The standard of living established in the marriage, and the likelihood that each party can maintain a reasonably comparable standard of living.
5. The earning capacities, educational levels, vocational skills, and employability of the parties.
6. The length of absence from the job market of the party seeking maintenance.
7. The parental responsibilities for the children.
8. The time and expense necessary to acquire sufficient education or training to enable the party seeking maintenance to find appropriate employment, and the opportunity for future acquisitions of capital assets and income.
9. The history of the financial and nonfinancial contributions to the marriage by each party including contributions to the care and education of the children and interruption of personal careers or educational opportunities.
10. The equitable distribution of property and any payouts on equitable distribution, directly or indirectly, out of current income—to the extent this consideration is reasonable, just, and fair.
11. The income available to either party through investment of any assets held by that party.
12. The tax treatment and consequences to both parties of any alimony award including the designation of all or a portion of the payment as a nontaxable payment.[a]

[a] N.J. Stat. Ann. § 2A: 34-23(b) (2003).

CASE 8.6 *Piscopo v. Piscopo,* 232 N.J. Super. 559, 557 A.2d 1040 (1989)

Facts: During the trial, the plaintiff, Joe Piscopo, claimed that the goodwill attributed to his celebrity status was not an asset subject to equitable distribution. Mrs. Piscopo, the defendant, asserted that the goodwill associated with the plaintiff's status as a celebrity was an intangible, but quantifiable, asset recognizable by analogy to well-accepted New Jersey case law, and therefore an equitably distributable marital asset. Irwin Marks, CPA, was appointed by the trial judge to value the plaintiff's business and pension interests and to calculate the value, if any, of celebrity goodwill and the actual disposable income.

Marks found that, substantially, all of the plaintiff's earned income flowed through Piscopo Productions, Inc., with the plaintiff's compensation from the corporation determined at the end of each year. Marks said the valuation of the plaintiff's business was analogous to valuing any other professional corporation. He used three out of five years of income from which to derive an average adjusted net income of $288,150 and average adjusted gross receipts of $635,452. Piscopo Productions, Inc., as the trial judge noted, was actually owned as follows: the plaintiff, 51%; the defendant, 48%; the plaintiff's father, 1%. Marks calculated the plaintiff's celebrity goodwill by taking 25% of his average gross earnings over the three-year period. Marks attributed to the plaintiff's celebrity goodwill a value of $158,863. The trial court agreed with Mrs. Piscopo. Mr. Piscopo appealed. On appeal, he conceded that celebrity goodwill could be a distributable marital asset, but he argued that his reputation as a celebrity could not be related to *probable* future earnings—only to *possible* future earnings.

Issue: Whether the marital property includes the plaintiff's celebrity goodwill.

Court's Reasoning: In the context of equitable distribution, the leading case holding that goodwill is a distributable asset is *Dugan v. Dugan,* 92 N.J. 423, 457 A.2d 1 (1983). In *Dugan,* the Supreme Court held that the goodwill attributed to the solely owned professional corporation of a lawyer was subject to equitable distribution, despite the fact that ethical considerations prevented the plaintiff from selling his practice. The court said that business goodwill existed, although the business depended entirely upon the skill of one person and had no book value. The court defined goodwill as *essentially a reputation that will probably generate future business.*

The court said further that goodwill does not exist at the time professional qualifications and a license to practice are obtained. A good reputation is earned after accomplishment and performance. Future earning capacity *per se* is not goodwill. However, when that future earning capacity has been enhanced because reputation leads to probable future patronage from existing and potential clients, goodwill may exist and have value. When that occurs, the resulting goodwill is property subject to equitable distribution.

The plaintiff distinguishes *Dugan* on the ground that a successful professional has a reliable future income, whereas show business is volatile. The *Dugan* court said, however, that the valuation of goodwill is not measured by future earnings, but by past earnings, which are undisputed.

The issue of valuation became moot. The parties stipulated $98,708.60 as the value of the plaintiff's celebrity goodwill. We agree with the lower court that the goodwill value of the plaintiff's business is a distributable marital asset.

Holding: Affirmed.

Case Discussion: If you are asking, "Who is Joe Piscopo?," you probably would agree that it's a good thing that Mrs. Piscopo got the value of Mr. Piscopo's mid-1980s celebrity goodwill, at the peak of his popularity, and not the value of Joe's celebrity goodwill today. This case is a good example of fame's fleeting nature. Joe does do a great Sinatra impression, though.

What Assets Are Considered Immune from Distribution?

An individually owned asset acquired before marriage by one spouse will remain a singularly owned asset of that spouse for purposes of equitable distribution, unless the asset has been commingled with the other spouse's assets during the marriage. The legal term for commingling of assets is *transmutation*. **Transmutation** is defined as changing one type of property interest into another. For example, suppose Heidi inherits $50,000 worth of mountain goats from her grandfather and, upon marrying, sells the goats to Peter and uses the $50,000 as a down payment to buy a house with her husband, Hapless Hal. Then, during the marriage, both spouses contribute to the maintenance of the house. Although Heidi's grandfather might not be pleased about it, the original $50,000 down payment will probably not be considered Heidi's assets once the money has been transmuted—or, in other words, *commingled*—with Hal's. Transmutation also occurred in Michael and Libby's case when Michael's inheritance was used to renovate the kitchen in the barn that they owned jointly.

When Courts Decide to Protect One Spouse from Another

Occasionally, the courts appear to be purposely protecting one spouse from another. The case of *Stallings v. Stallings* (see Case 8.7) involved one court's interpretation of equitable distribution. The *Stallings* court clearly stated that *equitable* distribution does not mean *equal* distribution.

ALIMONY

Alimony is defined as an allowance from one spouse to another that usually continues until the recipient spouse remarries or begins cohabiting with another partner. Typically, alimony payments terminate upon the death of either ex-spouse. Alimony is called *spousal maintenance* or *spousal support* in some states. Historically, alimony was viewed as a male-only responsibility. It was usually linked to spousal conduct during the marriage. This often necessitated an extensive he-said, she-said confrontation for the court to untangle. For example, an adulterous husband could face indefinite alimony payments to his innocent and wronged wife. On the other hand, an adulterous wife could face a loss of alimony if her adulterous behavior was proved. No-fault divorce reforms inspired the courts to look upon divorce as an opportunity for a fresh start for both spouses. Courts across the nation began to look upon permanent alimony awards as levying an unfair and lifelong burden upon the payer-spouse. The new no-fault thinking was that permanent alimony kept the spouses connected and prevented a new beginning. Instead, courts began to foster a fresh-start approach by granting alimony awards with a definite cutoff date. Most courts told spouses claiming a need for alimony that they should retrain themselves to become self-supporting.

The problem with attempting to retrain every divorcing spouse with a disparate financial position from that of her ex-spouse is that many spouses are never able to regain the economic status enjoyed before their divorce. For example, the long-term housewife who keeps the home fires burning so her husband can be free of household worries and pursue his career can never recoup those years spent at home. The judicial pendulum has ultimately swung to a middle ground when weighing the economic consequences of divorce. Today, courts award permanent alimony where the factual circumstances show that one spouse's long-term contributions (even if they are nonmonetary) were important and that failing to award permanent alimony to that spouse would be unjust considering her unequal earning capacity post-divorce.

So, how do courts determine how much alimony is reasonable and fair? They ask a five-part question: *When, why, how, how much,* and *for how long* should alimony be paid? The hunt for the answer to this question is complicated by the available subcategories of alimony generally used across the country. For example, subcategories available in most, but not all, states include alimony *pendente lite,* rehabilitative

CASE 8.7 *Stallings v. Stallings*, 393 N.E.2d 1065 (Ill. 1979)

Facts: The parties were married on June 17, 1972. Less than two months before their marriage, they purchased a home for $35,000 and took title as tenants in common. The couple had one child together, and the wife worked in a bank where she earned a total of $64,000 during the four-and-a-half-year marriage. Around 90 percent of her income was spent on family and household expenses, including the mortgage payments on the family home. During the marriage, the husband mainly remained at home and pursued a series of business misadventures and his earning for the same period were $13,000. The wife came into the marriage with assets of her own valued at around $125,000. Her financial assistance to her husband's floundering businesses caused a significant reduction in her assets. The husband came into the marriage with custody of five children from a previous marriage.

The wife was awarded the home, as well as household goods, bank stock, savings and checking accounts, a 1977 Oldsmobile, and the 1977 income tax refund. The court denied the husband's maintenance claim. The husband appealed the entire award and specifically claimed the court erred in awarding the home, purchased as tenants in common, to his wife.

Issue: Whether the court erred in failing to treat the house as a marital asset and failing to grant maintenance to the husband.

Court's Reasoning: The evidence was that this property was purchased in contemplation of the forthcoming marriage of the purchasers and with the intent that it would be their family home. Furthermore, all equity in the property, other than the $5,000 down payment, resulted from payments made by the wife during the marriage. The husband claims he is entitled to a fifty-fifty split of all marital property. We disagree, because if the legislature's intention was to split marital property equally, then the equitable distribution factors would not have been written. The husband dissipated the marital property and failed to contribute to the marriage and marital assets. The husband's credibility was successfully challenged by his admission to lying on federal bankruptcy and income tax forms, and thus, the trial court's complete award of marital property to the wife was not against the manifest weight of the evidence nor contrary to state law. With respect to the husband's argument that the trial court abused its discretion in denying him maintenance, an award of maintenance is indicated only when the court can find that a spouse is unable to support himself through appropriate employment or is otherwise without sufficient income. The husband was gainfully employed prior to the marriage.

Holding: Trial court affirmed.

Case Discussion: You can tell that neither the trial judge nor the appellate judges were buying anything the husband in this case was selling. Both courts based their decisions on the state's equitable distribution factors. If this case had happened in a community property state, it is unlikely that such a decision would have been made. Do you think the outcome would have been the same if the husband had been the one working in a bank and the wife had been home with the children and had been the one who dissipated assets through ill-advised financial schemes?

alimony, (or transitional support), lump-sum alimony (or alimony in gross), limited duration (or term alimony), reimbursement alimony, and permanent alimony.

Across the country, courts determine the monetary amount of alimony by weighing relatively *subjective* criteria. The judicial opinion in the *Lepis v. Lepis* case[3] provides an excellent explanation of one judicial determination on how much and for how long a dependent spouse should be paid alimony. The court in *Lepis* explained that when support of an economically dependent spouse is at issue, *the general considerations are the dependent spouse's needs, that spouse's ability to contribute to the fulfillment of those needs, and the supporting spouse's ability to pay and maintain the dependent spouse at the former living standard.*

Numerous economic and noneconomic factors can be considered by the courts when making an alimony award. All 50 states have an applicable statute pertaining to the economic and noneconomic factors the courts may consider. A minority of states still look to marital fault as one of the factors to be weighed. Typically, each case is viewed individually by the court because alimony is still a fact-sensitive issue. Read Exhibit 8.18 to review a relatively common list of alimony factors.

Alimony *Pendente Lite*

Recall, from your earlier reading, that **alimony *pendente lite*** (also called temporary alimony) is temporary monetary support payments made by one spouse to the other while they are waiting for their divorce to be finalized.

Rehabilitative Alimony

Rehabilitative alimony, sometimes called **transitional support,** is payable for a specific period of time and ceases when the supported spouse is able to be self-supporting. Typically, most states require the spouse seeking rehabilitative alimony to provide a plan of action for her rehabilitation. For example, a spouse seeking rehabilitative alimony may wish to return to college to finish a teaching degree and earn certification. The plan would explain the amount of alimony, tuition, and perhaps even job search time the spouse would need before the rehabilitative alimony was ended. The *Robinson* case (see Case 8.8) provides an excellent example of how one court determined the need for rehabilitative alimony to be ordered.

Lump-Sum Alimony

Lump-sum alimony, also called **alimony in gross,** entails a complete monetary payout of the total amount. Receiving lump-sum alimony does not preclude periodic alimony payments as well. Lump-sum alimony may be desirable for a client who wishes to sever the financial connections between herself and her spouse, and it also avoids dealing with collecting arrearages. **Arrearages** are defined as late payments. A trial court's refusal to grant lump-sum alimony is discussed in the case of *O'Neill v. O'Neill* (see Case 8.9).

Limited Duration Alimony

Limited duration alimony, also known as **term alimony,** is often utilized where rehabilitation of the dependent spouse is not necessary or where the marriage was of a short duration. Limited duration alimony is often granted where a grant of permanent alimony would not be warranted under a client's particular circumstances.

CASE 8.8 *In re Marriage of Donna J. Robinson v. Robinson*, 184 Ill. App. 3d 235, 539 N.E.2d 1365, 132 Ill. Dec. 559 (1989)

Facts: On May 26, 1983, the petitioner, Donna Robinson, filed a petition for dissolution of marriage. The court entered a memorandum on June 18, 1985, regarding property division. That decision awarded the wife maintenance, which was to be used to rehabilitate herself through education or job training to obtain gainful employment. The husband was ordered to pay $1500 per month, beginning July 1, 1985, for 24 months, and $750 per month, beginning July 1, 1987, for the next 36 months.

On July 12, 1985, the court's final judgment amended the previous memorandum to state that the payments beginning July 1, 1987, for $750 were to be paid for a total of 35 months instead of 36 months. This decision barred any further maintenance from the defendant. In addition, the court awarded a cash payment to the wife from the husband totaling $175,000, to be paid as follows: $10,000 by August 1, 1985; $15,000 by October 1, 1985; and $150,000 to be paid in ten annual principal installments of $15,000 each, plus annual interest payments at a rate of 10 percent payable from July 1, 1985, on the remaining balance and payable on the first of July of each year starting on July 1, 1986. The court placed a lien on the 400-acre farm allocated to the husband to secure these payments.

On October 1, 1987, the husband-respondent filed a petition to modify maintenance payments, stating that he had experienced a substantial reduction in income since the decree of dissolution. The court found that the maintenance could not be modified, since it was maintenance in gross and was thus nonmodifiable. The respondent appealed further.

The respondent argued that section 510 of the Illinois Marriage and Dissolution of Marriage Act (the Act) does not distinguish between maintenance and maintenance in gross, and further alleged that all maintenance is modifiable under certain circumstances. The petitioner responded that the maintenance was rehabilitative maintenance in gross.

The court found that the respondent did not correctly cite the law. It stated that the goal of the Act was to help and encourage a spouse seeking maintenance to regain dormant employment skills or to develop new ones. A specific termination date should not be set unless evidence supported that the dependent spouse would be able to support herself by the end of a specific time period.

Issue: Whether the trial court erred in determining that the original maintenance order was for maintenance in gross and as such was nonmodifiable.

Court's Reasoning: Circumstances revealed that it was not maintenance in gross that was ordered, but rehabilitative maintenance. The petitioner was married for 34 years. The petitioner was never employed outside of the home, nor did she ever receive her high school diploma because she had married when she was 16 years old. Therefore, as a woman in her 50s who had been solely dependent on her husband, rehabilitative maintenance was an incorrect decision and one that the statute was designed to recognize. This court finds that the maintenance is modifiable upon showing a change of circumstances. Furthermore, we hold that the petitioner, upon remand, may seek to have the court modify the automatic termination date.

Holding: Judgment reversed and remanded for further proceedings.

Case Discussion: This case is a good example of what can happen when you stir up a pot without knowing what is on the bottom! Mr. Robinson went to court to modify his ex-wife's alimony payment downward. The alimony was described by the original court as rehabilitative alimony. Mr. Robinson lost his first motion for modification and, not satisfied, he appealed that loss. The court in this case looked to the Illinois Marriage and Dissolution of Marriage Act and determined that Mrs. Robinson could return to court to *extend* the previously ordered payments because in her situation as an older woman who had been dependent on her spouse, she would have limited options in terms of rehabilitation.

CASE 8.9 *O'Neill v. O'Neill,* 13 Conn. App. 300, 536 A.2d 978 (1988)

Facts: The trial court awarded the plaintiff rehabilitative alimony in the amount of $200 per week for a duration of two years. The court did not award the plaintiff any lump-sum property settlement, nor did it order the defendant to pay the plaintiff's counsel fees. The plaintiff's appeal is based upon the limited two-year duration of the alimony and the trial court's refusal to award a lump-sum distribution as a property settlement.

Issue: Whether the trial court erred in limiting the rehabilitative alimony to two years, refusing to award a lump-sum property settlement, and failing to award counsel fees to the wife.

Court's Reasoning: The lower court denied the plaintiff's request for counsel fees on the ground that she had commenced the case. A trial court has the discretion to award counsel fees to parties in a dissolution action in accordance with their respective financial abilities. The undisputed facts show that the plaintiff did not have the funds available with which to pay for her counsel fees, whereas the defendant did. Courts ordinarily award counsel fees in divorce cases so that a party, usually the wife, may not be deprived of her rights because of a lack of funds.

A property division ought to accord value to those nonmonetary contributions of one spouse that enable the other spouse to devote substantial effort to paid employment, which, in turn, enables the family to acquire tangible marital assets. The investment of *human capital* in homemaking has worth and should be evaluated in a property division incident to dissolution of marriage.

The unambiguous purpose of rehabilitative alimony is to allow the recipient spouse to attain self-sufficiency. The trial court awarded rehabilitative alimony in order that the plaintiff might become a nurse. The alimony award was clearly for an insufficient duration. An award does not serve its purpose if it does not allow the plaintiff enough time in which to attain self-sufficiency.

Holding: The judgment of the trial court is set aside with respect to counsel fees, property division, and rehabilitative alimony, and the case is remanded for a new hearing on the financial issues.

Case Discussion: The *O'Neill* court reinforces several excellent points. A spouse would be effectively denied access to the courts if the payment of counsel fees was granted only to spouses responding to divorce complaints. Secondly, the alimony factors (and equitable distribution factors, too) require the courts to look at the nonfinancial contributions of a spouse to the marriage (plus numerous other factors) when determining whether the payment of alimony should be ordered.

Reimbursement Alimony

Reimbursement alimony is typically awarded in cases in which one party supported the other's pursuit of an advanced education. Recall the case of the young couple, Jack and Diane, who were planning to marry, but decided to go to Susan's law firm first to have a prenuptial agreement prepared. Diane was planning to work and pay for her future husband's expenses while he went to medical school. The couple agreed that if they divorced, Diane would be entitled to reimbursement alimony in the form of support while she attended graduate school. This factual scenario is similar to what happened in the case of *Woodworth v. Woodworth* (see Case 8.10), except the couple in that case had not planned ahead like Jack and Diane did.

CASE 8.10 *Woodworth v. Woodworth,* 126 Mich. App. 258, 337 N.W.2d 332 (1983)

Facts: After the plaintiff, Michael Woodworth, graduated from Central Michigan University with a bachelor's degree in secondary education, and the defendant, Ann Woodworth, graduated from Lancing Community College with an associate degree, the parties married on June 27, 1970. They moved to Jonesville, where the plaintiff worked as a teacher and coach for the high school and the defendant worked as a nursery school teacher. Michael left his job in Jonesville, and the family relocated to Detroit so he could attend law school. In Detroit, Ann sought and obtained full-time employment to support the family. Three years later, they moved to Lansing, where Michael took and passed the bar exam. He accepted a job as a research attorney with the Court of Appeals. Michael later became a partner in a Lansing law firm. The facts revealed that the plaintiff's law degree was the end product of a concerted family effort. Both parties planned their family life around the effort. The couple separated on August 25, 1980. The trial court held that the plaintiff's law degree was valued at $20,000 and awarded this amount to the defendant in payments of $2,000 over 10 years. The plaintiff contended that his law degree was not such a marital asset and appealed.

Issue: Whether plaintiff's law degree is marital property subject to distribution.

Court's Reasoning: The plaintiff quit his job and entered law school. The defendant secured employment so the plaintiff could become a professional with far greater earning capacity than he had previously, which would benefit him and their children. To permit, upon divorce, the benefit to go only to the party who secured the professional degree would be unconscionable. We agree that a marriage is not intrinsically a commercial enterprise. Instead, it is a relationship sanctioned by law and governed at its essence by fidelity and troth. Neither partner usually expects to be compensated for his efforts. However, *to allow a spouse to leave a marriage with all the benefits of additional education and a professional license without compensation to the spouse who bore much of the burdens incident to procuring these would be unfair.*

Therefore, the plaintiff's law degree was the result of mutual sacrifice and effort by both the plaintiff and the defendant. While the plaintiff studied and attended classes, the defendant carried her share of the burden as well as sharing vicariously in the stress of the experience known as the "paper chase." Clearly, in this case, the degree was a family investment, rather than a gift or a benefit to the degree holder alone. Treating the degree as such a gift would unjustly enrich the degree holder to the extent that the degree's value exceeds its cost.

We are unable to determine how the trial court reached the value of the law degree. Therefore, this case is remanded to the trial court to permit that court to revalue the degree in light of the following factors: (1) the length of the marriage after the degree was obtained; (2) the sources and extent of financial support given to the plaintiff during his years in law school; and (3) the overall division of the parties' marital property. In determining the degree's present value, the trial court should estimate what the person holding the degree is likely to make in that particular job market and subtract from that what he would probably have earned without the degree. The ultimate objective in a property distribution is to be fair. Both parties may present new evidence on these matters and the matter of valuation of the degree.

Holding: Remanded to the trial court for revaluation of the degree, and we order plaintiff to pay defendant reasonable attorney fees for this appeal. Costs to defendant.

Case Discussion: The irony in this case is that the husband never would have made it into a courtroom if his wife had not supported him through law school. Mr. Woodworth disagreed with the trial court's decision to place a $20,000 value on his law degree, and the court's subsequent award to his wife of $2,000 per year for 10 years for her role in supporting her husband and family during his years in law school and his early years of practice. Do you agree with the appellate court's decision?

Permanent Alimony

Permanent alimony is the alimony of choice where circumstances indicate that the dependent spouse is unlikely to be rehabilitated to a level that would allow her to reach the standard of living enjoyed during the marriage. Permanent alimony is often awarded to a spouse who has been a longtime homemaker with no employment experience. This was the scenario in the case of *Lash v. Lash* (see Case 8.11). The situation was different, however, in *D'Arc v. D'Arc* (see Case 8.12), where the case involved a wealthy spouse, an alleged attempted murder, and failure to impress the court that permanent alimony should be ordered.

Settlement Negotiations Stalled

Several weeks after going to court for the first relatively successful shot at settling, J. D. had no luck negotiating an end to the Smiths' divorce case with Howard Hughey. J. D. knew from his most recent conversation with Howard that Michael just did not want to budge on the alimony issue, although he would now agree to letting Libby and the children stay in the barn for two years. Michael has offered to give Libby a 60 percent share of the profits to offset the pension. This extra cash would help Libby put a larger down payment

---

CASE 8.11 *Lash v. Lash*, 307 So. 2d 241 (1975)

Facts: The parties were married 26 years. The wife was 44 years old, and the husband was 47 years old when they divorced. The husband was employed as executive director of the United Way of Pinellas County, Inc., for which he was paid an annual salary of approximately $29,000. The wife only worked alongside the husband while they were married and was unemployed at the time of the divorce. In the final judgment dated March 22, 1974, the wife was awarded rehabilitative alimony of $425 per month through December 1974. The wife appealed and argued that she should have been granted permanent alimony.

Issue: Whether the granting of permanent alimony was supported by the facts presented.

Court's Reasoning: The fact that the legislature authorized rehabilitative alimony did not do away with permanent alimony. Rehabilitative alimony presupposes the potential for self-support. Without this capacity, there is nothing to which one can be rehabilitated. Where the parties are still quite young and have been married only a short period of time, a judge is understandably reluctant to saddle the husband with the obligation of making permanent alimony payments for the rest of his life.

In this case, we have a wife who worked during part of her married life, but most of this was done in joint employment with her husband. At her husband's request, she did little outside work in recent years. By reason of her educational background and work experience, it is not likely that she will be able to obtain a job paying more than one quarter of what her husband now earns. In view of this, the husband should be required to assist in her support on a permanent basis, subject always to the right of obtaining relief under changed circumstances.

Holding: Reversed and remanded.

Case Discussion: The *Lash* decision was made in the 1970s. Do you think spouses should still expect permanent alimony to be an available option? In light of the fact that more than 50 percent of all American marriages end in divorce, do you think all spouses have adequate notice that they should be prepared to support themselves following a divorce? Should permanent alimony be awarded only in exceptional hardship cases?

CASE 8.12 *D'Arc v. D'Arc, 157 N.J. Super. 553, 385 A.2d 278 (1978)*

Facts: The trial court granted a dual divorce to both parties on the ground of an 18-month separation. Each party reserved the right to offer proof of marital fault that would be relevant and admissible on the issues of alimony and equitable distribution of marital assets. The husband had a private psychiatric practice in New York City prior to the marriage and earned $50,000 a year. After the marriage, he assumed management of his wife's (Mary Lea Johnson's) financial affairs and discontinued his private practice. The wife is the beneficiary of a substantial trust fund created by her father with stock in Johnson & Johnson. During this marriage, except for the small earnings of the husband shortly after the marriage, all the funds spent by the parties were provided by the wife. On the date of their separation, Dr. D'Arc typed a one-sheet agreement, which both promptly signed. The essential terms were that Miss Johnson agreed to pay her husband tax-free alimony of $10,000 per month indefinitely and, if he predeceased her, she would pay all the educational expenses of his two children by his first marriage.

Any chance at reconciliation was demolished in March and April 1976 when the wife received information that her husband was negotiating to arrange for her murder. The husband denied the charges and countered with the charge that his wife had solicited someone to murder him.

Issue: Whether Dr. D'Arc is entitled to receive alimony and an equitable distribution of marital assets.

Court's Reasoning: Did the wife prove by a preponderance of the evidence that her husband sought to solicit her murder? We must recognize that, while the charge is that of a serious criminal accusation, we are dealing with a civil case where the burden of proof is by a preponderance of the evidence, not proof beyond a reasonable doubt as in a criminal case. The court was very impressed with the credibility of the witnesses who identified the husband as the speaker in taped telephone conversations. Particularly credible was Olive Cohen, the housemaid, who testified that one day she heard the voice of Dr. D'Arc in another room, but when she entered, she learned to her surprise that a tape was being played and Dr. D'Arc was not present. Conversely, the court was not impressed with the credibility of the husband when he denied his complicity. Further, there were at least four comments made in the seven taped telephone conversations that corroborate the wife's charges because statements made could only be known by Dr. D'Arc, or someone extremely intimate with him.

The court is satisfied that Dr. D'Arc was the person on taped telephone conversations offering an individual $50,000 to murder his wife. Both parties clearly stipulated that proof of fault could be offered during the court's consideration of alimony and equitable distribution issues. Even if fault could not be considered, it is clear that on the merits, Dr. D'Arc is not entitled to alimony. He is a physician who is earning $40,000 per year and has earned more. While it is true that he will not be able to a maintain the same lavish level of living he enjoyed while married to Miss Johnson, it cannot be said on this record that Dr. D'Arc, in the space of approximately three and a half years, has become so accustomed to the style of living he enjoyed while married to her that he is now entitled to be maintained by her in that same style. Dr. D'Arc is not entitled to receive alimony from Miss Johnson. However, is he entitled to enforcement of the February 22, 1976, agreement in which Miss Johnson agreed to pay Dr. D'Arc $10,000 per month tax-free? Evidence of the unfairness and unjustness of the agreement was given by the attorney for Miss Johnson who testified that, because of Miss Johnson's income tax bracket, this agreement would cost her about $400,000 a year, a not insignificant portion of her one million trust fund income. Under these circumstances, the court finds that it would be unfair, unjust, and inequitable to enforce the February 22, 1976, agreement.

Before inquiring into what assets are subject to equitable distribution, the court questions whether fault should be taken into consideration when determining equitable distribution. The court concludes the answer is no. Equitable distribution requires that fault be excluded as a consideration. Fault may be merely a manifestation of a sick marriage and only reflect how a person reacted to a marital problem. A marriage is a partnership or shared enterprise with each contributing to the marital estate. We are merely giving to each what really belongs to him or her.

However, we are not dealing with the usual type of fault. To ignore the facts of this case would be tantamount to permitting Dr. D'Arc to obtain indirectly what he failed to obtain by a direct attack upon the life of his spouse. Considering all of the circumstances, the court finds that equity dictates that the vast bulk of assets be returned to Miss Johnson. Dr. D'Arc shall be permitted to retain the net proceeds of assets that he has already sold.

Case Discussion: The court ordered Miss Johnson to pay $15,000 of her husband's legal fees because she had the means to pay. Plus, the court explained that, although the husband had been charged with attempted murder, he may still have reasonably believed he was entitled to alimony and an equitable distribution of property because the state's law was unclear on the subject. Do you agree? This case shows that when determining equitable distribution of marital property, the court *normally* would not want to evaluate which spouse was more at fault for the ending of the marriage. Do you agree with the court's statement that in the space of approximately three years, a person would not have become used to a lavish lifestyle? How long would it take you to feel at home in a mansion? Do you think the court would have upheld the February 27th agreement if Dr. D'Arc had not tried to arrange his wife's murder?

on a condo so, subsequently, she would have a smaller mortgage. Unfortunately, the original problem still exists: Libby does not have a steady income, and it would be unlikely she could qualify for a mortgage.

J. D. Creates a Solution to the Settlement Stalemate

Following yet another negotiation call to Howard Hughey, J. D. was exasperated with the stalemate. Passing Susan at her desk, he stopped and asked, "Susan, I need a jolt of caffeine to figure out how we're going to settle the Smith case. Would you like to join me?"

Looking up from a gargantuan pile of interrogatories, Susan happily answered, "You bet!"

Companionably sipping their coffee in the lunchroom, J. D. asked, "You know the Smiths. Why do you think Mr. Smith is being so obstinate about alimony for Mrs. Smith?"

Thrilled to be asked her opinion, Susan waited a second to give the best answer she could think of. "I remember Mr. Smith once telling my dad that he didn't want to pay an increase in taxes for a new civic theater that was being planned because he didn't go to the theater and couldn't see why he should have to pay for something when he wasn't going to get anything out of the deal," she answered and looked to J. D. for his reaction.

J. D. sipped, and then it hit him. "Sue, I see what you're getting at. You sound a little like a Chinese riddle on the old Kung Fu television show, but I get it," he announced. "Mr. Smith will have to be *shown* how alimony paid to Mrs. Smith is going to benefit him directly."

Susan added, "I know Mr. Smith is sort of stubborn, and he'll probably push this thing to the bitter end unless someone comes up with a new idea."

Looking like he was still pondering a riddle, J. D. commented, "You know, if Mrs. Smith's art could pay off at a steady rate, then Mr. Smith's alimony payments, not to mention having to pay the full share of the child support, could go away."

More confused by the minute, Susan asked, "How would that happen exactly?"

J. D. responded, "If Mrs. Smith went back to school and used her artistic talent to become an art teacher, she could conceivably make enough to support herself, share in the kids' support, *and* lessen Mr. Smith's financial burden. It really would be the best thing for her, too. She's still young enough to earn a decent pension. Plus, I think if we went to court, a judge would come up with that idea, or at the very least put a limit on her alimony. She is still relatively young, and her children are school age already. Both those factors will be seriously looked at by the court as to why she shouldn't receive permanent alimony."

"During her interview Libby *did* say becoming an art teacher was the only thing she could see herself doing," Susan added. "Plus, she's starting to see that living in the barn and working so hard may not be how she wants to live forever. She mentioned that she's been thinking about how much easier life would be living in a condo."

"That's right," J. D. agreed. "I think I'll give Libby a call and see if she thinks this is an idea that will work for her."

Smiling, Susan stated, "I guess that means back to the interrogatories for me."

Rehabilitative Alimony Inspires New Career for Libby

"Hello. This is Libby."

"Hi, Libby. This is J. D. Dombroski."

"Hello, J. D. How are you?"

"I'm fine, thank you. How about yourself and the kids?"

"We're managing. Any news?" she inquired.

"Well, yes and no," J. D. answered. "I think I've figured out a way to push through the negotiations."

Libby quickly said, "Please, how? I'm all ears."

"You know," J. D. began. "Your soon-to-be ex-husband is a pretty stubborn character to negotiate with."

Libby commiserated, "You're telling me?"

J. D. explained, "I'd like to close this case, and the two sticking points are the questions of alimony and selling the barn. If we go to trial with this case, my opinion is that the judge will look at your age and intelligence and suggest you receive some training to help support yourself. I can honestly say that I don't think any judge is going to go for permanent alimony with your age and the family's financial situation. Michael's salary is not going to reach far enough to pay you permanent alimony and the children's support. My suggestion is that we should ask for rehabilitative alimony for your training as a teacher. I think you should think about staying in the barn only until you become eligible for a mortgage of your own. What do you think?"

Libby had quietly listened, "I've been doing a lot of my own thinking, too. I can't depend on my artwork. I need a steady income for our future. Plus, I'll need to think about a pension. Honestly, I've gotten really tired of all the work with the barn. I'd like to date, but I have no time with all the work involved in maintaining the place."

J. D. responded, "We could ask that you stay on until you have a job that would help you get your own mortgage."

Libby admitted, "I may have been so insistent on staying in the barn because Michael was so insistent that we sell it. I think I might like to rent for now, put my share of the barn sale in a safe investment, and concentrate on my kids and building a career."

J. D. responded, "It does sound like you've been doing some serious thinking. I think we'll try to use your change of heart to negotiate the best settlement possible. Michael has already agreed to

60 percent of the barn sale profits to offset the pension, and he has agreed to your staying in the barn for two years. The two years in the barn would probably cover three, or even four years, in a nice apartment. I'd like Michael to pay for your schooling, plus alimony, and the family's expenses for at least the next five years. I'm sure Howard Hughey will explain to Michael that the judge would probably eventually decide the same. It will probably take you that long to get a degree and get set up in your first job."

"It sounds like a plan I can live with," Libby said. "Plus, it sounds like a plan Michael could live with."

"Okay. Well, I guess I'll call Hughey and get the ball rolling," J. D. announced. "I'll talk to you as soon as I hear something."

SEEKING A MODIFICATION

When talking about alimony, the bottom line is that a judge's order to pay alimony is always subject to review and modification by the court. The spouse returning to court to seek an increase, decrease, or ending of alimony has the burden of proving that there are changed circumstances that warrant such modification. What will be considered a changed circumstance? Examples include: a change in income; a change in employment status; cohabiting with an adult sexual partner; and changes in a medical condition, to name a few. The *Waskin v. Waskin* case (see Case 8.13) puts an interesting spin on a request for alimony modification.

TERMINATION OF THE ALIMONY OBLIGATION

There are numerous factors for when a spouse should receive alimony, and there are numerous factors that could lead to a court terminating an alimony obligation. The four main reasons most courts will terminate alimony include: remarriage of the payee spouse; death of the payee or the payor spouse; cohabitation by the payee spouse; and disability of the payor spouse.

Cohabiting

Generally, alimony may be reduced or even terminated if a supported spouse begins cohabiting with a new romantic partner and the payor spouse can prove that the new roommate is financially aiding the supported spouse to the point of reaching a changed financial circumstance. Again, the magic words are *changed circumstances.*

Remarrying

Upon remarriage of the spouse receiving alimony, all states support the extinguishment of permanent or limited duration, also known as temporary, alimony. A rehabilitative or reimbursement alimony award typically continues even upon remarriage or cohabitation.

Disability

Severe disability of the payor spouse would very likely be considered a changed circumstance and result in a reevaluation of the alimony obligation.

CASE 8.13 *Waskin v. Waskin*, 484 So. 2d 1277 (1986)

Facts: As a result of Dr. Robert Waskin's conversations with Tretola, an undercover police officer, requesting that Tretola do away with the former Mrs. Waskin, Dr. Waskin was arrested and charged with conspiracy to commit murder. As a result of the charge, he hired an attorney and paid him $70,000. Dr. Waskin lost patients and institutional affiliations due to the case's publicity, and thus income. Dr. Waskin then went to court to modify his support payments downward because of that lost income.

Issue: Whether a husband was entitled to a modification of support payments based on a change of circumstance due to his illegal activity.

Court's Reasoning: The conversation between the Robert Waskin and Tretola, in actuality an undercover police officer, in the present case is, at the very least, susceptible of being understood by reasonable fact-finders as meaning that Waskin requested or encouraged, if not actually hired, Tretola to murder the ex–Mrs. Waskin. The facts that the time of performance was not agreed upon (or was postponed for several months) and that payment of money was not immediately made do not mean that no request or encouragement occurred, or even that no agreement (hiring) had taken place. Indeed, it appears that Waskin's request to postpone the hit was not occasioned by any disagreement about the figure of $10,000, but rather was motivated by Waskin's professed need to have sufficient time to amass the cash for payment without calling attention to his plan by borrowing.

We have little difficulty concluding that Waskin's voluntary action in seeking to do away with his ex-wife—the epitome of unclean hands—was the cause of his financial woes. What Waskin did to bring about his financial downfall is, quite obviously, far more condemnable than closing down a lucrative practice, failing to seek gainful employment, or going on spending sprees. It does not matter in this proceeding whether Waskin is ultimately convicted of the crime with which he is charged. What is important here is that the conversation between Waskin and Tretola indisputably occurred, that Waskin admittedly believed that Tretola was a hitman, and that, in the conversation, Waskin indisputably requested Tretola to do away with the ex-Mrs. Waskin. Under these circumstances, it can be readily said that Waskin's acts brought about his own arrest and prosecution, as well as the financial consequences of those events, whatever the outcome of the criminal proceeding.

We have no quarrel with the trial judge's finding that Robert Waskin showed "a substantial decrease in his financial ability dating back to October of 1983." The trial judge's conclusion, however, that this extraordinary expenditure on attorneys' fees and the reduction in income from the medical practice were matters beyond Waskin's control is, in our view, totally unwarranted.

Accordingly, we reverse the order below insofar as it reduced the alimony and child support payments and relieved Waskin of the responsibility to pay the monthly mortgage on the marital home. As counsel for the former wife correctly observes, the bitter irony of the trial court's ruling is that, in effect, it requires the children and former wife to defray the cost of Waskin's attorney, a result no less ironic than, as in the well-known anecdote, taking pity on the orphan who killed his parents.

Holding: Reversed and remanded.

Case Discussion: While the *Waskin* case is admittedly unusual, it does provide some basic guidance to a party wishing to modify the amount of spousal maintenance being paid by the party. Courts are not quick to modify payments if the request is being made due to the wrongful actions of the petitioner.

Death

All states provide that the death of the payor or payee spouse extinguishes alimony. However, back alimony owed will not be forgiven, and the supported spouse can look to the payor spouse's estate for arrearages.

THE SMITHS CALL IT A DAY

Michael and Libby's case headed toward a conclusion when a final judgment of divorce was granted by Judge Comfort, based on Libby's claim of extreme cruelty. If Michael had not withdrawn his counterclaim and had been able to prove the adultery claim, Judge Comfort could have granted a final judgment based on both the cause of action in Libby's complaint and Michael's cause of action in the counterclaim. The final judgment of divorce would then have been an example of a **dual divorce.**

Read the final judgment of divorce granted to Libby and Michael by Judge Comfort in Exhibit 8.19. This judgment incorporates the property settlement agreement negotiated between Michael and Libby with the assistance of their lawyers, which is provided in Exhibit 8.20.

FORGET THE FAT LADY SINGING: IT'S NOT REALLY OVER UNTIL THE LAST ALIMONY CHECK ARRIVES

The best of intentions and the highest of hopes may have prevailed on the day Libby and Michael's divorce was granted, but there is no guarantee in any divorce that the ex-spouses will not see each other again in a courtroom to deal with a postjudgment problem. You might think that, after all the hours of angst and negotiations (and all the money going to lawyers' fees rather than their children's college funds), Libby and Michael would never want to see the inside of a courtroom again. However, if either Libby or Michael defaults in any way on their settlement agreement, they could both end up back in court with the uncomfortable task of explaining the default to Judge Comfort.

Remedies for defaulting on such previously agreed-to matters as spousal and child support, child visitation, and property disbursement vary across the nation. While many states require a **petition for contempt** to be filed, other jurisdictions call the request for enforcement a *motion to enforce litigant's rights* or a *motion in aid of litigant's rights.* Inability to pay spousal support at the time it was due is a defense to the charge of contempt. However, the payor spouse who had the funds to pay at the time the support was due and failed to pay will not usually be allowed to plead inability to pay as a defense. If a court finds the payor spouse in civil contempt for nonpayment, the court may sentence the errant ex-spouse to some jail time. However, the court's main purpose is to get the ex-spouse on a payment schedule, and the civil contempt jail time can be withdrawn by the court if payment is made. Alternatively, criminal contempt charges will sometimes end in a fixed amount of jail time for the errant spouse and are designed more as a punishment mechanism for the truly recalcitrant ex-spouse than as inspiration for paying overdue support.

The spouse who deals with overdue alimony payments often also deals with overdue child support payments. Each state has what is known as a Title IV-D agency to deal with unpaid child support. Additionally, each state has enacted the Uniform Interstate Family Support Act (UIFSA) to enforce spousal and child support payments being made by former spouses who have moved across state lines. (More detail is provided about both Title IV-D agencies and UIFSA in Chapter 10 on child support.)

EXHIBIT 8.19 Michael and Libby's Final Judgment of Divorce

J. D. Dombroski, Esq.
Johnson & Webster, Esqs.
123 Main Street
Newton, New Jersey 12345
973-555-1212
Attorney for Plaintiff

ELIZABETH MOORE SMITH,	) SUPERIOR COURT OF NEW JERSEY
	) CHANCERY DIVISION-FAMILY PART
Plaintiff,	) SUSSEX COUNTY
	) Docket No. FM-12345-02
v.	) CIVIL ACTION
	)
MICHAEL SMITH,	)
	) JUDGMENT OF DIVORCE
Defendant.	)

This is an action coming to be heard in the presence of J. D. Dombroski, Esq., attorney for the plaintiff, and Howard Hughey, Esq., attorney for the defendant, before the Hon. Judge Comfort on the l5th day of September, 2003. Upon the Complaint and Answer and upon proofs being taken in open court, and the court having heard and considered the proofs in this action and the argument of counsel, and it appearing that the plaintiff and the defendant were joined in the bond of matrimony on or about the 14th day of February 1986, and that the parties have claimed extreme cruelty as alleged in the Complaint, and that there is no reasonable prospect of reconciliation, and that at the time the causes of action for divorce for such separation arose, the plaintiff and the defendant were bona fide residents of this state, and that the plaintiff and the defendant have continued so to be down to the time of the commencement of this action, and that the plaintiff and the defendant have been, for the one year next preceding the commencement of this action, bona fide residents of this state, and it further appearing that jurisdiction herein has been acquired by personal service of process upon the parties within this state; and it further appearing that each of the parties hereto have made out sufficient grounds for divorce against the other of them, entitling each of them to be granted a Judgment therefor, according to the statutes of this state, N.J.S.A 2A:34-2. The Property Settlement Agreement made and agreed to between the parties is hereby made a part of this final judgment.

It is this 30th day of September, 2003,

ORDERED AND ADJUDGED, and such court, by virtue of the power and authority of this court, and of the acts of the Legislature in such case made and provided, does hereby ORDER and ADJUDGE that the plaintiff, Elizabeth Moore Smith, and the defendant, Michael Smith, be and they are each divorced from the bond of matrimony for the causes aforesaid, and the parties, and each of them, be freed and discharged from the obligations thereof, and the marriage between the parties is hereby dissolved. The plaintiff will return to her maiden name, Elizabeth Moore, as of this day.

_____
Judge Comfort, J.S.C.

Consent is hereby given to the foregoing Judgment of Divorce as to all issues.

_____
J. D. Dombroski, Esq.
Johnson & Webster, Esqs.
Attorney for Plaintiff

_____
Howard Hughey, Esq.
Dewey, Hughey, & Lewey, Esqs.
Attorney for Defendant

EXHIBIT 8.20 Settlement Agreement of Elizabeth and Michael Smith

Settlement Agreement of Elizabeth and Michael Smith

This Agreement made the date hereinafter subscribed between Elizabeth Moore Smith, residing at 55 Main Street in the town of Newton, County of Sussex, and State of New Jersey, hereinafter referred to as the "Wife"; and Michael Smith, whose mailing address is 79 Carol Street in the town of Oak Ridge, County of Sussex, and State of New Jersey, hereinafter referred to as the "Husband."

WHEREAS, the parties were married on February 14, 1986, in a religious ceremony in Sparta, New Jersey; and

WHEREAS, two children were born of said marriage, to wit: Alphonse Smith, born March 21, 1993, and Brianna Smith, born April 21, 1991; and

WHEREAS, the parties intend to live separate and apart; and

WHEREAS, the parties to this Agreement are desirous of settling all questions relating to the disposition of their respective interest and the assets accumulated by them, or either of them, during the marriage, payment of obligations, alimony, support, maintenance of the parties, and disposition and determination of all claims of either party against the other, including equitable distribution; and

WHEREAS, the parties are independently represented by counsel of their own choice (Wife is being represented by the law firm Johnson & Webster, Attorneys at Law, J. D. Dombroski, Esq., appearing, of 123 Main Street, Newton, New Jersey 12345, and Husband is being represented by the law firm Dewey, Hughey, & Lewey, Attorneys at Law, Howard Hughey, Esq., appearing, of 52 Goody Lane, Glenwood, New Jersey 07461, and with the signing of this document agree that all property and financial questions, issues and problems arising out of the marital relationship are settled and determined;

NOW, THEREFORE, in consideration of the mutual promises and terms contained herein, the parties agree as follows:

ARTICLE 1 SEPARATION AND JOINT CUSTODY SEPARATION

1.1 SEPARATION. The parties shall at all times live separate and apart from each other. Each shall be free from interference and authority and control, either directly or indirectly, by the other as fully as if he or she were single and unmarried. Each may reside at such place or places as he or she may select. Neither party shall molest or annoy the other or compel or endeavor to compel the other to cohabit with him or her in any manner whatsoever.

1.2 CUSTODY. The parties shall share joint legal custody of the children of the marriage, to wit: Alphonse and Brianna. The primary custodial parent shall be the Wife subject to the reasonable parenting time of the Husband as set forth in this Agreement.

By joint legal custody, it is intended that the parties may, and the parties shall, confer as to major life decisions for the children, those affecting their health, education, and physical and moral welfare. By joint custody, the parties intend to provide the children with access to both parents and to grant both parents equal rights and responsibilities regarding the children.

1.3 PARENTING TIME. The Husband shall have reasonable and liberal rights of parenting time. The Husband's parenting times shall include, but are not limited to:

(a) One overnight each and every week at a time mutually agreed upon between the parties.
(b) Alternate weekend overnight parenting time commencing at 7:00 P.M. on Friday evening and ending at 7:00 P.M. the following Sunday evening.
(c) The parties shall alternate all federal and religious holidays except as otherwise provided for herein.
(d) The Husband shall have parenting time with the children the entire weekend upon which Father's Day falls. The children shall be with their mother the entire weekend on which Mother's Day falls.
(e) The Husband shall have parenting time with the children on his birthday.
(f) The children shall be with their mother on her birthday.
(g) The parties shall share time with the children on the children's birthdays, with the specific schedule to be determined by the parties.
(h) The Husband shall have extended parenting time for a minimum of two weeks during the summer and one week during the winter at times mutually agreed upon by the parties.

(continued)

EXHIBIT 8.20 *continued*

(i) The Wife and Husband will provide to one another current addresses and telephone numbers of their residences. In addition, the parties will provide to one another the telephone number at which they can be reached should they be away from their residence in excess of 24 hours, the purpose of said information being to facilitate emergency notices with regard to the children of the marriage.

(j) Wife and Husband will provide to each other addresses and telephone numbers for their locations when they are away from their residences overnight with the children. This information is to be communicated directly to the other parent and not through the children.

1.4 COOPERATION. Both parties will cooperate with each other in effectuating the rights of each to custody and parenting time with the children, and the dates and times of parenting time, which are not specifically provided for herein, shall be agreed upon by the parties, after reference to school schedules, the needs of the children, and reasonable notice of such parenting time on the part of the Husband.

Both parties shall have complete and free access to the children's school records and information as well as the right to consult with school officials on issues concerning the children. The Husband and Wife agree to confer together with regard to all such communications so as to maintain a consistent and cohesive approach to the education of the children.

1.5 WELFARE OF THE CHILDREN. It is expressly understood by both parties that neither shall do anything directly or indirectly to alienate the affection of the children for the other parent or to color the attitude of the children toward the other parent. The parents agree to consult and cooperate, and shall consult and cooperate, with respect to the children so as, in a maximum degree, to advance the health and both the emotional and physical well-being of the parties and the children and to give and afford the children the affection of both parties. Both parties shall conduct themselves in a manner that shall be best for the interest, welfare, and happiness of the children, and neither party shall do anything that shall affect the morals, health, and welfare of the children to the detriment of the children. The parents shall endeavor to guide the children so as to promote the affectionate relationship between the children and the parties. Each parent shall be entitled to and shall receive from the other parent complete and full information provided to them by any physician, dentist, consultant attending the children, or any teacher.

ARTICLE 2 SUPPORT AND MAINTENANCE

2.1 REHABILITATIVE ALIMONY (cross-referenced with Section 3.1—Marital Residence). The Husband shall continue to assume sole and exclusive responsibility for the monthly payments on the mortgage and utility bills of the marital home for a term of five (5) years in the form of rehabilitative alimony. Within said five (5) years, the Wife shall have the opportunity to complete a bachelor's degree and to obtain a job after said degree is obtained.

2.2 MEDICAL EXPENSES. From the date of the execution of this Agreement, the Husband is responsible for payment of the Wife's medical and dental expenses, also for a period of five (5) years. This is also in the form of rehabilitative alimony.

2.3 LIFE INSURANCE. The Husband shall maintain all life insurance policies currently maintained on his life for the benefit of the children of the marriage in the amount of $500,000. The Husband shall make his sister, Lisa Smith, the Trustee for the children until such time as the Husband's obligation for child support set forth in Section 2.4 shall cease.

2.4 CHILD SUPPORT. The Husband shall pay to the Wife $273 per week, as and for child support. Such payment shall be made on the first day of each and every week. All child support payments shall be made through the Probation Department, via certified check or money order, of the county within which the Husband resides and said payments shall be subject to a late interest charge at the rate prescribed by Rule 4:42-11(a). This obligation shall be enforced by an income withholding upon the commissions, earnings, salaries, wages, and other current or future income of the Husband, and any payment or installment for child support shall be enforceable and entitled to full faith and credit and shall be a judgment by operation of law on or after the date it is due. Pursuant to Rule 5:7-4:

A. If immediate income withholding is not ordered, the child support and child care provisions of this agreement are subject to income withholding when an arrearage has accrued in an amount equal to or in excess of the amount of support payable in fourteen (14) days. The withholding shall be effective against the defendant's current and future income from all sources authorized by law;

B. Any payment or installment provided for herein shall be fully enforceable and entitled to full faith and credit and shall be a Judgment by operation of law on or after the date it is due;

C. No payment or installment of this agreement that relates to child support shall be retroactively modified by the Court except for the period during which the party seeking relief has pending an application for modification as provided in N.J.S.A. 2A:176.23a;

D. The parties are required to notify the appropriate Probation Division of any change of employer or health insurance provider and to provide the address of each within ten (10) days of the change. Failure to provide such information shall be considered a violation of the JOD;

E. In accordance with N.J.S.A. 2A:34-3b, the custodial parent may require the noncustodial parent's health insurer to make payments directly to the health care provider by submitting a copy of the relevant sections of this agreement to the health care provider; and

F. Social Security numbers are collected and used in accordance with section 205 of the Social Security Act (42 U.S.C. § 405). Disclosure of an individual's Social Security number for Title IV purposes is mandatory. Social Security numbers are used to obtain income, employment, and benefit information on individuals through computer matching programs with federal and state agencies. Such information is used to establish and enforce child support under Title IV of the Social Security Act (42 U.S.C. § 651 *et seq.*)

2.5 SUPPORT TERM. The child support obligation referenced in Section 2.4 shall continue until the parties' children have reached majority (18 years of age) and are no longer enrolled in high school or other secondary education. After a child reaches majority (18 years of age) and completes secondary education, a support obligation for that child, if found by the court to be appropriate, shall be determined in accordance with N.J.S.A. 2A:34-23 and existing case law, unless an agreement as to the support of the child is reached by the parties. The Husband's child support obligation for the unemancipated child or children of the marriage shall be calculated in accordance with the New Jersey Child Support Guidelines.

2.6 CHILDREN'S MEDICAL EXPENSES. The Husband shall be responsible for all medical, surgical, hospitalization, drug, eye care, dental, orthodontic, psychiatric, and psychological expenses for the children of the marriage through his medical insurance coverage.

The term "medical, dental and hospital expenses" is intended to cover physicians' medical services, prescription drugs, psychiatric and/or counseling services, dental and orthodontic work, optical and eye care treatment and appliances, and all related expenses of a medical nature of the children.

The Husband shall provide the Wife with any and all identification cards required to process claims under said policy and will provide all forms that may be so required. The Husband shall cooperate with the Wife in the processing of all claims under the insurance policy and will submit those claims expeditiously. Pursuant to P.L. 1993, Chapter 14, the Wife may require the insurer to make payments directly to the health care provider by submitting a copy of the relevant sections of this Agreement to the insurer. The Husband shall cooperate with the Wife in facilitating this direct payment by the insurer to the health care provider.

2.7 COLLEGE OR HIGHER EDUCATION. If there are unemancipated children who are 18 years old or younger in the family in addition to college/postsecondary children, the New Jersey Child Support Guidelines shall first be applied to said unemancipated children before determining parental obligations for the costs of postsecondary education and/or the continued child support obligation for a child attending college/postsecondary education. Contributions toward college/postsecondary costs shall be determined based upon an application of current case law. In considering an amount of child support to be paid to the primary custodial parent for a child attending college/postsecondary education, same shall be determined in accordance with the factors set forth in N.J.S.A. 2A:34-23a.

The parties agree to consult with a view toward adopting a harmonious policy concerning the college education of the children. The children will apply for all grants, loans, scholarships, and the like in order to lessen the burden to their parents of the college education.

ARTICLE 3 REAL PROPERTY

3.1 MARITAL RESIDENCE. The Husband and Wife are presently vested with legal title to real property located at 55 Main Street in the town of Newton, County of Sussex, State of New Jersey, which premises were used in the past by the Husband and Wife as the marital home.

3.2 MORTGAGE. The mortgage held by Mortgages Are Us, Acct. No. 123456789, on the subject premises, which is held in the name of both Husband and Wife, is currently outstanding. The Husband shall continue to assume sole and exclusive responsibility for the monthly payments on the aforesaid mortgage (as set forth as rehabilitative alimony in Section 2.1) and shall indemnify and hold the Wife harmless for same.

3.3 OCCUPANCY. The Wife shall have sole and exclusive possession of this premises for five years from the date of this document. The marital home will be placed on the market for the appraised value four years and six months from the signing of this document. If the home is not sold within six months, the Wife may continue to reside in the residence at market rent payable to the Husband. The Wife will maintain the home in viewing condition for sale.

(continued)

EXHIBIT 8.20 *continued*

3.4 TAXES AND INSURANCE. The Husband shall be responsible for payment of all real estate taxes and homeowner's insurance for the marital residence.

3.5 REPAIRS. The Husband shall be responsible for any and all repairs, maintenance, and upkeep of the former marital residence during the period of time the Wife will be residing in the residence.

ARTICLE 4 PERSONAL PROPERTY

4.1 401K. The Husband has accumulated a 401K in the amount of $35,000. The Husband will keep 100%.

4.2 IRA. The Wife has accumulated an IRA in the amount of $15,000. Upon maturity of the IRA, the Wife will keep 100%.

4.3 DISTRIBUTION. The parties have divided between them, to their mutual satisfaction, the personal effects, household furniture and furnishings, bank accounts, automobiles, and all other articles of personal property that heretofore had been used or owned by them in common, and neither party will make claim as to any such items that are now in the possession or under the control of the other.

4.4 MARITAL FURNISHINGS. The Wife shall keep the property contained in the marital residence prior to August 15, 2003, and which is in her possession. The Husband shall keep the property removed from the marital residence as of August 15, 2003.

4.5 AUTOMOBILES. The Husband acquires all right and interest to the 1997 Honda Passport and shall be responsible for the expenses concerning that vehicle. The Wife shall acquire all rights, title, and interest to the 1995 Mitsubishi and shall be responsible for the expenses concerning that vehicle. Wife shall indemnify and hold Husband harmless in all matters regarding the Mitsubishi vehicle.

4.6 OTHER PROPERTY. The Husband and Wife by this Agreement become the owners of all tangible and intangible personal property such as, but not limited to, savings accounts, checking accounts, stocks and bonds presently in their respective names regardless of where these accounts are located or documents establishing such intangible property are kept, subject, however, to the terms contained herein.

4.7 BILL OF SALE. This Agreement shall constitute the Bill of Sale from each party to the other for all personal property distributed in accordance with this Agreement.

ARTICLE 5 BILLS AND OBLIGATIONS

5.1 MARITAL DEBTS. The marital debt shall be distributed as follows:

A.   Credit Card Debt. The Husband shall be responsible for the payment of the following credit card debts: Chadwick's (Acct. No. 000000000-34), a Mastercard (Acct. No. 00000000000-12), a Mastercard (Acct. No. 111111), and a Mastercard (Acct. No. 22222). There are no other credit card debts.

5.2 INDEMNIFICATION. All debts and obligations incurred by the respective parties, either prior to or subsequent to the date of the execution of this Agreement, and except as expressly otherwise provided herein, shall be the obligation of the party who incurred them and shall be paid solely by that party. If the nonobligated party, for any reason, pays said debts and obligations, that party shall be reimbursed or indemnified by the other party to that extent.

5.3 LIMITATION. Both parties agree that they have not and will not incur any debt affecting the other except as forth in this Agreement.

ARTICLE 6 TAX

6.1 TAX RETURNS. Commencing with tax year 2003, the parties shall file separate income tax returns. The Husband and the Wife both warrant and represent that all joint income tax returns, whether state or federal, heretofore filed by the parties are true, accurate, and complete; that all liabilities thereon have been fully paid; and that there is no pending audit or examination of those returns. All audits, examinations, suits, or other proceedings in connections with all joint returns heretofore filed by the parties jointly shall be handled at the parties' mutual expense and cost, said costs being divided fifty percent (50%) to each, and the parties agree that they will participate therein and execute any and all papers needed for such audits, examinations, suits, and other proceedings to the extent reasonably required by the Husband's or the Wife's counsel and/or accountants.

A.   The parties unequivocally agree that the Husband and the Wife shall hereafter file separate income tax returns.

B.   Any party receiving any notices of any kind from any taxing authority shall forthwith, within three (3) days after receipt of such notice, tender a complete copy to the other by first-class mail or personal delivery to the address first listed above or to any other address the Husband or the Wife designates.

C.   Both parties further agree not to assert a position in preparation and filing of their future income tax returns, whether singly or jointly with another, inconsistent with the terms and conditions of this Agreement.

6.2 DEDUCTIONS. The Husband shall have the right to take Alphonse and Brianna as dependents on his income tax return for a five-year period commencing with the date of this document. Upon the Wife's employment following rehabilitation, she will be entitled to take Brianna as a dependent. Commencing with tax year 2003, the Husband will file his income tax return making all relevant and proper deductions for the ownership and maintenance of the marital residence.

ARTICLE 7 WAIVER OF CLAIMS

7.1 COMPLETE DISCLOSURE. It is specifically represented that there has been complete disclosure of all assets subject to equitable distribution and that said complete disclosure is a condition precedent to the acceptance of the terms and agreements contained herein. If it is subsequently determined that there were assets not specifically referenced and disclosed in this Agreement, those assets will be subject to equitable distribution. The parties represent that reference has been made within this Agreement to all assets that were acquired during the marriage. The Husband and Wife further warrant and represent to the other that they are not now possessed or in control of any property subject to distribution other than that specifically mentioned in this Agreement.

7.2 DISCOVERY RIGHTS. Each party is aware and has been informed that under the law, they have broad financial discovery rights of the other party's finances, including, but not limited to, sworn net worth statements, sworn interrogatories, oral depositions under oath, the right to have accountants and appraisers conduct appraisals and examine books, records, documents, etc. The parties have exchanged current and complete Case Information Statements and are satisfied with the disclosures made in each. The parties further acknowledge that by entering into this Agreement, they are satisfied with the disclosures that have been made and are further satisfied that, under the circumstances, this Agreement is a fair, reasonable, and equitable resolution of all issues dividing the parties.

7.3 INDEPENDENT COUNSEL. The parties each acknowledge that they have retained separate and independent counsel of their own choice and that they have been separately and independently advised regarding every aspect of this Agreement. They acknowledge that the other party has in no sense participated in the selection of the individual counsel.

7.4 VOLUNTARY EXECUTION. The parties each acknowledge and represent that this Agreement has been executed by them, each of them, free from persuasion, fraud, undue influence, or economic, physical, or emotional duress of any kind, whatsoever, exerted by the other or by other persons.

7.5 ENTIRE AGREEMENT. This Agreement constitutes the entire understanding between the parties, and they each represent that there have been no representations, warranties, covenants, promises, or undertakings other than those set forth herein.

7.6 WAIVER OF PROPERTY RIGHTS. Except as herein to the contrary provided, each party may dispose of his or her property in any way and each hereby waives and relinquishes any and all right he or she may now have or hereafter acquire under the present or future laws of any jurisdiction to share in the property of the estate of the other party as a result of the marital relationship, including, but not limited to, equitable distribution of property pursuant to N.J.S.A. 2A:34:23, or other similar or statutory rights, dower, courtesy, statutory allowances, widow allowance, homestead rights, or rights under N.J.S.A. 3B:28-2 and N.J.S.A. 3B:28-3, right to take against or under any last will and testament of the other even if named as a beneficiary therein (unless such last will and testament is executed subsequent to the execution of this Agreement), and the right to act as administrator or executor of the other's estate even if named in such capacity.

7.7 GENERAL MUTUAL RELEASES. Except as herein to the contrary provided, the Husband and Wife hereby mutually remise, release, and forever discharge each other from any and all actions, suits, debts and claims, demands, and obligations whatsoever both in law in equity, which either of them ever had, now has, or may hereafter have against the other, upon or by reason of any matter, cause, or thing up to the date of the execution of this Agreement, it being the intention of the parties that henceforth there shall be as between them only such rights and obligations as are specifically provided in this Agreement.

ARTICLE 8 JUDICIAL PROCEEDINGS

8.1 NONCOLLUSIVE AGREEMENT. It is expressly understood that notwithstanding the provisions hereof, there have been no collusive agreements whatsoever made, either orally or in writing, or any representations by one party to the other with respect to the procurement of a divorce, or restraining or inhibiting the other from contesting or litigating any proceedings now pending or which may be instituted one against the other in any matrimonial action at any time.

8.2 INCORPORATION OF THE WITHIN AGREEMENT. This Agreement shall be offered in evidence in any proceedings instituted by either of the parties in any Court of competent jurisdiction in which a termination of the marriage by way of a divorce, annulment, or otherwise is sought, and shall, subject to the approval of the Court, be incorporated in any judgment in that action.

(continued)

EXHIBIT 8.20 *continued*

8.3 NONMERGER. Notwithstanding its incorporation and conformity with Section 8 into a judgment terminating the marriage, entered by a court of competent jurisdiction, the provisions of this Agreement shall not merge with, but shall survive such judgment in its entirety, in full force and effect, except as may be invalidated by a court of competent jurisdiction in a accordance with Section 8.4.

8.4 SEVERABILITY. Should any provision of this Agreement be held invalid or unenforceable by any court of competent jurisdiction, all other provisions shall nevertheless continue in full force and effect, to the extent that the remaining provisions are fair, just, and equitable.

8.5 MODIFICATION OR WAIVER. No modifications or waiver of any of the terms of this Agreement shall be valid unless made in writing and executed by the party to be changed. The failure of either party to insist upon strict performance of any of the provisions of this Agreement shall not be deemed a waiver of any subsequent breach or default of any provision contained in this Agreement.

ARTICLE 9 GENERAL PROVISIONS

9.1 COUNSEL FEES. The Husband shall be responsible for all counsel fees on his and the Wife's behalf, except as otherwise provided for herein—for all attorneys' fees, investigation fees, expert fees, or fees otherwise associated with the attendant matrimonial lawsuit.

9.2 DEFAULT. If either party fails to abide by the terms of this agreement, then the defaulting party will indemnify and hold the other harmless from all reasonable expenses and costs including attorneys' fees and disbursements incurred in successful enforcement of this Agreement, or asserting or defending his or her rights hereunder as against the other party or third parties.

9.3 CHANGE OF RESIDENCE. As long as any provision contained herein remains executory, each party shall keep the other informed of his or her residence and telephone numbers of such other places where he or she may readily receive communications, informing the other of any changes in residency or place of communication within five days of the actual change.

9.4 FURTHER DOCUMENTS. The parties each respectively agree that they will at any time hereafter, at a request, make, execute, and deliver any and all deeds, releases, or waivers, and any other instruments, papers, or documents, as the other party may reasonably require for the purpose of giving full effect to the covenants, promises, provisions, and terms contained within this Agreement, including, but not limited to, any documents specifically provided for herein.

9.5 SITUS. The laws of the State of New Jersey shall govern the execution, interpretation, and enforcement of this Agreement.

9.6 ORIGINAL DOCUMENTS. This Agreement shall be executed in three counterparts, one for each party—designated as H-1 for the Husband, W-1 for the Wife, and J-1 as a Court exhibit—and each counterpart shall be an agreement with the same effects as any other counterpart.

9.7 SURVIVORSHIP. This Agreement shall inure to the benefit of both parties and their heirs and assigns forever.

9.8 HEADINGS. Headings of the several subdivisions of sections of this Agreement are inserted solely for the convenience of reference and shall have no further meaning, force, and effect.

IN WITNESS WHEREOF, the parties have signed, sealed, delivered, and acknowledged this Agreement this _____ day of _____ 2003.

Witness

_____

_____   _____
                                                                    Elizabeth Smith

                                                                    _____
                                                                    Michael Smith

STATE OF NEW JERSEY)
COUNTY OF _____)   ss.
)
)
)

    I CERTIFY that on _____, Elizabeth Smith personally came before me and acknowledged under oath, to my satisfaction, that this person (or if more than one, each person): (a) is named in and personally signed this document; and (b) signed, sealed, and delivered this document as his or her act and deed.

_____
J. D. Dombroski, Esq.
Attorney at Law of the State of New Jersey

STATE OF NEW JERSEY)
COUNTY OF _____)   ss.
)
)
)

    I CERTIFY that on _____, Michael Smith personally came before me and acknowledged under oath, to my satisfaction, that this person (or if more than one, each person): (a) is named in and personally signed this document; and (b) signed, sealed, and delivered this document as his or her act and deed.

_____
Howard Hughey, Esq.
Attorney at Law of the State of New Jersey

CHAPTER SUMMARY

Divorce is big business in America in the twenty-first century. Legal costs for divorce rose to over one billion dollars as the nation entered the new century. The legal dismantling of a marriage can be achieved with simplicity or complexity. The choice is one to be mutually made by the divorcing spouses.

    Depending upon where the spouses live, they may meet the criteria for being granted an annulment. Some states allow spouses to remain married, but will grant the spouses a judicial separation. Depending on the state, a judicial separation may be called a legal separation, limited divorce, a divorce *a mensa et thoro,* separation from bed and board, or divorce from bed and board. A complete and final ending of a marriage without restriction is considered an absolute and full divorce. Some states use the term *dissolution of marriage* instead of divorce.

    Spouses seeking a divorce must have a valid cause of action. There are fault and no-fault causes of action. Historically, fault played a very large role in the legal system's determination of whether a couple could divorce. No-fault causes of action opened a new world in divorce litigation. The new legal terms *irreconcilable differences, irremediable breakdown,* and *incompatibility* were created by different states to describe the newly created grounds for divorce. The separation of the spouses for a statutorily mandated period of time is usually required with a no-fault cause of action. Some classic examples of fault grounds include adultery, impotence, insanity, imprisonment, physical cruelty, and mental cruelty. All 50 states have retained fault-based causes of action along with the no-fault cause of action option.

The first step for many couples who are seeking a divorce is hiring an attorney. A law firm's staff should understand how to maintain efficient appointment procedures and avoid conflict-of-interest problems for the firm's attorneys. The client's first interview with an attorney may involve an extensive interview or be an opportunity to determine if the client and attorney wish to work together. If they do decide to work together, it is a good idea to have both sign a retainer agreement.

A primary concern of the attorney should be ascertaining which court has personal jurisdiction over the parties and subject matter jurisdiction over the issues of the lawsuit. This is determined by the current domicile of the parties and where the parties' marital home was located.

The client interview will involve numerous questions. The questions will deal with financial support and property distribution, but also include custody and visitation issues if there are children involved. Temporary support issues are often a major concern for a divorcing spouse while awaiting the final order. If there are children, the issue of child support will be added to a temporary support motion to the court. Documents requesting temporary support are sometimes called interlocutory or *pendente lite* orders.

The initial pleading that begins a lawsuit is called the complaint (also called the petition in some states), and it is filed by the plaintiff (also called the petitioner in some states). The complaint should describe why the court has jurisdiction to hear the complaint, the legal reason why the plaintiff is seeking a divorce, and what the plaintiff wants in the way of a financial and property settlement. If there are children, the complaint should also detail the plaintiff's wishes pertaining to custody, support, and visitation. All 50 states have a requirement that a divorcing couple's finances and budget be detailed and submitted to the court. This financial document is often called a financial affidavit or a case information statement. The financial documents are usually submitted with the initial pleading. The defendant (also called the respondent in some states) should file either an answer or a waiver of service. If the defendant fails to respond to the complaint, the court will issue a default judgment. A defendant may also include a counterclaim in the answer. An important step is ensuring that the pleadings have been properly served upon the parties.

Spousal support that is paid to a spouse once the divorce has been granted is generally known as alimony or spousal maintenance. All 50 states have a variety of factors that their courts analyze to determine if alimony should be ordered in a particular case. Examples of these factors include: need and ability to pay; duration of the marriage; age of the parties; physical and mental health of the parties; standard of living during the marriage and likelihood that each party can maintain a reasonably comparable standard of living; earning capacities; educational levels; employability of the parties; parental responsibilities for children; history of the financial and nonfinancial contributions to the marriage; personal assets of each party; and property distribution to each party. A variety of types of alimony is available across the country. The types of alimony (depending upon the state) may include rehabilitative, lump-sum, maintenance in gross, limited duration or term, reimbursement, and permanent alimony. Alimony is always subject to review and modification by the court in the case of changed circumstances. Termination of alimony can occur if the payee spouse cohabits with a romantic partner or remarries, if the payor spouse becomes disabled, or if either ex-spouse dies.

Property distribution in all 50 states is dealt with in one of two ways, depending upon where the parties are domiciled. The majority of states have an equitable distribution concept for determining the financial settlement of divorcing spouses. A minority of states use the community property model. States using the equitable distribution concept based it on the belief that married people should deal fairly with each other when the marriage ends. Assets earned while the spouses were married are necessarily not split down the middle, but rather the emphasis is on a fair division based on the facts of the individual marriage. States using the community property concept split the property assets and debt acquired during the marriage equally between the spouses.

Creating and answering interrogatories, attending depositions, and sending and receiving notices to produce documents are parts of the discovery process in a typical divorce case. Experts, such as accountants and appraisers, may be hired to accurately determine the value of marital property. A contentious divorce case may ultimately lead to a trial, but trials only occur in a very small percentage of cases. Across the nation, courts encourage spouses to settle their cases without going to trial. This is fostered by many courts making mandatory settlement conferences a standard practice. When the divorcing spouses agree on a negotiated property settlement, the matters agreed to are memorialized on paper in a property settlement agreement. The court will schedule a hearing to have the parties publicly attest to the claims made in the complaint and to incorporate the property settlement agreement into the final judgment of divorce. The court can then grant an absolute divorce. Emotions often run high during a divorce case, and a paralegal should be aware of how emotionally draining a divorce can become for a client. A paralegal often takes on the role of the primary liaison between the client and the law firm.

Key Terms

interlocutory decree	divorce *a vinculo matrimonii*	rehabilitative alimony
bifurcated divorce	judicial separation	transitional support
divisible divorce	legal separation	lump-sum alimony
domicile	divorce *a mensa et thoro*	alimony in gross
permanent alimony	limited divorce	arrearages
absolute and full divorce	separate maintenance	limited duration alimony
collusive divorce	acknowledgement of service	term alimony
no-fault divorce statute	calendar tracking system	reimbursement alimony
living apart	equitable distribution	permanent alimony
irreconcilable differences	community property	dual divorce
incompatibility	transmutation	petition for contempt
irremediable breakdown	alimony *pendente lite*	

Surfing the Web

http://www.divorcenet.com This site, which claims to be the Net's largest divorce resource since May 1995, offers family law advice on divorce.

http://www.divorcelinks.com A divorce and child custody law directory with direct links to state and federal divorce law by topic (e.g., divorce, visitation, child custody, marriage, and so on).

http://www.divorce-forms.com Divorce forms and laws.

http://www.divorcelawinfo.com The Divorce Law Information Center offers do-it-yourself divorce forms, papers, and kits, as well as state-specific divorce and family law, child support calculators, custody and visitation information, and divorce and settlement information.

http://www.lawresearch.com The Internet law library, United States law, law search engine.

http://www.divorcesource.com Divorce laws by state, affairs and divorce, children and divorce, collect/pay child support, divorce, dollars and debts, lawyer-client relationship, military and divorce, parental alienation, pensions and divorce, surviving divorce, and more.

http://www.betterdivorce.com State divorce laws.

http://www.divorcedirect.com Read a list of FAQs, check out services, and become familiar with the divorce process.

ETHICS ALERT

1. Can an attorney represent both the husband and wife in their divorce?
2. Susan knew both Michael and Libby for years before Susan's boss took Libby on as a client. Should Susan have any ethical concerns regarding the Smiths being neighbors and Libby being a client of the law firm?

Review Questions

1. (a) What is it called when a party represents himself and has no attorney? (b) Should the parties in a divorce proceeding be separately represented by their own attorneys?
2. What should a client read and sign before an attorney begins working on the client's case?
3. What can be done to help clients meet their immediate financial needs?
4. How detailed should a client's financial statement be?
5. What is a bifurcated or divisible divorce?
6. What is the first step in determining a court's jurisdiction over a person?
7. What is the difference between *in personam* and *in rem* jurisdiction?
8. How is a person's domicile determined?
9. What is a no-fault divorce statute?
10. How many states now have no-fault divorce statutes?
11. Why do states still retain fault statutes?
12. What are the definitions of *irreconcilable differences, irremediable breakdown,* and *incompatibility?*
13. How do you prove irreconcilable differences or incompatibility?
14. Find and read your state's divorce statute.
15. What is a judicial separation?
16. What is a separate maintenance action?
17. What are the first two pleadings typically filed in a divorce proceeding?
18. What is the primary purpose of a settlement conference?
19. What are the differences between a property settlement that is determined using community property statutes versus one that is determined using equitable property division statutes?
20. List a variety of equitable distribution factors.
21. What assets are usually immune from distribution?
22. List the subcategories of alimony available in some, but not all, states.
23. How did rehabilitative alimony solve Libby and Michael's stalemate?
24. When will an alimony obligation be terminated?
25. What are an ex-spouse's options when a former spouse defaults on support payments or property disbursement?

Endnotes

1. Schramm, David, *What Could Divorce Be Costing Your State?,* Utah State University, June 25, 2003.
2. Sachs, Andrea, "No Fault Divorces," *Time* 161, no. 15 (2003): 96.
3. *Lepis v. Lepis,* 83 N.J. 139, 416 A.2d 45 (1980).

Chapter 9

Child Custody

WHAT IS BEST FOR THE CHILDREN?

It is sad when parties with at least above-average degrees of intelligence lose the ability to make reasonable decisions when it comes to child custody and visitation. Our years of handling such cases have proved the main result of the conflict is unnecessary damage to the children, the most valuable and continuing asset of the marriage relationship.

Justice Lund[1]

You do not have to be a psychologist to understand that when parents make the difficult decision to divorce and split up their family, their children may be the ones who are hardest hit. While divorce may be the best remedy for the adults, children often do not understand why Mom and Dad cannot live together anymore. Most parents are able to agree on custody and visitation issues without asking a judge to make the decisions for them. Many parents make every effort to ensure their children know that, while their family will be different after the divorce, a new version of their family will be built together. Unfortunately, some parents are either unable or unwilling to rise above their hostility for each other when making plans for their children's custody, visitation, and support.

It seems obvious that the trauma of divorce is intensified when children witness their parents arguing over child support and custody issues. Sadly, many parents not only argue in front of their children but also bring their intense hostility for each other to the negotiating table when discussing the future custody of their children. This hostility can prevent clear heads from prevailing and makes the work attorneys and paralegals do more difficult. During her first weeks at work, Susan has witnessed (and heard!) how hostility between parents can cause them to forget about the best interests of their children.

THE BATTLING BAXTERS: ONE FAMILY'S CUSTODY STRUGGLE

Their unwillingness to calmly reach an amicable custody decision was evident in Mr. and Mrs. Baxter's loud confrontational behavior during the settlement conference that was being held at Johnson & Webster. Susan and Pat were trying to have a relaxing lunch in the firm's employee lounge, but the yelling coming from the meeting room around the corner was spoiling their digestion.

"I really don't understand how parents can fight this much over their kids," lamented Susan.

"I know, I know, but these people obviously have lost the point of why they had children in the first place," Pat commented. "Why on earth did J. D. arrange for a conference *here* with those two?" she wondered aloud. Pat worked primarily for Anthony Dinsdale III, a senior partner in the firm whose clients were mostly corporate and quiet. "I think J. D. would have been better off using a courthouse meeting room for the Baxters," Pat added. "At least at the courthouse he'd be within earshot of a bailiff."

Worried, Susan asked, "Do you think things could get dangerous?"

Pat answered, "Well, I've been working for this firm for more than 15 years and haven't seen a drop of blood spilled yet, but I have heard of terrible things happening elsewhere." She munched on her salad and continued, "I know J. D. believes in trying to settle even his toughest cases without a trial. He's also a proponent of *mediation*. I remember he told me once that when people feel they've had a say in reaching a settlement, and it hasn't been forced down their throats by the judge, there's a higher chance of the parties keeping to the agreement down the road."

"I've heard of it, but what exactly is mediation?" Susan asked.

"*Mediation* is when an impartial third party, called a *mediator,* facilitates the solving of a dispute by promoting voluntary agreement by the parties. It's being used more and more in divorce situations. When it's used in a situation involving a family, it's often called *family mediation,*" Pat explained.

"I don't think family mediation would work with the Baxters. Do you know what happened to make them this angry?" Susan inquired.

Pat nodded her head conspiratorially as she sipped her diet soda. "Well, it *has* gotten around the office, and I helped prepare some motions for the Baxter case before you came aboard. It seems Mrs. Baxter got a little antsy at home alone with the kids and decided the Internet would be a great place to chat. One thing led to another, and eventually chatting wasn't enough—she started meeting her *friends* in person."

Susan asked, "What's wrong with that?"

Rolling her eyes, Pat responded, "Where have you been—playing Pac-Man?" She explained, "Mrs. Baxter met *men* through the Internet while our poor client was away on business."

Susan mouthed a big "Oh" and looked appropriately shocked.

"I know. It's shocking, but you learn pretty fast in a family law practice that human beings have inventive ways to basically screw up their lives, and they come here for help when they can't fix things themselves," Pat easily explained.

"I can't understand how anyone with children could put their family at risk," Susan stated.

Nodding in agreement, Pat added, "Me too, but as hard as it is sometimes, our job isn't to judge, but to do the work that needs to get done. Unfortunately, our client roster is *filled* with cases involving infidelity, violence, child endangerment, and addictions. I'm sure glad I do most of *my* work in the nice quiet world of corporate takeovers." Glancing at her watch, Pat said, "Look at the time, I've got to get back."

"Me too," Susan agreed. "I'm sure J. D. will want to talk after this conference. This place may not be the most relaxing place to work, but it sure isn't boring!"

THE COURT'S ROLE IN DETERMINING CUSTODY

The United States courts have a long history of supporting parents' right to decide what is best for their children. Although negotiations may become heated, having parents decide on the custody, visitation, and support issues, with limited interference by the court, makes the entire dissolution and post-judgment process go more smoothly for everyone—the parties, the attorneys, and the paralegals. When the parents proceed with the divorce, a family court judge will be asked to approve the parents' mutually agreed-to custody, visitation, and child support decisions. Some states have abolished the use of the term *child custody* and instead use the term *parental responsibility.* The judge's main job is to review the parents' decision to make sure the children's best interests, and not only the interests of the parents, have been seriously considered. The primary legal question asked by a judge who is hearing a custody matter is: What will be in the best interests of the child? This threshold question is known across the country as the **best interests of the child test.** Typically, judges approve what parents decide unless inadequacies are present. For example, if it appears that the parents have agreed to unfair visitation arrangements or insufficient financial support, the judge may not approve the parents' decision.

The majority of divorced parents do not leave child custody, visitation, and support issues to a judge to decide; but unfortunately, disagreements between the parents may necessitate that final decisions on these issues be made by the judge assigned to the divorce case. A dispute with custody, visitation, and support also may develop in a case in which the parents were never married to each other or post-judgment. Whatever the situation, the first thing to be determined is whether the court in which the matter will be heard has jurisdiction over the parties and their case. As explained earlier, this will involve determining whether the court has *in rem* and *in personam* jurisdiction over the subject matter and the parties involved in the dispute.

Judicial Decisions Should Be Gender-Neutral

The best interests of the child test used by American courts today is supposed to be gender-neutral, favoring neither the mother nor the father. The gender-neutral standard follows a long history of gender bias. This gender bias can be traced all the way back to the laws of ancient Rome. The Romans believed in the legal concept of *patria potestas.* The *patria potestas* concept gave males a superior legal and social position over females. Roman law considered wives and children to be the property of the father and gave him an absolute right over his children. Interestingly, during the early nineteenth century, courts *still* gave the father custody of the children if he requested it.

The legal supremacy of the father eventually faded as many men moved toward the industrial world and away from the home-based world of agriculture. As a result, women became more closely identified with the home and caring for the family. During most of the nineteenth and twentieth centuries, the best interests of the child were often automatically thought to be found by giving custody of young children to the mother. This presumption is known as the **tender years doctrine.**

Today, courts are much more likely to view each custody decision as a separate entity without any presumptions. According to a 1995 study of appellate court custody decisions, mothers won in 45 percent of the cases, and fathers won in 42 percent of the cases. Twelve percent involved some form of shared parental custody, and a third party was given custody in one percent of the cases.[2]

Reaching for Uniformity: The UCCJA Is Born

By the 1950s, America's child custody laws were like a patchwork quilt that was sewn together haphazardly. State courts were not required to respect each other's custody decisions, and one state's laws could differ radically from those of another. Judges, lawyers, scholars, and legislators knew that a more uniform way to deal with custody issues was needed for the sake of the nation's children. A group of professionals eventually got together to study the problem. The group, called the National Conference of Commissioners on Uniform State Laws (NCCUSL), studied the child custody laws in effect in all 50 states. Following years of work, a list of the most effective and responsible child custody legislation enacted throughout the United States was created.

This was how the **Uniform Child Custody Jurisdiction Act (UCCJA)** was ultimately produced in 1968. The UCCJA was promoted as a model child custody statute that should be put into effect in all

50 states. Eventually, all 50 states *did* adopt the UCCJA in an effort to bring a more standardized set of child custody laws to the United States. The main purpose of the UCCJA is to prohibit modification of custody orders made by other states; it requires the states to enforce original custody orders from other states. This standardization was intended to eliminate the possibility of parents removing or kidnapping their children to another state and then instituting a new custody hearing once they established the new state's jurisdiction over the children on the single test that the children were present in the state. Unfortunately, the UCCJA does not provide enforcement procedures for states to follow, and various sections of the UCCJA have been interpreted inconsistently across the country.

UCCJEA: Offspring of the UCCJA

The UCCJA was ultimately revised by the NCCUSL to reduce confusion. The result was the **Uniform Child Custody Jurisdiction and Enforcement Act (UCCJEA).** The UCCJEA provides newer, more uniform methods for expedited interstate enforcement of custody and visitation orders. Read the excerpts from the UCCJEA in Appendix F.

The UCCJEA amended the UCCJA to bring it into conformity with two newer federal statutes, the **Parental Kidnapping Prevention Act (PKPA)** and the **Violence Against Women Act (VAWA).** The purpose of the Parental Kidnapping Prevention Act, enacted in 1980, is to provide the necessary authority for states to give full faith and credit to their respective custody and visitation orders. In a nutshell, the PKPA requires courts to refrain from exercising jurisdiction over a custody case while another state is processing a custody case for the same child. Read excerpts from the PKPA in Appendix C. The VAWA is discussed in greater detail in Chapter 12 on domestic violence.

The UCCJEA has been adopted by 30 states, at least 6 states are in the process of passing it, and more states are expected to jump on the UCCJEA bandwagon. The UCCJEA requires that the first step in a custody dispute be *the determination of which state court has jurisdiction to hear the custody dispute.* Determining proper judicial jurisdiction is always the essential first step in undertaking any litigation, but before the UCCJA and the UCCJEA were adopted, state jurisdiction in custody matters was determined by asking where the child's domicile was located or if there was a significant connection between the child and the proposed court. Under the newer legislation, there are more specific requirements.

The first and most important requirement is to determine the child's *home state.* A state becomes a child's **home state** when the child has lived there for six months. Under the UCCJEA, once the home state is designated, that state has **continuing jurisdiction.** Even the absence of a child from the home state is immaterial, since what matters most is that a custodial parent or person acting as a parent continues to live in that state. A parent who is fighting the custodial parent for custody cannot alter the home state's designation by simply removing the child from the state and trying to get a new custody order in another state.

The second requirement is to determine whether the state in question has a significant connection with the child. Under the newer UCCJEA, however, establishing significant connection is not as important as determining what state has home state designation. A court with a significant connection jurisdiction under the UCCJEA will become the primary jurisdictional court *only* if the home state declines jurisdiction, if there are *forum non conveniens* grounds or misconduct grounds, or if there is no home state. *Forum non conveniens* is defined as an inconvenient court. For example, if two or more courts both have proper jurisdiction over a case, a judge may rule that a lawsuit must be brought in one of the courts rather than the other, either for convenience or to ensure fairness to the parties.

The third requirement to consider is whether the situation calls for a state to come forward and declare its jurisdiction over a child living in that state because of some kind of emergency situation.

TYPES OF CUSTODY

There are several different types of child custody arrangements. Relatively standard terms are used across the country when discussing custody arrangements, including *sole custody, split custody, joint custody, legal custody,* and *physical custody.*

Sole Custody

Sole custody is when only one parent is awarded custody of the parties' children. The parent without sole custody normally is awarded rights to visitation with the children. The parent with sole custody is responsible for making all the decisions regarding the children's upbringing, including those surrounding serious issues such as health, education, and religion. The parent with sole custody also has what is known as *legal custody* of the children. A parent with **legal custody** has the right to make decisions regarding *all* aspects of the children's upbringing.

Split Custody

Split custody occurs only when there are two or more children in a family. Each parent has sole custody of a different child or children, and each parent has visitation rights to the child or children in the custody of the other parent. Again, each parent with sole custody also has legal custody.

Joint Custody

With **joint custody,** both parents have equal legal custody of their children, but often only one parent has physical custody. The parent with physical custody has the child residing with him. Alternatively, both parents may have equal legal and physical custody. Joint custody is very popular because with this type of custody, both parents can have equal say in the upbringing of their children. The reality, however, is that where only one parent has physical custody, that parent will always carry a larger responsibility for the day-to-day upbringing of the children.

The Many Options of Child Custody

The mechanics of child custody arrangements are as varied as the families involved in a divorce situation. Parents may decide to alternate physical custody by the week, month, or year, with the children moving from one parent's home to the home of the other parent. Some parents are concerned that having the children change homes so often is not emotionally healthy for the children. A small minority of parents alternate living arrangements themselves; for example, the children may stay in the family home, while the parents alternately move between the family home and another home. This type of arrangement depends on the former spouses being unusually friendly and flexible.

The joint parental custody concept appears to be a more balanced alternative to a court granting one parent sole custody and the other only visitation rights. Critics of sole custody argue that it forces one parent to become essentially a *visitor* in her children's lives, with no significant parental influence, while the other parent's role becomes artificially larger with his designation as the sole custodial parent. Since the early 1980s, the majority of states have created legislation supporting joint custody arrangements.

As stated earlier, all custody arrangements are most effective when they are decided on by the parents themselves. Some states require that a court approve joint custody arrangements made voluntarily by parents without a court's intervention to ensure that they will be the best arrangements for the children involved. Some states support joint custody to such a degree that the courts in those states may decide in favor of a joint custody arrangement in spite of *objections* from the parents who have to live with the arrangement.

Court Provides Joint Custody over Parents' Objections

The case of *Beck v. Beck* (see Case 9.1) includes a good analysis of the pros and cons of courts foisting joint custody upon unwilling parents who are each battling for sole custody of their children. Note the use of the Latin term *sua sponte*. **Sua sponte,** as used in the *Beck* case, is defined as "on a judge's own motion," without a request from one of the parties.

THE BATTLING BAXTERS EXHAUST J. D.

Now that you are familiar with the varying kinds of custody arrangements, the next step is to understand how those custody arrangements are determined when the parents cannot agree on what type of custody arrangement is best for their children. This brings us back to the "Battling Baxters."

J. D. was in no mood to be pleasant. "Those Baxters are driving me nuts!" he complained, as he gulped down three aspirin. Having heard the Baxters yelling throughout her lunch with Pat, Susan knew it was probably best to say nothing until he calmed down. J. D. squeezed his magic stress ball in his right hand, while Susan laid out letters and documents on his desk.

"These need your review as soon as possible," Susan cautiously commented.

J. D. ignored the letters and asked, "Sue, you met the Baxters today. I was wondering if you had any new ideas for getting those two closer to an agreement."

Susan hated to tell J. D. that the chances of getting those two to agree did not look good, but she answered, "I just got really bad vibes from those two. I'd say they're headed for court."

J. D. nodded in agreement and squeezed his stress ball harder. "We have everything settled except for the kids," he lamented. "I'm really sick and tired of this case. I think psychologists and a *guardian ad litem* will have to be called in, or else *I* will need a therapist! If the Baxter's won't end this, I guess a judge will have to."

Weighing Child Support Factors: Where Is King Solomon When You Need Him?

By this point you should be clear on what the main legal issue in a disputed custody matter is. Simply put, it is whether the *best interests of the child or children* would be served by granting one parent's request for custody over the other parent's request.

The best interests of the child test is used by all 50 states as a guideline for the courts to follow. It sounds simple enough, right? However, the best interests of the child test can be determined in a multitude of ways by different state courts. So, it is important that, as a paralegal, you realize that your state may interpret the best interests test differently than a neighboring state. Generally, the best interests of a child are determined by a number of factors, which may include such things as the following: (1) investigating the emotional ties of the children to each parent; (2) the amount of child care each parent contributed in the past; (3) the wishes of the children; and (4) the lifestyle and moral beliefs of each parent. Read the lengthy and rather typical list of factors used in Illinois in Exhibit 9.1. (See ILL. ANN. STAT. ch 5, §§ 602, 602.1, 603.1, 610.) Obviously, with such general topics, there is a lot of room for judicial interpretation.

Child Custody Factors Analyzed

Speaking of judicial interpretation, the case of *Allen v. Farrow* (see Case 9.2) involving a well-known couple provides a superb explanation of the best interest factors as analyzed by a New York court. The court

CASE 9.1 *Beck v. Beck*, 86 N.J. 480 (1981)

Facts: The parties to this matrimonial action have two daughters, Lauren, age 12, and Kirsten, age 10. They were adopted in infancy. The parties were married in July 1963. In September 1977, the husband filed a complaint for divorce based on 18 months of separation. He sought liberal visitation rights, but not custody of the children. Defendant answered and counterclaimed for divorce on grounds of desertion. The husband is a successful commercial photographer. The wife works as a part-time student teacher supervisor at a local college. The girls have resided with their mother subject to periodic visitation by their father since Mr. Beck left the marital residence. The issue of custody appeared to be settled by the pleadings until April 12, 1979, when, in the course of its decision, the trial court decreed *sua sponte* that both legal and physical custody would be shared by the parties.

The lower court held that the children's ages presented no obstacle. The proximity of the parents' residences would enable continuity of schooling despite changes in physical custody. The prior visitation arrangement had been maintained with no difficulty whatever between the parties. Finally, because the girls were adopted, they needed the benefit, contact, and security of both parents.

Although neither party requested joint custody, the trial court nevertheless found such an arrangement to be in the best interests of the children.

Issue: Whether the trial court was within its discretion in granting joint legal and physical custody *sua sponte.*

Court's Reasoning: In the question of whether a trial court may make a *sua sponte* custody determination, the paramount consideration in child custody cases is to foster the best interests of the child. This standard has been described as one that protects the safety, happiness, and physical, mental, and moral welfare of the child.

At the root of the joint custody arrangement is the assumption that children in a unified family setting develop attachments to both parents and that the severance of either of these attachments is contrary to the child's best interests. Having established the joint custody arrangement's potential benefit to the children, the court must focus on the parents in order to determine whether they qualify for such an arrangement. Both parents must be physically and psychologically capable of fulfilling the parental role.

The necessity for at least minimal parental cooperation presents a thorny problem of judicial enforcement in a case such as this one where, despite the trial court's determination that joint custody is in the best interests of the child, one parent (the mother) contends that cooperation is impossible and refuses to abide by the decree. Despite the unfairness of allowing an uncooperative parent to flout a court decree, we are unwilling to sanction punishment of a recalcitrant parent if the welfare of the child will also suffer. When the actions of such a parent deprive the child of any kind of relationship with the other parent, removing the child from the custody of the uncooperative parent may well be appropriate as a remedy of the last resort.

Our review of the record indicates that the trial court gave proper consideration to the preference expressed by the children who were 8 and 10 years old at the time of trial. After interviewing them privately, the court stated for the record that the children were sincere and honest in their desire to remain with their mother. The court concluded that they had been persuaded to make their statements of preference and that the mother's negative attitude toward joint custody had consciously or unconsciously spilled over to the children. Given this conclusion, and the tender years of the children, a determination that did not fully accommodate their express wishes was not unreasonable.

(continued)

CASE 9.1 *continued*

Over two years have elapsed since the original decree of joint custody. Although we uphold that decree as originally made, we recognize that the facts and relationships upon which it was based may have changed dramatically. Therefore, we remand this case to the trial court for further fact-finding and a determination consistent with this opinion. We admonish the court to make a speedy, but thorough investigation into the present circumstances of the parties and their children—using whatever procedural mechanism and hearing what further testimony, if any, is deemed necessary—so that this matter may be expeditiously and properly laid to rest.

Holding: The decision is reversed and the case remanded to the trial court.

Case Discussion: Knowing that all American courts consider the best interests of the child in determining custody arrangements, can you make an argument that joint custody is more supportive of parental interests than a child's interests?

EXHIBIT 9.1 The State of Illinois Child Custody Factors

Sole or joint custody may be awarded, based upon the best interests of the child and upon the following factors:

(1) Preference of the child;
(2) Wishes of the parents;
(3) Child's adjustment to his or her home, school, and community;
(4) Mental and physical health of all individuals involved;
(5) Relationship of the child with parents, siblings, and other significant family members;
(6) Any history of violence or threat of abuse by a parent, whether directed against the child or against another person; and
(7) Willingness and ability of each parent to encourage a close and continuing relationship between the child and the other parent.

Additionally, for an award of joint custody, the court will also consider the following factors:

(1) Ability of the parents to cooperate effectively and consistently;
(2) The residential circumstance of each parent; and
(3) Any other relevant factor.

Wording taken from the Illinois state statutes.

looked closely to consider which parent was the *primary caregiver* to the children. A **primary caregiver** is the parent or other person who provides the care for the children the majority of the time. The court also discussed the father's supervised visitation of his son. **Supervised visitation,** which is typically ordered by a judge, requires that a parent's visits be supervised by a third party.

Court Asked: What's Best, Grandma's Babysitting or Day Care?

One widely publicized case involved a young Michigan woman fighting her daughter's father for custody. At first glance there does not seem to be anything unusual about the unmarried teenage parents in this case, whose daughter was born in 1991. Jennifer Ireland, the mother, who had always lived with her daughter, was a full-time student and resident at the University of Michigan. Steven Smith, the father, was a student who

CASE 9.2 *Allen v. Farrow*, 197 A.2d 327 (1994)

Facts: The petitioner (Allen) maintained that he was forced to commence the proceeding in order to preserve his parental rights to the three infant children because the respondent (Farrow) commenced, and continued to engage in, a campaign to alienate him from his children and to ultimately defeat his legal rights to them. From the inception of Mr. Allen's relationship with Ms. Farrow in 1980, until a few months after the adoption of Dylan O'Sullivan Farrow on June 11, 1985, Ms. Farrow claimed Mr. Allen wanted nothing to do with her children. However, following the adoption, Mr. Allen became interested in developing a relationship with the newly adopted Dylan. He also developed a relationship with Moses Farrow, who had been adopted by Ms. Farrow in 1980 and was 7 years old at the time of Dylan's adoption. However, Mr. Allen remained distant from Ms. Farrow's other six children.

In 1986, Ms. Farrow became pregnant with the couple's son, Satchel. The record supports the finding that Mr. Allen showed little or no interest in the pregnancy. It is not disputed that Ms. Farrow began to withdraw from Mr. Allen during the pregnancy and that afterward she did not wish Satchel to become attached to Mr. Allen. According to Mr. Allen, Ms. Farrow became inordinately attached to the newborn Satchel to the exclusion of the other children. Mr. Allen maintained that his interest in, and affection for, Dylan always has been paternal in nature and never sexual.

Issue: Whether a modification of the child custody order is in the best interests of the three children.

Court's Reasoning: The various psychiatric experts who testified or provided reports did not conclude that Mr. Allen's behavior toward Dylan prior to August of 1992 was explicitly sexual in nature. However, the clear consensus was that his interest in Dylan was abnormally intense in that he made inordinate demands on her time and focused on her to the exclusion of Satchel and Moses even when they were present. Mr. Allen's testimony showed he knew little about the daily activities of his children.

In 1991, at about the same time that the parties were growing distant from each other and expressing concerns about the other's relationship with their youngest children, Mr. Allen began acknowledging Ms. Farrow's daughter, Soon-Yi Previn. Previously he had treated Ms. Previn in the same way he treated Ms. Farrow's other children from her prior marriage. He rarely spoke to them. In December 1991, two events coincided. Mr. Allen's adoptions of Dylan and Moses were finalized, and Mr. Allen began his sexual relationship with their sister Soon-Yi Previn. His continuation of the relationship, viewed in the best possible light, shows a distinct absence of judgment. At the very minimum, it demonstrates an absence of any parenting skills. We recognize Mr. Allen's acknowledgment of the pain his relationship with Ms. Previn has caused the family. It is true that Ms. Farrow's failure to conceal her feelings from the rest of the family, and the acting out of her feelings of betrayal and anger toward Mr. Allen, enhanced the effect of the situation on the rest of her family. While the petitioner's testimony regarding his attempt to deescalate the dispute, and to insulate the family from it, displays a measure of concern for his three children, it is clear that he should have realized the inevitable consequence of his actions well before his relationship with Ms. Previn became intimate.

Although the evidence in support of the sexual abuse of Dylan by Mr. Allen remains inconclusive, it is clear that the investigation of the charges in and of itself could not have left Dylan unaffected. The weighing of the numerous factors to be considered *requires an evaluation of the testimony, character, and sincerity of all the parties involved in this type of dispute.* Although the investigation of the abuse allegations have not resulted in a conclusive finding, all the evidence received at trial supports the determination as to custody and visitation with respect to this child. There would be no beneficial purpose served in disturbing the custody

(continued)

CASE 9.1 *continued*

arrangement. Moreover, even if the abuse did not occur, it is evident that there are issues concerning Mr. Allen's inappropriately intense relationship with this child that can be resolved only in a therapeutic setting.

With respect to Satchel, the court denied the petitioner's request for unsupervised visitation. The record supports the conclusion that Mr. Allen may, if unsupervised, influence Satchel inappropriately and disregard the impact that exposure to his relationship with Satchel's sister, Ms. Previn, would have on the child. It has been held that the desires of the children are to be considered, but that it must be kept in mind that those desires can be manipulated. In considering the custody and visitation decision concerning Moses, who is a teenager, his expressed desire not to be compelled to see Mr. Allen cannot be ignored.

Holding: We hold that in view of the totality of the circumstances, the best interest of these children would be served by keeping them together in the custody of Ms. Farrow, with the parties abiding by the visitation schedule established by the trial court.

Dissenting Opinion: There is strong evidence in the record from neutral observers that Mr. Allen and Satchel basically have a warm and loving father-son relationship, but that their relationship is in jeopardy, in large measure, because Mr. Allen is being estranged and alienated from his son by the current custody and visitation arrangement. On one occasion when Satchel indicated that he wanted to stay with Mr. Allen longer than the allotted two-hour supervised visit, Satchel also said he could not stay longer because his mother had told him that two hours were sufficient. Perhaps most distressing, Satchel indicated to Mr. Allen that he was seeing a doctor who was going to *help him not see* Mr. Allen anymore. In contrast to what apparently is being expressed by Ms. Farrow about Mr. Allen to Satchel, Mr. Allen has been reported to say only positive things to Satchel about Ms. Farrow and conveys only loving regards to Moses and Dylan through Satchel. I do not believe that Mr. Allen's visitation with Satchel for a mere two hours, three times a week, under supervision is reasonable and meaningful under the circumstances or that exceptional circumstances are presented that warrant such significant restriction on his visitation with Satchel.

Case Discussion: The lifestyles of the rich and famous may not appear as enviable after you have read the *Allen* case. The lower court appeared to be highly influenced by Mr. Allen's apparent lack of knowledge regarding the children's daily activities, friends, and teachers. Do you think a parent who is not actively involved in the daily schedule of his children should have an equal opportunity to seek visitation and custody? The dissenting opinion discusses the behavior of Ms. Farrow as having a negative impact on Mr. Allen's relationship with his son. Such negative behavior, if intensified, can have such an impact on a parent's relationship with a child that it may develop into what is known as **parental alienation syndrome.**

resided with his parents. The case gained notoriety when the father pointed to the fact that the daughter attended daily day care on campus as the reason why he should gain custody. As an alternative babysitting arrangement, the father planned to have his mother care for his daughter. The trial court judge agreed with the father and granted Steven Smith sole custody. The mother appealed.

The appellate court ultimately overturned the lower court, but not before the media publicized this case as a possible legal turning point for all of America's working mothers.[3] Do you think that whether a parent will use day care, nonrelative babysitters, or babysitting by blood relatives should be a factor in determining which parent should gain custody? Do you think the ultimate outcome of the *Smith* case served the best interests of the child?

Religion's Role in Custody: In the Name of Faith

Parents have a fundamental constitutional right to teach their choice of religion to their minor children, and the courts have rarely interfered with this freedom of religious choice. When the courts have stepped in, the cases have usually involved health and safety issues concerning the children. Most freedom of religion cases involve two parents jointly fighting a children's services agency. A custody dispute concerning religion usually involves two parents fighting over what religion the children will be taught. Generally, most courts decide in favor of continuing the religious instruction that was in place prior to the custody dispute. Many courts allow parents with sole custody to make all decisions regarding the religious upbringing of the children. In the case of *Quiner v. Quiner* (see Case 9.3), the judges needed all of their King Solomon–like attributes to make their decision.

The Issue of Sexual Orientation in Custody Disputes

The *Nadler v. Superior Court* case (see Case 9.4) is a reflection of the numerous upheavals that have occurred in society in the area of traditional societal mores. This case moved away from past decisions that viewed homosexuality as a just cause for finding a parent unfit.

The Role of the Stepparent in Custody Disputes

Stepparents are a major component of family life in twenty-first-century America. In fact, it is estimated that one in every four children will live with a stepparent before reaching majority.[4] Although stepparents are recognized as a part of the extended family unit, their legal responsibility to their stepchildren is generally linked to the inability of the biological parents to care for their own children. Stepparenting may be here to stay, but legal recognition of the stepparent relationship in the United States is less than clear-cut.

A stepparent who fails to financially provide and assume responsibility for a stepchild may appear less than warm and hospitable, but the stepparent generally is not shirking a *legal* responsibility for the stepchild. A minority of states *do* impose financial responsibility upon the stepparent, but *do not* specifically require the continuance of such financial support in the event of a divorce between the stepparent and the biological parent. However, there is an exception applied when the stepparent has acted as a parent with respect to the care and supervision of a child. The ***in loco parentis* doctrine** is often applied by judges if the stepparent has *voluntarily assumed* a parental obligation. *In loco parentis* is Latin and literally means "in the place of a parent." States imposing financial obligations for stepchildren upon stepparents include Delaware, Hawaii, Iowa, Kentucky, Missouri, Montana, Nebraska, Nevada, New Hampshire, New York, North Carolina, North Dakota, Oregon, South Dakota, Vermont, and Washington.[5]

Courts Create Responsibility for Stepparents

In some cases, judges have used equitable estoppel and implied contract principles to impose a post-divorce duty of support on a stepparent. **Equitable estoppel** is defined as being stopped by your own prior acts from claiming a right against another person who has legitimately relied on those acts. An implied contract is a contract, the existence and terms of which are determined by the actions of the persons involved, not by their words. Judges have relied on equitable estoppel when the custodial parent has been able to prove that the stepparent's behavior interfered with a stepchild's relationship with his noncustodial biological parent *and* that this interference caused the biological parent not to financially support his child.

Another legal creation is the ***de facto* parent** concept, which gives limited recognition to the actual parenting done by a parent-type figure who is not necessarily a stepparent. This concept is applied most often in visitation disputes.

CASE 9.3 *Quiner v. Quiner,* 59 Cal. Rptr. 503 (1967)

Facts: The court found each parent to be of sound character, and the devotion of each to their 5-year-old son, John Edward, was not in issue. Edward Quiner sued for divorce on November 29, 1963, requesting custody of his son. The judgment, among other things, granted visitation rights to the mother, Linnea, but ordered her not to teach or inform her son of any religious belief concerning the Plymouth Brethren, including taking the child to any meetings, assemblies, or religious services of the Brethren. The depth of Linnea's desire to indoctrinate John Edward with the beliefs of her church was such that she admitted she would keep him away from his father if she could.

The trial court found that if John Edward lived with either parent, his physical needs would be well provided for, and that both parents were fit to be awarded custody. However, the child's mental welfare and his opportunities for intellectual, social, character, and personality growth were found by the trial court to be best served by granting custody to the father. In doing so, the trial court noted the following tenets of the Brethren's religion: The Brethren live separately and shun all social relationships with persons who are not members of their fellowship; Brethren members may not eat in any public or private place with nonmembers; Brethren may not vote; Christmas is not celebrated; children may not have dogs, cats, or other pets; the reading of all forms of literature, except for their bible, is discouraged; and all medical insurance is opposed.

Issue: Whether the mother was penalized for her religious beliefs by being deprived of the custody of her son.

Court's Reasoning: The conclusion seems inescapable that the mother was deprived of the custody of her child solely because she is a Jehovah's Witness. The trial court found that the beliefs of the followers of that faith are not in the best interests of their children. We find that a court cannot identify one way or another, with any degree of certainty, the sure road to personal security and happiness or to religious salvation. The evaluation of religious teaching, and its projected effect upon the physical, mental, and emotional well-being of a child, must be forcibly kept from judicial determinations. It appears to be the law that the parent having custody of a child has the right to bring up the child in the religion of such parent. There is no dispute that the appellant is a sincere believer in a bona fide faith. Deprivation of the custody of a child is a heavy penalty to pay for the exercise of a religious belief that is neither illegal nor immoral. The law is settled: All things being equal, the custody of a child of tender years should go to the mother.

However, if it is shown at any time in the future that the appellant is teaching John Edward not to love and respect his father, such direct indoctrination would undoubtedly require the application of sanctions. Further, if as a consequence of the teaching of the principle of separation to the child, it is shown that John Edward's physical, emotional, and mental well-being has been affected and jeopardized, or that the appellant is acting contrary to court order, even though the appellant's conduct may be compelled by her sincere religious beliefs, the courts of our state are open forums to which the father has ready access.

Holding: Reversed.

Case Discussion: The appellant court basically threw out any negative weight against the mother based on her religious beliefs. The court then applied the tender years doctrine and found that, because of the boy's age, the mother should be given custody. As stated earlier, the tender years doctrine has now basically been tossed aside by courts in favor of a non–gender-specific approach. Do you think that the father would have a better chance of getting custody in the twenty-first century? If you were the father, what argument could you make?

CASE 9.4 *Nadler v. The Superior Court of the State of California, in and for the County of Sacramento,* 255 Cal. App. 2d 523, 63 Cal. Rptr. 352 (1967)

Facts: This proceeding arose out of a divorce action brought by the petitioning wife. The custody of the petitioner's daughter, age 5, was awarded to the father. The basis of the order was explained by the court as follows: The court finds from the evidence and stipulations by counsel for the parties that (1) The plaintiff is a homosexual female engaging in sexual acts with other females, and (2) *the homosexuality of plaintiff as a matter of law constitutes her not a fit or proper person to have the care, custody, and control of the minor child.* The trial court found that it would be in the best interests and welfare of the child to place her in the custody of her father.

Both sides stipulated in the trial court that both the mother and father were able and willing to provide the child with physical care and support.

Issue: Whether the trial court failed to exercise its judicial discretion.

Court's Reasoning: In a divorce proceeding involving the custody of a child, primary consideration must be given to the welfare of the child. The good of the child must be regarded as the controlling force in directing the child's custody. It is also the rule that the matter of the custody of a minor is vested in the trial courts, and these courts are given a very broad discretion in determining the best interests of the child.

How the best interests of the child will be preserved is a question to be determined solely from the standpoint of the child. The feelings and desires of the contesting parties are not to be considered except insofar as they affect the best interests of the child. We are not saying that the trial court abused its discretion; rather, we are saying that the trial court failed in its duty to exercise the very discretion with which it is vested by holding that, as *a matter of law,* the petitioner is an unfit mother on the basis that she is a homosexual.

Holding: The Superior Court was ordered to vacate its order of October 5, 1967, and to exercise its discretion in awarding the custody of the child.

Case Discussion: The appellate court ordered that the case be returned to the trial court. The trial court was ordered to assess the evidence and to determine custody based on *all* the evidence, not just on the single fact that the mother is gay. Do you think the fact that a parent is homosexual should be considered a factor in determining custody?

Stepping Up to Responsibility

Not all stepparents must be brought to court before they will face their responsibilities to their stepchildren. Some stepparents seek to continue their relationships with their stepchildren after they have divorced their stepchildren's parent. However, those stepparents who wish to continue in the stepparent role post-divorce face serious legal hurdles. Procedural and substantive legal issues include the question of *legal standing* and the standards applied by the courts in weighing *biological versus stepparent rights.* The development in the late twentieth century of the *psychological parent doctrine* helped many courts recognize the importance of stepparents in the lives of their stepchildren. The **psychological parent doctrine** established that a psychological parent is a person who, on a day-to-day basis, through interaction, companionship, and mutual interest, fulfills a child's psychological need for an adult. Several states have recognized the psychological parent concept by enacting statutes that provide rights of visitation and custody to psychological parents.[6]

Parental Rights Doctrine: Biological Connection Versus Stepparent

Having standing to come to court to seek visitation or custody is only the first legal hurdle for a stepparent. Stepparents in the majority of states must face the *parental rights doctrine*. The **parental rights doctrine** gives the biological parent the superior right to custody of his child. This majority approach requires proving the biological parent's unfitness or abandonment of the child, plus proof must be provided that the welfare of the child requires custody to be given to a nonbiological adult. The *Simmons* case (see Case 9.5) deals with a visitation issue involving a stepparent. This case expands the stepparent position if the stepparent has developed an *in loco parentis* role in the child's life.

Joint Custody Awarded to Stepparent

Although a biological connection to a child is an important factor in determining child custody, it is not a foolproof defense to a custody claim by an adult who is not biologically related to the child if that adult has a strong connection to the child. The fact that an adult who is not biologically connected can gain court-ordered custody or visitation of a child is a scary, but realistic, possibility for American parents.

The subtitle of the case of *Stamps v. Rawlins* (see Case 9.6) should be "Biological Parents Beware." The stepdad and biological mother initially sought to establish a loving and secure home with two parents caring for the mother's biological son, Ryan, but their marriage went sour. This is another dispute involving a mother who learned too late that she put her sole custody of her son at risk by developing her new husband's *in loco parentis* role. This case provides a new word to add to your legal terminology arsenal: *de novo,* which is a Latin term that means new. A **trial *de novo*** is a new trial ordered by a judge when a previous trial was so flawed that it will be made void.

Grandparents' Role in Custody and Visitation

The reality of family life at the end of the twentieth-century America saw America's children living with only one parent in 28 percent of the country's households. This reality was evident in the developing role of third parties who began undertaking traditional parental responsibilities in many American households. For example, in 1998, approximately 4 million children lived with their grandparents.[7] Widespread enactment of third-party visitation statutes recognized that, in addition to their parents, children can also benefit from relationships with statutorily specified persons. All 50 states now have statutes that provide for grandparent visitation in some form. So far, you have read how the rights of children to benefit from relationships with stepparents and former partners of their biological parents have been protected. Now, you will read how the rights of children and grandparents to visit with each other have been interpreted in the courts.

Three cases are provided to demonstrate how the rights of grandparents and grandchildren to visit with each other have been interpreted by different state courts. The first case, *Bowers v. Matula* (see Case 9.7), concentrates on the question of a grandparent having standing to sue in order to seek visitation. The second case, *Dolman v. Dolman* (see Case 9.8), explains how simply having the biological connection as a grandparent will not ensure court-ordered visitation without a best interests of the child standard being applied to the facts of the individual case. Interestingly, a jury heard the *Dolman* case's custody dispute. (Texas is the exception in having juries hear child custody trials.) The third case, *Troxel v. Granvill* (see Case 9.9), was decided by the United States Supreme Court. *Troxel* steps away from statutorily ensured third-party visitation and supports the application of a more stringent fundamental liberty interest standard before third-party visitation can be provided by a court.

CASE 9.5 *In re the Marriage of Andrew W. Simmons v. JoEllen C. Simmons, 486 N.W.2d 788 (1992)*

Facts: Appellant JoEllen C. Simmons, now known as JoEllen C. Vasicheck, appealed the trial court's order granting her former husband, Andrew W. Simmons, structured visitation with her son from a previous relationship. The parties had stipulated the granting to Simmons of reasonable visitation with the child, and the stipulation was incorporated into judgment. Subsequently, Vasicheck argued that the trial court erred in ordering visitation over her objection.

The parties were married on May 22, 1989. Vasicheck had a 5-year-old son, M.V., at the time of the marriage. M.V.'s biological father had no contact with him and had surrendered his parental rights. The parties had one child during their marriage, a son, A.S., born September 14, 1989. M.V. lived with the parties until they separated in January 1991.

On February 22, 1991, the parties signed a stipulation settling all matters at issue between them. The parties were represented by separate counsel. They agreed to joint physical and legal custody of their son A.S. They also agreed that Simmons was *entitled to the right of reasonable visitation* with M.V. The stipulation included a notice provision pertaining to the parties' rights to have access to the minor child's records, to attend school conferences, to be informed of accident or serious illness, and to have reasonable telephone contact. A judgment incorporating the stipulation was entered on March 22, 1991.

After the judgment was entered, Vasicheck refused to allow Simmons any visitation with M.V. In September 1991, Simmons moved for structured visitation rights. In her response, Vasicheck moved for termination of Simmons's right to visit M.V. The trial court granted Simmons's motion, finding that Simmons was *in loco parentis* with M.V. throughout the 18-month period they lived together. The court granted Simmons visitation with M.V. every other weekend and on certain holidays, coinciding with the terms when Simmons had physical custody of A.S.

Issue: Whether the trial court erred in granting Simmons the right to visitation with his former stepson.

Court's Reasoning: Vasicheck argues that Simmons's right, if any, to seek visitation with M.V. is limited to Minn. Stat. § 257.022 (1990). This statute is entitled "Rights of Visitation to Unmarried Persons."

Since Simmons and M.V. resided together in the same house for 18 months, the two-year requirement under Minn. Stat. § 257.022, subd. 2b, was not met. Vasicheck contends that because Simmons is ineligible for visitation under the statute, the trial court lacked authority to grant visitation rights in the judgment. We disagree for two reasons: (1) Section 257.022, subd. 2b, does not preclude a former stepparent who was *in loco parentis* to the child from asserting a common law right to visitation, and (2) Vasicheck stipulated to the visitation.

In view of our supreme court's recognition of the *in loco parentis* doctrine, we hold that a former stepparent who was *in loco parentis* with a former stepchild may be entitled to visitation under the common law. Because Minn. Stat. § 257.022 does not contain any clause specifically repealing, restricting, or abridging a nonparent's common law visitation rights, we construe the statute to extend and supplement the common law rule. Because an *in loco parentis* relationship existed, the trial court had authority to award visitation, even though Simmons did not meet the requirements of Minn. Stat. § 257.022, subd. 2b. Moreover, the parties' stipulation granting Simmons visitation with M.V., approved by the trial court and incorporated in the judgment, created an enforceable right. *The parties to dissolution may impose obligations beyond the authority of the family court.*

(continued)

CASE 9.5 *continued*

The limited nature of Simmons's right to visitation with M. V. does not include access to M. V.'s confidential records or the other rights specified in Minn. Stat. § 518.17, subd. 3(b). These rights clearly apply only to a child's parents or a nonparent custodian. Because Simmons has only the right to visitation with M. V., and Vasicheck did not agree to any additional rights, the portion of the trial court's order granting Simmons the § 518.17, subd. 3(b), rights with respect to M. V. must be vacated.

Holding: Affirmed.

Case Discussion: What is your opinion of the Minnesota statute giving visitation rights to a person who resided with the child in question for more than two years? The court expanded the statute for a stepparent who lived with the child for less than the two-year statutory requirement by applying the *in loco parentis* doctrine. This may be understandable due to the original marital commitment to the biological parent. However, do you think most biological parents in Minnesota are aware that a possible right to their children, albeit to visitation and not to custody, is being created when their children live with another adult?

CASE 9.6 *Stamps v. Rawlins,* 297 Ark. 370, 761 S.W.2d 933 (1988)

Facts: A little over six months after the original divorce decree, the chancellor altered the original order giving sole custody to the mother. The biological mother and stepfather were awarded custody on an alternating weekly basis. In his findings of fact, the chancellor found that the stepfather was the only father that Ryan had ever had and that the stepfather treated Ryan as his own child. The mother appealed.

Issue: Whether the lower court erred in altering the custody arrangement.

Court's Reasoning: Almost all of the law in Arkansas regarding custody of children is common law. Arkansas has only one statute on custody, and it provides that the award shall be made solely on the basis of the welfare and best interests of the child and must be made without regard to the sex of the parent. The statute makes no reference to whom custody may be awarded. However, under case law, it is clear that a stepparent can be awarded custody of a minor child. Nevertheless, case law specifically establishes that a preference must prevail unless it establishes that the natural parent is unfit.

Here, the chancellor specifically found that the appellant mother was a fit and proper person for custody. The appellate court's *de novo* review of the decision sustains that finding. Therefore, custody of Ryan should have been left with the biological mother, and it was error for the court to rule otherwise. It makes no difference that split custody, rather than full custody, was awarded.

The chancellor manifested great understanding and patience in this custody dispute, but he erred when he proceeded to change the parties' original decree when the evidence reflected that no material circumstances had arisen to warrant a modification.

Holding: Overruled.

Case Discussion: Do you think that if the biological parent supports an *in loco parentis* role for a stepparent, the stepparent should then have an equal right to petition for custody without having to first prove that the biological parent is unfit? Would such a right be better or worse for the children involved? Biological parents would certainly have to think long and hard before bringing a new person into their children's lives.

CASE 9.7 *Bowers v. Matula*, 943 S.W.2d 536 (1997)

Facts: The maternal grandparents brought an action seeking access to their grandchild. The biological parents' rights were subsequently terminated, and the child was adopted by the paternal grandparents in a separate action. The paternal grandparents then moved to dismiss the maternal grandparents' action because they claimed the maternal grandparents lacked standing to request visitation.

Issue: Whether the maternal grandparents had standing to request visitation of their grandchild.

Court's Reasoning: This court finds that, under governing statutes, the line before which grandparents' requests for access to their grandchildren may be made, and after which such requests may not be made, is when all the parents' rights have been terminated and the grandchild has been adopted by someone other than a stepparent.

The statute is clear and unambiguous. The maternal grandparents had standing to request access to their grandchild when they filed their petition requesting access. The subsequent termination of the parents' rights and the grant of adoption to their paternal grandparents did not deprive the maternal grandparents of standing in their action seeking access. No parental rights had been terminated or adoption ordered when the maternal grandparents filed their petition.

Holding: Reversed and remanded.

Case Discussion: Do you see any possible problems with the maternal grandparents visiting with their grandchild, or do you see only a positive outcome as a result of the child being able to continue a relationship with a second set of grandparents? Following litigation, do you think the two sets of grandparents will bury the proverbial hatchet—or throw it at each other?

THE BAXTERS: A FAMILY STRUGGLES TO DETERMINE THE BEST INTERESTS OF THEIR CHILDREN

When it comes to their three children, there is absolutely nothing Leonard and Helen Baxter can agree on. For example, their parenting styles are as different as night and day. Married for 14 years, the Baxters are the parents of 12-year-old Leonard, Jr., 10-year-old Megan, and 8-year-old Michael.

The Baxters decided two years ago to live separate lives. This was not especially surprising, since Helen had embarked on a path of extramarital affairs via the Internet, and Leonard's energies for the previous five years had been totally concentrated upon the children to the exclusion of Helen.

The couple's financial state made it impossible for Leonard or Helen to move out of their family's comfortable split-level home, so in a somewhat odd arrangement, Leonard moved out of the upstairs bedroom he had shared with Helen and took over the lower level's family room. Leonard would not have moved out, even if they had been able to afford a separate apartment, because of his attachment to the children. Leonard is the boys' soccer coach, as well as Megan's softball coach.

Helen and Leonard finally decided to go through the legal requirements to get a divorce, and they have been battling over the custody issue ever since. A property settlement agreement was finally ironed out, except for child support, after several loud negotiating sessions. The problem is that both Helen and Leonard want full and sole custody of their three children, and they will go to any lengths to get it.

CASE 9.8 *Dolman v. Dolman*, 586 S.W.2d 606 (1979)

Facts: Carolyn F. Dolman was divorced from Denver Floyd in June 1967. The judgment awarded sole custody of Lise Nicole Dolman, an infant daughter, to Carolyn, with reasonable visitation privileges awarded to Denver.

In May 1978, Louise P. Dolman, the paternal grandmother of Lise, appearing *pro se,* filed a motion to modify the divorce judgment of June 1967 by seeking visitation rights pursuant to a state statute.

The case went to trial and was heard by a jury. The court's charge contained two special issues. The jury answered: (1) It was in the best interests of the child to grant the grandmother access rights to the child, and (2) one day each calendar month for eight consecutive hours was reasonable access. Access rights were defined in the jury charge to mean rights of visitation with the child.

The mother appealed and claimed that the state statute does not provide a grandparent with an independent cause of action for reasonable access rights to a child if the child is in the custody of a fit parent.

Issue: Whether the court erred in entering judgment for the paternal grandmother.

Court's Reasoning: Generally, an obligation of the custodial parent to permit visitation by a grandparent is a moral obligation, not a legal one, and courts will not enforce a right of visitation by a grandparent nor intervene in a relationship between a child and a custodial parent. Evidence in this case included the following: (1) the paternal grandmother had not seen the child, who was almost 12 years old, since the child was 19 months old; (2) she had never learned to pronounce the child's name correctly; (3) she had not written to the child since the child had learned to read; (4) she had once gone to the child's school in an attempt to visit her, but had erroneously determined that another student was her grandchild; and (5) the child's father did not want his mother to visit the child. This evidence was sufficient to show that the welfare and social needs of the child would not be served by the grandmother's visitation.

From our review of the record, we are convinced that the jury's answer is based upon little more than the well-accepted notion that it is just and right for a grandparent to know his grandchild. The paternal grandmother did not demonstrate by a *preponderance of the evidence* that the welfare or social needs of Lise would be served by the grandmother's visitation. Indeed, there is considerable support in the record that such visitation would not be in the best interests of Lise. Evidence indicated that allowing visitation by the paternal grandmother could be disruptive and emotionally detrimental to the child. In sum, the court, after considering all of the evidence, is of the opinion that the jury's decision was so contrary to the great weight and preponderance of the evidence as to be manifestly unjust.

Holding: Reversed and remanded for a new trial.

Case Discussion: The appellate court's decision clearly states that the best interests of the child must be weighed against the right of the grandparent to visit her grandchild. The court went further and wrote that the evidence appeared to show that such a visit in this case could be disruptive and emotionally detrimental to the child. Do you think a parent could negatively influence a child's visit with even the most wonderful of grandparents?

CASE 9.9 *Troxel v. Granville,*
520 U.S. 57, 120 S. Ct. 2054, 147 L. Ed. 2d 49 (2000)

Facts: Unmarried parents Tommie Granville and Brad Troxel had two daughters from a relationship that ended in June of 1991. Brad subsequently established a relationship between his daughters and his parents, the Troxels. Brad committed suicide in 1993. The Troxels commenced their case in December 1993 by filing a petition to obtain visitation rights with their granddaughters, Isabelle and Natalie. The Troxels filed their petition under Wash. Rev. Code § 26.10.160(3), which states: *Any person may petition the court for visitation rights at any time including, but not limited to, custody proceedings.* The Troxels requested two weekends of overnight visitation per month and two weeks of visitation each summer. The mother, Granville, did not oppose visitation altogether, but instead asked the court to order one day of visitation per month with no overnight stay. The original order gave the Troxels one weekend per month, one week during the summer, and four hours on both of the petitioning grandparents' birthdays.

The mother appealed, and the Washington Court of Appeals remanded the case back to the Superior Court. The Superior Court, on remand, again found quality-time visitation with their grandparents to be in the best interests of the girls.

Again, the mother appealed, but this time the Washington Court of Appeals reversed the lower court's visitation order, declaring that nonparents lack standing to seek visitation under the Washington statute in question unless a custody order is pending.

The Troxels then asked the Washington Supreme Court to review the case. Although the Washington Supreme Court disagreed with the appeals court and declared that the Troxels had standing to sue without a pending custody action, it agreed that visitation could not be ordered. Citing the United States Constitution, the Washington Supreme Court found that Wash. Stat. § 26.10.160(3) unconstitutionally infringed on the fundamental right of parents to rear their children.

The Troxels then sought the assistance of the United States Supreme Court by filing a *writ of certiorari.* The United States Supreme Court agreed to hear their case.

Issue: Whether third parties may petition a court for visitation rights at any time when that visitation serves the best interests of the child.

Court's Reasoning: The liberty interest at issue in this case—the interest of parents in the care, custody, and control of their children—is perhaps the oldest of the fundamental liberty interests recognized by this Court. In light of this extensive precedent, it cannot now be doubted that the due process clause of the Fourteenth Amendment protects the fundamental right of parents to make decisions concerning the care, custody, and control of their children.

The Washington statute in question contains no requirement that the court accord the parent's decision any presumption of validity or any weight whatsoever. Instead, the Washington statute places the best interest determination solely in the hands of the judge. Should the judge disagree with the parent's estimation of the child's best interests, the judge's view necessarily prevails. Thus, in practical effect, any Washington court can disregard and overturn any decision by a fit custodial parent concerning visitation whenever a third party affected by the parent's decision files a visitation petition. This compels our conclusion that § 26.10.160(3) as applied exceeded the bounds of the due process clause. First, the Troxels did not allege,

(continued)

CASE 9.9 *continued*

and no court has found, that Granville was an unfit parent. The Superior Court judge's comments instead suggest that the grandparents' request should be granted unless the children would be impacted adversely.

The Superior Court gave no weight to Granville having agreed to visitation even before the filing of any visitation petition. Many other states expressly provide by statute that courts may not award visitation unless a parent has denied visitation to the concerned third party. All the factors discussed by the Superior Court showed an unconstitutional infringement on Granville's fundamental right to make decisions concerning the care, custody, and control of her two daughters. The Washington Superior Court failed to accord the determination of Granville, a fit custodial parent, any material weight. The due process clause does not permit a state to infringe on the fundamental right of parents to make child-rearing decisions simply because a state judge believes a better decision could be made.

Holding: Affirmed.

Case Discussion: The *Troxel* case provides an excellent lesson in constitutional law. The freedom to parent is described as a *liberty interest.* This liberty interest is provided by the United States Constitution. The Fourteenth Amendment of the United States Constitution states: *No State shall deprive any person of life, liberty or property, without due process of law.* This amendment ensures that the rights provided in the federal Constitution are not taken away by a state through its courts or statutes.

This case is also a good example of the United States Supreme Court putting off for another day the job of defining the precise scope of parental due process rights in the visitation context. In other words, the 49 other states with grandparent visitation statutes were not told that their statutes are unconstitutional. Rather, the court simply stated that the constitutionality of any standard for awarding visitation depends on the specific manner in which that standard is applied. The Washington statute was found to be *breathtakingly broad* in that it allowed any fit custodial parent's decision to be overturned. In the context of a statute described as overly broad, the fear is that application of the statute will be seen as overreaching and as stepping on people's constitutional rights.

Asking Your Client the Right Questions

First, how much do you really know about Helen and Leonard? Not much, beyond a few rudimentary facts. A good offense, or defense, cannot be launched without having as much information as possible about the client's case. You learned about a type of legal question known as an interrogatory in a previous chapter. In the Baxter's case, each attorney has sent a set of interrogatories to the opposing party's attorney after completing interviews with the respective clients. Answers to interrogatories are usually based upon client interviews. If Helen were your firm's client, what questions would you want to ask her regarding custody? If Leonard were your firm's client, what questions regarding custody would you want to ask him? After interviewing Leonard and reading Helen's interrogatory answers, it has become apparent to J. D. and Susan that both parties think they have superior child-rearing skills.

Developing interview skills requires a lot of practice. A skilled and experienced interviewer can question a client and quickly adapt when the interviewee veers away from the interviewer's control of the interview. Many law firms have fine-tuned the art of client questioning by developing generic client questionnaires. A client file, however, will probably not be complete if all the questions are taken from a one-size-fits-all client questionnaire. Review Exhibit 9.2, which contains a sample of the type of interview ques-

---

EXHIBIT 9.2 Sample of Interview Questions to Ask in a Custody Dispute

1. How would you describe your children?
2. Since they were born, what role have you taken in their care?
3. Which parent has been primarily responsible for the children's everyday care (e.g., making meals, helping with homework, taking the children to the doctor, buying clothes)?
4. How do the children perform at school? What are their best and worst subjects?
5. Do the children play sports or participate in extracurricular activities?
6. Do you participate with the children in their extracurricular activities?
7. What are the names of the children's friends and teachers?
8. Do any of the children have any medical conditions and, if so, how do these conditions affect the children's behavior, schoolwork, and so on?
9. How do the siblings interact with each other?
10. What are your favorite activities with your children?

---

tions that may be utilized specifically in a custody dispute. These types of questions can also be used as interrogatories that are sent to the opposition.

Depositions Follow Interrogatories

In a previous chapter you learned about depositions, which are oral question-and-answer sessions conducted in the presence of a court reporter. The depositions of Helen and Leonard should have shed some light on the true nature of the family's life before the parents' separation. Unfortunately, during depositions, both parties are often determined not to back away from their own individual versions of the truth or give an inch in terms of their positions. In Helen and Leonard's case, both parties gave, in their individual depositions, responses that were not much different from the written responses they made to their interrogatories.

Following the depositions, as well as numerous court-mandated and voluntary settlement conferences, Helen and Leonard still cannot agree on the custody issue. Susan may have been right. The Baxter case might end up at trial because of the custody dispute.

Preparing for a Custody Trial

Pretrial hearings are designed to discuss issues that arise prior to any type of trial. In Helen and Leonard's case, the attorneys will explain to the judge that additional witnesses will be needed to support their clients' positions. Both Helen and Leonard have decided to hire psychologists to study their individual requests for custody. Additionally, unpaid witnesses may include family, friends, and clergy. The judge in the Baxter's case has also decided to order the appointment of a guardian *ad litem* to protect the children's interest, and he has appointed a court psychologist as well.

Advocating for the Children: The Guardian *Ad Litem*'s Role

A **guardian *ad litem*** (**GAL**) is the person who is appointed by a judge to look after the interests of the child or children whose parents are disputing their custody. A guardian *ad litem* may be appointed in *any* matter involving children or adults with special needs. Depending on the state, the guardian *ad litem* may be an attorney, social worker, psychologist, or volunteer who has been trained by the court system to get to the heart of a family's custody issues. The guardian *ad litem*, again depending on the state, may also be called an **advocate** or a children's advocate. In a custody dispute, the guardian *ad litem* should speak with anyone who can help sort out the family's background and give insight into the custody issues. He should speak with both parents, the child or children, the children's teachers, and the family's clergy; he also should visit the family home. In addition, the guardian *ad litem* should look at any psychology reports and speak with the professionals who prepared the reports. The guardian *ad litem* will prepare his own report to present to the judge, and that report should detail what custody arrangements he believes would be in the child or children's best interests. The judge uses the guardian *ad litem*'s report to assist in deciding on the final custody arrangements. The judge, however, is not bound by the guardian *ad litem*'s suggestions.

The Psychological Expert's Role

The guardian *ad litem* is not the only non–family member who gets to share an opinion with the court. Psychologists are often hired by battling spouses when custody is at issue. The psychologists hired by the parties may go through the process of being formally appointed by the judge hearing the case. A court order may be granted to ensure participation by the parties and the children involved. The judge hearing the custody dispute may also decide if an independent court-appointed psychologist should also be hired—with the court psychologist's bill to be paid by one or both of the warring parties.

Helen and Leonard's attorneys will need to follow certain guidelines when dealing with psychologists. The attorneys should first make sure that confidentiality waivers are signed by Helen and Leonard. A **confidentiality waiver** allows the psychologists to discuss matters that normally would be privileged information. The attorneys should also make sure that the psychologists conduct interviews with Leonard, Helen, the children, and anyone else with an important role in the children's lives. The psychologists should make home and school observations. They should administer psychological tests and procure any pertinent documents.[8] The case of *Shapiro v. Shapiro* (see Case 9.10) provides a good explanation of how many courts believe a psychologist's testimony can be extremely important.

BAXTERS DECLARE TRUCE

The Baxters did move forward and hire his-and-her psychologists. Additionally, the court appointed a guardian *ad litem* and a court psychologist. Quite a few weeks later, the reports were completed and delivered to the Johnson & Webster offices. J. D. is hoping that meeting with Leonard to review the recently delivered reports will put him in a settling mood.

Leonard arrived on time for his 10 A.M. appointment with J. D. While waiting in the firm's foyer, the angst of the extended custody dispute showed on his face. J. D. walked into the foyer and immediately saw the anxiety conveyed through Mr. Baxter's body language.

"Sorry for the sweaty palms," Leonard apologized as he shook J. D.'s hand. "I can't seem to shake the sweats ever since we started this whole thing."

J. D. smiled encouragingly and stated, "No problem. Let's go back to my office and review the reports. We have a lot to discuss."

Leonard couldn't wait until they got to J. D.'s office. "Well, is it okay? Did we win them over?" he anxiously asked.

J. D. was not going to share the results in the hallway. He told Leonard, "Let's sit down and give you a chance to read the reports."

"It's not good," Leonard stated through clenched teeth. "I can tell by your answer."

CASE 9.10 *Shapiro v. Shapiro,* 458 A.2d 1257 (1983)

Facts: Harry Shapiro, appellant, and Betty Sue Shapiro, appellee, were married February 14, 1969. The appellant filed for divorce in April 1977, and the parties were in continuous litigation for years. The chancellor heard the case in January 1981, and as part of a two-day hearing, he interviewed the couple's son, Lonnie, in his chambers with a court stenographer. An order was subsequently entered awarding temporary custody of Lonnie to his mother and directing Lonnie, the appellant, and the appellee to undergo psychiatric evaluation by Dr. Robert B. Lehman. The appellant was also ordered to undergo psychiatric treatment with Dr. Lehman in order to work on establishing a relationship between the father and son under Dr. Lehman's guidance. The mother was awarded permanent custody in a February 24, 1982, order. The order provided that the appellant would have no right of visitation with Lonnie until such time as Dr. Lehman *recommended that such visitation shall commence and such visitation shall be on the term as recommended by Dr. Lehman.* The appellant appealed the order.

Issue: Whether it was proper to connect the appellant's visitation with his son to Dr. Lehman's recommendation.

Court's Reasoning: The visitation aspects of the order give us concern. The appellant complains that the order denying him visitation until Dr. Lehman should recommend otherwise effectively denies him visitation permanently because of the doctor's refusal to participate in any further evaluation, consultation, or treatment until the balance of his fee is paid. The first problem with the order is that, in effect, it is a total suspension of visitation and a denial of all access for an indefinite period. Giving Dr. Lehman's recommendation such weight is an invalid delegation of authority by the court. Jurisdiction over custody and visitation, as well as guardianship, legitimation, maintenance, and support of children, is vested in the courts. There is no authority for the delegation of any portion of such jurisdiction to someone outside the court. We find that a provision for limited, structured visitation should be made—if necessary, under a third party designated by the chancellor.

Holding: Reversed and remanded for further proceedings in accordance with this opinion.

Case Discussion: The court can always base its decision on the opinions of others, but the final decision must always be the court's alone. Do you have any ethical concerns regarding the doctor's refusal to participate in any treatment without payment?

J. D. had never been so glad that his office was one of the first in a long hallway. "Here we are," he congenially announced, as he stepped aside to let Leonard enter. "Please sit, and I'll get us some coffee."

Leonard replied, "None for me, I'm as edgy as a cat in the rain. Just give it to me straight."

J. D. abandoned the coffee idea and sat down, preparing to give the news to Leonard "straight." He said, "Our psychologist was very positive about you, and her psychologist was very positive about her. That was expected. The bottom line of the court-appointed psychologist's report is that you and your wife are, and I quote, *inappropriately prioritizing their children's needs,* end quote." J. D. concluded, "The court psychologist thinks the whole family needs therapy to deal with the self-induced trauma of the divorce."

Leonard looked crushed by the news and inquired, "Does it get any better with the GAL?"

J. D. took a deep breath and answered, "The GAL supports the therapy suggestion and thinks joint custody may work, and I quote again, *if the parents can rise above their hate for each other and think about their kids*, end quote."

Leonard dejectedly inquired, "What now?"

J. D. answered, "Well, remember, your wife is hearing the same news. I'd like to talk to her attorney and do a little fishing to see if we can get together and support the GAL."

Leonard did not know if he was ready to give up. He asked, "You mean end this now?"

J. D. responded quickly, "I can't say with 100 percent certainty that the judge will follow the recommendations, but this judge usually gives the recommendations heavy consideration. If we can all agree, then we'll at least have a say in the custody decision rather than waiting for the unknown."

Leonard was bone-tired. His children were anxious all the time, and he knew his soon-to-be ex-wife was at her wit's end. Time had allowed him to realize his anger at his wife's affairs had colored his thinking about custody. He knew a trial would be the last straw for the family. He also felt that after a trial, whatever the outcome, there would be little likelihood of the family ever resuming anything resembling a normal life. "Okay," Leonard told J. D. "Please make it happen."

J. D. knew that all the Baxters had been riding an emotional rollercoaster for months, so he succinctly answered, "I'll do my best."

A week later, a mentally exhausted, not to mention financially depleted, Helen and Leonard finally decided on a custody arrangement that they thought would work for both them and their children. Helen and Leonard are still ironing out the final details, but they have agreed to decide between two custody arrangements jointly proposed by the psychologists and the guardian *ad litem*. Read the Proposed Custody Clauses A and B in Exhibit 9.3. Note that Helen is Party A and Leonard is Party B. Which custody clause do you think the Baxters will agree upon?

EXHIBIT 9.3 Write It Down: Proposed Custody and Visitation Clauses

Note: *Proposed Child Visitation Clause A is a typical clause that would be included in a settlement agreement if Sample Child Custody Clause A was used.*

Proposed Child Custody Clause A: *Party A and Party B agree that they will share joint legal custody of the minor children, Leonard, Jr., Megan, and Michael. The Parties agree that Part B will have physical custody of the children during the school year. The Parties agree that Party A will have physical custody of the children during the summer school recess and all other school holidays.*

Proposed Child Visitation Clause A: *The Parties agree that the children will visit Party A on every weekend, beginning at 10 A.M. Saturday morning and ending at 6 P.M. Sunday evening, while the children are residing with Party B. The Parties agree that Party A may telephone the children each evening while the children are residing with Party B. The Parties agree that when the children are residing with Party A, then Party B will have visitation with the children on every weekend, beginning at 10 A.M. Saturday morning and ending at 6 P.M. Sunday evening. The Parties agree that Party B may telephone the children each evening while the children are residing with Party A.*

Proposed Child Custody Clause B: *Party A and Party B agree that they will share joint legal and physical custody of the minor children, Leonard, Jr., Megan, and Michael. The parties understand that joint legal custody will give each parent equal say in the upbringing of the children. This includes decisions regarding the health, welfare, religious training, and schooling of the children. The children will each reside at their mother and father's homes, alternating weeks in residence. Party A and B plan to continue to reside in the same town so that the children may continue to attend their same schools. Both Party A and Party B agree that the children will alternate all holidays with their parents. The Parties agree that Party A may telephone the children each evening while the children are residing with Party B. The Parties agree that Party B may telephone the children each evening while the children are residing with Party A.*

LIVING WITH THE FINAL CUSTODY ORDER

The Baxters decided to use Proposed Child Custody Clause B as the foundation for their custody agreement. They still have to do some work to iron out the details, but at least the major decision has been made, and it will be smoother sailing for the exhausted Baxter family from now on.

The problem is, not every parent can with live the final custody order. Both parents may start off pleased with a jointly made custody decision, but later, one or both of them may have regrets. Even an experienced judge who is caught in the middle of two warring parents can arrive at a custody decision that looks good when it is made but in actuality does nothing to end the war. When one of the parents believes a change in custody or visitation is necessary, that parent can make a **motion for modification** of the child custody order. The request for a change is initiated by filing a motion with the court clerk and appearing before a judge for a scheduled hearing. The other parent receives a copy of the motion for modification of the custody order and has an opportunity to hire legal counsel and argue against the motion during the hearing.

Sometimes one of the parents returns to court not to modify a custody or visitation order, but to enforce his rights to custody or visitation. A parent who has a court order allowing visitation but is prevented by the other parent from seeing the children has the option of returning to court to have the original order enforced.

Requesting a Modification in Custody: One Court Is Slow to Change

The case of *Palmore v. Sidoti* (see Case 9.11) is a good example of just how slow change comes to some courts. This case involved a request for modification of custody based on the fact that the custodial parent's new partner, a black man, had moved into the home with the children. In light of the progress made in race relations in America, it is somewhat surprising that in the late twentieth century, a white mother could still fear losing her children because of her relationship with an African-American man. The United States Supreme Court stepped in to prevent the lower courts from ordering a change in custody, in effect sanctioning racial discrimination.

Effect of Sexual Orientation on Custody Modification

Society changed dramatically in the last half of the twentieth century, but not all courts chose to keep pace with societal shifts. The question in the case of *M.J.P. v. J.G.P.* (see Case 9.12) deals with the issue of whether a homosexual parent rather than a heterosexual parent should have custody of a 2½-year-old boy. Although this case took place years later, there does not seem to have been much movement away from the trial court's position in the earlier Nadler decision. (The trial court in *Nadler* was found to have erred in declaring that a homosexual person is not a fit or proper person to have custody of a child as a matter of law.)

The Child's Role in Modification: The Smallest Voice Heard

Generally, judges who are asked to decide a custody dispute ask the children involved whom they wish to live with. However, the age of the children is always taken into consideration, and there is no guarantee that Johnny, Jr., will get to live with his choice of parent. In *Goldstein v. Goldstein* (see Case 9.13, p. 298), the court decided to follow the wishes of a 9-year-old girl over the objections of her mother.

CASE 9.11 *Palmore v. Sidoti,* 466 U.S. 429, 104 S. Ct. 1979 (1984)

Facts: The biological father brought a petition for modification of the custody arrangement regarding the parties' daughter. The father's petition claimed the custody should be altered due to the mother cohabitating with, and planning to marry, an African American. Additionally, the father made several allegations of instances in which the mother had not properly cared for the child. The Florida trial court awarded custody, based on changed circumstances, to the father. The court concluded that the child's best interests would be served by the change in custody. The mother appealed. The Florida District Court of Appeals affirmed, and certiorari was granted by the United States Supreme Court.

Issue: Whether the race of a stepparent will warrant the modification of a custody order.

Court's Reasoning: Chief Justice Burger delivered the opinion to the court. After hearing testimony from both parties and considering a court counselor's investigative report, the court noted that the father had made allegations about the child's care, but the court made no findings with respect to these allegations. On the contrary, the court made a finding that *there is no issue as to either party's devotion to the child, adequacy of housing facilities, or respectability of the new spouse of either parent.* The court then addressed the recommendations of the court counselor. The court noted the counselor's recommendation for a change in custody because *the wife has chosen for herself, and for her child, a lifestyle unacceptable to the father and to society. The child will be subject to environmental pressures not of her choice.*

The lower court's opinion raised important federal concerns arising from the Constitution's commitment to eradicating discrimination based on race. The Florida court did not focus directly on the parental qualification of the natural mother or her present husband, or indeed on the father's qualifications to have custody of the child.

The lower court correctly stated that the child's welfare was the controlling factor. The court was entirely candid and made no effort to place its holding on any ground other than race. Taking the court's findings and rationale at face value, it is clear that the outcome would have been different had the petitioner married a Caucasian male.

A core of the Fourteenth Amendment was to do away with all governmental discrimination based on race. Classifying persons according to their race is more likely to reflect racial prejudice than legitimate public concerns. Such classifications are subject to the most *exacting scrutiny. They must be justified by a compelling governmental interest* and must be *necessary to the accomplishment of their legitimate purpose* to pass constitutional muster.

The goal of granting custody based on the best interests of the child is indisputably a substantial governmental interest for purposes of the equal protection clause. We would be ignoring reality to suggest that racial and ethnic prejudices do not exist, or that all manifestations of those prejudices have been eliminated. There is a risk that a child living with a stepparent of a different race may be subject to a variety of pressures and stress not present if the child were living with parents of the same racial or ethnic origin. The question, however, is whether the reality of private biases and the possible injury they might inflict are permissible considerations for removal of an infant child from the custody of its natural mother. We have little difficulty concluding that they are not. The Constitution cannot control such prejudices, but neither can it tolerate them. Private biases may be outside the reach of the law, but the law cannot, directly or indirectly, give them effect.

Holding: Reversed.

Case Discussion: Do you think that society's prejudicial reaction to a parent's lifestyle and its effect on the children should play a part in a court's custody analysis? If race is removed from the facts, do you think that a custody arrangement should be altered if a custodial parent decides to share his home with a new romantic partner? Do you think it would be a good idea for divorcing parents to include in their settlement agreement, and thus in their final judgment, that if either parent cohabits with a romantic partner without benefit of marriage, custody arrangements will have to be modified in a clearly defined way?

CASE 9.12 *M.J.P. v. J.G.P.,* 40 P.2d 966 (1982)

Facts: The parents were divorced in August 1978, and custody of the 2½-year-old child was given to the mother. The mother, along with the 2½-year-old son, moved into her lesbian lover's home to live with her lover and her lover's 12-year-old son. The 2½-year-old child, J., slept in the same bedroom with his mother and her lover, with only a screen separating the two beds. The two women were open about their homosexual relationship with everyone, including the 12-year-old child. They admitted to engaging in certain lovers' caresses in J.'s presence. The father of the younger child motioned for a change in custody based on his ex-wife's living arrangements being a significant change in circumstances.

Dr. Betsy Walloch, a specialist in child and adolescent psychiatry, testified at the custody hearing that children growing up in a homosexual environment were essentially no different with respect to their development from children growing up in a single-parent household. Furthermore, Dr. Walloch testified that in her professional opinion, children develop their sexual identity between the ages of 3 and 5 years old, and J. was masculine. However, Dr. Walloch did state that problems could occur for the child later if he were to be questioned by his grandparents, his father, or even his friends about his mother's homosexuality. Dr. Walloch testified that this type of confrontation between the morals set forth in society and the situation in which he grew up could be very detrimental to him.

Issue: Whether an acknowledged, open homosexual relationship involving the custodial parent was shown by the facts to be a sufficient change of circumstances to warrant modification of a child custody order.

Court's Reasoning: In any case involving a minor child, the standard on which the decision is to be based must remain steadfast as to what is best for the minor child. In this case, the change of residence in which the mother moved into her lover's home is enough to mandate a change in custody, in keeping what is in the best interests of the child. The fact that J. may at some point in his life be faced with a struggle to reject either society's morals, his own religious beliefs, or his mother's lifestyle forces the court to believe that to remain with his mother could be detrimental to him in some way. A change in custody is mandatory.

Holding: Affirmed.

Case Discussion: Do you think this case would have the same result if it were decided today, more than 20 years later?

CASE 9.13 *Goldstein v. Goldstein,* 115 R.I. 152, 341 A.2d 51 (1975)

Facts: This case has its roots in an August 4, 1970, decision granting the husband custody of Ann Robin and granting visitation rights to the wife. Shortly after the entry of that decree, the husband and child left Rhode Island to reside in Israel. For three years, the wife continued to request modification of the custody. Finally, in 1973, the husband appeared in Rhode Island to respond to the wife's modification motion. Again, the husband prevailed. The trial judge hearing the motion heard testimony from 9-year-old Ann and, based on her testimony, decided she should stay with her father. The mother appealed, and the case was then heard by the Rhode Island Supreme Court.

Issue: Whether the family court judge abused his discretion by giving weight to the preferences of a minor child.

Court's Reasoning: While in chambers with the judge, the child told the judge that she wished to return to Israel with her father. The child said she had no desire to visit with her mother, but agreed, after the trial judge's urgings, that it would be a fair bargain if he were to condition her being allowed to live with her father in Israel upon her willingly visiting with her mother for four weeks during each summer.

The wife argues that the trial judge, instead of considering all the circumstances of the case, allowed the child's choice to control his decision. It appears from the record that all pertinent facts were simply placed on the scale together, with the relevant considerations weighed by the trial judge, such as the parties' equal suitability to have custody, the psychiatric evidence of the child's emotional stability and intelligence, the child's demeanor with the judge, and the judge's obvious conclusion that her expressed desire to be with her father was not a mere whim and was entitled to substantial weight. In light of all this, the parents were so nearly in a state of equality that it does not seem to us that the judge abused his discretion.

Holding: Appeal denied.

Case Discussion: The trial judge provided that the cost of transporting Ann for the summer visit would be carried by the father and that the father would have to post a bond to ensure that this airfare would be paid. The judge also ordered that the custody and visitation arrangements would be reviewed after the 1975 visitation. Do you think the child's opinion should be weighed equally with all the other factors discussed? If so, can you foresee any problems that might occur as a result?

ENFORCEMENT OF CUSTODY AND VISITATION ORDERS

A family court judge who has invested the court's time, perhaps even through a trial, will not take kindly to a final judgment being ignored. A person who decides to ignore a court order regarding custody and visitation may find herself being hauled back into court to respond to contempt of court charges. A parent found guilty of contempt of court may face a monetary fine, jail time, or both.

Visitation Dispute Lands Mom in Jail

In the past few years, the media has reported several cases involving divorced mothers who refused to allow their children to visit with their fathers. One such case eventually landed on the desk of President George

Bush. The media reported that Dr. Elizabeth Morgan, a physician, believed that her ex-husband was sexually abusing their infant daughter during the daughter's visits with her father. The father vehemently denied the allegations. The father's visitation with the daughter was provided for in the court's final judgment of divorce. Dr. Morgan did not care. She hid her daughter. This angered the father, and he went back to court to enforce the visitation arrangements in the court's final judgment of divorce.

Apparently, Dr. Morgan was unable to positively prove the sexual abuse allegations, even with several specialists testifying, so the judge ordered her to allow the father visitation rights and to produce the missing daughter. Dr. Morgan refused and was sent to county jail for contempt of court. To some people, she became the symbol of a mother's love after spending a record number of days in jail because of a contempt of court charge. This is where President Bush came in. The president commuted her sentence without forcing her to produce her daughter. So where was the daughter all this time? Dr. Morgan had enlisted her parents' help, and her daughter had been secretly living with her grandparents in New Zealand.

Do you think Dr. Morgan should have been sent to jail for failing to disclose the whereabouts of her daughter to the judge? In the same circumstances, would you have been willing to go to jail?

Ignoring a Custody Order: Facing the Fear of Parental Kidnapping

The intent behind the UCCJA was to create uniformity in the handling of jurisdictional disputes in custody cases. The act achieved only limited success, however, because of the variations in the act as adopted by each of the states and the differences in interpretation from court to court. Consequently, forum shopping and the flow of children and cases from state to state continued. Federal legislation was needed to bolster the UCCJA in each state and to enhance uniformity in interpretation.

In 1980, the Parental Kidnapping Prevention Act (PKPA) was created. The title of the act is somewhat misleading, as it is not limited to criminal matters relating to kidnapping. Rather, one principal purpose of the PKPA was to protect the right of a decree-issuing state to exercise *exclusive continuing jurisdiction* over its child custody order. The act channels custody litigation into the court having continuing jurisdiction by requiring states (1) to give full faith and credit to the custody decrees of states retaining jurisdiction and (2) to refrain from issuing competing decrees. The PKPA has eliminated states' disregarding foreign decrees because of differences in the states' statutory enactments or jurisdictional interpretations. Most importantly, the PKPA has created a separate basis for exclusive continuing jurisdiction. As long as the original decree state continues to have jurisdiction under its own law, and remains the residence of the child or any party to the custody dispute, it has exclusive continuing jurisdiction over all future custody actions involving that child. Read the PKPA in Appendix C. The case of *Barndt v. Barndt* (see Case 9.14) provides an excellent example of how this act has been applied.

Dealing with International Parental Kidnapping

One especially difficult situation is created when a noncustodial parent who resides outside the United States kidnaps his child and takes the child back to his country. The legal drama this can cause was exemplified a few years ago when the film actress Sally Field brought the true-life story of Betty Mahmoody to the screen.[9] In the film entitled *Not Without My Daughter,* Field plays the wife of an Iranian doctor, Sayyed Bozorg Mahmoody, who was practicing medicine in Michigan. In 1984, on the pretext of taking the family for a two-week visit with his family in Iran, Moody, as he was called, took his American wife and young daughter, Mahtob, to Iran, having decided in advance that they would stay there and live under strict Muslim code. Field's character, Betty Mahmoody, went with her husband to Iran. There, she found that under Iran's fundamentalist Islamic law, she felt like a prisoner in her own home. She was also a prisoner of the country

CASE 9.14 *Barndt v. Barndt*, 580 A.2d 320 (1990)

Facts: Joel and Kathleen Barndt were married in 1977 and divorced in 1983. North Dakota had been the marital domicile. Joel adopted Kathleen's son, Michael, and the couple had a son, Kristopher, together. Kathleen had custody of the boys through a North Dakota order. Joel lived in North Dakota until December 1985, when he moved into his parents' home in Pennsylvania. In June 1986, the boys visited Pennsylvania, and Joel refused to return the children as agreed. Instead, he petitioned and received a modification of custody order from Columbia County Court in Pennsylvania. Kathleen appealed to the North Dakota courts, who declined to issue an order that would conflict with Pennsylvania's order. Kathleen was finally given an opportunity to appeal the Pennsylvania order in May 1988 in Columbia County.

Issue: Whether the courts of Pennsylvania had subject matter jurisdiction to hear the modification of custody petition of the father.

Court's Reasoning: The undisputed facts establish that even if subject matter jurisdiction could be asserted under Pennsylvania law, the PKPA, a federal statute, prevents jurisdiction under the facts of the case. The PKPA prevails over any contrary laws of the states in the area of recognition and modification of a sister state's custody decree.

Holding: Jurisdiction relinquished to the courts of North Dakota.

Case Discussion: The *Barndt* case clearly shows that the federal government wants each state to deal with custody and visitation matters. In fact, the promotion of the PKPA by the federal government and federal courts shows their unwillingness to take on the job of dealing with family law. Do you think one set of federal divorce laws would be a more efficient means of dealing with issues such as custody and visitation? Do you have any problem with the federal government usurping the states in an area of the law that historically has been left to the states?

because under Islamic law, her marriage to Moody made her a citizen of Iran, and Moody refused to allow her to leave the country with their daughter because he knew full well that they would never return. Risking brutal physical punishment and possibly even death, Betty decided to leave Iran and her husband at any cost. During her 18-month stay in Iran, she secretly planned her escape with her daughter. Her successful escape took place in harsh February weather and involved a five-day trek, by foot and on horseback, over the treacherous Iranian-Turkish mountains, along a smuggler's trail, into Turkey.[10]

Applying The Hague Convention

In the best of circumstances, Sally Field's character, Betty Mahmoody, should have been able to deal with the custody dispute via international law. Custody disputes involving parents who wish to reside in two different countries may involve the international law that was enacted at **The Hague Convention on the Civil Aspects of International Child Abduction** also known simply as *The Hague Convention* or *The Convention.* The international custody laws that were created and enacted through treaties between the signatory nations were the international community's answer to custody disputes.

The Hague Convention is part of United States federal law because the United States agreed to comply with The Hague Convention's requirements. The laws enacted at The Convention provide a detailed procedure to be followed by persons seeking the return of their children who have been wrongfully removed from the United States. Under Article Eight, the processing must be commenced by application to the Central Authority of the country where the children are believed to be. Upon receipt, the Central Authority must ascertain the location of the children and work toward their voluntary return.

The problem with The Hague Convention agreement in Betty Mahmoody's case was that when she was living in Iran and dealing with her custody problems, Iran was essentially closed to the rest of the world. Iran was not a signatory of The Hague Convention agreement. In the film, the mother deals with the problem by secretly taking her daughter across the Iranian border and then back to America. Although every parent may root for Fields's character while watching the movie, they should also note that *the mother took the daughter without a valid custody order from either an American or an Iranian court.*

In another case, *In the Matter of David S. v. Zamira S.* (see Case 9.15), The Hague Convention agreement was put into action effectively. In this case, the two parents were in dispute over which parent the child should reside with and, thus, in which country. Remember, a state court hearing a custody dispute, as the one in *David S.* did, must apply The Hague Convention laws to the situation. *The state must do this because federal law supercedes state law.* This is a fundamental part of constitutional law and the supremacy clause of the United States Constitution.

Read the portion of The Hague Convention agreement included in Appendix D. Note, in particular, its instructions to parents.

NEW QUESTIONS IN CUSTODY

As you continue your legal education, you will quickly learn that the laws in the United States are constantly changing and evolving. This constant current of change can be difficult to navigate. For example, until the early twentieth century, American women did not have the right to vote. This changed when the Twenty-First Amendment to the United States Constitution was passed and gave all women the right to vote. How did such a radical change occur in the law?

The changing opinions of the country's citizens helped make the lawmakers in 1920 see how right it was to add the Twenty-First Amendment to the United States Constitution. Thousands of citizens, women and men alike, campaigned for years all over the country. The women who campaigned for the vote were known as trend-setting *suffragists,* and by their critics as *Suffragettes* (a term meant to ridicule them). Once the Twenty-First Amendment passed, the suffragists evolved into the League of Women Voters. Now, in the twenty-first century, the League of Women Voters is an accepted and established part of American society.

A legal version of the classic question "Which came first—the chicken or the egg?" might be: Which came first—the evolving nature of the law with its constant changes, or the constantly changing and evolving nature of the American culture? Perhaps the evolving nature of the law is a natural response to the evolving nature and needs of the American culture. Unless the law keeps pace with the culture, the courts will be at a loss for dealing fairly with those in society. One developing area that constantly outdistances the law is the scientific community. Things that were once thought of as the dreams of science-fiction writers—and fantastic dreams at that—have now been brought startlingly close to home.

The concept of **assisted reproductive technology** is an example of a scientific development that has presented the need for new laws. Even half a century ago, who would have thought that surrogacy, *in vitro* fertilization, and frozen eggs and sperm would become viable reproductive options available to the average

CASE 9.15 *In the Matter of David S. v. Zamira S.,*
151 Misc. 2d 630, 574 N.Y.S.2d 429 (1991)

Facts: The parties were both Canadian nationals. They had two children. Their separation agreement provided that the mother *shall make the son available to the father within the Metropolitan Toronto vicinity.* Their daughter was not yet born when the couple separated. The mother and children left Ontario, and it was ascertained that they had moved to Brooklyn, New York. The father followed the procedures set forth in The Hague Convention to secure the return of the children. The Ontario Ministry of the Attorney General forwarded an application for the return of the children to the United States Department of State. This is the agency designated as the Central Authority pursuant to The Hague Convention with responsibility for carrying out its provisions. Subsequently, the Department of State communicated with the New York State Clearinghouse for Missing and Exploited Children. Meanwhile, the Supreme Court of Ontario had made a finding that the mother wrongfully and improperly removed the children from Ontario and evaded or refused service, although duly served with an order from their court. The mother appealed in a New York court, asking to be allowed to stay in Brooklyn.

Issue: Whether the petitioner has shown by a preponderance of the evidence that the removal of the children was wrongful.

Court's Reasoning: The mother was duly notified that there was a court order, but nonetheless, she left the country. The mother contended that the father was not entitled under The Hague Convention to have their son returned to Canada because the father had only visitation rights, not custody. This argument might have had merit, except for the mother's contemptuous conduct and the subsequent temporary custody order issued by the Ontario court. Plus, the separation agreement overlooked the custody of the unborn daughter. Upon her birth, the father had an equal right to custody when the mother left Ontario. The mother did not rebut the father's rights when she argued that her need to be in Brooklyn was greater than the father's rights because she *needs to be closer to the population of available Orthodox Jewish men and search for a new husband.* This court finds that the Ontario Supreme Court's order constituted a declaration that the removal or retention of the children was wrongful within the meaning of Article Three of The Hague Convention. Accordingly, this court gives full faith and credit to the orders of the Ontario court.

Holding: Petitioner wins. Both children should be returned to Ontario where a preliminary hearing may be held in accordance with the Ontario Supreme Court's order to determine the issues of interim custody and visitation. The father should immediately advise this court and the Central Authority upon the children's return.

Case Discussion: Note that the New York court did not determine the custody issue; they left that to the Ontario court. This case, with its application of The Hague Convention agreement, was all about jurisdiction.

American citizen? A relatively few years ago, a man and woman who wanted a child but were unable to conceive had only one option—adoption. Now the miracles of reproductive science have, for better or worse, expanded the options of an infertile couple beyond adoption. This is where the concept of surrogacy begins. **Surrogacy** in this context is the act of one female standing in for another female during pregnancy. A man who is physically able to be a father but whose female partner is unable to conceive can find hope in surrogacy. Using **artificial insemination,** the female **surrogate mother** conceives a child without having sexual intercourse with the father. The word *artificial* is used because there is no sexual contact between the biological parents.

During the last 25 years, thousands of American children have been born through *in vitro* fertilization, the best known of several methods of assisted reproduction. Specifically, the process known as *in vitro* **fertilization (IVF)** involves the mixing of sperm with retrieved eggs outside the womb. Once fertilized, the eggs can then be implanted in a uterus. Eggs that have been penetrated by sperm but have not yet been implanted in a uterus are called prezygotes. Today, tens of thousands of embryos are frozen annually and are routinely stored in liquid nitrogen canisters. Some have been in that state for more than 10 years, and some have been stored with no instructions for their use or disposal.[11]

How Does the Law Keep Up with Science?

While scientists continue to push the envelope, the law scurries to keep up. Where does that leave the legal professional who has been trained to argue a client's case using case precedent and applicable statutory authority? Imagine what thoughts would have raced through your mind if you had been a paralegal working on the very first surrogacy dispute. No applicable precedent existed yet. How could you begin to apply existing precedent and statutory authority to a fact pattern that had never been presented to a court? Recall that when a court has never ruled on the legal issue in a case, that case is known as a case of first impression.

The New Jersey case of *In the Matter of Baby M,* 109 N.J. 396, 537 A.2d 1227 (1988), was a case of first impression. At its most fundamental level, the *Baby M.* case (see Case 9.16) concerned a custody dispute between the unmarried mother and father of a child. The next level made the case more complicated. Mary Beth Whitehead had signed a contract agreeing to be artificially inseminated by the father, to carry the child to term, and then to terminate her parental rights to the child. The termination of parental rights would give the wife of the biological father freedom to adopt the child. When reading about the *Baby M.* case, keep in mind the arguments used in this case of first impression. The New Jersey Supreme Court granted direct certification. **Direct certification** means that the state's highest court will hear the appeal without the intermediate appellate court having to hear the case first.

At first glance, it appears that the miracle of birth would lead everyone involved to a happy ending. However, whenever science is several steps ahead of the law, problems are bound to occur. Mary Beth Whitehead, the surrogate mother, and William Stern, the father, entered relatively uncharted legal waters when they signed a surrogacy contract in the early 1980s.

Throughout the 1980s, the law in the United States was generally unsettled on the question of surrogacy. Meanwhile, the law in the United Kingdom has been settled on the surrogacy question since Parliament passed the Surrogacy Arrangements Act in 1985. The British act makes participating in a surrogacy contract, or even negotiating such a contract, a criminal act.

In the United States, three different decisions from New York, Kentucky, and Michigan exemplify the inconsistency of courts in dealing with surrogacy contracts. In 1986, a New York court approved an adoption in an uncontested surrogacy arrangement in the case of *In the Matter of Adoption of Baby Girl,* 132 Misc. 2d 972, 505 N.Y.S.2d 813 (1986). The New York court expressed concern regarding the morality of such an arrangement, but approved the adoption because it was in the best interests of the child. The Supreme Court of Kentucky, in *Surrogate Parenting Associates v. Commonwealth ex. rel. Armstrong,* 704 S.W.2d 209 (Ky. 1989), differentiated between surrogacy and the state's baby-selling statutes and found a surrogacy contract to be legal, as long as the surrogate mother had the right to void the contract if she changed her mind within a short period of time after the birth. The opposite result was reached by a Michigan court, however, when it found surrogacy contracts to be void and contrary to public policy.

CASE 9.16 *In the Matter of Baby M, a Pseudonym for an Actual Person,* 109 N.J. 396, 537 A.2d 1227 (1988)

Facts: William and Elizabeth Stern married in 1974 after meeting in graduate school. The Sterns decided to put off starting a family until after Elizabeth Stern finished her medical training (she later became a pediatrician) and the couple's finances were stabilized. Any thoughts of starting a family were put aside when Elizabeth Stern was diagnosed with multiple sclerosis. Testimony during the trial suggested that Mrs. Stern's anxiety over the perceived risk that pregnancy would precipitate blindness, paraplegia, or some other form of debilitation might have exceeded the actual risk. Mr. Stern's family had been destroyed in the Holocaust, and as the only survivor, Mr. Stern very much wanted to continue his bloodline.

Both the Sterns, Mary Beth Whitehead, and Richard Whitehead, Mary Beth's husband and the father of her two children, became aware of ICNY, an infertility clinic, from its advertising. Mrs. Whitehead contacted ICNY and was informed that a $10,000 fee was paid to surrogate mothers. The Whiteheads were suffering from severe financial problems. The Sterns and the Whiteheads met at ICNY, decided to enter the surrogacy contract, and a female child was born March 27, 1986. From the first moment the child was born, Mrs. Whitehead did not want to part with the child. However, she complied with the contract and gave the child to the Sterns. Mrs. Whitehead soon became extremely distraught. She asked the Sterns if she could care for the child for one week. The Sterns believed Mrs. Whitehead would return the child and turned the child over to her. Mrs. Whitehead refused to return the child after the one week, and Mr. Stern went to court for an order enforcing the surrogacy contract. The court granted Mr. Stern's motion for the court order. However, Mr. and Mrs. Whitehead had already fled to Florida with the child. Four months and *twenty* different residences later, the Whiteheads were forced by Florida police to turn over the child.

The Sterns then received a court order giving them custody of the child and giving Mary Beth Whitehead limited visitation with the child. The Sterns filed a complaint at the trial level seeking enforcement of the surrogacy contract. The contract had included language terminating Mary Beth Whitehead's parental rights to the child. A 32-day trial over a period of two months resulted in the surrogacy contract being found valid, Mrs. Whitehead's parental rights being terminated, and sole custody being given to Mr. Stern. Mrs. Stern was immediately allowed to adopt the child as per the surrogacy contract. Mrs. Whitehead appealed, and the New Jersey Supreme Court granted direct certification.

Issues: (1) Whether the surrogacy contract between Mary Beth Whitehead and William Stern should be upheld when it violates the existing statutes governing adoption, termination of parental rights, private placement adoptions, and the public policies of the state of New Jersey as expressed in its statutory and decisional law. (2) Whether a judgment of adoption can stand when parental rights were not legally terminated.

Court's Reasoning: The New Jersey Supreme Court concluded that the surrogacy contract was invalid based on its direct conflict with existing statutes and the public policies of the state of New Jersey as expressed in its statutory and decisional law. The court found that the surrogacy contract violated: (1) laws prohibiting the use of money in connection with adoptions when money was paid and accepted in direct violation of N.J.S.A. § 9:3-54c; (2) laws requiring proof of parental unfitness before termination of parental rights is ordered when the trial court affirmatively stated, in fact, that Mary Beth Whitehead was found to be a good mother to her other children; and (3) laws that make surrender of custody and consent to adoption revocable in private placement adoptions when the contract never gave Mary Beth Whitehead the option to rescind her decision. The trial court's award of specific performance of the original surrogacy contract reflected its view that the consent to surrender the child was irrevocable and, therefore, erroneous.

In regard to public policy of this state, this court found that the surrogacy contract was based on principles that are directly *contrary* to the objectives of New Jersey's laws. The surrogacy contract guaranteed permanent separation of the child from one of its natural parents, while the state's policy has long been that, to the extent possible, children should remain with, and be brought up by, both their natural parents.

Mrs. Whitehead's rights as a mother are restored, but are limited by the child's best interests being established by having the child live with Dr. Stern and his wife.

Holdings: (1) The surrogacy contract cannot be upheld because it directly conflicts with the existing statutes governing adoption, termination of parental rights, private placement adoptions, and the public policies of this state as expressed in its statutory and decisional law. (2) A judgment of adoption cannot stand when parental rights have not been legally terminated.

Case Discussion: The surrogacy contract was declared invalid. Furthermore, since the three experts appointed by the court, as well as the Stern's experts, unanimously and persuasively recommended custody by the Sterns, and since none of the Whiteheads' experts unequivocally stated, or even implied, that custody should be with the Whiteheads, the court gave sole custody to the Sterns and remanded the case back to the trial court for the sole purpose of determining the visitation rights of Mrs. Whitehead.

Mrs. Whitehead was found to have visitation rights to the child. She was granted some weekend, holiday, and summer visitation. Do you think the court should have granted the biological mother visitation rights? Despite the fact that the law did not permit the surrogacy contract used in this case, nowhere did it find any legal prohibition against surrogacy when the surrogate mother volunteers, without any payment, to act as a surrogate if given the right to change her mind and assert her parental rights. Moreover, the legislature remains free to deal with this most sensitive issue as it sees fit, subject only to constitutional restraints.

The increase in surrogacy contracts and the assortment of disputes arising from them led to the creation of the **Uniform Status of Children of Assisted Conception Act (USCACA)** in 1988. Interestingly, the USCACA presented two models for the states to choose from. One model regulated agreements and supported judicial review. The other model made surrogacy agreements against public policy. A little over a decade later, 25 states had developed statutory or case law on the issue.[12]

Genetic Versus Gestational Mothers: Defining Parental Rights in the New Millennium

The *Baby M.* case only addressed one issue—that of parental rights when a child is born because of a surrogacy arrangement. This issue involved the rights of the biological father versus the rights of the biological, but surrogate, mother. In the *Baby M.* case, Mary Beth Whitehead, the surrogate, used her own eggs and carried the fertilized egg in her uterus for nine months. In the next case, *McDonald v. McDonald* (see Case 9.17) the significant difference is that the gestational mother and the genetic mother were two *different* women. The husband attempted to use this difference to gain custody of his biological child. The court was asked by the husband to differentiate between a gestational and genetic mother.

CASE 9.17 *McDonald v. McDonald,* 608 N.Y.S.2d 477 (App. Div. 1994)

Facts: Mr. and Mrs. McDonald were married in 1988. The wife was unable to conceive naturally, but was able to conceive through *in vitro* fertilization (IVF). Specifically, the husband's sperm was mixed with the eggs of a female donor and implanted in the wife. The wife gave birth to twins in 1991. The couple then divorced, and the husband sued for sole custody and to sever all connection between the children and the former spouse. The husband sought to have the children declared illegitimate or to be found genetically and legally his on the grounds that he was the only genetic and natural parent available. He also requested that the children's surname on their birth certificates be changed from the wife's maiden name to his surname. The wife opposed and was granted temporary custody. The husband appealed.

Issue: Whether the wife is the natural mother of the children conceived by IVF from donor eggs and the husband's sperm.

Court's Reasoning: This court finds that in a true egg donation situation, where a woman gestates and gives birth to a child formed from the egg of another woman with the intent to raise the child as her own, the birth mother is the natural mother. The record shows that the husband is the genetic father of the children and that the interests of the children will be substantially promoted by changing their birth certificates to make their surnames the same as their father's.

Holding: Gestational mother wins, and a change in surnames on the birth certificates is ordered.

Discussion: Can you imagine the husband's shock when his children were not given his last name on their birth certificates? Do you think the birth certificates may have had something to do with the father's claims? Can you imagine the wife's shock when her husband claimed she had no genetic ties to the children and, therefore, he should be given sole custody? Do you agree with the outcome?

Birth Mother Seeks Custody

The case of *Johnson v. Calvert* (see Case 9.18) puts a different spin on facts similar to those in the *McDonald* case. In *Johnson*, the **surrogate gestational mother** agreed to carry the genetic child of Mr. and Mrs. Calvert. The surrogate gestational mother had no genetic link to the child she was carrying. Do you think the experience of carrying a child and giving birth gives a surrogate gestational mother a right to the child? Read the *Johnson* case to see if you agree with the court's decision. The term **genetic parents** is used in the case to define the individuals who provided the egg and sperm.

Assisted Reproductive Technology and the Law

What does one do with stored eggs, sperm, and prezygotes? A small minority of states have seen the legal writing on the wall and have attempted to head off problems by adopting statutes dealing with reproductive technology and disposition of stored genetic material. For example, Florida, a member of this minority, now requires couples to execute written agreements providing for the disposition of embryos in the event of the death, divorce, or other unforeseen circumstance involving the couple who stored the embryos. The statutes cannot be written fast enough to deal with the potential problems. For example, one embattled New Jersey couple's divorce was centered over the custody of prezygotes because the husband wanted the eggs

CASE 9.18 *Johnson v. Calvert,* 5 Cal. 4th 84 851 P.2d 776 (1993)

Facts: Mark and Crispina Calvert wanted to have a child. Unfortunately, Crispina was forced to have a hysterectomy in 1984. Her ovaries, however, remained capable of producing eggs, and the couple eventually considered surrogacy. In 1989, Anna Johnson heard about Crispina's plight from a coworker and offered to serve as a surrogate for the Calverts. On January 15, 1990, Mark, Crispina, and Anna signed a contract providing that an embryo created by the sperm of Mark and the egg of Crispina would be implanted in Anna. The agreement clearly stated that the child born would be taken into Mark and Crispina's home as their child. Anna agreed to relinquish all parental rights to the child in favor of Mark and Crispina. In return, Mark and Crispina agreed to pay Anna $10,000 in a series of installments, the last to be paid six weeks after the child's birth. Mark and Crispina were also to pay for a $200,000 life insurance policy with the beneficiary being Anna's 3-year-old daughter.

Unfortunately, relations deteriorated between the two sides. At the custody trial in October 1990, the parties stipulated that Mark and Crispina were the child's genetic parents. The trial court heard the evidence and ruled that the Calverts were the child's genetic, biological, and natural father and mother. The trial court terminated the visitation order Anna had been granted earlier and declared that Anna had no parental rights to the child. Anna appealed.

Issue: Whether being the gestational mother gives a woman parental rights.

Court's Reasoning: The passage of the Uniform Parentage Act clearly was not motivated by the need to resolve surrogacy disputes, which were virtually unknown in 1975. Yet, it applies to any parentage determination, including the rare case in which a child's maternity is in issue. Because two women each have presented acceptable proof of maternity, we do not believe this case can be decided without inquiring into the parties' intentions as manifested in the surrogacy agreement. Mark and Crispina are a couple who desired to have a child of their own genetic stock, but were physically unable to do so without the help of reproductive technology. The parties' aim was to bring Mark's and Crispina's child into the world, not for Mark and Crispina to donate a zygote to Anna. No reason appears why Anna's later change of heart should affect the fact that Crispina *is* the child's natural mother.

We conclude that, although the Uniform Parentage Act recognized both genetic consanguinity and giving birth as a means of establishing a mother-and-child relationship, when the two means do not coincide in one woman, then she who intended to procreate the child—that is, she who intended to bring about the birth of a child that she intended to raise as her own—is the natural mother under California law.

Holding: Appellant loses.

Case Discussion: Can you understand the gestational mother's attachment to the child she carried for nine months? The writers of the Uniform Parentage Act included giving birth as a way to determine the mother of a child. The court found itself in a situation of updating a statute to fit the scientific development of gestational surrogacy. This case is an excellent example of how the legal system must constantly deal with social and scientific changes.

for implantation in his *future* wife, and the current wife objected to that.[13] Meanwhile, across the country, a California couple litigated child support issues for a child born through a donor egg, donor sperm, and a surrogate mother. (See *Matter of Buzzanca v. Buzzanca,* 61 Cal. App. 4th 1410, 72 Cal. Rptr. 2d 280 (1998).)

What Do We Do with the Prezygotes?

Even though *in vitro* fertilization techniques had existed and been widely used for more than two decades, a dispute over the ownership of fertilized eggs did not reach the appellate level in New York until 1998. *Kass v. Kass* (see Case 9.19) is typical of the scant number of cases that have dealt with assisted reproductive technology issues because the court concluded that disposition of **prezygotes** does not implicate a woman's right of privacy or bodily integrity in the area of reproductive choice; nor are the prezygotes recognized as persons for constitutional purposes. In this case of first impression, although the court used the term *child custody*, the real dispute was over custody of *prezygotes*.

Who Gets the Embryo?

The case of *Davis v. Davis* (see Case 9.20) started as a run-of-the-mill divorce, but the custody issues being disputed soon drew the interest of the press. Mrs. Davis wanted custody of the couple's frozen embryos in order to become pregnant after she and Mr. Davis were divorced. The term *cryogenically preserved* is used in the case. **Cryogenic preservation** of embryos is a process whereby the embryos are frozen in such a way as to allow them to be used for implantation for the purpose of pregnancy.

Procreation Postmortem: Gone, but Not Forgotten

Two cases brought in the 1990s involved procreation postmortem, which is an odd, but interesting concept. In both *Hecht v. Superior Court* and *Hall v. Fertility Institute* (see Case 9.21 and 9.22) cases, children of

---

CASE 9.19 *Kass v. Kass*, 91 N.Y.2d 554 (1998)

Facts: The couple was married in 1988 and immediately began trying to conceive a child. The appellant was unable to become pregnant. The couple unsuccessfully tried artificial insemination and then enrolled in an IVF program. As a result of this process, five preembryos or prezygotes were frozen and stored. The couple signed a consent form for the eventual disposition of their frozen prezygotes. Prezygotes are defined in the court record as eggs that have been penetrated by sperm but have not yet been implanted in a uterus. In 1993, the couple divorced. They executed an uncontested divorce agreement that included a statement regarding the disposition of the five frozen prezygotes as outlined by their consent form. The wife later requested sole custody in order to undergo further pregnancy attempts and was awarded custody. The respondent appealed.

Issue: Whether the consent agreement signed by the parties should be binding as to the disposition of the five frozen prezygotes.

Court's Reasoning: Agreements between donors regarding disposition of their prezygotes should generally be presumed valid and binding and enforced in any dispute between the parties. This court finds that when the parties to an IVF procedure have themselves determined the disposition of any unused fertilized eggs, their agreement should control.

Holding: Appellee wins.

Case Discussion: The court decided this case on pure contract principles. Do you think the court should have rescinded the original contract if the former Mrs. Kass could have proven that the prezygotes were her last chance to become pregnant?

CASE 9.20 *Davis v. Davis*, 842 S.W.2d 588 (1992)

Facts: Beginning in 1985, Mary Sue and Junior Davis went through six attempts at IVF without conceiving. As a result of the IVF procedure, unused embryos were available for cryogenic preservation. The couple did not execute a written agreement specifying the disposition of the frozen embryos. The couple subsequently filed for divorce. The wife originally asked for control of the frozen embryos with the intent to have them transferred to her own uterus in order to become pregnant. The trial court awarded control to the wife. The husband appealed, and the court of appeals reversed and remanded the case to the trial court for entry of an order giving the couple joint control. The wife sought review, contesting the constitutional basis for the court of appeals' decision. However, both parties' positions shifted as both remarried in the interim. The former Mrs. Davis no longer wished to utilize the embryos herself, but wished to donate them to a childless couple. Mr. Davis opposed the donation and wished to have the embryos discarded.

Issue: How disposition of frozen embryos should be determined in the event of contingencies, such as the death of one or more of the parties, divorce, financial reversals, or abandonment of the program.

Court's Reasoning: Ordinarily, the party wishing to avoid procreation should prevail. This is assuming that the other party has a reasonable possibility of achieving parenthood by means other than use of the pre-embryos in question. If no other reasonable alternatives exist, then the argument in favor of using the pre-embryos to achieve pregnancy should be considered. However, if the party seeking control intends merely to donate them to another couple, the objecting party obviously has the greater interest and should prevail. Disputes involving the disposition of preembryos produced by IVF should be resolved, first, by looking to the preferences of the progenitors. If their wishes cannot be ascertained or if there is a dispute, their prior agreement concerning disposition should be carried out. If no prior agreement exists, the relative interests of the parties in using or not using the preembryos must be weighed.

Holding: Junior Davis prevails.

Case Discussion: Unless there was a written agreement otherwise, this court may have allowed the former Mrs. Davis to use the preembryos if she could have proven that this was her only opportunity to become a parent. Do you think this case is a good example of the power of a valid contract? Do you think Mrs. Kass from the case discussed previously would have won if these judges had heard her case?

---

deceased men were fighting to remain the only children while their late fathers' girlfriends were trying to increase size of the families by utilizing the late fathers' stored semen. The term *cryobank* is used in one case. A **cryobank** is a facility for the storage of human matter—in this case, the deceased's semen. Several other terms are used in these two cases, including *vel non, executrix, null,* and *contra bones mores. Vel non* and *contra bones mores* are both Latin terms. ***Vel non*** literally means "or not." ***Contra bones mores*** literally means "against good morals." The **executrix** is a female selected by a person making a will to administer the will and to distribute property after the person making the will dies. Today, the term *executor,* historically used to describe a male administrator of an estate, is often used to describe either a male or female in that role. **Null** means no longer having any legal effect or validity.

Is Artificial Insemination Natural?

The case of *C.M. v. C.C.* (see Case 9.23) has to fall under the heading "It Takes All Kinds." This was another case of first impression.

CASE 9.21 *Hecht v. Superior Court of the County of Los Angeles,* 50 Cal. App. 4th 1289 (1996)

Facts: Deborah Hecht was named in William Everett Kane's will as being bequeathed all right, title, and interest in any specimens of his sperm stored with any sperm bank. In this same will, his Statement of Wishes states that the sample of sperm was for use by Deborah Hecht to become impregnated. The adult children of the decedent blocked Hecht's access to the sperm vials, and thereby prevented her from conceiving a child.

Issue: Whether the beneficiary of the decedent's sperm may use the sperm for conceiving a child over the objections of the decedent's immediate family.

Court's Reasoning: Neither the court nor the decedent's adult children possess reason or right to prevent Hecht from implementing the decedent's preeminent interest in realizing his fundamental right to procreate with the woman of his choice. There is no question regarding the decedent's expressed intent. His will says he created and stored the sperm for the sole purpose of having a child with Hecht and instructs the cryobank preserving his sperm to deliver the sperm only to Hecht.

Holding: The court finds that the sperm must be turned over to Hecht.

CASE 9.22 *Hall v. Fertility Institute of New Orleans,* 647 So. 2d 1348 (La. App. 4th Cir. 1994)

Facts: Barry Hall died on October 29, 1993, of cancer. A sole heir, his son, survived Hall. Following diagnosis of his disease, Barry Hall and Christine St. John met with a doctor at the Fertility Institute to discuss the effects of contemplated chemotherapy on Hall's ability to father children and to find out about preserving his sperm deposits for St. John's artificial insemination at a later date. Hall and St. John executed what they called an Act of Donation before St. John's law partner, Michael Guarisco. This donation conveyed Hall's frozen semen deposits to St. John, in consideration of his *love and affection* for her.

Upon Hall's death, the executrix of Hall's estate, Barry's mother, Mary Alice Hall, sought to have the Act of Donation declared null and asked that the sperm be destroyed. Michael Hall, Hall's only child, provided an affidavit asserting his wish, as next of kin, to bury all his father's remains, including the semen deposits. Michael asserted his belief that had Hall wished to father children by St. John, Hall would have married her, impregnated her before undergoing treatment, or allowed her to be artificially inseminated while he was alive. He also declared that he was suffering extreme emotional upset, embarrassment, and anger at the prospect of the posthumous creation of blood relatives.

Hall's sister, Donna Hall-Whitlock, signed an affidavit declaring that Hall's surviving family was his son, his mother and his sisters, Marsha Hall Hartman, and herself. Donna declared that toward the end of his life, Hall was not responsible for his actions, was heavily sedated against pain, and was at all times under St. John's dominant influence. Donna also stated that she, her sister, and her mother were Hall's primary caretakers during the two years of his illness, and that St. John disclaimed responsibility for Hall. Donna said Hall told her the semen deposit was intended for use when he finished treatment and was cured. She also said that had Hall wished to marry and have a family with St. John, he would have done so.

Issue: Whether St. John has valid rights to the decedent's frozen semen.

Court's Reasoning: The sole issue relevant to disposition of the instant case is the validity *vel non* of the Act of Donation that purports to convey to St. John the decedent's 15 vials of sperm now on deposit with the Institute. This court is remanding the case back to the trial court to determine the factual issue of whether the decedent was competent and not under undue influence at the time the Act of Donation was executed. If the decedent is found to have been competent, the frozen semen is St. John's property, and she has full rights to its disposition.

We find no merit in the executrix's arguments that the Act of Donation should be set aside for reasons of public policy, and we reject the notion that St. John's proposed artificial insemination would be *contra bones mores* in this state.

Holding: St. John wins. Case remanded to the trial court.

Case Discussion: This case and the *Hecht* case are particularly interesting in that they deal with a relatively new technology that is affecting the settling of estates. Both cases are also good examples of how different areas of law can overlap—something the courts have to deal with frequently.

CASE 9.23 *C.M. v. C.C.,* 152 N.J. Super. 160 (1977)

Facts: C.C. and C.M. had been seeing each other for some time and were contemplating marriage. They discussed that C.C. wanted a child by C.M., but did not want to have intercourse with him before their marriage. C.C. learned of a procedure for artificial insemination using a glass syringe and a glass jar. Over a period of several months, the couple attempted the artificial insemination, and after several attempts C.C. conceived a child. C.M. assumed he would act toward the child in the same manner as most fathers act toward their children. However, C.C. did not agree with this, and their relationship broke off. C.M. petitioned for visitation rights as the child's natural father.

Issue: Whether C.M. should be considered the natural father although the sperm used to conceive was transferred to C.C. by other than natural means.

Court's Reasoning: It is in the child's best interests to have two parents whenever possible. In granting custody or visitation, this court will not make any distinction between a child conceived naturally or artificially. In this case, the man wants to take the responsibility of being a father to a child he helped conceive, and the court will not deny him that privilege.

Holding: The court finds C.M. to be the natural father of the child.

Case Discussion: This case's holding echoes the law that has been discussed so far in this text: The biological parent, in this case the father, has a primary right to his child, and the courts are loathe to take that right away. Do you agree?

CHAPTER SUMMARY

Most divorcing parents are able to mutually decide the custody and visitation arrangements for their children. A minority of parents are unable to come to such an agreement without the intervention of the courts. Courts asked to analyze a custody or visitation dispute use the *best interests of the child* test. Psychologists and guardians *ad litem* are among the professionals sometimes called to testify on custody and visitation issues.

There are a variety of types of custody, including: joint, split, shared, legal, and physical custody. Jurisdictional issues may arise during a custody and visitation dispute. The court hearing the dispute must have jurisdiction in the matter. An international custody dispute may involve application of The Hague Convention agreement. The Uniform Child Custody Jurisdiction Act (UCCJA) was enacted in the United States, followed by the enactment of a revised version called the Uniform Child Custody Jurisdiction and Enforcement Act (UCCJEA). Both the UCCJA and the UCCJEA were designed to combat the problem of enforcing child custody orders. The Parental Kidnapping Prevention Act (PKPA) forces every state to give full faith and credit to custody orders if the orders meet due process requirements.

The courts consider numerous factors before making child custody determinations. These factors include: the best interests of the child; biological connection; the *in loco parentis* role; social mores; and third-party rights. As the twentieth century came to a close and the country entered the new millennium, the definition of family continued to evolve. It is not unusual now to find single men and women fulfilling their wishes for children and family by adopting children or utilizing one of the available scientific techniques to aid in conception.

Law has never been static; it continually evolves to reflect changes in society. Scientists continue to push the envelope on what is possible in assisted reproductive technology, and the law scurries to keep up. *In vitro* fertilization (IVF), surrogate gestational mothers, egg donation, and viable prezygotes are all topics that have created new legal questions. The majority of states are enacting legislation to deal with the custody and disposition of frozen and stored prezygotes and other such questions. Most courts adhere to contract principles if a written contract has been created. Without a contract, some courts weigh all the options for each party involved in the dispute. Disputes involving the right to children born with assisted reproductive technology usually are decided in favor of a biological parent, unless the biological parent has agreed to be a surrogate.

Key Terms

best interests of the child
patria potestas
tender years doctrine
Uniform Child Custody
    Jurisdiction Act (UCCJA)
Uniform Child Custody
    Jurisdiction and
    Enforcement Act (UCCJEA)
Parental Kidnapping Prevention
    Act (PKPA)
Violence Against Women Act
    (VAWA)
home state

continuing jurisdiction
forum non conveniens
sole custody
split custody
legal custody
joint custody
physical custody
sua sponte
primary caregiver
supervised visitation
parental alienation syndrome
in loco parentis doctrine
equitable estoppel

de facto parent
psychological parent doctrine
parental rights doctrine
trial *de novo*
guardian *ad litem* (GAL)
advocate
confidentiality waiver
motion for modification
The Hague Convention on the
    Civil Aspects of
    International Child
    Abduction

assisted reproductive technology	direct certification	prezygote
surrogacy	Uniform Status of Children of Assisted Conception Act (USCACA)	cryogenic preservation
artificial insemination		cryobank
surrogate mother	surrogate gestational mother	*vel non*
in vitro fertilization (IVF)	genetic parents	*contra bone mores*
		executrix null

Surfing the Web

http://www.childcustody.org Child custody organizations, nationwide divorce and custody information, and resources for divorce and custody, including issues such as child custody, domestic violence, visitation, child abuse, blended families and child activities, as well as state-specific discussion forums.

http://www.custodysource.com State-by-state child custody and divorce resources.

http://www.acf.dhhs.gov The administration for Children and Families offers Office of Child Support Enforcement links, state and local Title IV-D agencies on the Web, and state-by-state information.

http://www.freeadvice.com Definition of legal terms (e.g., what is child visitation and a parenting plan?), plus links to other Web sites.

http://www.divorceinteractive.com Online Divorce Resources includes Find a Lawyer, Family Law, Child Support, and Mediation. This site covers many topics, including alimony; divorce; business appraisers; causes of divorce; certified divorce planners; child custody, support, and visitation; family therapists; and mediation

---

ETHICS ALERT

Susan could not believe J. D.'s luck. Just when he was feeling most discouraged about the Baxters' ability to settle their divorce, some very interesting news became available. Mrs. Baxter's attorney wrote some suggested settlement proposals for Mrs. Baxter on a memo and then accidentally faxed it to the Johnson & Webster office instead of sending it to Mrs. Baxter's fax machine. The memo contained not only the proposals but also what Mrs. Baxter should be willing to trade to Mr. Baxter if one of her proposals were accepted. Was this a stroke of luck for J. D.?

Review Questions

1. Name the types of child custody and briefly describe each.
2. What legal question is asked by every court that is asked to determine a custody issue?
3. What is a guardian *ad litem,* and when is one appointed?
4. (a) May custody determinations be modified? (b) If so, when and how?
5. (a) What acts (laws) have been passed to combat the problem of enforcing child custody orders? (b) Provide a description of each act.
6. (a) Why is the full faith and credit clause important to child custody issues? (b) What authority contains this clause?
7. What is the full name of The Hague Convention, and what was its purpose?

8. What is a case of first impression?
9. Is paid surrogacy pregnancy a legal option?
10. If you were planning to store your prezygotes for future use, what legal precautions would you take?

11. What rights does a gestational, but nonbiological, mother have to the child once the child is born?
12. Do you think the wishes of a deceased man who has left his semen to a friend for the purposes of procreation should usually be respected?

Endnotes

1. Justice Lund in *In re Marriage of Bush,* 191 Ill. App. 3d 249, 138 Ill. Dec. 423, 547 N.E.2d 590 (1989).
2. *Study of Appellate Decisions,* Justice Department, 1995.
3. Reske, Henry J., "Who's Minding Maranda?" *ABA Journal* (August 1996): 21.
4. Mason, Mary Ann, and Nicole Zayac, "Rethinking Stepparent Rights: Has the ALI Found a Better Definition?" *Family Law Quarterly* 36, no. 2 (Summer 2002): 227-53.
5. "Stepping in to Parent: The Legal Rights of Stepparents," *Family Advocate* 25, no. 1 (2002): 36.
6. Shuman, Daniel W., "The Role of Mental Health Experts in Custody Decisions: Science, Psychological Tests, and Clinical Judgment," *Family Law Quarterly* 36, no. 1 (Spring 2002): 135-62.
7. McCafferty, Dennis, "Who Should Decide Whether Grandparents Can Visit?" *USA Weekend,* January 7, 2000, 16.

8. Bricklin, Barry, "Getting Optimum Performance from a Mental Health Professional," *Family Law Quarterly* 29 (Spring 1995): 8.
9. Mahmoody, Betty, with William Hoffer, *Not Without My Daughter* (New York: St. Martin's Press, 1987).
10. Mahmoody, Betty, with Arnold D. Dunchock, *For the Love of a Child* (New York: St. Martin's Press, 1992).
11. *Family Law Quarterly* 35, no. 1 (2001): 78.
12. New York State, Task Force on Life and the Law, *Assisted Reproductive Technologies: Analysis and Recommendations for Public Policy* (Albany: State of New York, April 1998).
13. Custody seminar, New Jersey Institute for Continuing Legal Education, The Center, New Brunswick, NJ, 2002.

Chapter 10

Child Support

RESPONSIBILITY BEGINS AT HOME: PARENTS MUST SUPPORT THEIR CHILDREN

Parents are responsible for financially supporting their children. In fact, a parent who fails to provide for a child's *life necessities* can be held responsible for payment of such necessities, even if they are provided by others. **Life necessities** are usually considered food, shelter, and medical care.

This parental financial responsibility is defined through legislation that has been created by all 50 states. New York's legislation pertaining to this parental responsibility, which is typical, states: *The parents of a child under the age of twenty-one years are chargeable with the support of such child and, if possessed of sufficient means or able to earn such means, shall be required to pay for child support a fair and reasonable sum as the court may determine.*[1] **Child support** is defined as a legally mandated support obligation for one's child.

All states recognize a parental duty to their children until they reach adulthood. The majority of states define adulthood as 18 years old. A small minority of states (including New York) require parental financial support until a child is 21 years old. Most states also require parents to support adult disabled children *if* the disability occurred during childhood. Only a small minority (four states) ask parents to support adult children who become disabled in adulthood; these states are Alabama, California, Maryland, and Pennsylvania.[2] The only exception to these requirements is if the child has been granted a court-ordered emancipation or a court order stating otherwise. **Emancipation** is defined as "setting free." For example, a child is automatically emancipated when she reaches her state's statutorily defined age of adulthood. A child may be legally emancipated before reaching the state's statutorily defined age adulthood if a court orders that her parents have no further right to control nor obligation to support her.

STATE SUPPORT GUIDELINES: VARIATIONS ON A THEME

All 50 states follow legislatively created child support guidelines enacted to help parents and judges determine just *how much* child support should be ordered. In addition to the guidelines, all the states use income models to assist in determining the child support amount. Child support amounts for families with income over the top guideline are calculated using income models. Some states clearly use one type of model, while other states use a combination of models. These models include the following: the income-share model; the percentage-of-income model; and the Melson-Delaware income model.

The **income-share model** is based on the theory that children of divorce should receive the same share of their parents' income as they did when Mom and Dad were married. The problem with this theory is that when one of the parents leaves the family home, a large percentage of free help leaves the custodial parent, and the child as well. The loss of free help equals the need to pay for help with babysitting, household chores, and so on.

The **percentage-of-income model** is based on the theory that the noncustodial parent should pay a fixed percentage of his income based on how many children he has. The problem here is that the same amount of child support is paid regardless of whether the custodial parent works.

The **Melson-Delaware income model** looks to the basic financial needs of the noncustodial parent and puts this amount, called the **self-support reserve,** aside for the parent's self-support. Next, the children's basic needs are calculated, and the income is spread out among the children who need to be supported. Once the children's basic needs are met, some of any remaining income may be given to the children to raise their standard of living, and some may be allocated to the paying parent.

Review Exhibit 10.1, which shows a page from New Jersey's child support guidelines. The New Jersey child support guidelines chart, which is fairly typical, shows the number of children across the top, income in a column to the left, and the amount of child support recommended, based on income and number of children. The guidelines indicate how much monthly child support a parent is *expected* to provide. Note, however, that this expectation of what should be paid is a **rebuttable presumption,** which is defined as a conclusion that will be drawn unless evidence is presented to counter it.

Using the figures in Exhibit 10.1, you can calculate the weekly income of a New Jersey parent who earns $40,000 per year and determine that such a parent would be expected to pay monthly child support in the amount of $180 for one child, $261 for two children, and so forth. As indicated previously, a judge would be willing listen to that parent explain why he should pay less child support than that provided for in the guidelines, since the guidelines are rebuttable if the parent can convince the court that following them in his particular case would be unjust. If the judge finds that there is enough evidence to show that the presumption has been rebutted, the judge may order an amount lower than that recommended in the guidelines.

Over the Top: When Parental Income Is Above the Guidelines

In a perfect world, divorcing parents who could afford to do so would always amicably agree on a child support amount above that recommended in the guidelines. Most states only provide income guidelines up to a limited income. For example, New Jersey's child support guidelines stop at an annual income of $150,000. If a client earns more than the top guideline figure, the child support amount is likely to be a highly negotiated item between the divorcing parents. Again, judges step in and decide for parents who cannot reach an agreement on their own.

The higher a family's income (even if it still falls within the guidelines), the more likely it is that the courts will examine the family's lifestyle prior to the parents' separation. The needs of children in a family from a higher income bracket will still include such life necessities as food, shelter, and medical care, but may also include such things as private school, extracurricular lessons, camp, and orthodontia work.

This was the situation in one case in which the mother of a 3-year-old child was seeking child support of $320,000 per month from her wealthy ex-husband. Yes, you read that amount correctly. The court papers listed, among other things, $14,000 per month for parties and play dates, $144,000 per month for travel on private jets, and $436 per month for the care of the 3-year-old's pet bunny. Such requests may seem outlandish but are not necessarily unrealistic when Dad is a billionaire.[3]

EXHIBIT 10.1 New Jersey's Child Support Guidelines (Courtesy of the State of New Jersey)

New Jersey Child Support Guidelines

Combined Net Weekly Income	One Child	Two Children	Three Children	Four Children	Five Children	Six Children
580.00	23.8%	34.5%	40.8%	45.1%	48.8%	52.3%
590.00	23.7%	34.5%	40.7%	45.0%	48.8%	52.2%
600.00	23.7%	34.5%	40.7%	44.9%	48.7%	52.1%
610.00	23.7%	34.4%	40.6%	44.9%	48.6%	52.0%
620.00	23.7%	34.4%	40.5%	44.8%	48.6%	52.0%
630.00	23.7%	34.3%	40.5%	44.7%	48.5%	51.9%
640.00	23.6%	34.3%	40.4%	44.7%	48.4%	51.8%
650.00	23.6%	34.3%	40.4%	44.6%	48.4%	51.8%
660.00	23.6%	34.2%	40.3%	44.6%	48.3%	51.7%
670.00	23.6%	34.2%	40.3%	44.5%	48.3%	51.6%
680.00	23.6%	34.2%	40.2%	44.5%	48.2%	51.6%
690.00	23.6%	34.1%	40.2%	44.4%	48.2%	51.5%
700.00	23.5%	34.1%	40.2%	44.4%	48.1%	51.5%
710.00	23.5%	34.1%	40.1%	44.3%	48.1%	51.4%
720.00	23.5%	34.0%	40.1%	44.3%	48.0%	51.4%
730.00	23.5%	34.0%	40.0%	44.2%	48.0%	51.3%
740.00	23.5%	34.0%	40.0%	44.2%	47.9%	51.3%
750.00	23.5%	34.0%	40.0%	44.2%	47.9%	51.2%
760.00	23.4%	33.9%	39.9%	44.1%	47.8%	51.2%
770.00	23.4%	33.9%	39.9%	44.1%	47.8%	51.1%
780.00	23.4%	33.8%	39.8%	44.0%	47.7%	51.0%
790.00	23.3%	33.7%	39.6%	43.8%	47.5%	50.8%
800.00	23.2%	33.6%	39.5%	43.7%	47.3%	50.6%
810.00	23.1%	33.5%	39.4%	43.5%	47.2%	50.5%
820.00	23 0%	33.3%	39.3%	43.4%	47.0%	50.3%
830.00	22.9%	33.2%	39.1%	43.2%	46.9%	50.2%
840.00	22.9%	33.1%	39.0%	43.1%	46.7%	50.0%
850.00	22.8%	33.0%	38.9%	43.0%	46.6%	49.8%
860.00	22.7%	32.9%	38.8%	42.8%	46.4%	49.7%
870.00	22.6%	32.8%	38.7%	42.7%	46.3%	49.6%
880.00	22.6%	32.7%	38.6%	42.6%	46.2%	49.4%
890.00	22.5%	32.6%	38.4%	42.5%	46.0%	49.3%
900.00	22.4%	32.5%	38.3%	42.4%	45.9%	49.1%
910.00	22.4%	32.4%	38.2%	42.3%	45.8%	49.0%
920.00	22.3%	32.3%	38.0%	42.0%	45.6%	48.8%
930.00	22.1%	32.1%	37.8%	41.8%	45.3%	48.5%
940.00	22.0%	31.9%	37.6%	41.5%	45.0%	48.2%
950.00	21.9%	31.7%	37,4%	41,3%	44.8%	47.9%
960.00	21.8%	31.6%	37.2%	41.1%	44.5%	47.6%
970.00	21.7%	31.4%	36.9%	40.8%	44.2%	47.3%
980.00	21.6%	31.2%	36.7%	40.6%	44.0%	47.1%
990.00	21.5%	31.1%	36.5%	40.4%	43.8%	46.8%
1,000.00	21.4%	30.9%	36.3%	40.1%	43.5%	46.6%
1,010.00	21.3%	30.7%	36.1%	39.9%	.43.3%	46.3%
1,020.00	21.2%	30.6%	35.9%	39.7%	43.0%	46.1%
1,030.00	21.1%	30.4%	35.8%	39.5%	42.8%	45.8%

Working the Numbers: How to Calculate Child Support

Paralegals and attorneys in all 50 states utilize state-specific versions of a document often called a **child support worksheet,** as well as the case information statement or a **financial disclosure affidavit,** to calculate appropriate child support figures. These forms are used for families with incomes both within and above state guideline amounts. They assist paralegals and attorneys in determining the child support needs of clients' children. Recall the completed case information statement (which included the children's needs) that you reviewed for Libby Smith's case in Chapter 8 on divorce.

The financial forms required by most courts can be completed with convenient computer programs, which greatly eases the burden on paralegals and attorneys who need to prepare these calculations. The computer programs designed to complete mathematical calculations are especially helpful for those who have difficulty with math. A growing number of states have conveniently posted their state child support worksheets on the Internet. Review a typical child support worksheet in Exhibit 10.2.[4]

Determining What Expenses Will Be Included in Child Support

A proposed child support figure is determined initially by asking two questions: (1) What are the incomes of both parents? (2) What are the financial needs of each child? The majority of the states allow consideration of a variety of factors in addition to the numbers-based approach provided by state child support guidelines, although some states limit the number of factors that can be considered. A general list of factors that are considered across the United States includes:

1. all financial resources of the noncustodial parent, including the financial resources of a stepparent or new partner
2. all financial resources of the custodial parent, including the financial resources of a stepparent or new partner
3. all financial resources of the children
4. earning potential of both parents
5. financial needs of both parents
6. standard of living of the children before the parents' separation
7. age of the children
8. additional responsibility of the noncustodial parent to support other spouse and children
9. extraordinary expenses

Extraordinary expenses are those child-rearing costs that are outside daily living necessities but are appropriate to the raising of a particular child (e.g., orthodontia work, unusual medical costs, and educational enrichment beyond basic schooling).

Federal Law Supports Health Care

Federal law requires each state to have child support guidelines that allocate health care costs.[5] The federal law provides that employers must enroll their employees' children regardless of whether their employees are primary custodial parents or noncustodial parents who claim their children as income tax deductions.[6] If an employee-parent fails to enroll the children voluntarily, the custodial parent may do so by serving the health plan with a **qualified medical child support order (QMCSO).** The QMCSO should give the plan as much information as possible to ensure that the children are adequately covered.

EXHIBIT 10.2 Sample Child Support Worksheet (Courtesy of the State of Florida)

Florida Child Support Guidelines Worksheet

INTRODUCTION

This worksheet estimates the child support obligation that a court may order a parent to pay toward support of the child(ren) on a monthly basis. The court may deviate from the amount estimated depending on the circumstances of a particular case.

CASE INFORMATION

1. Mother's name:
2. Father's name:
3. Names of children addressed in this case:
4. Total number of children in this case

MONTHLY INCOME

		Mother	Father	Total
5	Gross Income	$	$	
6	Allowable Deductions	-	-	
7	Net Income — Income minus deduction Line 5 - Line 6	$ +	$ =	
8	% Share of Total — Each parent's net income divided by combined income	%	%	$

MONTHLY FINANCIAL NEED

					Total
9	Basic Need	You must use Table 1 to complete Line 9.			$
10	Child Care (75%)	Only for children included on Line 3. .75 x $ ____ per mo.			+
11	Insurance	Only for children included on Line 3.			+
12	Total Financial Need	Add Lines 9 + 10 + 11			=$

NONCUSTODIAL PARENTAL OBLIGATION

			Mother	Father	
13	Obligation	Line 8 x Total on Line 12 % share times total need	$	$	
14	Credit, Child Care	Only for the parent who actually pays and only for children listed on Line 3.	-	-	
15	Credit, Insurance		-	-	
16	Net Obligation		=$	=$	

(continued)

EXHIBIT 10.2 *continued*

INSTRUCTIONS FOR GUIDELINES WORKSHEET

General Information

Line 1   Enter the mother's name.

Line 2   Enter the father's name.

Line 3   List the names of children whose child support is addressed in this worksheet.

Line 4   Enter the total number of children listed on Line 3.

Monthly Income

Line 5   **Monthly Gross Income.** Use the list below to calculate monthly income before any deductions or taxes are taken. Convert all amounts to monthly amounts, using the Monthly Conversion Instructions, if needed.

1.	Salary and Wages	$_____	$_____
2.	Bonus, commissions, allowances, overtime, tips, etc.	$_____	$_____
3.	Self-employ/partnership/close corp. and independent contracts	$_____	$_____
4.	Disability benefits	$_____	$_____
5.	Worker's Compensation	$_____	$_____
6.	Unemployment compensation	$_____	$_____
7.	Pension, retirements or annuity payments	$_____	$_____
8.	Social Security benefits	$_____	$_____
9.	Spousal support received from previous marriage	$_____	$_____
10.	Interest and dividends	$_____	$_____
11.	Rental income	$_____	$_____
12.	Income from royalties, trusts or estates	$_____	$_____
13.	Reimbursed expenses or in-kind payments	$_____	$_____
14.	Capital gains	$_____	$_____

Add items 1 through 14 for the **Gross Income** $_____ $_____
Enter these amounts on Page 1, Line 5

Line 6   **Allowable Deductions**. Use the list below to calculate deductions. Convert all amounts to monthly amounts, using the Monthly Conversion Instructions, if needed.

1.	Federal, state, and local income taxes	$_____	$_____
2.	Fed. insurance contributions or self-employment tax	$_____	$_____
3.	Mandatory union dues	$_____	$_____
4.	Mandatory retirement	$_____	$_____
5.	*Health insurance paid for family members **not** included on Line 3	$_____	$_____
6.	Court ordered support for other children actually paid	$_____	$_____
7.	Court ordered spousal support actually paid	$_____	$_____

Add items 1 through 7 for the **Allowable Deductions** $_____ $_____
Enter this amount on Page 1, Line 6.

*Insurance Deductions. Parents who pay health and dental insurance for family members not included on Line 3 may deduct part or all of the insurance premium from their income. This deduction is available to both parents. If a parent pays insurance for other family members but does not cover any child from Line 3, enter the total monthly insurance premium. If part of a parent's premium pays for children listed on Line 3, click here.

Link for insurance footnote.

If a parent pays an insurance premium that includes any children on Line 3, only the part of the premium paid for other family members is deducted on Line 6, item 5. The part of the premium paid for children included in Line 3 will be given credit on Line 15. First, figure the per person premium for the insurance by dividing the monthly premium by the total number of persons covered.

> For example: The father has $300 deducted from his salary for family insurance that covers him, his current spouse, 2 children of his current marriage, and 2 children included on Line 3, the insurance premium would cover 6 individuals. In this example, the total monthly premium ($300) must be divided by 6 to determine the monthly premium for each person ($50).
>
> | Monthly insurance premium | divided by | Total number of persons insured | equals | Per person premium |
> |---|---|---|---|---|
> | $300 | / | 6 | = | $50 |
>
> The number of *"other"* family members covered is 4, excluding the 2 children in Line 3. The deduction amount is 4 times $50 (the per person premium), for a total deduction of $200. He would enter $200 for item 5 of Line 6.

Line 7   **Net Income**

To calculate monthly net income, subtract allowable deductions (Line 6) from gross income (Line 5). Enter the monthly net income on Line 7 for the mother and father. Add the net income of both parents and enter it in the last column of Line 7.

Line 8   **Percentage (%) Share of Total**

Line 8 calculates the percentage (part) of the total support for each parent, based on both parents' income. Divide each parent's Net Income by the combined net income from the last column on Line 7, to determine the percentage. Enter this percentage on Line 8.

> For example: The mother's net monthly income is $1,212. The father's net income is $2,064. Their combined income is $3,276. Divide the mother's income ($1,212) by the total combined monthly income ($3,276) to determine the % share for the mother. $1,212 / $ 3,276 = 37%

Monthly Financial Need

Line 9   **Basic Need**

Using Table 1, find the row for your monthly combined net income (Line 7) and total number of children (Line 4) to look up the basic monthly financial need. If the Combined Net Income is more than $10,000 a month, complete the box at the bottom right of Table 1. Enter the total on Line 9. The dollar amounts included in the guidelines table represent the minimum amount of support required to maintain the child(ren)'s standard of living if both parents' incomes were available to provide for their financial needs.

Line 10   **75% of Child Care.**

Seventy-five percent of child care for children on Line 3 may be added to the financial need, regardless of which parent is responsible for paying. The child care costs must be related to a parent's job, job search or education planned to result in employment or improve the income from the current job of either parent. The child care costs shall not exceed the level required for quality care from a licensed source and must be paid on a consistent basis throughout the year. If child care is paid on a schedule that is not monthly, use the Monthly Conversion Instructions. Multiply the monthly child care cost times .75. Enter the amount on Line 10.

> For example: The mother pays $160 monthly for child care for 2 children while she attends night classes. Enter $120 on Line 10. $160 x .75 = $120

(continued)

EXHIBIT 10.2 *continued*

Line 11   **Child's Insurance.**

If neither parent pays health or dental insurance for the children on Line 3, enter 0 on Line 11.

If one or both parents pay insurance for children on Line 3, enter the total amount paid for those children, based on the per person premium(s). Click here

Line 12   **Total Financial Need**

Add Lines 9 + 10+ 11. Enter the total on Line 12.

Noncustodial Parental Obligation

Line 13   **Obligation**

The obligation should be calculated for the noncustodial parent. If there is a third party caregiver, Line 13 should be completed for both parents. Multiply the total monthly financial need from Line 12 by the percent share from Line 8. Enter the totals on Line 13 for each parent.

> For example: Multiply the total financial need of the 2 children from Line 12 ($1,295) by the mother's percentage (37% or .37). $1,295 X .37 = $479 per month.
>
> Multiply the monthly financial need of the 2 children from Line 10 ($1,075) by the father's percentage (63% or .63). $1,295 X .63 = $876 per month.

Line 14 and 15   **Credit, Child Care**

If a noncustodial parent pays for the children's work-related child care or insurance, the amount can be credited against their obligation. Subtract 75% of any child care (Line 10) paid by that parent and any amounts the noncustodial parent pays for insurance (from Line 11) from the noncustodial parent's monthly obligation. For the noncustodial parent(s), enter the child care amount on Lines 14 and insurance on Line15 .

Line 16   **Net Obligation**

For the noncustodial parent, subtract any credits for child care or insurance paid by that parent from the obligation on Line 13. This is the net obligation for that parent.

> For example: the noncustodial father's obligation is $876 per month. He is credited for the $100 he pays every month for health insurance. $876 - $100 = $776.
> His child support obligation is $776 each month.

Additional Calculations

Insurance

Figure the per person premium for the insurance by dividing the monthly premium by the total number of persons covered. For example, if the father has $300 deducted from his salary for family insurance that covers him, his current spouse, 2 children of his current marriage, and 2 children included on Line 3, the insurance premium would cover 6 individuals. In this example, the total monthly premium ($300) must be divided by 6 to determine the monthly premium for each person ($50).

Monthly insurance premium	divided by	Total number of persons insured	equals	Per person premium
$300	/	6	=	$50

The number of children included on Line 3 and covered by this insurance is 2. The insurance need amount is 2 times $50 (the per person premium), for a total of $100. Enter $100 on Line 11.

Return to Instruction

TABLE 1. CHILD SUPPORT, MONTHLY FINANCIAL NEED

Monthly Combined Net Income	One	Two	Three	Four	Five	Six
650.00	74	75	75	76	77	78
700.00	119	120	121	123	124	125
750.00	164	166	167	169	171	173
800.00	190	211	213	216	218	220
850.00	202	257	259	262	265	268
900.00	213	302	305	309	312	315
950.00	224	347	351	355	359	363
1000.00	235	365	397	402	406	410
1050.00	246	382	443	448	453	458
1100.00	258	400	489	495	500	505
1150.00	269	417	522	541	547	553
1200.00	280	435	544	588	594	600
1250.00	290	451	565	634	641	648
1300.00	300	467	584	659	688	695
1350.00	310	482	603	681	735	743
1400.00	320	498	623	702	765	790
1450.00	330	513	642	724	789	838
1500.00	340	529	662	746	813	869
1550.00	350	544	681	768	836	895
1600.00	360	560	701	790	860	920
1650.00	370	575	720	812	884	945
1700.00	380	591	740	833	907	971
1750.00	390	606	759	855	931	996
1800.00	400	622	779	877	955	1022
1850.00	410	638	798	900	979	1048
1900.00	421	654	818	923	1004	1074
1950.00	431	670	839	946	1029	1101
2000.00	442	686	859	968	1054	1128
2050.00	452	702	879	991	1079	1154
2100.00	463	718	899	1014	1104	1181
2150.00	473	734	919	1037	1129	1207
2200.00	484	751	940	1060	1154	1234
2250.00	494	767	960	1082	1179	1261
2300.00	505	783	980	1105	1204	1287
2350.00	515	799	1000	1128	1229	1314
2400.00	526	815	1020	1151	1254	1341
2450.00	536	831	1041	1174	1279	1367
2500.00	547	847	1061	1196	1304	1394
2550.00	557	864	1081	1219	1329	1420
2600.00	568	880	1101	1242	1354	1447
2650.00	578	896	1121	1265	1379	1473
2700.00	588	912	1141	1287	1403	1500
2750.00	597	927	1160	1308	1426	1524
2800.00	607	941	1178	1328	1448	1549
2850.00	616	956	1197	1349	1471	1573
2900.00	626	971	1215	1370	1494	1598
2950.00	635	986	1234	1391	1517	1622
3000.00	644	1001	1252	1412	1540	1647
3050.00	654	1016	1271	1433	1563	1671
3100.00	663	1031	1289	1453	1586	1696
3150.00	673	1045	1308	1474	1608	1720
3200.00	682	1060	1327	1495	1631	1744
3250.00	691	1075	1345	1516	1654	1769
3300.00	701	1090	1364	1537	1677	1793
3350.00	710	1105	1382	1558	1700	1818
3400.00	720	1120	1401	1579	1723	1842
3450.00	729	1135	1419	1599	1745	1867
3500.00	738	1149	1438	1620	1768	1891
3550.00	748	1164	1456	1641	1791	1915
3600.00	757	1179	1475	1662	1814	1940
3650.00	767	1194	1493	1683	1837	1964
3700.00	776	1208	1512	1702	1857	1987
3750.00	784	1221	1520	1721	1878	2009
3800.00	793	1234	1536	1740	1899	2031
3850.00	802	1248	1553	1759	1920	2053
3900.00	811	1261	1570	1778	1940	2075
3950.00	819	1275	1587	1797	1961	2097
4000.00	828	1288	1603	1816	1982	2119
4050.00	837	1302	1620	1835	2002	2141
4100.00	846	1315	1637	1854	2023	2163
4150.00	854	1329	1654	1873	2044	2185
4200.00	863	1342	1670	1892	2064	2207
4250.00	872	1355	1687	1911	2085	2229
4300.00	881	1369	1704	1930	2106	2251
4350.00	889	1382	1721	1949	2127	2273
4400.00	898	1396	1737	1968	2147	2295
4450.00	907	1409	1754	1987	2168	2317
4500.00	916	1423	1771	2006	2189	2339
4550.00	924	1436	1788	2024	2209	2361
4600.00	933	1450	1804	2043	2230	2384
4650.00	942	1463	1821	2062	2251	2406
4700.00	951	1477	1838	2081	2271	2428
4750.00	959	1490	1855	2100	2292	2450
4800.00	968	1503	1871	2119	2313	2472
4850.00	977	1517	1888	2138	2334	2494
4900.00	986	1530	1905	2157	2354	2516
4950.00	993	1542	1927	2174	2372	2535
5000.00	1000	1551	1939	2188	2387	2551
5050.00	1006	1561	1952	2202	2402	2567
5100.00	1013	1571	1964	2215	2417	2583
5150.00	1019	1580	1976	2229	2432	2599
5200.00	1025	1590	1988	2243	2447	2615
5250.00	1032	1599	2000	2256	2462	2631
5300.00	1038	1609	2012	2270	2477	2647
5350.00	1045	1619	2024	2283	2492	2663
5400.00	1051	1628	2037	2297	2507	2679
5450.00	1057	1638	2049	2311	2522	2695
5500.00	1064	1647	2061	2324	2537	2711
5550.00	1070	1657	2073	2338	2552	2727
5600.00	1077	1667	2085	2352	2567	2743
5650.00	1083	1676	2097	2365	2582	2759
5700.00	1089	1686	2109	2379	2597	2775
5750.00	1096	1695	2122	2393	2612	2791
5800.00	1102	1705	2134	2406	2627	2807
5850.00	1107	1713	2144	2418	2639	2820
5900.00	1111	1721	2155	2429	2651	2833
5950.00	1116	1729	2165	2440	2663	2847
6000.00	1121	1737	2175	2451	2676	2860
6050.00	1126	1746	2185	2462	2688	2874
6100.00	1131	1754	2196	2473	2700	2887
6150.00	1136	1762	2206	2484	2712	2900
6200.00	1141	1770	2216	2495	2724	2914
6250.00	1145	1778	2227	2506	2737	2927
6300.00	1150	1786	2237	2517	2749	2941
6350.00	1155	1795	2247	2529	2761	2954
6400.00	1160	1803	2258	2540	2773	2967
6450.00	1165	1811	2268	2551	2785	2981
6500.00	1170	1819	2278	2562	2798	2994
6550.00	1175	1827	2288	2573	2810	3008
6600.00	1179	1835	2299	2584	2822	3021
6650.00	1184	1843	2309	2595	2834	3034
6700.00	1189	1850	2317	2604	2845	3045
6750.00	1193	1856	2325	2613	2854	3055
6800.00	1196	1862	2332	2621	2863	3064
6850.00	1200	1868	2340	2630	2872	3074
6900.00	1204	1873	2347	2639	2882	3084
6950.00	1208	1879	2355	2647	2891	3094
7000.00	1212	1885	2362	2656	2900	3103
7050.00	1216	1891	2370	2664	2909	3113
7100.00	1220	1897	2378	2673	2919	3123
7150.00	1224	1903	2385	2681	2928	3133
7200.00	1228	1909	2393	2690	2937	3142
7250.00	1232	1915	2400	2698	2946	3152
7300.00	1235	1921	2408	2707	2956	3162
7350.00	1239	1927	2415	2716	2965	3172
7400.00	1243	1933	2423	2724	2974	3181
7450.00	1247	1939	2430	2733	2983	3191
7500.00	1251	1945	2438	2741	2993	3201
7550.00	1255	1951	2446	2750	3002	3211
7600.00	1259	1957	2453	2758	3011	3220
7650.00	1263	1963	2461	2767	3020	3230
7700.00	1267	1969	2468	2775	3030	3240
7750.00	1271	1975	2476	2784	3039	3250
7800.00	1274	1981	2483	2792	3048	3259
7850.00	1278	1987	2491	2801	3057	3269
7900.00	1282	1992	2498	2810	3067	3279
7950.00	1286	1998	2506	2818	3076	3289
8000.00	1290	2004	2513	2827	3085	3298
8050.00	1294	2010	2521	2835	3094	3308
8100.00	1298	2016	2529	2844	3104	3318
8150.00	1302	2022	2536	2852	3113	3328
8200.00	1306	2028	2544	2861	3122	3337
8250.00	1310	2034	2551	2869	3131	3347
8300.00	1313	2040	2559	2878	3141	3357
8350.00	1317	2046	2566	2887	3150	3367
8400.00	1321	2052	2574	2895	3159	3376
8450.00	1325	2058	2581	2904	3168	3386
8500.00	1329	2064	2589	2912	3178	3396
8550.00	1333	2070	2597	2921	3187	3406
8600.00	1337	2076	2604	2929	3196	3415
8650.00	1341	2082	2612	2938	3205	3425
8700.00	1345	2088	2619	2946	3215	3435
8750.00	1349	2094	2627	2955	3224	3445
8800.00	1352	2100	2634	2963	3233	3454
8850.00	1356	2106	2642	2972	3242	3464
8900.00	1360	2111	2649	2981	3252	3474
8950.00	1364	2117	2657	2989	3261	3484
9000.00	1368	2123	2664	2998	3270	3493
9050.00	1372	2129	2672	3006	3279	3503
9100.00	1376	2135	2680	3015	3289	3513
9150.00	1380	2141	2687	3023	3298	3523
9200.00	1384	2147	2695	3032	3307	3532
9250.00	1388	2153	2702	3040	3316	3542
9300.00	1391	2159	2710	3049	3326	3552
9350.00	1395	2165	2717	3058	3335	3562
9400.00	1399	2171	2725	3066	3344	3571
9450.00	1403	2177	2732	3075	3353	3581
9500.00	1407	2183	2740	3083	3363	3591
9550.00	1411	2189	2748	3092	3372	3601
9600.00	1415	2195	2755	3100	3381	3610
9650.00	1419	2201	2763	3109	3390	3620
9700.00	1422	2206	2767	3115	3396	3628
9750.00	1425	2210	2772	3121	3402	3634
9800.00	1427	2213	2776	3126	3408	3641
9850.00	1430	2217	2781	3132	3414	3647
9900.00	1432	2221	2786	3137	3420	3653
9950.00	1435	2225	2791	3143	3426	3659
10000.00	1437	2228	2795	3148	3432	3666

Over $10,000 a month income.

If the combined income on Line 7 exceeds $10,000 an additional calculation is required. Subtract $10,000 from the amount on Line 7. $_____

Multiply this answer by 5% for 1 child, 7.5% for 2, 9.5% for 3, 11% for 4, 12% for 5 or 12.5% for 6. $_____

Add this to the amount from the table for an income of $10,000 for the appropriate number of children. Total $_____

Enter this total on Line 9.

For example: If the combined monthly net income on the last column of Line 7 is $3,276 per month, and the total number of children (Line 4) is 2. Therefore $1,075 should be entered on Line 9.

(continued)

EXHIBIT 10.2 *continued*

MONTHLY CONVERSION WORKSHEET

If you are paid or make payments on a schedule that is not monthly, you must convert those amounts. These formulas may be used for income and expenses.

Return to Instruction

If you are:	
Paid by the Hour	hourly x hours = weekly x 52 weeks = yearly divide by 12 months = MONTHLY
	amount per week amount amount AMOUNT
Sample	$7.50 x 40 = $300 x 52 = $15,600 / 12 = $1,300
Your Calculation	$_____ x _____ = $_____ x _____ = $_____ / _____ = $_____ .
Paid by the Day	daily x days = weekly x 52 weeks = yearly **divide by** 12 months = MONTHLY
	amount per week amount amount AMOUNT
Sample	$80 x 5 = $400 x 52 = $20,800 / 12 = $1,733
Your Calculation	$_____ x _____ = $_____ x _____ = $_____ / _____ = $_____
Paid by the Week	Weekly amount x 52 weeks = Yearly amount divide by 12 months = MONTHLY AMOUNT
Sample	$200 x 52 = $10,400 / 12 = $650
Your Calculation	$_____ x_____ = $_____ / _____ = _____ $ _____
Paid Every 2 Weeks	Bi-weekly amount x 26 = Yearly amount **divide by** 12 months = MONTHLY AMOUNT
Sample	$600 x 26 = $15,600 / 12 = $2,300
Your Calculation	$_____ x 26 = $_____ / _____ 12 = $_____
Paid Twice per Month	Semi-monthly amount x 2 = Monthly Amount
Sample	$550 x 2 = $1,100
Your Calculation	$_____ x 2 = $_____

Return to Instruction

Additional Insurance Calculation

Figure the per person premium for the insurance by dividing the monthly premium by the total number of persons covered. For example, if the father has $300 deducted from his salary for family insurance that covers him, his current spouse, 2 children of his current marriage, and 2 children included on Line 3, the insurance premium would cover 6 individuals. In this example, the total monthly premium ($300) must be divided by 6 to determine the monthly premium for each person ($50).

Monthly insurance premium	divided by	Total number of persons insured	equals	Per person premium
$300	/	6	=	$50

The number of children included on Line 3 and covered by this insurance is 2. The insurance need amount is 2 times $50 (the per person premium), for a total of $100. Enter $100 on Line 11.

Florida Child Support Worksheet and Guidelines

Florida Statute (s. 61.30, F.S.) requires guidelines to be used in establishing new child support obligations or modifying child support in a Florida court. All states are required to have statutory guidelines but they vary greatly among states. The Florida guidelines must take into consideration all income and earnings of both parents and the children's health care needs. This worksheet provides an estimate of the amount a court may order, depending on individual circumstances.

The court may deviate from the guidelines if there is a written finding in the court record that the guidelines in the particular case would be inappropriate. The finding must include the amount of support that would have been required under the guidelines and a reason why the order varies.

Monthly income, insurance and child care information for both the mother and father will be necessary to complete the forms.

Is Johnny Going to College?

Imagine that you are 18 years old and you want to go to college a thousand miles away from home, but your parents have decided they will only pay your way only if you stay at home and go to the local college. If your parents are married, there is not much you can do to force them to pay for your education at Party University, but if Mom and Dad are divorced, you may be in for a piece of fiscal good luck. In a large number of states, if a parent moves out of the family home, the courts are allowed to order that parent to pay a percentage of the cost of a private college.

As noted previously, in most states, parents can bid a financial good-bye to their children when the children reach 18 years of age. At that point, a parent's legal support obligation ends. However, 20 states give judges discretion to order divorced parents of children past the age of majority to help support the children or pay their college tuition.[7] Interestingly, the American Academy of Matrimonial Lawyers cites a United States Department of Education study of 25,000 students that found that children from divided homes face greater obstacles in pursuing higher education than children from intact homes.[8] Although arguments have been made that to impose a college support obligation on divorced parents but not on married parents is a violation of the equal protection clause, these arguments have not, for the most part, been successful.

Questions to Ask

As you can see, many questions must be answered when determining the amount of child support and the circumstances surrounding how the child support should be paid. For example, will college expenses be paid by the parents? If so, what percentage will be paid for and by which parent? Do the parents agree to an escalation clause being included in the final order? An **escalation clause** describes the amount of an automatic increase in child support. How do the parents feel about the increase in child support being connected to the Consumer Price Index? Have the costs of extracurricular activities been figured into the child support agreement? Will there be a reduction of the child support that is paid to the custodial parent when the children are visiting with the noncustodial parent or away from home for any length of time? For example, will a stay at camp for a week be a red flag to the payor-parent to reduce the child support paid to the custodial parent? Should the child support payment be the total amount the paying parent should expect to pay, or should the parents also expect to split clothing costs, dental bills, and music lessons. These are examples of just some of the details that must be considered.

Typically, a judge will order temporary child support because of a *pendente lite* motion being filed by one of the parents. (Refer to Chapters 1 and 8 to refresh your recollection of what a typical motion and application for *pendente lite* support, a plaintiff's certification, and a *pendente lite* order look like.) A temporary support order will only be in effect until the final judgment is granted. Often, the child support ordered in the final judgment is based on the temporary amount that was ordered.

A parent who is ordered to pay child support may present evidence to the judge to prove that his income is lower than it was prior to the separation or that the cost of maintaining a separate household is imposing a burden that prevents maintaining the same sort of lifestyle the children enjoyed prior to their parents' separation. If the parents disagree on the child support issue, they can choose to return to court or to have their dispute heard by an arbitrator or a mediator. Mediation is a process in which an impartial third party, a mediator, facilitates the settling of a dispute. Arbitration is different from mediation. It is defined as the resolution of a dispute by a person other than a judge (called an arbitrator) whose decision is often binding. More information about mediation and arbitration will be provided in a later chapter.

The final judgment of divorce ultimately includes the final child support order, as well as the final decisions regarding custody, spousal support, and the distribution of any assets and debts. Although the word *final* is used to describe the final judgment, either party can return to court to request an alteration to the financial support provided. Later in this chapter, you will read about how some courts have viewed such requests.

Earning Above the State Guidelines: Parent Disputes Amount Ordered

The case of *Bush v. Bush* (see Case 10.1) centered on two physicians who had a problem healing the rift between them. This case concerned disputed child support figures and highlights how difficult a case can be when former spouses have serious difficulties in dealing with each other. This case also provides an excellent example of a situation where the parties earn significantly more than the child support guidelines of Illinois specifically provide for.

Equitable Estoppel's Role in Determining Child Support

The case of *County of Erie on Behalf of Karin T. v. Michael T.* (see Case 10.2) may bring to mind the old saying, "Be careful what you ask for, you might get it." Michael T. was unable to physically impregnate his wife Karin and agreed to Karin being artificially inseminated. In fact, Karin's physician wanted to ensure that Michael was voluntarily participating in his wife's artificial inseminations, so he had Michael sign a consent form. Michael T. wanted to participate in the raising of Karin's two children conceived from the insemination and did so until the couple decided to divorce.

Once the couple decided to divorce, Michael did not want to support the two children born during their marriage. Michael decided to answer his wife's petition for child support by claiming an affirmative defense. An *affirmative defense* is defined as that part of a defendant's answer to a complaint that goes beyond denying the facts and arguments of the complaint. It sets out new facts and arguments that might win the case for the defendant even if everything claimed by the plaintiff in the complaint is true.

This case was a case of first impression for Pennsylvania. The court discusses the doctrine of equitable estoppel, which is usually applied by the courts in cases where a party is being stopped by her own prior acts from claiming a right against another person who legitimately relied on those acts.

The issue in this case is whether Michael T. must support the two children born to Karin T. Does this seem like an easy question? If so, throw in another wrinkle: Michael T. claims he is a female and could not possibly have fathered the children and therefore, does not have any responsibility toward them. Make sure you read this interesting case.

CASE 10.1 *Bush v. Bush,* 191 Ill. App 3d 249, 138 Ill. Dec. 423, 547 N.E.2d 590 (1989)

Facts: The parties, both physicians, were married in 1982. The parties had one child, Alan, born October 1983. The mother (petitioner) testified that the father (respondent) physically and mentally abused her before and during her pregnancy. The father's gross salary was $156,000, and the mother's gross monthly salary was $7,200.

During the two years between issuance of the temporary and final orders, the father paid $4,833 to the mother as temporary child support. By March of 1988, temporary child support arrearages totaled $12,567. The father admitted he did not make temporary child support payments as ordered and gave five reasons for refusing to pay—none of them related to his ability to pay. First, he alleged the mother denied him visitation rights, as he did not know the whereabouts of his son for seven weeks following the petitioner's marriage to Dr. Lawrence Webster. Second, the father cited two brief confrontations between himself and the mother in August and September of 1986. Testimony from each party indicated that they occurred when the father had the child pursuant to court-ordered visitation. There was confusion or disagreement over the length of the child's stay with his father on each occasion, and the mother entered the father's home uninvited to remove the child. Physical confrontations resulted. The third reason given for refusing to pay child support was that the mother never told the father how she intended to use the monies to support the child. The fourth reason was that the father claimed he should not pay temporary child support because he had custody of Alan eight days each month and contributed directly to Alan's support during those days. Finally, the father refused to pay temporary child support because he believed all the child's needs were already being met by the mother. The father did establish a $1,600 certificate of deposit (CD) in the child's name in 1986, pursuant to the court's order that he place $200 per month in trust.

The court entered its final order on September 20, 1988. The court awarded joint custody, with physical custody awarded to the mother during the school year. During the school year, Alan would visit his father on alternate weekends and would live with his father for approximately two months each summer. During summer visitation, the mother would have absolutely no visitation rights. This visitation schedule would begin when the child entered kindergarten. Until then, the visitation schedule established under the temporary order would remain in effect. The court ordered the father to obtain a $100,000 life insurance policy to guarantee payment of child support and to name the mother as beneficiary of the trust he had been directed to establish for temporary child support arrearages. The court also ordered the father to establish a trust fund of $18,767 on behalf of the child. This amount included temporary child support arrearages, the CD, and monies in the trust fund the father had already established pursuant to the temporary order.

Issues: (1) Whether the trial court abused its discretion in ordering arrearages to be placed in a trust fund for the child rather than ordering the arrearages paid to the payee custodial parent. (2) Whether the child support award was excessive.

Court's Reasoning: We now turn to the issues involving child support, custody, and visitation. The mother argues the trial court abused its discretion when it ordered the father to place child support arrearages in a trust fund for the child. We agree. The law in this state is clear: *Past due installments of child support are the vested right of the designated recipient.* The lower court lacked the authority to modify those amounts that had already accrued.

(continued)

CASE 10.1 *continued*

The lower court's order requiring the father to establish a trust fund with the arrearages was not legally justified and deprived the mother of a vested right. The mother argues that the trial court erred on March 15, 1988, when it did not find the father in contempt for his refusal to pay temporary child support as ordered. The mother argues that this decision was against the manifest weight of the evidence and urges this court to reverse and find the father in contempt. We decline to do so. Enforcement of support payments by contempt is in the sound discretion of the court. As a reviewing court, we will not disturb the trial court's decision unless contrary to the manifest weight of the evidence or an abuse of discretion.

The next issue raised on appeal by both parties concerns the child support award. The respondent argues that the child support award is excessive because it is far more than the amount necessary to meet the child's reasonable and necessary support needs, particularly in light of each parent's separate abilities to financially care for the child. The mother argues that the award is insufficient because according to her calculations, $800 per month is only 6 percent of the father's monthly net income.

In making child support awards, trial courts are to consider the following factors: (1) the financial resources of the child; (2) the financial resources and needs of the custodial parent; (3) the standard of living the child would have enjoyed had the marriage not been dissolved; (4) the physical and emotional condition of the child; (5) the child's educational needs; and (6) the financial resources and needs of the noncustodial parent.

The amount of the award of child support is a matter within the sound discretion of the trial court, and the award will not be disturbed on appeal absent an abuse of discretion. The trial court's overall award of 20 percent of the father's net income was excessive for a child of such tender years and, as such, constituted an abuse of discretion.

The testimony is that the respondent's net monthly income is approximately $13,000 monthly, or $156,000 annually. An award of 20 percent of the respondent's income is approximately $30,000 per year, or more than the average income of most Americans.

We now hold that where the individual incomes of both parents are more than sufficient to provide for the reasonable needs of the parties' children, and taking into account the lifestyle the children would have had absent the dissolution, the court is justified in setting a figure below the guideline amount. Certainly, there will be instances where a high child support figure will be warranted. A child support figure approaching 20 percent might be justified if the situation involved high medical expenses or if the child attended an expensive, private grammar school.

Despite the requirement that a court consider a child's station in life, the courts are not required to automatically open the door to a windfall for children where one or both parents have large incomes. The facts in the present case do not establish the special circumstances justifying the use of a trust.

Holding: We remand this issue to the trial court for determination of a reasonable monthly support amount. Additionally, we hold it was improper to order the creation of a trust in this case.

Case Discussion: Do you agree with the court's decision? Does the court's decision impose an additional burden on the custodial parent to return to court to prove extra expenses for her son? Does this case ignore the generally accepted notion that the court should look to the lifestyle the child would have enjoyed had the parents not divorced?

CASE 10.2 *County of Erie on Behalf of Karin T. v. Michael T.,* 127 Misc. 2d 14, 484 N.Y.S.2d 780 (1985)

Facts: To a routine-appearing child support petition, Michael T. filed an answer that set forth an affirmative defense as follows: *Michael T. is female and not the father of the said children and that the children were born due to artificial insemination.* Michael T. requested the court to dismiss the petition on the grounds that it failed to state a cause of action.

Michael was born a female on August 16, 1948, and was named Marlene A.T. In her 20s, Marlene became increasingly unhappy with her feminine identity and attempted to change that identity and to live like a man. She changed her name from Marlene to Michael, dressed in men's clothing, and obtained employment that she regarded as "men's work." At some time prior to May of 1977, Michael T. and Karin T. commenced a relationship. Karin and Michael obtained a marriage license in the village of Spencerport in Monroe County in May 1977. At that time, no birth certificate was requested of either party, and a marriage license was issued. Subsequently, Karin and Michael participated in a marriage ceremony performed by a minister in Parma, Monroe County. This marriage was evidenced by a marriage certificate executed by the minister.

Thereafter, two children were born by means of artificial insemination. The physician, prior to engaging in the procedure, had both parties execute an agreement, which was presented as evidence to the court. David T. was born October 8, 1980, and Falin T. was born January 17, 1983, as a result of the artificial insemination performed by the physician. Subsequent to the birth of the second child in 1983, the parties separated.

Issue: Whether the respondent should be considered a parent and, therefore, responsible for the support of her partner's biological children.

Court's Reasoning: Although a question arose as to whether the respondent had become transsexual, this court finds that, for the purposes of this proceeding only, Michael is a female. Karin and Michael lived together in the same household and both contributed to the support of the family and to the two children from 1977 through 1983. This court acknowledges there is a pending action to declare Karin and Michael's marriage null and void.

Neither counsel for the parties nor the court found any authority similar to the fact situation in this case. This is a case of first impression, and its resolution carried the court through *uncharted legal waters.* As a general rule, only biological or adoptive parents are liable for the support of children. Where extraordinary circumstances require, courts have held nonparents responsible for the support of children.

It is conceded that the children involved in this proceeding were born only after the respondent affixed her name to the agreement indicating that she was the husband. The agreement stated in part: *a. That such child or children so produced are his own legitimate child or children and are the heirs of his body, and b. That he hereby completely waives forever any right, which he might have to disclaim such child or children as his own.*

The plaintiff's primary obligation rests upon dual foundations of an implied contract to support the children, and equitable estoppel. Michael signed the insemination agreement by which these children were brought into the world, and this should give rise to a situation that must provide these two children with

(continued)

CASE 10.2 *continued*

remedies. To hold otherwise would be to allow this respondent to completely abrogate her responsibilities for the support of the children involved and to allow her to benefit from her own fraudulent acts that induced their birth as much as if she were indeed the natural father of these children. The respondent is, of course, free to engage and live in any lifestyle she feels is appropriate; however, by her course of conduct in this case, which brought into the world two innocent children, she should not be allowed to benefit from those acts to the detriment of these children and of the public generally. The court finds that under the unique facts in this case, the respondent is indeed a *parent* to whom such responsibility attaches.

The respondent is chargeable with the support of these children, and this case is referred to the hearing examiner to determine the level of such support. We leave it to another forum to decide, at another time, on the rights and remedies of the respondent and the mother of these children concerning custody, visitation, inheritance rights, and other issues.

Holding: Karin T. wins.

Case Discussion: In deciding the outcome of the *Karin T.* case, the court did not want to get involved with the question of whether two women could be parents of the same children. Instead, the court fell back on classic contract law principles (admittedly, easier to understand) and let the concept of equitable estoppel support its findings. Do you think the concept of equitable estoppel applied to the facts in this case?

NOT SET IN STONE: SEEKING A MODIFICATION OF CHILD SUPPORT

The courts in all 50 states retain the right to hear requests for modification of child support payments. *Modification* is a change or alteration to a child support order. Typically, courts only modify an original decree when there has been a **material and substantial change in circumstances.** Reasons for requests for modification usually involve increased costs for supporting the children or a financial hardship hitting the parent who is paying the child support. The *burden rests on the petitioner requesting the modification* of the child support order to establish the substantial change in circumstances by a preponderance of the evidence. *Preponderance of the evidence* is defined as the greater weight of evidence, not as to quantity, as in the number of witnesses or facts, but as to quality, as in the believability and greater weight of important facts proved. It is not as high a standard as *clear and convincing evidence* or *beyond a reasonable doubt.* The next few cases discussed in this chapter highlight the machinations some parents go through to prove there have been material and substantial changes in the circumstances of the parents or children.

Requesting an Upward Modification

Karin and Michael's case demonstrated that one does not have to be a biological parent to be found responsible for child support. The facts clearly supported Michael being found responsible for the two children born during his and Karin's marriage. In *Mears v. Mears* (see Case 10.3), a biological father was fighting the mother's request for an increase in his child support payments. Before jumping to any conclusions about what kind of father he must have been, note that the increase was requested to help meet the increased costs of maintaining his children in their new standard of living after the children's mother had remarried an upwardly mobile business owner.

CASE 10.3 *Mears v. Mears,* 213 N.W.2d 511 (1973)

Facts: Robert and Carla Mears were divorced July 28, 1965. The divorce decree was modified July 8, 1968, reducing the child support payments payable to Carla. Carla filed an application May 24, 1971, asking that those payments be increased. She then appealed from the court's order dismissing her application. The original decree awarded custody of the two minor children of the parties, Robert Brett Mears, born July 1959, and Kenton Bradley Mears, born in October 1960, to Carla and required Robert to pay $100 per week for the first 26 weeks after the court entered its decree. Thereafter, Robert was required to pay $62.50 per week toward the support and maintenance of both children until the children attained the age of 21, married, or became self-supporting.

At the time of the divorce, Carla was employed and self-supporting. A later modification of the decree reduced the child support to $25 per week July 8, 1968. It was further provided that the defendant should have the right to have the children with him during the summer months of every year commencing with the first week after the end of the regular school year. The defendant was to pay the transportation costs for the children to and from his place of residence during vacation periods. No child support payments were required of the defendant while the children were with him.

Carla remarried in November 1969. She is now a housewife with no personal earnings. The defendant also remarried and lives with his wife and her five children from a previous marriage in Calmar, Iowa. He is a schoolteacher and coach and had been offered a contract for the 1971–72 school year at a salary of $12,450. His wife is a secretary and has an income of $4,500 a year. She also receives $200 per month in child support for the five children from their father.

The plaintiff applied on May 24, 1971, for a modification of the court's order of July 8, 1968. She sought a minimum of $100 per week, alleging there had been certain material changes in the circumstances of the parties, including: (1) both parties had remarried; (2) the plaintiff had sustained a loss of personal income following her remarriage; (3) the children had grown older and had additional needs; and (4) the defendant's income had increased. The plaintiff wanted the child support to be increased from the current $25 per week to $100 per week.

Following a hearing, the trial court denied the plaintiff any increased support payments. In doing so, the court found: (1) that the remarriage of both parties, the additional needs of the children, the increase in the defendant's income, and the plaintiff's loss of income *were within the knowledge and contemplation of the court* when the modified order was entered in 1968, as they are all natural occurrences and as such could be foreseen by the court; and (2) that the plaintiff's present husband, as the stepfather of the children, stood *in loco parentis* to them and was obligated to provide for their needs as long as they were in his home should the defendant's contribution be insufficient.

Issue: Whether the defendant-father should be required to increase his child support payments in order to help meet the increased costs of maintaining his children in their new standard of living.

Court's Reasoning: The power of the court to modify child support exists only when there has been a *material and substantial change in circumstances* since the date of the original decree. Not every change of circumstances is sufficient for modification of support provisions. An award entered in a final decree is not to be regarded as a variable sum, to be adjusted either upward or downward with each fluctuating change in the conditions of the respective parties. Such a decree is entered at the time with a view to reasonable and ordinary changes that may be likely to occur in the relations of the parties. When this is done,

(continued)

CASE 10.3 *continued*

the decree is conclusive and should not be disturbed unless it is made to appear that enforcement of the decree will be attended by positive wrong or injustice because of changed conditions. The burden rests on the petitioner for the modification of child support provisions to establish such a change of circumstances by a *preponderance of the evidence.*

We consider first the plaintiff's contention that her remarriage in November 1969, followed by a loss of personal income due to her assuming the full-time duties of a housewife, was such a material and substantial change of circumstances as to justify modification of the child support provision of the 1968 order, since her remarriage was not within the knowledge and contemplation of the court when the modified order was entered. It is a fair inference to be drawn from a reading of the record that she is an attractive, well-dressed woman. Remarriage appears to be a common occurrence in the present day and was likely within the contemplation of the court when the last order was made.

The plaintiff also alleges that the additional needs of the children as they grow older are such a change in the circumstances of the parties as to justify modification of the 1968 order. The trial court, in denying the plaintiff's petition, found that what the plaintiff contended were additional needs of the boys as they grew older were *within the knowledge and contemplation of the court when the modified order was entered, and they are all natural occurrences and as such could be foreseen by the court.* The plaintiff expressed the view that *as boys grow older they get rougher and tougher and go through clothes awfully fast.* The plaintiff's observation describes such an ordinary and reasonable change in circumstances that we are convinced the trial court at the 1968 modification hearing anticipated and took into consideration that the boys would grow older, get rougher, and be tougher on clothes in fixing the support payments at $25 per week. The plaintiff relied principally on the orthodontia work she felt the boys needed in support of her contention. The plaintiff did provide an estimate of $2,000 for orthodontia work for the two boys. In describing what the plaintiff insisted were additional needs of the boys, she told of her unsuccessful attempt to have their father contribute to the expense of the two boys attending a summer camp at a cost of $320 per child. There was also an occasion when one son wanted a minibike to use in the riding area near the plaintiff's present home; she had asked the father to pay $50 toward the $119 purchase of this bike, but he did not do so. Since October 1969, the two boys have had dental work costing $196, which was paid for by the plaintiff's present husband.

The expense of the orthodontia work desired by the mother for the sons cannot reasonably be said to fall within the category of unusual or unanticipated medical expenses brought about by accident, poor health, or mental deficiencies of a child which this court has recognized as constituting a change in circumstances justifying modification.

It is commendable that the mother wants certain advantages for her children, but this is not the problem before the court. The trial court based its dismissal of the plaintiff's application at least in part on the theory that the plaintiff's present husband stood *in loco parentis* to the children and was bound to support them as long as they were in his home if the defendant's contributions were insufficient. The plaintiff contends this was error. This court recently provided the following description of one who is *in loco parentis: The term* in loco parentis, *according to its generally accepted common law meaning, refers to a person who has put himself in the situation of a lawful parent by assuming the obligations incident to the parental relation without going through the formalities necessary to legally adopt.*

The record justifies the inference that plaintiff's desire for at least some of the benefits she now seeks for the boys is due to the higher standard of living presently enjoyed by her and her boys.

Where a stepfather has taken into his home his wife's children by a former marriage, which has ended in divorce or dissolution, the question of his duty to support his wife's children while in his home should be limited to the extent that their being in his home may have increased the cost of their maintenance by reason of a higher living scale than that experienced during the marriage of their father and mother.

The plaintiff's contention that the increase in the defendant's income justifies modification of the 1968 order has merit. At the time of the divorce in 1965, the defendant had a yearly income of $20,000. At the time of the 1968 modification hearing, a reduction was justified in view of the defendant's decrease in income. Now that the defendant's income has been increased by $3,450, which is substantial, it is equitable that other or different terms be imposed. This court has judicially noticed the diminished purchasing power of the dollar, as well as the fact that the impact of inflation in the past 10 years has disastrously eroded the dollar's actual value.

Holding: Based on the standard of living experienced by the children before their mother's remarriage, and upon consideration of the defendant's increased ability to pay, it is our conclusion that the payments required of the defendant toward support of the children should be increased by $20 per week per child.

Case Discussion: Can you list circumstances in which you would agree to child support being modified? You can learn quite a lot from reading the *Mears* case. Would it have been a good idea for Carla's original divorce attorney to have negotiated the inclusion of a cost-of-living adjustment for the boys' support? Perhaps it would have been best had the attorney erred on the side of caution by assuming that the Mears boys would need orthodontia work and negotiating the sharing of that cost during the original divorce. What did you think of the comment regarding Mrs. Mears' attractiveness and good chance of remarrying? Do you think that comment would be acceptable today?

Watch for the court's application of the *in loco parentis* doctrine to the wealthier stepfather. This doctrine applies to situations where the facts show that a person, other than a child's biological parent, has stepped in and affirmatively performed the role of a parent to the child. Applying the *in loco parentis* doctrine in a stepparent scenario is one option for the courts. Alternatively, a minority of states have statutes that allow the courts to impose a support obligation on stepparents.[9]

Modifying Child Support Downward

As stated earlier, child support orders can be modified up or down when a paying or receiving parent can show that a material and substantial change in circumstances has occurred. The case of *McQuiddy v. McQuiddy* (see Case 10.4) also concerned a request for modification of a child support order, but the twist in this case is that the father, according to a doubting judge's dissenting opinion, may have been playing a financial hide-and-seek game with his ex-wife. The parents originally settled the amount of child support to be paid by the father via a consent order. A **consent order** is one in which both parties have agreed to the terms in the order and have presented the order to the judge for her signature.

Yours, Mine, and Ours: Recalculating Child Support When Parents Have More Children

Usually, remarriage or repartnering alters the amount of income available for household expenses. Although this may appear to be a material and substantial change in circumstances, a voluntary increase in the parent's living expenditures is not usually considered by the courts as relevant to a child support guidelines calculation. For example, suppose a noncustodial parent has now remarried and has bought a larger home to

CASE 10.4 *McQuiddy v.McQuiddy,* 238 Pa. Super. 390, 358 A.2d 102 (1976)

Facts: The parties were divorced in February of 1974 and entered into a separation agreement dated October 11, 1973. They agreed that $90 per week would be paid by the father (appellee) for the support of the two children and the wife (appellant). Pursuant to their agreement, the amount was to have been increased to $100 weekly on September 1, 1974.

The father reduced the payment to $50 in August 1974. The father then filed a petition on August 5, 1974, seeking modification of the consent support order. The Bucks County rules required a preliminary conference with a domestic relations officer prior to a hearing, and the conference was held on September 20, 1974. At the conference, the parties developed a preliminary record of income, expenses, assets, and other matters helpful to the lower court in subsequent hearings. The lower court conducted hearings on November 22, 1974, and December 5, 1974, and at the conclusion of those hearings reduced the support order to $50 per week. The order reducing the support was the subject of this appeal.

The father was earning a gross weekly salary of $200 and a net salary of $165 per week. In addition, the lower court found that at the time he had a $50 weekly income from other sources, which translated into a total net income of $215 per week. In December 1973, the father, an attorney, left the shelter of salaried employment and entered the private practice of law. The father's practice then became his sole source of income. It was found that after almost a year in the private practice, he had current net earnings of approximately $100 per week.

Issue: Whether the trial court was correct in finding a substantial and material change of financial circumstances that warranted a reduction in support payments.

Court's Reasoning: This court asks whether the trial court is chargeable with an abuse of discretion. This case is a portrait of a tragic and all-too-common consequence of the separation of young married people who have children. The alleged expenses of each are modest indeed. There is little doubt that the mother requires more income to sustain her and her children under her present circumstances than she now receives from her employment and the contributions of the father. A material change in such circumstances appears clear in this case. The court must look beyond actual earnings and consider earning power and the nature and extent of the father's property and other financial resources. It is hoped that the latent earning power to be found in every young lawyer will emerge with the passage of time and will inure to the benefit of the father's minor children, as well as to himself. That earning power should not be equated to the higher earnings that he might be able to command as a salaried employee at the expense of abandoning his professional career. We do not find any abuse of discretion on the part of the lower court.

Holding: The order entered by the lower court is affirmed.

Dissenting Opinion: Although I recognize the very narrowly circumscribed appellate review of support orders, I cannot agree that the reduction should stand. The testimony of the defendant-appellee in this case was *faltering and evasive*. It was crucial to determine what other assets might be available to the appellee for payment of support. I find the appellee's testimony on this important issue unsatisfactory. For example, on direct examination, appellee testified that he owned a one-fifth interest, worth roughly $2,800, in the office building in which he practiced law. The property was actually owned by a corporation in which the appellee was one of the five principals. It was purchased February of 1974, less than two months after the appellee entered the private practice of law, and during the period in which the appellee was required to make a weekly support payment of $90. The appellee's capital contribution was $2,000, $800 of which was paid in cash or its equivalent, and $1,200 of which was obtained as a loan from the woman who subsequently became the appellee's second wife. It is incongruous that the appellee should have access to such sums of money in February 1974 and plead poverty in August, only six months later. The appellee testified that $350 of his capital contributions was financed by legal services that he rendered to the corporation. During the early part of 1974, the appellee also wrote a check for $6,500 that was applied toward the purchase of an apartment building in Columbia, South Carolina. Had the appellee refrained in early 1974 from making these investments in real estate, he might not have had to testify, at the November 22 hearing: *I would have liked to pay more than $50 per week support. I would love to afford to pay more, but I do not make much money.*

More importantly, it clearly appeared on cross-examination that the appellee had not disclosed his interest in the office building at the preliminary mandatory conference held on September 20, 1974. The appellee's explanation of the omission is quite unconvincing when it is considered that the appellee is an attorney. I can understand the appellee's desire to enter the individual practice of law. His professional aspirations, however, must be balanced against the needs of his two young children. I consider that the balance must be struck in favor of the children. It is noteworthy that the appellee's status as a lawyer was due in no small part to the appellant, who worked as a bank teller during the years in which the appellee was a law student. In her effort to support her children adequately since her separation, she has worked in a Burger King restaurant and in a cocktail lounge in Doylestown, Pennsylvania. For the foregoing reasons, I would vacate the order below and remand with instructions to conduct a further hearing consistent with this opinion.

Case Discussion: The dissent in this case is included to bring a little more light onto the *McQuiddy* case. The dissenting judge clearly explains that he does not believe the appellee simply overlooked his interest in the practice's office building or the new apartment building. Further, the dissenting judge explains that Mrs. McQuiddy worked when her husband was a law student. What do you think of this decision? Do you agree with the majority or the dissent?

more comfortably house his new wife and her children from her first marriage. The guideline calculation for a noncustodial parent with a larger mortgage payment would be the same as for a noncustodial parent with a low rent payment, *even if both had the same income.* The new lifestyle of noncustodial parents will not typically alter their court-ordered responsibilities to children born of previous marriages. There are practical reasons why the legislature created a rule allowing a parent to reduce the expenses of other support obligations only in limited circumstances. Child support obligations that have been previously imposed by a court have been determined to be both a necessary and reasonable amount in proper judicial proceedings. In the case of *Ainsworth v. Ainsworth* (see Case 10.5), the court is asked to balance the needs of a first and subsequent family.

THE PROBLEM OF TRACKING DOWN A NONPAYING PARENT

The question of just how much child support should be paid usually causes some level of disagreement between divorcing parents even if the parents can calmly decide the custody and visitation issues. The best-case scenario would involve parents who have jointly and amicably agreed to the custody and child support arrangements. Such amiability makes the entire decision process much easier on everybody,

CASE 10.5 *Ainsworth v. Ainsworth,* 154 Vt. 103, 574 A.2d 772 (1990)

Facts: The parties were divorced on April 30, 1986. They stipulated at that time that Mr. Ainsworth (defendant) was to pay child support in the amount of $35 per week for each of their two children, totaling $70 per week. Mr. Ainsworth remarried on August 15, 1987, and established a home with his new wife and her son at that time. On September 21, 1987, the plaintiff filed a motion for modification pursuant to the recently revised child support guidelines. She sought increased support in an amount to be determined under the new guidelines. The new statute provided that the new guidelines could be applied to any previous divorce order that varied more than 15 percent from the amount that would be required to be paid under the new guidelines.

A hearing on the motion was held on November 3, 1987. The parties agreed that since the preexisting order amount was more than 15 percent lower than an amount calculated under the new guideline, the plaintiff had shown a change of circumstances as required by the new statute, and a new amount could be calculated by the court. The trial court held that a departure downward from the new guideline amount of $141 per week for the two children was warranted because under the circumstances (the defendant had a new second family to support), the new amount would not leave sufficient financial resources for the needs of the defendant. The trial ordered that the new total support obligation should be $90 per week. This new amount was $20 more than the plaintiff had been receiving before the guidelines were revised, but the plaintiff still appealed the decision.

Issue: Whether the expenses for a second family should enter into the determination of child support for the preexisting family.

Court's Reasoning: If a noncustodial parent is subject to two child support orders, the amount paid under the first order is always deductible from that parent's income in determining the amount of the second order. This is so even if the child covered by the second order might have been born *before* the child covered by the first order. It would be unfair, however, to consider amounts paid under existing support obligations only when they are the subject of court orders. The legislature must have intended that the courts use their discretion to consider the expenses connected with second families. The use of discretion in this area prevents the guideline system from being wholly arbitrary. Support for dependents without an order does not have a judicial evaluation, and therefore, the noncustodial parent must prove that the amounts paid are reasonable and necessary under the circumstances.

Holding: Reversed in favor of the first Mrs. Ainsworth.

Case Discussion: A question of how to determine child support arises when newly married spouses bring another child into the family, and then subsequently divorce. It would appear from this case that the first child, *if there's a child support order in place,* takes priority. Do you think it would be more equitable to split any available support equally among the children?

including the judge. The parties who cannot agree are asking an impersonal judicial system for help with very personal matters.

Unfortunately, the newest case to enter Susan's law office could never be described as a best-case scenario. Clara and Clay Cleaver are divorced, and the post-divorce financial situation is not pretty because Clay has left town while owing child support without leaving a forwarding address.

Show Me the Money

Johnson & Webster's client Clara Cleaver has a classic "he says, she says" problem. *She* says her ex-husband should have plenty of money to pay the court-ordered child support, and the last time Clara saw him, *he* said he did not. Clara was a stay-at-home mother of two boys who faced her recent divorce without a job or proverbial nest egg. She is now working in a grocery store and studying to be a nurse. Her ex-spouse is somewhat suspiciously claiming poverty, and his whereabouts are uncertain.

"Susan, could you come in here for a minute?" Alyssa called from her office.

"Sure, Alyssa, I just want to save this," Susan answered. Ever since she'd lost work on her computer during her first week at Johnson & Webster's, Susan *always* saved her work to the network drive before moving on to the next task. Walking into Alyssa's office, Susan grinned and asked, "What's up?"

"I know you're working on several things right now, but I need some help with a nonpayment of support matter. I represented Mrs. Clara Cleaver in her divorce, and unfortunately, Mr. Clay Cleaver has been less than diligent in paying his child support."

"Why doesn't the court go after him?" Susan asked.

"They've tried," Alyssa answered. "The original order included that all payments were to be made to the Probation Department so that the contempt orders for nonpayment would be automatic, and Mrs. Cleaver wouldn't have to go hunting for the boys' child support," Alyssa explained. "However, the sheriff's office can't serve an order on a person who has left the area, has no local bank accounts, and whose employment isn't local. In the past, Mr. Cleaver has claimed he had very little. Mrs. Cleaver always claimed he had more, but we've never been able to prove as much as she claimed."

"How did you get a child support order from the judge without proving Mr. Cleaver's income?" Susan asked.

"We were able to produce an estimate of Mr. Cleaver's income, but it wasn't easy," Alyssa explained. "Mr. Cleaver is self-employed, so we had to base our estimate on the amount of income it took to support the Cleaver family. We even produced paid bills to help show the minimum that Mr. Cleaver must have earned to support his family as he did. We didn't even have any income tax records or W-2 forms to produce. We presented our evidence to the judge, and he *imputed* income to Mr. Cleaver."

"What does **imputed income** mean?" Susan asked.

Alyssa explained, "The court will attribute income to someone in several situations. For example, if a noncustodial parent purposely quits a job to avoid the initial child support obligation order, the judge will look to how much the parent was earning before he quit. Another classic example is when a payor-parent voluntarily becomes what the court considers underemployed despite having more advanced training. We asked the court to look to the lifestyle of the Cleavers before the separation to impute an estimate of his earnings. The problem is that Mr. and Mrs. Cleaver have two young boys, Thomas and Woodrow (Woodchuck is his nickname), and Mrs. Cleaver and the children had been solely supported by Mr. Cleaver."

"What can *I* do to help?" Susan asked.

"I need you to track down Mr. Cleaver's income. We'll need to find out where he is spending his money, if he has any. He left the area without any forwarding address. He's staying somewhere. Does he have a girlfriend? Who is he spending his money on? You get the idea," Alyssa replied. Then she added, "You can ask Mrs. Cleaver where she thinks the money went, and then from right here, in the safety of the office, you can use the phone and computer to follow Mrs. Cleaver's leads. Do you want to give it the old college try?"

Susan was interested. "I've never done anything like this before," she told Alyssa. "But I love a good mystery. I'll certainly give it a go."

"Good," Alyssa responded. "The overwhelming majority of moms and dads provide for their children, and I just hate to see a parent abdicate his responsibility. Those Cleaver kids have been through enough. I've known Clara Cleaver and her family for years, and she needs our help. Just think of it as financial hide-and-seek, and let's get this guy."

CHECK IS IN THE MAIL?:
REPRESENTING A CLIENT SEEKING ENFORCEMENT

The majority of the five million mothers and fathers who have court-ordered child support obligations *do* pay their child support, but the federal government's entry into the child support punishment arena has provided another layer of defense in the war on nonpaying parents.[10] For its part, the federal government has made an effort to encourage payment of child support by creating the Deadbeat Parents Punishment Act in 1998. The **Deadbeat Parents Punishment Act** ensures that the seriousness of not supporting one's children will be understood by a nonpaying parent by providing that the nonpaying parent can be sentenced to jail for 6 to 24 months for nonpayment.

Suppose your client has a child support order gripped tightly in her hand and has begun to hang out daily at her mailbox. The child support check is a no-show. What now? Along with the governmental support, a family practice can be very helpful to their clients tracking down child support. When child support is not being paid, one of the first questions to ask the custodial parent is whether the obligated parent is living in the same state with the children, out of the state, or out of the country. It is admittedly more difficult to retrieve child support from a nonpaying out-of-state parent, but not impossible.

First, let's take the case of the client whose obligated ex-spouse resides in the same state, but has failed to pay court-ordered child support. The following questions are really just common sense. Where is the deadbeat parent living? Do we know where the parent is working? Do we know the parent's Social Security number? One of the most successful ways to collect child support from a nonpaying parent is by direct *wage withholding* from the obligated parent's paycheck, also known as **wage garnishment.** Most child support orders will state that it requires the obligated parent's employer to withhold the child support that is ordered, and to send it to the local Child Support Enforcement Program for disbursement. Another way is for federal and state income tax refunds to be withheld to collect unpaid child support. This is known as a **tax refund intercept.**

Overdue child support may be collected in interesting places if you can think outside the proverbial box. Several years ago, single-mom Susan Brotchie founded *Advocates for Better Child Support* in Massachusetts to help people establish child support or collect overdue payments. Brotchie heard that a group of prisoners at the state penitentiary had won $2.3 million from the state as a result of a lawsuit based on overcrowded prison conditions. This motivated Brotchie to investigate whether any of the prisoners involved in the lawsuit also owed back child support. Brotchie's efforts resulted in over $300,000 of the lawsuit winnings being seized by the state for overdue child support.[11]

A final order of divorce should provide the legal mechanism for ensuring that child support obligations are met. The judge may decide to include the mechanism, or hopefully the parties agree to such mechanisms in the case of a default. Sanctions may also be included in the final order. For example, the public sanctions for nonpayment of financial obligations could include hearings for civil contempt and criminal contempt (also known as criminal nonsupport). **Civil contempt** is when the sentence can be purged (removed from a person's record) by paying the overdue amount to the receiving spouse. **Criminal contempt** (or criminal nonsupport) will be more punitive in nature toward the nonpaying payor. The civil mechanisms for ensuring payment could include *liens* on property owned by the payor, *trusts* clearly designed to ensure payment to the payees, and *life insurance* paid in the event of the death of the payor to the payees. A **lien** is defined as a claim against specific property that can be enforced in court to secure payment of a judgment, duty, or debt. A **trust** is an arrangement by which one person holds legal title to money or property for the benefit of another. The **life insurance** will typically be in large enough amounts that financial loss of the payor-parent will still allow the child to be supported until adulthood.

The courts may also order the sale of property with the proceeds applied to the support debt. To do that, a court order called a *writ of execution* must be issued permitting a court official to take the debtor's property to pay the debt. Additionally, many states routinely report child support debts to credit bureaus.

Getting Serious: Feds Step In to Enforce Child Support Orders

During the latter half of the twentieth century, divorce filings increased, illegitimate births rose, and in too many instances parents abandoned financial responsibilities. Looking for a reason behind the increasing number of children needing public assistance programs and the increasing need for federal funding, the United States Senate in 1974 studied the growing problem.

The results of the study were reported in Senate Report 93-1356, which stated: *The problem of welfare in the United States is, to a considerable extent, a problem of nonsupport of children by their absent parents. The eleven million recipients, who are now receiving Aid to Families with Dependent Children (AFDC), are on the rolls because four out of five children have been deprived of the support of a parent who has absented himself from the home.* The Senate Report also found that a fundamental problem appeared to be the lack of a cohesive national policy to ensure that errant parents were forced to face their financial responsibilities to their children. This is why the federal government stepped in to deal with the problem.

The Senate Report was presented in preparation for the enactment of **Title IV-D of the Social Security Act.** Title IV-D called for an improvement in child support enforcement programs in all 50 states and for an increase in federal monitoring of the state programs. Title IV-D was also designed to connect the effectiveness of a state's child support enforcement program with the federal funding the state would receive for its *Aid to Families with Dependent Children (AFDC) program.* The eventual passage of the Title IV-D legislation had a huge national impact because Title IV-D required that each state's legislature would have to create legislation directing their family courts to expeditiously and uniformly deal with child support enforcement matters.

Although the *Child Support Recovery Act of 1992* made it a federal crime to willfully fail to pay support for a child living in another state, the abandonment of parental financial responsibilities still places the burden of aiding millions of insufficiently supported children upon the individual states. Each state, with assistance from federal funding, has supported its needy children through the AFDC program, which began as a small part of the Social Security Act and was originally designed solely to help widows support their children. The AFDC subsequently mushroomed in the 70-odd years after it was initiated and was replaced with a program named *Transitional Assistance to Needy Families (TANF)* in 1996. Every year each state receives a significant portion of the funding needed to support their public assistance programs from the federal government.

All states now require that any parent receiving TANF support *assign* their right to uncollected child support to the state. When you **assign** a right, you give another your right through a legal and formal transfer. Additionally, all government assistance programs will consider the income of a custodial parent's new spouse, or adult partner, in residence when determining benefit eligibility. Title IV-D agencies must also provide assistance to custodial parents who are seeking to obtain or enforce a child support award. A small service fee is charged by the states offering such assistance. The agency's help is especially useful when a custodial parent cannot afford a lawyer to assist in enforcing a court order.

The Title IV-D state agency is also required to operate a **Parent Locator Service** within its child support enforcement program. If an individual state's Parent Locator Service cannot find the nonpaying parent, a state can ask the **Federal Locator Service** to use its national computer network or ask for help from such state agencies as the Department of Motor Vehicles. The national computer network is linked with Social Security, employment, and tax information.

The access to finding where a nonpaying parent has relocated has never been greater. Unfortunately, the problem is that when all this computer-generated information gets in the hands of the wrong person or is accessed for the wrong reasons, serious ramifications can occur. For example, a victim of domestic violence may purposely be hiding from an attacker who could fraudulently attempt to access information on a victim's location utilizing the state or federal locator systems. The state and federal locator systems are necessary tools and as such cannot be shut down. However, a protection mechanism has been instituted, and now **domestic violence indicators** are placed on personal files that need to be flagged for disclosure protection.

URESA to the Rescue: Law Provides Jurisdictional Authority

The Social Security Act's Title IV-D legislation was not the only legislation written to combat the problem of collecting unpaid court-ordered child support payments. A group of law professors, politicians, and practicing family law attorneys first gathered together in the 1950s to contemplate the jurisdictional problems of following a nonpaying parent from one state to another. This group originated from the *National Conference of Commissioners on Uniform State Laws.* Developed from this group's discussions was a uniform statute written to help solve the jurisdictional problems.

The first line of the **Uniform Reciprocal Enforcement of Support Act of 1968 (URESA)** explained that it was created *to improve and extend by reciprocal legislation the enforcement of duties of support.* More bluntly stated, URESA was born to combat the problem of a parent abdicating his monetary child support obligations by not only skipping town, but also skipping the *state.* A 1968 amended version of URESA became the **Revised Uniform Reciprocal Enforcement of Support Act (RURESA).**

Prior to URESA, a nonpaying parent could leave the state where the child support order had been signed and then relax because his new state would not have jurisdiction to hear a contempt of court case against the new resident for nonpayment of a child support order from another state. The eventual passage of URESA or RURESA by all 50 states means that a nonpaying parent now may face civil contempt penalties, or even arrest on criminal charges, for leaving a child support responsibility in another state. Once the nonpaying parent is found in his new state, the court in the new state can proceed to order enforcement of the original order by requiring that all child support payments be made by the nonpaying parent directly to his new state's Title IV-D agency. This state agency is often the probation department of the county where the previously nonpaying parent currently resides. This helps to ensure that if nonpayment occurs again, a contempt of court arrest warrant can go out as soon as possible from the new state's probation department. The nonpaying parent can then be brought to court without the former spouse having to file a request for payment of child support all over again.

UIFSA: New and Improved Statute Facilitates Interstate Issues

The relatively recently enacted **Uniform Interstate Family Support Act (UIFSA)** facilitates interstate child support case processing today. The UIFSA was partly created in response to a January 1992 U.S. Accounting Report that concluded that 30 percent of all child support cases are interstate and that children in interstate cases are less likely than in-state children to receive support payments. The **Full Faith and Credit for Child Support Orders Act (FFCCSOA)** was another recent addition to the federal arsenal of laws enacted to ensure that each state will respect the child support orders written in other states. The UIFSA updates the Revised Uniform Reciprocal Enforcement of Support Act of 1968 discussed in the case of *Kulko v. Kulko* (see Case 10.6). Although there may be some state-specific alterations, all 50 states have enacted a version of the UIFSA. (The states did not have much choice, since the passage of UIFSA was connected

CASE 10.6 *Kulko v. Kulko,*
436 U.S. 84, 98 S. Ct. 1690 (1978)

Facts: The appellant, Ezra Kulko, married the appellee, Sharon Kulko Horn, in 1959 during the appellant's three-day stopover in California en route from a military base in Texas. Both parties resided in and were residents of New York. The parties had two children and resided as a family in New York until March 1972, when the Kulkos separated.

Following the separation, Sharon Kulko moved to San Francisco, California. The separation agreement was drawn up in New York. Sharon flew to New York to sign the agreement in September 1972.

The agreement provided that the children would spend the school year with their father in New York and their vacations with their mother in California. While the children were with their mother, she would receive $3,000 per month from Ezra for the support of their children. Immediately after the execution of the separation agreement, Sharon flew to Haiti and procured a divorce there. She then returned to California and remarried, taking the name of Horn.

In December of 1973, one of the two children informed Ezra, just as she was about to leave to visit her mother, that she wished to remain in California with her mother after her vacation. Her father, the appellant, purchased a one-way plane ticket for his daughter, and she commenced living in California with her mother and vacationing with her father in New York. In January 1976, the appellant's other child called his mother and informed her that he also wished to live with her. The appellee sent him a plane ticket to come live with her; however, the appellant was unaware of this decision at this time. Less than one month after the appellee's second child came to live with her, she brought this action in California against the appellant to enforce the Haitian divorce, modify the custody order, and increase the support obligations.

Issue: Whether the California state courts in an action for child support may exercise *in personam* jurisdiction over a nonresident, nondomiciliary parent of minor children domiciled within the state.

Court's Reasoning: The due process clause of the Fourteenth Amendment operates as a limitation on the jurisdiction of state courts to enter judgments affecting rights or interests of nonresident defendants. It has long been the rule that a valid judgment imposing a personal obligation or duty in favor of the plaintiff may be entered only by a court having *in personam* jurisdiction over the person of the defendant. In this case, the court finds that having his children in the state does not constitute the adequate contact with the state in order to have that state assert personal jurisdiction over him. This is the case whether or not the appellant had given permission to his children to move out to California with their mother. The Court holds that the exercise of such jurisdiction would violate the due process clause of the Fourteenth Amendment, and therefore, any action that needs to be taken by the appellee can be done through the Uniform Reciprocal Enforcement of Support Act of 1968. This act provides a mechanism for communication between court systems in different states in order to facilitate the procurement and enforcement of child support decrees where dependent children reside in a state that cannot obtain personal jurisdiction over the defendant.

Holding: Appellant wins.

Case Discussion: The Reciprocal Enforcement of Support Act of 1968 has been revised since the *Kulko* decision and was followed by the UIFSA. The revised act and UIFSA still provide for situations involving child support and parents residing in different states. Do you agree with the court's explanation that having your children reside in a state does not create a threshold connection to that state by a nondomiciliary? The father may have won the case because of the jurisdictional issue, but the court has still given the mother the option to seek her modifications through a New York court. It is unlikely that Mr. Kulko would not have to pay increased child support now that his children live in California with their mother.

to whether the federal government would supply child support funding to the states.) Check where your state's version of the UIFSA statute is located in Exhibit 10.3, and read the original UIFSA in Appendix G.

U.S. Supreme Court Decides Jurisdictional Issue

The case of *Kulko v. Kulko* (see Case 10.6) pulled the United States Supreme Court into the jurisdictional fray. It may be hard to believe, but a request for modification of child support that started out in a California family court ended up with the illustrious United States Supreme Court deciding a disputed issue of *in personam* jurisdiction. Recall from your earlier reading that *in personam* jurisdiction is defined as the authority a court has over the person about whom the court has the power to make decisions that are legally binding. The *Kulko* case also involves an attempt at **long-arm jurisdiction,** which is when a state claims jurisdiction over persons outside the state. A court will not have long-arm jurisdiction unless the person sued has certain minimum contacts with the state.

SUSAN PLAYS DETECTIVE

Susan wanted to do her best to help the Cleaver family. Alyssa had told Susan to check out Mrs. Cleaver's file first. Her first step after pulling the office file was to review the Cleaver's child support order. Next, she wanted to check the order against the file's check-off sheet. Alyssa had explained to Susan on her first day on the job that all of the office files included check-off sheets. The check-off sheets acted as a safety net to ensure that all necessary actions were completed on each file.

Susan could see by reading the order that the child support order was quite inclusive. The Cleaver order included the following: (1) income of the parents; (2) the support figure based on the child support guidelines; (3) duration of the support obligation; (4) the date on which child support is due each month; (5) the requirement that medical insurance be provided; (6) provisions for a QMSCO; (7) a provision for life insurance coverage; (8) allocation of deductibles and copayments; (9) allocation of tax deductions; (10) allocation of reasonable and necessary expenses for the boys' college expenses; (11) payment to be made through the court system; and (12) a cost-of-living adjustment.[12]

As far as Susan could tell, the problem clearly wasn't the order, but a nonpaying Mr. Cleaver. Susan knew she'd have to find Mr. Cleaver if the Cleaver kids were ever going to see another dollar of their support. Susan thought, "I really need to speak with the person who may unwittingly know where he is—Mrs. Cleaver." Susan decided to telephone Mrs. Cleaver.

"Hi, Mrs. Cleaver, it's Susan," she began. "I know that Alyssa already went over this with you, but do you have any more ideas about where your ex-husband could be?"

Clara quickly answered, "Believe me, I've called all his friends and family, and no one has heard from him."

"Do you think any of those friends and family are tight enough with him that they'd lie for him?" Susan asked.

"Honestly, I don't think so." Clara paused, and then added, "He burned a lot of bridges and borrowed money from a lot of those people. I think they'd like to get ahold of him, too."

Susan continued, "Can you think of any contacts he may have that you haven't checked? Perhaps, you've overlooked someone because you assumed Mr. Cleaver wouldn't go to that person."

Clara was quiet for a minute. "Well, now that I think about it, there is his brother, Cletus, in California, but none of us have spoken to him in years. Clay's brother left over 10 years ago himself, and he owed Clay and me quite a lot of money, too."

"California!" Susan thought. Aloud she said, "Blood *is* thicker than water—plus, what easier way to pay off a debt than letting your own brother stay with you?" Susan continued, "Do you have any idea where Cletus lives in California?"

EXHIBIT 10.3 State UIFSA Statutes

Uniform Interstate Family Support Act

State	Code	State	Code
Alabama	Ala. Code § 30-3A-101	Montana	Mont. Code Ann. § 40-5-101
Alaska	Alaska Stat. § 25.25.101	Nebraska	Neb. Rev. Stat. § 42-701
Arizona	Ariz. Rev. Stat. § 25-621	Nevada	Nev. Rev. Stat. § 130.0902
Arkansas	Ark. Code Ann. § 9-17-101	New Hampshire	N.H. Rev. Stat. Ann. § 546-B:1
California	Cal. Fam. Code § 4900 (West)	New Jersey	N.J. Stat. Ann. § 2A:4-30.65
Colorado	Colo. Rev. Stat. Ann. § 14-5-101	New Mexico	N.M. Stat. Ann. § 40-6A-101
Connecticut	Conn. Gen. Stat. Ann. § 46b-212	New York	N.Y. Dom. Rel. § 580-101
Delaware	Del. Code Ann. tit. 13, § 601	North Carolina	N.C. Gen. Stat. § 52C-1-100
District of Columbia	D.C. Code Ann. § 30-341.1	North Dakota	N.D. Cent. Code § 14-12.2-01
Florida	Fla. Stat. Ann. § 88.0011	Ohio	Ohio Rev. Code Ann. § 3115.01
Georgia	Ga. Code Ann. § 19-11-100	Oklahoma	Okla. Stat. Ann. tit. 43, § 601-100
Hawaii	Haw. Rev. Stat. § 576B-101	Oregon	Or. Rev. Stat. tit. § 110.303
Idaho	Idaho Code § 7-1001	Pennsylvania	Pa. Stat. Ann. tit. 23, § 7101
Illinois	Ill. Rev. Stat. ch. 750, para. 22/100	Rhode Island	R.I. Gen. Laws § 15-23.1-101
Indiana	Ind. Code Ann. § 31-18-1-1 (West)	South Carolina	S.C. Code Ann. § 20-7-960
Iowa	Iowa Code Ann. § 252K.101 (West)	South Dakota	S.D. Cod. Laws § 25-9B-101
Kansas	Kan. Stat. Ann. § 23-9, 101	Tennessee	Tenn. Code Ann. § 36-5-2001
Kentucky	Ky. Rev. Stat. Ann. § 407.5101	Texas	Tex. Fam. Code Ann. § 159.001
Louisiana	La. Rev. Stat. Ann. art. 1301.1	Utah	Utah Code Ann. § 78-45f-100
Maine	Me. Rev. Stat. Ann. tit. 19, § 2801	Vermont	Vt. Stat. Ann. tit. 15B, § 101
Maryland	Md. Code Ann. Family Law § 10-301	Virginia	Va. Code Ann. § 20-88.32
Massachusetts	Mass. Gen. Laws Ann. ch 209D, § 1-101	Washington	Wash. Rev. Code Ann. § 26.21.005
Michigan	Mich. Comp Laws Ann. § 552	West Virginia	W. Va. Code § 48B-1-101
Minnesota	Minn. Stat. Ann. § 518C.101	Wisconsin	Wis. Stat. Ann. § 769.101
Mississippi	Miss. Code Ann. § 93-25-1	Wyoming	Wyo. Stat. Ann. § 20-4-139
Missouri	Mo. Ann. Stat. § 454.850		

Mrs. Cleaver answered, "Honestly, I haven't a clue. Clay's mom died a few years back, but Cletus didn't even come back for the funeral."

"If you think of any leads, please give me a call," Susan requested.

"I most certainly will," Clara answered. She added, "And Susan, thanks for helping us out. I really appreciate it. I didn't know where else to turn."

Susan said a quick good-bye. She was eager to do some sleuthing and see if she could trace Mr. Cleaver to California.

Tracking Down a Deadbeat Parent: Susan Gets Her Man

Susan's next telephone call was to the state Parent Locator Service. The service had tried, with no success, to locate Mr. Cleaver when he had first failed to pay. Now Susan, armed with a possible California location, wanted the state to help again. Only a state Title IV-D agency can ask the federal locator service to join in the search. Additionally, Susan had learned that new state and federal laws required all new employees to be reported to a new-hire registry on the state and national levels. The new-hires directories are part of the federal Parent Locator Service. The federal service was able to track down Clay through his car registration.

Within a few days, Susan received notification that Clay Cleaver had registered his snazzy new sports car in California. Bingo!

Next, Alyssa directed Susan to prepare a Notice of Motion for Enforcement, a Certification of the Plaintiff, and an Order for Enforcement. All states are required to pursue out-of-state child support cases in the same way they pursue in-state cases. The Cleaver's situation was exactly the situation the UIFSA was designed to assist with. Susan quickly finished the papers for Alyssa's review and thought, "A threat of a little jail time should loosen the change from Mr. Cleaver's wallet." The state where the request for child supports originates is called the **initiating state.** The state where the nonpaying parent resides is the **responding state.** Read the documents Susan prepared in Exhibits 10.4, 10.5, and 10.6. Notice that Clara has been called the *defendant* in these papers. This is because Mr. Cleaver was the plaintiff in the original divorce action. In addition, review the warrant for Mr. Cleaver's arrest shown in Exhibit 10.7.

All's Well That Pays Well

Alyssa excitedly called Susan into her office and told her, "Susan, I'm thrilled to report that Mr. Cleaver has seen the light. The warrant for his arrest must have worked."

"Has he paid a good chunk of the arrearages?" Susan inquired.

"Better than that," Alyssa announced. "The California judge must not have liked the idea that he'd bought a new car, hid out, *and* hadn't paid a dime of support. Good old Clay had to pay the whole thing before the judge let him out of the county jail!"

Susan was thrilled for the Cleavers and responded with enthusiasm, "I'm sure glad I had the UIFSA to help me out. It must have been hard to track a deadbeat parent before the feds got involved and computers were so handy."

Alyssa answered, "You can say that again. Susan, you did a great job. Your work will have a very positive affect on the Cleaver family."

"Thanks, Alyssa," Susan beamed. She couldn't help but smile all the way back to her desk.

CHAPTER SUMMARY

Any child support issue begins with the basic premise that parents are responsible for providing life necessities for their children until they reach majority or are emancipated. All 50 states have statutorily created child support guidelines. The guidelines typically match a parent's income with the amount of child support the parent should have to pay. Each state also includes a number of factors that their courts will consider before determining the final child support figure. The guidelines usually stop at a certain level of income. When parents make more income than is listed on the income guidelines, the following general list of factors is considered by United States courts: (1) all financial resources of the noncustodial parent, including the financial resources of a stepparent or new partner; (2) all financial resources of the custodial parent, including the financial resources of a stepparent or new partner; (3) all financial resources of the children; (4) the earning potential of both parents; (5) the financial needs of both parents; (6) the standard of living of children before the parents' separation; (7) the age of the children; (8) additional responsibility of the noncustodial parent to support other spouse and children; and (9) extraordinary expenses. Different income models are used to calculate child support; these include the income-share model, the percentage-of-income model, and the Melson-Delaware income model.

The federal government has become extensively involved in the pursuit of unpaid child support for our nation's children. One example of that involvement is the Deadbeat Parents Punishment Act. The federal government also enacted Title IV-D of the Social Security Act. Title IV-D requires an improvement in child support enforcement programs in all 50 states or a state could risk the lost of federal aid to their state-run

EXHIBIT 10.4 Notice of Motion for Enforcement

Alyssa Jensen, Esq.
Johnson & Webster, Esqs.
123 Main Street
Newton, New Jersey 12345
973-555-1212
Attorney for Defendant

CLAY CLEAVER,
 	
           Plaintiff,
 	
v.
 	
CLARA CLEAVER,
 	
           Defendant.
	) SUPERIOR COURT OF NEW JERSEY
	) CHANCERY DIVISION-FAMILY PART
	) SUSSEX COUNTY
	) Docket No. FM-19-456-03
	) CIVIL ACTION
	)
	) NOTICE OF MOTION FOR
	) ENFORCEMENT
	)

TO: Clay Cleaver, pro se
909 Runaway Lane
Loserville, CA 99999
Plaintiff

SIR:

PLEASE TAKE NOTICE that on Friday, June 13, 2003, at 9 o'clock in the forenoon or as soon thereafter as counsel may be heard, the under-signed attorney for the Defendant, Clara Cleaver, shall move before the Superior Court of New Jersey, Chancery Division, Family Part, located at 43-47 High Street, County of Sussex, Newton, New Jersey, for an order:

1. Finding Plaintiff in willful and knowing contempt of Court.
2. Finding Plaintiff to be in violation of litigants' rights for failure to comply with the Final Judgment of Divorce and Separation and Property Settlement Agreement.
3. Issuing an immediate warrant for Plaintiff's arrest for his continuing and willful violation of the Final Judgment of Divorce and Separation and Property Settlement Agreement.
4. Holding Plaintiff incarcerated until all sums due and owing the Defendant are paid in full.
5. Directing Plaintiff to pay any and all arrears in child support in full.
6. Directing Plaintiff to pay any and all medical expenses in full.
7. For counsel fees and costs of this application.
8. For such further relief as the Court may deem equitable and just.

PLEASE TAKE FURTHER NOTICE that annexed hereto is a Certification in support hereof.

PLEASE TAKE FURTHER NOTICE that oral argument with regard to this motion is requested given the nature of the relief sought and the complexity of the issues involved.

Alyssa Jensen, Esq.
Attorney at Law

By: _____
Alyssa Jensen

DATED: _____

The undersigned hereby certifies that the within pleading was signed within the time permitted by the rules.

_____

Alyssa Jensen, Esq.
Johnson & Webster, Esqs.
123 Main Street
Newton, New Jersey 12345
973-555-1212
Attorney for Defendant

EXHIBIT 10.5 Order of Enforcement

Alyssa Jensen, Esq.
Johnson & Webster, Esqs.
123 Main Street
Newton, New Jersey 12345
973-555-1212
Attorney for Defendant

CLAY CLEAVER,
 	
              Plaintiff,
 	
 v.
 	
 CLARA CLEAVER,
 	
           Defendant.
	SUPERIOR COURT OF NEW JERSEY
	 CHANCERY DIVISION-FAMILY PART
	 SUSSEX COUNTY
	 Docket No. FM-19-456-03
	 CIVIL ACTION
	
	 ORDER FOR ENFORCEMENT

This matter having come to the attention of the court on June 13, 2003, on application of the Defendant, Alyssa Jensen, Esq., attorney for the Defendant, and on notice to Plaintiff, Clay Cleaver, and the court having read the papers filed on behalf of the Defendant, and the court having heard oral argument and the court having considered same, and for good cause shown:

It is, on this 13th day of June, 2003,

ORDERED, as follows:

1. Plaintiff is hereby found to be in willful and knowing contempt of this Court.

2. Plaintiff is hereby found to be in violation of litigants' rights for failure to comply with the Final Judgment of Divorce and Separation and Property Settlement Agreement.

3. A warrant for Plaintiff's arrest is hereby issued and executed for his continuing and willful violation of the Final Judgment of Divorce and Separation and Property Settlement Agreement.

4. Plaintiff will hereby be held incarcerated until all sums due and owing are paid in full.

5. Plaintiff is to pay $3,000 for full satisfaction of child support arrears.

6. Plaintiff is to pay $550 for full satisfaction of medical arrears.

7. Defendant is hereby ordered to pay the sum of $_____ to Alyssa Jensen, Esq., for the benefit of the Defendant, Clara Cleaver, within fifteen (15) days of entry hereof.

_____
Judge Jonathan Faire, J.S.C.

Consent as to form:

_____
Clay Cleaver
Pro Se

_____
Alyssa Jensen, Esq.
Attorney for Defendant

EXHIBIT 10.6 Certification of Defendant

Alyssa Jensen, Esq.
Johnson & Webster, Esqs.
123 Main Street
Newton, New Jersey 12345
973-555-1212
Attorney for Defendant

CLAY CLEAVER,	)	SUPERIOR COURT OF NEW JERSEY
	)	CHANCERY DIVISION-FAMILY PART
Plaintiff,	)	SUSSEX COUNTY
	)	Docket No. FM-19-456-03
v.	)	CIVIL ACTION
	)	
CLARA CLEAVER,	)	CERTIFICATION OF DEFENDANT
Defendant.	)	

I, Clara Cleaver, of full age do hereby certify and say:

1. I am the Defendant in the above-captioned matter. I make this Certification in support of my application for Enforcement of child support.

2. By way of background, Plaintiff and I were married on February 14, 1989, in a civil ceremony in Las Vegas, Nevada. There were two children born of this marriage: Woodrow, age 10, and Thomas, age 12.

3. Plaintiff and I were divorced on April 26, 2001, by way of a Final Judgment of Divorce and Separation and Property Settlement Agreement, annexed hereto as Exhibits A and B, respectively.

4. Pursuant to Section IV, paragraph A, of our Separation and Property Settlement Agreement, Plaintiff was to pay $250 per week in child support for the benefit of the minor children, Woodrow and Thomas. This is far below what the Plaintiff should be paying.

5. Plaintiff is a self-employed contractor. In addition, Plaintiff has his black seal for boilers, his plumber's license, and his electrician's license. The child support was set at an amount based on his imputed income. As the Court is well aware, there are many ways a self-employed person can get paid cash income that is unreported to the Internal Revenue Service.

6. Nevertheless, Plaintiff has failed to make his support payments, and when he did they were very sporadic. Plaintiff has now accrued arrears exceeding $3,000 which is over 12 months of nonpayment of support. In addition, Plaintiff has failed to pay any of the unreimbursed medical expenses for the children, which exceed $500.

7. I am a clerk at the local grocery store. I am not able to support myself and the children on my income alone. I need the support from the Plaintiff to make ends meet. I have had to borrow money from my friends and family members, including Plaintiff's mother and cousin, to make ends meet and to make sure the boys, Woodrow and Thomas, do not go without the necessities.

8. It has been discovered that Plaintiff has recently purchased a new car. How is it that Plaintiff can afford to buy new things that benefit him, but does not support his children? Plaintiff should make the children a priority, but he told me the last time I saw him that he feels the support is my *play* money. I only want the Plaintiff to be responsible for his obligations to me and the children.

9. Plaintiff has shown blatant disregard for the court-ordered child support. I am begging the Court to take action against the Plaintiff and enforce the Separation and Property Settlement Agreement. I am asking the Court to issue a warrant for Plaintiff's arrest and to keep that warrant active for the lifetime of the child support obligation. The Court knows how this works. A bench warrant will be issued; Plaintiff will pay; the warrant will be withdrawn; Plaintiff will then stop paying again; and back to Court we come. I cannot afford to incur any more legal fees.

10. I am asking the Court to make Plaintiff responsible for my legal fees for this application for enforcement. I cannot afford to pay my household bills without Plaintiff's support, and it is his fault that I have to bring this application to the Court.

Certification

I certify that the foregoing statements made by me are true. I am aware that if any of the foregoing statements made by me are willfully false, I am subject to punishment.

DATED: _____

Clara Cleaver

EXHIBIT 10.7 Warrant For Arrest

Alyssa Jensen, Esq.
Johnson & Webster, Esqs.
123 Main Street
Newton, New Jersey 12345
973-555-1212
Attorney for Defendant

CLAY CLEAVER,	)	SUPERIOR COURT OF NEW JERSEY
	)	CHANCERY DIVISION-FAMILY PART
Plaintiff,	)	SUSSEX COUNTY
	)	Docket No. FM-19-456-03
v.	)	CIVIL ACTION
	)	
	)	
CLARA CLEAVER,	)	WARRANT FOR ARREST
	)	
Defendant.	)	

TO: Sheriff of Deadbeat County
        123 Law Way
        Abiding Citizens, CA 55875

YOU ARE HEREBY COMMANDED to arrest Clay Cleaver, at his California residence, 909 Runaway Lane, Loserville, California, or at such place as he is physically present in the State of California upon notice by Defendant, Clara Cleaver, of his location, and bring him forthwith before a Judge of the Superior Court to await further Order of the Court in this matter in connection with his willful violation of the Final Judgment of Divorce and Separation and Property Settlement Agreement of this Court.

DATED: _____

            WITNESS, _____, J.S.C., this 13th day of June, 2003.

                                                                    _____
                                                                    Hon. Jonathan Faire, J.S.C.

_____   _____
Alyssa Jensen, Esq.   Deputy Clerk of the
Attorney for Defendant   Superior Court

Transitional Assistance to Needy Families (TANF) programs. The Uniform Reciprocal Enforcement of Support Act of 1968 (URESA), and a later revised version, developed into the Uniform Interstate Family Support Act (UIFSA). The uniform acts, eventually passed into law by all 50 states, with some variations, were especially needed to assist in the retrieving of child support from parents who live in a different state from that where their children reside. For example, a mother and children residing in New York can receive a child support order in New York for payment by the father who lives in California. If the father fails to pay the child support order, the mother can file a motion in New York for arrearages. The New York court will send the motion to California for its judicial system to deal with. Prior to the uniform acts, the mother would usually have to travel to California to try to have a California court deal with the nonpayment of child support. The Internal Revenue Service also has become more involved by collecting child support arrearages through the withholding of tax refunds via a tax refund intercept.

Private enforcement measures for ensuring that child support payments are made include liens, trusts, and life insurance. Sanctions for nonpayment can include civil and criminal contempt. Wage garnishment may be another way to ensure that child support is paid. Requests for modification, either for an increase or a decrease, of the child support amount ordered can be made to the court at any time. The parent requesting the modification must have evidence of a material and substantial change in circumstances. The first child support order takes precedence when calculating any subsequent child support orders. Federal law requires each state to have child support guidelines that allocate health care costs. If an employee-parent fails to enroll her child in her employer's plan, as ordered by the court, the custodial parent may do so by serving the employer's health plan with a qualified medical child support order (QMCSO).

Key Terms

life necessities
child support
emancipation
income-share model
percentage-of-income model
Melson-Delaware income model
self-support reserve
rebuttable presumption
child support worksheet
financial disclosure affidavit
extraordinary expenses
qualified medical child support
   order (QMCSO)
escalation clause
material and substantial change
   in circumstances

consent order
imputed income
Deadbeat Parents Punishment
   Act
wage garnishment
tax refund intercept
civil contempt
criminal contempt
lien
trust
life insurance
Title IV-D of the Social
   Security Act
assign
Parent Locator Service
Federal Locator Service

domestic violence indicatiors
Uniform Reciprocal
   Enforcement of Support Act
   (URESA)
Revised Uniform Reciprocal
   Enforcement of Support Act
   (RURESA)
Uniform Interstate Family
   Support Act (UIFSA)
Full Faith and Credit for Child
   Support Orders Act
   (FFCCSOA)
long-arm jurisdiction
initiating state
responding state

Surfing the Web

http://www.supportguidelines.com Comprehensive resource for the interpretation and application of child support guidelines in the United States that provides both resources and links.

http://www.childsupport.com Support laws and calculator, CSN in the news, links to sites of interest, nationwide service.

http://www. nationalchildsupport.com National Child Support specializes in helping custodial parents get the child support payments they are legally entitled to receive. The site provides resources and information, a child support calculator, and information on paternity testing.

http://www.acf.hhs.gov The Administration for Children and Families (ACF) is a federal agency that assists state, territory, local, and tribal organizations in providing family assistance (welfare) and other programs relating to children and families through funding, policy direction, and information services. This site contains links to sites regarding adoption and foster care, child abuse and neglect, child care and support, disabilities, energy assistance, and so on.

http://www.acf.hhs.gov/programs/cse The Office of Child Support Enforcement details federal provisions for child support enforcement, including how businesses as employers can help to ensure that children receive proper support from their parents. The site also provides links to state child support agencies and to research on the quality of child care services and projects.

http://singleparents.about.com Articles on child support and visitation and on divorce and spousal support.

ETHICS ALERT

Susan could not believe what she had overheard in the lunchroom. One of the wealthiest professional athletes in the state was denying paternity and all claims for child support made by the mother of his alleged infant daughter. Apparently, the new mom was a cheerleader for the athlete's team. She had called Johnson & Webster's for representation in seeking child support. The financially strapped mom was coming in that afternoon because she had heard that the law firm would agree to a contingency fee arrangement only when dealing with paternity and child support actions. Do you think the cheerleader heard right?

Review Questions

1. What are life necessities?
2. (a) Name the income models. (b) What are the differences between these models?
3. The expectation of what should be paid is a rebuttable presumption. What does this mean?
4. What financial document must be filed to prove that child support calculations are correct? (The name of the document will depend on what state you are in.)
5. A majority of states allow the consideration of a variety of factors in addition to the numbers approach of the child support guidelines. What general factors may be considered?
6. What is the name of the federally mandated health care order?
7. What is an escalation clause?
8. What is the role of equitable estoppel in determining child support?
9. (a) What do you have to prove if you make a motion for modification of child support? (b) What is the standard of proof when seeking a modification?
10. How do most courts balance the needs of first and subsequent families when calculating child support?
11. What are some of the mechanisms used for collecting child support?
12. What is UIFSA?
13. Why was *in personam* jurisdiction such a big deal in the *Kulko* case?
14. Susan reviewed the Cleaver file and discovered that the original child support order was quite inclusive. What was included in the original order?
15. Describe the documents Susan prepared in the Cleaver case.

Endnotes

1. N.Y. Fam. Ct. Act § 413 1(a) (2003).
2. "Ties Cannot Be Unknotted," *ABA Journal* (February 2002): 28.
3. Kuczynski, Alex, "Can a Kid Squeeze by on $320,000 a Month?" *New York Times,* January 20, 2002, 9-1.
4. State of Florida Child Support Guidelines Worksheet.
5. 42 U.S.C. § 652(f) (1988).
6. 42 U.S.C. § 1396(g-1) (1988).
7. Lowe, Alexandra Dylan, "Divorced Dads Challenge Tuition Law," *ABA Journal* (August 1995): 23.
8. *Id.* at 25.
9. *Family Advocate* (Fall 2002): 42.
10. Thompson, Dianna, and Glenn Sacks, "Divorced from Reality on Child Support," *Star Ledger,* January 10, 2001, 21.
11. "The Scourge of Deadbeat Dads," *Newsweek,* March 29, 1995, 34.
12. "Child Support Checklists," *Family Advocate* 25, no. 1 (Summer 2002): 35.

Chapter 11

Divorce and Tax: No Shelter for the Weary

TAX RAMIFICATIONS OF DIVORCE AND SEPARATION

The **Internal Revenue Service** (popularly known by its abbreviation, **IRS**) is the federal agency that is empowered by our federal government to collect taxes. It may not seem fair to the spouse who receives temporary spousal support or alimony, but the IRS usually considers such payments to be taxable income. Meanwhile, the spouse who has agreed to, or has been ordered to, make these payments may have the last laugh because the IRS usually considers them tax-deductible.

Payments made by a client to support a separated or former spouse, however, are not automatically considered tax-deductible. Several statutory requirements must be fulfilled in order to be eligible for tax-deductible status. The attorneys negotiating clients' property settlement must be aware of these statutory requirements in order to negotiate the best property and support agreement possible for their clients. Failure to understand the tax ramifications of a settlement can cause lasting financial damage for a client and can lead an attorney precipitously close to a malpractice claim.

SUSAN LEARNS A TAX TIP

The Smiths' last negotiating session was held in a Johnson & Webster conference room. Susan had been asked by J. D. to take notes to make sure there would be a record of the numerous decisions that were being made. During the session, the Smiths and their attorneys ironed out the final details so that a draft of the settlement and property agreement could be prepared by Susan for review by the attorneys and clients. Ultimately, the settlement and property agreement would be submitted to Judge Comfort for the final hearing. The group had finished relatively quickly, considering the earlier difficulties. However, Susan left the meeting somewhat confused.

Susan planned to ask J. D. to clear up her confusion once Libby, Michael, and Howard Hughey left the office. Susan politely walked Libby to the office foyer after the session and then quickly returned to J. D.'s office to ask her question. "J. D., excuse me, but can I ask you a question?" Susan inquired.

"Sure, what's up?" J. D. answered.

"Why did you laugh when Mr. Hughey suggested that Mr. Smith pay a larger alimony payment to Mrs. Smith in return for paying a lower child support payment?" Susan asked.

J. D. smiled as he recalled his response. "I actually guffawed, didn't I?"

"Well, to be honest, yes," Susan agreed.

"The Internal Revenue Service really provided the punch line for me," J. D. explained. More confused than ever, Susan responded with only a baffled look. Seeing that Susan was still confused, J. D. said, "Okay, let me explain. You probably put tax out of your mind after graduating, but I'm sure your family law professor mentioned that alimony is *tax-deductible* to the spouse paying it and *taxable* to the spouse receiving it. Mrs. Smith isn't required to pay taxes on any child support payments, but she *is* expected to pay taxes on any alimony received. Oh, and you have to remember, child support payments aren't tax-deductible for Mr. Smith. Decreasing the child support and increasing the alimony would mean *more taxes* for Mrs. Smith, and I just couldn't allow that."

Susan sheepishly responded, "Now that you mention it, I do remember something like that."

Laughing, J. D. stated, "It's okay, I'm used to people getting a blank expression where tax is concerned." He continued, "While I've never had a case with Hughey before, he is known for being wily. He *must* know that it's an old trick to try to negotiate a larger *deductible* alimony payment for your client, and that's what made me laugh."

Susan asked, "Was Mr. Hughey being ethical in trying that?"

"What Hughey tried wasn't really illegal or unethical because the job of an attorney *is* to try to negotiate the best outcome without stepping over the line, but I had to do *my* job in negotiating for Mrs. Smith," J. D. explained. "By the way, I want to tell you that you did a great job assisting me with Mrs. Smith's case," he added.

Beaming, Susan answered, "Thank you, I'm glad I could help. I enjoyed applying what I learned in class to a real case."

HOW TO RESEARCH A TAX ISSUE

Where would you begin if you were working as a paralegal and were asked to find the statute that listed the IRS requirements that must be met before alimony or separate maintenance payments can be considered tax-deductible? As a federal agency, the IRS has rules that it lives by. The collected rules of an agency are known as a *code*. The Internal Revenue Service works with its own set of rules known as the **Internal Revenue Code.** The Internal Revenue Code is split into subject categories called *sections*. Your first research stop should be to look up your category within a section of the Code. Do not forget that the sections of the Internal Revenue Code are usually revised in some way each year. Therefore, any tax research must involve checking for recent revisions or precedent-setting court decisions.

The Code explains that an individual taxpayer may deduct an amount of alimony equal to the amount he has paid during any given tax year. This is a simple statement with clear intent. However, difficulties may occur when trying to determine what payments will be eligible to be considered alimony by the IRS. The Internal Revenue Code's **section 71(b)** lists the six requirements that must be met in order for a client's payments to be considered eligible as a tax deduction. You should know some of the fundamental vocabulary used in the Code before reading a description of the requirements. A **payor** is the spouse who is making the monetary payments, and the **payee** is the spouse who is receiving the monetary payments.

The Six IRS Must-Haves

1. The payment must be made in *cash*. The payment will still be considered cash if made by check or money order. Services provided by the payor do not qualify as cash. *(So, for example, Michael cannot go to the barn and clean out the chicken coop and have the value of that service be considered alimony.)* Payments in the form of property also do not comply with the rule. *(In this case, Michael*

also will not be considered to have paid alimony if he brings 20 pounds of chicken feed to the barn.)

2. The cash payment must be made to a payor's separated or divorced spouse according to a written divorce or separation agreement. The payor can give the cash payments to a third party that is owed money by the payee spouse. *(For example, if Michael, the payor spouse, sends a payment to the finance company holding a lien on Libby's car the payment would be considered a cash payment to Libby, the payee spouse.)*

3. If a written and signed divorce or separation agreement (whether temporary or final) clearly designates that the payments are not allowable as a deduction under section 71(b)(1), then the payment will not qualify.

4. When a couple is legally separated under a court order of divorce or separate maintenance but the two people are still living in the same household, the payor's payments to the payee will not be tax-deductible. An exception to this is when the spouses only have a temporary support order in place. Then the payments should be considered tax-deductible. *(This example would not apply to Michael, since he left the barn prior to the* pendente lite *order being issued.)*

5. If the payor-spouse is required to make *even one payment* to the payee's estate after the payee spouse dies, none of the previous payments are eligible as tax deductions. *(This is an attempt by the IRS to differentiate between support payments and a property settlement. This should definitely be a malpractice red flag, and J. D. has wisely ensured that no such payment is included in the separation and property agreement.)*

6. The payments cannot be a disguised version of child support. *(Child support is not tax-deductible because parents have a responsibility to care for their children, even if they do not have physical custody of the children. Again, J. D. was watching out for this during settlement negotiations.)*

Attempting to Disguise Child Support

In several situations, a payor-spouse may attempt to call a payment an alimony or spousal support payment, when in reality, that spouse is playing hide-and-seek with child support. Remember, alimony or spousal support will be tax-deductible for the payor spouse and taxable income for the payee-spouse, but child support is not considered tax-deductible for the payor-spouse or income to the payee-spouse. A telltale sign of child support being disguised as alimony occurs when the amount of spousal support is connected to an event occurring in the child's life. For example, say Harry is to pay Gladys $250 per week in alimony until Harry Junior leaves home. Upon Harry Junior's leaving home Gladys's alimony will be reduced to $200 per week. The $50 difference in alimony would be considered by the IRS to be child support and not tax-deductible. The remaining $200 would still be considered tax-deductible for Harry, the payor-spouse, and income for Gladys, the payee-spouse.

The game of hide-and-seek becomes slightly more complicated when the divorcing parties agree that the alimony or temporary spousal support payments are to be reduced upon certain dates that may or may not be related to their children. For example, Suppose Edsel and Agnes were married and had two children, Little Edsel and Little Agnes. Edsel agrees to pay Agnes $1,000 per month in alimony for the five years following their divorce, then $800 per month in alimony for the next five years, and finally $600 per month in alimony for the next five years. Now suppose Little Agnes is 16 years old at the time of the divorce and will be 20 years and six months old at the time the alimony payment will be reduced to $800. Little Edsel is 13 years old at the time of the divorce and will be 23 years old when the second reduction in alimony is to be made. The problem with the first reduction is that it will be made *less* than six months before Little Agnes is to reach the age of majority in their home state. Therefore, the IRS could make the assumption that the reduction is connected to an event happening in the child's life—in this case, Little Agnes turning 21.

The second reduction faces another problem. The IRS's red flag goes up when spousal support payments are to be reduced two or more times. If the multiple reductions occur within the year before, or after, the payor-spouse's children reach between the ages of 18 and 24, the IRS will often assume that the reductions are contingent upon the children reaching a certain age, even if additional child support is being paid apart from the spousal support. In the previous example, the difference in the amounts would be considered child support and, therefore, would not be tax-deductible. This could require a payor-spouse who wrongly claimed that payments were alimony and not child support to pay back taxes with interest.

The Recapture Rule

Prior to the Tax Reform Act of 1984, the recapture rule existed only in the imagination of tax accountants. The recapture rule lessened the pre-1984 constraints on what could be considered child support. Any final divorce order or separate maintenance order executed after December 31, 1984, is subject to the tax revisions. Any final orders executed prior to January 1, 1985, remain subject to the law in effect at the time of execution. Although you need to be aware of the existence of the Tax Reform Act of 1984, it is not necessary to spend time learning the pre-1984 rules, since the majority of your work as a paralegal will involve post-reform cases.

Tax Consequences of Transferring Property

When a husband and wife decide to divorce, the process is usually complicated by the real and personal property the spouses own together. A divorce between two spouses who do not have children or own any property can be a relatively simple legal process. This is usually not the case when divorcing spouses begin to negotiate which one gets which piece of property or which property, if any, will be sold. The old tax law made the transferring of property from one spouse to the other complicated and onerous. For example, if Annie purchased some shares of Disney Company stock many years ago for $500, but the stock was worth $5,000 when she transferred it to her husband Andy pursuant to a property settlement agreement, she would be facing a *capital gains tax*. The **capital gain** is the apparent profit between the $500 investment and the $5,000 value of the stock. Thus, the capital gains tax would be based on what appears to be a $4,500 profit. The problem is: Annie did not sell the stock, so she did not make any real money from the transfer. Transferring spouses used to be faced with the problem of coming up with the cash needed to pay the capital gains tax for property they had transferred without any real cash profit for themselves.

The new law takes a more realistic look at the transferring of property from one spouse to the other. Whether a couple is divorcing or happily married, the transfer of property by one spouse to the other does not now generate capital gains taxes. The current law applies whether the property is real or personal and whether the property was separately owned by one spouse or jointly owned by the spouses.

When divorcing spouses are negotiating their property settlement, there are still some tax liabilities of which the spouse contemplating the receipt of transferred property should be made aware. For instance, in the previous example, Andy may be thrilled to receive the Disney stock now, but if he plans to sell the stock, he will be the one who has to pay the capital gains tax. And here is a big surprise: The IRS never forgets capital gains taxes. The capital gains tax is just postponed until the receiving spouse decides to sell the transferred property. The receiving spouse may not have to pay tax if the property sells for less than the amount for which it was originally purchased. If the property sells for less than the purchase price, a loss can be claimed.

Here is another possible tax concern for the divorcing couple. What if Andy had received $5,000 in United States savings bonds when he graduated from college? Suppose he and Annie agree to exchange the Disney stock for the bonds. The IRS does not create an exception for the interest income on transferred property. Andy would be still liable for any interest from the bonds that accrued during the transfer year.

Transferring Property to a Third Party

A property transfer is not always made by one spouse to the other. Sometimes a property transfer is made by one spouse to a third party on behalf of the other spouse. The spouse who receives the benefit of the transfer is called the **beneficiary spouse.** This is often done to pay off the debts of the spouse benefiting from the transfer. In the eyes of the IRS, there are really two transfers occurring, even though the transferring spouse is transferring the property directly to a third party. The IRS allows the tax exemptions for the transfer between the spouses, but the beneficiary spouse is liable for any profit shown after the property is transferred to the third party. To ensure the tax exemption for the spousal transfer, three basic IRS requirements must be met: (1) the transfer must be made pursuant to a divorce or separation agreement; (2) the transfer must be made pursuant to a written request of the beneficiary spouse; and (3) the transferring spouse must receive a written acceptance of the property transfer after the property has been transferred.

Retirement Plans and Property Settlements

Generally, the two largest assets that most people have are their homes and their retirement plans. Retirement plans come in different forms and are often created through a person's place of employment. A retirement plan is intended to provide income to the retiree following retirement. The **intended beneficiary** of a retirement plan is known as the payee of the retirement plan. There are many different types of retirement plans, for example, **pensions, individual retirement plans (IRAs), profit sharing, Keogh plans, 401K plans,** and **403B plans.** Since a retirement plan is often one of the largest assets built up during a marriage, it often will be part of the property settlement between divorcing spouses.

A tax problem can arise if a retirement plan participant attempts to withdraw funds from a plan before he is entitled to. A participant who withdraws funds too early will face a tax penalty on those funds. Early withdrawal will reduce the value of the plan as well. The tax penalties and value reduction should be considered when negotiating any property settlement that would require the premature withdrawal of funds.

UNDERSTANDING QUALIFIED DOMESTIC RELATIONS ORDERS

The court that has jurisdiction over a couple's divorce has the authority to issue an order requesting that a retirement plan's benefits be paid to someone other than the intended payee. The person paid benefits from another's retirement plan is called an **alternate payee.** Such an order is known as a **qualified domestic relations order (QDRO).** A retirement plan's manager will not release any portion of a retirement plan to an alternate payee spouse without a QDRO. Although the majority of retirement plans are subject to such orders, QDROs are not applicable to some government and church plans that do not choose to be covered by the Employee Retirement Income Security Act of 1974 (ERISA). ERISA is a federal law that is specifically intended to protect retirement benefits. Those government or church plans have their own rules as to how a retirement benefit may be divided. The United States military will honor QDROs ordering pension division only if the divorcing spouses have been married at least 10 years and the division is no more than 50 percent.

Steps to Take When Seeking Retirement Benefits for an Alternate Payee Spouse

In order to save time asking a judge to revise a QDRO he previously signed, it is best to check on the proper required wording *before* the first request is made for the QDRO. When seeking a transfer of the retirement benefits from the intended payee spouse to the alternate spouse, the following steps are required:

1. Contact the retirement plan administrator to ensure the QDRO granted by the court includes the language the plan requires. If a plan administrator believes the court order does not contain the

correct language, the administrator is entitled, within a reasonable time, to refuse to acknowledge the order as a QDRO; and

2. Request a QDRO from the court that includes language that states that it is the intention of the intended payee and the court that an alternate payee is entitled to a certain benefit from the retirement plan.

Preparing a Qualified Domestic Relations Order

As a paralegal, you may be asked to handle the task of researching the proper wording for the QDRO and then preparing the QDRO. The best-case scenario occurs when attorneys for both spouses agree on the wording of the QDRO before going to court to have the QDRO signed by the judge. See Exhibit 11.1 to read a sample QDRO.

EXHIBIT 11.1 Sample Qualified Domestic Relations Order

This sample QDRO is provided by the Littlest Widget Company, Inc., as an example of an order the company will treat as a QDRO. You may include the language in a separate order or as part of the divorce decree itself. The company does not give individual tax advice or advice about the marital property rights of either party.

1. Pursuant to Section 414(p) of the Internal Revenue Code, this qualified domestic relations order ("Order") assigns a portion of the benefits payable in the Littlest Widget Company, Inc., Annuity Plan ("the Plan") from _____ (Member's Name) (Member No._____) to _____ (Spouse's Name) in recognition of the existence of his/her marital rights in _____ (Member's Name)'s retirement benefits.

2. The Member in the Plan is _____ (Member's Name), whose last known mailing address is _____ , Social Security no. _____ .

3. The Alternate Payee is _____ (Spouse's Name), whose last known mailing address is _____ , Social Security no. _____ .

   [Use the following paragraph if the Member is *not* already receiving retirement benefits:]

4. Littlest Widget Company, Inc., is hereby ORDERED to assign a portion of the accumulations so that each party as of the date of the assignment has a retirement account of approximately the same value. The date of assignment is _____ .

   [Use the following paragraph if the Member *is* already receiving retirement benefits:]

5. Littlest Widget Company, Inc., is hereby ORDERED to make monthly payments equal to one-half of the amount payable to _____ (Member's Name) directly to _____ (Spouse's Name). These direct payments to _____ (Spouse's Name) shall be made beginning after the date of this Order and ending at _____ (Member's Name)'s death.

6. This qualified domestic relations order is not intended to require the Plan to provide any type or form of benefits or any option not otherwise provided by the Plan, nor shall this Order require the Plan to provide for increased benefits not required by the Plan. This Order does not require the Plan to provide benefits to the Alternate Payee that are required to be paid to another alternate payee under another order previously determined to be a qualified domestic relations order.

7. All benefits payable under the Littlest Widget Company, Inc., Annuity Plan other than those payable to _____ (Spouse's Name) shall be payable to _____ (Member's Name) in such manner and form as he/she may elect in his/her sole and undivided discretion, subject only to plan requirements.

8. _____ (Spouse's Name) is ORDERED AND DECREED to report any retirement payments received on any applicable income tax return. The Plan Administrator of Littlest Widget Company, Inc., is authorized to issue the appropriate Internal Revenue Form for any direct payment made to _____ (Spouse's Name).

9. While it is anticipated that the Plan Administrator will pay directly to _____ (Spouse's Name) the benefit awarded to her, _____ (Member's Name) is designated a constructive trustee to the extent he receives any retirement benefits under the Plan that are due to _____ (Spouse's Name) but paid to _____ (Member's Name).

   _____ (Member's Name) is ORDERED AND DECREED to pay the benefit defined above directly to _____ (Spouse's Name) within three days after receipt by him.

   _____   _____
   (Name of Court)   (Name of Judge)

Which Spouse Is Taking the Dependency Exemptions?

Any divorcing or separating spouses who have children must determine which spouse is entitled to the allowable **dependent exemptions.** The IRS allowed a $3,050 tax exemption per child for parents earning less than a total of $103,000 per year in 2003. For a parent, this means that $3,050 will be deducted from the total available income on which she can be taxed. These exemptions can only be taken once a year for each child. Each state that has an income tax also allows a state deduction for each child. This exemption is worth negotiating. For example, a parent in a 28 percent federal tax bracket would have a federal tax exemption worth approximately $600 for each child.

The general rule is that the parent who has custody of the children the majority of the year is entitled to use the exemption. However, this can be negotiated between the parents. If the noncustodial parent is given the right to use any exemptions, the custodial parent must sign *IRS Form 8332.* The noncustodial parent's right to use the exemptions is usually related to the amount of child support the noncustodial parent has agreed to pay. The IRS Form 8332 is one more document the attorney and paralegal must complete and make part of the client's case file.

Are Legal Fees Tax-Deductible?

Fees paid to law firms for work done by attorneys or paralegals in connection with a separation or divorce are not deductible. However, if an attorney or accountant provides tax advice, the fees attributable to such advice are tax-deductible.

Who Is Head of the Household Now?

A person who pays for over half the cost of maintaining a household without children is considered the head of the house by the IRS. If there are children, there is a three-step test that must be passed by a spouse who wishes to claim **head of household** status. First, the claiming spouse must provide over half the cost of maintaining a household. Secondly, the house must have been the children's main residence during the tax year. Thirdly, the claiming spouse's spouse must not have lived in the household during the last six months of the taxable year.

Tax Ramifications of Selling the Marital Home

The major property divided in most divorce situations is the family home. Once more, there are pitfalls to be navigated around. Here is a typical scenario. Andy and Annie bought a house in a small suburban town two years after they were married. Neither one wants to stay in the house now that their marriage is over. Andy has already moved to an apartment in a nearby city. Annie has had a hard time maintaining both the interior and exterior of the house. Eventually, she wants to buy a smaller townhouse without all the upkeep. Both have agreed to sell the house and split any profit down the middle. This profit is known as capital gains. They both feel that splitting the profit will be the fairest way for each of them to get an equal share.

The problem in Andy and Annie's case is that tax ramifications from the sale may not ensure that both get equal shares. The IRS allows any taxes on the profit made on a house sale to be waived if the parties were domiciled in the house for at least two out of the last five years prior to the sale. If Andy moves out and the house is not sold within the allotted time—in this case, three years are left—then Andy will have to pay capital gains taxes on his share. Remember, the IRS does not currently provide any such waiver of capital gains taxes unless the house in question is the primary residence. Investment property and vacation homes are not included in the waiver.

One Option Is Filing Separately

It is not hard to imagine a divorcing client not wanting to sign a joint tax return with her soon-to-be ex-spouse. The alternative to a client signing a joint return is for the client and other spouse to file *married, filing separately* IRS forms. The problem to watch out for is that filing separately may put the spouses in a higher tax bracket—and that means paying more taxes. A sample of the type of clauses that can be included in a typical divorce settlement agreement is included in Exhibit 11.2.

DOES DECLARING BANKRUPTCY END A SUPPORT OBLIGATION?

Asking if bankruptcy ends a support obligation is an appropriate question considering the financial hardships that follow many divorces. When it comes to child support or spousal support, the United States Bankruptcy Code, 11 U.S.C. § 523, clearly states that such support is nondischargeable. Dischargeable means an order from the bankruptcy court can remove the debt. There are still a few rain clouds to watch for, however. An obligation arising out of a divorce settlement (e.g., property division) *may* be discharged in bankruptcy under certain circumstances. This nasty possibility is the reason it is a good idea to walk out of court with the property split instead of a graduated plan for one spouse to pay off the other spouse over time. This is how it works: Usually property distribution is not dischargeable unless the payor-spouse can prove that the detriment from paying the debt outweighs the benefit to the payee-spouse. Additionally, Chapter 13 (a type of bankruptcy that allows for a restructuring of the debt and payments made over time) does allow for discharging a property distribution. A payee-spouse can object to any attempt at discharging.

EXHIBIT 11.2 Tax Clauses

1. Tax-Deductible or Taxable Income

The Parties have negotiated this Agreement based upon the prevailing tax laws that, as of the date of this Agreement, allow spousal support payments to be considered a tax deduction for the spouse making the payment and taxable income for the spouse receiving the payment. If current law to this effect changes, both Parties may agree to renegotiate this paragraph or return to the negotiating table for binding arbitration.

2. Deficiencies and Refunds

In the event the Internal Revenue Service or the Division of Taxation of the State of _____ claims there has been a deficiency in the income taxes paid after the signing of this Agreement, all costs will be paid for by the husband/wife. In the event the Internal Revenue Service or the Division of Taxation of the State of _____ returns any refunds after the signing of this Agreement, all refunds shall be the property of the husband/wife.

3. Agreement to File Separate Returns

The Parties will file separately any federal or state income tax returns required after the signing of this Agreement.

4. Agreement to File Joint Returns

The Parties will file any federal or state income tax returns jointly after the signing of this Agreement in the event joint filing will lower the tax liability and such joint filing is allowed by law. The Parties request the joint filing to lower the tax liability. The party requesting the joint filing will notify the other party of the request by certified mail. And this, unlike the liability for such joint return, shall be allocated according to the proportion which each party's liability on a separate return bears to the total of the party's separate return. In computing his or her separate return liability, each party shall take into account such income, deductions, exemptions, and credits as are in accordance with then prevailing laws.

5. Exemptions for Federal and State Income Tax Purposes

The Parties agree that as long as the husband/wife pays child support, the husband/wife will claim the children (names of children inserted here) as exemptions on federal and state income tax returns. The husband/wife agrees to sign any federal and state income tax forms as may be required.

CHAPTER SUMMARY

Divorce can result in numerous tax ramifications for the ex-spouses. The Internal Revenue Service will consider the temporary or permanent financial support received by a spouse as a result of a divorce or separation to be taxable income. The spouse receiving the support is called the payee-spouse. The paying spouse, called the payor-spouse, may treat the spousal support as tax-deductible. Child support payments will not be considered taxable income or tax-deductible.

The Internal Revenue Code section 71(b) lists six requirements that must be met in order for payor-spouse's payments to be considered eligible as a tax deduction: (1) The payment must be made in cash; (2) the cash payment must be made to the separated or divorced spouse according to a written divorce or settlement agreement; (3) any payments that are clearly designated as not deductible in a written and signed divorce or settlement agreement will not qualify; (4) the spouses cannot be living in the same residence; (5) no payments are to be made to a spouse's estate; and (6) a payment cannot be a disguised as a child support payment.

Generally, the two largest assets that most people have are their homes and their retirement plans. There are tax consequences when property is transferred from one spouse to the other. A tax problem can arise if a retirement plan participant attempts to withdraw funds from the plan before the participant is entitled to withdraw those funds. A court order directing a retirement plan to pay to an alternate payee is known as a qualified domestic relations order (QDRO).

The general rule pertaining to dependent exemptions is that the parent who has custody of the children for the majority of the year is entitled to use the exemption, unless one parent pays more than half of the support of the children or the spouses agree otherwise. Legal fees are not tax-deductible, but tax advice is deductible. Support obligations are never dischargeable in bankruptcy. However, a property division obligation may be dischargeable under certain factual circumstances. A property division obligation is always dischargeable under a Chapter 13 bankruptcy. The payee-spouse may always object to any discharge.

Key Terms

Internal Revenue Service (IRS)	intended beneficiary	403B plans
Internal Revenue Code	pension	alternate payee
section 71(b)	individual retirement plan	qualified domestic relations
payor	(IRA)	order (QDRO)
payee	profit sharing	dependent exemption
capital gain	Keogh plans	head of household
beneficiary spouse	401K plans	

Surfing the Web

http://www.irs.gov Internal Revenue Service Web site for all your tax questions.

http://www.divorcesource.com Do you think you have it all covered in your divorce? You had better check on all the tax aspects of divorce.

http://www.benderlaw.com Understanding how alimony is subject to tax for both spouses and how it has been tested in court. Explained in an interesting site from the Bender Law offices in North Carolina.

http://www.betterdivorce.com Within this site find information dealing with the financial aspects of divorce.

http://www.rrbb.com Web site for an independent accounting firm and services they offer with regard to a divorce.

ETHICS ALERT

The computer age has definitely come to Johnson & Webster. The firm recently hired a consultant to maintain the firm's Web site. The Web site is informative and highlights the talents of the firm's attorneys. Susan has heard that the Web site seems to generate a lot of business. Alyssa and J. D. get many e-mails from possible clients on a daily basis. Susan has been asked to monitor the incoming e-mails whenever Alyssa and J. D. do not have a chance to get to their mail. Susan has noticed that quite a few of the e-mails delve into the senders' *very private* business. Increasingly, Susan has begun to wonder if these senders should expect an attorney-client privacy privilege for the e-mails they send. What do you think? Is Susan starting to become a worrier for no reason?

Review Questions

1. (a) What section of the Internal Revenue Code lists the six requirements that must be met in order for a client's payments to be considered eligible as a tax deduction? (b) List the six requirements.
2. Describe the hide-and-seek game that can occur with alimony or spousal support payments.
3. What are capital gains taxes?
4. Which spouse owes capital gains taxes when the spouse who received the transferred property eventually sells the property?
5. What is a QDRO?
6. When is a QDRO necessary?
7. What specific language should be included in a QDRO?
8. Which spouse usually takes dependency exemptions?
9. What three things must be proved to the IRS in order for a person to be considered the head of a household?
10. Are legal fees for work done in connection with a divorce tax-deductible?

Chapter 12

Domestic Violence

DOMESTIC VIOLENCE FACTS

Domestic violence is the single greatest cause of injury to American women, exceeding car accidents, rapes, and muggings combined.[1] Over 95 percent of reported domestic violence victims are women.[2] Between 1959 and 1975, 58,000 American soldiers were killed in Vietnam. During that same period, 51,000 American women were killed by their male partner.[3] Battering crosses all economic, educational, ethnic, sexual orientation, age, and racial lines in equal proportions. There is no typical victim.[4]

These facts speak volumes. It is no longer a dark secret that domestic violence permeates all levels of society. From 1.8 to 4 million women will become a domestic violence victim in their lifetime, and boys who witness domestic violence are more likely to continue the cycle than boys raised in nonviolent homes, according to a 1992 report from the United States Surgeon General's Office. The havoc caused by domestic violence has damaging effects on our country's health, welfare, and economy. Untold billions of dollars are spent each year on the physical and mental health costs stemming from violence. It is estimated that over $5 billion a year is lost in the United States alone each year because of missed work and reduced productivity.[5]

Just as there is no typical victim, there also is no typical batterer. Batterers are found in every social, ethnic, religious, and economic class of society. The majority of batterers are productive members of society. Batterers go to work, serve as community volunteers, and go to houses of worship. Yet, at home, they use violence to gain control over their victims' actions, thoughts, and feelings.

ONE WOMAN'S STORY

Maggie unconsciously sighed as she looked over the menu. Susan sat across from Maggie and sneaked a peek at her childhood friend. Susan didn't like what she saw. Maggie had another artfully hidden bruise on her left cheekbone. Susan thought no matter how much foundation and blush Maggie used, the emotional scars would always be there to deal with—if what Susan suspected was true.

Joining in with an unconscious sigh of her own, Susan thought to herself, "I've brought up the subject of domestic violence several times over the last few years, and Maggie has never confided that such things are going on in her home. She's always blamed clumsiness for her bruises. Maybe, I should just stay out of it." Susan shook her head as if to clear her mind of her suspicions, but the idea of her friend as a victim of domestic violence wouldn't go away. Her thoughts continued, "After all, I've never actually *seen* Maggie's husband Tim lose his temper. Maybe I should just keep my nose out of other people's business." While Maggie studied the menu as if it were an exam, Susan had time to ponder further. She thought, "Maggie is a successful, dynamic realtor. She just isn't the type you'd think would be a victim. And anyway, she'd tell her minister or the police about any domestic violence, I'm sure."

Coming back to the matter at hand, lunch, Susan said a bit too brightly, "The salads are great here. I'm going to have one. How about you, Maggie?" She'd known Maggie for a long time —since second grade—and she could tell Maggie was having trouble pulling herself together and putting on a cheerful face.

"To tell you the truth, I'm not very hungry," Maggie admitted. "I wasn't feeling very well this morning and was almost going to cancel, but you know how you always cheer me up." Maggie stopped speaking and called the waitress to the table so she and Susan could order beverages.

Agreeing that iced tea would be fine, Susan pondered to herself, "I almost thought she was going to tell me something just then." After ordering a salad, Maggie asked Susan questions about her new job at Johnson & Webster and Susan's new apartment. As the salads were cleared away, coffee ordered, dessert rejected, and the check delivered, Maggie kept Susan busy answering her questions. The two women were in the parking lot before Susan realized she had not had a chance to delve into her suspicions about Maggie's relationship with Tim.

Turning to give Maggie a good-bye hug, Susan announced, "Well, I feel like the rudest person. I never got a chance to ask you how everybody at your house is doing these days."

"Please don't feel that way," Maggie answered. "I'm the one who kept you talking about all those interesting cases you're working on. An hour lunch goes by fast, and we haven't seen each other in weeks."

Susan scratched her head and responded, "I think it's actually been at *least* four months."

The two old friends looked at each other in amazement. "Has it been that long?" Maggie asked. "I just don't really get to see *anybody* outside of work these days," she explained. "When I get home, Tim wants his dinner to be on the table at 7:00 sharp. Then there's the laundry and chauffeuring little Tim to Little League." Promising to see each other soon, the old friends gave each other one last hug and drove off.

As she hummed along with the radio, Susan's mind kept returning to Maggie. "I can't help it, but I feel like something terrible is going to happen," she thought.

A Victim Reaches Out for Help

"Hello, Sue?" Maggie whispered. "It's Maggie."

Susan could barely hear her friend. "Can you speak up? I can hardly hear you."

"Oh, I'm sorry. I'm so used to whispering when I use the phone that it's second nature. Tim has already left for work."

Susan was immediately concerned and asked, "Are you all right?" Maggie did not answer immediately, which worried Susan more. "Maggie are you there?" Susan asked, beginning to panic.

"Yes, yes, I'm here—and no, I'm not all right," Maggie said almost without emotion. "I've had it with Tim."

Now Susan was really worried because she was afraid she knew what Maggie was going to tell her. She asked her friend, "What do you mean?"

"I've never told you, but I know you know me too well not to have guessed," Maggie began. "Tim has been hitting me for a long time, even back in high school, and I guess, well, I was just too ashamed to tell you—or anyone." Susan knew that this was a huge step forward for Maggie but that she'd have to treat Maggie in exactly the right way to keep her from retreating backward. While Susan tried to think of what advice she could give Maggie, Maggie started crying and repeating, "I feel so stupid, I feel so stupid."

Susan did not know what to say, but responding to her friend's pain, she blurted, "Why on earth do *you* feel stupid, when it's that idiot Tim who's been hurting you?"

Maggie sniffled, "I know, I know, but I can't help the way I feel."

"Boy, oh boy," Susan thought. "This is the first time I wish I was living back with Mom and Dad instead of in my own apartment. I could use some help." She wanted to ask Maggie why she had finally decided to say something, but was afraid of what she'd be told. She decided to muddle forward and asked, "Are you hurt now?"

Maggie quickly responded, "No, he hasn't touched me since the day before I met you for lunch, but the straw that broke the camel's back is that Tim Junior, is beginning to copy his dad's behavior."

Susan could not stifle her immediate reaction of shock and said, "Oh Maggie, I'm so sorry! What did Timmy do?"

"I asked him to come in from playing softball in the yard, but he just wouldn't come in for his bath," Maggie said, and then paused. "I guess I was sort of impatient—it was getting dark, and he was refusing to come in, and. . . ." She started to cry again.

Susan wished she could hug her friend through the phone and said, "Go on, Hon."

Maggie took a deep breath and finished, "He started to hit me with the bat and call me stupid. I mean, the bat's plastic, thank goodness, but a 5-year-old can hit pretty hard."

Susan had instinctively raised her hand to her mouth as she listened. Now she asked, "What do you want to do?"

"I want to leave Tim before little Tim learns any more bad behavior from him," Maggie said. She added tearfully, "I just hope it isn't too late for him."

Susan knew when action was needed. She said, "Look, the first thing you should do is see a lawyer."

Maggie sadly answered, "Okay."

Susan continued, "You know I'm at Johnson & Webster. I was just leaving for work. You're lucky you found me home. I'm sure I can get you an emergency appointment right away." She looked at her watch and said, "It's early still, and you have hours before Tim gets home. You should get as many important papers together as possible to take to the lawyer, just in case he needs that stuff—and I'd go to the bank, too. I'd have your mom or sister pick up Tim after school."

"Okay," Maggie said.

Susan continued, "I'll go to work, talk to my boss about an appointment today, and then call you on your cell phone. Don't worry. We'll figure this whole thing out."

Maggie was slightly overwhelmed, but thankful that Susan knew what to do. She asked nervously, "You'll call as soon as possible, right?"

Susan quickly responded, "Yes, of course—of course I will."

"Suze, I can't thank you enough for this. I'm so relieved to have finally told someone," Maggie said gratefully.

"I'm glad you called me," said Susan. "Now, remember what I said. Get those papers together and get out of there. I'll call you soon, Maggie."

Domestic Violence and the Law Office

It should come as no surprise that domestic violence is present in some of the divorce cases a law firm handles. Any attorney who ignores the fact that domestic violence could have been a part of a client's life experience is figuratively placing her head in the sand. Ignoring domestic violence issues when handling a client's divorce is not only inadequate representation, but could be potentially dangerous for the client, the attorney, and the law firm's staff. Therefore, the first question that should be asked of all clients, both women and men, is: *Are you safe?* [6]

Representing a Victim of Domestic Violence

What should an attorney and paralegal do when faced with a client who describes a litany of violent domestic episodes? Whether the violent spouse has remained in the family home or has moved out, the attorney representing the battered spouse can prepare a domestic violence complaint and request that the court provide a **protective order** preventing the husband from approaching his wife, and possibly his children. Exhibit 12.1 shows instructions for filing a petition for protection against domestic violence. Most states require that the party filing the petition also submit an affidavit or Declaration in Support of the TRO along with the complaint. The court's order in this scenario may be called a **temporary restraining order (TRO).** A sample form can be reviewed in Exhibit 12.2. This sample is fairly typical. A TRO can generally be requested from a county or municipal court *ex parte* because of the emergency nature of the request. *Ex parte* is Latin and is defined as "with only one side present." A client may also go to the local police department first and file a domestic violence report and follow up the report with the filing of a domestic violence complaint in the county or municipal court.

When preparing a TRO motion, do not ask for protection in a general fashion but request the *assurance of safety for the victim wherever she may be*—not just at home. This is usually called a **stay-away order.** In some states, if a judge has ordered the alleged perpetrator to avoid all contact with a victim, the order may be called a **no-contact order.** In addition, most states allow that the request include: (1) supervised child visitation to prevent the manipulation of the children; (2) the surrendering of any weapons in the allegedly violent spouse's possession; (3) addressing the issue of temporary financial support, if necessary; and (4) the vacating of the family home by the abusive spouse. When a judge orders an alleged perpetrator of violence out of the home he shares with his victim, the order is usually called a **vacate order.**

A court will have jurisdiction to hear the domestic violence complaint if the complaint is filed where the defendant or plaintiff resides or where the violence occurred. The failure of a violent spouse to respect a TRO can lead the offending spouse to face a **contempt of court** charge with possible fines and jail time for willfully disobeying an official court order. Following the issuing of the TRO, the parties will be asked to appear in court (usually within 10 to 20 days if the TRO was issued *ex parte*) to determine whether a **final restraining order,** an extension of the TRO (usually at least a year or longer), or the temporary order should be vacated. In some states, the hearing is not automatically scheduled and the respondent must request a hearing. It is during this second hearing that both parties will have an opportunity to present evidence and testimony to the court.

Although in some instances the TRO can be a wake-up call to a violent spouse, it is not an effective tool when dealing with a violent spouse who has ceased to care how civilized society views him and whose intent is to commit violence against his spouse and anyone he believes is assisting her.

Representing Maggie

That very same afternoon, Susan and Maggie were sitting in J. D. Dombroski's office at Johnson & Webster. Susan had agreed to Maggie's request for her to stay during the appointment for moral support. J. D. had patiently listened to Maggie's laundry list of violent acts she had suffered since she was 15 years old and had first dated Tim. Susan had done her best to hide her shock. J. D. asked questions about her son, the financial situation of the family, and the possible reactions she thought Tim might have when he learned his violence had been uncovered. Finally, J. D. asked what Maggie wanted.

"I want this to be over," Maggie whispered while looking down at her hands clenched in her lap. Raising her head and her voice, she repeated, "I want this to be over for little Tim and me. I want a divorce. I want Tim to stay away from me, and I don't want to lose my house."

EXHIBIT 12.1 Instructions for Filing a Petition for Protection Against Domestic Violence

(1) There is created a cause of action for an injunction for protection against domestic violence.

   (a) Any person described in paragraph (e), who is either the victim of domestic violence as defined in § 741.28 or has reasonable cause to believe he or she is in imminent danger of becoming the victim of any act of domestic violence, has standing in the circuit court to file a sworn petition for an injunction for protection against domestic violence.

   (b) This cause of action for an injunction may be sought whether or not any other cause of action is currently pending between the parties. However, the pendency of any such cause of action shall be alleged in the petition.

   (c) In the event a subsequent cause of action is filed under chapter 61, any orders entered therein shall take precedence over any inconsistent provisions of an injunction issued under this section which addresses matters governed by chapter 61.

   (d) A person's right to petition for an injunction shall not be affected by such person having left a residence or household to avoid domestic violence.

   (e) This cause of action for an injunction may be sought by family or household members. No person shall be precluded from seeking injunctive relief pursuant to this chapter solely on the basis that such person is not a spouse.

   (f) This cause of action for an injunction shall not require that either party be represented by an attorney.

   (g) Any person, including an officer of the court, who offers evidence or recommendations relating to the cause of action must either present the evidence or recommendations in writing to the court with copies to each party and their attorney, or must present the evidence under oath at a hearing at which all parties are present.

   (h) Nothing in this section shall affect the title to any real estate.

   (i) The court is prohibited from issuing mutual orders of protection. This does not preclude the court from issuing separate injunctions for protection against domestic violence where each party has complied with the provisions of this section. Compliance with the provisions of this section cannot be waived.

   (j) Notwithstanding any provision of chapter 47, a petition for an injunction for protection against domestic violence may be filed in the circuit where the petitioner currently or temporarily resides, where the respondent resides, or where the domestic violence occurred. There is no minimum requirement of residency to petition for an injunction for protection.

(2) (a) Notwithstanding any other provision of law, the assessment of a filing fee for a petition for protection against domestic violence is prohibited effective October 1, 2002. However, subject to legislative appropriation, the clerk of the circuit court may, on a quarterly basis, submit to the Office of the State Courts Administrator a certified request for reimbursement for petitions for protection against domestic violence issued by the court, at the rate of $40 per petition. The request for reimbursement shall be submitted in the form and manner prescribed by the Office of the State Courts Administrator. From this reimbursement, the clerk shall pay any law enforcement agency serving the injunction the fee requested by the law enforcement agency; however, this fee shall not exceed $20.

   (b) No bond shall be required by the court for the entry of an injunction.

   (c) I. The clerk of the court shall assist petitioners in seeking both injunctions for protection against domestic violence and enforcement for a violation thereof as specified in this section.

      2. All clerks' offices shall provide simplified petition forms for the injunction, any modifications, and the enforcement thereof, including instructions for completion.

      3. The clerk of the court shall advise petitioners of the availability of affidavits of insolvency or indigence in lieu of payment for the cost of the filing fee, as provided in paragraph (a).

      4. The clerk of the court shall ensure the petitioner's privacy to the extent practical while completing the forms for injunctions for protection against domestic violence.

      5. The clerk of the court shall provide petitioners with a minimum of two certified copies of the order of injunction, one of which is serviceable and will inform the petitioner of the process for service and enforcement.

      6. Clerks of court and appropriate staff in each county shall receive training in the effective assistance of petitioner as provided or approved by the Florida Association of Court Clerks.

      7. The clerk of the court in each county shall make available informational brochures on domestic violence when such brochures are provided by local certified domestic violence centers.

      8. The clerk of the court in each county shall distribute a statewide uniform informational brochure to petitioners at the time of filing for an injunction for protection against domestic or repeat violence when such brochures become available. The brochure must include information about the effect of giving the court false information about domestic violence.

(3) (a) The sworn petition shall allege the existence of such domestic violence and shall include the specific facts and circumstances upon the basis of which relief is sought.

(b) The sworn petition shall be in substantially the following form:

Petition for Injunction for Protection Against Domestic Violence

Before me, the undersigned authority, personally appeared Petitioner (Name), who has been sworn and says that the following statements are true:

(a) Petitioner resides at: (address)

(Petitioner may furnish address to the court in a separate confidential filing if, for safety reasons, the petitioner requires the location of the current residence to be confidential.)

(b) Respondent resides at: (last known address)

(c) Respondent's last known place of employment: (name of business and address)

(d) Physical description of respondent:

Race _____
Sex _____
Date of birth _____
Height _____
Weight _____
Eye color _____
Hair color _____
Distinguishing marks or scars _____

(e) Aliases of respondent: _____

(f) Respondent is the spouse or former spouse of the petitioner or is any person related by blood or marriage to the petitioner or is any other person who is or was residing within a single dwelling unit with the petitioner, as if a family, or is a person with whom the petitioner has a child in common, regardless of whether the petitioner and respondent are or were married or residing together, as if a family.

(g) The following describes any other cause of action currently pending between the petitioner and respondent:

_____

_____

The petitioner should also describe any previous or pending attempts by the petitioner to obtain an injunction for protection against domestic violence in this or any other circuit, and the results of that attempt:

_____

_____

Case numbers should be included if available.

(h) Petitioner is either a victim of domestic violence or has reasonable cause to believe he or she is in imminent danger of becoming a victim of domestic violence because respondent has (mark all that apply and describe in the spaces below the incidents of violence or threats of violence, specifying when and where they occurred, including, but not limited to, locations such as a home, school, place of employment, or visitation exchange): _____

_____ committed or threatened to commit domestic violence defined in § 741.28, Florida Statutes, as any assault, aggravated assault, battery, aggravated battery, sexual assault, sexual battery, stalking, aggravated stalking, kidnapping, false imprisonment, or any criminal offense resulting in physical injury or death of one family or household member by another. With the exception of persons who are parents of a child in common, the family or household members must be currently residing or have in the past resided together in the same single dwelling unit.

_____ previously threatened, harassed, stalked, or physically abused the petitioner.

_____ attempted to harm the petitioner or family members or individuals closely associated with the petitioner.

_____ threatened to conceal, kidnap, or harm the petitioner's child or children.

_____ intentionally injured or killed a family pet.

_____ used, or has threatened to use, against the petitioner any weapons such as guns or knives.

_____ physically restrained the petitioner from leaving the home or calling law enforcement.

(continued)

EXHIBIT 12.1 *continued*

_____ a criminal history involving violence or the threat of violence (if known).

_____ another order of protection issued against him or her previously or from another jurisdiction (if known).

_____ destroyed personal property, including, but not limited to, telephones or other communication equipment, clothing, or other items belonging to the petitioner.

_____ engaged in any other behavior or conduct that leads the petitioner to have reasonable cause to believe he or she is in imminent danger of becoming a victim of domestic violence.

  (i) Petitioner alleges the following additional specific Facts: (mark appropriate sections)

_____ Petitioner is the custodian of a minor child or children whose names and ages are as follows: _____

_____ Petitioner needs the exclusive use and possession of the dwelling that the parties share.

_____ Petitioner is unable to obtain safe alternative housing because: _____

_____ Petitioner genuinely fears that respondent imminently will abuse, remove, or hide the minor child or children from petitioner because: _____

  (j) Petitioner genuinely fears imminent domestic violence by respondent.

  (k) Petitioner seeks an injunction: (mark appropriate section or sections)

_____ immediately restraining the respondent from committing any acts of domestic violence.

_____ restraining the respondent from committing any acts of domestic violence.

_____ awarding to the petitioner the temporary exclusive use and possession of the dwelling that the parties share or excluding the respondent from the residence of the petitioner.

_____ awarding temporary custody of, or temporary visitation rights with regard to, the minor child or children of the parties, or prohibiting or limiting visitation to that which is supervised by a third party.

_____ establishing temporary support for the minor child or children or the petitioner.

_____ directing the respondent to participate in a batterers' intervention program or other treatment pursuant to § 39.901, Florida Statutes.

_____ providing any terms the court deems necessary for the protection of a victim of domestic violence, or any minor children of the victim, including any injunctions or directives to law enforcement agencies.

 (c) Every petition for an injunction against domestic violence shall contain, directly above the signature line, a statement in all capital letters and bold type not smaller than the surrounding text, as follows:

I HAVE READ EVERY STATEMENT MADE IN THIS PETITION AND EACH STATEMENT IS TRUE AND CORRECT. I UNDERSTAND THAT THE STATEMENTS MADE IN THIS PETITION ARE BEING MADE UNDER PENALTY OF PERJURY, PUNISHABLE AS PROVIDED IN SECTION 837.01, FLORIDA STATUTES.

_____
Signature of Petitioner

 (d) If the sworn petition seeks to determine issues of custody or visitation with regard to the minor child or children of the parties, the sworn petition shall be accompanied by or shall incorporate the allegations required by § 61.522 of the Uniform Child Custody Jurisdiction and Enforcement Act.

(4) Upon the filing of the petition, the court shall set a hearing to be held at the earliest possible time. The respondent shall be personally served with a copy of the petition, financial affidavit, uniform child custody jurisdiction and enforcement act affidavit, if any, notice of hearing, and temporary injunction, in any, prior to the hearing.

(5) (a) When it appears to the court that an immediate and present danger of domestic violence exists, the court may grant a temporary injunction *ex parte,* pending a full hearing, and may grant such relief as the court deems proper, including an injunction:

  1. Restraining the respondent from committing any acts of domestic violence.

  2. Awarding to the petitioner the temporary exclusive use and possession of the dwelling that the parties share or excluding the respondent from the residence of the petitioner.

3. On the same basis as provided in § 61.13(2), (3), (4), and (5), granting to the petitioner temporary custody of the minor child or children.

(b) In a hearing *ex parte* for the purpose of obtaining such *ex parte* temporary injunction, no evidence other than verified pleadings or affidavits shall be used as evidence, unless the respondent appears at the hearing or has received reasonable notice of the hearing. A denial of a petition for an *ex parte* injunction shall be by written order noting the legal grounds for denial. When the only ground for denial is no appearance or an immediate and present danger of domestic violence, the court shall set a full hearing on the petition for injunction with notice at the earliest possible time. Nothing herein affects a petitioner's right to promptly amend any petition, or otherwise be heard in person on any petition consistent with the Florida Rules of Civil Procedure.

(c) Any such *ex parte* temporary injunction shall be effective for a fixed period not to exceed 15 days. A full hearing, as provided by this section, shall be set for a date no later than the date when the temporary injunction ceases to be effective. The court may grant a continuance of the hearing before or during a hearing for good cause shown by any party, which shall include a continuance to obtain service of process. Any injunction shall be extended if necessary to remain in full force and effect during any period of continuance.

(6) (a) Upon notice and hearing, when it appears to the court that the petitioner is either the victim of domestic violence as defined by § 741.28 or has reasonable cause to believe he or she is in imminent danger of becoming a victim of domestic violence, the court may grant such relief as the court deems proper, including an injunction:

1. Restraining the respondent from committing any acts of domestic violence.
2. Awarding to the petitioner the exclusive use and possession of the dwelling that the parties share or excluding the respondent from the residence of the petitioner.
3. On the same basis as provided in chapter 61, awarding custody or temporary visitation rights with minor child or children.

Courtesy of the state of Florida.

EXHIBIT 12.2 Sample Order for Protection

COURT OF WASHINGTON

FOR ___

Petitioner ___ DOB ___

vs.

Respondent ___ DOB ___

NO. ___

ORDER FOR PROTECTION
(ORPRT) (All Cases)
(Clerk's Action Required)
Court Address ___

Telephone Number: (___) ___

The court has jurisdiction over the parties, the minors, and the subject matter. ☐ If minors are involved, this state ☐ has exclusive continuing jurisdiction ☐ is the home state; ☐ no other state has exclusive continuing jurisdiction; ☐ other: ___

Notice of this hearing was served on the respondent by ☐ personal service ☐ service by mail pursuant to court order ☐ service by publication pursuant to court order ☐ other ___

(continued)

EXHIBIT 12.2 *continued*

This order is issued in accordance with the Full Faith and Credit provisions of VAWA: 18 U.S.C. § 2265.

Identification of Minors: ☐ No minors involved.

Name (First, Middle Initial, Last)	Age	Race	Sex

Based upon the petition, testimony, and case record, the court finds that the respondent committed domestic violence as defined in RCW 26.50.010 and represents a credible threat to the physical safety of petitioner, and IT IS THEREFORE ORDERED THAT:

	1 Respondent is RESTRAINED from causing physical harm, bodily injury, assault, including sexual assault, and from molesting, harassing, threatening, or stalking ☐ petitioner ☐ the minors named in the table above ☐ these minors only:
	2 Respondent is RESTRAINED from coming near and from having any contact whatsoever, in person or through others, by phone, mail, or any means, directly or indirectly, except for mailing or service of process of court documents by a 3rd party or contact by Respondent's lawyer(s) with ☐ petitioner ☐ the minors named in the table above ☐ these minors only: If both parties are in the same location, respondent shall leave.
	3 Respondent is EXCLUDED from petitioner's ☐ residence ☐ workplace ☐ school; ☐ the day care or school of ☐ the minors named in the table above ☐ these minors only: ☐ Other ☐ Petitioner's address is confidential. ☐ Petitioner waives confidentiality of the address which is:
	4. Petitioner shall have exclusive right to the residence that petitioner and respondent share. The respondent shall immediately VACATE the residence. The respondent may take respondent's personal clothing and tools of trade from the residence while a law enforcement officer is present. ☐ This address is confidential. ☐ Petitioner waives confidentiality of this address, which is:

5. Respondent is PROHIBITED from knowingly coming within, or knowingly remaining within _____ (distance) of: ☐ petitioner's residence ☐ workplace ☐ school; ☐ the day care or school of ☐ the minors named in the table on page one ☐ these minors only:

☐ other:

6. Petitioner shall have possession of essential personal belongings, including the following:

7. Petitioner is granted use of the following vehicle:

Year, Make & Model _____ License No. _____

8. Other:

9. Respondent shall participate in treatment and counseling as follows:
   ☐ domestic violence perpetrator treatment program approved under RCW 26.50.150 or counseling
   at: _____
   ☐ parenting classes at: _____
   ☐ drug/alcohol treatment at: _____
   ☐ other:

10. Petitioner is granted judgment against Respondent for $_____ fees and costs.

11. Parties shall return to court on _____, at _____ ___.m. for review.

Complete only if the protection ordered involves children

12. Petitioner is GRANTED the temporary care, custody, and control of ☐ the minors named in the table above ☐ these minors only:

13. Respondent is RESTRAINED from interfering with petitioner's physical or legal custody of ☐ the minors named in the table above ☐ these minors only:

14. Respondent is RESTRAINED from removing from the state ☐ the minors named in the table above ☐ these minors only:

(continued)

EXHIBIT 12.2 *continued*

15. The respondent will be allowed visitations as follows: _____

_____

_____

_____

_____

_____

_____

_____

Petitioner may request modification of visitation if respondent fails to comply with treatment or counseling as ordered by the court.

If the person with whom the child resides a majority of the time plans to relocate the child, that person must comply with the notice requirements of the Child Relocation Act. Persons entitled to time with the child under a court order may object to the proposed relocation. See RCW 26.09, RCW 26.10 or RCW 26.26 for more information.

WARNINGS TO THE RESPONDENT: Violation of the provisions of this order with actual notice of its terms is a criminal offense under chapter 26.50 RCW and will subject a violator to arrest. If the violation of the protection order involves travel across a state line or the boundary of a tribal jurisdiction, or involves conduct within the special maritime and territorial jurisdiction of the United States, which includes tribal lands, the defendant may be subject to criminal prosecution in federal court under 18 U.S.C. §§ 2261, 2261A, or 2262.

Violation of this order is a gross misdemeanor unless one of the following conditions apply: Any assault that is a violation of this order and that does not amount to assault in the first degree or second degree under RCW 9A.36.011 or 9A.36.021 is a class C felony. Any conduct in violation of this order that is reckless and creates a substantial risk of death or serious physical injury to another person is a class C felony. Also, a violation of this order is a class C felony if the respondent has at least 2 previous convictions for violating a protection order issued under Titles 10, 26 or 74 RCW.

Effective immediately, and continuing as long as this protection order is in effect, the respondent may not possess a firearm or ammunition. 18 U.S.C. § 922(g)(8). A violation of this federal firearms law carries a maximum possible penalty of 10 years in prison and a $250,000 fine. An exception exists for law enforcement officers and military personnel when carrying department/government-issued firearms. 18 U.S.C. § 925(a)(1). If the respondent is convicted of an offense of domestic violence, the respondent will be forbidden for life from possessing a firearm or ammunition. 18 U.S.C. § 922(g)(9); RCW 9.41.040.

YOU CAN BE ARRESTED EVEN IF THE PERSON OR PERSONS WHO OBTAINED THE ORDER INVITE OR ALLOW YOU TO VIOLATE THE ORDER'S PROHIBITIONS. You have the sole responsibility to avoid or refrain from violating the order's provisions. Only the court can change the order upon written application.

Pursuant to 18 U.S.C. § 2265, a court in any of the 50 states, the District of Columbia, Puerto Rico, any United States territory, and any tribal land within the United States shall accord full faith and credit to the order.

It is further ordered that the clerk of the court shall forward a copy of this order on or before the next judicial day to _____ ☐ County Sheriff's Office ☐ Police Department WHERE PETITIONER LIVES which shall enter it in a computer-based criminal intelligence system available in this state used by law enforcement to list outstanding warrants.

☐ The clerk of the court shall also forward a copy of this order on or before the next judicial day to ☐ County Sheriff's Office ☐ Police Department WHERE RESPONDENT LIVES which shall personally serve the respondent with a copy of this order and shall promptly complete and return to this court proof of service.

☐ Petitioner shall serve this order by ☐ mail ☐ publication.
☐ Petitioner has made private arrangements for service of this order.
☐ Respondent appeared and was informed of the order by the court; further service is not required.

☐ The law enforcement agency where ☐ petitioner ☐ respondent lives shall:
    ☐ assist petitioner in obtaining:
        ☐ Possession of petitioner's ☐ residence ☐ personal belongings located at: ☐ the shared residence ☐ respondent's
           residence ☐ other: _____
        ☐ Custody of the above-named minors, including taking physical custody for delivery to petitioner.
        ☐ Use of above-designated vehicle.
        ☐ Other: _____
    ☐ Other: _____

THIS ORDER FOR PROTECTION EXPIRES ON _____
[date].

If the duration of this order exceeds one year, the court finds that an order of less than one year
 will be insufficient to prevent further acts of domestic violence.

DATED _____ at _____ a.m./p.m.

                                    _____
                                    JUDGE/COURT COMMISSIONER

Presented by:

                                    I acknowledge receipt of a copy of this
                                    Order for Protection:

_____   _____
Petitioner   Date   Respondent   Date

Courtesy of the state of Washington.

"Okay," J. D. replied. "That's coming in loud and clear, and I think I can help you. I want to explain the options you have. A victim of domestic violence may have a variety of remedies available because of her particular situation. For example, if Tim is physically violent with you, then those actions may also lead to criminal charges for battery or assault. Plus, there are situations where victims have sued for monetary damages against their batterers."

Maggie looked worried. She told J. D., "I don't really want to get into all of that, if I don't have to."

"I understand," J. D. commented. "I just want to make sure you know your options. I'm sure you realize that Tim will probably be in shock to hear that you're standing up to him, and a temporary restraining order will probably be necessary. I can ask the judge to order Tim out of the family home. I'll also want to file a divorce complaint based on the violence, and then a temporary financial support order called a *pendente lite* application to make sure you'll have enough money to tide you and Timmy over in the family home."

Maggie's head was swimming with all the new information. "I'm sure you know what I should do. I'm depending on your experience with this type of case."

J. D. solemnly nodded and further explained, "A domestic violence claim may be a little difficult to prove since you've never called the police to report the violence, but your medical records will show the pattern of injuries you've suffered over the years."

It was decided that Maggie and Timmy would stay with Susan until the situation could be better assessed. Luckily, Tim did not know where Susan's new apartment was located, and she had an unlisted number.

Post TRO: Maggie Takes One Step at a Time

Maggie was so nervous about going to court that J. D. agreed to let Susan act as Maggie's victim advocate. A **victim advocate** (states may use different titles) is loosely defined as a person who provides assistance to a victim of domestic violence. A victim of domestic violence may be accompanied by an advocate to hearings. Advocates may include social workers, counselors, domestic violence shelter workers, and volunteers.

The court gave Maggie her TRO, and she moved back into her home with Timmy after her husband moved out. Maggie was shocked at the condition of the house. Being served with the legal papers had angered Tim, and without Maggie being there to absorb his anger, he had taken his anger out on the furniture. Subsequently, Maggie agreed to meet with Tim at a family counselor's office after he had been in therapy by himself for several weeks. J. D. had moved ahead with the filing for divorce and motioning for temporary support. Tim had moved in with his brother and was also getting counseling from his minister.

Susan, typically, was being a strong shoulder to lean on for her old friend. Months after having her worst suspicions confirmed, Susan finally was beginning to feel like the clouds were lifting. She had spoken with Maggie almost every day, but now the conversations were becoming less frequent and more upbeat. However, she was a bit worried about their last conversation. Maggie had called Susan at the office.

"Hi, Sue, it's me," Maggie began.

"Hi! How are you and little Timmy doing?" Susan asked.

"We're doing really well. We've continued the family counseling with the therapist and Reverend Hatch. Tim has gone to that anger management class that the court ordered, too. Even his mom came to a session. I think the shame of what he has done is starting to dawn on him," Maggie said. She paused, and then quietly added, "Oh, Sue, Tim was crying like a baby at the therapist's office. He's so sorry for putting us through everything."

"Didn't your counselor say that the typical domestic violence cycle involves the batterer feeling really sorry for what he's done?"

"Yeah, and I know she's probably right," Maggie answered. "He's always been really sorry afterward, but Sue, he's never acted like this before."

"So what? Is it going to change your mind about a divorce, the TRO, and everything we've talked about for months?" Susan anxiously asked.

"No, it's not. It's just . . .." Maggie paused, and then continued, "It's just that for the first time I'm hoping we can all move ahead—you know, to have a fresh start."

Susan was worried, "You don't mean starting fresh with Tim?"

Maggie quickly answered, "Oh, no! Don't worry. I'm not putting myself or Timmy through that again!"

Susan was relieved and told Maggie, "That's good to hear. You've come a long way, and I know you'll do great now that you don't have to hide behind fear or face your situation alone."

DEFINING DOMESTIC VIOLENCE

The first step in dealing with domestic violence is becoming aware of how it is defined across the United States. The abuse prevention statutes are all designed to protect one person from another person with whom there has been some type of *special relationship*. What is a special relationship? Minnesota's statutory definition is an example of a relatively inclusive statute. It states: *Domestic violence is the infliction of fear or actual physical harm, bodily injury, assault, terroristic threats, and criminal sexual conduct between family or household members.*[7] Minnesota's statute defines family or household members as spouses, former spouses, parents, children, blood relatives, cohabitants, and persons who have a child in common, whether or not they have ever been married or lived together.

States with more inclusive type statutes might expand the definition to include dating partners. States with less inclusive statutes might limit the list to spouses and relatives, and fail to include protection to unmarried individuals with a child in common, dating couples, or same-sex couples. The national trend is toward the inclusion of different types of special relationships.

However, a *legal* definition does not adequately describe the full picture of domestic violence. Most domestic violence victims are women, and most perpetrators are men; however, domestic violence can be inflicted by women against men, by women against women in same-sex relationships, by men against men in same-sex relationships, and by the caretakers of the elderly against their elderly charges. In addition, though outside the scope of this chapter, one of the most heinous crimes is domestic violence by adults against children.

What Conduct Is Considered Domestic Violence?

Domestic violence can be defined as actual physical violence, but also includes *attempts* at physical violence. A *verbal threat* of violence can be considered domestic violence. However, if the victim of a verbal threat wishes to be granted a TRO, most courts will require a statement that the victim was fearful of *imminent harm* as a follow-up to the verbal abuse. Many states include harassment within their definition of domestic violence. **Harassment** consists of words and actions that unlawfully annoy or alarm another. Harassment may include anonymous, repeated, offensively coarse, and/or late-night telephone calls and insulting, taunting, or physically challenging approaches. Often accompanying domestic violence of some sort, the act of stalking is clearly criminal behavior. **Stalking** is the crime of repeatedly following, threatening, or harassing another person in ways that lead to a legitimate fear of physical harm.

Psychological Abuse Is Usually Present

Psychological abuse usually accompanies physical or sexual abuse. Examples of psychological abuse include such behavior as the following: (1) threatening to hurt or kill the battered person; (2) intimidation; (3) isolating the battered person from others or from transportation; (4) using a child's safety to control the battered woman; (5) blaming others for the violence; (6) refusing access to information or assistance; (7) degrading the battered person; and (8) using economic superiority against the victim.[8]

Fears of the Battered Spouse

Statistically, we now know that the majority of domestic violence is inflicted by the husband or male partner and suffered by the wife or female partner, and sometimes by the children. You may question why a battered woman would not leave her batterer. Many reasons may prevent a battered woman from leaving. The abused woman often loves her batterer partner. It is the abuse she hates, not the abuser. She often feels she has no place to go if she leaves. She may believe that the abuse is her fault and that she can find a way to make things right *if only she tries hard enough.* Usually she is ashamed of having other people find out she is abused. She may be afraid that no one will believe she is battered or abused because her partner is so nice to everyone else. Perhaps her partner has threatened to harm her, or even her children, if she leaves.[9]

Sometimes a client makes the decision to divorce and hires an attorney, but fails to share the extent of the violence against her, or even that there is violence occurring at home. Why would a woman who has made the decision to leave a violent marriage still refuse to acknowledge to her attorney that such violence occurred? To determine the answer to that question there must be some understanding of the psychological reaction of some women who suffer through violence inflicted by a spouse. Some battered women may refuse to publicly admit their battering because they fear their spouse's reaction will lead to more violence against themselves and their children. Also, many battered women have kept the secret of their battering for so many years that telling their secret has become a larger hurdle to jump with each ensuing year of battering.

If you find yourself working on a client's case that involves domestic violence, you must be aware of the very real possibility that your battered client may feel so humiliated that she may find it nearly impossible to admit to the battering, even to her attorney. The psychological impact of being battered can make the victim highly emotional, often displaying symptoms of psychological trauma. In fact, the battered woman's reaction often results in a post-traumatic stress disorder.[10] **Post-traumatic stress disorder** can be defined as the residual effects of an emotionally disturbing episode or continual series of episodes.

If a battered client comes to your law firm, it is important to realize that there is a bright side to representing a battered spouse. When she enters your law firm, the battered spouse has bravely taken a giant step forward in seeking to extricate herself and her children from their cycle of misery. The representation she receives at your law firm may be her lifeline.

Do Not Be Afraid to Ask if Domestic Violence Occurs

So, what is the best way to make sure each client seeking a divorce is helped to the utmost ability of each attorney and paralegal working on the client's case? As sensitive as the question may be, each client should be asked if domestic violence was present at any time during the marriage. By learning to watch the client for telltale signs of recognition and nervousness, an attorney or paralegal can delve more deeply into the serious topic of domestic violence. Remember, what attorneys and paralegals should not do is think a domestic relations practice can exist without some cases involving domestic violence. Such ignorance can lead to inadequate efforts being made to protect the client, the attorney, and his staff. What also must be realized is that sometimes the very action of a battered spouse attempting to extricate herself from domestic violence can lead to an escalation of violence by the abusive spouse.

How Does Domestic Violence Happen?

Anyone planning to work in domestic relations law should have some understanding of *why* domestic violence occurs. Someone who has never experienced domestic violence may think it is easy to take the position that the first time such violence happens, the victim should leave immediately and never turn back. However, what often occurs is that the violence does not begin until after the victim, usually a woman, is in love, marries, and, perhaps, has children. A batterer often follows violence with what appears to be sincere and profuse apologies. This cycle is the precursor to the dissipation of the wife's self-esteem to the point of nonexistence. The batterer batters to show control over his wife and children. If a battered spouse seeks an end to violence through divorce, the attorney and paralegal representing the battered spouse must be aware that the violent spouse faced with separation and divorce often becomes a wild card whose actions cannot be guaranteed.[11]

Unfortunately, separation and impending divorce seldom bring an end to domestic violence. Attorneys must do everything possible to remove batterers from the lives of their clients and their clients' children. This is made more difficult when a batterer denies that domestic violence has occurred, which batterers typically do.

Child Custody Issues

The pervasiveness of domestic violence has been the catalyst for a majority of states to statutorily ensure that their court judges consider the presence of violence when determining child custody issues. However, not so long ago, many battered spouses were faced with the problem of child custody issues that were decided by courts that would not consider spousal abuse *allegations* when deciding custody matters. During the pendency of divorce proceedings, the battered spouse was required to supply the current address of herself and the children to the court and to her husband. If a battered spouse and her children left the state to escape the possibility of violence while the divorce was being heard, she could face kidnapping and contempt of court charges.

Prior to relatively recent statutory changes designed to protect battered spouses and their children, the battered spouse often found herself in an untenable position. As if it was not difficult enough for a spouse to deal with domestic violence, she also had to deal with the court system's somewhat "split personality." On the one hand, the courts wanted to be seen as a protector of battered spouses. On the other hand, those same courts wanted to protect the constitutional right of accused batterers to be considered innocent until proven guilty, and fathers' fundamental right to see their children.

Historically, a father's right to see his children was vigorously protected even if the court found that the father of a child had actually been guilty of battering the child's mother. As long as the batterer was not accused of violence against his children, the batterer's custody and visitation rights were often considered sacred. A more modern view is that a child's best interest may not be served by encouraging visitation with a father who has battered the child's mother. The bottom line is that statutory changes encourage and require the courts to weigh the needs of the battered wife *over* the rights of the father seeking custody or visitation with his children. The problem with the new statutory changes is that if a father has been falsely accused by his wife of being a batterer, he now has the responsibility of disproving the allegations. Unfortunately, while attempting to disprove false charges, a father may not be allowed to know where his children are residing or may not be allowed visitation.

As stated in the chapter on custody, there is a statutory preference for joint custody and frequent contact with the children by both parents. This preference for joint custody is diminished when domestic violence is a factor in a divorce case. The psychotherapy and pediatric communities do not recommend awarding joint custody in cases involving highly emotional conflicts between the parents.

The majority of states now provide some statutory guidelines for attorneys who wish to argue against joint custody when domestic violence is present. In fact, 35 states require their family courts to consider the presence of domestic violence when determining the best interests of the children. Other states either require, or simply suggest, that their family courts also discern each parent's ability to deal with the other in a friendly and ongoing relationship during a custody dispute. This is known as a **friendly parent provision.** Advocates of battered women, including the American Bar Association's Center on Children and the Law, find such provisions to be inappropriate because a battered spouse often appears uncooperative while trying to ensure her and her children's safety.

Some states have moved toward a more progressive *child-focused* way of dealing with custody disputes. For example, Texas has moved the focus away from parents' rights to a focus on whether each parent has shown by his/her *actions* that he/she takes the children's best interests seriously. *Texas Family Code* § 153.004 clearly states that a history of domestic violence will be evaluated. Section 153.004 provides: (1) In determining whether to appoint a party as sole or joint managing conservator, the court shall consider evidence of the intentional use of abusive physical force by a party against the party's spouse or against any person younger than 18 years of age committed within a two-year period preceding the filing of the suit or during the pendency of the suit; (2) the court may not appoint joint managing conservators if credible evidence is presented of a history or pattern of past or present child neglect, or physical or sexual abuse by one parent directed against the other parent, a spouse, or a child; and (3) the court shall consider the commission of family violence in determining whether to deny, restrict, or limit the possession of a child by a parent who is appointed as a possessory conservator.

Creating a Client Safety Plan and Protecting Important Documents

Attorneys and paralegals should be prepared to help their battered clients develop a **client safety plan** for escaping their workplace or home, if needed. On the job, you can gently assist in this endeavor by keeping a list of the area's safe havens and emergency numbers for distribution to all clients. Additionally, clients should be instructed on how to protect their important documents. The attorney should advise the client to keep important documents in a safe place outside her home. Documents to protect include: (1) identification; (2) driver's license; (3) car registration; (4) court orders, such as restraining orders; (5) birth certificates for the client and her children; (6) police reports and any documentation of previous abuse; (7) money, bank books, or at least bank account numbers, checkbooks, credit cards, and an ATM card; (8) any lease or house deed; (9) medical, life, and auto insurance papers; (10) house keys and car keys; (11) medications; and (12) small saleable items.[12] Read Exhibit 12.3 to review a client safety plan.

The Importance of Confidentiality

The importance of confidentiality cannot be overstated when discussing domestic violence. In some situations, if a battered spouse is unable to keep her location secret, the possibility of violence looms constantly overhead. The problem of maintaining confidentiality most often arises when the battered spouse takes her children with her to a location unknown to her spouse. Since the threat is very real, it is of the utmost importance that the following records and information be guarded and kept strictly confidential: (1) new address;

EXHIBIT 12.3 Client Safety Plan

1. The client should know how to get out of her home as quickly as possible and plan her escape from different locations throughout the house.
2. The client should keep important items such as her keys and wallet in an accessible area.
3. The client should notify neighbors to call the police if the neighbors see any suspicious movement around the client's house.
4. The client should teach the children to call the police when they are fearful that domestic violence will occur.
5. The client should know of several safe places to go when violence is feared.
6. The client should know how to get to a battered women's shelter if the client does not have any other safe place to go.

---

(2) school records; (3) medical records; (4) postal service records; (5) motor vehicle records; (6) voter registration; (7) name changes; and (8) Social Security number changes.

Changing Identity

You may need to advise clients on the procedures for changing their Social Security numbers. Some victims seeking to elude their abusers and reduce the risk of further violence choose to establish new identities. As part of that effort, it may be helpful to obtain a new Social Security number. The Social Security Administration (SSA) joins with other federal agencies to provide assistance to victims of domestic violence. Your clients can apply in person at any Social Security office for a new number, but they must produce evidence of their age, identity, and either United States citizenship or lawful alien status. According to the SSA, changing one's name is one of the most important steps a domestic violence victim needs to take for personal protection. If your client is changing her name, she will have to submit a request with her name along with the application for the new Social Security number.

Violence Against Women Act of 1994

The tough job of balancing national preference and issues of domestic violence has forced the majority of states to make changes in their state statutes and fostered major changes in federal law. Numerous policies and laws, both civil and criminal, address the systemic issues in domestic violence. Examples include the federal Violence Against Women Act of 1994, the Uniform Full Faith and Credit of Protection Orders Act, gun prohibition acts, and evidentiary rules for custody cases. The **Violence Against Women Act (VAWA)** was created to provide a new, more effective tool for preserving women's safety in domestic violence cases, as well as for any category of gender-based violence against women in our society.[13] Important from the perspective of trying to prove that a crime occurred under the VAWA is that proof of specific intent is not required. Instead, an *objective* showing of the history of a violent spouse is sufficient to reach the threshold required by the VAWA. This change in proof is important. Historically, there was always a requirement that the specific intent to commit a crime was necessary to find a defendant guilty of a crime.

Creation of the VAWA was especially important because it mandated a new *federal approach* to how states must react to protection orders that are issued by another state's courts. Under VAWA, federal law mandates that all states must recognize and respect another state's protection orders. Also, the VAWA makes it a federal crime to cross state lines to injure or threaten a spouse. It is also a federal crime to cross state lines and violate a state protection order.

In addition to removing the legal obstacles in prosecuting a violent spouse, the mandate is assisted in its effective application by VAWA's added bonus of providing restitution to battered women whose abusive spouses are found guilty under VAWA. **Restitution** is defined as giving a financial payment to the victim of a criminal act. New Hampshire's state statute is a good example of one that follows the intent of the VAWA. The statute is called the New Hampshire Protection of Persons from Domestic Violence Act. Section 173-B:1 of the state's statute includes the following relief:

> *Upon a showing of abuse of the plaintiff by a preponderance of the evidence, the court shall grant such relief as is necessary to bring about a cessation of abuse, which relief may include: (1) Directing the defendant to refrain from abusing or interfering in any way with the person or liberty of the plaintiff; (2) Enjoining the defendant from entering the premises wherein the plaintiff resides, unless the defendant exclusively owns or leases and pays for the premises and the defendant has no legal duty to support the plaintiff or minor children on the premise; (3) Enjoining the defendant from contacting the plaintiff at, or entering, plaintiff's place of employment or school; (4) Enjoining the defendant from harassing, intimidating, or threatening the plaintiff, the plaintiff's relatives, regardless of their place of residence, or plaintiff's household members in any way; and (5) Enjoining the defendant from taking, converting, or damaging property in which the plaintiff may have a legal or equitable interest. Additional relief includes granting to the plaintiff the exclusive right of use and possession of the household furniture, furnishings and automobiles unless the defendant exclusively owns such personal property and the defendant has no legal duty to support the plaintiff or minor children.*

Was Spousal Abuse Victim Also Child Abuser?

The case entitled *In the Interest of Betty J. W.* (see Case 12.1) involved an interesting twist to the typical domestic violence case. The question in this case was whether, under the facts presented, a victim of domestic violence could be held responsible when her abusive spouse had injured her children, but she failed to report the injuries immediately. As you read the facts, imagine yourself in the mother's position. Do you excuse her delay in reporting injuries? The appellate court hearing the appeal described Betty J.W., the wife and mother, as a classic example of a person suffering from the "battered wife syndrome." The **battered wife syndrome** had previously gained much publicity as a legal defense used in cases involving alleged female victims of domestic violence. These victims, charged with killing their battering husbands, claimed that the continual emotional and physical violence affected their ability to comprehend right from wrong.

Victim Fights In-Laws

In the domestic violence case of *Lewelling v. Lewelling* (see Case 12.2), the victim found herself battling for her son's custody, not with her abuser, but with his parents. The term *battered woman's syndrome* was used by the court in this case to describe the behavior of the typical battered woman. Describing the syndrome, the court explained that the victim of domestic violence often does not want to end an abusive relationship because her personal willpower has been beaten into submission by the life of continuous fear she has lived.

Violence Claim Used as Strategic Weapon

The court in the case of *Cesare v. Cesare* (see Case 12.3) did not believe the heinous crime of domestic violence had occurred between the two parties. Rather, they feared a great injustice occurred when the defendant's nonviolent behavior and verbal statements were found by the trial court judge to rise to the level of *terroristic* threats. As you read the case, note how the appellate court judges preferred to view the defendant's behavior and statements.

CASE 12.1 *In the Interest of Betty J.W.,*
Dorothy N.W., James E.W., Sandra K.W., and Cassie A.W.,
179 W. Va. 605, 371 S.E.2d 326 (1988)

Facts: Mary W. and her husband J.B.W. are the parents of five minor children. On April 30, 1985, J.B.W. sexually abused and assaulted his 17-year-old daughter, B.J. When Mary W. intervened, she was beaten and threatened with a knife. On the second day after the assault, while her husband was absent, Mary W. paid a neighbor to take her and her children to her parents' residence. That same day she reported the abuse to the West Virginia Department of Human Services (DHS) and requested help and a safe place for her family to stay. She also obtained a warrant against her husband for the abuse.

After the incident, J.B.W. left the house and did not return until June 1, 1985, at which time he stayed overnight. His overnight stay immediately prompted the DHS to file a petition on June 4, 1985, to terminate parental rights alleging that J.B.W. had habitually physically abused his children and that Mary W. had failed to protect her children from his abuse. A hearing was held on June 10, 1985, with a guardian *ad litem* appointed for the five children. At this hearing, Mary W. made a motion for an improvement period in which she would be appointed the guardian of her children. However, the court denied the motion, stating that the alleged history of abuse by her husband was a compelling circumstance justifying the denial of an improvement period. On August 1, 1985, the Circuit Court of Mingo County ordered the DHS to take legal and physical custody of the children and denied a second motion by the parents for an improvement period. Mary W. appealed.

Issue: Whether Mary W.'s parental rights were improperly terminated.

Court's Reasoning: The lower court again denied Mary W.'s request for an improvement period at the final hearing on September 17, 1985. It based its decision on their findings that Mary W. was a classic example of a victim of the battered wife syndrome whose continued contact with her husband was indicative of her inability to break the pattern of abuse. Therefore, allowing an improvement period would put the children at great risk. On that basis, the court concluded that there was no less drastic alternative than to terminate their parental rights. Mary W. argues that she was unlawfully denied a statutory improvement period before her parental rights were terminated.

In deciding the case, we must weigh a natural parent's constitutional rights to the custody of her children until the unfitness of that parent is proven. We refer to *In re Willis,* 157 W. Va. 225 (1973), which recognized that a natural parent has a constitutional right to the custody of her children and, before a final hearing, is entitled to an improvement period of three to twelve months in order to remedy the alleged circumstances. This is a fundamental personal liberty protected and guaranteed by the due process clauses of the West Virginia and United States constitutions. This court has a role as the ultimate protector of minors. *This* parens patriae *interest in promoting the welfare of the child favors preservation, not severance, of natural family bonds, a proposition that is echoed in our child welfare statute.* Furthermore, we find that the record did not support the trial court's legal conclusion that Mary W. *knowingly allowed* the sexual abuse. When J.B.W. attempted to sexually abuse the daughter on the day of the assault, Mary W. interceded and was beaten and threatened with a knife. *Certainly a parent charged with an act of omission who takes reasonable steps to protect her child and who does not defend the abuser or condone the abusive conduct, does not knowingly allow the abuse.* It is obvious to the court that the reason for the one-day delay

(continued)

CASE 12.1 *continued*

in removing her children from her husband's presence centered on her opportunity to get away from him and her inability to drive.

There was no showing that an improvement plan had been developed and had not been followed by Mary W. In fact, the record indicates that Mary W., after reporting the sexual abuse incident the day after it happened to the authorities, was left to fend for herself and her family. There is no indication in the record that the DHS acted under W. Va. Code § 40-6A-9 (1977) to bring into play its family protective services to assist Mary W. and her family.

Holding: Judgment reversed and case remanded.

Case Discussion: The appellate court remanded the case back to the trial court in order for the court to supervise what the appellate judges called a *family improvement period.* The social service agency within the family's county was to create an appropriate family case plan to help the family deal with their situation. Do you think the mother should have another chance, considering the facts of this case?

Representing a Defendant in a Domestic Violence Complaint

A family law office usually has a number of defendants who are fighting false allegations of domestic violence. As was discussed in the court's opinion in the *Cesare* case, a small percentage of domestic violence complaints may be less-than-truthful allegations that are being used by the plaintiff to gain leverage in a pending divorce. On the other hand, the domestic violence may have actually occurred, in which case the defendant needs legal counsel to assist in his defense. Unlike a criminal case where a person is provided with due process, and if guilty may receive probation and/or a monetary fine, a domestic violence finding allows judges to issue far-reaching orders.

As discussed earlier, a final hearing is usually held within 10 to 20 days of the filing of an *ex parte* complaint. After the hearing, and usually without benefit of financial statements, family court judges in many states are permitted to grant substantial relief to the complainant. Typically, American courts may award some or all of the following types of relief: (1) an order restraining the defendant from subjecting the victim to domestic violence, as defined in state law; (2) an order granting exclusive possession of the residence or household to the victim, regardless of whether the residence or household is jointly or solely owned by the parties or jointly or solely leased by the parties; (3) an order providing for custody of any children to the victim and visitation to the defendant; (4) an order requiring the defendant to pay the victim monetary compensation for losses suffered as a direct result of the act of domestic violence; (5) an order restraining the defendant from entering the residence, property, school, or place of employment of the victim or other family or household members of the victim; (6) an order restraining the defendant from any communication with the victim that is likely to cause annoyance or alarm; (7) an order requiring that the defendant make or continue making rent or mortgage payments on the residence occupied by the victim; (8) an order granting temporary possession of specified property, such as an automobile, checkbook, documentation of health insurance, identification, a specific document, a key, and other personal effects; and (9) an order awarding emergency monetary relief to the victim and other dependents, if any.

Unlike criminal and family proceedings, most court rules involving domestic violence allegations do not explicitly provide for any discovery. Your office may have to prepare a formal request in writing for a copy of the complaint and other documents. Also, if necessary, your office may have to send discovery letters asking for any discoverable information to the local police department and prosecutor's office.

CASE 12.2 *Brenda Lewelling v. Carl and Melba Lewelling,* 796 S.W.2d 164 (Tex. 1994)

Facts: Six months after the birth of their son, Jesse, in April 1987, Brenda Lewelling initiated divorce proceedings against her husband, Billy, alleging that he had physically abused her throughout their relationship. Although Billy did not seek custody of Jesse and even wanted the child to remain with Brenda, his parents, Melba and Carl Lewelling, intervened in the divorce proceedings, seeking to be named managing conservators of Jesse. Brenda testified that Billy had beaten her badly enough that she required hospitalization on several occasions, and that this abuse continued during the time she was pregnant with Jesse. The El Paso Court of Appeals affirmed the trial court's appointment of Carl and Melba Lewelling as managing conservators, basing its decision on the fact that Brenda continued to see Billy after suffering several incidents of physical abuse, and after she testified to the fact that she might consider reconciling with him if he received counseling. Brenda Lewelling appealed again, and the Texas Supreme Court heard the case.

Issue: Whether the fact that someone is a victim of domestic violence should have a negative impact on that victim in a custody dispute.

Court's Reasoning: The appointment of a nonparent as a conservator of a child requires the nonparent to affirmatively prove by a preponderance of the evidence that the appointment of the natural parent as managing conservator would significantly impair the child either physically or emotionally. We find no evidence to establish that the appointment of Brenda as managing conservator would significantly impair Jesse's health or emotional development. Brenda's behavior is characteristic of a woman with the battered woman syndrome. By finding against Brenda, we can only deter battered spouses from reporting their suffering for fear they will lose their children. Finally, in a custody battle between two parents in which there is any evidence of abusive physical force by one parent against the other, *Texas Family Code* § 14.01(c)(22) creates a preference that the nonviolent, rather than the violent, parent be appointed managing conservator. The court concluded that the abuser could not take advantage of his acts of abuse in a custody battle with the abused, and neither could the abuser's parents benefit from that abuse.

Holding: Appellant wins.

Case Discussion: Do you think the grandparents' efforts to keep their grandchild away from the parents involved in a domestic violence situation was admirable? Can you think of any other effort they could have made instead of seeking custody?

Using Domestic Violence as the Basis for a Civil Action

A fundamental legal concept in the American legal system is the belief that when one person injures another, the injured person has the right to recover monetary damages from the person who injured him. This is known as the tort law concept. Historically, the tort law concept could not be applied in a domestic violence situation because under the common law in the majority of states, spouses were not allowed to sue each other. Generally known as the **doctrine of interspousal tort immunity,** the immunity against being sued by a family member was supposed to support family cohesiveness and prevent possible frauds. Intrafamily tort actions are now a growing area of practice, however, due to the nearly complete statutory removal of the prohibition against these tort actions. This currently leaves the domestic violence victim with the possible option of suing her attacker.

CASE 12.3 *Cesare v. Cesare,*
154 N.J. 394, 713 A.2d 390 (1998)

Facts: The plaintiff testified that on the evening of July 9, 1996, she and the defendant got into an argument because she wanted to end the marriage. During the argument, the pair discussed the custody of the children. The plaintiff testified that the defendant said that he was not going to sell the house and give her half of the proceeds. The plaintiff informed the defendant that he might not have a choice if a court ordered it. She said, *I said to him that if we went through the system did he think he'd have a choice?* The plaintiff said he responded, *I've told you before, I do have a choice, and you will not get either of those things.* She interpreted this statement as a threat because *in the past he has told me that he will kill me before I get custody of our children, and before he gives me any part of our assets.* The argument lasted perhaps an hour and ended when the defendant said he felt sick and went upstairs to bed. The plaintiff said her husband did not use any profane language during the exchange.

After he was upstairs for about five minutes, the defendant started asking his wife to come upstairs. She said that he sounded agitated and angry, and shouted from the top of the stairs, *What are you still doing down there? Why don't you come up here?* At this time, two of the children were apparently sleeping upstairs in the house, with the third child at a friend's house. After persistent pleas by the defendant for the plaintiff to come upstairs, she said she responded, *Why? Do you want to shoot me now?* In reaction, the defendant apparently glared at her for perhaps five or ten seconds. She said her fear was *that he had gotten a gun out upstairs and that he wanted me upstairs so he could use it. There were guns in the house.* Fearful for her own safety, she then put a jacket on over her pajamas and left the house and children to go to the police department. There she signed a complaint under the New Jersey Domestic Violence Act. According to the plaintiff, during their marriage, her husband had made a number of threats to kill her as follows: *We have railroad tracks behind our house. He has told me he could, you know, make it look like I was taking a walk and somehow secure me to the railroad tracks until the train came. He has told me that he would put me in our shed, make it look like some kind of gas propane explosion. He said that he can make it look like a suicide.* Henry A. Phillips, the plaintiff's father, testified on behalf of his daughter that the defendant told him that he did not intend to carry out his threats to take the plaintiff's life, but admitted making such statements.

Issue: Whether the surrounding circumstances of the events of July 9, 1996, would have made a reasonable person fear a threat of any kind of violence.

Court's Reasoning: At trial, on July 18, 1996, the judge considered, without referring to any specific criminal statute being violated, whether the proofs before him were sufficient to constitute an act of domestic violence. The judge appeared to find a threat, presumably a terroristic threat, rather than harassment. The judge noted that in seeking a restraining order, some people come to court with the intent of gaining an advantage in an impending divorce action in order to obtain custody of the children or possession of the home or both. The judge acknowledged that both parties told conflicting stories and that the defendant denied ever threatening the life or safety of the plaintiff. The judge felt that the testimony of the plaintiff's father, Phillips, essentially tipped the balance in her favor because the judge could not comprehend what Phillips would gain by testifying, even though it was on behalf of his daughter. The judge considered that the defendant's words, *I do have a choice,* had implications beyond the literal meaning of those words. Thus, the judge issued a restraining order and ordered an evaluation of the defendant with regard to custody and visitation.

Aside from the legal issues, our scope of review is normally limited to whether there was sufficient credible evidence to support the trial judge's finding that an act of domestic violence had been committed. To support such a finding, where there is no actual physical abuse, the court must find by a preponderance of the evidence that the defendant committed one of the enumerated classes of prohibited conduct. Plus, there must have been a previous history of violence between the parties, including previous threats, harassment, and physical abuse. We do not generally disturb a judge's fact-finding unless there was a palpable abuse of discretion—that is, unless the findings are so wide of the mark that a manifest denial of justice resulted.

The judge's finding here of an act of domestic violence on July 9, 1996, resulted in a manifest denial of justice. An ordinary person in those circumstances would not perceive the defendant's statement on that occasion as a threat of any kind of violence. The defendant's statement that he had *choices* was made in response to his wife's assertion that he would be powerless to gain custody of the children and the marital home. The defendant was entitled to a response in that discussion. We are mindful that the dissolution of a marriage is often acrimonious, but such acrimony should not be used as a weapon to gain a strategic advantage in a matrimonial court, thus trivializing and distorting the beneficial purpose of the Domestic Violence Act to protect against regular abusive behavior.

Holding: Appellant wins.

Case Discussion: The appellate court was quite upset with the treatment Mr. Cesare had received by the trial court judge. Do you think Mrs. Cesare may have honestly misconstrued Mr. Cesare's statements? Do you agree with the court's determination that the domestic violence complaint was simply a strategic weapon used in an acrimonious divorce?

CHAPTER SUMMARY

Domestic violence knows no boundaries. It does not care about color of the skin or the economic standing of its victims. It is cold; it is harsh; and it exists regardless of whether society chooses to acknowledge it. Partners, wives, children, and the elderly are all its victims; however, women are its chief victims. Society pays for the moral and financial costs of domestic violence in our country.

Attorneys and paralegals must be prepared to deal with clients whom they suspect have been abused. Legal professionals need to be knowledgeable of victims' rights and all that can be done to help ensure the safety of such clients and their families. The legal professional has to ask questions about the home situation of the client and must not be hesitant about asking whether there has been violence between the partners during the course of the relationship. Temporary restraining orders (TROs) and orders of temporary support can provide the victim with the added protection and financial support needed to maintain the family.

The majority of states have enacted statutes to ensure that domestic violence in a relationship is taken into account when deciding matters of child custody. Under the Violence Against Women Act of 1994, victims have protections that make it a federal crime for a batterer to cross state lines and violate a state protection order. Funds are available through VAWA for the abuse victim to use for transitional housing and supervised visitation. Funds are also available for the training of law enforcement and other professionals to help them better deal with domestic violence situations.

The legal professional must be knowledgeable about domestic violence and take whatever steps are within her power to ensure the safety and welfare of her firm's clients and their children. This can be done by assisting with the creation of a client safety plan, assisting with a change in name and Social Security number, and keeping a list of safe houses and other places where domestic violence victims can get help.

Key Terms

protective order
temporary restraining order
   (TRO)
stay-away order
no-contact order
vacate order
contempt of court

final restraining order
victim advocate
domestic violence
harassment
stalking
post-traumatic stress disorder
friendly parent provision

client safety plan
Violence Against Women Act
   (VAWA)
restitution
battered wife syndrome
doctrine of interspousal tort
   immunity

Surfing the Web

http://www.dawnonline.org A not-for-profit organization that offers assistance to women and children of domestic violence.

http://www.ncadv.org This site is run by the National Coalition Against Domestic Violence. Includes information on how to obtain a new Social Security number if you are a victim of domestic violence.

http://www.feminist.org Are you a victim of domestic violence and don't know where to turn? Look no further than the Feminist Majority site.

http://www.ojp.usdoj.gov Do you think you are the only victim of domestic violence? Click here for statistics from the Bureau of Justice.

http://www.fbi.gov Obtain updates from the Federal Bureau of Investigation.

http://www.vaw.umn.edu Do you want to find the federal Domestic Violence laws and the "how-to" of enforcement? Check this Web site to find online resources on the topic of violence against women.

http://www.judicial.state.ia.us Iowa's domestic violence laws.

ETHICS ALERT

Alyssa is representing Noelle Wood in her divorce case. Noelle has given to Alyssa a detailed litany of the abuse inflicted on her by her husband. Alyssa knows that Noelle's husband is a big shot in town and would not want anyone to know about the domestic violence. Should Alyssa grab this opportunity to use this information as a negotiating tool to get a larger financial settlement for her client? Do you see an ethical dilemma arising from these facts?

Review Questions

1. What is the greatest single cause of injury to American women?
2. What is the definition of a typical batterer?
3. Why do you think a woman who has made the decision to leave a violent marriage would still refuse to acknowledge to her attorney that violence occurred?
4. When faced with a client who describes a history of domestic violence, what can an attorney do to protect the client?
5. What kind of protection should a TRO ask for?
6. Is the TRO an effective tool in dealing with a violent spouse, and what happens to a violent spouse when he fails to respect a TRO?
7. What does VAWA stand for, and why was it created?
8. If a battered spouse with a valid protection order from the state of Missouri moves to Pennsylvania with her children, how does the VAWA help?
9. Suppose the abusive spouse of the woman in question 8 ignored the protection order and assaulted his wife in a shopping mall in Pennsylvania. Suppose further that he pummeled her with his fist badly enough for her to require hospitalization, but there were no witnesses to the incident. How does the VAWA help the battered spouse prove the charges against her violent spouse? What if the battered spouse was inundated with medical bills and lost two weeks of work? How else can the VAWA help her?
10. How important is confidentiality in domestic violence cases, and just what records must be guarded and kept secret from the abuser?

Endnotes

1. Uniform Crime Reports, FBI-1991, Domestic Abuse Women's Network, http://www.cybergrrl.com and http://www.dawnonline.org.
2. U.S. Department of Justice (2000).
3. U.S. Department of Justice.
4. Novella, Antonia, *Battered Women* (Bureau of Justice Statistics National Crime Victimization Survey, U.S. Department of Justice, 1995), http://www.famvi.com.
5. *Report to the Nation on Crime and Justice* (Bureau of Justice Statistics, U.S. Dept. of Justice, October 1983), http://www.cybergrrl.com.
6. Barnett, Martha W., *"Ending Domestic Violence," American Bar Association Journal* (November 2000): 6.
7. MINN. STAT. § 518(B)(01) (2002).
8. DiCamillo, Angelo, "Dynamics and Principles of Domestic Violence," (Essentials of Domestic Violence, Institute for Continuing Legal Education Seminar, New Jersey, April 23, 2000).
9. Nadkarni, Lavita I., and Jessica P. Greenwald O'Brien, "Domestic Violence Under the Microscope Implications for Custody and Visitation," *Family Advocate* 3, no. 1 (Summer 2000).
10. Brinegar, Jerry, "What to Do If You're Being Abused," http://www.negia.net.
11. Miller, Janice Davis, "Dynamics of Domestic Violence— Representing the Victim." (Essentials of Domestic Violence, Institute for Continuing Education Seminar, New Jersey, April 23, 2002).
12. Lehrman, F., "Factoring Domestic Violence into Custody Cases," *Trial,* (February 1996): 32–39.
13. Paone, John P., *Representing Persons Falsely Accused of Domestic Violence* (Essentials of Domestic Violence, Institute for Continuing Legal Education Seminar, New Jersey, April 23, 2000).

Chapter 13

Alternative Dispute Resolution

Discourage litigation. Persuade your neighbors to compromise whenever you can. Point out to them how the nominal winner is often a real loser—in fees, expenses and waste of time. As a peace-maker, the lawyer has a superior opportunity of being a good man. There will still be business enough.

Abraham Lincoln (1846)[1]

FINDING AN ALTERNATIVE TO LITIGATION

As long as there have been people who wanted to go to court to fight a legal battle, there have been others who have sought every possible alternative to the classic courtroom-based confrontation. **Alternative dispute resolution (ADR)** is a concept whose purpose is to provide that alternative. Modern ADR developed mainly as a cost-cutting and time-saving option for individuals who did not want to face the daunting prospect of courtroom-centered litigation, whatever the subject matter may be.

Historically, ADR can trace its roots back to ancient societies, both religious and secular. A community's elders or religious leaders often would be asked to help resolve its citizen's problems without involving the formal judicial system.[2] During the American colonial period, ADR was the preferred alternative for settling disputes. Gradually, the new society matured and moved away from ADR, shifting toward the courtroom as the preferred method for settling disputes. It has been argued that the American passion for individual liberties is best protected by the country's courts, and not by ADR. After all, the courtroom is where one precedent-setting decision can ultimately affect all of society. By its very nature, ADR *is* a private process between the parties and usually happens outside the public view. It was not until the late nineteenth century that the country again began to turn to ADR in any significant number of cases. The reintroduction of ADR had its roots in the private sector as a cost-efficient measure and primarily dealt with labor disputes.

A complete turnaround in popularity occurred as twentieth-century America increasingly learned how to file lawsuits in alarming numbers. In fact, by 1989, 18 million new civil cases were filed in the United States. Amazingly, the federal court system saw its case numbers tripled in 30 years from 90,000 in 1960 to 250,000 in 1990.[3] The volume of litigation during the last half of the twentieth century led the courts, attorneys, and the general public to scrutinize the complexities of our judicial system and search for alternatives. This is why America returned to the less complex, problem-solving methodologies of ADR. The end of the twentieth century saw an explosion in both federal and state laws requiring the creation of ADR programs within the federal and state court systems.

The state of California was a leader in promoting ADR more than 25 years ago when the state made a push toward ADR with the passage of progressive legislation. The legislation requires mediation of *all* child custody and visitation disputes. California's success with ADR encouraged other states to pass legislation that expanded to include *all* areas of conflict within a family.[4] In 1996, lending momentum to this approach, the United States Commission on Child and Family Welfare recommended that all courts *adopt a series of measures, including mandatory mediation, to help resolve parenting disputes and the development of plans by parents together to determine their future involvement in the lives of their children when they live apart.*[5]

America in the twenty-first century has already seen ADR become embedded within the judicial structure and viewed as the viable alternative it is. In fact, ADR has been called the *second legal system.*[6] All 50 states and the District of Columbia have established ADR requirements in differing degrees for their judicial systems.

What Exactly Is ADR?

Alternative dispute resolution (ADR) is an umbrella term that includes numerous alternatives to traditional courtroom-centered litigation involving *all* subject areas. There are a number of ADR alternatives.[7] All of the ADR alternatives have their place, but mediation and arbitration can be considered the two main types of ADR used in most disputes. **Mediation** is a process whereby parties who have a dispute are helped by an individual called a **mediator** to settle their dispute themselves. Mediation is based on the principle of self-determination by the participants. The process relies upon the ability of participants to make their own voluntary and informed decisions.[8] Mediation is the ADR method most closely associated with divorce and other family-related disputes. **Arbitration** is the resolution of a dispute by a person other than a judge whose decision is binding. This person is called an **arbitrator.**[9] While arbitration is mostly used in commercial-type disputes, it is also used in resolving family law matters, although to a lesser extent than mediation.

The Paralegal's Role in ADR

The same job skills paralegals use in supporting litigation can be transferred directly to some forms of ADR.[10] Paralegals can conduct interviews of parties and witnesses, review documents and depositions during discovery, organize all information and exhibits, and communicate with the court, witnesses, and parties. The ADR method can offer career opportunities for paralegals to participate in dispute resolution in various venues. Some ADR is conducted under the auspices of the state or federal courts. Other ADR opportunities are independent of the courts.

The question of whether a paralegal can fill the mediator's role depends upon the state. Some state statutes specifically limit who can act as a mediator. For example, Florida limits mediators to attorneys, accountants, and licensed professional counselors.[11] Other states clearly promote mediation by providing mediation training for nonattorneys. There is no question that a paralegal can assist an attorney who provides mediation services. Duties or tasks performed can be similar to those required of a paralegal working in litigation. The paralegal may need to interview witnesses, research procedural and substantive legal issues, and draft documents. Those documents may include a motion for referral to mediation, an order to mediate, or the mediated settlement agreement. A *motion for referral to mediation* is a request to the court by a party to a legal dispute to have the matter mediated. The *order to mediate* is given by a judge directing parties to a disputed matter to mediate the case. The **mediated settlement agreement** is the end product of parties mediating their dispute.

Using Mediation to Deal with Family Law Issues

For many married couples, the joy of their wedding day is not matched by the days that follow. The fact that spouses do not stay together until *death do us part* means that a significant portion of your legal career may be spent assisting with the daunting task of untangling lives that were intentionally entangled in happier times. Unfortunately, the high costs of litigation can translate into a couple's divorce costing more than their wedding.

What can be done about lowering the financial drain of divorce? More importantly, what can be done to lessen the emotional and psychological trauma to the millions of spouses and children who go through the divorce process every year in the United States? The answer may be mediation. Mediation can be very effective in the divorce scenario because it empowers the participants and can sensitively deal with emotional issues.

The process of divorce mediation brings the husband and wife together to mutually decide on how the marriage shall end. The choices are discussed with the assistance of the impartial mediator. The mediator does not make the decision for the parties; thus, the parties are responsible for coming to a mutually satisfactory decision.

Mediation differs from the standard scenario of each spouse hiring an attorney to protect their individual interests and negotiating a settlement on their behalf. For example, suppose Brad wants to divorce Jennifer and keep custody of their two kids, Joey and Monica. First, Brad hires an attorney to represent him. This adversarial approach would often begin with Brad's attorney writing a long list of demands on behalf of his client because he knows that if he starts out asking for everything earned during the marriage, as well as custody, child support, and spousal maintenance, he will beat the other side to the punch. This will inevitably send Jennifer in a mad dash to an attorney, who will also ask for custody and probably twice as much for the financial settlement. Both attorneys will then roll up their sleeves and set to work negotiating who gets *what stuff* that in all likelihood is not worth as much as their combined legal fees.

This type of approach often complicates matters. Brad and Jennifer may soon speak to each other only through their attorneys, and tempers may escalate. After all, you would probably get mad if it seemed you were being asked to give up a large portion of what you had earned, plus possibly face the loss of custody of your children. This "war of the spouses" scenario will certainly have no winner, and the emotional toll can be heavy. Unfortunately, for the divorcing couple, the legal expenses can deplete their savings or even force the sale of the family home.

A more satisfying alternative for some couples is to sit down with a mediator and discuss how their children can best be served and their property divided. This process is mostly for couples who have some open channels of communication and are willing to go forward for the benefit of all concerned.

When Not to Mediate

On the other hand, the adversarial approach may be the only way out of a marriage when the two parties cannot stand being in the same room with one another, when one spouse is intent on taking advantage of the other, or when domestic violence is present. Mediation is almost impossible when *only one spouse* has information about the family's finances. A spouse who is dealing with mental illness or is taking medication that affects mental acuity may not have the mental capacity to participate in mediation sessions. The bottom line is: An individual should not mediate unless the person believes himself to be *informed, capable, supported,* and *safe.*[12]

Suggested Mediation Guidelines

The American Bar Association (ABA) approved the *Model Standards of Practice for Family and Divorce* (Model Standards) in 2001. This meant that the legal profession was recognizing that the mediation process has again become an accepted and successful methodology for resolving disputes. According to the Model Standards, a mediator should possess four qualifications: (1) knowledge of family law; (2) knowledge of and training in the impact of family conflict on parents, children, and interested third parties, including knowledge of child development and domestic abuse; (3) education and training specific to the process of mediation; and (4) the ability to recognize the impact of culture and diversity. The ABA's Model Standards are just one set of mediation guidelines. Already in place were numerous state and local regulations governing family mediators and court-connected family mediation programs. Read the ABA's Model Standards in their entirety in Exhibit 13.1.

What Family Mediation Can and Cannot Do

The ABA's Model Standards help to clarify that mediation is a dispute resolution process, and not mental health therapy, family counseling, or legal representation. Even if the mediator is a mental health professional, the goal of the mediator should be facilitation of the couple's self-resolution of the dispute, and not mental health therapy. Mediation serves society by promoting self-determination. Self-determination often reduces emotional trauma and financial costs because it limits intrusion into the family. Thus, mediation makes for more satisfied families. This conclusion is supported by studies that report that parents mediating disputes reach resolution more quickly than litigating parents.[13] Additionally, mediated agreements tend to be more specific and detailed than those negotiated by attorneys alone. Studies also report that mediated agreements result in higher rates of children's contact with both parents following divorce and higher rates of compliance with parenting plans and child support agreements compared to agreements reached by adversarial-type negotiations.

Susan's Progress Continues: J. D. Teaches the ABCs of Family Mediation

Recall that J. D. and Alyssa have been generally pleased with Susan's work. She has prepared motions, pleadings, and memorandums of law. The *Yanov* appellate brief appeared daunting at first, but Susan was proud of what she and Pat produced. However, the true reward was meeting Mr. Yanov and his young son when they came in to visit and share in the success of his appeal. Another heartfelt moment was sharing in the Mahoney's joy at finally having a child to call their own.

As wonderful as those moments may have been, Susan was still getting used to the constant telephone calls, questions from clients, and frequent interruptions. Perhaps her most effective moment was in reaching out to her friend Maggie and being able to direct her to J. D. for some long-overdue help with her violent situation at home. While assisting J. D. with Maggie's legal problems, Susan realized that the petty annoyances at Johnson & Webster (lost work while she learned a new computer system, the necessity of multitasking, and acclimating to life in a former broom closet, albeit temporarily) seemed insignificant when weighed against the positive help she had given. She had especially enjoyed *playing detective* and tracking down Clay Cleaver. The child support money provided to Clara and her kids made an enormous change in their lives. Susan also had fended off ethical dilemmas. When both of Susan's friends, Michelle and Tara, wanted legal advice, she was able to redirect their inquiries to attorneys at her firm.

EXHIBIT 13.1 The American Bar Association's Model Standards of Practice for Family and Divorce Mediation

ABA General Standards of Practice for Family and Divorce Mediation

Standard I: A family mediator shall recognize that mediation is based on the principle of self-determination by the participants.

Standard II: A family mediator shall be qualified by education and training to undertake the mediation.

Standard III: A family mediator shall facilitate the participants' understanding of what mediation is and assess their capacity to mediate before the participants reach an agreement to mediate.

Standard IV: A family mediator shall conduct the mediation process in an impartial manner. A family mediator shall disclose all actual and potential grounds of bias and conflicts of interest reasonably known to the mediator. The participants shall be free to retain the mediator by an informed, written waiver of the conflict of interest. However, if a bias or conflict of interest clearly impairs a mediator's impartiality, the mediator shall withdraw regardless of the express agreement of the participants.

Standard V: A family mediator shall fully disclose and explain the basis of any compensation, fees and charges to the participants.

Standard VI: A family mediator shall structure the mediation process so that the participants make decisions based on sufficient information and knowledge.

Standard VII: A family mediator shall maintain the confidentiality of all information acquired in the mediation process, unless the mediator is permitted or required to reveal the information by law or agreement of the participants.

Standard VIII: A family mediator shall assist participants in determining how to promote the best interests of children.

Standard IX: A family mediator shall recognize a family situation involving child abuse or neglect and take appropriate steps to shape the mediation process accordingly.

Standard X: A family mediator shall recognize a family situation involving domestic abuse and take appropriate steps to shape the mediation process accordingly.

Standard XI: A family mediator shall suspend or terminate the mediation process when the mediator reasonably believes that a participant is unable to effectively participate or for some other compelling reason.

Standard XII: A family mediator shall be truthful in the advertisement and solicitation for mediation.

Standard XIII: A family mediator shall acquire and maintain professional competence in mediation.

From "Model Standards of Practice for Family and Divorce Mediation," *Family Law Quarterly* 35, no. 1 (Spring 2001). Reprinted by permission.

The partners at Johnson & Webster have decided to allow J. D., a mediation proponent, to handle more mediation cases. Alyssa and Susan will still be working with J. D., but Alyssa will now concentrate a bit more on the litigation cases, and Susan will continue to assist both attorneys. It has been decided that Susan's next training will focus on J. D.'s newest mediation case. With the Baxter's child custody dispute, Susan saw firsthand how much J. D. believed in settlement by the parties. He did everything he could think of to have the Baxters settle on their own terms, rather than leaving the decision to a judge. J. D.'s newest case will hopefully go more smoothly, since the new clients have sought out J. D. to mediate their divorce. J. D. has decided to give Susan a mediation lesson over a pizza.

Susan's First Mediation Lesson

Downing his third slice of pizza, J. D. announced, "I'm glad we could grab some time to give you a review of how we're going to run the mediation side of our work."

"Me, too," Susan stated. "Pardon me, but what exactly *does* a mediator do?"

"My job is to be a neutral third party and let the couple come to their own conclusions," J. D. explained.

Susan chewed and looked perplexed at the same time. Between bites, she asked, "But won't they spend most of the session yelling or fighting because they're so personally involved in their own problems?"

"I hope not!" J. D. laughed. He explained, "Well, I'm supposed to establish an environment for the negotiations to be productive. I establish rules."

"Like, they'll each be polite to each other during a session?" Susan asked.

"Exactly," J. D. affirmed, and then added, "Although, I'm there to smooth out the rough spots, too. The presence of a mediator often acts as a buffer to arguments between the spouses."

"What if one spouse is a talker and the other is shy?" Susan wondered.

"That's where I'm really needed," J. D. enthusiastically answered. "I have to make sure the more reticent spouse doesn't feel pushed into speaking, but is still given a chance to speak his or her mind. A couple should expect the mediation process to produce a less adversarial feeling between them. It allows each spouse to voice his or her concerns while the mediator promotes an atmosphere of reasonableness."

"I know a lot of couples who may not have divorced if you'd been around to provide some of your therapy when they argued!" she exclaimed.

J. D. quickly responded, "The role of a mediator is *not* that of a marriage counselor. A marriage counselor is usually trying to help spouses learn how to keep the marriage working. The mediator's purpose is to assist the couple who has thoughtfully made the decision to *stop working* on the marriage and get a divorce." He paused and added, "However, while mediation isn't therapy *per se,* it does give the parties an opportunity to separate emotional from substantive issues. This is where the feeling of empowerment comes in for the parties. I'll provide a summary of the laws pertaining to divorce in our state and a summary of the applicable portions of the Internal Revenue Code. Plus, I'll talk about how divorce, in my experience, can affect the children and the spouses."

"Mediation really sounds like a good idea for many couples," Susan stated.

"Absolutely," J. D. agreed. "Plus, if it doesn't work, the couple can still proceed toward the litigation route."

Looking at her watch, Susan said, "Lunch flew by. We have clients coming into the office in 10 minutes!"

"It did go fast—and lunch is on the firm today, Susan. When I get on the subject of mediation, I do get on a roll!" J. D. said, laughing. Getting a receipt, J. D. grabbed a pocketful of mints from the bowl on the counter and hurried out of the restaurant with Susan.

One Family Struggles to Mediate a Settlement

This is the story of Doris and Peter Williams who, after 15 years of marriage, want to divorce. Peter is a quiet man who hates to argue. Doris admits she is argumentative and aggressive at times and wants to see this thing over with so she can "get on with her life." The Williams have two children, Peter, Jr., who is 13 years old, and Janet, who is 10 years old. Doris learned about mediation through a soon-to-be divorced friend. This friend told Doris that her mediator, J. D. Dombroski, pointed the couple in the right direction and allowed the *couple* to take charge of the decisions. Doris loves being in charge, thinks mediation should save money, and is ready to go.

Doris and her husband have agreed to schedule an appointment with J. D. to begin the mediation process. Doris is being her usual gung-ho self and has already thought out her position on most issues without having discussed anything with Peter. Peter is being typically reticent. So far nothing much is new with how the couple deals with important issues. However, Peter has taken a shine to, how he puts it, "this mediation thing." He hopes mediation will prove to be the least disruptive way to deal with Doris and the "divorce thing." Meanwhile, Susan has sent an introductory letter to Peter and Doris to get things started off on the right foot. Read the introductory letter J. D. asked Susan to send in Exhibit 13.2, and then read the Mediation Questionnaire in Exhibit 13.3 that he told Susan to enclose with the letter.

Filling Out the Questionnaire

Depending on the mediator, or just how ready the couple is to proceed, the mediation questionnaire can be filled out in the office with the mediator during the first visit, at home after the first visit, or it can be sent to the parties prior to the first visit. This last alternative really saves time and money. It also allows a couple who wants to jump right into negotiating during the first visit to do so.

Peter commented that the questionnaire appeared long and involved, he was correct. The preparation for a mediated settlement agreement is no less intense than the preparation for any divorce that includes issues involving marital property and children. The requested information is essential to a successful negotiation. It needs to be clearly conveyed to the couple that if one spouse tries to hide any property from the other, any settlement will be tainted. If such fraudulent behavior is discovered, a court of law can, and likely

---

EXHIBIT 13.2 Mediator's Introductory Letter

November 25, 2003

Dear Mr. and Mrs. Williams:

This is a follow-up letter to my telephone conversation with Doris this morning and confirms your first appointment on November 19, 2003, at 3:00 p.m. in my office.

I am glad you have made the decision to reach out for assistance during what must be a very difficult time in your personal lives. Your choice of mediation will hopefully make the divorce process less stressful for both of you.

As you know, mediation is the vehicle through which two spouses sit down and negotiate their own settlement agreement. My role as mediator is really to be a facilitator. My efforts will concentrate on making the negotiation process run more smoothly. Finally, I will collate your decisions and produce a mediated settlement agreement. A mediated settlement agreement is the written documentation of all of your mutual decisions regarding all issues pertinent to your divorce.

To protect your legal rights, each of you is encouraged to seek advice from counsel. There is no limitation on the right to seek such advice at any time before, during, or after the mediation process.

I have enclosed a questionnaire that you should review prior to our first appointment. It is very important that all information provided by you and listed on the questionnaire be correct, as it will be a primary information resource during the settlement negotiations.

Should the spouses begin discussing the custody and property issues prior to visiting the mediator? Yes. It is only by discussing such issues that a couple will know if they are good candidates for mediation. If neither spouse can discuss a topic openly and reasonably with the other, then mediation may not be the right decision for the couple. I have also enclosed a document checklist that I ask you to read. If you have any of the documents on the list, please make copies (no originals, please) and bring them to the first appointment as well.

If you have any further questions prior to our first appointment, please do not hesitate to call.

Very truly yours,

J. D. Dombroski, Esq.

Encls.

EXHIBIT 13.3 Mediation Questionnaire

Part I Mediation Questionnaire

1. Current name and any former names of wife:
2. What name does wife want to use following divorce:
3. What is the wife's Social Security number:
4. Wife's current address:
5. Wife's address during the last two years:
6. Wife's telephone number:
7. Was wife previously married:
8. If yes, how was previous marriage(s) terminated:
9. Husband's full name:
10. What is the husband's Social Security number:
11. Husband's address:
12. Husband's address during the last two years:
13. Husband's telephone number:
14. Was husband previously married:
15. If yes, how was previous marriage(s) terminated:
16. Date spouses were married:
17. Where spouses were married:
18. The last address where both spouses resided together:
19. Have spouses separated:
20. If yes, what is the date of separation:
21. List names and ages of children born or adopted during this marriage:

Part II Personal Property

1. Make and model of car:
2. Whose name is on title:
3. Value:
4. Loan amount:
5. Monthly loan payment:
6. Make and model of car:
7. Whose name is on title:
8. Value:
9. Loan amount:
10. Monthly loan payment:
11. Other vehicles, if any:
12. Appliances:
13. Sports equipment:
14. Jewelry:
15. Electronic equipment:
16. Tools:
17. Furniture:
18. Any monthly payments on personal property:
19. Checking accounts:
20. Savings accounts:
21. Safe deposit boxes:
22. Certificates of deposit:

23. Money market accounts:
24. Bonds:
25. Stocks:
26. Business assets:
27. Describe type of business:
28. Location of business:
29. Who owns business:
30. Value of business:
31. Business loan:
32. Monthly loan payment:
33. Retirement/investment plans:
34. Pension plan:
35. Whose fund:
36. Company:
37. Value:
38. Stock option plan:
39. Whose fund:
40. Company:
41. Value:
42. Profit-sharing plan:
43. Whose fund:
44. Company:
45. Value:
46. IRA accounts:
47. Named owner:
48. Bank:
49. Value:
50. Insurance—auto/medical/dental/life/homeowner's/disability:
51. Auto insurance:
52. Identify car:
53. Company policy number:
54. Premium amount:
55. Dental insurance:
56. On whom:
57. Company:
58. Policy number:
59. Premium amount:
60. Medical insurance:
61. On whom:
62. Company:
63. Policy number:
64. Premium amount:
65. Life insurance:
66. On whom:
67. Company:
68. Policy number:
69. Premium amount:
70. Homeowner's insurance:

(continued)

EXHIBIT 13.3 *continued*

71. Property address:
72. On whom:
73. Company:
74. Policy number:
75. Premium amount:
76. Debts:
77. Credit cards:
78. In whose name:
79. Name of company:
80. Balance due:
81. Monthly payments:
82. In whose name:
83. Name of company:
84. Balance due:
85. Monthly payments:
86. Other debts:
87. In whose name:
88. Name of company:
89. Reason for debt:
90. Balance of debt:
91. Monthly payment:

92. Separately owned property:
93. Value:
94. List all the property that was owned by either spouse prior to the marriage:
95. Owner:
96. Description of property:
97. Value:
98. List all the property that was either inherited or given to either spouse:
99. Owner:
100. Description of property:
101. Value:

Part III Please make a copy of the following documents:

1. Appraisals of any property
2. Safe deposit box inventory list
3. Auto insurance policy
4. Health insurance policies
5. Life insurance policies
6. Homeowner's insurance policy
7. Income tax records for the last 3 years

will, *declare any mediated settlement agreement invalid.* A safety clause for the mediator preparing a mediated settlement agreement could include a statement to the effect that *all property owned by either party has been included and distributed in the settlement agreement signed by the parties.*

The First Mediation Appointment

Sitting in the Johnson & Webster waiting room, both Peter and Doris had begun to realize that they had voluntarily made an appointment with a stranger in order to "air their dirty laundry." This realization made them both nervous and edgy. J. D. greeted the tense couple and invited them into his office. Comfortably furnished, the office had three chairs away from J. D.'s desk to promote conversation. J. D. launched into the short introduction he gave to every mediating couple.

Introduction to Mediation

J.D. began, "I like to begin with a short overview of how I see my role in your mediation process. During our meeting today, we can make a definitive decision regarding your suitability for mediation. Sometimes a couple thinks mediation is for them, but it may not be."

Doris knowingly responded, "We've already reviewed the plusses and negatives of mediation."

Peter cleared his throat and nodded, "Yeah, we're sure it's for us."

J. D. smiled and responded, "I'm glad to hear that. I'd also like to use today to begin collecting all necessary information and determining the issues for each of you. I'm going to assist you in preparing budgets and in obtaining evaluations of property, businesses, and retirement plans and insurance. I understand you have children?"

Doris answered, "Yes, Peter, Jr., who is 13, and Janet who is 10."

J. D. said his biggest concern in any divorce case was for the children involved. He explained, "Because you have children, we'll be discussing custody, visitation, and child support along with all the other issues. Any agreement you come to will still have to be approved by the court, especially any agreement on issues regarding the children."

Peter had something on his mind. He hesitantly interjected, "Your questionnaire asked for quite a few documents. It sure seems like a lot."

Nodding his head in sympathetic agreement, J. D. explained, "I'd have to agree with you about that. A couple planning to mediate their settlement should expect to produce numerous supporting documents and information. The documents and information listed in the mediation questionnaire may seem a bit lengthy, but this same information would be necessary if you had gone to attorneys first instead of to a mediator. Only then everything would need to be copied twice!" he finished with a smile.

Doris straightforwardly asked, "What is the typical cost of mediating a divorce?"

J. D. wanted to be clear. He stated, "My fee is $150 dollars per hour. My paralegal, Susan, may be able to work on some of your case as well. Her fee is $75 per hour. A mediator's fee depends on how many hours the spouses take to agree to a fair settlement. Additional factors include the area of the country in which the mediator is practicing, child custody issues, and the amount of property to be divided. In most cases, one mediator's fee will be less than the cost of hiring two attorneys to handle the individual interests of the spouses during the negotiating phase."

Doris was convinced. She stated, "I know I want to go ahead with mediation."

Hoping it would all be over as quickly as possible, Peter added, "I've made my decision to go forward, too."

J. D. stated in response, "In that case, I'd like to ask you to read and sign a mediation retainer agreement. We can move forward today if this agreement is fine with you." (Review this agreement in Exhibit 13.4.)

Back to Session One

Once the retainer was signed, J. D. began the session in earnest. Doris, true to form, again took the initiative. She had filled the form herself even though J. D.'s introductory letter clearly asked that the couple answer the questionnaire together with equality in mind. J. D. sensed this was going to be a bumpy ride.

J. D. gently inquired, "Doris, I was wondering if you and Peter filled out the questionnaire together. Peter, I only ask because it makes the entire mediation experience run more smoothly. Your mutual cooperation is what mediation is all about."

Doris defensively answered, "The form was on the dining room table for over a week, and Peter never even picked it up once to fill it out!"

Trying not to appear judgmental, J. D. asked, "Peter, is there any particular reason you didn't want to fill out the form?"

After a moment, he responded, "I guess I'm ticked off that I can't afford to move out and pay the house bills at the same time."

J. D. could see that Peter felt silly explaining his irrational behavior. Peter could see there was no connection between not filling out the form and his financial difficulties, but J. D. knew that unless the questionnaire was filled out by both parties, there wouldn't be much movement on financial decisions during the first session. J. D. decided to switch the subject.

Nodded understandingly, J. D. said, "Perhaps, it's best if we move to the custody issue. Have you discussed the type of custody arrangement you would prefer for your children? Peter, could you begin?"

Peter was much more comfortable with the custody issue. "Sure. I think Doris is a good mother and the children should stay with her during the week, but I want to see my kids on the weekends and during holidays," Peter declared.

Doris smiled. "Thank you, Peter, I think you're a good father, too." She added, "I do think the children should stay with me in the family home."

EXHIBIT 13.4 Mediation Retainer Agreement

A.   Peter Williams and Doris Williams (the parties) have jointly requested J. D. Dombroski, Esq. (the mediator), to act as their mediator. This shall serve as the agreement between the two of you and between each of you and me with respect to mediation of your divorce negotiations.

B.   The controversy between the parties concerns the terms of a separation agreement. The parties agree to negotiate in good faith toward such settlement and to provide the mediator with full and accurate information about the case. I agree to serve as mediator to facilitate direct negotiation between you in an attempt to help you agree on all outstanding issues of your divorce including, but not limited to, parenting, visitation, child support, spousal support, and equitable distribution of the marital assets.

C.   The mediator has accepted the parties' request and will provide mediation services to them on an impartial basis. I will serve at all times as an impartial facilitator of your negotiations. The time and place of mediation will be set at the convenience of the parties. Good faith negotiation requires full disclosure of all information relevant to the issues to be negotiated. You each agree to produce any and all pertinent documents that I request or that either of you request of each other. If there is a dispute between you with respect to whether a particular item or document is relevant, I will decide. If documents and information requested by me is not forthcoming, I reserve the right to terminate the mediation.

D.   The mediator has advised the parties that conflicts are likely to arise between them during the course of negotiations. In order to protect their legal rights, each party is encouraged to seek advice from counsel. There is no limitation on the right to seek such advice at any time during the mediation. Each party should advise the mediator of the name and telephone number of counsel. If I feel at any time that either of you needs separate legal counsel, you agree to obtain such advice.

E.   The mediator has also advised the parties that they may terminate the mediation at any point, paying the mediator only what has accrued to that time. The mediator in turn reserves the right to resign from the case at any time.

F.   The mediator acknowledges that all information received by the mediator during this procedure will be confidential. The mediator will not divulge such information to any third person without the written consent of both parties so that there can be full and candid exchanges.

G.   The parties agree not to hold the mediator liable or to include the mediator in any judicial proceedings involving the mediation or the parties' relationship. The mediator agrees not to represent or give support to either party in any subsequent matter or proceeding. The mediator will not provide any legal opinion as to the law or any other aspect of the case. Under no conditions will I represent either or both of you at any time during the divorce.

H.   To preserve the integrity of the mediation process it is agreed that neither I nor any of my records shall be subject to subpoena by either of you or anyone acting on your behalf should you choose to litigate this matter subsequent to mediation. Each of you makes this covenant with the other as a condition of your agreement with each other to attempt mediation. Each of you also makes this covenant with me to induce me to agree to serve as your mediator.

I.   It is agreed that if the services of other professionals are required to appraise or otherwise evaluate your assets and income that you will retain neutral experts for each task and that you will promptly pay their respective fees. This may include an accountant, appraiser, pension expert, tax expert, or, in child custody matters, a mental health professional. If requested, I will recommend professionals whose opinions I respect.

J.   It is up to the parties themselves to negotiate their own agreement. If the parties are able to reach an agreement, the mediator will prepare a mediated settlement agreement recording your understanding, which may then be submitted to the parties' personal attorneys for incorporation into a formal separation agreement.

K.   Each party agrees, during the course of the mediation, to respect the privacy of the other and not to transfer disputed property or assume additional debts without mutual consent. All interim agreements will be discussed with the mediator before being entered into.

L.   The mediator's fees are $150 per hour, plus any costs incurred. Each party will be billed monthly for the entire outstanding amount for which they will be jointly liable. My fee for services rendered by me shall include all times I spend with you, as well as all time I spend reviewing documents, preparing a memorandum of understanding, on telephone conferences and on correspondence. Unless we have agreed otherwise before we begin, you will pay me at the end of each mediation session for that session and any time spent by me since the previous session. Any work done by a paralegal will be billed at $75 per hour.

M.   It is agreed that if you cancel an appointment less than 24 hours in advance, you will be charged a cancellation fee of $50.

_____ Mediator   _____ Date

_____ Party   _____ Date

_____ Party   _____ Date

Peter's facial muscles visibly tightened. He angrily responded, "See, there she goes again. We can't afford to keep the house and get me a decent apartment."

In a matter of moments, the couple's compliments had turned into a discussion of who should retain possession of what is probably the marriage's biggest asset, the house. J. D. decided to steer the conversation toward something positive. He asked the couple to acknowledge that deciding the custody question was a big step forward and that until the budget had been worked through, the living arrangements must be left up in the air.

J. D. calmly asked, "Doris, have you any ideas on how you and the children can stay in the family home and Peter can afford an apartment that has room for the children?"

Doris had a surprise for Peter. She had been trying to figure out how they could afford an apartment for Peter. She quickly answered, "I've been thinking that I'd like to work full-time, but the only jobs I'm qualified for right now pay poorly. I'd like to finish my nursing training and then work full-time. I've also thought that maybe my mom could move in with us and help share the expenses, but I haven't asked her yet."

Peter's face showed that he was hearing this information for the first time. Grinning, he said, "I'm totally surprised, but it's a great idea. That may work."

J. D. decided that the Williams needed to fill out a questionnaire and a form breaking down monthly expenses before the mediation could go much further. He told the couple that Doris's idea may seem like a good one, but Doris's mother would have to agree first, and then the financial numbers would tell them if it could be pulled off. As the first session ended, the couple promised to come back in a week with the information J. D. had requested.

Session Two: Concentrating on the Financial Ramifications of Divorce

The Williams returned for the next session weighted down with folders filled with papers.

As she plopped into one of J. D.'s chairs, Doris exclaimed, "I never knew we could make our lives so complicated!"

Peter sat down and added, "Insurance, mortgage, bills—and the list goes on and on!"

J. D. took a deep breath and joined them in the conversation area. He firmly stated, "Well, let's just dive into the paperwork."

Typically, what would follow would be each party giving and taking over each issue. The process can be arduous, or it may be as simple as writing down the choices. Doris and Peter are amazed at where their money goes and quickly realize that even if Doris's mother moves in, some luxury items will have to go so Peter can afford an apartment as close as possible to the children. J. D. has calculated the child support that Peter would be asked to pay based upon the state's child support guidelines. Several hours and numerous decisions later, they called it a day and planned to meet again in a week.

Session Three: Moving Steadily Toward Agreement

Session Three depended heavily on the filled-out questionnaire, which proved to be invaluable. Neither Peter nor Doris could believe how much had to be decided upon. J. D. shared the tax ramifications of each financial decision. Steadily, the threesome moved through the accumulation of 15 years of marriage. The hours invested in Sessions Two and Three resulted in firm financial decisions. The couple's next step would be to concentrate on the children. They decided to schedule the next session to discuss the children exclusively.

Session Four: Concentrating on the Children

J. D. has been keeping a running log of who gets what and has written down all the decisions made by the Williams concerning their property. Susan has been putting the information onto a disk to prepare for the creation of the mediated settlement agreement. The next step is to clear up the details concerning the Williams' children.

A few minutes into Session Four, Peter dropped a bombshell, saying, "I want the children to spend their birthdays and Christmas with me, since they will spend most of the year with their mother."

Doris loudly responded, "I'm so totally *not* happy with that. I'll get their daily grind of laundry and cooking, and you'll get the fun times of being a parent!"

Peter felt strongly and firmly explained, "I'm not going to see a lot of their growing up like you. I don't want to just be a visitor in their lives."

Calmly, J. D. asked, "Let's put the holidays aside for a minute. Do you think that you would be able to both be together with your kids on their birthdays?"

Doris nodded, "That might work."

Again, Peter was firm as he replied, "I'd *make* it work because I think the kids would like it."

Relieved, J. D. responded, "Okay, very good. What are your feelings on the children's relationships with third parties? You know, new romantic partners, grandparents, cousins, and friends. Any problems?"

Doris began, "I don't have a problem with any of Pete's friends or family. However, I certainly wouldn't want the kids to know any new girlfriends Pete may have. It would be too confusing for them."

Peter lifted his eyebrows and asked, "Would it be okay if they knew I was remarried?"

Doris pursed her lips and told Peter, "You don't have to be sarcastic. You know what I mean."

Peter was starting to get angry. "Hey, this divorce wasn't really *my* idea to begin with. I'm not going to stop having a life because you say so. I don't like the idea of anyone staying overnight with *either* of us if the kids are home—unless, of course, it's a new spouse."

Doris was surprised at Peter's emotion and decided not to argue. She simply replied, "Okay, I could live with that."

"Let's get back to the holiday question," J. D. suggested. "Peter, you don't really want the children to have every holiday without their mother, do you?"

Peter looked somewhat impatient at J.D's question. "Okay, okay," he grudgingly nodded. "I get your point. I'll be agreeable to switching the holidays."

"You mean, like I get them one year for Christmas and you get them the next?" Doris asked.

"Yeah, okay," Peter nodded.

"Great," J. D. commented. "I'll make sure to include that in the draft."

J. D. concluded the session by scheduling another meeting for the next week to have Doris and Peter review the draft of the mediated settlement.

Including the Children

Some parents include their children in the mediation sessions that concern custody and visitation rights. This can work well if the children are old enough to have the patience to sit through a session. This inclusion makes some children feel that their parents are thinking of the children's wishes. A caveat should be given: Children should not be *forced* to attend a mediation session or be a witness to arguing between the parents. The session with the children may be best thought of as an informative session for the children, and not a session for heavy mediation. Also, a mediation session is not a good place for children who need the constant attention of a parent. An alternative is for the children to come to a session after the parents have made the majority of the custody and visitation schedule decisions. The parents may assist the children in feeling included by leaving a decision or two to be made as a family.

Session Five: The Mediated Settlement Agreement Reviewed

As promised, J. D. prepared a draft of the mediated settlement agreement so Doris and Peter could review each line. The next meeting would concentrate on a review of the agreement. Many of the kinks had been worked out already because J. D. had Susan prepare an updated draft of the decisions made during each session for the couple's review before starting the next session. The time for changes or questions would be during this last session. They made one change before the final session: After Session Four, Peter and Doris decided that Peter would visit with the children every weekend at his apartment and that Peter could telephone the children each day and drive the children to school each morning.

Where to Go from Here: *Pro Se* or Attorney?

After reading the settlement agreement, Doris asked, "I'm a little confused about what we do now. Do we each retain counsel to file the necessary legal documents and to represent us in court for a final hearing?"

Hoping to save a bit of money, Peter asked, "Should Doris and I proceed on our own and represent ourselves *pro se?* It seems like it wouldn't be necessary to hire two attorneys when all the hard work, that is, the settlement agreement—is done."

Without letting J. D. answer, Doris asked, "Why don't we just hire one attorney and save half the cost?"

J. D. wanted to be clear. He thoughtfully answered, "A single attorney should not represent the interests of two parties, even if the parties are the most agreeable of divorcing couples. I want you both to understand that successfully completing mediation and producing a settlement agreement is not the end of the divorce process, but it *is* an achievement. The decision to represent oneself during this latter stage should not be made lightly. If you can research how pleadings are to be written, follow up on the details, and you won't freeze up in a new surrounding, the *pro se* representation may be for you. Admittedly, it *will* save money. However, the attorneys hired to review the settlement agreement, file the paperwork with the court, and appear before the judge on your behalf can also make sure that we've all done our jobs during our mediation sessions. These attorneys are often called **review attorneys.**"

Mediators should be careful not to give legal advice to mediation clients, especially nonattorney mediators, since practicing law without a license is a criminal act. The lawyer-mediator should also be careful, since giving legal advice may leave the lawyer-mediator open to charges of malpractice.

Following the last session, Doris and Peter decided to each seek individual legal counsel to review the mediated settlement agreement, file the pleadings, and appear at the final hearing. The real measure of how well mediation works is the satisfaction level of the clients. Here, Doris and Peter left the last session with a mediated settlement agreement that left both feeling that they had been fairly treated by the other.

ARBITRATION INSTEAD OF THE COURTHOUSE?

Mediation is not the only way to avoid the courthouse. Arbitration has been used for years as a method of resolving domestic disputes. As you read earlier, arbitration is a process in which one or more neutral third parties are selected by the participants to hear testimony, take evidence, and issue a decision or award.

For example, when child custody, support requests, or other details spelled out in a separation agreement are not adhered to, many turn to arbitration. A separation agreement can contain an arbitration clause such as that shown in Exhibit 13.5. Without such a clause, parties cannot automatically resort to arbitration to resolve their differences. Arbitration is a very powerful tool for getting to the heart of a matter without the numerous delays often faced in courthouse litigation. This is because arbitration works differently than litigation.

Broad Powers

Arbitrators have broader powers than judges and are not limited by strict rules of evidence. They can hear all relevant testimony when making an award, including some forms of hearsay evidence that would likely be excluded in a regular court.

EXHIBIT 13.5 Sample Arbitration Clause

Any claim or controversy arising among or between the parties and any claim or controversy arising out of or respecting any matter contained in this Agreement, or the breach of any understanding arising out of or in connection with this Agreement, including but not limited to the obligation to pay child support, or modify the obligation of child support, or any differences as to the interpretation of any of the provisions of this Agreement, shall be settled by arbitration in _____ (name of the town) by three arbitrators under the then prevailing rules of the American Arbitration Association. The decision of the arbitrators shall be binding on all parties.

Arbitrators have the authority to hear witnesses out of order. Their decision is usually final and cannot be appealed. This is what is known as a **binding arbitration** decision. If the arbitrated matter involves child custody or child support, the courts will retain jurisdiction. Both parties should agree to the arbitration process in writing to avoid claims of unfairness after the decisions are made by an unhappy party.

Positives Versus Negatives of Arbitration

Substantial savings can be achieved through arbitration. Attorney fees are reduced because the average hearing is shorter than the average trial. Time-consuming and expensive pretrial procedures are usually eliminated. Out-of-pocket expenses are reduced because stenographic fees, transcript costs, and other expenses are not incurred.

In arbitration hearings, final awards regarding property settlements, support payments, and other domestic relations matters are usually reached quickly. Cases are usually decided in a matter of weeks, compared with months or years in formal litigation.

The arbitration hearing is held in a private conference room rather than a courtroom. Unlike a trial, the hearing cannot be attended by the general public. Thus, some privacy is assured.

Arbitrators, like mediators, usually have special training in the areas of divorce litigation and separation agreements. Most arbitrators are lawyers.

The party who is unhappy with an arbitration decision will be stymied by the fact that arbitrators, unlike judges, need not give formal reasons for their decisions. They are not required to maintain a formal record of the proceedings. The arbitrator's decision is usually binding. This means that an appeal cannot be made if a party loses the case or disagrees with the size of the award. The only exception is in the few extraordinary circumstances where an arbitrator's misconduct, dishonesty, or bias can be proved.

There are two ways of selecting an arbitration panel or a single arbitrator. The first way is for each party to choose an arbitrator from a list each provides to the other. The third arbitrator can be chosen by the attorneys jointly. The second way is for the attorneys to agree on one arbitrator from a random list of arbitrators provided by the local American Arbitration Association office.

A strong negative is the fact that in many cases one spouse has possession of all the documents and records that the other spouse needs to prove her case. In a dispute over assets acquired during the marriage, the spouse with control of the assets often does not voluntarily supply all the information necessary to reach a fair and equitable share of the assets. In the trial process, lawyers have the legal right and ample opportunity to view the private books and records of an adversary long before going to court. This is accomplished by pretrial discovery devices designed to obtain documents for inspection, including tax returns, back records, and other private financial documents. However, pretrial discovery is not as readily available to parties arbitrating a dispute. In many instances, records are not viewed until the day of the arbitration hearing. And to make matters even less desirable, it is often up to the arbitrator's discretion whether to grant an adjournment for the purpose of reviewing such records. Thus, it would be prudent to avoid arbitration if one party is dependent upon a difficult spouse supplying valuable information.

In making the decision to choose mediation, arbitration, or the courthouse, the concerned individual would want to weigh all the factors to determine the best choice for his particular set of facts. If both spouses have been forthcoming in providing information or the couple's financial or custody issues do not need much documentation, a combination of mediation and arbitration may fit nicely. Neither mediation nor arbitration would be the appropriate avenue if the spouses are failing to provide each other with necessary information or using the divorce process as a way to hurt each other. Mediation and arbitration work best when the spouses involved are committed to treating each other fairly.

COLLABORATIVE LAW: A LEGAL HYBRID

Collaborative law is a legal hybrid because it combines the mediation-based principle of a nonlitigated settlement with strong attorney participation. The attorneys and parties who agree to a collaborative law–based approach often sign collaborative law participation agreements. Such an agreement clarifies the roles of the parties and their attorneys in the process. The sole purpose of the attorneys in a collaborative law scenario is to guide the settlement; they do not represent the parties in court. In fact, most agreements state that if the settlement process breaks down and the case ends up in court, new attorneys must be hired. The idea is that by taking away the adversarial approach and the fear that one party will lose, the middle ground of compromise can be reached.

Collaborative law has mostly been applied to divorce cases, but can be effective in all areas. It is different from mediation because the parties rely on their attorneys to conduct the settlement. One plus is that the role of the review attorney (used in mediation) can be incorporated into the role of the collaborative attorney. As with mediation, parties who do not want to participate in a collaborative process will end up in court.[14]

CHAPTER SUMMARY

Alternative dispute resolution (ADR) is a cost-cutting and time-saving option for individuals who do not want to face the daunting prospect of courtroom-centered litigation, whatever the subject matter may be. There are many varieties of ADR, but the two ADR methods used most in family law are mediation and arbitration.

Mediation is a process where parties who have a dispute are assisted by a third party, called a mediator, in an effort to settle their dispute themselves. Mediation is based on the principle of self-determination by the participants. Divorcing spouses who decide to utilize a mediator's assistance will mutually participate in all decisions, including those regarding spousal support, child support, child custody, and property distribution. The mutually agreed upon terms will be incorporated by the mediator into a document called a mediated settlement agreement. Unless a couple is committed to a nonadversarial approach to their divorce, mediation is not the best method for negotiating settlement terms. Utilizing a mediator should provide several positive benefits compared to the typical nonmediated divorce handled by two attorneys. These benefits include: (1) increased client participation and say in the outcome; (2) lower cost; and (3) possibly more efficient closure of the divorce.

Arbitration is similar to mediation, but in the case of divorce, it is more typically used after the final judgment. For example, when the settlement agreement has not been adhered to, the arbitration process may be used. Arbitrators have broader powers than judges and are not limited by strict rules of evidence. They can hear all relevant testimony when making an award, including some forms of hearsay evidence and questionable copies of documents that may be excluded in a regular court. Arbitrators have the authority to hear witnesses out of order. Their decision is usually final and cannot be appealed unless the arbitrator's misconduct, dishonesty, or bias can be proved. This is what is known as binding arbitration. Like mediation, substantial savings are achieved through arbitration. Attorney fees are reduced because the average hearing is shorter than the average trial. The arbitration hearing is held in a private conference room rather than a courtroom. Unlike a trial, the hearing cannot be attended by the general public. Thus, some privacy is assured. The negatives of arbitration over the courtroom include: (1) Arbitrators, unlike judges, do not need to give formal reasons for their decisions; (2) no formal record must be kept of the proceedings; (3) arbitrated decisions are typically binding (unless the arbitrated matter involves child custody or child support) without an appeal available; and (4) arbitrators, unlike judges, are paid by the parties.

Collaborative law is a legal hybrid because it combines the mediation-based principle of a nonlitigated settlement with strong attorney participation. The attorneys and parties who agree to a collaborative law–based approach often sign collaborative law participation agreements.

Key Terms

alternative dispute resolution (ADR)	arbitration	review attorney
mediation	arbitrator	binding arbitration
	mediated settlement agreement	collaborative law

Surfing the Web

http://www.adr.org The American Arbitration Association site offers information on mediation, arbitration, and all methods of dispute resolution.

http://www.collaborative-law.ca This site promotes the dignified collaborative law approach.

http://www.adrr.com What is mediation? For an explanation, check out this site, which is promoted by a mediator.

http://www.promediation.com For more information on mediation surf over to this Professional Mediation Association site.

ETHICS ALERT

Mitzi and Maynard have decided to "call it a day"—to stop talking about a divorce and to actually get divorced. Living more like brother and sister after 15 years of marriage, they amiably agree to find a mediator to figure out who should get what and how much. They both agree that they want to go the mediator route in order to save money and time. Both Mitzi and Maynard want to have enough cash to spend on single ads in their search for new mates after the divorce. Their plan is to hire one mediator to handle the mediation and those annoying legal papers that need to be filed with the county court. They have reached out to J. D. Dombroski, but Susan is the one who handles the telephone call for J. D. What do you think Susan's response should be to Mitzi and Maynard?

Review Questions

1. What are the alternatives to the typical adversarial approach when a couple has decided to divorce?
2. Is the adversarial approach ever warranted in divorce proceedings?
3. Describe the mediation process.
4. What factors determine the mediator's fee? How does a mediator's fee compare to the cost of hiring two attorneys to handle the individual interests of the spouses?
5. Why should divorcing spouses be completely honest when mediating a property settlement agreement?
6. Should children of divorcing parents always be included in mediation sessions involving custody and visitation issues?
7. When is arbitration an effective tool?
8. What are some of the advantages of choosing arbitration instead of taking the more typical litigation route?
9. What is a major disadvantage of choosing arbitration over the more typical litigation route?
10. What is the collaborative law process?

Endnotes

1. Abraham Lincoln, *Notes for a Law Lecture, in Life and Writings of Abraham Lincoln* 328 (Philip V.D. Stern, ed. 1940, as quoted in Schepard, Andrew, "An Introduction to the Model Standards of Practice for Family and Divorce Mediation," *Family Law Quarterly* 35, no. 1 (Spring 2001): 23).
2. Chasen, Andrea Nager, "Defining Mediation and Its Use for Paralegals," *Journal of Paralegal Education* 9 (1999): 61–75.
3. U.S. Department of Commerce, *Statistical Abstract of the United States* (1991).
4. Jandt, Fred E., *Alternative Dispute Resolution* (Cincinnati, OH: Anderson, 1997).
5. Henley, Rita, *American Bar Association Journal* (February 1997).
6. Plapinger, Elizabeth, and Stienstra, "ADR in the Federal District Courts: A Practitioner's Guide," *Dispute Resolution Magazine* (Spring 1996): 7.
7. The variety of alternative dispute resolution options that exists includes: negotiation, mediation, arbitration, minitrial, summary jury trial, moderated settlement conference, Med-Arb, private judging, early neutral evaluation, conciliation, and collaborative law.
8. *Model Standards of Practice for Family and Divorce Mediation,* Standard I (2001).
9. Patterson, Susan, and Seabolt, *Essentials of Alternative Dispute Resolution* (Dallas, TX: Pearson, 1997).
10. Chasen, *supra* note 2, at 67.
11. ADR Act of 1987, FLA. STAT. §§ 44.1011 to 44.1011 (1989), as cited at Chasen, *supra* note 2, at 71.
12. Schepard, Andrew, "An Introduction to the Model Standards of Practice for Family and Divorce Mediation," *Family Law Quarterly* 35, no. 1 (Spring 2001): 22.
13. *Id.* at 5.
14. Pollak, Rita, "Collaborative Law," *Family Advocate* 24, no. 4 (2002): 29.

Appendix A

Paralegal and Legal Assistant Associations

NATIONAL ORGANIZATIONS

National Federation of Paralegal Associations (NFPA)

http://www.paralegals.org
2517 Eastlake Avenue East, Suite 200
Seattle, WA 98102
E-mail: infor@paralegals.org

National Paralegal Association

http://nationalparalegal.org/
P.O. Box 406
Solebury, PA 18963
Phone: (215) 297-8333
Fax (215) 297-8358
E-mail: admin@nationalparalegal.org

National Association of Legal Assistants, Inc. (NALA)

http://nala.org/
1516 S. Boston, Suite 200
Tulsa, OK 74119
Phone: (918) 587-6828

STATE ORGANIZATIONS

Alabama	Gulf Coast Paralegal Association http://www.paralegals.org P.O. Box 66705 Mobile, AL 36660
Alaska	Alaska Association of Paralegals http://www.alaskaparalegals.org P.O. Box 101956 Anchorage, AK 99510-1956 Phone: (907) 646-8018 E-mail: info@alaskaparalegals.org
Arizona	Arizona Association of Professional Paralegals, Inc. P.O. Box 430 Phoenix, AZ 85001 Phone: (602) 258-0121 E-mail: Arizona@paralegals.org
California	Sacramento Valley Paralegal Association http://www.svpa.org/ P.O. Box 453 Sacramento, CA 95812-0453 Phone: (916) 763-7851 E-mail: Sacramento@paralegals.org San Diego Association of Legal Assistants http://www.sdparalegals.org P.O. Box 87449 San Diego, CA 92138-7449 Phone: (619) 491-1994 E-mail: SanDiego@paralegals.org San Francisco Paralegal Association http://www.sfpa.com P.O. Box 2110 San Francisco, CA 94126-2110 Phone: (415) 777-2390 Fax: (415) 586-6606 E-mail: SanFrancisco@paralegals.org

Los Angeles Paralegal Association
http://www.lapa.org
P.O. Box 71708
Los Angeles, CA 90071
Phone: (310) 921-3094
E-mail: info@lapa.org

Colorado

Rocky Mountain Paralegal Association
http://www.rockymtnparalegal.org
P.O. Box 481864
Denver, CO 80248-1864
Phone: (303) 370-9444
E-mail: webmaster@rockymtnparalegal.org

Connecticut

Central Connecticut Paralegal Association, Inc.
http://www.paralegals.org
P.O. Box 230594
Hartford, CT 06123-0594
E-mail: CentralConnecticut@paralegals.org

Connecticut Association of Paralegals, Inc.
http://www.paralegals.org
P.O. Box 134
Bridgeport, CT 06601-0134
E-mail: Connecticut@paralegals.org

New Haven County Association of Paralegals, Inc.
http://www.paralegals.org
P.O. Box 862
New Haven, CT 06504-0862
E-mail: NewHaven@paralegals.org

Delaware

Delaware Paralegal Association
P.O. Box 1362
Wilmington, DE 19899
Phone: (302) 426-1362

District of Columbia (Washington, D.C.)

National Capital Area Paralegal Association (NCAPA)
http://www.ncapa.com
P.O. Box 27607
Washington, DC 20038-7607

Georgia

Georgia Association of Paralegals, Inc.
http://www.gaparalegal.org
1199 Euclid Avenue N.E.
Atlanta, GA 30307-1509
Phone: (404) 522-1457

Hawaii

Hawaii Paralegal Association
http://www.hawaiiparalegal.org
P.O. Box 674
Honolulu, HI 96809

Illinois

Illinois Paralegal Association
http://www.ipaonline.org
P.O. Box 452
New Lenox, IL 60451-0452
Phone: (815) 462-4620
Fax: (815) 462-4696
E-mail: IPA@ipaonline.org

Indiana

Indiana Paralegal Association
http://indianaparalegals.org
Federal Station
P.O. Box 44518
Indianapolis, IN 46204
Phone: (317) 767-7798
E-mail: Indiana@paralegals.org

Michiana Paralegal Association
http://www.paralegals.org
P.O. Box 11458
South Bend, IN 46634
E-mail: Michiana@paralegals.org

Northeast Indiana Paralegal Association, Inc.
http://www.paralegals.org
P.O. Box 13646
Fort Wayne, IN 46865
E-mail: NortheastIndiana@paralegals.org

Kansas

Kansas Paralegal Association
http://www.accesskansas.org
P.O. Box 1675
Topeka, KS 66601

Kentucky

Greater Lexington Paralegal Association, Inc.
P.O. Box 574
Lexington, KY 40586
E-mail: Lexington@paralegals.org

Kentucky Paralegal Association
http://www.kypa.org
P.O. Box 2675
Louisville, KY 40201-2675

Louisiana

New Orleans Paralegal Association
http://paralegals.org
P.O. Box 30604
New Orleans, LA 70190
Phone: (504) 467-3136
E-mail: neworleans@paralegals.org

Maryland

Maryland Association of Paralegals, Inc.
http://paralegals.org
550 M Ritchie Highway PMB #203
Severna Park, MD 21146
Phone: (410) 576-2252
E-mail: Maryland@paralegals.org

Massachusetts

Central Massachusetts Paralegal Association
P.O. Box 444
Worcester, MA 01614
E-mail: CentralMassachusetts@paralegals.org

Massachusetts Paralegal Association
http://www.paralegals.org
P.O. Box 1381
Marblehead, MA 01945
Phone: (800) 637-4311
E-mail: Massachusetts@paralegals.org

Western Massachusetts Paralegal Association
http://www.paralegals.org
P.O. Box 30005
Springfield, MA 01103
E-mail: WesternMassachusetts@paralegals.org

Minnesota

Minnesota Paralegal Association
http://mnparalegals.org
1711 W. County Road B, #300N
Roseville, MN 55113
Phone: (651) 633-2778
Fax: (651) 635-0307
E-mail: info@mnparalegals.org

Missouri

Kansas City Paralegal Association (KCPA)
http://paralegals.org
1912 Clay Street
North Kansas City, MO 64116
Phone: (816) 421-0302
Fax: (816) 421-1991
E-mail: KansasCity@paralegals.org

Nebraska

Rocky Mountain Paralegal Association (covers states other than Colorado)
http://www.rockymtnparalegal.org
P.O. Box 481864
Denver, CO 80248-1864
Phone: (303) 370-9444
E-mail: webmaster@rockymtnparalegal.org

Nevada

Paralegal Association of Southern Nevada
P.O. Box 1752
Las Vegas, NV 89125-1752
E-mail: SouthernNevada@paralegals.org

New Hampshire

Paralegal Association of New Hampshire (PANH)
http://www.panh.org
P.O. Box 728
Manchester, NH 03105-0728

New Jersey

South Jersey Paralegal Association
http://paralegals.org
P.O. Box 355
Haddonfield, NJ 08033
E-mail: SouthJersey@paralegals.org

New York

Capital District Paralegal Association
P.O. Box 12562
Albany, NY 12212-2562
E-mail: Capital District@paralegals.org

Long Island Paralegal Association
1877 Bly Road
East Meadow, NY 11554-1158
E-mail: LongIsland@paralegals.org

Manhattan Paralegal Association, Inc.
http://www.paralegals.org
P.O. Box 4006
Grand Central Station
New York, NY 10163
Phone: (212) 330-8213
E-mail: Manhattan@paralegals.org

Paralegal Association of Rochester
http://par.itgo.com
P.O. Box 40567
Rochester, NY 14604
Phone: (716) 234-5923
E-mail: Rochester@paralegals.org

West/Rock Paralegal Association
P.O. Box 668
New City, NY 10956
E-mail: WestRock@paralegals.org

Western New York Paralegal Association, Inc.
http://www.wnyparalegals.org
P.O. Box 207
Niagara Square Station
Buffalo, NY 14201
Phone: (716) 635-8250
E-mail: WesternNewYork@paralegals.org

Ohio

Cincinnati Paralegal Association
http://www.cincinnatiparalegals.org
P.O. Box 1515
Cincinnati, OH 45201
Phone: (513) 244-1266
E-mail: Cincinnati@paralegals.org

Cleveland Association of Paralegals
http://www.capohio.org
P.O. Box 14517
Cleveland, OH 44114-0517
Phone: (216) 556-5437
E-mail: Cleveland@paralegals.org

Greater Dayton Paralegal Association
http://www.paralegals.org
P.O. Box 515
Mid-City Station
Dayton, OH 45402
E-mail: Dayton@paralegals.org

Northeastern Ohio Paralegal Association
http://www.paralegals.org
P.O. Box 80068
Akron, OH 44308-0068
E-mail: NorthEasternOhio@paralegals.org

Paralegal Association of Central Ohio
http://www.pacoparalegals.org
P.O. Box 15182
Columbus, OH 43215-0182
Phone: (614) 224-9700
E-mail: CentralOhio@paralegals.org

Oregon

Oregon Paralegal Association
http://paralegals.org
P.O. Box 8523
Portland, OR 97207
Phone: (503) 796-1671
E-mail: bab@canbylaw.com

Pennsylvania

Central Pennsylvania Paralegal Association
http://www.paralegals.org
P.O. Box 11814
Harrisburg, PA 17108
E-mail: CentralPennsylvania@paralegals.org

Chester County Paralegal Association
P.O. Box 295
West Chester, PA 19381-0295
E-mail: ChesterCounty@paralegals.org

Lycoming County Paralegal Association
P.O. Box 991
Williamsport, PA 17701
E-mail: Lycoming@paralegals.org

Montgomery County Paralegal Association
http://www.paralegals.org
P.O. Box 1765
Blue Bell, PA 19422
E-mail: Montgomery@paralegals.org

Philadelphia Association of Paralegals
http://www.philaparalegals.com
P.O. Box 59179
Philadelphia, PA 19102-9179
Phone: (215) 545-5395
E-mail: Philadelphia@paralegals.org

Pittsburgh Paralegal Association
http://66.200.75.105/pghparalegals/index.php
P.O. Box 2845
Pittsburgh, PA 15230
Phone: (412) 344-3904
E-mail: Pittsburgh@paralegals.org

Rhode Island

Rhode Island Paralegals Association
http://paralegals.org
P.O. Box 1003
Providence, RI 02901
E-mail: RhodeIsland@paralegals.org

South Carolina

Palmetto Paralegal Association
http://paralegals.org
P.O. Box 11634
Columbia, SC 29211-1634
Phone: (803) 252-0460
E-mail: Palmetto@paralegals.org

South Dakota

Rocky Mountain Paralegal Association (covers states other than Colorado)
http://www.rockymtnparalegal.org
P.O. Box 481864
Denver, CO 80248-1864
Phone: (303) 370-9444
E-mail: webmaster@rockymtnparalegal.org

Tennessee

Memphis Paralegal Association
http://www.paralegals.org
P.O. Box 3646
Memphis, TN 38173-0646
E-mail: Memphis@paralegals.org

Middle Tennessee Paralegal Association
P.O. Box 198006
Nashville, TN 37219
E-mail: MiddleTennessee@paralegals.org

Texas

Dallas Area Paralegal Association
http://www.dallasparalegals.org
P.O. Box 12533
Dallas, TX 75225-0533
Phone: (972) 991-0853

Utah

Rocky Mountain Paralegal Association (covers states other than Colorado)
http://www.rockymtnparalegal.org
P.O. Box 481864
Denver, CO 80248-1864
Phone: (303) 370-9444
E-mail: webmaster@rockymtnparalegal.org

Vermont

Vermont Paralegal Organization
http://paralegals.org
P.O. Box 5755
Burlington, VT 05402
E-mail: Vermont@paralegals.org

Virginia

Fredericksburg Paralegal Association
http://paralegals.org
P.O. Box 7351
Fredericksburg, VA 22404
E-mail: Fredericksburg@paralegals.org

Washington

Washington State Paralegal Association
http://www.wspaonline.com
P.O. Box 58530
Seattle, WA 98138
Phone (within Washington): (800) 288-WSPA (9772)

Wisconsin

Paralegal Association of Wisconsin
http://www.wisconsinparalegal.org
P.O. Box 510892
Milwaukee, WI 53203-0151
Phone: (414) 272-7168
E-mail: info@WisconsinParalegal.org

Wyoming

Rocky Mountain Paralegal Association (covers states other than Colorado)
http://www.rockymtnparalegal.org
P.O. Box 481864
Denver, CO 80248-1864
Phone: (303) 370-9444
E-mail: webmaster@rockymtnparalegal.org

Appendix B

Model Standards and Guidelines for Utilization of Legal Assistants

Copyright 1997; Adopted 1984; Revised 1991, 1997.
National Association of Legal Assistants, Inc.

Table of Contents:

INTRODUCTION

The purpose of this annotated version of the National Association of Legal Assistants, Inc. Model Standards and Guidelines for the Utilization of Legal Assistants (the "Model," "Standards" and/or the "Guidelines") is to provide references to the existing case law and other authorities where the underlying issues have been considered. The authorities cited will serve as a basis upon which conduct of a legal assistant may be analyzed as proper or improper.

The Guidelines represent a statement of how the legal assistant may function. The Guidelines are not intended to be a comprehensive or exhaustive list of the proper duties of a legal assistant. Rather, they are designed as guides to what may or may not be proper conduct for the legal assistant. In formulating the Guidelines, the reasoning and rules of law in many reported decisions of disciplinary cases and unauthorized practice of law cases have been analyzed and considered. In addition, the provisions of the American Bar Association's Model Rules of Professional Conduct, as well as the ethical promulgations of various state courts and bar associations have been considered in the development of the Guidelines.

These Guidelines form a sound basis for the legal assistant and the supervising attorney to follow. This Model will serve as a comprehensive resource document and as a definitive, well-reasoned guide to those considering voluntary standards and guidelines for legal assistants.

I

PREAMBLE

Proper utilization of the services of legal assistants contributes to the delivery of cost-effective, high-quality legal services. Legal assistants and the legal profession should be assured that measures exist for identifying legal assistants and their role in assisting attorneys in the delivery of legal services. Therefore, the National Association of Legal Assistants, Inc., hereby adopts these Standards and Guidelines as an educational document for the benefit of legal assistants and the legal profession.

COMMENT

The three most frequently raised questions concerning legal assistants are (1) How do you define a legal assistant; (2) Who is qualified to be identified as a legal assistant; and (3) What duties may a legal assistant perform? The definition adopted in 1984 by the National Association of Legal Assistants answers the first question. The Model sets forth minimum education, training and experience through standards which will assure that an individual utilizing the title "legal assistant" has the qualifications to be held out to the legal community and the public in that capacity. The Guidelines identify those acts which the reported cases hold to be proscribed and give examples of services which the legal assistant may perform under the supervision of a licensed attorney.

These Guidelines constitute a statement relating to services performed by legal assistants, as defined herein, as approved by court decisions and other sources of authority. The purpose of the Guidelines is not to place limitations or restrictions on the legal assistant profession. Rather, the Guidelines are intended to outline for the legal profession an acceptable course of conduct. Voluntary recognition and utilization of the Standards and Guidelines will benefit the entire legal profession and the public it serves.

II

DEFINITION

The National Association of Legal Assistants adopted the following definition in 1984:

> Legal assistants, also known as paralegals, are a distinguishable group of persons who assist attorneys in the delivery of legal services. Through formal education, training, and experience, legal assistants have knowledge and expertise regarding the legal system and substantive and procedural law which qualify them to do work of a legal nature under the supervision of an attorney.
>
> Comment - More on definition

COMMENT

This definition emphasizes the knowledge and expertise of legal assistants in substantive and procedural law obtained through education and work experience. It further defines the legal assistant or paralegal as a professional working under the supervision of an attorney as distinguished from a non-lawyer who delivers services directly to the public without any intervention or review of work product by an attorney. Statutes, court rules, case law and bar associations are additional sources for legal assistant or paralegal definitions. In applying the Standards and Guidelines, it is important to remember that they were developed to apply to the legal assistant as defined herein.

Lawyers should refrain from labeling those who do not meet the criteria set forth in this definition, such as secretaries and other administrative staff, as legal assistants.

For billing purposes, the services of a legal secretary are considered part of overhead costs and are not recoverable in fee awards. However, the courts have held that fees for paralegal services are recoverable as long as they are not clerical functions, such as organizing files, copying documents, checking docket, updating files, checking court dates and delivering papers. As established in *Missouri v. Jenkins*, 491 U.S.274, 109 S.Ct. 2463, 2471, n.10 (1989) tasks performed by legal assistants must be substantive in nature which, absent the legal assistant, the attorney would perform.

There are also case law and Supreme Court Rules addressing the issue of a disbarred attorney serving in the capacity of a legal assistant.

III

STANDARDS

A legal assistant should meet certain minimum qualifications. The following standards may be used to determine an individual's qualifications as a legal assistant:

> 1. Successful completion of the Certified Legal Assistant ("CLA") certifying examination of the National Association of Legal Assistants, Inc.;

> 2. Graduation from an ABA approved program of study for legal assistants;

> 3. Graduation from a course of study for legal assistants which is institutionally accredited but not ABA approved, and which requires not less than the equivalent of 60 semester hours of classroom study;

> 4. Graduation from a course of study for legal assistants, other than those set forth in (2) and (3) above, plus not less than six months of in-house training as a legal assistant;

> 5. A baccalaureate degree in any field, plus not less than six months in-house training as a legal assistant;

6. A minimum of three years of law-related experience under the supervision of an attorney, including at least six months of in-house training as a legal assistant; or

7. Two years of in-house training as a legal assistant.

For purposes of these Standards, "in-house training as a legal assistant" means attorney education of the employee concerning legal assistant duties and these Guidelines. In addition to review and analysis of assignments, the legal assistant should receive a reasonable amount of instruction directly related to the duties and obligations of the legal assistant.

COMMENT

The Standards set forth suggest minimum qualifications for a legal assistant. These minimum qualifications, as adopted, recognize legal related work backgrounds and formal education backgrounds, both of which provide the legal assistant with a broad base in exposure to and knowledge of the legal profession. This background is necessary to assure the public and the legal profession that the employee identified as a legal assistant is qualified.

The Certified Legal Assistant ("CLA") examination established by NALA in 1976 is a voluntary nationwide certification program for legal assistants. The CLA designation is a statement to the legal profession and the public that the legal assistant has met the high levels of knowledge and professionalism required by NALA's certification program. Continuing education requirements, which all certified legal assistants must meet, assure that high standards are maintained. The CLA designation has been recognized as a means of establishing the qualifications of a legal assistant in supreme court rules, state court and bar association standards and utilization guidelines.

Certification through NALA is available to all legal assistants meeting the educational and experience requirements. Certified Legal Assistants may also pursue advanced specialty certification ("CLAS") in the areas of bankruptcy, civil litigation, probate and estate planning, corporate and business law, criminal law and procedure, real estate, intellectual property, and may also pursue state certification based on state laws and procedures in California, Florida, Louisiana and Texas.

IV

GUIDELINES

These Guidelines relating to standards of performance and professional responsibility are intended to aid legal assistants and attorneys. The ultimate responsibility rests with an attorney who employs legal assistants to educate them with respect to the duties they are assigned and to supervise the manner in which such duties are accomplished.

COMMENT

In general, a legal assistant is allowed to perform any task which is properly delegated and supervised by an attorney, as long as the attorney is ultimately responsible to the client and assumes complete professional responsibility for the work product.

ABA Model Rules of Professional Conduct, Rule 5.3 provides:

With respect to a non-lawyer employed or retained by or associated with a lawyer:

(a) a partner in a law firm shall make reasonable efforts to ensure that the firm has in effect measures giving reasonable assurance that the person's conduct is compatible with the professional obligations of the lawyer;

(b) a lawyer having direct supervisory authority over the non-lawyer shall make reasonable efforts to ensure that the person's conduct is compatible with the professional obligations of the lawyer; and

(c) a lawyer shall be responsible for conduct of such a person that would be a violation of the rules of professional conduct if engaged in by a lawyer if:

(1) the lawyer orders or, with the knowledge of the specific conduct ratifies the conduct involved; or

(2) the lawyer is a partner in the law firm in which the person is employed, or has direct supervisory authority over the person, and knows of the conduct at a time when its consequences can be avoided or mitigated but fails to take remedial action.

There are many interesting and complex issues involving the use of legal assistants. In any discussion of the proper role of a legal assistant, attention must be directed to what constitutes the practice of law. Proper delegation to legal assistants is further complicated and confused by the lack of an adequate definition of the practice of law.

Kentucky became the first state to adopt a Paralegal Code by Supreme Court Rule. This Code sets forth certain exclusions to the unauthorized practice of law:

For purposes of this rule, the unauthorized practice of law shall not include any service rendered involving legal knowledge or advice, whether representation, counsel or advocacy, in or out of court, rendered in respect to the acts, duties, obligations, liabilities or business relations of the one requiring services where:

A. The client understands that the paralegal is not a lawyer;

B. The lawyer supervises the paralegal in the performance of his or her duties; and

C. The lawyer remains fully responsible for such representation including all actions taken or not taken in connection therewith by the paralegal to the same extent as if such representation had been furnished entirely by the lawyer and all such actions had been taken or not taken directly by the attorney. Paralegal Code, Ky.S.Ct.R3.700, Sub-Rule 2.

South Dakota Supreme Court Rule 97-25 Utilization Rule a(4) states:

The attorney remains responsible for the services performed by the legal assistant to the same extent as though such services had been furnished entirely by the attorney and such actions were those of the attorney.

Guideline 1

Legal assistants should:

1. Disclose their status as legal assistants at the outset of any professional relationship with a client, other attorneys, a court or administrative agency or personnel thereof, or members of the general public;

2. Preserve the confidences and secrets of all clients; and

3. Understand the attorney's Rules of Professional Responsibility and these Guidelines in order to avoid any action which would involve the attorney in a violation of the Rules, or give the appearance of professional impropriety.

COMMENT

Routine early disclosure of the legal assistant's status when dealing with persons outside the attorney's office is necessary to assure that there will be no misunderstanding as to the responsibilities and role of the legal assistant. Disclosure may be made in any way that avoids confusion. If the person dealing with the legal assistant already knows of his/her status, further disclosure is unnecessary. If at any time in written or oral communication the legal assistant becomes aware that the other person may believe the legal assistant is an attorney, immediate disclosure should be made as to the legal assistant's status.

The attorney should exercise care that the legal assistant preserves and refrains from using any confidence or secrets of a client, and should instruct the legal assistant not to disclose or use any such confidences or secrets.

The legal assistant must take any and all steps necessary to prevent conflicts of interest and fully disclose such conflicts to the supervising attorney. Failure to do so may jeopardize both the attorney's representation of the client and the case itself.

Guidelines for the Utilization of Legal Assistant Services adopted December 3, 1994 by the Washington State Bar Association Board of Governors states:

> "Guideline 7: A lawyer shall take reasonable measures to prevent conflicts of interest resulting from a legal assistant's other employment or interest insofar as such other employment or interests would present a conflict of interest if it were that of the lawyer."

In Re Complex Asbestos Litigation, 232 Cal. App. 3d 572 (Cal. 1991), addresses the issue wherein a law firm was disqualified due to possession of attorney-client confidences by a legal assistant employee resulting from previous employment by opposing counsel.

The ultimate responsibility for compliance with approved standards of professional conduct rests with the supervising attorney. The burden rests upon the attorney who employs a legal assistant to educate the latter with respect to the duties which may be assigned and then to supervise the manner in which the legal assistant carries out such duties. However, this does not relieve the legal assistant from an independent obligation to refrain from illegal conduct. Additionally, and notwithstanding that the Rules are not binding upon non-lawyers, the very nature of a legal assistant's employment imposes an obligation not to engage in conduct which would involve the supervising attorney in a violation of the Rules.

The attorney must make sufficient background investigation of the prior activities and character and integrity of his or her legal assistants.

Further, the attorney must take all measures necessary to avoid and fully disclose conflicts of interest due to other employment or interests. Failure to do so may jeopardize both the attorney's representation of the client and the case itself.

Legal assistant associations strive to maintain the high level of integrity and competence expected of the legal profession and, further, strive to uphold the high standards of ethics.

NALA's Code of Ethics and Professional Responsibility states "A legal assistant's conduct is guided by bar associations' codes of professional responsibility and rules of professional conduct."

Guideline 2

Legal assistants should not:

> 1. Establish attorney-client relationships; set legal fees; give legal opinions or advice; or represent a client before a court, unless authorized to do so by said court; nor

> 2. Engage in, encourage, or contribute to any act which could constitute the unauthorized practice law.

COMMENT:

Case law, court rules, codes of ethics and professional responsibilities, as well as bar ethics opinions now hold which acts can and cannot be performed by a legal assistant. Generally, the determination of what acts constitute the unauthorized practice of law is made by State Supreme Courts.

Numerous cases exist relating to the unauthorized practice of law. Courts have gone so far as to prohibit the legal assistant from preparation of divorce kits and assisting in preparation of bankruptcy forms and, more specifically, from providing basic information about procedures and requirements, deciding where information should be placed on forms, and responding to questions from debtors regarding the interpretation or definition of terms.

Cases have identified certain areas in which an attorney has a duty to act, but it is interesting to note that none of these cases state that it is improper for an attorney to have the initial work performed by the legal assistant. This again points out the importance of adequate supervision by the employing attorney.

An attorney can be found to have aided in the unauthorized practice of law when delegating acts which cannot be performed by a legal assistant.

Guideline 3

Legal assistants may perform services for an attorney in the representation of a client, provided:

> 1. The services performed by the legal assistant do not require the exercise of independent professional legal judgment;
>
> 2. The attorney maintains a direct relationship with the client and maintains control of all client matters;
>
> 3. The attorney supervises the legal assistant;
>
> 4. The attorney remains professionally responsible for all work on behalf of the client, including any actions taken or not taken by the legal assistant in connection therewith; and
>
> 5. The services performed supplement, merge with and become the attorney's work product.

COMMENT:

Legal assistants, whether employees or independent contractors, perform services for the attorney in the representation of a client. Attorneys should delegate work to legal assistants commensurate with their knowledge and experience and provide appropriate instruction and supervision concerning the delegated work, as well as ethical acts of their employment. Ultimate responsibility for the work product of a legal assistant rests with the attorney. However, a legal assistant must use discretion and professional judgment and must not render independent legal judgment in place of an attorney.

The work product of a legal assistant is subject to civil rules governing discovery of materials prepared in anticipation of litigation, whether the legal assistant is viewed as an extension of the attorney or as another representative of the party itself. Fed. R. Civ. P. 26 (b)(2).

Guideline 4

In the supervision of a legal assistant, consideration should be given to:

1. Designating work assignments that correspond to the legal assistant's abilities, knowledge, training and experience;

2. Educating and training the legal assistant with respect to professional responsibility, local rules and practices, and firm policies;

3. Monitoring the work and professional conduct of the legal assistant to ensure that the work is substantively correct and timely performed;

4. Providing continuing education for the legal assistant in substantive matters through courses, institutes, workshops, seminars and in-house training; and

5. Encouraging and supporting membership and active participation in professional organizations.

COMMENT:

Attorneys are responsible for the actions of their employees in both malpractice and disciplinary proceedings. In the vast majority of cases, the courts have not censured attorneys for a particular act delegated to the legal assistant, but rather, have been critical of and imposed sanctions against attorneys for failure to adequately supervise the legal assistant. The attorney's responsibility for supervision of his or her legal assistant must be more than a willingness to accept responsibility and liability for the legal assistant's work. Supervision of a legal assistant must be offered in both the procedural and substantive legal areas. The attorney must delegate work based upon the education, knowledge and abilities of the legal assistant and must monitor the work product and conduct of the legal assistant to insure that the work performed is substantively correct and competently performed in a professional manner.

Michigan State Board of Commissioners has adopted Guidelines for the Utilization of Legal Assistants (April 23, 1993). These guidelines, in part, encourage employers to support legal assistant participation in continuing education programs to ensure that the legal assistant remains competent in the fields of practice in which the legal assistant is assigned.

The working relationship between the lawyer and the legal assistant should extend to cooperative efforts on public service activities wherever possible. Participation in pro bono activities is encouraged in ABA Guideline 10.

Guideline 5

Except as otherwise provided by statute, court rule or decision, administrative rule or regulation, or the attorney's rules of professional responsibility, and within the preceding parameters and proscriptions, a legal assistant may perform any function delegated by an attorney, including, but not limited to the following:

1. Conduct client interviews and maintain general contact with the client after the establishment of the attorney-client relationship, so long as the client is aware of the status and function of the legal assistant, and the client contact is under the supervision of the attorney.

2. Locate and interview witnesses, so long as the witnesses are aware of the status and function of the legal assistant.

3. Conduct investigations and statistical and documentary research for review by the attorney.

4. Conduct legal research for review by the attorney.

5. Draft legal documents for review by the attorney.

6. Draft correspondence and pleadings for review by and signature of the attorney.

7. Summarize depositions, interrogatories and testimony for review by the attorney.

8. Attend executions of wills, real estate closings, depositions, court or administrative hearings and trials with the attorney.

9. Author and sign letters providing the legal assistant's status is clearly indicated and the correspondence does not contain independent legal opinions or legal advice.

COMMENT:

The United States Supreme Court has recognized the variety of tasks being performed by legal assistants and has noted that use of legal assistants encourages cost-effective delivery of legal services, *Missouri v. Jenkins*, 491 U.S.274, 109 S.Ct. 2463, 2471, n.10 (1989). In *Jenkins*, the court further held that legal assistant time should be included in compensation for attorney fee awards at the rate in the relevant community to bill legal assistant time.

Courts have held that legal assistant fees are not a part of the overall overhead of a law firm. Legal assistant services are billed separately by attorneys, and decrease litigation expenses. Tasks performed by legal assistants must contain substantive legal work under the direction or supervision of an attorney, such that if the legal assistant were not present, the work would be performed by the attorney.

In *Taylor v. Chubb*, 874 P.2d 806 (Okla. 1994), the Court ruled that attorney fees awarded should include fees for services performed by legal assistants and, further, defined tasks which may be performed by the legal assistant under the supervision of an attorney including, among others: interview clients; draft pleadings and other documents; carry on legal research, both conventional and computer aided; research public records; prepare discovery requests and responses; schedule depositions and prepare notices and subpoenas; summarize depositions and other discovery responses; coordinate and manage document production; locate and interview witnesses; organize pleadings, trial exhibits and other documents; prepare witness and exhibit lists; prepare trial notebooks; prepare for the attendance of witnesses at trial; and assist lawyers at trials.

Except for the specific proscription contained in Guideline 1, the reported cases do not limit the duties which may be performed by a legal assistant under the supervision of the attorney.

An attorney may not split legal fees with a legal assistant, nor pay a legal assistant for the referral of legal business. An attorney may compensate a legal assistant based on the quantity and quality of the legal assistant's work and value of that work to a law practice.

CONCLUSION

These Standards and Guidelines were developed from generally accepted practices. Each supervising attorney must be aware of the specific rules, decisions and statutes applicable to legal assistants within his/her jurisdiction.

Addendum

For further information, the following cases may be helpful to you:

Duties:

Taylor v. Chubb, 874 P.2d 806 (Okla. 1994)
McMackin v. McMackin, 651 A.2d 778 (Del.Fam Ct 1993)

Work Product:

Fine v. Facet Aerospace Products Co., 133 F.R.D. 439 (S.D.N.Y. 1990)

Unauthorized Practice of Law

Akron Bar Assn. V. Green, 673 N.E.2d 1307 (Ohio 1997)
In Re Hessinger & Associates, 192 B.R. 211 (N.D. Calif. 1996)
In the Matter of Bright, 171 B.R. 799 (Bkrtcy. E.D. Mich)
Louisiana State Bar Assn v. Edwins, 540 So.2d 294 (La. 1989)

Attorney/Client Privilege

In Re Complex Asbestos Litigation, 232 Cal. App. 3d 572 (Calif. 1991)
Makita Corp. V. U.S., 819 F.Supp. 1099 (CIT 1993)

Conflicts

In Re Complex Asbestos Litigation, 232 Cal. App. 3d 572 (Calif. 1991)
Makita Corp. V. U.S., 819 F.Supp. 1099 (CIT 1993)
Phoenix Founders, Inc., v. Marshall, 887 S.W.2d 831 (Tex. 1994)
Smart Industries v. Superior Court, 876 P.2d 1176 (Ariz. App. Div.1 1994)

Supervision

Matter of Martinez, 754 P.2d 842 (N.M. 1988)
State v. Barrett, 483 P.2d 1106 (Kan. 1971)

Fee Awards

In Re Bicoastal Corp., 121 B.R. 653 (Bktrcy.M.D.Fla. 1990)
In Re Carter, 101 B.R. 170 (Bkrtcy.D.S.D. 1989)
Taylor v. Chubb, 874 P.2d 806 (Okla.1994)
Missouri v. Jenkins, 491 U.S. 274, 109 S.Ct. 2463, 105 L.Ed.2d 229 (1989) 11 U.S.C.A. '330
McMackin v. McMackin, Del.Fam.Ct. 651 A.2d 778 (1993)

Miller v. Alamo, 983 F.2d 856 (8th Cir. 1993)
Stewart v.Sullivan, 810 F.Supp. 1102 (D.Hawaii 1993)
In Re Yankton College, 101 B.R. 151 (Bkrtcy. D.S.D. 1989)
Stacey v. Stroud, 845 F.Supp. 1135 (S.D.W.Va. 1993)

Court Appearances

Louisiana State Bar Assn v. Edwins, 540 So.2d 294 (La. 1989)

In addition to the above referenced cases, you may contact your state bar association for information regarding guidelines for the utilization of legal assistants that may have been adopted by the bar, or ethical opinions concerning the utilization of legal assistants. The following states have adopted a definition of "legal assistant"or "paralegal" either through bar association guidelines, ethical opinions, legislation or case law:

Legislation:	**Guidelines**	**Bar Associations (Cont.)**
California	Colorado	Massachusetts
Florida	Connecticut	Michigan
Illinois	Georgia	Minnesota
Indiana	Idaho	Missouri
Pennsylvania	New York	Nevada
	Oregon	New Mexico
Supreme Court Cases or Rules:	Utah	New Hampshire
	Wisconsin	North Carolina
		North Dakota
Kentucky	**Bar Association Activity:**	Ohio
New Hampshire		Oregon
New Mexico	Alaska	Rhode Island
North Dakota	Arizona	South Carolina
Rhode Island	Colorado	South Dakota
South Dakota	Connecticut	Tennessee
Virginia	Florida	Texas
	Illinois	Virginia
Cases	Iowa	Wisconsin
	Kansas	
Arizona	Kentucky	
New Jersey		
Oklahoma		
South Carolina		
Washington		

Parental Kidnapping Prevention Act

Title 28, Part V, Chapter 115, § 1738A

SEC. 1738A.—Full faith and credit given to child custody determinations

(a)

The appropriate authorities of every State shall enforce according to its terms, and shall not modify except as provided in subsections (f), (g), and (h) of this section, any custody determination or visitation determination made consistently with the provisions of this section by a court of another State.

(b)

As used in this section, the term—

(1)

"child" means a person under the age of eighteen;

(2)

"contestant" means a person, including a parent or grandparent, who claims a right to custody or visitation of a child;

(3)

"custody determination" means a judgment, decree, or other order of a court providing for the custody of a child, and includes permanent and temporary orders, and initial orders and modifications;

(4)

"home state" means the state in which, immediately preceding the time involved, the child lived with his parents, a parent, or a person acting as parent, for at least six consecutive months, and in the case of a child less than six months old, the State in which the child lived from birth with any of such person. Periods of temporary absence of any of such persons are counted as part of the six-month or other period;

(5)

"modification" and "modify" refer to a custody or visitation determination which modifies, replaces, supersedes, or otherwise is made subsequent to, a prior custody or visitation determination concerning the same child, whether made by the same court or not;

(6)

"person acting as a parent" means a person, other than a parent, who has physical custody of a child and who has either been awarded custody by a court or claims a right to custody;

(7)

"physical custody" means actual possession and control of a child;

(8)

"State" means a State of the United States, the District of Columbia, the Commonwealth of Puerto Rico, or a territory or possession of the United States; and

(9)

"visitation determination" means a judgment, decree, or other order of a court providing for the visitation of a child and includes permanent and temporary orders and initial orders and modifications.

(c)

A child custody or visitation determination made by a court of a State is consistent with the provisions of this section only if—

(1)

such court has jurisdiction under the law of such State; and

(2)

one of the following conditions is met:

(A)

such State

(i)

is the home State of the child on the date of the commencement of the proceeding, or

(ii)

had been the child's home State within six months before the date of the commencement of the proceeding and the child is absent from such State because of his removal or retention by a contestant or for other reasons, and a contestant continues to live in such State;

(B)

(i)

it appears that no other State would have jurisdiction under subparagraph (A), and it is in the best interest of the child that a court of such State assume jurisdiction because

(I)

the child and his parents, or the child and at least one contestant, have a significant connection with such State other than mere physical presence in such State, and

(II)

there is available in such State substantial evidence concerning the child's present or future care, protection, training, and personal relationships:

(C)

the child is physically present in such State, and

(i)

the child has been abandoned, or

(ii)

it is necessary in an emergency to protect the child because the child, a sibling, or parent of the child has been subjected to or threatened with mistreatment or abuse;

(D)

(i)

it appears that no other State would have jurisdiction under subparagraph (A), (B), (C), or (E) or another State has declined to exercise jurisdiction on the ground that the State whose jurisdiction is in issue is the more appropriate forum to determine the custody or visitation of the child, and

(ii)

it is in the best interest of the child that such court assume jurisdiction; or

(E)

the court has continuing jurisdiction pursuant to subsection (d) of this section.

(d)

The jurisdiction of a court of a State which has made a child custody or visitation determination consistently with the provisions of this section continues as long as the requirement of subsection (c)(1) of this section continues to be met and such State remains the residence of the child or of any contestant.

(e)

Before a child custody or visitation determination is made, reasonable notice and opportunity to be heard shall be give to the contestants any parent whose parental rights have not been previously terminated and any person who has physical custody of a child.

(f)

A court of a State may modify a determination of the custody of the same child made by a court of another State,

(1)

it has jurisdiction to made such a child custody determination; and

(2)

the court of the other State no longer has jurisdiction, or it has declined to exercise such jurisdiction to modify such determination.

(g)

A court of a State shall not exercise jurisdiction in any proceeding for a custody or visitation determination commenced during the pendency of a proceeding in a court of another State where such court of that other State is exercising jurisdiction consistently with the provisions of this section to make custody or visitation determination.

(h)

A court of a State may not modify a visitation determination made by a court of another State unless the court of the other State no longer has jurisdiction to modify such determination or has declined to exercise jurisdiction to modify such determination.

International Parental Child Abduction

Revised July 2001
Department of State Publication 10862
Bureau of Consular Affairs

Introduction
Part I: Prevention—How to Guard Against International Child Abduction
Part II: What the State Department Can and Cannot Do When a Child Is Abducted Abroad
Part III: How to Search for a Child Abducted Abroad
Part IV: The Best Solution: Settling Out of Court
Part V: One Possible Solution: The Hague Convention
Part VI: Legal Solutions When the Hague Convention Does Not Apply
Part VII: Using the Criminal Justice System
Part VIII: References
       Uniform State and Federal Laws on Custody, Parental Child Abduction, and Missing Children
       Reading List
Appendix 1—Questionnaire for Non-Hague Convention Parents
Appendix 2—Instructions for Completing the Hague Convention Application
Appendix 3—Children's Passport Issuance Alert Program

PART I: PREVENTION

How to Guard Against International Child Abduction

How Vulnerable Is Your Child?

You and your child are most vulnerable when your relationship with the other parent is troubled or broken, the other parent has close ties to another country, and/or the other country has traditions or laws that may be prejudicial against a parent of your gender or to non-citizens in general. However, anyone can be vulnerable.

Cross-Cultural Marriages: Should You or Your Child Visit the Country of the Other Parent?

Many cases of international parental child abduction are actually cases in which the child traveled to a foreign country with the approval of both parents, but was later prevented from returning to the United States. Sometimes the marriage is neither broken nor troubled, but the foreign parent, upon returning to his or her country of origin, decides not to return to the U.S. or to allow the child to do so. A person who has assimilated a second culture may find a return to his or her roots disturbing and may feel pulled to shift loyalties back to the original culture. Furthermore, a person's behavior may change when he or she returns to the culture where he or she grew up.

In some societies, children must have their father's permission and a woman must have her husband's permission to travel. If you are a woman, to prevent your own or your child's detention abroad, find out about the laws and traditions of the country you plan to visit or plan to allow your child to visit, and consider carefully the effect that a return to his traditional culture might have on your child's father; in other societies, children need the permission of both parents to travel and the refusal of one parent to give that permission may prevent the departure of a child from that country. For detailed advice in your specific case, you may wish to contact an attorney in your spouse's country of origin. Many U.S. Embassies/Consulates list attorneys on their Web sites, accessible via **http://travel.state.gov**.

Precautions That Any Parent Should Take

In international parental child abduction, an ounce of prevention is worth a pound of cure. Be alert to the possibility and be prepared:

- ❏ Keep a list of the addresses and telephone numbers of the other parent's relatives, friends, and business associates both here and abroad;
- ❏ Keep a record of important information about the other parent, including: physical description, passport, social security, bank account, and driver's license numbers, and vehicle description and plate number;
- ❏ Keep a written description of your child, including hair and eye color, height, weight, fingerprints, and any special physical characteristics; and
- ❏ Take full-face color photographs and/or videos of your child every six months—a recent photo of the other parent may also be useful.

If your child should be abducted, this information could be vital in locating your child.

In addition, the National Center for Missing and Exploited Children (NCMEC), **http://www.missingkids .org**, at telephone (800) 843-5678, suggests that you teach your child to use the telephone, memorize your home phone number, practice making collect calls, and instruct him or her to call home immediately if anything unusual happens. Discuss possible plans of action with your child in the case of abduction. Most important, however, if you feel your child is vulnerable to abduction, seek legal advice. Do not merely tell a friend or relative about your fears.

The Importance of a Custody Decree

Under the laws of the United States and many foreign countries, **if there is no decree of custody prior to an abduction, both parents may be considered to have equal legal custody of their child.** (IMPORTANT: Even though both parents may have custody of a child, it still may be a crime for one parent to remove the child from the United States against the other parent's wishes.) If you are contemplating divorce or separation, or are divorced or separated, or even if you were never legally married to the other parent, ask your attorney, as soon as possible, if you should obtain a decree of sole custody or a decree that prohibits the travel of your child without your permission or that of the court. If you have or would prefer to have a joint custody decree, you may want to make certain that it prohibits your child from traveling abroad without your permission or that of the court.

Reminder: *Obtain several* **certified** *copies of your custody decree from the court that issued it. Give a copy to your child's school and advise school personnel to whom your child may be released.*

PART V: ONE POSSIBLE SOLUTION

The Hague Convention

One of the most difficult and frustrating elements for a parent of a child abducted abroad is that United States laws and court orders are not automatically recognized abroad and therefore are not directly enforceable abroad. Each country has jurisdiction within its own territory and over people present within its borders. No country can tell another country how to decide cases or enforce laws. Just as foreign court orders are not automatically enforceable in the United States, United States court orders are not automatically enforceable abroad.

At the Hague Conference on Private International Law in 1976, 23 nations agreed to draft a treaty to deter international child abduction. Between 1976 and 1980, the United States was a major force in preparing and negotiating the Hague Convention on the Civil Aspects of International Child Abduction (Hague Convention or the Convention). The Convention was incorporated into U.S. law and came into force for the United States on July 1, 1988. As of July 2001, the Convention is in force between the United States and 50 other countries. The Convention applies to wrongful removals or retentions that occurred on or after the date the treaty came into force between those two countries. The dates vary for each country and more countries are considering signing on to the Convention all the time. Check the most recent list prepared by the Office of Children's Issues to learn whether the Convention was in force in a particular county at the time of the wrongful removal or retention.

PART VIII: REFERENCES

Directory—Where to Go for Assistance

Consular Assistance

United States Department of State
The Office of Children's Issues
2401 E Street N.W., Room L127
Washington, D.C. 20522
Phone: (202) 736-7000
Fax: (202) 312-9743
Fax-on-demand: (202) 647-3000
After hours: (202) 647-5225
Web site: http://travel.state.gov/children's_issues.html

Children's Passport Issuance Alert Program

United States Department of State
The Office of Children's Issues
2401 E Street N.W., Room L127
Washington, D.C. 20037
Phone: (202) 736-7000
Fax: (202) 312-9743
Fax-on-demand: (202) 647-3000
Web site: http://travel.state.gov/children's_issues.html

National Center for Missing and Exploited Children (NCMEC)

699 Prince Street
Alexandria, VA 22314-3175
Phone: (703) 522-9320
Fax: (703) 235-4067
Web site: http://www.missingkids.org
24-hour hot line for emergencies: 1-800-THE-LOST
TTD: 1-800-826-7653

For American Bar Association Publications

American Bar Association (ABA)
750 North Lake Shore Drive
Chicago, IL 60611
Phone: (312) 988-5555
Web site: http://www.abanet.org/store/catalog.html

Federal Parent Locator Service (FPLS)

Note: The FPLS can be accessed through local and state Child Support Enforcement offices. The names of those offices are available in telephone books and from the address below.

Department of Health and Human Services

Office of Child Support Enforcement
Federal Parent Locator Service (FPLS)
370 L'Enfant Promenade S.W.
Washington, D.C. 20447
Phone: (202) 401-9267
Web site: http://www.acf.dhhs.gov/programs/cse/

Office of Victims of Crime (OVC)

United States Department of Justice
633 Indiana Avenue N.W.
Washington, D.C. 20531
Phone: 1-800-627-6872
Web site: http://www.ojp.usdoj.gov/ovc/

International Social Services/American Branch

700 Light Street
Baltimore, MD 21230
Phone: (410) 230-2734
Web site: http://www.iss-usa.org

UNIFORM STATE AND FEDERAL LAWS ON CUSTODY, PARENTAL CHILD ABDUCTION, AND MISSING CHILDREN

Uniform Child Custody Jurisdiction Act (UCCJA) (9 ULA at 123): Determines when a state has jurisdiction to make a custody order and provides procedures for interstate enforcement of orders in custody conflicts.

Uniform Child Custody Jurisdiction and Enforcement Act (UCCJEA) (9 ULA at 115, Part 1): Enhances the UCCJA by awarding priority to the child's home state, clarifies the limits of emergency jurisdiction, and grants exclusive jurisdiction to the state making the original custody determination.

Missing Children Act (28 USC § 534): Requires law enforcement to enter complete descriptions of missing children into the National Crime Information Center's (NCIC) Missing Person File, even if the abductor has not been charged with a crime.

National Child Search Assistance Act (42 USC §§ 5779 and 5780): Mandates elimination of waiting periods before law enforcement takes a missing child report, including family abduction cases; requires immediate entry of information into the NCIC Missing Person file; requires close liaison with the National Center for Missing and Exploited Children (NCMEC).

International Child Abduction Remedies Act (42 USC § 11601 *et seq.*): Establishes procedures to implement the Hague Convention. Empowers state and federal courts to hear cases under the Convention and allows the Central Authority access to information in certain American records regarding the location of a child and abducting parent.

Parental Kidnapping Prevention Act (PKPA) (28 USC § 1738A): Requires authorities of every state to enforce and not modify orders made by the state court exercising proper jurisdiction. Authorizes the use of the Unlawful Flight to Avoid Prosecution (UFAP) warrant and the Federal Parent Locator Service (FPLS) in family abductions.

International Parental Kidnapping Crime Act (IPKCA) (18 USC § 1204): Makes it a federal felony to remove a child under 16 from the United States, or to retain a child outside the United States with the intent to obstruct the lawful exercise of parental rights.

Fugitive Felon Act (18 USC § 1073): Enhances the ability of states to pursue abductors beyond state and national borders; permits the FBI to investigate cases that would otherwise be under state jurisdiction and authorizes use of UFAP warrants in parental kidnapping cases.

Extradition Treaties Interpretation Act of 1998 (18 U.S.C. § 3181): Authorizes the United States to interpret extradition treaties listing "kidnapping" as encompassing the offense of parental kidnapping.

APPENDIX 2

Instructions for Completing the Hague Convention Application

To invoke the Hague Convention, submit two completed applications for each child. The application form may be photocopied. Type or print all information in black or blue ink. Furnish as much of the information called for as possible, using an additional sheet of paper if you need more space. If you have further questions about the form, you may wish to refer to the text of the Convention. You may also call CA/OCS/CI at 202-736-7000.

Translation of the supporting documents into the official language of the requested country may be necessary. Translations can speed up the overall process. Foreign attorneys and judges tend to respond more favorably with such documents. Ask CA/OCS/CI for more information about supporting documents.

You may fax your Hague application to CA/OCS/CI, fax number 202-312-9743. Send originals and supporting documents by mail, express mail, or courier service to: Department of State CA/OCS/CI, Room L127 2401 E Street N.W. Washington, D.C. 20522.

Be sure to sign and date the application.

CHECKLIST AND INSTRUCTIONS FOR COMPLETING THE HAGUE APPLICATION

Information Block and Details Needed

I. Identity of Child and Parents

Child's Name—The child's full name: last name, first, middle
Date of Birth—Month/Day/Year
Place of Birth—City/State/Country
Address—Child's address in the country of habitual residence **at the time of** the abduction or removal.
United States Social Security Number—A nine-digit number: 000-00-0000 (if known)
Passport/Identity Card—Issuing country and passport or I.D. number (if known)

Nationality—Include all nationalities of the child (e.g., U.S., Canadian)
Height—Feet and inches
Weight—Pounds
Sex—Male or female
Color of Hair—Child's hair color
Color of Eyes—Child's eye color (include color photo, if available)

Father

Name—Full name of father: last name, first, middle
Date of Birth—Month/Day/Year
Place of Birth—City/State/Country
Nationality—Include all nationalities
Occupation—Usual or last known
Passport/Identity Card—Issuing country and number (if known)
Current Address and Tel.—Include zip code as well as telephone and fax numbers for work and home.
United States Social Security Number—A nine-digit number: 000-00-0000 (if known)
Country of Habitual Residence—Of the father **before** the abduction or retention, particularly if different from that of the child.
Date and Place of Marriage and Divorce, if applicable—Indicate date and location of marriage and divorce or the parent of the child. It is important to clearly state the marital status at the time of the abduction or retention.

Mother

Name—Full name of mother of child: last name, first, middle (include maiden name)
Date of Birth—Month/Day/Year
Place of Birth—City/State/Country
Nationality—Include all nationalities
Passport/Identity Card—Issuing country and number (if known)
Current Address and Tel.—Include zip code as well as telephone and fax numbers for work and home.
Occupation—Usual or last known
United States Social Security Number—A nine-digit number: 000-00-0000 (if known)
Country of Habitual Residence—Of the mother **before** the abduction or retention, particularly if different from that of the child.
Date and Place of Marriage and Divorce, if applicable—Indicate date and location of marriage and divorce, as applicable, of the parents of the child. It is important to clearly indicate the parents' marital status at the time of the abduction or retention.

II. Person Seeking Return of/Access to Child

This section is for information concerning the person or institution applying for the return of the child to the United States.

Name—Provide the full name of the person or institution asking for the child to be returned.
Nationality—Of the requester
Relationship to Child—Relationship of the requester to the child (e.g., mother, father)
Current Address and Telephone Number—Include home, work, and fax numbers.

Occupation—Of the requester (if a person)

Name, Address, and Telephone Number of Legal Adviser, if any—Include zip code as well as telephone and fax numbers. *Some of this information may be the same as that already given.*

III. Information Concerning the Person Alleged to Have Wrongfully Removed or Retained Child

The information about the abducting parent is needed to assist in locating the child. Please provide all requested information and any additional facts that may help authorities locate the child.

Name—Full name of parent who has abducted or wrongfully retained the child

Relationship to Child—Relationship of the abductor to the child (e.g., mother, father)

Known Aliases—Any other names the abductor may use

Date of Birth—Month/Day/Year

Place of Birth—City/State/Country

Nationality—Include all nationalities

Occupation, Name and Address of Employer—Provide any employment information that may be helpful in locating the abductor, such as usual type of work, potential employers or employment agencies.

Passport/Identity Card—Country and number

United States Social Security Number—A nine-digit number: 000-00-0000 (if known)

Current Location—Of the abductor in the country where the child was taken

Height—Feet and inches

Weight—Pounds

Color of Hair—Abductor's hair color

Color of Eyes—Abductor's eye color

Other Persons with Possible Additional Information—Provide names, addresses and telephone numbers of anyone in the Information Relating to the Whereabouts of country to which the child was taken who could give the Central Authority in that country information on the child's location.

IV. Time, Place, Date, and Circumstances of the Wrongful Removal or Retention

Provide the date, to the best of your knowledge, that the child left the United States or when the wrongful retention began. Include the place from which the child was taken. Describe the legal relationship existing between you and the abducting parent when the child was removed. What were the circumstances leading up to the removal or retention? How did you learn of the removal/retention? Did the other parent take the child during a scheduled visitation? Did the other parent take the child for what you believed would be a short visit and then inform you that they were staying? Did they purchase round-trip air tickets to show that they intended to return? Had you and your family moved to the other country, and then you decided to return to the United States?

Take this opportunity to tell your story. Try to anticipate what claims the other parent may make and provide your explanation.

Do not limit yourself to the space provided on the form.
Additional pages may be attached to fully narrate the circumstances.
However, please be concise.

V. Factual or Legal Grounds Justifying Request

Provide information and documentation establishing that you had, and were exercising, a right of custody at the time of the child's removal. Generally, a right of custody is created by a custody order when parents are divorced, or by operation of state law when parents are still married or were never married when the child was taken. As stated, the Convention defines "rights of custody" as including "rights relating to the care of the child and, in particular, the right to determine the child's place of residence." Thus, you may have a "right of custody" as defined by the Convention even if you do not have court-ordered joint or sole custody of the child.

IMPORTANT

If there is no applicable court order, please provide a copy of the state statute, case law or an affidavit of law prepared by an attorney that establishes your right of custody at the time of the child's removal. This provision of the law may sometimes be found in the estate and wills section of the state code. Remember, you are not attempting to show that you would have an equal right to obtain custody in a subsequent custody proceeding, but that you **had** and were exercising a right of custody when the child was taken.

SEND IN YOUR HAGUE APPLICTION IMMEDIATELY
Do NOT wait to get an order of custody. Orders issued after removal/retention are irrelevant in a Hague hearing.

VI. Civil Proceeding in Progress, If Any

Indicate any civil action (in the United States or abroad) that may be pending (e.g., custody, divorce). Name court and hearing dates.

VII. Child Is to Be Returned to:

Name—Of person to whom child will be returned
Date of Birth—Of person to whom child will be returned
Place of Birth—Of person to whom child will be returned
Address—Of person to whom child will be returned
Telephone Number—Of person to whom child will be returned
Proposed Arrangements for Return—Provide means by which you propose the child will return to the United States if this is ordered. For example, would you travel to pick up the child, or would someone go in your place? Is the child old enough to travel by him or herself? Is there someone in the foreign country who could return with the child? Would the child travel by car, train, airplane? Be specific.

VIII. Other Remarks

State here whether you are applying for return or access under the Convention. You should include here any additional information that you believe may be pertinent to the Hague application.

Sign and date the application in black or blue ink.

HAGUE APPLICATION CHECKLIST

(Check with country officer for specific requirements.)

_____ **Application form—signed original, one for each child.** Note: Country may require use of special application form.

_____ **Marriage certificate** (if applicable)—May need to be certified copy

_____ **Birth certificate of child**—May need to be certified copy

_____ **Divorce decree** (if applicable)—May need to be certified copy

_____ **Evidence of custodial right**

- ❒ Custody order, or
- ❒ Copy of state statute, or
- ❒ Affidavit of law regarding presumption of custody under state law, or
- ❒ Article 15 determination by state court

_____ **Other pertinent court documents**

_____ **Photographs of taking parent and child**

_____ **Statement regarding circumstances of removal or retention**

_____ **Other documents specifically required by receiving country** (e.g., Article 28 statement—power of attorney to foreign Central Authority)

_____ **Translations** (if applicable)

_____ **Application for legal assistance** (if applicable)

State Child Support Enforcement Agencies

Alabama

Child Support Enforcement Division
50 North Ripley Street
P.O. Box 304000
Montgomery, AL 36130
800-284-4347
http://www.dhr.state.al.us/csed/default.asp

Alaska

Child Support Enforcement Division
550 West 7th Avenue, Suite 310
Anchorage, AK 99501
800-478-3300
http://www.csed.state.ak.us

Arizona

Department of Economic Security
3443 North Central, 021A
P.O. Box 40458
Phoenix, AZ 85012
800-882-4151
http://www.de.state.az.us/links/dcse/index.html

Arkansas

Office of Child Support Enforcement
P.O. Box 3278
Little Rock, AR 72203
800-264-2445
http://www.state.ar.us/dfa/childsupport/index.html

California

Department of Child Services Support
744 P. Street MS 17-29
Sacramento, CA 95814
800-952-5253
http://www.childsup.cahwnet.gov/Default.htm

Colorado	Division of Child Support Enforcement 1575 Sherman Street, 2nd Floor Denver, CO 80203 303-866-5994 http://www.childsupport.state.co.us
Connecticut	State of Connecticut Child Support Enforcement Bureau 25 Sigourney Street Hartford, CT 06105 800-842-1508 http://www.dss.state.ct.us/svcs/csupp.htm
Delaware	Division of Child Support Enforcement 1901 North DuPont Highway P.O. Box 904 New Castle, DE 19720 302-577-7171 http://www.state.de.us/dhss/dcse/index.html
District of Columbia	Child Support Enforcement 441 4th Street NW Washington, DC 20001 888-689-6088 http://www.csed.dcgov.org
Florida	Department of Revenue P.O. Box 8030 Tallahassee, FL 32314 800-622-KIDS http://www.sun6.dms.state.fl.us/dor/childsupport
Georgia	Division of Family and Children Services P.O. Box 38450 Atlanta, GA 30334 800-227-7993 http://www.acf.dhhs.gov/programs/cse/extinf.htm#exta
Hawaii	Child Support Enforcement Agency 601 Kamokila Boulevard, Suite 251 Kapolei, HI 96707 888-317-9081 http://kumu.icsd.hawaii.gov/csea.htm

Idaho

Department of Health and Welfare
450 West State Street
Boise, ID 83720
800-356-9868
http://www.idahochild.org

Illinois

Department of Public Aid
201 South Grand Avenue East
Springfield, IL 62763
800-447-4278
http://www.state.il.us/dpa/html/cs_child_support_news.htm

Indiana

Bureau of Child Support
IGC-South, Room W360
402 West Washington
P.O. Box 7083
Indianapolis, IN 46207
800-622-4932
http://www.state.in.us/fssa/children/support/index.html

Iowa

Child Support Enforcement
1305 East Walnut
Des Moines, IA 50319
515-281-5767
http://www.dhs.state.ia.us?HomePages?DHS?csrunit.htm

Kansas

Child Support Enforcement
415 SW 8th
Topeka, KS 66603
888-219-7801
http://www.srskansas.ord/srslegalservice.html

Kentucky

Division of Child Support Enforcement
275 East Main Street
Frankfort, KY 40621
800-248-1163
http://www.law.state.ky.us/childsupport/Default.htm

Louisiana

Department of Social Services
P.O. Box 3776
Baton Rouge, LA 70821
800-256-4650
http://www.dss.state.la.us

Maine	Bureau of Family Independence 11 State House Station Whitten Road Augusta, ME 04333 800-371-3101 http://www.state.me.us/csea/index.htm
Maryland	Child Support Enforcement Administration 200 North Howard Road Baltimore, MD 21201 800-332-6347 http://www.dhr.state.md.us/csea/index.htm
Massachusetts	Department of Revenue Child Support Enforcement 51 Sleeper Street P.O. Box 9492 Boston, MA 02205 800-332-2733 http://www.state.ma.us/cse/cse.htm
Michigan	State Court Administration 309 North Washington Square P.O. Box 30048 Lansing, MI 48909 800-524-9846 http://www.mfia.state.mi.us/CHLDSUPP/CS-INDEX.htm
Minnesota	Child Support Enforcement Division 121 7th Plaza St. Paul, MN 55155 800-672-3954 http://www.dhs.state.mn.us/ecs/Program/csed.htm
Mississippi	Division of Child Support Enforcement 750 North State Street Jackson, MS 39205 800-948-4010 http://www.mdhs.state.ms.us/cse.html
Missouri	Division of Child Support Enforcement 3418 Knipp Drive, Suite F P.O. Box 2320 Jefferson City, MO 65102 800-585-9234 http://www.dss.state.mo.us/cse/cse.htm

Montana	Child Support Enforcement Division 3075 North Montana Avenue Helena, MT 59601 800-346-KIDS http://www.dphhs.state.mt.us/divisions/cse/csed.htm
Nebraska	Child Support Enforcement P.O. Box 94728 Lincoln, NE 68509 800-831-4573 http://www.hhs.state.ne.us/cse/cseindex.htm
Nevada	Child Support Enforcement 2527 North Carson Street Carson City, NV 89706 800-992-0900 http://www.state.nv.us/ag/agpub/chldsupp.htm
New Hampshire	Office of Program Support 6 Hazen Drive Concord, NH 03301 800-371-8844
New Jersey	Division of Family Development P.O. Box 716 Trenton, NJ 08625 800-621-5437 http://www.njchildsupport.org
New Mexico	Child Support Enforcement Division P.O. Box 2348 Santa Fe, NM 87504 800-288-7207 http://www.state.nm.us/hsd/csed.html
New York	Division of Child Support Enforcement 1 Commerce Plaza P.O. Box 14 Albany, NY 12260 800-343-8859 http://www.dfa.state.ny.us/csms

North Carolina

Office of Child Support Enforcement
Social Services Division
325 North Salisbury Street
Raleigh, NC 27603
800-992-9457
http://www.dhhs.state.nc.us/dss/cse/cse_mission.htm

North Dakota

Child Support Enforcement
1929 North Washington Street
Bismarck, ND 58501
800-755-8530
lnotes.state.nd.us/dhs/dhsweb.nsf?ServicePages?ChildSupportEnforcement

Ohio

Office of Child Support
50 West Broad Street
Columbus, OH 43206
800-686-1556
http://www.state.oh.us/odhs/ocs

Oklahoma

Child Support Enforcement Division
2400 North Lincoln Boulevard
P.O. Box 25352
Oklahoma City, OK 73125
800-522-2922
http://www.okdhs.org/childsupport

Oregon

Division of Child Support
1162 Court Street
Salem, OR 97310
800-850-0228
http://www.afs.hr.state.or.us/rss/childsupp.html

Pennsylvania

Child Support Enforcement Bureau
P.O. Box 8018
Harrisburg, PA 17105
800-932-0211
http://www.pachildsupport.com

Rhode Island

Child Support Enforcement
77 Dorrance St.
Providence, RI 02903
800-768-5858
http://www.state.sd.us/social/CSE/index.htm

South Carolina

Department of Social Services
1535 Confederate Avenue
P.O. Box 1015
Columbia, SC 29202
800-827-6078
http://www.state.sc.us/dss/csed

South Dakota

Division of Child Support Enforcement
700 Governers Drive
Pierre, SD 57501
800-827-6078
http://www.state.sd.us/social/CSE/index.htm

Tennessee

Child Support Enforcement
400 Deadrick Street
Nashville, TN 37248
800-827-6078
http://www.state.tn.us/humanserv

Texas

Child Support Enforcement Division
P.O. Box 12548
Austin, TX 78711
800-252-8014
http://www.oag.state.tx.us/child/mainchil.htm

Utah

Office of Recovery Services
515 East 100 South
Salt Lake City, UT 84102
800-257-9156
http://www.ors.state.ut.us

Vermont

Office of Child Support
103 South Main Street
Waterbury, VT 05671
800-786-3214
http://www.ocs.state.vt.us

Virginia

Division of Child Support Enforcement
730 East Broad Street
Richmond, VA 23219
800-468-8894
http://www.dss.state.va.us/division/childsupp

Washington

Division of Child Support
P.O. Box 45860
Olympia, WA 98504
800-457-6202
http://www.wa.gov/dshs/dcs/index.html

West Virginia

Bureau of Child Support Enforcement
1900 Kanawha Boulevard East
Charleston, WV 25305
800-249-3778
http://www.wvdhhr.org/bcse

Wisconsin

Bureau of Child Support
1 West Wilson Street
Madison, WI 53707
888-300-4473
http://www.dwd.state.wi.us/bcs

Wyoming

Child Support Enforcement
2300 Capitol Avenue
Cheyenne, WY 82002
800-970-9258
http://dfsweb.state.wy.us/csehome/cs.htm

Uniform Child Custody Jurisdiction and Enforcement Act

GENERAL PROVISIONS

SECTION 102. DEFINITIONS. In this [Act]:

(1) "Abandoned" means left without provision for reasonable and necessary care or supervision.

(2) "Child" means an individual who has not attained 18 years of age.

(3) "Child-custody determination" means a judgment, decree, or other order of a court providing for the legal custody, physical custody, or visitation with respect to a child. The term includes a permanent, temporary, initial, and modification order. The term does not include an order relating to child support or other monetary obligation of an individual.

(4) "Child-custody proceeding" means a proceeding in which legal custody, physical custody, or visitation with respect to a child is an issue. The term includes a proceeding for divorce, separation, neglect, abuse, dependency, guardianship, paternity, termination of parental rights, and protection from domestic violence, in which the issue may appear. The term does not include a proceeding involving juvenile delinquency, contractual emancipation, or enforcement under [Article] 3.

(5) "Commencement" means the filing of the first pleading in a proceeding.

(6) "Court" means an entity authorized under the law of a State to establish, enforce, or modify a child-custody determination.

(7) "Home State" means the State in which a child lived with a parent or a person acting as a parent for at least six consecutive months immediately before the commencement of a child-custody proceeding. In the case of a child less than six months of age, the term means the State in which the child lived from birth with any of the persons mentioned. A period of temporary absence of any of the mentioned persons is part of the period.

(8) "Initial determination" means the first child-custody determination concerning a particular child.

(9) "Issuing court" means the court that makes a child-custody determination for which enforcement is sought under this [Act].

(10) "Issuing State" means the State in which a child-custody determination is made.

(11) "Modification" means a child-custody determination that changes, replaces, supersedes, or is otherwise made after a previous determination concerning the same child, whether or not it is made by the court that made the previous determination.

(12) "Person" means an individual, corporation, business trust, estate, trust, partnership, limited liability company, association, joint venture, government; governmental subdivision, agency, or instrumentality; public corporation; or any other legal or commercial entity.

(13) "Person acting as a parent" means a person, other than a parent, who:

(A) has physical custody of the child or has had physical custody for a period of six consecutive months, including any temporary absence, within one year immediately before the commencement of a child-custody proceeding; and

(B) has been awarded legal custody by a court or claims a right to legal custody under the law of this State.

(14) "Physical custody" means the physical care and supervision of a child.

(15) "State" means a State of the United States, the District of Columbia, Puerto Rico, the United States Virgin Islands, or any territory or insular possession subject to the jurisdiction of the United States.

[(16) "Tribe" means an Indian tribe or band, or Alaskan Native village, which is recognized by federal law or formally acknowledged by a State.]

(17) "Warrant" means an order issued by a court authorizing law enforcement officers to take physical custody of a child.

SECTION 103. PROCEEDINGS GOVERNED BY OTHER LAW. This [Act] does not govern an adoption proceeding or a proceeding pertaining to the authorization of emergency medical care for a child.

SECTION 104. APPLICATION TO INDIAN TRIBES.

(a) A child-custody proceeding that pertains to an Indian child as defined in the Indian Child Welfare Act, 25 U.S.C. § 1901 et seq., is not subject to this [Act] to the extent that it is governed by the Indian Child Welfare Act.

[(b) A court of this State shall treat a tribe as if it were a State of the United States for the purpose of applying [Articles] 1 and 2.]

[(c) A child-custody determination made by a tribe under factual circumstances in substantial conformity with the jurisdictional standards of this [Act] must be recognized and enforced under [Article] 3.]

SECTION 105. INTERNATIONAL APPLICATION OF [ACT].

(a) A court of this State shall treat a foreign country as if it were a State of the United States for the purpose of applying [Articles] 1 and 2.

(b) Except as otherwise provided in subsection (c), a child-custody determination made in a foreign country under factual circumstances in substantial conformity with the jurisdictional standards of this [Act] must be recognized and enforced under [Article] 3.

(c) A court of this State need not apply this [Act] if the child custody law of a foreign country violates fundamental principles of human rights.

SECTION 106. EFFECT OF CHILD-CUSTODY DETERMINATION. A child-custody determination made by a court of this State that had jurisdiction under this [Act] binds all persons who have been served in accordance with the laws of this State or notified in accordance with Section 108 or who have submitted to the jurisdiction of the court, and who have been given an opportunity to be heard. As to those persons, the determination is conclusive as to all decided issues of law and fact except to the extent the determination is modified.

SECTION 107. PRIORITY. If a question of existence or exercise of jurisdiction under this [Act] is raised in a child-custody proceeding, the question, upon request of a party, must be given priority on the calendar and handled expeditiously.

SECTION 108. NOTICE TO PERSONS OUTSIDE STATE.

(a) Notice required for the exercise of jurisdiction when a person is outside this State may be given in a manner prescribed by the law of this State for service of process or by the law of the State in which the service is made. Notice must be given in a manner reasonably calculated to give actual notice but may be by publication if other means are not effective.

(b) Proof of service may be made in the manner prescribed by the law of this State or by the law of the State in which the service is made.

(c) Notice is not required for the exercise of jurisdiction with respect to a person who submits to the jurisdiction of the court.

SECTION 109. APPEARANCE AND LIMITED IMMUNITY.

(a) A party to a child-custody proceeding, including a modification proceeding, or a petitioner or respondent in a proceeding to enforce or register a child-custody determination, is not subject to personal jurisdiction in this State for another proceeding or purpose solely by reason of having participated, or of having been physically present for the purpose of participating, in the proceeding.

(b) A person who is subject to personal jurisdiction in this State on a basis other than physical presence is not immune from service of process in this State. A party present in this State who is subject to the jurisdiction of another State is not immune from service of process allowable under the laws of that State.

(c) The immunity granted by subsection (a) does not extend to civil litigation based on acts unrelated to the participation in a proceeding under this [Act] committed by an individual while present in this State.

SECTION 110. COMMUNICATION BETWEEN COURTS.

(a) A court of this State may communicate with a court in another State concerning a proceeding arising under this [Act].

(b) The court may allow the parties to participate in the communication. If the parties are not able to participate in the communication, they must be given the opportunity to present facts and legal arguments before a decision on jurisdiction is made.

(c) Communication between courts on schedules, calendars, court records, and similar matters may occur without informing the parties. A record need not be made of the communication.

(d) Except as otherwise provided in subsection (c), a record must be made of a communication under this section. The parties must be informed promptly of the communication and granted access to the record.

(e) For the purposes of this section, "record" means information that is inscribed on a tangible medium or that is stored in an electronic or other medium and is retrievable in perceivable form.

SECTION 111. TAKING TESTIMONY IN ANOTHER STATE.

(a) In addition to other procedures available to a party, a party to a child-custody proceeding may offer testimony of witnesses who are located in another State, including testimony of the parties and the child, by deposition or other means allowable in this State for testimony taken in another State. The court on its own motion may order that the testimony of a person be taken in another State and may prescribe the manner in which and the terms upon which the testimony is taken.

(b) A court of this State may permit an individual residing in another State to be deposed or to testify by telephone, audiovisual means, or other electronic means before a designated court or at another location in that State. A court of this State shall cooperate with courts of other States in designating an appropriate location for the deposition or testimony.

(c) Documentary evidence transmitted from another State to a court of this State by technological means that do not produce an original writing may not be excluded from evidence on an objection based on the means of transmission.

SECTION 112. COOPERATION BETWEEN COURTS; PRESERVATION OF RECORDS.

(a) A court of this State may request the appropriate court of another State to:

(1) hold an evidentiary hearing;

(2) order a person to produce or give evidence pursuant to procedures of that State;

(3) order that an evaluation be made with respect to the custody of a child involved in a pending proceeding;

(4) forward to the court of this State a certified copy of the transcript of the record of the hearing, the evidence otherwise presented, and any evaluation prepared in compliance with the request; and

(5) order a party to a child-custody proceeding or any person having physical custody of the child to appear in the proceeding with or without the child.

(b) Upon request of a court of another State, a court of this State may hold a hearing or enter an order described in subsection (a).

(c) Travel and other necessary and reasonable expenses incurred under subsections (a) and (b) may be assessed against the parties according to the law of this State.

(d) A court of this State shall preserve the pleadings, orders, decrees, records of hearings, evaluations, and other pertinent records with respect to a child-custody proceeding until the child attains 18 years of age. Upon appropriate request by a court or law enforcement official of another State, the court shall forward a certified copy of those records.

[ARTICLE] 2
JURISDICTION

SECTION 201. INITIAL CHILD-CUSTODY JURISDICTION.

(a) Except as otherwise provided in Section 204, a court of this State has jurisdiction to make an initial child-custody determination only if:

(1) this State is the home State of the child on the date of the commencement of the proceeding, or was the home State of the child within six months before the commencement of the proceeding and the child is absent from this State but a parent or person acting as a parent continues to live in this State;

(2) a court of another State does not have jurisdiction under paragraph (1), or a court of the home State of the child has declined to exercise jurisdiction on the ground that this State is the more appropriate forum under Section 207 or 208, and:

(A) the child and the child's parents, or the child and at least one parent or a person acting as a parent, have a significant connection with this State other than mere physical presence; and

(B) substantial evidence is available in this State concerning the child's care, protection, training, and personal relationships;

(3) all courts having jurisdiction under paragraph (1) or (2) have declined to exercise jurisdiction on the ground that a court of this State is the more appropriate forum to determine the custody of the child under Section 207 or 208; or

(4) no court of any other State would have jurisdiction under the criteria specified in paragraph (1), (2), or (3).

(b) Subsection (a) is the exclusive jurisdictional basis for making a child-custody determination by a court of this State.

(c) Physical presence of, or personal jurisdiction over, a party or a child is not necessary or sufficient to make a child-custody determination.

SECTION 202. EXCLUSIVE, CONTINUING JURISDICTION.

(a) Except as otherwise provided in Section 204, a court of this State which has made a child-custody determination consistent with Section 201 or 203 has exclusive, continuing jurisdiction over the determination until:

(1) a court of this State determines that neither the child, the child's parents, and any person acting as a parent do not have a significant connection with this State and that substantial evidence is no longer available in this State concerning the child's care, protection, training, and personal relationships; or

(2) a court of this State or a court of another State determines that the child, the child's parents, and any person acting as a parent do not presently reside in this State.

(b) A court of this State which has made a child-custody determination and does not have exclusive, continuing jurisdiction under this section may modify that determination only if it has jurisdiction to make an initial determination under Section 201.

SECTION 203. JURISDICTION TO MODIFY DETERMINATION. Except as otherwise provided in Section 204, a court of this State may not modify a child-custody determination made by a court of another State unless a court of this State has jurisdiction to make an initial determination under Section 201(a)(1) or (2) and:

(1) the court of the other State determines it no longer has exclusive, continuing jurisdiction under Section 202 or that a court of this State would be a more convenient forum under Section 207; or

(2) a court of this State or a court of the other State determines that the child, the child's parents, and any person acting as a parent do not presently reside in the other State.

SECTION 204. TEMPORARY EMERGENCY JURISDICTION.

(a) A court of this State has temporary emergency jurisdiction if the child is present in this State and the child has been abandoned or it is necessary in an emergency to protect the child because the child, or a sibling or parent of the child, is subjected to or threatened with mistreatment or abuse.

(b) If there is no previous child-custody determination that is entitled to be enforced under this [Act] and a child-custody proceeding has not been commenced in a court of a State having jurisdiction under Sections 201 through 203, a child-custody determination made under this section remains in effect until an order is obtained from a court of a State having jurisdiction under Sections 201 through 203. If a child-custody proceeding has not been or is not commenced in a court of a State having jurisdiction under Sections 201 through 203, a child-custody determination made under this section becomes a final determination, if it so provides and this State becomes the home State of the child.

(c) If there is a previous child-custody determination that is entitled to be enforced under this [Act], or a child-custody proceeding has been commenced in a court of a State having jurisdiction under Sections 201 through 203, any order issued by a court of this State under this section must specify in the order a period that the court considers adequate to allow the person seeking an order to obtain an order from the State having jurisdiction under Sections 201 through 203. The order issued in this State remains in effect until an order is obtained from the other State within the period specified or the period expires.

(d) A court of this State which has been asked to make a child-custody determination under this section, upon being informed that a child-custody proceeding has been commenced in, or a child-custody determination has been made by, a court of a State having jurisdiction under Sections 201 through 203, shall immediately communicate with the other court. A court of this State which is exercising jurisdiction pursuant to Sections 201 through 203, upon being informed that a child-custody proceeding has been commenced in, or a child-custody determination has been made by, a court of another State under a statute similar to this section shall immediately communicate with the court of that State to resolve the emergency, protect the safety of the parties and the child, and determine a period for the duration of the temporary order.

SECTION 205. NOTICE; OPPORTUNITY TO BE HEARD; JOINDER.

(a) Before a child-custody determination is made under this [Act], notice and an opportunity to be heard in accordance with the standards of Section 108 must be given to all persons entitled to notice under the law of this State as in child-custody proceedings between residents of this State, any parent whose parental rights have not been previously terminated, and any person having physical custody of the child.

(b) This [Act] does not govern the enforceability of a child-custody determination made without notice or an opportunity to be heard.

(c) The obligation to join a party and the right to intervene as a party in a child-custody proceeding under this [Act] are governed by the law of this State as in child-custody proceedings between residents of this State.

SECTION 206. SIMULTANEOUS PROCEEDINGS.

(a) Except as otherwise provided in Section 204, a court of this State may not exercise its jurisdiction under this [article] if, at the time of the commencement of the proceeding, a proceeding concerning the custody of the child has been commenced in a court of another State having jurisdiction substantially in conformity with this [Act], unless the proceeding has been terminated or is stayed by the court of the other State because a court of this State is a more convenient forum under Section 207.

(b) Except as otherwise provided in Section 204, a court of this State, before hearing a child-custody proceeding, shall examine the court documents and other information supplied by the parties pursuant to Section 209. If the court determines that a child-custody proceeding has been commenced in a court in another State having jurisdiction substantially in accordance with this [Act], the court of this State shall stay its proceeding and communicate with the court of the other State. If the court of the State having jurisdiction substantially in accordance with this [Act] does not determine that the court of this State is a more appropriate forum, the court of this State shall dismiss the proceeding.

(c) In a proceeding to modify a child-custody determination, a court of this State shall determine whether a proceeding to enforce the determination has been commenced in another State. If a proceeding to enforce a child-custody determination has been commenced in another State, the court may:

(1) stay the proceeding for modification pending the entry of an order of a court of the other State enforcing, staying, denying, or dismissing the proceeding for enforcement;

(2) enjoin the parties from continuing with the proceeding for enforcement; or

(3) proceed with the modification under conditions it considers appropriate.

SECTION 207. INCONVENIENT FORUM.

(a) A court of this State which has jurisdiction under this [Act] to make a child-custody determination may decline to exercise its jurisdiction at any time if it determines that it is an inconvenient forum under the circumstances and that a court of another State is a more appropriate forum. The issue of inconvenient forum may be raised upon motion of a party, the court's own motion, or request of another court.

(b) Before determining whether it is an inconvenient forum, a court of this State shall consider whether it is appropriate for a court of another State to exercise jurisdiction. For this purpose, the court shall allow the parties to submit information and shall consider all relevant factors, including:

(1) whether domestic violence has occurred and is likely to continue in the future and which State could best protect the parties and the child;

(2) the length of time the child has resided outside this State;

(3) the distance between the court in this State and the court in the State that would assume jurisdiction;

(4) the relative financial circumstances of the parties;

(5) any agreement of the parties as to which State should assume jurisdiction;

(6) the nature and location of the evidence required to resolve the pending litigation, including testimony of the child;

(7) the ability of the court of each State to decide the issue expeditiously and the procedures necessary to present the evidence; and

(8) the familiarity of the court of each State with the facts and issues in the pending litigation.

(c) If a court of this State determines that it is an inconvenient forum and that a court of another State is a more appropriate forum, it shall stay the proceedings upon condition that a child-custody proceeding be promptly commenced in another designated State and may impose any other condition the court considers just and proper.

(d) A court of this State may decline to exercise its jurisdiction under this [Act] if a child-custody determination is incidental to an action for divorce or another proceeding while still retaining jurisdiction over the divorce or other proceeding.

SECTION 208. JURISDICTION DECLINED BY REASON OF CONDUCT.

(a) Except as otherwise provided in Section 204 [or by other law of this State], if a court of this State has jurisdiction under this [Act] because a person seeking to invoke its jurisdiction has engaged in unjustifiable conduct, the court shall decline to exercise its jurisdiction unless:

(1) the parents and all persons acting as parents have acquiesced in the exercise of jurisdiction;

(2) a court of the State otherwise having jurisdiction under Sections 201 through 203 determines that this State is a more appropriate forum under Section 207; or

(3) no court of any other State would have jurisdiction under the criteria specified in Sections 201 through 203.

(b) If a court of this State declines to exercise its jurisdiction pursuant to subsection (a), it may fashion an appropriate remedy to ensure the safety of the child and prevent a repetition of the unjustifiable conduct, including staying the proceeding until a child-custody proceeding is commenced in a court having jurisdiction under Sections 201 through 203.

(c) If a court dismisses a petition or stays a proceeding because it declines to exercise its jurisdiction pursuant to subsection (a), it shall assess against the party seeking to invoke its jurisdiction necessary and reasonable expenses including costs, communication expenses, attorney's fees, investigative fees, expenses for witnesses, travel expenses, and child care during the course of the proceedings, unless the party from whom fees are sought establishes that the assessment would be clearly inappropriate. The court may not assess fees, costs, or expenses against this State unless authorized by law other than this [Act].

SECTION 209. INFORMATION TO BE SUBMITTED TO COURT.

(a) Subject to [local law providing for the confidentiality of procedures, addresses, and other identifying information in] a child-custody proceeding, each party, in its first pleading or in an attached affidavit, shall give information, if reasonably ascertainable, under oath as to the child's present address or whereabouts, the places where the child has lived during the last five years, and the names and present addresses of the persons with whom the child has lived during that period. The pleading or affidavit must state whether the party:

(1) has participated, as a party or witness or in any other capacity, in any other proceeding concerning the custody of or visitation with the child and, if so, identify the court, the case number, and the date of the child-custody determination, if any;

(2) knows of any proceeding that could affect the current proceeding, including proceedings for enforcement and proceedings relating to domestic violence, protective orders, termination of parental rights, and adoptions and, if so, identify the court, the case number, and the nature of the proceeding; and

(3) knows the names and addresses of any person not a party to the proceeding who has physical custody of the child or claims rights of legal custody or physical custody of, or visitation with, the child and, if so, the names and addresses of those persons.

(b) If the information required by subsection (a) is not furnished, the court, upon motion of a party or its own motion, may stay the proceeding until the information is furnished.

(c) If the declaration as to any of the items described in subsection (a)(1) through (3) is in the affirmative, the declarant shall give additional information under oath as required by the court. The court may examine the parties under oath as to details of the information furnished and other matters pertinent to the court's jurisdiction and the disposition of the case.

(d) Each party has a continuing duty to inform the court of any proceeding in this or any other State that could affect the current proceeding.

(e) If a party alleges in an affidavit or a pleading under oath that the health, safety, or liberty of a party or child would be jeopardized by disclosure of identifying information, the information must be sealed and may not be disclosed to the other party or the public unless the court orders the disclosure to be made after a hearing in which the court takes into consideration the health, safety, or liberty of the party or child and determines that the disclosure is in the interest of justice.

SECTION 210. APPEARANCE OF PARTIES AND CHILD.

(a) In a child-custody proceeding in this State, the court may order a party to the proceeding who is in this State to appear before the court in person with or without the child. The court may order any person who is in this State and who has physical custody or control of the child to appear in person with the child.

(b) If a party to a child-custody proceeding whose presence is desired by the court is outside this State, the court may order that a notice given pursuant to Section 108 include a statement directing the party to appear in person with or without the child and informing the party that failure to appear may result in a decision adverse to the party.

(c) The court may enter any orders necessary to ensure the safety of the child and of any person ordered to appear under this section.

(d) If a party to a child-custody proceeding who is outside this State is directed to appear under subsection (b) or desires to appear personally before the court with or without the child, the court may require another party to pay reasonable and necessary travel and other expenses of the party so appearing and of the child.

[ARTICLE] 3
ENFORCEMENT

SECTION 301. DEFINITIONS. In this [article]:

(1) "Petitioner" means a person who seeks enforcement of an order for return of a child under the Hague Convention on the Civil Aspects of International Child Abduction or enforcement of a child-custody determination.

(2) "Respondent" means a person against whom a proceeding has been commenced for enforcement of an order for return of a child under the Hague Convention on the Civil Aspects of International Child Abduction or enforcement of a child-custody determination.

SECTION 302. ENFORCEMENT UNDER HAGUE CONVENTION. Under this [article] a court of this State may enforce an order for the return of the child made under the Hague Convention on the Civil Aspects of International Child Abduction as if it were a child-custody determination.

SECTION 303. DUTY TO ENFORCE.

(a) A court of this State shall recognize and enforce a child-custody determination of a court of another State if the latter court exercised jurisdiction in substantial conformity with this [Act] or the determination was made under factual circumstances meeting the jurisdictional standards of this [Act] and the determination has not been modified in accordance with this [Act].

(b) A court of this State may utilize any remedy available under other law of this State to enforce a child-custody determination made by a court of another State. The remedies provided in this [article] are cumulative and do not affect the availability of other remedies to enforce a child-custody determination.

SECTION 304. TEMPORARY VISITATION.

(a) A court of this State which does not have jurisdiction to modify a child-custody determination, may issue a temporary order enforcing:

(1) a visitation schedule made by a court of another State; or

(2) the visitation provisions of a child-custody determination of another State that does not provide for a specific visitation schedule.

(b) If a court of this State makes an order under subsection (a)(2), it shall specify in the order a period that it considers adequate to allow the petitioner to obtain an order from a court having jurisdiction under the criteria specified in [Article] 2. The order remains in effect until an order is obtained from the other court or the period expires.

SECTION 305. REGISTRATION OF CHILD-CUSTODY DETERMINATION.

(a) A child-custody determination issued by a court of another State may be registered in this State, with or without a simultaneous request for enforcement, by sending to [the appropriate court] in this State:

(1) a letter or other document requesting registration;

(2) two copies, including one certified copy, of the determination sought to be registered, and a statement under penalty of perjury that to the best of the knowledge and belief of the person seeking registration the order has not been modified; and

(3) except as otherwise provided in Section 209, the name and address of the person seeking registration and any parent or person acting as a parent who has been awarded custody or visitation in the child-custody determination sought to be registered.

(b) On receipt of the documents required by subsection (a), the registering court shall:

(1) cause the determination to be filed as a foreign judgment, together with one copy of any accompanying documents and information, regardless of their form; and

(2) serve notice upon the persons named pursuant to subsection (a)(3) and provide them with an opportunity to contest the registration in accordance with this section.

(c) The notice required by subsection (b)(2) must state that:

(1) a registered determination is enforceable as of the date of the registration in the same manner as a determination issued by a court of this State;

(2) a hearing to contest the validity of the registered determination must be requested within 20 days after service of notice; and

(3) failure to contest the registration will result in confirmation of the child-custody determination and preclude further contest of that determination with respect to any matter that could have been asserted.

(d) A person seeking to contest the validity of a registered order must request a hearing within 20 days after service of the notice. At that hearing, the court shall confirm the registered order unless the person contesting registration establishes that:

(1) the issuing court did not have jurisdiction under [Article] 2;

(2) the child-custody determination sought to be registered has been vacated, stayed, or modified by a court having jurisdiction to do so under [Article] 2; or

(3) the person contesting registration was entitled to notice, but notice was not given in accordance with the standards of Section 108, in the proceedings before the court that issued the order for which registration is sought.

(e) If a timely request for a hearing to contest the validity of the registration is not made, the registration is confirmed as a matter of law and the person requesting registration and all persons served must be notified of the confirmation.

(f) Confirmation of a registered order, whether by operation of law or after notice and hearing, precludes further contest of the order with respect to any matter that could have been asserted at the time of registration.

SECTION 306. ENFORCEMENT OF REGISTERED DETERMINATION.

(a) A court of this State may grant any relief normally available under the law of this State to enforce a registered child-custody determination made by a court of another State.

(b) A court of this State shall recognize and enforce, but may not modify, except in accordance with [Article] 2, a registered child-custody determination of a court of another State.

SECTION 307. SIMULTANEOUS PROCEEDINGS. If a proceeding for enforcement under this [article] is commenced in a court of this State and the court determines that a proceeding to modify the determination is pending in a court of another State having jurisdiction to modify the determination under [Article] 2, the enforcing court shall immediately communicate with the modifying court. The proceeding for enforcement continues unless the enforcing court, after consultation with the modifying court, stays or dismisses the proceeding.

SECTION 308. EXPEDITED ENFORCEMENT OF CHILD-CUSTODY DETERMINATION.

(a) A petition under this [article] must be verified. Certified copies of all orders sought to be enforced and of any order confirming registration must be attached to the petition. A copy of a certified copy of an order may be attached instead of the original.

(b) A petition for enforcement of a child-custody determination must state:

(1) whether the court that issued the determination identified the jurisdictional basis it relied upon in exercising jurisdiction and, if so, what the basis was;

(2) whether the determination for which enforcement is sought has been vacated, stayed, or modified by a court whose decision must be enforced under this [Act] and, if so, identify the court, the case number, and the nature of the proceeding;

(3) whether any proceeding has been commenced that could affect the current proceeding, including proceedings relating to domestic violence, protective orders, termination of parental rights, and adoptions and, if so, identify the court, the case number, and the nature of the proceeding;

(4) the present physical address of the child and the respondent, if known;

(5) whether relief in addition to the immediate physical custody of the child and attorney's fees is sought, including a request for assistance from [law enforcement officials] and, if so, the relief sought; and

(6) if the child-custody determination has been registered and confirmed under Section 305, the date and place of registration.

(c) Upon the filing of a petition, the court shall issue an order directing the respondent to appear in person with or without the child at a hearing and may enter any order necessary to ensure the safety of the parties and the child. The hearing must be held on the next judicial day after service of the order unless that date is impossible. In that event, the court shall hold the hearing on the first judicial day possible. The court may extend the date of hearing at the request of the petitioner.

(d) An order issued under subsection (c) must state the time and place of the hearing and advise the respondent that at the hearing the court will order that the petitioner may take immediate physical custody of the child and the payment of fees, costs, and expenses under Section 312, and may schedule a hearing to determine whether further relief is appropriate, unless the respondent appears and establishes that:

(1) the child-custody determination has not been registered and confirmed under Section 305 and that:

(A) the issuing court did not have jurisdiction under [Article] 2;

(B) the child-custody determination for which enforcement is sought has been vacated, stayed, or modified by a court having jurisdiction to do so under [Article] 2;

(C) the respondent was entitled to notice, but notice was not given in accordance with the standards of Section 108, in the proceedings before the court that issued the order for which enforcement is sought; or

(2) the child-custody determination for which enforcement is sought was registered and confirmed under Section 304, but has been vacated, stayed, or modified by a court of a State having jurisdiction to do so under [Article] 2.

SECTION 309. SERVICE OF PETITION AND ORDER. Except as otherwise provided in Section 311, the petition and order must be served, by any method authorized [by the law of this State], upon respondent and any person who has physical custody of the child.

SECTION 310. HEARING AND ORDER.

(a) Unless the court issues a temporary emergency order pursuant to Section 204, upon a finding that a petitioner is entitled to immediate physical custody of the child, the court shall order that the petitioner may take immediate physical custody of the child unless the respondent establishes that:

(1) the child-custody determination has not been registered and confirmed under Section 305 and that:

(A) the issuing court did not have jurisdiction under [Article] 2;

(B) the child-custody determination for which enforcement is sought has been vacated, stayed, or modified by a court of a State having jurisdiction to do so under [Article] 2; or

(C) the respondent was entitled to notice, but notice was not given in accordance with the standards of Section 108, in the proceedings before the court that issued the order for which enforcement is sought; or

(2) the child-custody determination for which enforcement is sought was registered and confirmed under Section 305 but has been vacated, stayed, or modified by a court of a State having jurisdiction to do so under [Article] 2.

(b) The court shall award the fees, costs, and expenses authorized under Section 312 and may grant additional relief, including a request for the assistance of [law enforcement officials], and set a further hearing to determine whether additional relief is appropriate.

(c) If a party called to testify refuses to answer on the ground that the testimony may be self-incriminating, the court may draw an adverse inference from the refusal.

(d) A privilege against disclosure of communications between spouses and a defense of immunity based on the relationship of husband and wife or parent and child may not be invoked in a proceeding under this [article].

SECTION 311. WARRANT TO TAKE PHYSICAL CUSTODY OF CHILD.

(a) Upon the filing of a petition seeking enforcement of a child-custody determination, the petitioner may file a verified application for the issuance of a warrant to take physical custody of the child if the child is immediately likely to suffer serious physical harm or be removed from this State.

(b) If the court, upon the testimony of the petitioner or other witness, finds that the child is imminently likely to suffer serious physical harm or be removed from this State, it may issue a warrant to take physical custody of the child. The petition must be heard on the next judicial day after the warrant is executed unless that date is impossible. In that event, the court shall hold the hearing on the first judicial day possible. The application for the warrant must include the statements required by Section 308(b).

(c) A warrant to take physical custody of a child must:

(1) recite the facts upon which a conclusion of imminent serious physical harm or removal from the jurisdiction is based;

(2) direct law enforcement officers to take physical custody of the child immediately; and

(3) provide for the placement of the child pending final relief.

(d) The respondent must be served with the petition, warrant, and order immediately after the child is taken into physical custody.

(e) A warrant to take physical custody of a child is enforceable throughout this State. If the court finds on the basis of the testimony of the petitioner or other witness that a less intrusive remedy is not effective, it may authorize law enforcement officers to enter private property to take physical custody of the child. If required by exigent circumstances of the case, the court may authorize law enforcement officers to make a forcible entry at any hour.

(f) The court may impose conditions upon placement of a child to ensure the appearance of the child and the child's custodian.

SECTION 312. COSTS, FEES, AND EXPENSES.

(a) The court shall award the prevailing party, including a State, necessary and reasonable expenses incurred by or on behalf of the party, including costs, communication expenses, attorney's fees, investigative fees, expenses for witnesses, travel expenses, and child care during the course of the proceedings, unless the party from whom fees or expenses are sought establishes that the award would be clearly inappropriate.

(b) The court may not assess fees, costs, or expenses against a State unless authorized by law other than this [Act].

SECTION 313. RECOGNITION AND ENFORCEMENT. A court of this State shall accord full faith and credit to an order issued by another State and consistent with this [Act] which enforces a child-custody determination by a court of another State unless the order has been vacated, stayed, or modified by a court having jurisdiction to do so under [Article] 2.

SECTION 314. APPEALS. An appeal may be taken from a final order in a proceeding under this [article] in accordance with [expedited appellate procedures in other civil cases]. Unless the court enters a temporary emergency order under Section 204, the enforcing court may not stay an order enforcing a child-custody determination pending appeal.

SECTION 315. ROLE OF [PROSECUTOR OR PUBLIC OFFICIAL].

(a) In a case arising under this [Act] or involving the Hague Convention on the Civil Aspects of International Child Abduction, the [prosecutor or other appropriate public official] may take any lawful action, including resort to a proceeding under this [article] or any other available civil proceeding to locate a child, obtain the return of a child, or enforce a child-custody determination if there is:

(1) an existing child-custody determination;

(2) a request to do so from a court in a pending child-custody proceeding;

(3) a reasonable belief that a criminal statute has been violated; or

(4) a reasonable belief that the child has been wrongfully removed or retained in violation of the Hague Convention on the Civil Aspects of International Child Abduction.

(b) A [prosecutor or appropriate public official] acting under this section acts on behalf of the court and may not represent any party.

SECTION 316. ROLE OF [LAW ENFORCEMENT]. At the request of a [prosecutor or other appropriate public official] acting under Section 315, a [law enforcement officer] may take any lawful action reasonably necessary to locate a child or a party and assist [a prosecutor or appropriate public official] with responsibilities under Section 315.

Comment

SECTION 317. COSTS AND EXPENSES. If the respondent is not the prevailing party, the court may assess against the respondent all direct expenses and costs incurred by the [prosecutor or other appropriate public official] and [law enforcement officers] under Section 315 or 316.

Comment

One of the major problems of utilizing public officials to locate children and enforce custody and visitation determinations is cost. This section authorizes the prosecutor and law enforcement to recover costs against the non-prevailing party. The use of the term "direct" indicates that overhead is not a recoverable cost. This section cannot be used to recover the value of the time spent by the public authorities' attorneys.

[ARTICLE] 4
MISCELLANEOUS PROVISIONS

SECTION 401. APPLICATION AND CONSTRUCTION. In applying and construing this Uniform Act, consideration must be given to the need to promote uniformity of the law with respect to its subject matter among States that enact it.

SECTION 402. SEVERABILITY CLAUSE. If any provision of this [Act] or its application to any person or circumstance is held invalid, the invalidity does not affect other provisions or applications of this [Act] which can be given effect without the invalid provision or application, and to this end the provisions of this [Act] are severable.

SECTION 405. TRANSITIONAL PROVISION. A motion or other request for relief made in a child-custody proceeding or to enforce a child-custody determination which was commenced before the effective date of this [Act] is governed by the law in effect at the time the motion or other request was made.

Appendix G

Uniform Interstate Family Support Act

ARTICLE 1. GENERAL PROVISIONS

SECTION 101. DEFINITIONS. In this [Act]:

(1) "Child" means an individual, whether over or under the age of majority, who is or is alleged to be owed a duty of support by the individual's parent or who is or is alleged to be the beneficiary of a support order directed to the parent.

(2) "Child-support order" means a support order for a child, including a child who has attained the age of majority under the law of the issuing State.

(3) "Duty of support" means an obligation imposed or imposable by law to provide support for a child, spouse, or former spouse, including an unsatisfied obligation to provide support.

(4) "Home State" means the State in which a child lived with a parent or a person acting as parent for at least six consecutive months immediately preceding the time of filing of a [petition] or comparable pleading for support and, if a child is less than six months old, the State in which the child lived from birth with any of them. A period of temporary absence of any of them is counted as part of the six-month or other period.

(5) "Income" includes earnings or other periodic entitlements to money from any source and any other property subject to withholding for support under the law of this State.

(6) "Income-withholding order" means an order or other legal process directed to an obligor's employer [or other debtor], as defined by [the income-withholding law of this State], to withhold support from the income of the obligor.

(7) "Initiating State" means a State from which a proceeding is forwarded or in which a proceeding is filed for forwarding to a responding State under this [Act] or a law or procedure substantially similar to this [Act], the Uniform Reciprocal Enforcement of Support Act, or the Revised Uniform Reciprocal Enforcement of Support Act.

(8) "Initiating tribunal" means the authorized tribunal in an initiating State.

(9) "Issuing State" means the State in which a tribunal issues a support order or renders a judgment determining parentage.

(10) "Issuing tribunal" means the tribunal that issues a support order or renders a judgment determining parentage.

(11) "Law" includes decisional and statutory law and rules and regulations having the force of law.

(12) "Obligee" means:

(i) an individual to whom a duty of support is or is alleged to be owed or in whose favor a support order has been issued or a judgment determining parentage has been rendered;

(ii) a State or political subdivision to which the rights under a duty of support or support order have been assigned or which has independent claims based on financial assistance provided to an individual obligee; or

(iii) an individual seeking a judgment determining parentage of the individual's child.

(13) "Obligor" means an individual, or the estate of a decedent:

(i) who owes or is alleged to owe a duty of support;

(ii) who is alleged but has not been adjudicated to be a parent of a child; or

(iii) who is liable under a support order.

(14) "Register" means to [record; file] a support order or judgment determining parentage in the [appropriate location for the recording or filing of foreign judgments generally or foreign support orders specifically].

(15) "Registering tribunal" means a tribunal in which a support order is registered.

(16) "Responding State" means a State in which a proceeding is filed or to which a proceeding is forwarded for filing from an initiating State under this [Act] or a law or procedure substantially similar to this [Act], the Uniform Reciprocal Enforcement of Support Act, or the Revised Uniform Reciprocal Enforcement of Support Act.

(17) "Responding tribunal" means the authorized tribunal in a responding State.

(18) "Spousal-support order" means a support order for a spouse or former spouse of the obligor.

(19) "State" means a State of the United States, the District of Columbia, Puerto Rico, the United States Virgin Islands, or any territory or insular possession subject to the jurisdiction of the United States. The term includes:

(i) an Indian tribe; and

(ii) a foreign jurisdiction that has enacted a law or established procedures for issuance and enforcement of support orders which are substantially similar to the procedures under this [Act], the Uniform Reciprocal Enforcement of Support Act, or the Revised Uniform Reciprocal Enforcement of Support Act.

(20) "Support enforcement agency" means a public official or agency authorized to seek:

(i) enforcement of support orders or laws relating to the duty of support;

(ii) establishment or modification of child support;

(iii) determination of parentage; or

(iv) to locate obligors or their assets.

(21) "Support order" means a judgment, decree, or order, whether temporary, final, or subject to modification, for the benefit of a child, a spouse, or a former spouse, which provides for monetary support, health care, arrearages, or reimbursement, and may include related costs and fees, interest, income withholding, attorney's fees, and other relief.

(22) "Tribunal" means a court, administrative agency, or quasi-judicial entity authorized to establish, enforce, or modify support orders or to determine parentage.

SECTION 102. TRIBUNAL OF STATE. The [court, administrative agency, quasi-judicial entity, or combination] [is the tribunal] [are the tribunals] of this State.

SECTION 103. REMEDIES CUMULATIVE. Remedies provided by this [Act] are cumulative and do not affect the availability of remedies under other law.

ARTICLE 2. JURISDICTION

Part 1. Extended Personal Jurisdiction

SECTION 201. BASES FOR JURISDICTION OVER NONRESIDENT. In a proceeding to establish, enforce, or modify a support order or to determine parentage, a tribunal of this State may exercise personal jurisdiction over a nonresident individual [or the individual's guardian or conservator] if:

(1) the individual is personally served with [citation, summons, notice] within this State;

(2) the individual submits to the jurisdiction of this State by consent, by entering a general appearance, or by filing a responsive document having the effect of waiving any contest to personal jurisdiction;

(3) the individual resided with the child in this State;

(4) the individual resided in this State and provided prenatal expenses or support for the child;

(5) the child resides in this State as a result of the acts or directives of the individual;

(6) the individual engaged in sexual intercourse in this State and the child may have been conceived by that act of intercourse;

[(7) the individual asserted parentage in the [putative father registry] maintained in this State by the [appropriate agency];] or

(8) there is any other basis consistent with the constitutions of this State and the United States for the exercise of personal jurisdiction.

SECTION 202. PROCEDURE WHEN EXERCISING JURISDICTION OVER NONRESIDENT. A tribunal of this State exercising personal jurisdiction over a nonresident under Section 201 may apply Section 316 (Special Rules of Evidence and Procedure) to receive evidence from another State, and Section 318 (Assistance with Discovery) to obtain discovery through a tribunal of another State. In all other respects, Articles 3 through 7 do not apply and the tribunal shall apply the procedural and substantive law of this State, including the rules on choice of law other than those established by this [Act].

Part 2. Proceedings Involving Two or More States

SECTION 203. INITIATING AND RESPONDING TRIBUNAL OF STATE. Under this [Act], a tribunal of this State may serve as an initiating tribunal to forward proceedings to another State and as a responding tribunal for proceedings initiated in another State.

SECTION 204. SIMULTANEOUS PROCEEDINGS IN ANOTHER STATE.

(a) A tribunal of this State may exercise jurisdiction to establish a support order if the [petition] or comparable pleading is filed after a pleading is filed in another State only if:

(1) the [petition] or comparable pleading in this State is filed before the expiration of the time allowed in the other State for filing a responsive pleading challenging the exercise of jurisdiction by the other State;

(2) the contesting party timely challenges the exercise of jurisdiction in the other State; and

(3) if relevant, this State is the home State of the child.

(b) A tribunal of this State may not exercise jurisdiction to establish a support order if the [petition] or comparable pleading is filed before a [petition] or comparable pleading is filed in another State if:

(1) the [petition] or comparable pleading in the other State is filed before the expiration of the time allowed in this State for filing a responsive pleading challenging the exercise of jurisdiction by this State;

(2) the contesting party timely challenges the exercise of jurisdiction in this State; and

(3) if relevant, the other State is the home State of the child.

SECTION 205. CONTINUING, EXCLUSIVE JURISDICTION.

(a) A tribunal of this State issuing a support order consistent with the law of this State has continuing, exclusive jurisdiction over a child-support order:

(1) as long as this State remains the residence of the obligor, the individual obligee, or the child for whose benefit the support order is issued; or

(2) until all of the parties who are individuals have filed written consents with the tribunal of this State for a tribunal of another State to modify the order and assume continuing, exclusive jurisdiction.

(b) A tribunal of this State issuing a child-support order consistent with the law of this State may not exercise its continuing jurisdiction to modify the order if the order has been modified by a tribunal of another State pursuant to this [Act] or a law substantially similar to this [Act].

(c) If a child-support order of this State is modified by a tribunal of another State pursuant to this [Act] or a law substantially similar to this [Act], a tribunal of this State loses its continuing, exclusive jurisdiction with regard to prospective enforcement of the order issued in this State, and may only:

(1) enforce the order that was modified as to amounts accruing before the modification;

(2) enforce nonmodifiable aspects of that order; and

(3) provide other appropriate relief for violations of that order which occurred before the effective date of the modification.

(d) A tribunal of this State shall recognize the continuing, exclusive jurisdiction of a tribunal of another State which has issued a child-support order pursuant to this [Act] or a law substantially similar to this [Act].

(e) A temporary support order issued ex parte or pending resolution of a jurisdictional conflict does not create continuing, exclusive jurisdiction in the issuing tribunal.

(f) A tribunal of this State issuing a support order consistent with the law of this State has continuing, exclusive jurisdiction over a spousal-support order throughout the existence of the support obligation. A tribunal of this State may not modify a spousal-support order issued by a tribunal of another State having continuing, exclusive jurisdiction over that order under the law of that State.

SECTION 206. ENFORCEMENT AND MODIFICATION OF SUPPORT ORDER BY TRIBUNAL HAVING CONTINUING JURISDICTION.

(a) A tribunal of this State may serve as an initiating tribunal to request a tribunal of another State to enforce or modify a support order issued in that State.

(b) A tribunal of this State having continuing, exclusive jurisdiction over a support order may act as a responding tribunal to enforce or modify the order. If a party subject to the continuing, exclusive jurisdiction of the tribunal no longer resides in the issuing State, in subsequent proceedings the tribunal may apply Section 316 (Special Rules of Evidence and Procedure) to receive evidence from another State and Section 318 (Assistance with Discovery) to obtain discovery through a tribunal of another State.

(c) A tribunal of this State which lacks continuing, exclusive jurisdiction over a spousal-support order may not serve as a responding tribunal to modify a spousal-support order of another State.

Part 3. Reconciliation of Multiple Orders

SECTION 207. RECOGNITION OF CONTROLLING CHILD-SUPPORT ORDER.

(a) If a proceeding is brought under this [Act] and only one tribunal has issued a child-support order, the order of that tribunal controls and must be so recognized.

(b) If a proceeding is brought under this [Act], and two or more child-support orders have been issued by tribunals of this State or another State with regard to the same obligor and child, a tribunal of this State shall apply the following rules in determining which order to recognize for purposes of continuing, exclusive jurisdiction:

(1) If only one of the tribunals would have continuing, exclusive jurisdiction under this [Act], the order of that tribunal controls and must be so recognized.

(2) If more than one of the tribunals would have continuing, exclusive jurisdiction under this [Act], an order issued by a tribunal in the current home State of the child controls and must be so recognized, but if an order has not been issued in the current home State of the child, the order most recently issued controls and must be so recognized.

(3) If none of the tribunals would have continuing, exclusive jurisdiction under this [Act], the tribunal of this State having jurisdiction over the parties shall issue a child-support order, which controls and must be so recognized.

(c) If two or more child-support orders have been issued for the same obligor and child and if the obligor or the individual obligee resides in this State, a party may request a tribunal of this State to determine which order controls and must be so recognized under subsection (b). The request must be accompanied by a certified copy of every support order in effect. The requesting party shall give notice of the request to each party whose rights may be affected by the determination.

(d) The tribunal that issued the controlling order under subsection (a), (b), or (c) is the tribunal that has continuing, exclusive jurisdiction under Section 205.

(e) A tribunal of this State which determines by order the identity of the controlling order under subsection (b)(1) or (2) or which issues a new controlling order under subsection (b)(3) shall state in that order the basis upon which the tribunal made its determination.

(f) Within [30] days after issuance of an order determining the identity of the controlling order, the party obtaining the order shall file a certified copy of it with each tribunal that issued or registered an earlier order of child support. A party who obtains the order and fails to file a certified copy is subject to appropriate sanctions by a tribunal in which the issue of failure to file arises. The failure to file does not affect the validity or enforceability of the controlling order.

SECTION 208. MULTIPLE CHILD-SUPPORT ORDERS FOR TWO OR MORE OBLIGEES. In responding to multiple registrations or [petitions] for enforcement of two or more child-support orders in effect at the same time with regard to the same obligor and different individual obligees, at least one of which was issued by a tribunal of another State, a tribunal of this State shall enforce those orders in the same manner as if the multiple orders had been issued by a tribunal of this State.

SECTION 209. CREDIT FOR PAYMENTS. Amounts collected and credited for a particular period pursuant to a support order issued by a tribunal of another State must be credited against the amounts accruing or accrued for the same period under a support order issued by the tribunal of this State.

ARTICLE 3. CIVIL PROVISIONS OF GENERAL APPLICATION

SECTION 301. PROCEEDINGS UNDER [ACT].

(a) Except as otherwise provided in this [Act], this article applies to all proceedings under this [Act].

(b) This [Act] provides for the following proceedings:

(1) establishment of an order for spousal support or child support pursuant to Article 4;

(2) enforcement of a support order and income-withholding order of another State without registration pursuant to Article 5;

(3) registration of an order for spousal support or child support of another State for enforcement pursuant to Article 6;

(4) modification of an order for child support or spousal support issued by a tribunal of this State pursuant to Article 2, Part 2;

(5) registration of an order for child support of another State for modification pursuant to Article 6;

(6) determination of parentage pursuant to Article 7; and

(7) assertion of jurisdiction over nonresidents pursuant to Article 2, Part 1.

(c) An individual [petitioner] or a support enforcement agency may commence a proceeding authorized under this [Act] by filing a [petition] in an initiating tribunal for forwarding to a responding tribunal or by filing a [petition] or a comparable pleading directly in a tribunal of another State which has or can obtain personal jurisdiction over the [respondent].

SECTION 302. ACTION BY MINOR PARENT. A minor parent, or a guardian or other legal representative of a minor parent, may maintain a proceeding on behalf of or for the benefit of the minor's child.

SECTION 303. APPLICATION OF LAW OF STATE. Except as otherwise provided by this [Act], a responding tribunal of this State:

(1) shall apply the procedural and substantive law, including the rules on choice of law, generally applicable to similar proceedings originating in this State and may exercise all powers and provide all remedies available in those proceedings; and

(2) shall determine the duty of support and the amount payable in accordance with the law and support guidelines of this State.

SECTION 304. DUTIES OF INITIATING TRIBUNAL.

(a) Upon the filing of a [petition] authorized by this [Act], an initiating tribunal of this State shall forward three copies of the [petition] and its accompanying documents:

(1) to the responding tribunal or appropriate support enforcement agency in the responding State; or

(2) if the identity of the responding tribunal is unknown, to the state information agency of the responding State with a request that they be forwarded to the appropriate tribunal and that receipt be acknowledged.

(b) If a responding State has not enacted this [Act] or a law or procedure substantially similar to this [Act], a tribunal of this State may issue a certificate or other document and make findings required by the law of the responding State. If the responding State is a foreign jurisdiction, the tribunal may specify the amount of support sought and provide other documents necessary to satisfy the requirements of the responding State.

SECTION 305. DUTIES AND POWERS OF RESPONDING TRIBUNAL.

(a) When a responding tribunal of this State receives a [petition] or comparable pleading from an initiating tribunal or directly pursuant to Section 301(c) (Proceedings Under this [Act]), it shall cause the [petition] or pleading to be filed and notify the [petitioner] where and when it was filed.

(b) A responding tribunal of this State, to the extent otherwise authorized by law, may do one or more of the following:

(1) issue or enforce a support order, modify a child-support order, or render a judgment to determine parentage;

(2) order an obligor to comply with a support order, specifying the amount and the manner of compliance;

(3) order income withholding;

(4) determine the amount of any arrearages, and specify a method of payment;

(5) enforce orders by civil or criminal contempt, or both;

(6) set aside property for satisfaction of the support order;

(7) place liens and order execution on the obligor's property;

(8) order an obligor to keep the tribunal informed of the obligor's current residential address, telephone number, employer, address of employment, and telephone number at the place of employment;

(9) issue a [bench warrant; capias] for an obligor who has failed after proper notice to appear at a hearing ordered by the tribunal and enter the [bench warrant; capias] in any local and state computer systems for criminal warrants;

(10) order the obligor to seek appropriate employment by specified methods;

(11) award reasonable attorney's fees and other fees and costs; and

(12) grant any other available remedy.

(c) A responding tribunal of this State shall include in a support order issued under this [Act], or in the documents accompanying the order, the calculations on which the support order is based.

(d) A responding tribunal of this State may not condition the payment of a support order issued under this [Act] upon compliance by a party with provisions for visitation.

(e) If a responding tribunal of this State issues an order under this [Act], the tribunal shall send a copy of the order to the [petitioner] and the [respondent] and to the initiating tribunal, if any.

SECTION 306. INAPPROPRIATE TRIBUNAL. If a [petition] or comparable pleading is received by an inappropriate tribunal of this State, it shall forward the pleading and accompanying documents to an appropriate tribunal in this State or another State and notify the [petitioner] where and when the pleading was sent.

SECTION 307. DUTIES OF SUPPORT ENFORCEMENT AGENCY.

(a) A support enforcement agency of this State, upon request, shall provide services to a [petitioner] in a proceeding under this [Act].

(b) A support enforcement agency that is providing services to the [petitioner] as appropriate shall:

(1) take all steps necessary to enable an appropriate tribunal in this State or another State to obtain jurisdiction over the [respondent];

(2) request an appropriate tribunal to set a date, time, and place for a hearing;

(3) make a reasonable effort to obtain all relevant information, including information as to income and property of the parties;

(4) within [two] days, exclusive of Saturdays, Sundays, and legal holidays, after receipt of a written notice from an initiating, responding, or registering tribunal, send a copy of the notice to the [petitioner];

(5) within [two] days, exclusive of Saturdays, Sundays, and legal holidays, after receipt of a written communication from the [respondent] or the [respondent's] attorney, send a copy of the communication to the [petitioner]; and

(6) notify the [petitioner] if jurisdiction over the [respondent] cannot be obtained.

(c) This [Act] does not create or negate a relationship of attorney and client or other fiduciary relationship between a support enforcement agency or the attorney for the agency and the individual being assisted by the agency.

SECTION 308. DUTY OF [ATTORNEY GENERAL]. If the [Attorney General] determines that the support enforcement agency is neglecting or refusing to provide services to an individual, the [Attorney General] may order the agency to perform its duties under this [Act] or may provide those services directly to the individual.

SECTION 309. PRIVATE COUNSEL. An individual may employ private counsel to represent the individual in proceedings authorized by this [Act].

SECTION 310. DUTIES OF [STATE INFORMATION AGENCY].

(a) The [Attorney General's Office, State Attorney's Office, State Central Registry or other information agency] is the state information agency under this [Act].

(b) The state information agency shall:

(1) compile and maintain a current list, including addresses, of the tribunals in this State which have jurisdiction under this [Act] and any support enforcement agencies in this State and transmit a copy to the state information agency of every other State;

(2) maintain a register of tribunals and support enforcement agencies received from other States;

(3) forward to the appropriate tribunal in the place in this State in which the individual obligee or the obligor resides, or in which the obligor's property is believed to be located, all documents concerning a proceeding under this [Act] received from an initiating tribunal or the state information agency of the initiating State; and

(4) obtain information concerning the location of the obligor and the obligor's property within this State not exempt from execution, by such means as postal verification and federal or state locator services, examination of telephone directories, requests for the obligor's address from employers, and examination of governmental records, including, to the extent not prohibited by other law, those relating to real property, vital statistics, law enforcement, taxation, motor vehicles, driver's licenses, and social security.

SECTION 311. PLEADINGS AND ACCOMPANYING DOCUMENTS.

(a) A [petitioner] seeking to establish or modify a support order or to determine parentage in a proceeding under this [Act] must verify the [petition]. Unless otherwise ordered under Section 312 (Nondisclosure of Information in Exceptional Circumstances), the [petition] or accompanying documents must provide, so far as known, the name, residential address, and social security numbers of the obligor and the obligee, and the name, sex, residential address, social security number, and date of birth of each child for whom support is sought. The [petition] must be accompanied by a certified copy of any support order in effect. The [petition] may include any other information that may assist in locating or identifying the [respondent].

(b) The [petition] must specify the relief sought. The [petition] and accompanying documents must conform substantially with the requirements imposed by the forms mandated by federal law for use in cases filed by a support enforcement agency.

SECTION 312. NONDISCLOSURE OF INFORMATION IN EXCEPTIONAL CIRCUMSTANCES. Upon a finding, which may be made ex parte, that the health, safety, or liberty of a party or child would be unreasonably put at risk by the disclosure of identifying information, or if an existing order so provides, a tribunal shall order that the address of the child or party or other identifying information not be disclosed in a pleading or other document filed in a proceeding under this [Act].

SECTION 313. COSTS AND FEES.

(a) The [petitioner] may not be required to pay a filing fee or other costs.

(b) If an obligee prevails, a responding tribunal may assess against an obligor filing fees, reasonable attorney's fees, other costs, and necessary travel and other reasonable expenses incurred by the obligee and the obligee's witnesses. The tribunal may not assess fees, costs, or expenses against the obligee or the support enforcement agency of either the initiating or the responding State, except as provided by other law. Attorney's fees may be taxed as costs, and may be ordered paid directly to the attorney, who may enforce the order in the attorney's own name. Payment of support owed to the obligee has priority over fees, costs and expenses.

(c) The tribunal shall order the payment of costs and reasonable attorney's fees if it determines that a hearing was requested primarily for delay. In a proceeding under Article 6 (Enforcement and Modification of Support Order After Registration), a hearing is presumed to have been requested primarily for delay if a registered support order is confirmed or enforced without change.

SECTION 314. LIMITED IMMUNITY OF [PETITIONER].

(a) Participation by a [petitioner] in a proceeding before a responding tribunal, whether in person, by private attorney, or through services provided by the support enforcement agency, does not confer personal jurisdiction over the [petitioner] in another proceeding.

(b) A [petitioner] is not amenable to service of civil process while physically present in this State to participate in a proceeding under this [Act].

(c) The immunity granted by this section does not extend to civil litigation based on acts unrelated to a proceeding under this [Act] committed by a party while present in this State to participate in the proceeding.

SECTION 315. NONPARENTAGE AS DEFENSE. A party whose parentage of a child has been previously determined by or pursuant to law may not plead nonparentage as a defense to a proceeding under this [Act].

SECTION 316. SPECIAL RULES OF EVIDENCE AND PROCEDURE.

(a) The physical presence of the [petitioner] in a responding tribunal of this State is not required for the establishment, enforcement, or modification of a support order or the rendition of a judgment determining parentage.

(b) A verified [petition], affidavit, document substantially complying with federally mandated forms, and a document incorporated by reference in any of them, not excluded under the hearsay rule if given in person, is admissible in evidence if given under oath by a party or witness residing in another State.

(c) A copy of the record of child-support payments certified as a true copy of the original by the custodian of the record may be forwarded to a responding tribunal. The copy is evidence of facts asserted in it, and is admissible to show whether payments were made.

(d) Copies of bills for testing for parentage, and for prenatal and postnatal health care of the mother and child, furnished to the adverse party at least [ten] days before trial, are admissible in evidence to prove the amount of the charges billed and that the charges were reasonable, necessary, and customary.

(e) Documentary evidence transmitted from another State to a tribunal of this State by telephone, telecopier, or other means that do not provide an original writing may not be excluded from evidence on an objection based on the means of transmission.

(f) In a proceeding under this [Act], a tribunal of this State may permit a party or witness residing in another State to be deposed or to testify by telephone, audiovisual means, or other electronic means at a designated tribunal or other location in that State. A tribunal of this State shall cooperate with tribunals of other States in designating an appropriate location for the deposition or testimony.

(g) If a party called to testify at a civil hearing refuses to answer on the ground that the testimony may be self-incriminating, the trier of fact may draw an adverse inference from the refusal.

(h) A privilege against disclosure of communications between spouses does not apply in a proceeding under this [Act].

(i) The defense of immunity based on the relationship of husband and wife or parent and child does not apply in a proceeding under this [Act].

SECTION 317. COMMUNICATIONS BETWEEN TRIBUNALS. A tribunal of this State may communicate with a tribunal of another State in writing, or by telephone or other means, to obtain information concerning the laws of that State, the legal effect of a judgment, decree, or order of that tribunal, and the status of a proceeding in the other State. A tribunal of this State may furnish similar information by similar means to a tribunal of another State.

SECTION 318. ASSISTANCE WITH DISCOVERY. A tribunal of this State may:

(1) request a tribunal of another State to assist in obtaining discovery; and

(2) upon request, compel a person over whom it has jurisdiction to respond to a discovery order issued by a tribunal of another State.

SECTION 319. RECEIPT AND DISBURSEMENT OF PAYMENTS. A support enforcement agency or tribunal of this State shall disburse promptly any amounts received pursuant to a support order, as directed by the order. The agency or tribunal shall furnish to a requesting party or tribunal of another State a certified statement by the custodian of the record of the amounts and dates of all payments received.

ARTICLE 4. ESTABLISHMENT OF SUPPORT ORDER

SECTION 401. [PETITION] TO ESTABLISH SUPPORT ORDER.

(a) If a support order entitled to recognition under this [Act] has not been issued, a responding tribunal of this State may issue a support order if:

(1) the individual seeking the order resides in another State; or

(2) the support enforcement agency seeking the order is located in another State.

(b) The tribunal may issue a temporary child-support order if:

(1) the [respondent] has signed a verified statement acknowledging parentage;

(2) the [respondent] has been determined by or pursuant to law to be the parent; or

(3) there is other clear and convincing evidence that the [respondent] is the child's parent.

(c) Upon finding, after notice and opportunity to be heard, that an obligor owes a duty of support, the tribunal shall issue a support order directed to the obligor and may issue other orders pursuant to Section 305 (Duties and Powers of Responding Tribunal).

ARTICLE 5. ENFORCEMENT OF ORDER OF ANOTHER STATE WITHOUT REGISTRATION

SECTION 501. EMPLOYER'S RECEIPT OF INCOME-WITHHOLDING ORDER OF ANOTHER STATE. An income-withholding order issued in another State may be sent to the person or entity defined as the obligor's employer under [the income-withholding law of this State] without first filing a [petition] or comparable pleading or registering the order with a tribunal of this State.

SECTION 502. EMPLOYER'S COMPLIANCE WITH INCOME-WITHHOLDING ORDER OF ANOTHER STATE.

(a) Upon receipt of an income-withholding order, the obligor's employer shall immediately provide a copy of the order to the obligor.

(b) The employer shall treat an income-withholding order issued in another State which appears regular on its face as if it had been issued by a tribunal of this State.

(c) Except as otherwise provided in subsection (d) and Section 503, the employer shall withhold and distribute the funds as directed in the withholding order by complying with terms of the order which specify:

(1) the duration and amount of periodic payments of current child-support, stated as a sum certain;

(2) the person or agency designated to receive payments and the address to which the payments are to be forwarded;

(3) medical support, whether in the form of periodic cash payment, stated as a sum certain, or ordering the obligor to provide health insurance coverage for the child under a policy available through the obligor's employment;

(4) the amount of periodic payments of fees and costs for a support enforcement agency, the issuing tribunal, and the obligee's attorney, stated as sums certain; and

(5) the amount of periodic payments of arrearages and interest on arrearages, stated as sums certain.

(d) An employer shall comply with the law of the State of the obligor's principal place of employment for withholding from income with respect to:

(1) the employer's fee for processing an income-withholding order;

(2) the maximum amount permitted to be withheld from the obligor's income; and

(3) the times within which the employer must implement the withholding order and forward the child support payment.

SECTION 503. COMPLIANCE WITH MULTIPLE INCOME-WITHHOLDING ORDERS. If an obligor's employer receives multiple income-withholding orders with respect to the earnings of the same obligor, the employer satisfies the terms of the multiple orders if the employer complies with the law of the State of the obligor's principal place of employment to establish the priorities for withholding and allocating income withheld for multiple child support obligees.

SECTION 504. IMMUNITY FROM CIVIL LIABILITY. An employer who complies with an income-withholding order issued in another State in accordance with this article is not subject to civil liability to an individual or agency with regard to the employer's withholding of child support from the obligor's income.

SECTION 505. PENALTIES FOR NONCOMPLIANCE. An employer who willfully fails to comply with an income-withholding order issued by another State and received for enforcement is subject to the same penalties that may be imposed for noncompliance with an order issued by a tribunal of this State.

SECTION 506. CONTEST BY OBLIGOR.

(a) An obligor may contest the validity or enforcement of an income-withholding order issued in another State and received directly by an employer in this State in the same manner as if the order had been issued by a tribunal of this State. Section 604 (Choice of Law) applies to the contest.

(b) The obligor shall give notice of the contest to:

(1) a support enforcement agency providing services to the obligee;

(2) each employer that has directly received an income-withholding order; and

(3) the person or agency designated to receive payments in the income-withholding order or if no person or agency is designated, to the obligee.

SECTION 507. ADMINISTRATIVE ENFORCEMENT OF ORDERS.

(a) A party seeking to enforce a support order or an income-withholding order, or both, issued by a tribunal of another State may send the documents required for registering the order to a support enforcement agency of this State.

(b) Upon receipt of the documents, the support enforcement agency, without initially seeking to register the order, shall consider and, if appropriate, use any administrative procedure authorized by the law of this State to enforce a support order or an income-withholding order, or both. If the obligor does not contest administrative enforcement, the order need not be registered. If the obligor contests the validity or administrative enforcement of the order, the support enforcement agency shall register the order pursuant to this [Act].

ARTICLE 6. ENFORCEMENT AND MODIFICATION OF SUPPORT ORDER AFTER REGISTRATION

Part 1. Registration and Enforcement of Support Order

SECTION 601. REGISTRATION OF ORDER FOR ENFORCEMENT. A support order or an income-withholding order issued by a tribunal of another State may be registered in this State for enforcement.

SECTION 602. PROCEDURE TO REGISTER ORDER FOR ENFORCEMENT.

(a) A support order or income-withholding order of another State may be registered in this State by sending the following documents and information to the [appropriate tribunal] in this State:

(1) a letter of transmittal to the tribunal requesting registration and enforcement;

(2) two copies, including one certified copy, of all orders to be registered, including any modification of an order;

(3) a sworn statement by the party seeking registration or a certified statement by the custodian of the records showing the amount of any arrearage;

(4) the name of the obligor and, if known:

(i) the obligor's address and social security number;

(ii) the name and address of the obligor's employer and any other source of income of the obligor; and

(iii) a description and the location of property of the obligor in this State not exempt from execution; and

(5) the name and address of the obligee and, if applicable, the agency or person to whom support payments are to be remitted.

(b) On receipt of a request for registration, the registering tribunal shall cause the order to be filed as a foreign judgment, together with one copy of the documents and information, regardless of their form.

(c) A [petition] or comparable pleading seeking a remedy that must be affirmatively sought under other law of this State may be filed at the same time as the request for registration or later. The pleading must specify the grounds for the remedy sought.

SECTION 603. EFFECT OF REGISTRATION FOR ENFORCEMENT.

(a) A support order or income-withholding order issued in another State is registered when the order is filed in the registering tribunal of this State.

(b) A registered order issued in another State is enforceable in the same manner and is subject to the same procedures as an order issued by a tribunal of this State.

(c) Except as otherwise provided in this article, a tribunal of this State shall recognize and enforce, but may not modify, a registered order if the issuing tribunal had jurisdiction.

SECTION 604. CHOICE OF LAW.

(a) The law of the issuing State governs the nature, extent, amount, and duration of current payments and other obligations of support and the payment of arrearages under the order.

(b) In a proceeding for arrearages, the statute of limitation under the laws of this State or of the issuing State, whichever is longer, applies.

Part 2. Contest of Validity or Enforcement

SECTION 605. NOTICE OF REGISTRATION OF ORDER.

(a) When a support order or income-withholding order issued in another State is registered, the registering tribunal shall notify the nonregistering party. The notice must be accompanied by a copy of the registered order and the documents and relevant information accompanying the order.

(b) The notice must inform the nonregistering party:

(1) that a registered order is enforceable as of the date of registration in the same manner as an order issued by a tribunal of this State;

(2) that a hearing to contest the validity or enforcement of the registered order must be requested within [20] days after notice;

(3) that failure to contest the validity or enforcement of the registered order in a timely manner will result in confirmation of the order and enforcement of the order and the alleged arrearages and precludes further contest of that order with respect to any matter that could have been asserted; and

(4) of the amount of any alleged arrearages.

(c) Upon registration of an income-withholding order for enforcement, the registering tribunal shall notify the obligor's employer pursuant to [the income-withholding law of this State].

SECTION 606. PROCEDURE TO CONTEST VALIDITY OR ENFORCEMENT OF REGISTERED ORDER.

(a) A nonregistering party seeking to contest the validity or enforcement of a registered order in this State shall request a hearing within [20] days after notice of the registration. The nonregistering party may seek to vacate the registration, to assert any defense to an allegation of noncompliance with the registered order, or to contest the remedies being sought or the amount of any alleged arrearages pursuant to Section 607 (Contest of Registration or Enforcement).

(b) If the nonregistering party fails to contest the validity or enforcement of the registered order in a timely manner, the order is confirmed by operation of law.

(c) If a nonregistering party requests a hearing to contest the validity or enforcement of the registered order, the registering tribunal shall schedule the matter for hearing and give notice to the parties of the date, time, and place of the hearing.

SECTION 607. CONTEST OF REGISTRATION OR ENFORCEMENT.

(a) A party contesting the validity or enforcement of a registered order or seeking to vacate the registration has the burden of proving one or more of the following defenses:

(1) the issuing tribunal lacked personal jurisdiction over the contesting party;

(2) the order was obtained by fraud;

(3) the order has been vacated, suspended, or modified by a later order;

(4) the issuing tribunal has stayed the order pending appeal;

(5) there is a defense under the law of this State to the remedy sought;

(6) full or partial payment has been made; or

(7) the statute of limitation under Section 604 (Choice of Law) precludes enforcement of some or all of the arrearages.

(b) If a party presents evidence establishing a full or partial defense under subsection (a), a tribunal may stay enforcement of the registered order, continue the proceeding to permit production of additional relevant evidence, and issue other appropriate orders. An uncontested portion of the registered order may be enforced by all remedies available under the law of this State.

(c) If the contesting party does not establish a defense under subsection (a) to the validity or enforcement of the order, the registering tribunal shall issue an order confirming the order.

SECTION 608. CONFIRMED ORDER. Confirmation of a registered order, whether by operation of law or after notice and hearing, precludes further contest of the order with respect to any matter that could have been asserted at the time of registration.

Part 3. Registration and Modification of Child Support Order

SECTION 609. PROCEDURE TO REGISTER CHILD-SUPPORT ORDER OF ANOTHER STATE FOR MODIFICATION. A party or support enforcement agency seeking to modify, or to modify and enforce, a child-support order issued in another State shall register that order in this State in the same manner provided in Part 1 if the order has not been registered. A [petition] for modification may be filed at the same time as a request for registration, or later. The pleading must specify the grounds for modification.

SECTION 610. EFFECT OF REGISTRATION FOR MODIFICATION. A tribunal of this State may enforce a child-support order of another State registered for purposes of modification, in the same manner as if the order had been issued by a tribunal of this State, but the registered order may be modified only if the requirements of Section 611 (Modification of Child-Support Order of Another State) have been met.

SECTION 611. MODIFICATION OF CHILD-SUPPORT ORDER OF ANOTHER STATE.

(a) After a child-support order issued in another State has been registered in this State, the responding tribunal of this State may modify that order only if Section 613 does not apply and after notice and hearing it finds that:

(1) the following requirements are met:

(i) the child, the individual obligee, and the obligor do not reside in the issuing State;

(ii) a [petitioner] who is a nonresident of this State seeks modification; and

(iii) the [respondent] is subject to the personal jurisdiction of the tribunal of this State; or

(2) the child, or a party who is an individual, is subject to the personal jurisdiction of the tribunal of this State and all of the parties who are individuals have filed written consents in the issuing tribunal for a tribunal of this State to modify the support order and assume continuing, exclusive jurisdiction over the order. However, if the issuing State is a foreign jurisdiction that has not enacted a law or established procedures substantially similar to the procedures under this [Act], the consent otherwise required of an individual residing in this State is not required for the tribunal to assume jurisdiction to modify the child-support order.

(b) Modification of a registered child-support order is subject to the same requirements, procedures, and defenses that apply to the modification of an order issued by a tribunal of this State and the order may be enforced and satisfied in the same manner.

(c) A tribunal of this State may not modify any aspect of a child-support order that may not be modified under the law of the issuing State. If two or more tribunals have issued child-support orders for the same obligor and child, the order that controls and must be so recognized under Section 207 establishes the aspects of the support order which are nonmodifiable.

(d) On issuance of an order modifying a child-support order issued in another State, a tribunal of this State becomes the tribunal having continuing, exclusive jurisdiction.

SECTION 612. RECOGNITION OF ORDER MODIFIED IN ANOTHER STATE. A tribunal of this State shall recognize a modification of its earlier child-support order by a tribunal of another State which assumed jurisdiction pursuant to this [Act] or a law substantially similar to this [Act] and, upon request, except as otherwise provided in this [Act], shall:

(1) enforce the order that was modified only as to amounts accruing before the modification;

(2) enforce only nonmodifiable aspects of that order;

(3) provide other appropriate relief only for violations of that order which occurred before the effective date of the modification; and

(4) recognize the modifying order of the other State, upon registration, for the purpose of enforcement.

SECTION 613. JURISDICTION TO MODIFY CHILD-SUPPORT ORDER OF ANOTHER STATE WHEN INDIVIDUAL PARTIES RESIDE IN THIS STATE.

(a) If all of the parties who are individuals reside in this State and the child does not reside in the issuing State, a tribunal of this State has jurisdiction to enforce and to modify the issuing state's child-support order in a proceeding to register that order.

(b) A tribunal of this State exercising jurisdiction under this section shall apply the provisions of Articles 1 and 2, this article, and the procedural and substantive law of this State to the proceeding for enforcement or modification. Articles 3, 4, 5, 7, and 8 do not apply.

SECTION 614. NOTICE TO ISSUING TRIBUNAL OF MODIFICATION. Within [30] days after issuance of a modified child-support order, the party obtaining the modification shall file a certified copy of the order with the issuing tribunal that had continuing, exclusive jurisdiction over the earlier order, and in each tribunal in which the party knows the earlier order has been registered. A party who obtains the order and fails to file a certified copy is subject to appropriate sanctions by a tribunal in which the issue of failure to file arises. The failure to file does not affect the validity or enforceability of the modified order of the new tribunal having continuing, exclusive jurisdiction.

ARTICLE 7. DETERMINATION OF PARENTAGE

SECTION 701. PROCEEDING TO DETERMINE PARENTAGE.

(a) A tribunal of this State may serve as an initiating or responding tribunal in a proceeding brought under this [Act] or a law or procedure substantially similar to this [Act], the Uniform Reciprocal Enforcement of Support Act, or the Revised Uniform Reciprocal Enforcement of Support Act to determine that the [petitioner] is a parent of a particular child or to determine that a [respondent] is a parent of that child.

(b) In a proceeding to determine parentage, a responding tribunal of this State shall apply the [Uniform Parentage Act; procedural and substantive law of this State,] and the rules of this State on choice of law.

ARTICLE 8. INTERSTATE RENDITION

SECTION 801. GROUNDS FOR RENDITION.

(a) For purposes of this article, "governor" includes an individual performing the functions of governor or the executive authority of a State covered by this [Act].

(b) The governor of this State may:

(1) demand that the governor of another State surrender an individual found in the other State who is charged criminally in this State with having failed to provide for the support of an obligee; or

(2) on the demand by the governor of another State, surrender an individual found in this State who is charged criminally in the other State with having failed to provide for the support of an obligee.

(c) A provision for extradition of individuals not inconsistent with this [Act] applies to the demand even if the individual whose surrender is demanded was not in the demanding State when the crime was allegedly committed and has not fled therefrom.

SECTION 802. CONDITIONS OF RENDITION.

(a) Before making demand that the governor of another State surrender an individual charged criminally in this State with having failed to provide for the support of an obligee, the governor of this State may require a prosecutor of this State to demonstrate that at least [60] days previously the obligee had initiated proceedings for support pursuant to this [Act] or that the proceeding would be of no avail.

(b) If, under this [Act] or a law substantially similar to this [Act], the Uniform Reciprocal Enforcement of Support Act, or the Revised Uniform Reciprocal Enforcement of Support Act, the governor of another State makes a demand that the governor of this State surrender an individual charged criminally in that State with having failed to provide for the support of a child or other individual to whom a duty of support is owed, the governor may require a prosecutor to investigate the demand and report whether a proceeding for support has been initiated or would be effective. If it appears that a proceeding would be effective but has not been initiated, the governor may delay honoring the demand for a reasonable time to permit the initiation of a proceeding.

(c) If a proceeding for support has been initiated and the individual whose rendition is demanded prevails, the governor may decline to honor the demand. If the [petitioner] prevails and the individual whose rendition is demanded is subject to a support order, the governor may decline to honor the demand if the individual is complying with the support order.

ARTICLE 9. MISCELLANEOUS PROVISIONS

SECTION 901. UNIFORMITY OF APPLICATION AND CONSTRUCTION. This [Act] shall be applied and construed to effectuate its general purpose to make uniform the law with respect to the subject of this [Act] among States enacting it.

Glossary

A

absolute and full divorce A complete and final, without any restrictions, ending of a marriage by court order.

acceptance (1) Agreeing to an offer and thus forming a contract. (2) Taking something offered by another person with the intention of keeping it.

acknowledged father A father who registers with a Registry of Paternity or a biological father whose name is placed on a child's birth certificate by the child's mother.

action to determine paternity Each state is required by federal law to have a simple civil process for voluntarily acknowledging paternity and a civil procedure for establishing paternity in contested cases.

addendum A document providing information that is attached to an original document, often a contract.

adjudication of paternity Judicial decision declaring a man to be the father of a child.

adoption To formally accept a child of another as one's own, with all the rights and duties there would have been if the child had been one's own.

adoption agency negligence A cause of action that requires the defendant to have breached a duty by failing to supply plaintiffs with information the defendant possessed and had available regarding adoptable children.

advance sheets Unbound copies of case decisions that will later be printed with other cases in bound form.

advocate A person who speaks on behalf of another person.

affidavit A written statement sworn to before a person officially permitted by law to administer an oath.

affirmative defenses The part of a defendant's answer to a complaint that goes beyond denying the facts and arguments of the complaint. It sets out new facts and arguments that might win for the defendant even if everything in the complaint is true.

agreement An intention of two or more persons to enter into a contract with one another combined with an attempt to form a valid contract.

alienation of affection Taking away the love, companionship, or help of another person's husband or wife.

alimony Payments by a divorced spouse to his or her ex-spouse for personal support.

alternate payee A payment made to a third party on behalf of another.

alternative dispute resolution Different methods, such as arbitration and mediation, used to resolve legal problems without litigating the matter.

Amended complaint A complaint that has been altered after it was first filed because of some change in the case.

American Arbitration Association An organization that publishes arbitration rules and supplies arbitrators to help settle labor and other disputes.

American Bar Association (ABA) The largest voluntary organization of lawyers in the country. Its branches and committees are involved in almost every area of legal practice and governmental activity.

American Jurisprudence (Am Jur) A multivolume legal encyclopedia that is cross-referenced with *American Law Reports.*

annotation A note or commentary intended to explain the meaning of a passage in a book or document; usually consists of an explanation of a case, including a comparison to other similar cases, and follows the text of the decision in a collection of cases.

annulment The act of making something void or wiping it out completely. The annulment of a marriage "wipes the marriage off the books," as opposed to divorce, which only ends the marriage.

anomalous contract An unusual contract.

answer The first pleading by the defendant in a lawsuit, responding to the charges and demands of the plaintiff's complaint.

antenuptial agreement A contract between persons about to marry; also called a prenuptial agreement.

antimiscegenation laws Statutes banning interracial marriage and relationships.

appearance The coming into court as a party to a lawsuit.

appellant The person who appeals a case to a higher court.

appellate brief A written statement prepared by an attorney to explain to the appellate court why her client's negative result at the trial level should be reversed on appeal.

appellate level Refers to a higher court that can hear appeals from a lower court, or refers to an appeal.

appellee The person against whom an appeal is made (usually, but not always, the winner in the lower court).

arbitration Resolution of a dispute by a person (other than a judge) whose decision is binding. This person is called an arbitrator. Submission of the dispute for decision is often the result of an agreement (an arbitration clause) in a contract. If arbitration is required by law, it is called compulsory.

arbitrator A person who conducts arbitration. This person is usually not a public official, is often chosen by the persons having the dispute, and is often an impartial expert in the field or one trained in the law.

arranged marriages Predominant primarily in societies that place great importance on property inheritance, linkages between lineage, or in which elders think that young people are unable to make sound choices.

arrearages Unperformed, overdue obligations, including money owed.

artificial insemination The act of inseminating a woman without intercourse.

assault An intentional threat, show of force, or movement that could reasonably make a person feel in danger of physical attack or harmful physical contact. It can be a crime or tort.

assets Money, property, and money-related rights (such as money owed) owned by a person or an organization.

assisted reproductive technology The medical field that assists men and women who are seeking to procreate.

associate A licensed attorney working in a salaried position in a law firm.

attorney-client privilege The principle that a lawyer will not reveal any information provided by a client, unless it concerns the future commission of a crime.

attorney work-product privilege The principle that a lawyer need not show the other side in a case any facts or things gathered for the case unless the other side can convince the judge that it would be unjust for the things to remain hidden and that there is a special need for them.

a vinculo matrimonii A Latin term that means "from the marriage bonds"; a complete divorce or an annulment.

B

battered wife syndrome (battered woman syndrome) The resulting psychological harm that continuing domestic violence may have upon a victim.

batterer An individual who uses violence to gain control over his victim's actions, thoughts, and feelings.

bench warrant Order by a judge to have the party named in the bench warrant picked up by the police and brought before the judge for punishment (e.g., time in the county jail or monetary fines).

beneficiary spouse A spouse who receives a property transfer made by one spouse to a third party on behalf of the other spouse.

best interests of the child test The legal test used by judges in custody disputes.

bifurcated A case in which separate hearings are held for different issues in the case.

bigamy The crime of being married to two or more husbands or wives at the same time.

binding arbitration The final and unappealable decision of an arbitrator.

breach of contract Failure, without legal excuse, to live up to a significant promise made in a contract.

breach of promise Refers to a breach of promise to marry.

C

calendar number A term used in some states to describe the number assigned to a legal case to identify the case as it moves throughout the state's court system.

capital gain The money made that is the difference between the purchase price and the selling price of the thing in question. A tax is usually imposed on the profit resulting from the sale of a capital asset.

case briefing (1) A written summary or condensed statement of a series of ideas or of a document. (2) A written statement prepared by one side in a lawsuit to explain its case to the judge. It usually contains a face summary, a law summary, and an argument about how the law applies to the facts.

case digest system A collection of books divided into volumes by time periods, usually giving not only summaries, but also excerpts and condensations. It collects head notes (summaries given at the top of each case) and is arranged by subject categories.

case information statement (CIS) A detailed statement of the plaintiff's and defendant's financial budgets that is required by most states to be filed with every answer and complaint.

case of first impression A case that presents an entirely new legal problem to a court and cannot be decided by precedent.

cause of action (1) Facts sufficient to support a valid lawsuit (e.g., a cause of action for battery must include facts to prove intentional, physical contact without permission). (2) The legal theory upon which a lawsuit or action is based.

child support Required financial support for a child in a fair and reasonable sum determined by the court.

citation A reference to a legal authority and where it is found.

civil contempt A public sanction used in child support cases that can be purged from a person's record once the person has paid the overdue child or spousal support.

civil marriage Legal union as husband and wife.

civil rights law The rights of all citizens that are guaranteed by the Constitution and other laws.

civil union Marriage of two people of the same sex; the concept falls short of full equal status with marriage, but does provide some of the benefits and protections of civil marriage.

clear and convincing evidence Stronger evidence than a preponderance of the evidence (evidence that something is more likely to be true than false) but not as strong as beyond a reasonable doubt.

client safety plan A list of actions that may be taken by a victim of domestic violence when the victim wishes to remove herself from the presence of the perpetrator of the violence.

closed adoption An adoption whereby the adoptive parents and the biological parents do not know each other's identities.

closing argument A review of the entire case that explains how the testimony and evidence presented clearly provides reasons for deciding the case in the attorney's client's favor.

code (1) A collection of laws. (2) A complete, interrelated, and exclusive set of laws.

coercion Making a person act against free will.

cohabitation (1) Living together. (2) Living together and having a sexual relationship.

cohabitation agreement A contract that clearly outlines the assets and responsibilities of each of the participants.

collaborative adoption An adoption in which the birth parents place their child directly with the adoptive parents.

collaborative law The process by which two attorneys agree to put their efforts into mediating a legal matter rather than taking the more adversarial route to court.

collusive divorce A divorce that is based on an agreement between the husband and wife that one of them will commit (or appear to commit) an act that will allow the other one to get a divorce. This tactic was used more often in the past when divorces were only granted based on fault causes.

common law (1) Either all case law or the case law that is made by judges in the absence of relevant statutes. (2) The legal system that originated in England and is composed of case law and statutes that grow and change as they are influenced by ever-changing customs and traditions.

common law marriage A legally binding marriage that occurs without license or ceremony under the laws of some states when a man and a woman hold themselves out as married (or live together as if married) for a specified time period.

community property Refers to those states that call most property acquired during a marriage the property of both partners, no matter whose name it is in.

compensatory damages Damages awarded for the actual loss suffered by a plaintiff.

complaint (1) The first main paper filed in a civil lawsuit that includes, among other things, a statement of the wrong or harm done to the plaintiff by the defendant, a request for specific help from the court, and an explanation of why the court has the power to do what the plaintiff wants. (2) Any official complaint in the ordinary sense (e.g., a complaint to the police about a noisy party). (3) In criminal law, a format document that charges a person with a crime.

computer-assisted legal research Abbreviated as CALR, the research conducted with the assistance of the World Wide Web and services that provide access to information, usually for a fee.

concurring opinion When a judge agrees with the result reached in an opinion by another judge in the same case, but not necessarily with the reasoning that the other judge used to reach the conclusion.

condition precedent An event that creates or destroys rights and obligations.

confidentiality waiver A waiver that allows psychologists or others to discuss matters that would normally be confidential.

confidential relationship Any relationship where one person has a right to expect a higher than usual level of care and faithfulness from another person (e.g., an attorney and client).

conflict of interest Being in a position where one's own needs and desires could possibly lead one to violate one's duty to a person who has a right to depend on one, or being in a position where one tries to serve two competing clients.

consanguinity Having a blood relationship to another.

consent order A court order that is presented to a judge for her signature once both parties have agreed to the terms in the order.

consideration The reason or main cause for a person to make a contract; something of value received or promised to induce (convince) a person to make a deal. Without consideration, a contract is not valid. The concept of consideration has two parts: valuable (can be valued in money) and good (legally sufficient). Consideration for a valid contract between close relatives, however, can be good even if not valuable because their "love and affection" may be legally sufficient even if it cannot be valued in money.

consortium The right of a husband or wife to the other's love and services.

constructive trust A situation in which a person holds legal title to property, but the property should, in fairness, actually belong to another person (because the title was gained by fraud, by a clerical error, etc.). In this case, the property may be treated by a court as if the legal owner holds it in trust for the "real" owner.

contempt of court (1) An act that obstructs a court's work or lessens the dignity of the court (usually criminal contempt). (2) A willful disobeying of a judge's command or official court order. Contempt can be direct (within the judge's notice) or indirect (outside the court and punishable only after proved to the judge).

contingency fee Payment to a lawyer of a percentage of the "winnings," if any, from a lawsuit rather than payment of a flat fee or payment according to the number of hours worked.

continuing jurisdiction The power of a court to continue to control a matter even after the court has decided the case, used especially in cases involving child custody and support.

contra bones mores A Latin term meaning "against good morals" or "offending the public conscience."

contract An agreement that affects or creates legal relationships between two or more persons. To be a contract, an agreement must involve at least one promise, consideration (something of value promised or given), persons legally capable of making binding agreements, and a reasonable certainty about the meaning of the terms.

Corpus Juris Secundum **(CJS)** A legal encyclopedia that is cross-referenced with the American Digest System.

counterclaim A claim made by the defendant in a civil lawsuit that, in effect, "sues" the plaintiff.

court clerk A court official who keeps court records and other official files.

court reporter A person who records court proceedings in court and later makes good copies of some of them.

covenant marriage Marriage entered into after agreeing that divorce will be made more difficult for the parties. *Covenant* means a formal promise to some restriction.

criminal contempt Also known as criminal nonsupport; public and punitive sanction for failing to pay court-ordered child and spousal support.

criminal conversation Causing a married man or woman to commit adultery; considered to be a tort.

cross-examination The questioning of an opposing witness during a trial or hearing.

cryobank Preserves genetic material for later use in procreation.

D

Deadbeat Parents Punishment Act A federal law designed to punish parents who fail to pay court-ordered child support.

declaration of nullification The Catholic Church's version of a religious annulment.

default judgment Failure to perform a legal duty, observe a promise, or fulfill an obligation. Failure to take a required step in a lawsuit can sometimes lead to a default judgment.

defendant The person against whom a legal action is brought.

Defense of Marriage Act Known by its abbreviated name DOMA, this act was designed to allow individual states to decide separately whether they will acknowledge the legalization of same-sex marriages in other states and thereby apply the full faith and credit and the equal protection clauses of the United States Constitution.

demand for production of documents The formal request for documents.

de novo A Latin term that means "new." For example, a trial *de novo* is a new trial ordered by a judge when a previous trial is so flawed that it will be made void.

deoxyribonucleic acid (DNA) test A test used to determine inherited characteristics and declare paternity.

dependent exemption The tax exemption for children allowed by the IRS and usually given to the parent who has custody of the children the majority of the year.

deposition (1) The process of taking a witness's sworn out-of-court testimony. The questioning is usually done by a lawyer, with the lawyer from the other side given a chance to attend and participate. (2) The written record of the deposition process.

deposition summary The process of taking the deposition transcript and highlighting the important part of the testimony for use in trial preparation.

deposition transcript The official, written copy of a deposition.

designated adoption An adoption in which the birth parents place their child directly with the adoptive parents.

digest A collection of books, usually giving not only summaries, but also excerpts and condensations. For example, the American Digest System covers the decisions of the highest court of each state and of the Supreme Court. It is divided into volumes by time periods, collects head notes (summaries given at the top of each case), and is arranged by subject categories.

direct certification When a state's highest court will hear an appeal without the intermediate appellate court having to hear the case first.

direct examination The first questioning in a trial of a witness by the side that called the witness.

discovery (1) The formal and informal exchange of information between sides in a lawsuit. Two types of discovery are interrogatories and depositions. (2) Finding out something previously unknown. For example, in patent law, a discovery is finding out something new rather than inventing a device or process. Also, the discovery of a fraud or medical malpractice occurs when the person harmed finds out the problem (or should have found out, if careful.)

dissenting opinion A judge's formal, written disagreement with the decision of the majority of the judges in a lawsuit.

dissolution of marriage A formal, legal ending of a marriage other than by annulment.

divisible divorce Where one court is able to divorce the parties but, because of a lack of personal jurisdiction over the parties, cannot determine the property and support settlement.

divorce The ending of a marriage by court order.

docket number A number assigned to a case to identify it throughout the court system.

doctrine of interspousal immunity The legal principle describing when spouses are not allowed to sue each other.

doctrine of *stare decisis* A Latin term that means "let the decision stand"; the rule that when a court has decided a case by applying a legal principle to a set of facts, the court should stick by the principle and apply it to all later cases with clearly similar facts unless there is a strong reason not to, and courts below must apply the same principle in similar cases as well.

domestic partners Sometimes used to describe same-sex couples who reside together.

domestic violence The infliction of fear or actual physical harm and bodily injury, assault, terroristic threats, and criminal sexual conduct between family or household members.

domestic violence indicators A protection mechanism placed on personal files within state and federal locator services.

domicile A person's legal residence.

due process clause of the Fourteenth Amendment A constitutional requirement that no person be deprived of life, liberty, or property without due process of the law.

duress Unlawful pressure on a person to do what the person otherwise would not have done. It includes force, threats of violence, physical restraint, and so on.

E

ecclesiastical court A religious court.

election Choosing from among legal rights. For example, a husband or wife may have to elect (choose) between what was left in a will by the other one and what state law reserves as a minimum share of a husband or wife's estate.

enticement action An old form of lawsuit brought because of the seduction or taking away of a wife.

equal protection clause A constitutional requirement that a state government not treat equal unequally, set up illegal categories to justify treating a person unfairly, or give unfair or unequal treatment to person based on that person's race, religion, disability, color, sex, age, or national origin.

equitable remedy A solution that is just, fair, and right for a particular situation. Used by the courts to apply fairness in a particular situation. The courts have the power to do justice where specific laws do not cover the situation.

escalation clause Describes the amount of an automatic increase in child support.

estoppel Being stopped by one's own prior acts from claiming a right against another person who has legitimately relied on those acts.

executrix A female executor of a will.

exhibit (1) Any object or document offered and marked as evidence (in a trial, hearing, deposition, audit, etc.) (2) Any document attached to a pleading, affidavit, or other formal papers.

ex parte A Latin term that means "with only one side present." For example, an *ex parte* order is one made at the request of one side in a lawsuit when the other side fails to appear in court. The *ex parte* order may be made because the other side has failed to appear, because the other side does not need to be present for the order to issue, or because there is no other side.

expectation damages Money awarded in breach-of-contract lawsuits to replace the profits that probably would have been made from a deal that fell through.

expert A person possessing special knowledge or experience who is allowed to testify at a trial not only about facts (like an ordinary witness) but also about the professional conclusions he draws from the facts.

express contract A contract with terms stated orally or in writing.

extraordinary expenses Those child-rearing costs that are outside daily living necessities.

F

family violence indicator (FVI) A notation made on a file at the national and state parent locator services indicating that a spouse has been violent and therefore the other spouse's whereabouts should not be freely given.

federal locator service A national computer network system designed to assist in locating people.

final judgment A final decision that is based on the facts of the case and made at the end of a trial.

final order The ruling that a judge makes at the conclusion of a hearing or a trial.

final order of adoption An order signed by a judge following testimony by a social worker and the adoptive parents.

final restraining order An order that is issued after a temporary restraining order and is either a limited or permanent order.

financial disclosure affidavit A detailed accounting of a person's financial affairs that is sworn to by the person. All states require individuals who are divorcing, separating, or dealing with child custody and support issues to file a detailed accounting of the family's finances. Some states call such an accounting a case information statement or a budget statement.

forum non conveniens A Latin term that means "inconvenient court." If two or more courts both have proper venue for a case, a judge may rule that a lawsuit must be brought in one court or the other court for the sake of convenience and fairness to the parties.

forum shopping Choosing one court, among two or more that may legally handle a lawsuit, that a person believes will look most favorably at that person's side.

401(K) A type of retirement plan.

403(B) A type of retirement plan.

fraud Any kind of trickery used to cheat another of money or property.

friendly parent provision States either require or simply suggest that their family courts discern each parent's ability to deal with the other in a friendly and ongoing relationship during a custody dispute.

full disclosure Completely revealing something that is secret or not well understood.

Full Faith and Credit for Child Support Orders Act (FFCCSOA) Another addition to the federal arsenal of laws enacted to ensure that each state will respect child support orders written in other states.

G

genetic parent A biological parent who is genetically linked to a child.

guardian *ad litem* A person who is appointed by a court to oversee the interests of another person during a lawsuit involving that person.

H

Hague Convention on the Civil Aspects of International Child Abduction The international custody laws created and enacted via treaties between the signatory nations that are the international community's answer to custody disputes; also known as The Hague Convention or The Convention.

harassment Words and actions that unlawfully annoy or alarm another.

head of the household Refers to the Internal Revenue Service's requirement for designating a person as the head of a family.

heart-balm statutes State laws that either eliminate or restrict lawsuits based on alienation of affection, breach of promise to marry, criminal conversation, and seduction of an adult.

holding The core of a judge's decision in a case; that part of the judge's written opinion that applies the law to the facts of the case and about which can be said "the case means no more and no less than this." When later cases rely on a case as precedent, only the holding is used to establish the precedent. A holding may be less than the complete comments of the judge. If the judge made broad, general statements, the holding is limited to only that part of the generalizations that directly applies to the facts of the particular case.

home state A state in which a child has lived for six months according to the UCCJEA.

home study report A report based on a study of the home of adoptive parents conducted to ensure the safety of the adoptive child. It is required by all 50 states before an independent, public, or private adoption can take place.

horn book A book summarizing the basic principles of one legal subject, usually for law students.

I

identified adoption An adoption in which the birth parents place their child directly with the adoptive parents.

illegitimate child An outmoded term that was used to describe children born outside of marriage.

implied contract A contract with existence and terms determined by the actions of the persons involved, not by their words.

improvement period A term used in child custody cases whereby a judge gives parents a time period within which to improve their parenting skills in order to retain custody of their children.

imputed income Income that is imputed to a person for tax or other purposes based on certain kinds of activities.

income-share model A model based on the theory that children of divorce should receive the same share of their parents' income as they did when their parents were married.

independent adoption An adoption in which the biological mother creates the requirements she wants to meet with the adoptive parents of her child.

Indian Child Welfare Act Federal law that was created at the urging of the Indian Nations in order to curtail the adoption of Indian children by non-Indian adoptive parents.

individual retirement plan Popularly known as an IRA; a self-funded retirement plan.

in loco parentis A Latin term that means "in the place of a parent"; acting as a parent with respect to the care and supervision of a child.

in personam **jurisdiction** Describes the court's authority over a person, as opposed to one brought to enforce rights in a thing against the whole world.

in rem **jurisdiction** Describes the court's authority over things as opposed to authority over a person.

intended beneficiary The payee of a retirement plan.

interlocutory decree of adoption A provisional (i.e., temporary) court order.

Internal Revenue Code The primary United States tax laws.

Internal Revenue Service (IRS) The federal agency that is empowered by our federal government to collect taxes.

international adoption The type of adoption that occurs when the child and the adoptive parents are from two different countries.

interpret To explain the meaning of, understand, or translate.

interrogatories (1) Written questions sent from one side in a lawsuit to another, attempting to get written answers to factual questions or seeking an explanation of the other side's legal contentions. These are part of the formal discovery process in a lawsuit and usually take place before the trial. (2) In some states, written questions addressed to any witness.

Interstate Compact on the Placement of Children Designed to protect children who are born in one state and taken to another state to be adopted.

intestate Without a will. Dying intestate is dying without having a valid will that covers all of the dead person's property.

investment tax credit A tax credit for property (e.g., buildings and major machines) bought for a business.

in vitro **fertilization (IVF)** The medical technology that permits the retrieval of eggs from a female, the fertilization of those eggs in a laboratory, and the implanting of those fertilized eggs into a uterus.

involuntary termination of parental rights Occurs when a judge finds that a parent or both parents have failed to properly care for their child to the extent that the child's physical and/or mental welfare has been gravely compromised.

irreconcilable differences Grounds for a divorce in some states because the marriage has simply broken down.

irremediable breakdown A no-fault ground for divorce.

irrevocable Incapable of being called back, stopped, or changed.

J

joint custody A custody arrangement in which both parents have equal legal custody of their children, but only one parent has physical custody of the children.

judgment The official decision of a court about the rights and claims of each side in a lawsuit; usually refers to a final decision that is based on the facts of the case and made at the end of a trial.

judicial notice The act of a judge in recognizing the existence or truth of certain facts without bothering to make one side in a lawsuit prove them.

judicial opinion A judge's statement of the decision she has reached in a case.

judicial surrender A statement of the biological parents' intention to have their child adopted.

jurisdiction (1) The geographical area within which a court (or a public official) has the right and power to operate. (2) The persons about whom and the subject matters about which a court has the right and power to make decisions that are legally binding.

K

Keogh plan A tax-free retirement account for persons with self-employment income.

key facts The essential facts in a case (e.g., who, what, when, where, and how).

kinship adoption A type of adoption whereby the adoptive parents are biologically related to the child to be adopted.

L

law review or law journal A publication that is produced by a law school or bar association and contains articles on legal topics.

legal citation A reference to a legal authority and where it is found.

legal custody Rightful possession; a general term meaning care and keeping. Parents normally have custody of their children.

legal error A mistake made by a judge in the procedures used at trial, or in making legal rulings during the trial.

legal malpractice Bad, incomplete, or unfaithful work done by a lawyer.

legal separation A husband and wife living apart by agreement, either before divorce or instead of getting a full divorce.

legislative history The background documents and records of hearings related to the enactment of a bill.

legitimate Lawful or legal, or to make lawful or legal.

liabilities A broad word for legal obligation, responsibility, or debt.

lien A claim against specific property that can be enforced in court to secure payment of a judgment, duty, or debt.

life insurance Money paid to a designated beneficiary when the insured dies.

life necessities Those material essentials that one needs to survive (e.g., food, shelter, and medical care).

living apart A cause of action that requires spouses to be living apart a statutorily mandated amount of time before filing a complaint.

long-arm jurisdiction A state law that allows the courts of a state to claim jurisdiction over (decide cases directly involving) a person outside the state because that person has committed a wrong inside the state. The person in question must have certain minimum contacts with the state.

M

majority opinion An opinion that is written when more than half the judges in a case agree about both the result and the reasoning used to reach that result.

Married Women's Property Acts Statutes enacted in the latter half of the nineteenth century that removed the majority of a wife's legal disabilities.

Martindale-Hubbell Short for the *Martindale-Hubbell Law Directory,* a multivolume book that lists many lawyers by location and type of practice.

material and substantial change in circumstances A reason that courts will modify an original decree of child support payments.

mediated settlement agreements The written and memorialized result of a third-party mediator assisting parties in settling a dispute.

mediation Using the services of a third party to assist in settling a dispute.

mediation retainer agreement A written agreement between an individual acting as a mediator and at least two parties (e.g., a divorcing couple will create such an agreement to clarify how they want to mutually end their marriage).

mediator The person who helps in settling a dispute. Mediation is different from arbitration in that a mediator can only persuade, not force, people into a settlement.

Melson-Delaware Income Model A model based on the theory that the basic financial needs of the parent should be calculated, and then the children's needs.

mental capacity The ability to make a rational decision.

modification A change or alteration; often a minor change, but a modification of judgment under most court rules also includes changing a judgment in major ways and for major reasons such as fraud.

monogamy Two-person marriage.

motion A request that a judge make a ruling or take some other action. For example, a motion to dismiss is a request that the court throw the case out; a motion for more definite statement is a request that the judge require an opponent in a lawsuit to file a less vague or ambiguous pleading; a motion to strike is a request that immaterial statements or other things be removed from an opponent's pleading; and a motion to suppress is a request that illegally gathered evidence be prohibited. Motions are either granted or denied by the judge.

motion for modification A motion that is filed when one of the parents involved in a child custody order believes a change in custody or visitation is needed.

N

negligence The failure to exercise a reasonable amount of care in a situation that causes harm to someone or something.

no-contact order Some states use this term when a perpetrator of domestic violence is ordered to avoid all contact with the victim.

no-fault divorce A divorce that is granted upon proof that a husband and wife have lived apart without marital relations for a period of time, usually six months, a year, or more.

nondomiciliary A person residing outside a particular state.

notice To make an individual formally aware of an upcoming legal action involving that individual.

notice of alleged paternity Notice of impending adoption that should not only inform the biological father of the upcoming adoption, but should also provide the date, time, and place of any scheduled adoption hearing.

null No longer having any legal effect or validity.

O

offer A proposal that is presented for acceptance or rejection. In contract law, a proposal to make a deal. To be capable of acceptance, the offer must be communicated from the person making it to the person to whom it is made, and it must be reasonably definite and certain in its terms.

on point Law or a prior case that directly applies to the facts of the present case.

on the papers When a judge makes a decision by reading the documents filed with the court without oral argument by the attorneys.

open adoption An adoption whereby the biological parents and the adoptive parents meet each other and exchange information.

opening a file Creating a new client file.

opening statement An introductory statement made at the start of a trial by the lawyers for each side. The lawyers typically explain the version of the facts best supporting their side of the case, how these facts will be proved, and how they think the law applies to the case.

order A written command or direction given by a judge.

P

pain and suffering damages Money awarded to a plaintiff for emotional pain inflicted as a result of a defendant's actions.

palimony Support payments between persons who are not and never were married; any payments based on an express or implied contract between two persons who lived together in a sexual relationship. The law as to the validity of these contracts is still changing.

paralegal A person, also known as a legal assistant, with special education, training, or work experience who works under a lawyer's supervision on substantive legal work that the lawyer otherwise would do.

parallel citation An alternate reference to a case or other legal document that is published in more than one place. A citation to the (usually one) official publication of a court case or a statute is the official or primary citation, and all others are parallel citations.

parens patriae A Latin term that means "ultimate protector of minors."

Parentage Registry Some states require an unmarried biological father to list his name in such a registry to ensure notification in the event his child is placed for adoption by the biological mother.

parental alienation syndrome When one parent has a negative and influential impact on the relationship his child has with the other parent.

Parental Kidnapping Prevention Act A federal law enacted to assist in the retrieval of a child taken by a parent without a valid custody order from the parent with custody.

parental rights doctrine A legal concept that gives the biological parent the superior right to custody of his child.

Parent Locator Service A service provided by the states and the federal government to assist in locating a parent who has failed to comply with a court order.

parole evidence The principle that the meaning of a written agreement, in which the parties have expressly stated that it is their complete and final agreement, cannot be changed by using prior oral or written statements or agreements as evidence. Exceptions to the rule include situations in which there was duress, fraud, or mistake.

partner A member of a partnership. A "full" or "general" partner participates fully in running the firm and sharing the profits and losses.

patria potestas The ancient Roman legal concept that gave males a superior legal and social position over females.

payee A person who is receiving monetary payments.

payor A person who is making monetary payments.

pendente lite A Latin term that means "during the pending lawsuit." For example, support pendente lite is temporary support while a divorce case is in progress.

pendente lite **application** A request made to a court to issue a temporary order for support while divorce litigation is pending.

pendente lite **order** A court order granting temporary financial support until a final divorce decree is signed by a presiding judge.

pension A plan set up by an employer to pay employees after retirement.

percentage-of-income model A model based on the theory that the noncustodial parent should pay a fixed percentage of his income based on the number of children he has.

permanent alimony Payments made by a divorced spouse to his former spouse for ongoing support.

petition A written request to a court that it take a particular action. In some states, the word is limited to written requests made when there is no other side in a case, and in some states, it is used in place of the term *complaint*.

physical custody The parent with whom the child actually lives has physical custody.

plaintiff A person who brings a lawsuit against another person.

pleading The process of making formal, written statements of each side of a civil case (e.g., complaint, answer, or the papers in which such statements are made). The *pleadings* are the sum of all the papers in a case.

pocket part An addition to a law book that updates it until a bound supplement or a new edition comes out. It is usually found inside the back cover, secured in a pocket, and should always be referred to when doing legal research.

polyandry marriage Union of several husbands with one wife.

polygamy Plural marriage with one husband and more than one wife.

post-nuptial agreement An agreement between spouses.

post-placement home study An investigation of the home environment of an adoptive child after the child is placed with the adoptive parents. The study is usually conducted by a social worker and concentrates on the acclimation of the child and parents to each other.

post-traumatic stress disorder A mental health condition that is diagnosed a significant amount of time after an individual has suffered a severe emotional trauma.

practice manual A legal practice manual for your state.

precedent A court decision on a question of law (how the law affects that case) that is binding authority on lower courts in the same court system for cases in which those courts must decide a similar question of law involving similar facts. The United States court system is based on judges making decisions supported by past precedent, rather than by the logic of the judge alone.

preliminary injunction A judge's order to a person to do or to refrain from doing a particular thing.

prenuptial agreement A contract created between two engaged individuals prior to their marriage.

preplacement home study A home study done to ensure the safety of the adoptee before a child is placed with a family for adoption.

preponderance of evidence The greater weight of evidence, not as to quantity (in number of witnesses or facts) but as to quality (believability and greater weight of important facts proved). This is a standard of proof that is generally used in civil lawsuits. It is not as high a standard as clear and convincing evidence or beyond a reasonable doubt.

presumed father A man considered to be the father of a child, usually because he is married to the mother or he has openly acknowledged the child as his own.

pretrial hearing or pretrial conference A meeting of lawyers and a judge to narrow the issues of a lawsuit, agree on what will be presented at the trial, and make a final effort to settle the case without a trial.

prezygote A fertilized human egg prior to implantation in the uterus.

prima facie **case** A Latin term that means "at first sight" or "on the face of it." It describes something that will be considered to be true unless disproved by contrary evidence (e.g., a *prima facie* case is a case that a party will win unless the other side comes forward with evidence to disprove it).

primary authority (1) Binding authority. (2) Laws, court decisions, regulations, and other similar sources of law, as opposed to the interpretive or indirect information found in legal encyclopedias, treatises, and so on.

primary caregiver A parent or other person who cares for a child the majority of the time.

private adoption An adoption that is supported by fees collected by adoption agencies and through donations.

procedural law The rules of carrying on a civil lawsuit or a criminal case, as opposed to substantive law.

process server A person who personally gives a copy of the complaint with summons to the defendant.

profit sharing A plan established by an employer to distribute part of the firm's profits to some or all of its employees.

pro se A Latin term that means "for himself" or "on his or her own behalf." If a person is without attorney representation in a legal matter and is representing himself, he is said to be *pro se*.

protective order (1) A court order that protects an individual from any type of harassment or stalking. (2) A court order that temporarily allows one side in a lawsuit to hold back from showing the other side documents or other things that have been requested.

psychological parent doctrine A concept that describes a parental-type relationship between an adult and a child. The adult is usually fulfilling the duties and role of the parent.

public adoption An adoption supported by tax dollars; public adoption agencies are responsible for the adoption of all children under the guardianship of the child's home county or state of residence.

punitive damages Extra money given to punish the defendant and to keep a particularly bad act from happening again.

putative marriage A marriage in which a technical legal defect, unknown to the husband and wife, is discovered. These marriages are usually considered to be still valid.

Q

qualified domestic relations order (QDRO) A court judgment, decree, or order that gives a spouse, ex-spouse, or dependent child rights to the spouse's or parent's pension plan. This is an exception to the pension protection rules of ERISA.

qualified medical child support order (QMCSO) A court judgment, decree, or order that requires a parent's health plan to enroll the parent's children in his plan.

quash To overthrow, annul, or completely do away with; usually refers to a court stopping a subpoena, an order, or an indictment.

quasi-contract An obligation similar to a contract that is created, not by an agreement, but by law. The principle of quasi-contract is used to bring about a fair result when a person's actions or the relationship between persons makes it clear that one should owe an obligation to the other that is similar to a contract. Quasi-contract is also called constructive contract and implied-in-law contract.

R

ratification Confirmation and acceptance of a previous act done by oneself or another person.

rationale, reasoning The judges' reasons for deciding as they did.

rebuttable presumption A conclusion that will be drawn unless evidence is presented to counter it.

reciprocal beneficiaries Law first created in Hawaii permitting any two adults residing together who are barred from marrying each other to register for benefits that are not as encompassing as those provided by marriage.

reconciliation agreement A contractual agreement between spouses who were previously separated but have since decided to reunite as spouses.

re-cross One step in the order of questioning a witness, which usually moves from direct examination (by the side that called the witness), to cross-examination (by the other side), and then to re-direct, re-cross, and so on.

re-direct The opportunity for the plaintiff's attorney to ask questions again of his witnesses after they have been cross-examined.

regional reporter A reporter that contains the state court opinions of one region of the United States. A regional digest summarizes these opinions.

registered partnership A procedure whereby same-sex or opposite-sex partners may officially register either with their state or municipality (if such a registry exists). Registries fall short of providing full equal status with those who are married, but do provide some of the benefits and protections of a civil marriage.

rehabilitative award A term used to describe alimony that is provided so that the spouse receiving the award can become trained for self-sufficiency.

reliance damages Money awarded for the expenditures a plaintiff made in reliance on a broken promise (i.e., the breach) of a defendant.

religious annulment An annulment that has no legal standing. The couple is considered not to have been validly married, according to the rules of whatever religious group is granting the annulment.

relinquishment The act of surrendering parental rights to another.

reporters (1) Hardcover books containing judicial opinions. (2) A court reporter, which is the person who records legal proceedings and later creates transcripts of those proceedings.

rescission To cancel a contract and wipe it out as if it had never been.

residual A term used to describe the part of a person's estate that is not specifically bequeathed.

respondent The person against whom an appeal is taken. This person might have been either the plaintiff or the defendant in the lower court.

response A court paper that directly answers the points raised by the other side's pleading.

resume A document that details a person's education and employment history.

retainer (1) Employment of a lawyer by a client. (2) The specific agreement between a lawyer and a client who hired her. (3) The first payment by a client to a lawyer either for one specific case or so the lawyer will be available for unspecified future cases.

retirement plan One of the largest assets that most people have. Retirement plans come in different forms and are often created through a person's place of employment.

review attorney An attorney who is often hired to review mediated settlement agreements, file paperwork for divorces, and appear in court.

Revised Uniform Reciprocal Enforcement of Support Act (RURESA) An act under which a nonpaying parent may be forced to pay or face civil contempt penalties or even arrest on criminal charges for failing to support his minor children pursuant to a court order.

S

sample portfolio A collection of work gathered together for review by prospective employers.

sanction A penalty or punishment attached to a law to make sure it is obeyed.

secondary authority (1) Persuasive authority. (2) Writings about the law, such as articles, treatises, and encyclopedias.

sections A subdivision of law, regulation, or other document (e.g., a subdivision of an article of the United States Constitution or a chapter of a book).

Section 71B Part of the Internal Revenue Code that lists six requirements that must be met in order for a client's payments to be considered eligible as a tax deduction.

series A set of law books in numerical order; new (e.g., second, third, etc.) series follow, but do not replace, older ones.

service of process The delivery (or its legal equivalent, such as publication in a newspaper in some cases) of a legal document, such as a complaint, by an authorized person in a way that meets certain formal requirements.

71(b) Part of the Internal Revenue Code that lists six requirements that must be met in order for a client's payments to be considered eligible as a tax deduction.

sham marriage A marriage in which one of the parties takes the marriage vows without the intent to fulfill the responsibilities of marriage.

shepardizing Using *Shepard's Citations* to ascertain an authority's current state. For example, using the *Shepard's* citator helps to determine whether a case has been followed, overruled, or distinguished and whether a statute is still current law.

sole custody Custody of a child by only one parent.

split custody A custody arrangement that can occur when there are more than two children in the family under which each parent has sole custody of a different child or children, and the other parent has visitation rights to the child or children not in that parent's sole custody.

stalking The crime of repeatedly following, threatening, or harassing another person in ways that lead to a legitimate fear of physical harm.

statute of frauds Any of various state laws, modeled after an Old English law, that requires many types of contracts to be signed and in writing to be enforceable in court.

statutory law The law that is created within the state's elected bodies and Congress.

stay-away order A protection order that does not permit the perpetrator of violence to approach the victim.

stipulation An agreement between lawyers on opposite sides of a lawsuit.

sua sponte A Latin term that means "of his or her own will; voluntarily." Refers to something being based on a judge's own motion, without a request from one of the parties.

substantive law The basic law of rights and duties, as opposed to procedural law.

summary judgment motion A request that a judge make a final judgment for one side in a lawsuit without a trial, when the judge finds, based on pleadings, depositions, affidavits, and so on, that there is no genuine factual issue in the lawsuit.

summons (1) A writ (a notice delivered by a sheriff or other authorized person) informing a person of a lawsuit against her. It tells the person to show up in court at a certain time or risk losing the suit without being present. (2) Any formal notice to show up in court (as a witness, juror, etc.).

supervised visitation Visitation usually ordered by a judge in which a parent may only visit his child when a third party is present to watch the visitation.

supplemental pocket part An addition to a law book that updates it until a bound supplement or new edition comes out. It is found inside the back (or occasionally the front) cover, secured in a pocket, and should always be referred to when doing legal research.

surrogacy The act of one female standing in for another female during pregnancy.

surrogate gestational mother A woman who has agreed to have a fertilized egg implanted, carry the child to term, and give the child up for adoption. Such a mother has no genetic connection to the child.

surrogate mother A woman who has agreed to provide an egg for fertilization, carry a child, and give the child up to another to parent.

T

tax refund intercept An action whereby the Internal Revenue Service will not deliver a refund check to a parent who is in arrears with child support but will instead redirect the check for payment of the back child support.

temporary child support A temporary order of child support until the final divorce decree is signed by the presiding judge.

temporary restraining order (TRO) A judge's order to a person to not take a certain action during the period prior to a full hearing on the rightfulness of the action.

tender years doctrine The presumption that custody of very young children should be given to the mother unless the mother is unfit. A gender-neutral standard is now prevalent in the courts.

termination of parental rights The court-ordered termination of any and all parental rights one may have to one's child.

Title IV-D of the Social Security Act This federal law required each state's legislature to create legislation directing their family courts to expeditiously and uniformly deal with child support enforcement matters.

tort A civil wrong, other than a breach of contract. For an act to be a tort, there must be: a legal duty owed by one person to another, a breach of that duty, and harm done as a direct result of the action.

trial *de novo* A new trial ordered by a judge when a previous trial was so flawed it is made void.

trust An arrangement by which one person holds legal title to money or property for the benefit of another.

U

UCCJA Uniform Child Custody Jurisdiction Act.

UCCJEA Uniform Child Custody Jurisdiction and Enforcement Act. An act that revised and improved the Uniform Child Custody Jurisdiction Act, particularly in terms of enforcement mechanisms.

UIFSA Uniform Interstate Family Support Act.

unconscionable Grossly unfair.

undue influence Pressure that takes away a person's free will to make decisions.

Uniform Interstate Family Support Act (UIFSA) An act that facilitates interstate child support case processing. UIFSA should also be used to establish and enforce a support order, modify a support order, and determine parentage, with or without an accompanying establishment of support.

Uniform Premarital Agreement Act A statute that describes the general requirements for creating a valid prenuptial agreement.

Uniform Reciprocal Enforcement of Support Act (URESA) An act created to improve by reciprocal legislation the enforcement of the duty of support.

Uniform Status of Children of Assisted Conception Act (USCACA) An act that offers two models for states to refer to when dealing with surrogacy contracts.

unjust enrichment Obtaining money or property unfairly and at another's expense. This does not include merely driving a hard bargain or being lucky in a deal. The law provides several ways to avoid unjust enrichment, such as by imposition of quasi-contract.

URESA Uniform Reciprocal Enforcement of Support Act.

V

vacate To annul, set aside, or take back (e.g., when a judge vacates a judgment, it is wiped out completely).

victim advocate A person who provides assistance to a victim of domestic violence. Some states may use other terms to refer to such people.

Violence Against Women Act (VAWA) Created to provide a new, more effective tool for preserving women's safety in domestic violence cases and other instances of gender-based violence against women in our society.

void ab initio A Latin term that means "void from the very beginning."

voidable Something that can be made void; something that is in force, but can be legally avoided.

voluntary parental surrender The act of relinquishing one's parental rights to one's child.

W

wage garnishment An arrangement by which a portion of a person's income is withheld because of support payments being in arrears.

waiver The voluntary giving up of a right.

waiver of service Acknowledgment by the defendant or her lawyer that she has received the complaint and agrees to the court's jurisdiction without requiring official service of process.

without prejudice A term used to describe a right given to one of the parties that prevents the court from denying the party the right to return to court to appeal.

words and phrases A large set of law books that defines legal (and many nonlegal) words by giving actual quotations from cases.

writ of certiorari A Latin term that means "to make sure." A request for *certiorari* (or *cert.* for short) is like an appeal, but one that the higher court is not required to take for decision. It is literally a writ from the higher court asking the lower court for the record of the case.

Index